The Peoples of Canada

A Pre-Confederation History

The Peoples of Canada

A Pre-Confederation History

THIRD EDITION

J.M. Bumsted

OXFORD
UNIVERSITY PRESS

OXFORD
UNIVERSITY PRESS

70 Wynford Drive, Don Mills, Ontario M3C 1J9
www.oupcanada.com

Oxford University Press is a department of the University of Oxford.
It furthers the University's objective of excellence in research, scholarship,
and education by publishing worldwide in

Oxford   New York

Auckland   Cape Town   Dar es Salaam   Hong Kong   Karachi
Kuala Lumpur   Madrid   Melbourne   Mexico City   Nairobi
New Delhi   Shanghai   Taipei   Toronto

With offices in

Argentina   Austria   Brazil   Chile   Czech Republic   France   Greece
Guatemala   Hungary   Italy   Japan   Poland   Portugal   Singapore
South Korea   Switzerland   Thailand   Turkey   Ukraine   Vietnam

Oxford is a trade mark of Oxford University Press
in the UK and in certain other countries

Published in Canada by Oxford University Press

Library and Archives Canada Cataloguing in Publication

Bumsted, J. M., 1938–
The peoples of Canada : a pre-Confederation history / J.M. Bumsted. — 3rd ed.

Includes bibliographical references and index.
ISBN 978-0-19-542340-2

1. Canada—History—To 1763 (New France).   2. Canada—History—1763–1867.
3. Native peoples—Canada—History.   4. Canada—Historiography.   I. Title.

FC162.B85 2009   971   C2009-904787-X

This book is printed on permanent (acid-free) paper ∞.
Printed and bound in Canada.

1 2 3 4 — 13 12 11 10

Contents

Introduction: Understanding History   vii

Part I: To 1760

Introduction   1
1. The Peoples of Early North America   3
2. Contacts and Encounters   21
3. Early European Approaches   40
4. The Atlantic Region to 1670   59
5. Canada to 1663   79
6. Canada 1663–1763: Government, Military, Economy   104
7. Canada 1663–1763: Population, Society, Culture   123
8. The Peripheries of the Empires, 1670–1760   141
9. A Century of Conflict, 1660–1760   170
   Writing about Aboriginal Peoples' History   192

Part II: 1760–1840

Introduction   197
10. The Expansion and Contraction of British North America, 1760–1782   199
11. Loyalties and Loyalists, 1775–1791   223
12. Colonial Politics, War, and Rebellion, 1791–1840   246
13. Peopling British North America, 1791–1860   273
14. The Colonial Economy, 1791–1840   295
15. Colonial Society, 1791–1840   317
16. Colonial Culture, 1791–1840   340
   Writing about Women's History   360

Part III: 1840–1870

Introduction   365
17. Political and Administrative Reform, 1840–1860   367
18. Reorientation: British North America and the Empire after 1840   388
19. Reorientation: British North America and the Continent after 1840   411
20. The West and the North, 1821–1868   432
21. Early Victorian Society, 1840–1870   453
22. Early Victorian Culture, 1840–1870   473
23. Industrialization, 1850–1870   499
24. Unification, 1862–1867   522
   Writing about the History of Confederation   542

Part IV: 1867–1885

Introduction   547
25. The Completion of Confederation, 1867–1873   548
26. Envisioning the New Nation, 1867–1885   572

Notes   599
Index   621

MAPS

Beringia: the 'land bridge' at its greatest extent   6

Distribution of Aboriginal peoples and language areas in the sixteenth century   9

L'Anse aux Meadows site   42

Cartier's first and second voyages   49

A map by Willem Barents, 1598, showing European explorations into Arctic Circle   51

The Descelliers map, 1546   62

'Newfoundland described by Captaine John Mason', 1617   65

Champlain's map of New France, 1632   68

Acadia and environs to 1670   74

'The country of the Five Nations' in the mid-eighteenth century   82

'Novae Franciae Accurata Delineatio, 1657'   90

The Île d'Orléans, 1709   114

New France in 1688   126

European possessions in North America after the peace of Utrecht   143

French territorial claims in Acadia, c. 1720   149

British territorial claims in Acadia, c. 1720   150

French territorial claims in North America, c. 1755   151

British territorial claims in North America, c. 1755   152

'The South Part of Nova Scotia and its Fishing Banks', 1750   153

A map by Thomas Jefferys showing the British claims to Acadia   155

Territory west of Lake Superior, 1754   167

The war in 1755   178

'Wilderness through which General Arnold marched to attack Quebec', 1775   212

Peter Pond's map of the HBC Territory, 1785   216

'A Map of the Great River St John & Waters', 1788   240

Southwestern Lower Canada in 1837   266

British North America in 1825   278

The Oregon Territory   301

Canadian canals   313

Railroads in Canada West   402

British North America in 1849   413

Canada in 1873   569

Canada in 1882   577

The numbered treaties, 1871–1921   590

■ Understanding History

■ Every experienced historian has at some point encountered someone from a totally different disciplinary background who assumes that 'anyone can do history'. In the sense that anyone can research, write, and even publish historical work without specialized training, that assumption is correct. History is one of those fields—creative writing is another—where the standards of achievement can be flexible and intuitive, and where much of the methodology is based on plain common sense. History's accessibility to almost all of us, not simply as readers but as actual researchers, is one of its great charms and greater merits. And many people do engage in historical research without calling it by that name. Everyone who tries to trace her ancestry through the labyrinth of historical records (often called 'genealogy') is involved in a form of historical research. Everyone who tries to research the background to a business project as part of a report on its present status, or to explain how a sports team achieved a championship season, is in a sense 'doing history'. Every criminal trial (and almost every civil one) is at some level a historical reconstruction, although the rules of evidence are somewhat different. The historical mode is one of the most common ways through which we attempt to understand the world we live in.

To say that nearly all of us engage in some form of historical reconstruction, often uncon-sciously, is not to say there are no fundamental rules to such activity. Most of us know instinctively that witnesses can be biased or mistaken, that human motivation is complex, and that in the chronological sequence of events—the establishment of which many non-professional historians regard as the centre of the enterprise—the cause must precede the effect. But history is not a laboratory science. Even the simplest rules of evidence and argument can be difficult to apply in specific situations, particularly if the researcher is operating intuitively. Understanding what causes these difficulties is important, and becoming sensitive to the problems of history is one of the chief benefits of formal historical study.

A good many Canadians (probably nearly as many as commonly read fiction or poetry) read history, for recreation and for information. Unfortunately, general readers often approach historical writing in much the same way they approach fiction, judging a work's value by its success in telling 'a good story'. But of course storytelling is only one of numerous ways in which history can be written. Although, as with fiction, there is great pleasure to be had from reading history simply at the level of entertainment, to remain at that level would be to miss much of the best modern historical writing. It is possible without training or formal critical tools to recognize that a Harlequin romance offers a far less complex view of the world than a Margaret Atwood novel; it is somewhat more difficult to appreciate a parallel difference in history. Readers who expect writers of fiction to have distinctive voices and world views still often assume that all historians participate equally in the effort to recover the truth of the past through application of some unspecified 'scientific' method: if history is about truth, then all historical writing must be more or less equally true, at least if the historian has 'the facts' right. The ordinary reader is frequently unable to distinguish between 'facts' and 'truth', failing to appreciate on one level that factual accuracy is in itself a complex issue and on another level that it has limited value as a critical test.

In addition, many readers fail to distinguish between history as everything that has happened before the present moment (also commonly known as 'the past') and history as the record (usually written) of the unfolding of some event(s) in that past. Yet that past can never be recovered, for reasons I shall discuss. All we can do is attempt to recreate and analyze discrete parts of that past, refracted through the historian's prism. Only this history can be studied and investigated. As a further confusion, history can mean not only the historian's account of the past, but the systematic study of the past as a discipline or a craft. The study of either the work of individual historians or the discipline itself is often known as historiography. Just as filmmakers make a surprising number of movies about the process of making movies, so historians devote more of their energy to examining the making of history than they do to any other single project.

The processes of both reading and researching history can obviously be greatly enhanced by some understanding of the problems that engage historians as they pursue their craft. Before we turn to some of those problems, however, it might be well to consider the question of the value of history.

THE VALUE OF HISTORY

Once upon a time, especially in the nineteenth and earlier twentieth centuries, most people did not question the value of historical study or wonder how it was relevant to their lives. They did not doubt the value of the liberal arts or the humanities, much less debate the benefits of studying languages like Greek or Latin. There are really two separate but related issues inherent in the 'value of history' question. One is whether or not historical study has a sufficient grip on truth and meaning in our modern world to have any value at all, intrinsic or extrinsic. Ultimately, this question involves us in high philosophy and theory, but it also has a particular Canadian edge. The other question is whether or not historical work has a sufficiently attractive vocational pay-off to justify its study at the university. Perhaps we should turn to the latter question first, since it is easier to answer and may be of more interest to the beginning historian.

For many centuries, the opportunity to attend a university was available only to those of outstanding intellectual abilities or privileged socio-economic standing. In a world that did not question the importance of religion, the original purpose of universities was to educate clerics. The university gradually became the centre of humanistic scholarship and enterprise generally, but so long as society valued education for its own sake—chiefly because it was something available only to the privileged few—its specific vocational role was quite insignificant. Universities turned out educated and 'cultured' men (not women until well into the nineteenth century) into a world that took it for granted that such people were important to the society. Specific occupational training was not part of the university's function, and preparation even for such elevated professions as law or medicine was done outside its doors. Yet gradually the notion of vocational training did enter the cloistered world of the university, particularly in North America, and by 1940 it was possible to prepare for nearly any occupation through specialized studies at a university, although such opportunities were still limited to members of the elites. Despite the new vocational bent of the university, occupational studies were largely confined to the post-graduate level; most undergraduate students at universities (as opposed to acknowledged vocational centres such as teachers' training colleges) still expected An Education rather than A Vocation.

The great change in the nature of the university really came after 1945, when the idea took hold that all Canadians were entitled to attend university, and the number of university places was greatly expanded. A dynamic relationship has existed between the democratization of the university and the introduction of the idea that there should be some demonstrable economic value to a university degree. Thus, specific occupational training now starts at the undergraduate rather than the graduate level. Today at many universities it is likely that the majority of students are enrolled in such programs, and even those who are not in such programs themselves commonly expect a university education to provide some kind of occupational entrée or advantage. In the new occupational sweepstakes, a field like history is of less obvious relevance than one like management or accounting or pharmacy or computers. Some historians would prefer to ignore the question of occupational relevance altogether, but the days of a simple liberal arts education for most university students are probably gone forever. History may not ever compete with accounting or pharmacy or medical school as preparation for employment, but it is still superb preparation for many professional programs (assuming that they do not insist on specialization from day one). And one can do more in the workforce with a history specialization than most students might at first think.

There are any number of history-related occupations besides teaching. They include work in archives, libraries, and museums, as well as in government service. 'Heritage' in itself is a major industry in Canada. Other occupations, such as law, journalism, and some branches of the civil service (the diplomatic corps, for example) have traditionally recruited heavily among history graduates, but any job requiring the ability to gather and analyze evidence and then communicate the findings is ideally suited to someone with a background in history. One individual with a graduate degree in history, Mike Smith, has become the general manager of several National Hockey League teams. What students have to do is learn to translate their historical training into the jargon of the contemporary job market. 'Researching term essays in history', for example, can be translated into 'using documentary resources to abstract and analyze complex information'. (At one recent 'interview' for a summer job with a government department, the student applicant was simply asked to summarize a complex document quickly and accurately.) To the extent that history is a discipline that teaches students both to think and to communicate, it should improve their qualifications for almost any job.

Beyond developing essential skills in research, analysis, and communication, what are the uses of history? Certainly few historians today believe—if they ever did—in the use of historical 'laws' of human conduct for predictive purposes. Most historians who have employed historical laws, such as Arnold Toynbee in *A Study in History*, Oswald Spengler in *The Decline of the West*, or Karl Marx in *Capital*, have done so on such an abstract level that it is difficult to translate those laws into specific terms. Toynbee's notion that civilizations pass through recognizable stages paralleling the human life cycle is attractive, but it does not tell us when our civilization will die. Employing the insights of Karl Marx, no reader could have concluded that the 'dictatorship of the proletariat' would come first in Russia, or that it would eventually lead not to a classless society but to the collapse of the Soviet Union. No discipline has worked harder than economics to achieve scientific status, but the whole world has come to appreciate that economists constantly disagree on even the most general level of prediction and analysis.

Yet if history cannot predict, it can help us to understand the difficulty of prediction. In the same way it can help us to recognize the recurrent and ongoing nature of many of society's problems. By and large, historians were far more sanguine about the outcome of the 1992 referendum on the Charlottetown constitutional accord than were the scaremongers on either side of the debate or many of the journalists covering the 'crisis'. Indeed, those with an understanding of Canadian history, constitutional and otherwise, were bound to find the very concept of a 'crisis' suspect, just as they would any other popular journalistic concept, such as 'conspiracy'. The historical record tells us that there have been crises and conspiracies, but equally that these terms have so often been used without justification that they have lost any real meaning. Seen within a historical context, the recent financial collapse and recession, while real enough, seem less frightening, for they have happened many times before.

History provides us not only with a social context but with a personal one as well. The genealogical search for 'roots' has become important for many Canadians seeking to trace their family backgrounds and to understand the circumstances that drove their ancestors across the ocean, or the ways their ancestors' lives changed as a result of the newcomers' arrival. Nor is the question of personal identity merely an individual matter. It is no accident that as minority groups in Canada work to develop themselves as collectivities, they need to establish and assert their historical experience. Over the past 30 years some Canadians have lost interest in the historical mode, adopting what we might call 'the irrelevance of history' position. But this has not been the case with collective 'minorities' such as women, Native peoples, blacks, and ethnic minorities. For these groups, establishing their rightful place in Canadian history has been an absolutely primary function. That these groups' interpretations of their histories have often run counter to the traditional versions of Canadian history does not render them any less consequential—or less historical.

THE ELUSIVE FACT

More than 40 years ago, a television series called *Dragnet* became famous for a catchphrase used by one of its characters, a police detective named Sergeant Joe Friday. When questioning witnesses, Friday always repeated the same request, delivered in an emotionless monotone: 'All I want is the facts, just give me the facts.' The monotone was intended to indicate Friday's objectivity and to extract from his witness a response devoid of personal bias and coloration. Of course, he seldom got 'just the facts'—which from our perspective is exactly the point. Somehow, just as the popular mind in the 1950s associated Joe Friday with facts, so it has more recently come to think of historians as dealing in the same coin. The equation of facts and history has doubtless been assisted by the traditional way of teaching history in the schools, by marching out one name, date, event after another for students to commit to memory and regurgitate at the appropriate time in the course of an examination. Certainly, historians do rely on facts as their basic building blocks; but they do not think of them the way Sergeant Friday did, nor do they use them the way common opinion believes they do.

The *Canadian Oxford Dictionary* offers several meanings for 'fact'. The most familiar is probably number 1: 'a thing that is known to have occurred, to exist, or to be true', although number 4—'truth, reality'—is also very common. Facts, as *Dragnet* suggested, are true things, unsullied by any process of interpretation or conclusion. Such things may exist, but they are much harder to come by than one might expect, for several reasons. One problem is the language in which 'facts' must be stated. Another is the context in which they become significant.

Over the last century we have become increasingly aware that language is not a neutral instrument, but one that carries with it a heavy freight of cultural experience and usage. 'John Cabot discovered Newfoundland in 1497' may seem a straightforward statement of fact, but at least half of the words in it conjure up a whole host of meanings. One of those words is 'discovered'. The implication is that what Cabot found was previously unknown—but of course an Aboriginal population had been living in the area for millennia. Even qualifying the word 'discovered' with the phrase 'by Europeans' doesn't help much, since we now know that the Vikings had settled at L'Anse aux Meadows in the eleventh century, and even they may not have been the first Europeans to cross the Atlantic. 'Discovery' is a complex concept. The term 'Newfoundland' is equally problematic, since in modern geographic terms Cabot was not at all precise about his movements, and the land he sighted may not have been part of the island that we know as Newfoundland today. Indeed, Cabot called the land he saw 'the New-Founde Land', and it was only later that the label was applied to the island. Moreover, Cabot's sightings were not confirmed by anything other than vague self-declarations. To top matters off, there are questions about the identity of John Cabot himself, who started in Italy as Giovanni (or Zuan) Caboto and became John Cabot Montecalunya, a resident of Valencia, in the early 1490s, before he called himself John Cabot of Bristol. Almost all but the most simplistic statements are subject to the same difficulties. Philosophers have spent thousands of years trying to formulate 'true' statements, with very little success, and historians are unlikely to do much better. Almost any 'factual' statement worth making has to be expressed in a language heavily weighted with values and contexts. Language is only one of the challenges in the quest for the fact.

Even if facts could be expressed in a neutral language, such as numbers, we would still need to decide which facts are important. At any given moment there exists a virtual infinity of pieces of information that could be isolated and stated. Most 'historical facts' are simply labels of events and dates, names and movements, which by themselves do not tell us very much. They are not statements in which anything is asserted, and therefore they have no standing as facts. Only when their significance is implicitly or explicitly understood do they acquire any utility or susceptibility to truth. 'The Battle of Vimy Ridge' is not a fact, since it does not assert anything capable of being either true or false. 'The Battle of Vimy Ridge in 1917 was won by the Canadian army' is an assertion the validity of which can be assessed. Whether it is false or true (and hence 'a fact') is another matter entirely. The validity of the statement requires a detailed account of the battle in the context of the war.

One of the chief benefits of modern historical study is that it promotes a healthy skepticism about the neutrality and ultimate truth of the notorious fact. Taken by itself, in isolation, the fact has little meaning. It is only when facts are arranged into some larger picture—some sort of interpretive account—that they acquire significance. Those interpretive pictures themselves are subject to change over time. Anyone today who reads a Canadian history textbook written 40 years ago will be struck by the almost complete absence of any reference to women as important historical figures. Yet 40 years ago the majority of readers—even female readers—took that absence for granted. The absence of women does not mean that women were not present. It simply means that historians of that generation did not regard their activities as worthy of attention. The historian can uncover whole constellations of new facts simply by asking a new question of the historical record, as happened when some scholar asked: 'What about the women?' History is not the study of something eternally fixed, of something that can be 'discovered', but rather the continual dynamic re-investigation and re-evaluation of the past. Moreover, current interpretations have a distinct tendency to mimic society's assumptions about itself. Thus, many historians today find evidence of multiculturalism in Canada's past.

If historians can recover new facts, however, they are still limited to those facts that have been recorded in some way. The records need not be in written form; sometimes they take the form of oral history, sometimes of artifacts. Whatever form the evidence takes, it has to have been preserved. Preservation may be deliberate or serendipitous, but in either case certain biases may be observed. If we think about our own personal history, we realize that not every part of it has been recorded, let alone recorded with equal care; and much of the individual record that does exist has been preserved not through personal choice but to serve bureaucratic purposes. Not every society keeps public records, however, and even in the record-keeping societies, not everyone produces an equal quantity of evidence. Only a relative handful of historical actors, for example, have left behind their own written accounts. Personal evidence tends to be limited to those involved in self-consciously important activity, as defined by any particular society. Such recorders usually represent that society's elite, and what they record represents what the elites think needs recording. We know far more about taxation in the Middle Ages than we do about sexual behaviour, for example. Whatever their limitations, it is with the records that historians must start. They are the primary sources for historical investigation, as distinguished from secondary sources (usually other historians' research gleanings and interpretations). In working with primary sources, historians face two problems: the first one of authenticity, the second one of credibility.

For understandable reasons, historians have to be certain that the records they study are genuine. Historians thus prefer to work with original documents, the so-called 'manuscript' sources (although not all manuscripts are necessarily hand-written). The republication of such material often raises questions of accuracy, which become even more problematic when the docu-

ments have been translated from one language to another. Even the most scrupulous of editors may subtly alter the meaning of a document through changes in punctuation or spelling, and until our own time the editors of historical documents often intervened in other ways as well. A famous editor of Shakespeare named Thomas Bowdler expurgated material that he considered to be in bad taste (his name is now commemorated in the verb 'to bowdlerize'). Other editors silently rewrote texts to what they regarded as the advantage of their authors. Even the appearance of authenticity is no guarantee; many skilful forgeries have been designed to pass close inspection. The famous Shroud of Turin (supposedly showing the imprint of the body of Christ) is not necessarily a deliberate forgery, but recent scientific investigation has found that it could not be authentically associated with the crucifixion. As for the supposedly fifteenth-century 'Vinland Map', discovered in the 1960s, it still has not been satisfactorily authenticated, and many scholars think it is a forgery.

Even if we are dealing with an 'authentic' document, there are still many potential problems to face before we can use it as evidence. Many documents cannot be precisely dated or attributed to a specific author. But these questions must be addressed before the historian—acting all the parts in a court of law except that of witness—can determine the document's credibility. Was the author in a position to be authoritative? Are there reasons, obvious or subtle, for suspecting bias of some kind? Bias may appear in many forms. Authors may seek to justify themselves; they may place their interpretation of events in a context resulting from their place in society or from their ideological assumptions; they may report hearsay; they may adjust their accounts for literary reasons, or simply to tell 'a good story'. Evidence is best if it can be corroborated by more than one source; but supporting evidence is not always available, particularly for specific details. Like the 'facts' derived from them, the documents themselves are seldom unassailable as sources.

Historians work with probabilities rather than certainties, and the more evidence is available, the more likely it is that there will be complications. In any event, students of history need to be both skeptical and critical of what they read, whether documentary evidence itself or interpretations of such material.

THE CONVENTIONS OF HISTORY

Historians have developed a series of conventions for dealing with their raw data. Historical information presented in its unexplicated form—as a series of unrelated facts—is not history as historians understand it, and insufficient attention to interpretation and context is one of the most common faults of beginning historians. Traditionally, the chief mode for historians has been narrative, the recounting of past events in the sequence in which they occurred. Like all aspects of historical work, narrative requires selection—cutting into the seamless web of the past to isolate a particular sequence of events involving a limited number of characters. Narrative deals with the passage of time, and—since it is axiomatic that cause and effect must be in the right sequence—chronology is critical to historical understanding. Many great historians of the past concentrated almost exclusively on narrative, appropriately embellished with description and context; an example is Francis Parkman, who wrote extensively on the early conflict of the French and British in North America. But most modern historians would agree with Arthur Marwick that 'the historian must achieve a balance between narrative and analysis, between a chronological approach and an approach by topic, and, it should be added, a balance between both of these, and, as necessary, passages of pure description "setting the scene", providing routine but essential information, conveying the texture of life in any particular age and environment.'[1] Some historians have even dropped narrative entirely, although the sequence of events remains implicitly crucial to their work.

Despite the common use of the term 'causation' in historical writing, particularly among beginners, philosophers of history have long emphasized that historians really do not deal much in the sort of cause-and-effect relationships usually associated with scientific work. The past is too complex to isolate factors in this way. Instead, historians talk about 'explanation', which is not quite the same as scientific causation. Explanation requires the inclusion of enough context and relevant factors to make it clear that the events in question were neither totally predetermined nor utterly capricious. As E.H. Carr has observed:

> . . . no sane historian pretends to do anything so fantastic as to embrace 'the whole of experience'; he cannot embrace more than a minute fraction of the facts even of his chosen sector or aspect of history. The world of the historian, like the world of the scientist, is not a photographic copy of the real world, but rather a working model which enables him more or less effectively to understand it and to master it. The historian distils from the experience of the past, or from so much of the experience of the past as is accessible to him, that part which he recognizes as amenable to rational explanation and interpretation, and from it draws conclusions.[2]

In their efforts at narrative and/or explanation, historians also use many other conventions. Among them, let us focus on periodization. The division of the past into historical 'periods', while in some ways artificial, serves purposes beyond the organization of a teaching curriculum. By focusing attention on larger units of time, periodization serves to narrow and limit the range of material to be considered and helps to provide a structure for what would otherwise be a meaningless jumble of events and dates. The choice of beginning and end dates for larger historical sequences is hardly arbitrary, but it is still a matter of interpretation. Take, for example, the standard decision to divide Canadian history at

1867, the year of Confederation. This fundamental periodization reflects the assumption not only that political and constitutional development shaped everything else, but also that the creation of a national state called the Dominion of Canada was the critical point in that development. But it makes little sense for many other themes in Canadian history. Historians of Canada continually debate the question of relevant periods. The authors of the first survey of the history of women in Canada, for example, were forced to find a new way of periodizing their account, since the standard political and constitutional periodization reflected a chronology mainly masculine in emphasis.

NEW INTERPRETATIONS

Like all academic disciplines, history is constantly reinterpreting its subject matter. Some of the pressure for reinterpretation is a simple matter of growth: within the past quarter-century, the number of academic positions for historians in Canada has more than quadrupled, with the result that more individuals are now researching and writing within the field. At the same time, technological advances (in computers and photocopiers, for example) and the advent of the relatively inexpensive airline ticket have made it possible for historians to examine and process documentary materials in ways and quantities that would have been unthinkable at the beginning of the 1960s. Other pressures for revision, of course, come from changes in the social context, which is continually raising new questions for historians to explore, and shifts in the climate of opinion.

In history, revisionist movements usually arise out of new developments in three (often related) areas: subject matter, conceptual frameworks, and methodologies. A new development in any one of these areas may be enough on its own to provoke significant revision. When two or three come together (as is often the case), they can completely alter our understanding of the past.

Addressing new subject matter involves asking new questions about hitherto neglected aspects of the past. In Canadian history, with its traditional focus on the political and constitutional ways in which a national state was created, the opportunities for new questions have been quite substantial. Out of a variety of new subjects, we can perhaps offer three examples: women, Aboriginal peoples, and ethnic groups. While each of these subjects would today be regarded as central to any contemporary understanding of Canadian history, they were virtually neglected until recent years. As we have seen, lack of attention to women in the past did not reflect lack of information, but lack of interest on the part of historians. With the simple act of focusing attention on women, a new field of study was opened. In the case of Aboriginal peoples, the subject had not been entirely neglected, but it had virtually always been approached from the perspective of the developing national state. Thus, many of the new questions raised today are aimed at understanding the First Nations' perspectives. As for ethnic groups, research has tended to involve scholars from a variety of disciplines, such as sociology and geography, and has been encouraged by the availability of grant money from governmental agencies at both the federal and provincial levels. Ethnic studies have proved to be politically popular within Canada.

New areas of study often suggest—if not require—new conceptual contexts. In general, all three of the new areas noted above fall under the rubric of 'social history'. As early as 1924, an article on 'The Teaching of Canadian History' advocated the study of the 'actual life of the Canadian people' in 'their efforts to secure a livelihood and then to provide for the higher demands of mind and spirit'.[3] Until recent years, however, much of the research in the social history area concentrated on the upper echelons of society in Canada, the so-called 'elites'. Broadening the social base to include individuals outside the ranks of those whose lives were normally documented (women, Aboriginal people, racial and ethnic minorities, ordinary working men) involved a substantial reconceptualization of the nature of Canada's past.

Studying those 'inarticulate' groups often required new methodologies as well. Perhaps the most important methodological innovation was quantification: generating new data sets by processing existing information not previously practicable for historical purposes out of data such as name-by-name census returns. At its worst, quantification could be little more than mindless number-crunching, but at its best it enabled historians to open up whole categories of hitherto unusable documentation. The information collected by the Dominion Bureau of the Census or the various provincial departments of Vital Statistics has provided much new insight into the way ordinary Canadians have lived (and loved) in the past. Computers have made it easier for historians to process large amounts of aggregate information— although the axiom 'Garbage In, Garbage Out' continues to apply. The complex processes of collecting and analyzing new categories of data have been contentious, and beginning historians should understand that the apparently simple act of producing a new set of information involves many steps and many disagreements. 'Hard' numbers and percentages are no more sacrosanct than information that appears 'softer'. Moreover, quantified data still require interpretation, and are subject to all the standard rules that apply to historical explanation.

In many respects, the most important single innovation in historical study over the past generation has been the general acceptance of non-documentary sources, which make it possible for us to recover some notion of the lives of those who did not live in a world of documents. The role of Aboriginal land claims in this shift is important, but not the only factor. Women and other groups have also benefited greatly from the substantial broadening of the data base.

Where the Aboriginal past has had special impact is in the realm of authority. The philosophical problems of expert testimony in court trials are perhaps even more serious than is generally realized. Most historical arguments and interpretations are judged in the free market of opinion by one's historical peers, and there is seldom a 'final judgement'. In court cases, however, the judge pronounces a verdict that appears to rely on and thus to validate one or more particular historical interpretations or methodological approaches. Does the court's approval mean that the historical evidence or technique employed takes on the truth? Has something actually been validated?

Although explicit controversies do arise within the field of Canadian history, especially in the courts, they are probably less common than controversies among historians of other nations, notably the United States and Great Britain. To some extent the profession in Canada has avoided confrontations by allowing each practitioner his or her own area of specialization (or 'turf'). This has made good sense because the number of questions not yet adequately explored in the history of Canada is considerable. Whatever the reasons for the muting of controversy, disagreements in Canadian historiography have had less to do with specific points and interpretations within a single tradition than with first principles and underlying assumptions. Thus, Canadian historians tend to disagree only at the macro level, as in the current debate over Canadian 'national history', which is really a debate among scholars with two totally different sets of assumptions about the role of narrative in the past. Those on the moving frontier of scholarship are in some ways far less embattled than those still working in older traditions, since they can simply add their 'new' interpretations onto the old ones.

Because history is a cumulative subject, students should not think that the latest books and journal articles are necessarily better simply by virtue of their dates of publication. Many older works of historical scholarship can still be regarded as the best treatments of their topics. This is particularly true in traditional areas of study that have not attracted much attention from modern scholars, such as the military history of the War of 1812. Earlier generations were fond of publishing editions of documents, which if well-transcribed, translated, and edited are just as valuable today as they were a century ago. The complete (and most commonly used) edition of the *Jesuit Relations* in English was published between 1896 and 1901. On some topics our only sources are earlier documents; for example, Richard Hakluyt's sixteenth-century accounts are still essential for any study of English overseas voyages.

By now it should be clear that both the writing and the reading of history are extremely complicated enterprises. Whole books with titles like *Understanding History* or *The Nature of History* have been devoted to introducing students to the complexities of the craft, and in the space of a few pages it is impossible to explore all the potential dimensions. In any case, readers of this book should understand that every work of history involves a series of decisions to hold various contradictions in dynamic tension. Among the most important issues held in tension in this book are the following:

1. *Interpretive complexity versus authority.* Virtually every sentence in this work (or any other work of history) could be hedged in with conflicting evidence and interpretation. The result would almost certainly be incomprehensible. I have chosen to favour readability over total academic accuracy. This is not to say that I do not recognize the issues of interpretive complexity. Rather, I have consciously addressed them in two ways: by introducing questions of interpretation into the text on a regular basis, and by including essays on historiography (one for each of the book's three sections).

2. *Individual biography versus groups and forces.* One problem that all historians face (or ought to face) is how to make the material interesting to readers. As any newspaper editor will tell you, readers like their stories to have people in them. This work uses the experiences of individual people to represent and suggest the complex groups and forces that lie behind them. I do not subscribe to the Great Person theory of history, but I do believe in personalizing history as much as possible.

3. *Overarching master narrative versus the complex voices of social and cultural history.* Whether or not Canadian history has a single narrative is a hotly debated issue today, sometimes posed in the form of the question 'Is there a national history?' The single narrative is also related to the problem of authority, although the two are not the same. A coherent and connected single narrative could be based on the concept of the development of the nation, or on viewing events from the perspective of that nation, or on something quite different. The point is that any such narrative line represents an abstraction. Critics of the abstract, single-narrative approach associate it with the imposition of a hegemonic 'master principle' that in turn is often taken to represent the sequence of events preferred by the 'men in suits' or the 'ruling class' or the 'politicians in Ottawa'. Many groups are commonly left outside such a master narrative: workers, racial and cultural minorities, women, inhabitants of marginalized regions, inhabitants of alienated regions (e.g., Quebec for much of the twentieth century). Over the past 40 years, Canadian historians have concentrated on recovering the voices of these groups. But if those voices were all we heard, telling their own stories in their own tongues, the resulting cacophony would be unintelligible; and to establish chronology and meaningful periodization, we need a structure that will provide some common reference points. Hence a master narrative of some kind is still essential.

The master narrative around which this book is structured, into which all the other stories are woven, is a highly abstract one that may be labelled 'the history of Canada'. I hope this discussion will help readers to understand the chapters that follow.

THE SIGNIFICANCE OF 1885

Using watershed dates to separate major periods of historical development is always problematic, but there is something compelling about 1885 as a symbolic year for dividing the formative from the modern period in Canadian history. Unlike the more traditional dividing point of 1867, which marks the beginning of the confederated Canada, 1885 is significant for containing not just one event but several events of far-reaching importance. It marks the completion of Canada's first intercontinental transportation system, connecting the entire nation from sea to sea. Politically crucial, the Canadian Pacific Railway was also visible evidence of the establishment of an integrated Canadian economy that would experience further industrialization over the ensuing decades. The year 1885 also marks the firm establishment of Canada's control over the West, with the military defeat of the Métis and their Native allies. The execution of Louis Riel provided Canada with a major political martyr, and the frenzied public debate surrounding his case brought to the surface a deep division between anglophone Canada (chiefly Ontario) and francophone Canada (chiefly Quebec). Moreover, Riel's execution in 1885, and that of his Indian ally Wandering Spirit, began to symbolize the attitude to its minorities of the Canadian government of the time, as did the decision of Ottawa that same year to impose a head tax on every Chinese person entering the country.

Canada would change enormously after 1885. Indeed, the very rate of change would be speeded up. A British North American of 1785 could probably have functioned in the Canada of 1885, despite many changes. But that a Canadian of 1885 could easily adapt to the Canada of 1985 is most unlikely.

J.M. Bumsted
Winnipeg, 2009

A confrontation between Inuit and English sailors, 1577. The artist, John White, was a member of Martin Frobisher's expedition in search of a northwest passage. © Copyright The British Museum.

PART ONE

■ To 1760

■ In the beginning were the Paleolithic people who migrated to North America, probably from Siberia, sometime around 15,000 BCE (Before the Common Era). Gradually their descendants spread out across the continent from west to east. Although life for the First Peoples was not idyllic, for the most part they lived in harmony with nature. Occasional visitors began arriving from Europe perhaps simultaneously with the Siberians, certainly as early as 1000 CE (Common Era),[1] but their presence had no serious consequences until the end of the fifteenth century. Then the trickle of Europeans turned into a flood, bringing new diseases, technologies, and cultural influences that had a profound—often devastating—impact on the indigenous people. In many ways, the single most important theme of the period before 1750 was the complex interaction between the First Peoples and the intruders.

Several European nations spent the sixteenth century searching the northern part of the continent for sources of wealth comparable to those found by the Spanish and Portuguese to the south. Finally they realized that if they were to exploit North America effectively, they would have to establish year-round settlements. Serious colonization began in the seventeenth century. In the territory that would become Canada, the two imperial nations were England (later Great Britain) and France.

The English initially established themselves on Newfoundland, where they concentrated on extracting wealth from the sea in the form of fish, especially cod. Over the following decades they founded colonies all down the eastern seaboard. The French settled first in the coastal region of the mainland (Acadia) but soon moved up the St Lawrence River, and in 1608 they established a settlement at Quebec as a base from which to exploit the furs available through trade with the local First Nations. Thus the colony of Canada began its life dependent on the Aboriginal people who supplied the furs. Even after the struggling colony was taken over by the French Crown, in 1663, the fur trade continued to be a central influence on its development. Leading the French into alliances with the northern peoples, and permanent warfare with the Iroquois, the fur trade also spurred them to continue searching for new sources of furs, first to the west and then to the south, down the Mississippi Valley as far as the

Gulf of Mexico. Inevitably, such expansion brought the French into conflict with the British, whose colonies along the eastern seaboard were much more populous than those of New France, and extremely dynamic economically.

Conflict was endemic in the years before 1760, involving the First Nations, the French, and the English in various combinations. In 1713 Britain gained control of most of the Atlantic region, and for several decades it tolerated the French-speaking, Roman Catholic inhabitants of Acadia—now renamed Nova Scotia. But by the mid-1750s the two European rivals were once again at war, and the British expelled the Acadians. The fate of the continent was decided at Quebec in 1759, and after 1760 the British were the political masters of most of North America. Whether they could maintain their control was an open question.

CHAPTER ONE

The Peoples of Early North America

■ Until very recently, most textbooks on Canadian history began with the arrival of Europeans on the Atlantic coast at the end of the fifteenth century. The standard justification for choosing this starting point was that 'history' could not exist without written records. Accordingly, the period before 1500 was labelled 'pre-history' and set aside for specialists in disciplines such as archaeology, anthropology, or linguistics, when it was covered at all. Over the last few decades, however, historians have become less concerned about the absence of written records documenting the early history of humankind in North America. They have come to appreciate that there are other kinds of historical evidence, and that the distinction between 'pre-history' and 'history' was an artificial construct helping to perpetuate many misconceptions about the continent's First Peoples.

This chapter has three major aims. The first is to outline the evidence that does exist regarding the early human presence in North America. The second is to identify some of the major problems of interpretation presented by that evidence. The third is to offer a very brief survey of the major cultural groups who by 1500 had already inhabited the northern part of North America for many thousands of years.

THE CREATION OF THE WORLD

According to the Plains Cree, the world was created in three stages.[1] In the first stage the Creator, with the help of the Sun and other spirits, produced *Manitowitisin*—a being part spirit and part human who was able to talk with the animals. But his descendants strayed from the Creator's plan for reasons so terrible they could not be talked about, so the Creator destroyed them and started anew. This time he made *Asiskiwiyin*, Earthen Man, and gave him intelligence and knowledge; the Fire Spirit provided fire to cook with and Pointed Arrow supplied tools and weapons. When a giant people from another planet arrived on their island, however, conflict developed. The Creator decided that humans were ruining the world with their intelligence, and he punished them. The earth shook and began to flood. One of the people—*Wisahkecahk*, or 'Like a Spirit'—had a vision showing him how to build a great raft, which he used to rescue many of the smaller animals in pairs. Also on the raft was *Omistikos*, the first man to inhabit the new island that emerged out of the flood. The descendants of *Omistikos*—the *iyiniwak*—lived on that island (the present earth), and as their numbers grew they extended the area of their habitation to the prairies.

TIMELINE

30,000–15,000 BCE
Humans cross Beringia land bridge from Siberia to North America.

12,000 BCE
Human occupation of site near Clovis, New Mexico.

9000 BCE
Spread of fluted stone points in North America. Salmon fishing culture emerges among Northwest Coast peoples.

7000 BCE
Gourds grown in Mexico.

6500 BCE
Dogs first appear in North America.

6000 BCE
North American landforms, climate, and sea level have stabilized. Plano (ripple-flaked) points appear in North America. Early Archaic peoples from Eastern Woodlands migrate to the Plains.

3200 BCE
Ceramics made in Peru. Sumerian civilization at its height. First evidence of written language.

3000 BCE
Plains peoples hunt bison by driving them over cliffs. North American forest reaches its northernmost extension.

2500 BCE
The first libraries established, in Egypt.

2000 BCE
Paleo-Eskimos begin spreading from Alaska to Greenland.

500 BCE
Greek city-state civilization at its height.

500 CE
Corn is cultivated in what is now southern Ontario.

600
Dorset population disappears from Newfoundland. Europe invaded by 'barbarians'.

1000
Tobacco and ceramic pots appear in southern Ontario.

1525
Modern horses introduced to North America.

This Cree story, or creation myth, was passed down orally through many generations. Other First Nations have their own traditional accounts of the creation. (For three other Aboriginal legends, see pp. 12, 16, and 19.) More examples of these stories are available. For many years, myths and legends of this kind were regarded with suspicion; the only accounts considered worthy of study were those recorded in writing. Today, academic views have shifted and oral traditions are being examined with new interest. Even so, science still depends on material evidence, and for the far distant past most of the material evidence we have consists of human artifacts (usually of stone, which survives better than leather or wood) found and identified by archaeologists. The dates assigned to such artifacts typically depend on radiocarbon-dating of organic materials associated with them.

THE EARLY RECORD

According to the standard academic view, the First Nations peoples probably came to North America from Asia during one (or more) of the most recent ice ages, when the sea was low enough to expose a strip of land called Beringia, linking Siberia and Alaska. Since the northern part of the continent was still covered by glaciers, the migrants would have had to find a gap between the ice sheets and follow it south.[2] The earliest indisputable evidence of a human presence in North America was discovered in the 1930s in Clovis, New Mexico, in the form of flint spear points dated at roughly 12,000 BCE, although most archaeologists would date the first migrants' arrival on the continent much earlier, to allow time for them to get to New Mexico.[3]

It is an axiom of science that the simplest explanation fitting the known facts is usually the most accurate one, and the simplicity of the Beringia theory has been one of the greatest arguments in its favour. Another is the fact that many North American Aboriginal people do share some physical characteristics, such as blood types and dental features, with Asian peoples. In the absence of any hard evidence to the contrary—in particular, evidence of an earlier occupation or a different time sequence—gradually the idea of a Siberian origin was accepted as the conventional wisdom. Nevertheless, in recent years the Beringia theory has come under increasing attack. As new evidence pushes the dates for human occupation elsewhere in the world ever farther back, many critics find it unlikely that the Americas could have remained without human inhabitants for so long. Others point to the fact that very few early human remains have been found in the northwestern part of the continent, where the first immigrants supposedly arrived from Siberia; yet many extremely old remains have been uncovered on Canada's east coast, more than 6,000 km from Beringia. The few specimens of early humans found on the west coast of North America have

not shown a close resemblance to contemporary Aboriginal people; this was notably the case with 'Kennewick Man', found in Washington state in 1996 and recently dated at about 8000 BCE. A skull recently found in Brazil, of about the same age as the Clovis find, suggests African rather than Asian features.[4] And a skull found in Mexico in the 1950s and studied carefully at the beginning of the twenty-first century (dubbed 'Peñon Woman') has also proven to be of Clovis age or older, and resembles Kennewick Man much more than the Siberians. Archaeologists in Chile have unearthed artifacts that predate the Clovis evidence by thousands of years,[5] and a recent find in South Carolina has been dated sometime before the last Ice Age. In addition, recent studies of blood types and teeth across the Americas suggest that a single origin in Siberia cannot account for the diversity that exists today.

The hard documentation available is still insufficient to disprove the Beringia theory, but softer evidence does tend to undermine it. For example, linguists point to the striking variety of Aboriginal languages found in the Americas— more than 50 in Canada alone—and argue that 14,000 years is simply not long enough for such diversification to occur. A number of alternative theories have been proposed, most of which posit pre-Beringia intrusions by various peoples, mainly (though not exclusively) from Europe. According to these theories, Europeans, Africans, and Asians had been making unrecorded visits to America for thousands of years. Although earlier generations of mainstream scholars categorically dismissed those theories as products of a crackpot amateur fringe, many experts now think that such contacts quite likely did occur, but were without great significance except locally. Other explanations for North American settlement patterns, such as a theory that early immigrants floated down the west coast in small boats, have also gained increasing credibility. So, too, have views that early humankind, leaving no documentable traces, crossed an ice or land bridge many thousands of years before the date assigned to Clovis.[6]

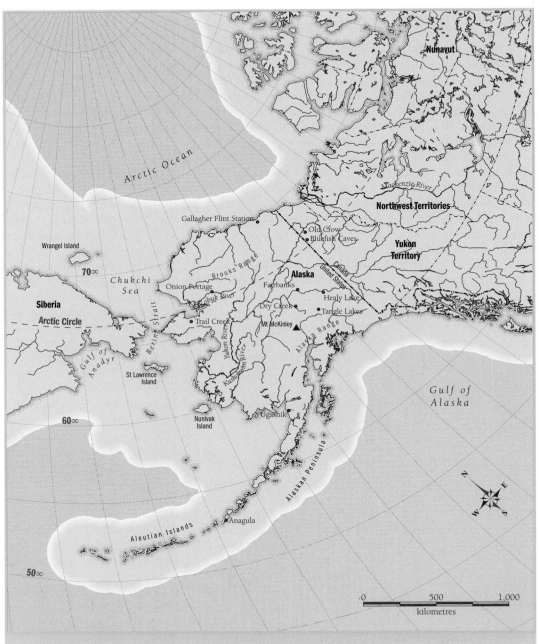

Beringia: The shaded area shows the 'land bridge' at its greatest extent, approximately 20,000 years ago. Adapted from Brian M. Fagan, *The Great Journey: The Peopling of Ancient North America* (London: Thames and Hudson, 1987), 100.

At this stage it seems unlikely that the Beringia theory will ever be entirely disproved: there is simply too much genetic and linguistic evidence to support the view that most of today's First Nations are closely related to Asian peoples, but equally, too much evidence has accumulated to deny categorically other intrusions. Perhaps a large wave of Siberian migrants did arrive as the Beringia theory proposes, but had been preceded by other people arriving from different places by different routes; or perhaps some people came from Siberia in a much earlier period than the present model allows. It is also possible that new discoveries will force a wholesale rethinking of the question.

In any event, even if the human presence in North America is pushed back as far as 50,000 years, we are still looking at a relatively recent phenomenon in relation to the age of the earth. The glacial record shows that human habitation was possible for only the last few long-term climate cycles. For the period in which humans have lived on the continent, the dominant ecological factor was the climate: the naturally occurring complexes of meteorological patterns found in defined regions.[7]

The indisputable evidence of an ice age as recently as 10,000 years ago reminds us that climatic conditions on our earth are constantly changing. For our purposes, the millennia since the first documented human presence in America can be divided into four periods. The first, lasting from 11,000 BCE to 8000 BCE, was a period of rapid glacial retreat during which plants and animals reoccupied the land that had been covered by the ice. From 8000 to 5000 BCE the climate was warmer and drier than before, with rapid changes in climate and vegetation. From 5000 to 500 BCE, the continent was very warm, and the forest reached its northernmost extension around 3000 BCE.[8]

Since 500 BCE climatic conditions have been relatively stable, although minor shifts likely produced substantial change along the borders between climatic zones. The period between 500

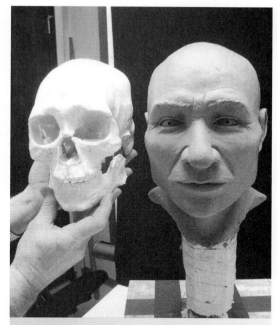

■ 'Kennewick Man': a re-creation of his facial features based on the skull. Photo André Ranieri, *Tri-City Herald*.

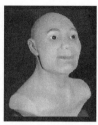

■ Skull and re-creation of Peñon Woman. The skull was discovered in Mexico in the 1950s and is believed to be of Clovis age or earlier.

BCE and 400 CE was one of severe changes from winter to summer, while from 400 to 900 more moderate conditions prevailed and the forest again extended northwards. Between 1200 and 1500 the climate turned cooler and drier, again driving the tree line south; and from 1550 to 1850 further cold reduced the growing season and sent the forests still farther south. The low point of this period was reached in 1816, the infamous 'year without a summer' during which much of the northern hemisphere failed to produce any harvestable crops. Since 1850 Canada has experienced slight warming trends within a generally stable climate, although there have been regional variations in factors such as rainfall. Today, many scientists think that another major shift may have begun in the 1980s. (The long-term history of climate change is one reason why some experts are reluctant to place the principal responsibility for the apparent warming trend of recent years on the 'greenhouse effect'.)

Human activities on the continent roughly correspond to climatic patterns. Over time, as the climate stabilized, humans would become increasingly adept at modifying their environment. However, the first people to inhabit North America, the Paleo-Indians, had to adapt to local conditions. Gradually moving across the continent, these Paleo peoples depended mainly on large mammals such as bison, caribou, and, in some areas, woolly mammoth.

In the same period, however, the last ice age was coming to an end. Melting glaciers caused sea levels to rise and altered weather patterns, and these changes in turn affected the habitats on which plants and animals depended. Paleo-Indian people adapted to these environmental changes by effectively transforming themselves. Although small family-based bands continued to follow a pattern of seasonal migration, with the end of the ice age (around 8000 BCE) they began to exploit a much broader range of resources. In the process they adapted existing tools and techniques and, where necessary, developed new ones—nets and baskets, for example, to take

advantage of the fish and shellfish available in coastal areas. And, since a more diverse subsistence base meant that less territory was needed to support the band, individual groups were able to become increasingly specialized in their own local areas—and increasingly differentiated from other groups. Together, these developments mark the transition from Paleolithic to Archaic culture. Although archaeologists place the Archaic period between 8000 and 500 BCE, some groups would continue to practise Archaic ways of life well into the nineteenth century.[9]

Environmental conditions dictated that the southern part of the continent would be more welcoming to humans than the northern. Nevertheless, substantial populations belonging to three major linguistic families—Algonquian (by far the largest), Iroquoian, and Athapaskan—established themselves across much of what is now southern Canada. Archaeological evidence of materials such as sea shells, or Great Lakes copper, at sites hundreds of kilometres from their places of origin shows that extensive exchange networks were already in place thousands of years ago, providing access to many more resources than were available in any one region. And trade goods were not the only things that travelled from one group to another: so did information.

FIRST PEOPLES: A REGIONAL OVERVIEW

What follows is a very brief introduction to the major Aboriginal groups as they existed across the northern part of the continent around the year 1500, focusing here on means of subsistence; broader questions of culture will be discussed in Chapter 2. Nevertheless, one cultural issue that has to be addressed from the start is the fact that in many cases the names these groups have come to be known by are not what they called themselves, but what Europeans called them. Sometimes the European terms were rough approximations, as in 'Micmac', 'Nishka', or 'Kutchin'; today those names are more accurately rendered 'Mi'kmaq', 'Nisga'a',

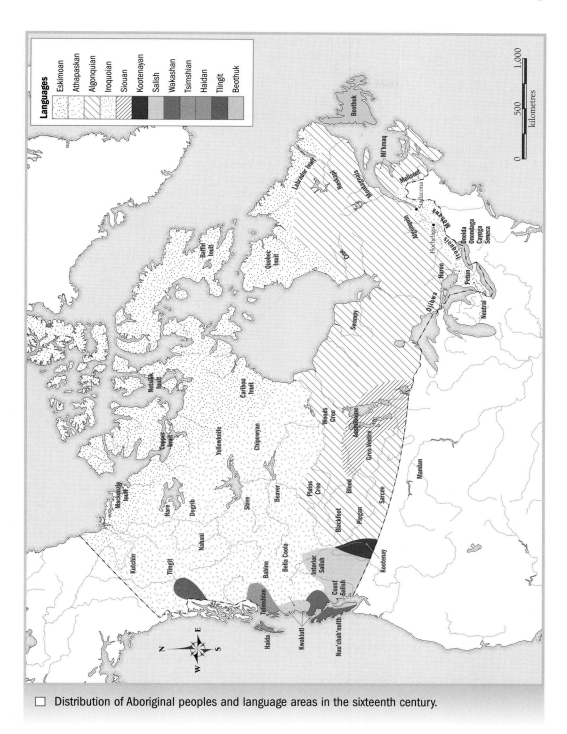

Languages

Eskimoan
Athapaskan
Algonquian
Iroquoian
Siouan
Kootenayan
Salish
Wakashan
Tsimshian
Haidan
Tlingit
Beothuk

0   500   1,000
kilometres

Beothuk

Mi'kmaq

Maliseet

Stadacona

Mohawk

Labrador Inuit

Naskapi

Montagnais

Hochelaga

Abenaki

Iroquois

Oneida
Onondaga
Cayuga
Seneca

Huron

Petun

Ojibwa

Neutral

Baffin Inuit

Quebec Inuit

Cree

Swampy

Netsilik Inuit

Caribou Inuit

Woods Cree

Assiniboine

Gros Ventre

Copper Inuit

Yellowknife

Chipewyan

Mandan

Mackenzie Inuit

Hare

Dogrib

Slave

Beaver

Plains Cree

Blood

Piegan

Sarcee

Blackfoot

Kutchin

Tlingit

Nahani

Babine

Bella Coola

Interior Salish

Kootenay

Tsimshian

Coast Salish

Haida

Kwakiutl

Nuu'chah'nulth

N E S W

☐ Distribution of Aboriginal peoples and language areas in the sixteenth century.

and 'Gwich'in'. Sometimes the Europeans adopted a term used by a different Native group: 'Maliseet' was a Mi'kmaq term for the people who call themselves 'Wuastukwiuk', and many of us were taught that 'Eskimo' originated as an Ojibwa name for the Inuit (though this derivation is no longer accepted).[10] In other cases people came to be known by European names that had nothing to do with any Aboriginal language. 'Huron', for instance, comes from a French term referring to rough hair;

■ 'Homme acadien': a Mi'kmaq hunter. Hand-coloured etching, c. 1788–96, from original by Jacques Grasset de Saint-Sauveur, published in *Tableaux des principaux peuples de l'Europe, de l'Asie, de l'Afrique, de l'Amérique et les découvertes des Capitaines Cook, La Pérouse, etc.* (Paris et Bordeaux, 1796–8). LAC, C-21112.

the 'Hurons' themselves—actually a confederacy of several nations—used the name 'Wendat'.

THE ATLANTIC REGION

The earliest traces of a human presence on the eastern seaboard come from near Cobequid Bay, Nova Scotia, where the remains of a Paleo-Indian site—perhaps a seasonal camp for caribou hunters—have been dated to roughly 8,600 BCE.[11] Archaeological evidence can be hard to find in the Atlantic region because rising sea levels have washed away many coastal settlements, but we know that the Paleo-Indians were followed by a succession of Archaic cultures (Early, Middle, and Late). By approximately 500 BCE, Maritime cultures were moving into the Woodland or Ceramic period, marked by the manufacture of clay pots for cooking and storage. Different groups developed their own combinations of hunting, fishing, and gathering, depending on their location.

The first people to inhabit the island that we know as Newfoundland belonged to the Maritime Archaic tradition and arrived there from Labrador at least 5,000 years ago. In time, two successive Paleo-Eskimo peoples would follow the same route across the Strait of Belle Isle, the second of which, known to us as the Dorset (after an archaeological find at Cape Dorset), are thought to have disappeared around 600 CE. By then another people had settled on the island as well. The origins of these people, who came to be known as the Beothuk, are obscure, and although it has been suggested that their language belonged to the Algonquian family, even that is subject to debate. Like the Paleo-Eskimos, the Beothuk relied on the sea for much of the year, following the caribou migrations inland in the depths of winter.

By 1500 the modern Maritime provinces and Gaspé Peninsula were home to the Mi'kmaq, the northernmost speakers of Eastern Algonquian. Subject to severe winters, this region of heavy forests, tidal rivers, and coastal harbours was not well suited to agriculture, and although the Mi'kmaq did grow some tobacco, they were primarily hunters and fishermen who used the region's extensive river system to travel between the interior and the coast. In summer they would gather in groups of up to 200 at traditional locations along the water to fish (using weirs) and collect shellfish. In winter, smaller bands regularly hunted their own traditional territories.

A little to the west of the Mi'kmaq lived two other Algonquian peoples: the Wuastukwiuk (Maliseet) around the Saint John River basin and the Passamaquoddy around the Bay of Fundy and Passamaquoddy Bay in the present state of Maine. The dialects spoken by these two peoples were mutually comprehensible, but quite distinct from the Mi'kmaq language. By 1500 the Wuastukwiuk had begun growing corn—a reflection of the richness of the land along the Saint John, as well as influences from the horticulturalists to the south—but were still principally hunters. So, too, were the Passamaquoddy, though of sea mammals rather than game.[12]

A MI'KMAQ LEGEND
GLOOSCAP'S ORIGIN

This text was collected by the Baptist missionary Silas Tertius Rand (1810–89) sometime during a 40-year association with the wandering Mi'kmaq people of Nova Scotia. He heard this story about the supernatural character Glooscap from Gabriel Thomas of Fredericton. Rand had learned the language in 1846, and translated the legends into English in his posthumously published book *Legends of the Micmacs* (1894).

Glooscap was one of twins. Before they were born, they conversed and consulted together how they would better enter the world. Glooscap determined to be born naturally; the other resolved to burst through his mother's side. These plans were carried into effect. Glooscap was first born; the mother died, killed by the younger as he burst the walls of his prison. The two boys grew up together, miraculously preserved.

After a time the younger inquired of Glooscap how the latter could be killed. Glooscap deemed it prudent to conceal this, but pretended to disclose the secret, lest his brother, who had slaughtered the mother, should also kill him. But he wished at the same time to know how the younger one could be despatched, as it might become convenient to perform the same operation upon him. So he told his brother very gravely that nothing would kill him but a blow on the head dealt with the head of a cat-tail flag. Then the brother asked, 'And how could you be killed?' 'By no other weapon,' was the answer, 'than a handful of bird's-down.'

One day the younger brother tried the experiment. Procuring a cat-tail flag, he stepped up slyly behind his friend, and gave him a smart blow on the head, which stunned him; he left him on the ground for dead. But after a while he came to; and now it was his turn. So he collected a handful of down, and made a ball of it; and with this ball he struck his younger brother and killed him.

Glooscap had many enemies, visible and invisible. The wolves were his dogs; and their dolorous howl and the scream of the loon were notes of lamentation. These animals and birds were lamenting for their master, now that he was gone away.

SOURCE: Silas Tertius Rand, *Legends of the Micmacs* (New York and London: Longmans, Green, and Co., 1894), 339-40.

THE SHIELD

To the north, climatic and vegetation boundaries had continued to shift throughout the time of human occupation, but one constant was the vast expanse of the Pre-Cambrian (Canadian) Shield. Across the sprawling territory above the St Lawrence, between what is now Labrador and the drainage area of James Bay, lived the Innu (Montagnais–Naskapi). A region inhospitable to agriculture could not support large numbers of human inhabitants. Even small hunting bands had to travel huge distances in pursuit of the species on which their lives depended: moose and caribou.

Farther west lived several groups that the Europeans would call 'Algonquins', and to their west—north of the Great Lakes as far as the prairies—the Ojibwa or Chippewa. Humans living in this region had always been hunters, presumably of caribou. But as the climate warmed and the forests began to move north, the herds disappeared and the people were forced to adapt to a new environment of mixed hardwood forests, which covered central and eastern Canada between 6000 and 4000 BCE. In these woodlands a culture emerged based on a much wider variety of species. The Ojibwa supplemented their predecessors' diet of game and fish with plant foods—ranging from berries to wild rice to maple syrup–and as a result were able to increase their numbers relatively quickly. Even this more hospitable environment, however, did not lend itself to agriculture. If they were to remain alive, the Ojibwa could not stay in one place. Thus, their basic social unit remained the hunting band.

THE GREAT LAKES

South of the Ojibwa, in the more temperate, fertile woodlands around the lower Great Lakes, lived several peoples belonging to the Iroquoian language family. The Huron lived south of Georgian Bay in what is now northern Simcoe County, Ontario. The Petun resided to their west, the Attiwandaronk (Neutrals) along the north shore of Lake Erie, and the Five Nations Iroquois (Mohawk, Oneida, Onondaga, Cayuga, and Seneca) south of the lakes, in present-day New York State. Beginning about 1,500 years ago, these peoples adopted a practice already in wide use to the south, in the Mississippi Valley: they began to grow corn. The consequences were dramatic. Because domesticated plants provided a more stable food supply than hunting, they made it possible for a small area to support a relatively large population. People might still hunt and fish, but they no longer needed to travel great distances in pursuit of game. Once it became possible to settle in one area more or less permanently, the Iroquoians began to establish villages made up of longhouses—large communal homes, usually housing between five and ten nuclear families. A large village might contain upwards of 100 longhouses and some 3,000 people. Smaller villages were more common, however.[13]

In the slash-and-burn style of agriculture that the Iroquoians practised, the land was cleared for fields by cutting the trees and burning off the ground cover; seeds (first corn, then beans, squash, sunflowers, and tobacco) were planted in holes made with a digging stick; then earth was hoed up around the plants into mounds—up to 6,000 per hectare in fields as much as 25 hectares in area. Once the land had been cleared by the men, planting, cultivation, and harvesting were the responsibility of women and children. The soil, a sandy loam, was relatively easy to work, but after several years of steady production it would become exhausted. At that point the entire community would move to another site with more fertile soil.

Land was treated as a unit of production; it did not confer status or wealth, and unused land was held in common. But families possessed their own farm plots, as large as they could reasonably cultivate. Thus, unlike hunting and gathering peoples, horticulturalists were able to accumulate possessions, particularly food sup-

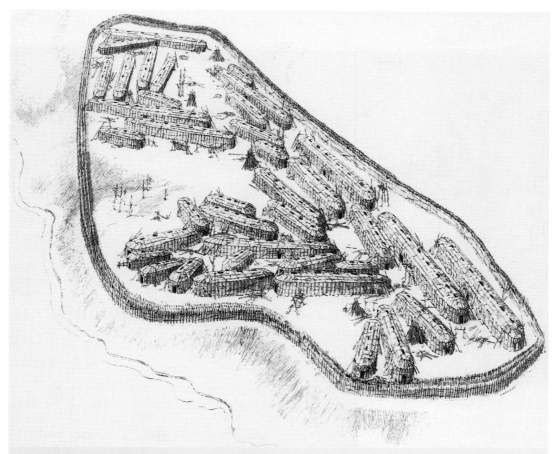

■ This reconstruction of the Draper site, east of Toronto, shows a Huron village in the sixteenth century. A large longhouse—up to 7.5 metres wide and perhaps 30 metres long—would contain several hearths, each shared by two families. A large village might consist of more than a hundred longhouses and some 3,000 people. Drawing by Ivan Kocsis. Courtesy London (Ont.) Museum of Archaeology.

plies for the winter, and to that extent agricultural produce did represent a form of wealth. Hoarding was discouraged, however, and goods were shared through games of chance and ceremonies such as gift-giving. Artifacts discovered hundreds of kilometres from their presumed points of origin indicated the development of complex trading patterns among the early Eastern Woodland peoples;[14] in particular,

Iroquoian corn was traded with the Algonquian groups to the north. Apart from corn, shells and chert (a crystalline quartz) were the most highly prized trade goods.

PLAINS AND PARKLAND

In the huge expanse between the Great Lakes and the Rockies, large mammals remained the centre

■ 'Indian Hunters. Pursuing the Buffalo in the Early Spring', Peter Rindisbacher, 1824 or earlier. These men are Assiniboine, but the artist later repainted the scene, adding a feather headdress and identifying the hunters as Blackfoot instead. LAC, C-114467.

of human economies. When the mammoth, the earliest prey, became extinct, it was replaced by species more familiar to our own time, including the Plains buffalo (or bison). With the arrival of the horse—introduced to southwestern North America by the Spanish in the 1500s and gradually moving north over the next two centuries—the Plains peoples would develop one of the world's great equestrian cultures, but until then they hunted on foot, often stampeding the animals over cliffs or herding them into gullies or 'pounds' where they could be killed with spears or stone hammers. Head-Smashed-in Buffalo Jump in present-day Alberta (today a UNESCO World Heritage Site) was used by four cultures in succession over more than 5,000 years.[15] Because they needed to follow the herds as they moved in search of forage, the Plains cultures did not establish permanent habitations. Instead, they developed the highly portable hide tipi, and used dogs as pack animals.

Changes in spear- and arrow-points indicate that the Plains cultures were influenced by developments to the south.[16] Burial practices also suggest southern influences, and graves containing goods from far distant regions, such as shells and copper, point to the existence of elaborate trade networks. Although horticulture was practised at times in several areas of the prairies, recurring droughts made hunting and gathering a more reliable survival strategy.

Not all of the region between the Great Lakes and the Rockies was prairie, however. Between the Shield and the southern Plains was a zone of heavy forest alternating with open clearings covered with high grasses. This parkland, as it came to be called, extended west from the Red River to the north branch of the Saskatchewan, and ultimately into the Peace River country. The lives of people in this region had more in common with those of the eastern hunters than of the buffalo hunters to the south.

A CREE LEGEND
HOW CHAHKABESH SNARED THE SUN

This legend was recorded over the winter of 1955–6 at the home of C. Douglas Ellis at Albany Post. The storyteller was Simeon Scott, a resident of Fort Albany and a native speaker of Swampy Cree. The text was translated into English by Ellis.

Now, once more, another story about Chahkabesh. . . . One morning Chahkabesh went off walking about in his search to sustain himself. At last he reached a very high mountain. It was then that . . . he saw as though someone had trudged over the ridge, as it looked, making a trail over the ridge. He didn't know who it was who was doing it, so he started thinking about setting a snare. And there Chahkabesh snared. When he returned home, however, he did not tell at home what he had done. He always lived only with his sister, of course, after they were supposed to have been orphaned. But he did not . . . tell her what . . . he had been doing, when he arrived. So, . . . when it began to get dark they started to go to bed, since they slept together which they always did.

Then, at the point when it would begin to dawn, dawn never came. Not even a little bit. At last they got tired waiting for it to dawn. Then his sister started thinking about him. 'What in the world must you have been up to again when you went away?' she said to him. Then he suddenly remembered . . . , remembered that he had set a snare on the trail made by someone going over that high hill. So he told his older sister that he had done that. Then he went there. So, when he began to get close to where he had set his snare, at that very point light was showing at a distance right in his snare.

Now he remembered what had happened. 'I imagine I must have snared the sun,' he thought. Then in truth, as he was nearing it, he saw the sun caught in the snare. He was caught by the neck. Then, . . . he thought, he couldn't go there. It was too hot there at the fire. So, . . . he went looking for a creature to bite through that line. . . . The animals were not able to do it. They got scorched. Because it was too hot there he couldn't manage to undo it himself either. So, the small mouse with the pointed nose, so he said to him, '[See i]f you can't somehow do it . . .' [and] he threw him there.

But that mouse, he hurriedly gnawed it through, that mouse with the pointed nose. It was then that . . . it became light and the sun suddenly rose. That thing came off where the sun had been snared. That mouse, however, you will see looking as though he was singed, looking like that. And the reason he looks that way, they say, is that he went into the fire. But he was certainly able to gnaw through that line where the sun got snared.

So he went home; and then he told his sister. 'I shnared [sic] the sun, Big Sister,' he shaid [sic] to her. 'That's why it didn't even dawn. But there was nothing for it, I threw the very littlest mouse in there, and he gnawed through that line. The rabbit could not do it. The rabbit tried; but the rabbit wasn't able.' That's what he said to her. So then his older sister spoke to him that he should never do that again,—and that he should never again misuse anything. His older sister spoke to him a great deal because she was frightened of course that it didn't even dawn,—and it was his fault.

That then is the length of the story.

SOURCE: C. Douglas Ellis, ed., *Cree Legends and Narratives from the West Coast of James Bay* (Winnipeg: University of Manitoba Press, 1995), 15–17.

■ Haida village at Skidegate, Queen Charlotte Islands, 1878. Photographed by George M. Dawson, a member of the Geological Survey of Canada who made the first survey of northern British Columbia and the Yukon. LAC, PA-037756.

The two largest groups in the western interior were the Assiniboine and the Cree; the former were based mainly in the buffalo country and the latter mainly in the woodlands. Linguistically, both of these peoples belonged to the Algonquian family, as did their western neighbours the Blackfoot. The Gros Ventre and the Sarcee—who, with the Blackfoot, inhabited what is now Alberta—spoke Athapaskan languages.

THE PACIFIC COAST AND PLATEAU

On the Pacific slope, rivers and coastal waters teeming with fish and marine mammals made possible a more varied economy than was the case for the bison-centred cultures east of the Rockies. Nevertheless, one fish and one tree became central to the cultures of the northwest coast: the salmon—fresh, smoked, and dried—provided a year-round food supply, while the towering cedar of the coastal rain forest furnished the material for everything from large houses and sea-going dugout canoes to totem poles and ceremonial masks to baskets and clothing woven from the trees' bark and roots. In this rich environment, with the gentlest climate of any in the northern part of the continent, there was little need to follow a migratory food supply, and relatively large populations were able to settle in one place. Over time they developed highly complex social systems with sharp class divisions based on kinship and wealth,

A HAIDA MYTH

This text was collected in the Queen Charlotte Islands between September 1900 and August 1901 by John Swanton (1873–1958) while he was part of the Jesup North Pacific Expedition. Swanton recorded the text in the Skidegate dialect. It was translated by John Enrico in the 1990s. Terms in boldface type are names, exclamations, and other untranslated expressions. The symbol resembling the figure '7' represents a glottal stop.

hlraxiid town was in existence, they say. They say that sometimes the townspeople used to go out fishing for herring with nets. Sometimes they used to catch a porpoise in the net. They would land and the town chief would have a slave go to the house into which those who had killed it had returned and [say], 'The chief orders that not one drop of the porpoise's blood make a spot on the floor.' They say he used to take away the porpoise immediately. The chief treated the townspeople like property [slaves].

The chief's nephew was a child. His little nephew used to see that the chief despised the boy's maternal uncles. He used to see that the chief in the town would take the porpoise from his uncles after they had stayed awake getting it, though the people were hungry. And one day the boy left with his grandmother, they say. After they had walked for a while, they came to **tll7aal**.

He and his grandmother built a house there. They say that the boy began to bathe for strength there. After he bathed for a while, he became strong. He made a bow for himself. They say he shot a goose with an arrow. Then he skinned it and cut a hole in the skin's front. He put his head in it and it was fine. Then he dried it, they say.

There were many geese in the water and he put his head into the skin and swam toward them, they say. He pulled them underwater from below. He wrung their necks right away. He did the same to their wings too. He took them to his grandmother and his grandmother plucked them. She dried the goose meat right . . .

Then one time he went beachcombing northward. . . . He came to lying on the edge of the planks lining the housepit of a house. Someone said about him in that house, 'Throw him out. Throw with him the thing that he wanted.' Then he forgot himself again. He came to lying at the water's edge. A whale lay near him.

He cut it up and twisted a good-sized spruce tree and tied it to the whale. Then he towed it into the inlet and towed it home to the front of his grandmother's house and his grandmother cut it up. When she finished cutting it up, she steamed it. And after she/he had strung it on sticks, he had his grandmother weave a big seaweed basket, they say. It was ready.

He packed the food into it. He packed into it every kind of berry, and salmon, and lupine roots and sedum. When it was ready, he went into [the] inlet with his grandmother, they say. He hid the basket at the edge of the town. He went into his uncle's house, they say.

After his uncles had fished for the herring a while, they came back with a porpoise again. Then a slave came in and said to not let one drop of the porpoise's blood spot the floor. Then the chief came in to get it and took off with it. As he went out the door with it, **qunaads** grabbed it and took it back in. The cedar floor planks at the back of the house where the chief became angry went [to pieces] as when a person tears something up with his nails.

The chief took it back. When he left with it again, **qunaads** let him go out with it. Then he twisted the chief's head around outside. The chief said, '**7wa-a-a, 7wa-a-a**.' When the chief got to the edge of the village, '**7wa-a-a**, he makes me leave by beating me up!' When his voice disappeared up in the woods, qunaads had a crowd of people go for the seaweed basket. They were unable to bring it. Then he went for it. He brought it inside. Then he began to give feasts, they say. He gave a feast the next day, and the next.

They say **qunaads** became town chief at that town. The one whom he chased away by beating him up is The One Who Travels Up in the Woods, they say.

SOURCE: *Skidegate Haida Myths and Histories*, collected by John R. Swanton, edited and translated by John Enrico (Skidegate, BC: Queen Charlotte Islands Museum Press, 1995), 173-7.

both material and immaterial (e.g., rights to cultural property such as dances, songs, or rituals). Peoples such as the Haida, Nuu-chah-nulth, Kwakwaka'wakw, and Tsimshian also owned slaves, often prisoners of war taken in raids on less powerful peoples such as the Salish of southern Vancouver Island. A strong aesthetic sensibility expressed itself in all aspects of these cultures, and the linguistic diversity of the region—of the 12 Aboriginal language families in Canada, half are found only in present-day British Columbia[17]—suggests that it has been occupied for a very long time.

The peoples of the Interior Plateau were heavily influenced by the coastal societies, with clan-based social organization and hierarchical divisions between chiefs, nobles, commoners, and slaves. In their economies, however, groups such as the Interior Salish, Kootenay, Chilcotin, and Okanagan were more closely akin to the hunting and gathering societies of eastern Canada. Semi-migratory, dependent on hunting and fishing, most of these peoples spoke Athapaskan languages.

THE WESTERN SUBARCTIC AND THE ARCTIC

In the basins of the Mackenzie and Yukon rivers, north of the 56th parallel, lived several other Athapaskan-speaking woodland peoples. The lives of the Chipewyan, Dogrib, and Gwich'in were centred on a constant search for game: moose, caribou, bear, beaver, and smaller mammals. Historically, their direction of movement

was southward, away from the Barrens—that vast bleak area stretching from northern Manitoba to the shore of Coronation Gulf (an arm of the Arctic Ocean). In the west they had gradually extended into the interior of British Columbia, but to the southeast they had found their way blocked by other groups. Their lives were hard and insecure; the sparse, difficult terrain could not support a dense population, and their social organization was that of the small hunting band.

Finally, the earliest human occupants of the High Arctic and Subarctic coasts, known to us as Paleo-Eskimos, had been land-based hunters of caribou and muskoxen. As the climate became more moderate and the sea level stabilized, producing a more reliable food supply based on marine mammals, beginning about 2000 BCE they expanded eastward from Alaska, eventually reaching as far as northern Greenland. The Paleo-Eskimos were succeeded by the Dorset culture and the Dorset by the Thule, the direct ancestors of the modern Inuit.[18]

Survival in the intractable environment of the Far North demanded extreme ingenuity. Without trees for building, the Inuit used the materials at hand, which varied with region and time of year but were largely derived from the animals they hunted for food: caribou, seal, and whale. Boats were made of animal skins stretched over driftwood or whalebone frames; sled runners of animal bones; tools and weapons (including the toggling harpoon) of bone and ivory; and dwellings either of snow blocks (igloos) or rocks, sod, and skins. For transportation by water they

■ Sadlermiut man paddling a walrus-skin boat, by an unknown artist, c. 1830. LAC, W304 (Peter Winkworth Collection of Canadiana).

used both the small, speedy kayak and the large, flat-bottomed umiak; for land travel, the dogsled. Most of their clothing was made of caribou skins, which provided a warmth unknown in other materials. As in other societies reliant on the hunt, political organization was simple, based on the extended family, although individual bands would come together briefly, especially in winter, for activities such sealing.

CONCLUSION

Exactly where the First Peoples came from and when they arrived in North America may never be known for certain, but there can be no doubt that by 1500 they had been on the continent for many thousands of years. The physical environment across much of the northern part of the continent was anything but welcoming to humans. Yet, over the millennia individual groups had developed all the adaptive strategies they needed to live and flourish in their particular territories. In many cases they had also established communication networks that enabled them to exchange goods and information with other groups in distant regions. Even so, nothing in their experience could have prepared them for the invasion of their homeland by people from the other side of the world, who brought with them a radically different set of cultural assumptions.

SHORT BIBLIOGRAPHY

Adovasio, J.M. *The First Americans: In Pursuit of Archaeology's Greatest Mystery*. New York, 2002. A semi-popular account of recent archaeology.

Bryan, Liz. *The Buffalo People: Prehistoric Archaeology on the Great Plains*. Edmonton, 1991. A recent synthesis of archaeology for one important region of Canada.

Carlson, Roy, and Luke Dalla Bona. *Early Human Occupation in British Columbia*. Vancouver, 1995. A summary of the complex early history of First Nations in British Columbia before 5000 BCE.

Dewar, Elaine. *Bones: Discovering the First Americans*. Toronto, 2001. A recent journalistic excursion into the scientific debates over the origins of humankind in the Americas, sympathetic to the revisionists.

Dickason, Olive Patricia, with David T. McNab. *Canada's First Nations: A History of Founding Peoples from Earliest Times*, 4th edn. Toronto, 2009. The best general history of the First Nations, detailed and carefully written.

Dillehay, Tom, *The Settlement of the Americas: A New Prehistory*. New York, 2000. The story by one of the revisionists.

Fagan, Brian. *The Great Journey: The Peopling of Ancient America*. New York, 1987. An introduction to the problem of early occupation by a conservative scholar.

Greenberg, Joseph. *Language in the Americas*. Stanford, Calif., 1987. A survey of a complex question.

Hare, F.K., and M.K. Thomas. *Climate Canada*. Toronto, 1979. Perhaps the best overview of the history of the Canadian climate.

McGhee, Robert. *Ancient People of the Arctic*. Vancouver, 1996. A recent account of the early history of the Arctic.

McMillan, Alan D., ed. *Native Peoples and Cultures of Canada*, 2nd edn. Vancouver, 1995. A collection of useful essays focusing on various themes and topics in the analysis of First Nations in Canada.

Wright, J.V. *A History of the Native Peoples of Canada*, 3 vols. Ottawa, 1995–2000. Dense and hard to read, but absolutely essential.

STUDY QUESTIONS

1. Many recent scholars have rejected the term 'pre-history'. Why? Do you agree with their decision?

2. What evidence would you require to believe that travellers or settlers visited America long before the earliest recorded contact?

3. In what ways did the horticultural societies of southern Ontario differ from others in pre-contact North America?

4. What do the Cree, Haida, and Mi'kmaq legends reproduced in this chapter tell us about those cultures?

CHAPTER TWO

Contacts and Encounters

Today it is not uncommon to describe the arrival of Europeans in North America as an intrusion. Not so many decades ago, however, the notion that Europe forced its way into an environment where it was not necessarily welcome would not have occurred to most Canadians; for them, the 'discovery' of America seemed a perfectly natural and desirable development of the Renaissance—as indeed it was, from the perspective of the Europeans. Nor would many scholars have thought that the interactions between newcomers and indigenous residents (and their respective cultures) in themselves constituted a subject worth careful study. Yet, in fact, the dynamics of cultural contact would prove one of the most revealing topics in the early period of Canadian history.

That the intrusion of Europeans had a profound impact on North America's First Peoples is obvious. At the same time, we can never know very much about how the Aboriginal people really responded to that contact because, for centuries to follow, virtually everything written about the indigenous peoples of Canada reflected the European perspective.[1] Even for indigenous oral traditions in the contact period, we must depend on the accounts written down by Europeans, whose ability to understand the Native peoples' languages, let alone their broader cultural references, was severely constrained. The fact that no First Nations names appear on the list of major explorers of North America points us towards a hard truth: that history as we understand the term is monopolized by those with the tools to record it.

Any scholar would delight in being able to observe that definitive moment when a group of people totally untouched by any earlier European presence encountered their first new arrivals. But such moments were rare, and even more rarely recorded. Over the centuries it took for Europeans to penetrate the continent there were innumerable episodes of 'first contact'. But in the relatively isolated and fragile ecosystems of North America, European influences travelled far in advance of the first European travellers—a point that the term 'first contact' tends to obscure. When Jacques Cartier arrived in the Gulf of St Lawrence there were a number of fishing vessels in the area, and he found the people there eager to trade, probably because they were already familiar with European visitors. More than two centuries later, when British exploration had only just reached the Pacific slope, Captain James Cook indulged himself in the thought that he and his party were the first Europeans to visit the 'Nootka' (Nuu-chah-nulth), although Spaniards had been travelling

TIMELINE

1000
Norse in Newfoundland are attacked by 'Skraelings'.

1497
John Cabot makes landfall at Newfoundland and sees human figures in the distance.

1501
Gaspar Corte-Real captures 57 Beothuk and takes them to Portugal.

1502
Three Aboriginal captives from the 'Newe Found Ileland' are taken by English fishermen to Britain clothed in 'beasty skinnys'.

1534
Jacques Cartier meets with Donnacona on the Gaspé Peninsula and kidnaps his two sons.

1535
Domagaya and Taignoagny lead Cartier to Stadacona and Hochelaga, where he is received by a chief called Agona.

1576
Martin Frobisher brings a 'strange man and his bote' back from Baffin Island.

1577
Inuit fight a pitched battle with members of Frobisher's expedition.

1605
Membertou meets French at Port-Royal.

1608
Champlain establishes the 'habitation' at Quebec and contacts local First Nations.

1609
Champlain leads armed party of Algonquin, Huron, and Montagnais against the Iroquois.

1615
First Récollet missionaries arrive in Huronia.

1621
Étienne Brulé reaches Lake Superior.

1634
Jean Nicollet smokes pipe of peace with Winnebagos at Green Bay.

1660
Radisson and Groseilliers reach Hudson Bay drainage system and commence trade with local people.

1668
English make trade treaties with Cree at Hudson Bay.

1672
Marquette and Joliet reach mouth of Arkansas River.

1682
LaSalle arrives at Gulf of Mexico.

1690
Henry Kelsey travels to the Canadian Plains.

1735
La Vérendrye establishes fur-trading forts on prairies.

1738
La Vérendrye reaches Mandan country in modern North Dakota.

1742
La Vérendrye enters lower Saskatchewan River.

1770
Matonnabee and Samuel Hearne follow Coppermine River to Arctic.

1778
Nuu-chah-nulth ('Nootka') meet James Cook on Vancouver Island.

the west coast for centuries. On the other hand, it is important to recognize that, in Canada, first encounters between individual Native groups and Europeans were still occurring well into the twentieth century, though later meetings differed from earlier ones in that word of the newcomers and evidence of their presence would virtually always precede their actual arrival in a region.

One European scholar has identified three basic types of contact—short-lived peaceful meetings; collisions; and longer-term relationships for trade or evangelization—each of which can be further subdivided.[2] As we will see, the Canadian experience has included many examples of each type. First, however, this chapter will provide a context for those events by looking at some of the broader issues involved in first encounters between radically different cultures.

THE IMPACT OF DISEASE

The question of demography is one of the most contentious in the literature of early America. Before the 1950s, scholars assumed that Aboriginal numbers were invariably small, because the early explorers did not come into contact with large populations. Then, in response to discoveries in Mexico suggesting that contagious diseases had devastated indigenous populations, scholars began revising the numbers upward.[3] Some of the first revised calculations seemed to assume that the Americas had never known contagious disease before the arrival of the Europeans, and recent estimates have tended to take a more conservative view of pre-contact demographics.

Even so, there can be little doubt that Aboriginal populations were sharply reduced within a few decades of the Europeans' arrival. However rapidly trade goods may have travelled ahead of the newcomers, disease spread even faster.[4] Geographically, North America in the sixteenth century was relatively isolated. A host of communicable diseases common to the 'known world' of international trade and commerce either did not exist or were not so virulent on the American continent, and the population had had no occasion to develop immune responses to them. Communicable diseases were not unknown, but measles, smallpox, typhus, typhoid, mumps, and venereal disease—the last perhaps first contracted by Europeans in the Caribbean region—were all introduced to North America by Europeans. They spread like wildfire through populations without natural resistance to them, helped along by the already established links between different Native peoples, friendly (trade) or unfriendly (war, including the custom of adopting captured women and children to compensate for population losses). These contacts carried the virulent new diseases far beyond the regions where Europeans themselves had set foot. In fairness to the newcomers, they did not understand that engaging in sexual relations with Native people, or kidnapping them as informants or prize specimens to be displayed in Europe, was potentially devastating to the indigenous people. Nor is there is any reason to assume that the newcomers deliberately exposed Native people to diseases that would be fatal for them: in this earliest period of contact, Europeans themselves did not understand how disease was transmitted.

Native populations were devastated nonetheless. It is now generally accepted that the pre-contact population of Canada was substantially larger than the sum total of all the most generous estimates of all the early European observers. On the east coast, the Mi'kmaq people alone may have numbered 100,000 before the introduction of epidemic disease in the sixteenth century, and demographic disaster preceded the Europeans right across the country.[5] At the same time, it is important to recognize that there never was a 'Golden Age' in which pre-European America was free of contagious disease. Moreover, the inadvertent introduction of 'germs' was not the only cause of the ultimate reduction (in size and in power) of Aboriginal populations: Europeans also undertook many deliberate actions towards the same end.[6]

■ John White, 'The manner of their fishing'.
© Copyright The British Museum.

WHAT ABORIGINAL PEOPLE KNEW AND EUROPEANS HAD TO LEARN

Over the last few decades we have had several opportunities to observe how the advanced nations of the world operate in space and on the moon. Although sophisticated technologies have been developed to enable humans to function in what are, after all, alien environments for them, no one who has watched astronauts in action on television could describe them as being fully in control of their new environments. Unlike those astronauts, the first Europeans who came to North America were able to breathe the same air they did at home, experience the same pull of gravity, and function according to the same physical laws (even if they did not yet understand them very well). Nevertheless, the 'New World' was truly a strange place for the newcomers, and the people who understood best how it worked were those who had lived there for thousands of years.

To survive in their new environment, the newcomers needed to learn what was common knowledge to the people who had lived there since time immemorial. The Aboriginal people knew how the local wildlife behaved. They knew how to hunt and trap game for food and furs. They knew where the fish could be found, and when, and how to catch and, in some cases, preserve them. Those living in temperate regions knew what seeds to plant and how to cultivate them in order to harvest crops. Such knowledge became particularly important to Europeans when supply ships failed to arrive, or imported seeds failed to germinate (as they usually did). The indigenous people also knew the physical geography of their territory. They knew where the rivers ran and where the trails led, and they were able to draw maps describing the landscape far beyond the ability of the eye to see. They also knew the most efficient ways of travelling across difficult terrain, constructing small, light-weight, shallow-draft boats out of readily available materials; not only were their canoes capable of navigating the thousands of lakes and rivers in the new country, but they could be carried across land from one water system to another. Equally valuable were snowshoes, which made it possible to move around even in the deep snows of winter. The First Nations knew how to dress warmly in winter, using animal skins, and the advantages of light-weight moccasins instead of heavy boots. The indigenous peoples also understood how to wage war against enemies who did not necessarily position themselves in fortified structures or fight en masse in the open. In the early days, the influence of North America on Europeans was at least as dramatic as the European influence on North America.

■ Native hunters in winter. The author of the work in which this woodcut appeared, André Thevet, described their snowshoes as 'rackets'. From his *Cosmographie universelle* (Paris, 1558), fol. 1013r. The John Carter Brown Library at Brown University.

THE PROBLEM OF COMMUNICATION

In the beginning, communication between Europeans and Native North Americans was likely more difficult than the contemporary documents suggest.[7] For one thing, neither Europeans nor Native peoples spoke a single language among themselves. There were as yet no generally comprehensible national languages in Europe, and even between two French speakers (for instance), differences of dialect could make communication difficult at best. The great sea captains, many of whom had connections at the royal courts of Europe, were likely to use different pronunciations and vocabularies than the common sailors, even when technically both spoke the same language. The Aboriginal people of North America, for their part, spoke several hundred different local languages in a myriad of dialects. Within a language family like Algonquian, the differences between local languages could be as great as the differences between

FIRST NATIONS EXPLORERS

❖

The contributions made to European 'exploration' by Aboriginal peoples have traditionally been ignored in much the same way that the labour of the Europeans' servants has been ignored. Yet, historians of exploration have long known that Native people not only served as guides, interpreters, and canoe paddlers, but provided a great deal of geographical information, often including maps.

In 1770, for example, an 'Indian guide' named Matonabbee accompanied the Hudson's Bay Company fur trader Samuel Hearne when he left Prince of Wales Fort on Hudson Bay to travel north in his third effort to find a reputed source of pure copper. But Matonabbee was considerably more than a mere assistant. He had already visited the region that Hearne was to 'discover', and had even brought back to Prince of Wales Fort a map sufficiently accurate that scholars have been able to align it with actual orientations and locations in the North.[8] And Matonabbee's service to Hearne extended well beyond his personal knowledge of the country's geography. He provided Hearne with proper clothing—'a good warm suit of otter and other skins'—and helped him make temporary snowshoes and sledges. He also insisted that the reason Hearne's earlier expeditions had failed was that they had not included any women to do the cooking, sewing, and carrying.[9]

For the next 32 months Hearne would travel in Matonabbee's entourage, which included his seven wives, as it followed the seasonal movements of the caribou and buffalo herds—virtually the only source of food available in the remote country of the Barrens.[10] As one of Hearne's biographers points out, his suc-

cess as an explorer 'was largely the result of his adaptation' to the Aboriginal 'way of life and movement'.[11] But even the *Dictionary of Canadian Biography* describes Matonabbee

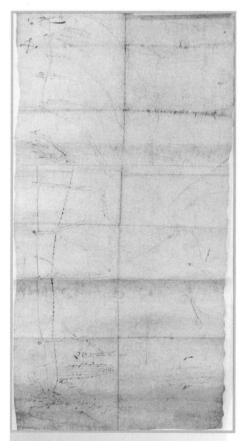

■ Matonabbee's map. Hudson's Bay Company Archives, Provincial Archives of Manitoba, G.2/27.

merely as a 'leading Indian', not an 'explorer'.[12] The tendency to give the Europeans the credit for exploration and discovery while treating the Native participants as—at best—resource people has been all too common in Canadian his-tory. This approach not only reduces First Nations men to secondary status, it also virtu-ally eliminates First Nations women from the historical record.[13] Without the contributions of both, the Europeans would not have got far.

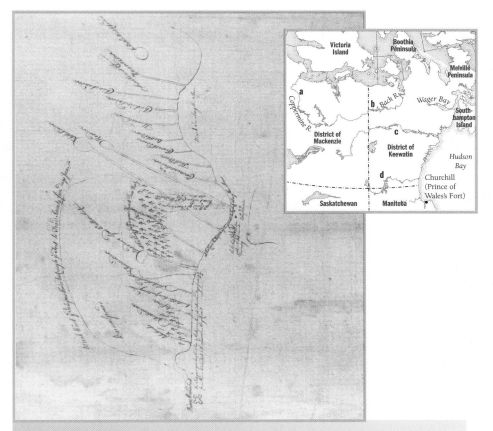

■ Early untitled map showing rivers flowing into marine waters north of Churchill Fort; drawn c. 1716–17 either by Chipewyan informants themselves or from their reports by James Knight of the HBC. Inset is a modern map of the same territory, based on June Helm, 'Matonabbee's Map', *Arctic Anthropology* 26, 2 (1989). River A is the Coppermine; B is the Back; C is probably the Thelon; and D is the Thlewiaze. Hudson's Bay Company Archives, Provincial Archives of Manitoba, G.1/19.

REPORT OF THE SIEUR DE LA VÉRENDRYE TOUCHING UPON THE DISCOVERY OF THE WESTERN SEA, 10 OCTOBER 1730

In 1730, the fur-trader Pierre Gaultier, Sieur de la Vérendrye, wrote a report on his geographical findings to the governor-general of New France. La Vérendrye was searching for the 'western sea', the short route to Asia that the French government dearly wanted to discover. Canadien officials may have been more interested in the fur trade.

(Annexed to the Letter of M. de Beauharnois, of 10 October 1730)

A savage named Pako, Chief of Lake Nipigon, Llefoye, and Petit Jour his brother, Cree chiefs, reported to me that they had been beyond the height of land and reached a great river which flows straight towards the setting sun, and which widens continually as it descends; that in this great river there are only two rapids about three days' journey from its source, and that wood is only found along about two hundred leagues of its course, according to the estimate they made in their travel.

They give a great account of that country, saying that it is all very level, without mountains, all fine hard wood with here and there groves of oak; that everywhere there are quantities of fruit trees, and all sorts of wild animals; that the savage tribes are there very numerous, and always wandering, never staying in any fixed place, but carrying their cabins with them continually from one place to another and always camping together to form a village. They call these nations Assiniboin and Sioux because they all speak the Sioux languages. The nations about three hundred leagues lower down are sedentary, raise crops, and for want of wood make themselves mud huts. The wood comes to an end on the shore of a great lake formed by the river about two hundred leagues from its source; on the left as you follow down, at the outlet of the lake,

you come to a little river the water of which looks red like vermilion, and is held in great esteem by the savages. . . . As I am going to report such new facts as I have learnt this year, 1729, respecting the country I have just been speaking about, I conclude by mentioning the other particulars which I learnt last year so as to give a more exact account of them on the testimony of other savages who have explored the same river.

Having neglected nothing, Monsieur, since I arrived last autumn as commander of the Northern post, that could help to give me the fullest possible knowledge of the fine and mighty river which flows straight to the west and the route to be taken to get to it, I have taken care also to secure a savage able to conduct a party thither in case, with the consent of His Majesty, you should be so good as to honour me with our commands to discover it, and, on the strength of the new information I have received, I can now positively state as follows: The savages of the interior have knowledge for the most part of this river; some speak as having been there, others have heard of it, and all agree in what they say about it. . . . Tacchigis, a chief of the Cree, told me then that he had been as far as the lake of the great river of the West, and several times afterwards he told me the same story that the others had already done. He then gave me a statement in regard to several other larger rivers that he had seen from a height of land sloping to the south-west. . . . With a piece of charcoal he made me a map of those regions, and placed these rivers on them according to his marks.

I am expecting this spring some savages who, I am assured, have been very far down the river of the West, and who will be able to supply a map of the road to the places at which they have been.

SOURCE: Lawrence J. Burpee, ed., *Journals and Letters of Pierre Gaultier de Varennes et de la Vérendrye and his Sons with Correspondence between the Governors of Canada and the French Court, Touching the Search for the Western Sea* (Toronto: Champlain Society, 1927), 43-7.

Spanish and Portuguese. Even a local patois would vary from place to place.

The very first attempts at communication would have depended entirely on gestures and body language. But these modes are not necessarily straightforward. For example, various body parts carry quite different connotations in different cultures, and similar gestures can mean very different things. Even with a more or less universal gesture, such as pointing, it may not always be clear what is being pointed at. And though pointing probably worked well for learning the names of concrete things, such as a knife or a fire, that method would have been no use at all for abstractions. Notions like climate and weather were hard enough to conceptualize, and ideas like truth, justice, law, or property were virtually impossible to articulate. Imagine a game of charades with people from an entirely different world, who not only speak a language unrelated to any you have ever encountered, but who do not share any cultural referents in common with you. Even after the parties involved had acquired some of one another's vocabulary, therefore, early linguistic exchanges were conducted on the simplest and most concrete levels.

In time, some Native people would learn to speak and understand European languages very well, and a few Europeans who grew up in Native societies (often as captives) became equally adept at the local tongues. But for centuries most people would communicate in new 'pidgin' languages that, amalgamating elements from various European and Aboriginal languages,[14] eliminated the potentially inflammatory problem of choosing which people's language to speak. One very venerable 'pidgin' was spoken on the coasts of the Gulf of St Lawrence, where Basque fishermen had traded with local Natives from the early sixteenth century. 'Since their languages were completely different', wrote one observer in 1710, 'they created a form of lingua franca composed of Basque and two different languages of the Indians, by means of which they could understand each other very well.'[15] In the early seventeenth century, the Mi'kmaq spoke to the French in a simplified version of Mi'kmaq mixed with 'much Basque'.[16] Later, as the fur trade moved into the interior of the continent, complex pidgins would develop, combining elements of French, Gaelic, and English with Assiniboine and Cree.[17]

As relations between Europeans and Aboriginal peoples became more formalized and negotiations more complex, the need for skilled interpreters became urgent. An interpreter who could be trusted by both sides to translate accurately both formal meaning and more subtle nuance was highly prized. As late as 1873, when Treaty Six was negotiated between the Canadian government and the Saskatchewan Cree, the issue of translation remained critical. The government had brought two interpreters of its own, and argued that it was unnecessary to use the services of the translator brought by the Cree. The Cree chief answered, 'Very good. You keep your interpreters and we will keep ours. We will pay our own man and I already see that it will be well for us to do so.'[18]

SOVEREIGNTY

The assumption of sovereignty by European states in the early period of exploration consisted chiefly of the performance of various symbolic acts or ceremonies of possession. Such ceremonies were intimately bound up with the culture and language of a particular nation, so that no two nations meant quite the same thing by their actions. The Portuguese, for example, thought that mere discovery was sufficient to establish legitimate dominion, and the word 'discovery' in Portuguese carried that nuanced meaning, while other nations had quite different concepts of what produced a legitimate right to rule. For the English, settlement in the form of 'first building and habitation' was one important test, as was 'replenishing and subduing' a land that had previously existed in common and was seemingly undeveloped.[19] Every European nation had its own understanding of the meaning of possession. This question still continues today, both in terms of the 'ownership' of the High Arctic and Antarctica and that of outer space.

Among those European powers that explored in North America, the French were the most likely to take into account the feelings of the indigenous peoples they encountered. Indeed, the French—whose monarchical political customs at home relied heavily on the use of ritual and ceremony—often incorporated the consent of the Aboriginals into their ceremonies as a central component. The early French explorers assumed that physical gestures and body language could be universally understood, and made sure that the Aboriginal people either gave appropriate signs of agreement, or better still, actually participated in the ceremonies of possession. Thus, the French explorers did not simply raise objects of possession like crosses and pillars, but sought to communicate something of their meaning to the Native witnesses and interpreted Native responses as evidence of acceptance of or even enthusiasm for the French ceremonialism.

French accounts of ceremonies usually include detailed descriptions of the bodily movements and sounds of the indigenous observers, which were taken to mean formal consent. For the English, on the other hand, cultural symbols of land possession usually involved signs of successful occupation, such as housing, fencing, and cultivation of the land. Such actions had their own justification. Since the local inhabitants in most places obviously did not exhibit such signs of permanent occupation, they were not regarded as having proper jurisdiction over the country in which they resided.[20]

MUTUAL ASSUMPTIONS OF SUPERIORITY

From the start, the newcomers to North America were convinced that they were superior to the indigenous inhabitants by virtue of their technology, their emerging capitalistic economic order, their new political organization into nation-states, and especially their Christian system of values and beliefs. This conviction was to a considerable extent unwarranted. The veneer of civilization covering the visitors was thin at best, and it often wore away quickly. Although the master mariners and expedition leaders who left most of the written observations during the sixteenth century were usually men of some education—they could write, for example, which set them apart from their compatriots—and were often well-connected at the royal courts, they lived in a nasty and brutish age. Most Europeans, including the ordinary sailors on board the visiting ships, still ate with their fingers, bathed rarely, and enjoyed such amusements as bear baiting, in which dogs were pitted against captive bears in fights to the death. The institutions of the ruling classes allowed heretics to be tortured in the name of Jesus Christ, witches to be burned alive, and

■ A seventeenth-century European view of some Natives of New France. From Joannis de Laet, *Americae utriusque Descriptio*, 1633. Samuel de Champlain described the large round shield being carried by the man in the centre as being made of boiled leather. The Huron warrior on the right is wearing armour made of wooden slats laced together with fibre. The warrior at the left is supposed to be a Montagnais. (Photo courtesy The Newberry Library, Chicago)

thousands of others to be executed at the convenience of those in power. Public executions were guaranteed crowd-pleasers, especially if the victim was to be hanged, drawn, and quartered before being burnt at the stake. In some parts of Europe a popular entertainment at fairs was to watch blind men in pens try to beat each other to death with clubs.[21] Garbage and excrement were piled high in the streets of European cities, and 'piss-pots' were emptied in the streets, where their contents assisted in the spread of contagious disease. One of the major motivations behind European expansion was the search for new spices and perfumes to help disguise the stench of daily life. To the modern

mind, Europe's use of the word 'sauvages' to refer to the people of North America can be seen as richly ironic.

Many Native Americans appear to have assumed that the first Europeans they saw were supernatural beings. Once they realized the newcomers were humans like themselves, in many cases they were not impressed. A missionary in the Atlantic region noted that the Mi'kmaq 'greatly underrate us, regarding themselves as our superiors'.[22] Physically, the differences in appearance were striking. The Europeans were short—the height of the doorways in Renaissance-era buildings suggests that the average man stood only a little over five feet tall—often bearded, and had eyes and hair of many hues. The Aboriginal people were considerably taller and more physically fit, with straight black hair on their heads, black eyes, and little body or facial hair. Socially, too, Aboriginal peoples found European ways strikingly different from their own. Iroquoian men did not display emotion, did not interject their own views when another was speaking, and did not do 'women's work'. By contrast, the Europeans were quick to anger, often interrupted one another in conversation, and, without women to do menial chores for them, carried their own firewood. From the Native point of view, they were greedy, violent, and generally ill-mannered. No wonder the Hurons found the French 'less intelligent than they', and the Mi'kmaq considered themselves 'better, more valiant and more ingenious than the French'.[23]

A further complication in relations between Aboriginal people and Europeans was the ambiguous image in which Europe cast the indigenous populations of America. This equivocal picture was especially prevalent among the French, who had the closest contact with Native peoples in the early years. On the one hand, many Europeans considered the New World a kind of natural Eden, populated by 'natural savages' who might be untutored barbarians but were nevertheless—as Montaigne put it—'not at all behind us in natural brightness of mind and pertinence', and hence capable of conversion to Christianity and assimilation into the French way of life. This view, promulgated by Samuel de Champlain in his 1603 book *Des Sauvages, ou voyage du Samuel Champlain de Brouage, fait en France Nouvelle*, was the one with which most of the early missionaries started. On the other hand, many Europeans also believed the tales they heard of naked 'wild men' living like animals in the forest, and stories of scalping and torture circulated widely. Some missionaries whose colleagues had suffered at the hands of Native people came to see them as instruments of the devil.

In 1668, after nearly two decades of teaching Native children, the head of the Ursuline school at Quebec expressed frustration:

> It is a very difficult thing, not to say impossible, to make the little Savages French or civilized. . . .We find docility and intelligence in these girls, but, when we are least expecting it, they clamber over our wall and go off to run with their kinsmen in the woods, finding more to please them there than in all the amenities of our French houses. . . . We have had . . . Hurons, Algonkins, and Iroquois; these last are the prettiest and the most docile of all. I do not know whether they will be more capable of being civilized than the others. . . . I do not expect it of them, for they are Savages and that is sufficient reason not to hope.[24]

And a priest who worked among the Mi'kmaq in the 1670s later wrote that 'the number of those who abide by the rule of Christianity and who do not fall back into the irregularities of a brutal and savage life is very small, either because of the natural insensibility of these people to matters of salvation or because of drunkenness, their delusions, their superstitions and other great defects to which they are addicted.'[25] There is no evidence that European missionaries ever considered the possibility that Aboriginal people's preference for their own way of life did not necessarily mark them as inferior, or that their resistance to European control was both natural and legitimate.

In the eighteenth century an idealized, romanticized view of Aboriginal society became a kind of literary convention, frequently used by philosophers and others to criticize contemporary European society. As Peter Moogk has pointed out, press censorship, particularly in France, made it advisable to use fictitious foreigners, often North Americans, to express negative opinions about church or state.[26] An early example was a character in a popular 1703 novel by Baron de Lahontan: Adario, a supposed 'Huron', observes that the ten commandments are routinely ignored in France, while his own people exemplify innocence, love, and tranquillity of mind. Further developed by Voltaire and Rousseau, the notion of the 'noble savage' or 'bon sauvage' as the antithesis of Old World corruption and greed was central to the Enlightenment in Europe, but as an analytical tool for understanding North American society it was not very useful.

TECHNOLOGY, ECONOMY, AND SOCIETY

By the sixteenth century, Europe had advanced to a new level of technology based on the book and the wheel. Although that technology undoubtedly contributed to Europeans' sense of superiority, much of it was useless in the wilderness of the New World. The importance of the gun, for example, has been vastly overrated. In fact, muskets were not widely available, and they were so unreliable that, as tools for hunting and warfare, they were far inferior to the bow and arrow. As a result, they were probably not widely adopted by Native people before 1670. Yet by then a mythology was already in place, according to which Europeans felt they had to be prepared to defend themselves against Native people heavily armed with guns.[27] Here, as elsewhere, the newcomers' tendency to assess indigenous people's intentions and behaviour by reference to European models led to misunderstandings that would continue to poison relations for centuries to come.

The economies of most Native societies, especially those centred on the hunt, were relatively simple, but they were also logical, and the behaviour of those who operated within them was entirely rational. Semi-nomadic hunter-gatherers, dependent on the seasonal availability of various foods, had no incentive to acquire material possessions that would only have to be abandoned at the next move—which was always imminent. The movements of game animals had certain rhythms, but were at least potentially capricious. When food was available, the people sprang into action, gathering as much as possible

and then consuming it in what Europeans perceived as orgies of overindulgence. When food supplies ran out, the search to replenish them did not necessarily begin at once. Intimately familiar with the general patterns of life among the plants and animals they depended on, Aboriginal people knew when it made sense to go hunting, or fishing, or berry-picking, and when it did not.

In any event, such economies did not put a premium on the disciplined pursuit of goals, or on the deferral of expectations. Nor did they encourage the sort of unremitting hard labour to which Europeans, rural and urban alike, were accustomed. Even after the Europeans had introduced new elements into Native economies— specifically guns, alcohol, and tobacco—consumer demand tended to be (in the language of the modern economist) inelastic. Native people could not be persuaded to continue producing furs and pelts—the currency with which they could purchase trade goods—once their limited desires had been satisfied.[28] To Europeans, however, the extended periods of leisure that followed brief periods of concentrated activity seemed shiftless and indolent rather than economically sensible.

Similarly, Native societies did not require political institutions on a European scale. Semi-sedentary people had no need for political organizations larger than the band, based on a few family units. If a group had too many members, they could not travel together. Even where the practice of horticulture permitted the establishment of semi-permanent villages, political structures were not elaborate by European standards. 'Chiefs' were not kings, although the visitors treated them as such; they may not even have been 'head men' in any European sense. These concepts were introduced and imposed on indigenous societies by the newcomers.

Amerindian and European ways of thinking about property were dramatically different. Although some Native societies could conceive of territory as 'belonging' to them in the sense that it

JOHN GYLES'S CAPTIVITY

A small book entitled *Of Odd Adventures, Strange Deliverances, Etc., in the Captivity of John Gyles, Esq., Commander of the Garrison of St. George River, in the District of Maine, written by Himself* was published in Boston in 1736. Gyles had been captured at age nine by people from the Penobscot nation and spent some years with the Aboriginals before being 'sold' to the French. His adventures were told in a matter-of-fact way. In later years he was a famous soldier and interpreter.

After some weeks had passed, we left this village and went up St. John's river about ten miles to a branch called *Medockseenecasis*, where there was one wigwam. At our arrival an old squaw saluted me with a yell, taking me by the hair and one hand, but I was so rude as to break her hold and free myself. She gave me a filthy grin, and the Indians set up a laugh, and so it passed over. Here we lived upon fish, wild grapes, roots, &c, which was hard living to me.

When the winter came on we went up the river, till the ice came down, running thick in the river, when, according to the Indian custom, we laid up our canoes till spring. Then we traveled sometimes on the ice, and sometimes on the land, till we came to a river that was open, but not fordable, where we made a raft and passed over, bag and baggage. I met with no abuse from them in the winter's hunting, though I was put to great hardships in carrying burdens and for want of food. But they underwent the same difficulty, and would often encourage me, in broken English, '*By and by great deal moose.*' Yet they could not answer any questions I asked them. And knowing little of their customs and way of life, I thought it tedious to be constantly moving from place to place, though it in some respects were an advantage; for it ran still in my mind that we were travelling to some settlement; and when my burden was over-heavy, and the Indians left me behind, and the still evening coming on, I fancied I could see through the bushes, and hear the people of some great town; which hope, though some support to me in the day, yet I found not the town at night.

Thus we were hunting three hundred miles from the sea, and knew no man within fifty or sixty miles of us. We were eight or ten in number, and had but two guns, on which we wholly depended for food. If any disaster had happened, we must all have perished. Sometimes we had no manner of sustenance for three or four days; but God wonderfully provides for all creatures. In one of these fasts, God's providence was remarkable. Our two Indian men, who had guns, in hunting started a moose, but there being a shallow crusted snow on the ground, and the moose discovering them, ran with great force into a swamp. The Indians went round the swamp, and finding no track, returned at night to the wigwam, and told what had happened. The next morning they followed him on the track, and soon found him lying on the snow. He had, in crossing the roots of a large tree, that had been blown down, broken through the ice made over the water in the hope occasioned by the roots of the tree taking up the ground, and hitched one of his hind legs among the roots, so fast that by striving to get it out he pulled his thigh bone out of its socket at the hip, and thus extraordinarily were we provided for in our great strait. . . . When one supply was spent we fasted till further success.

SOURCE: Samuel Drake, ed., *Indian Captivities* (Boston: Antiquarian Bookstore and Institute, 1839), 81–2.

was available for their use, this understanding had nothing to do with European ideas of ownership. Equally foreign was the notion of 'sovereignty', or supreme authority over a country, as exercised by a ruler. Symbolic ceremonies of possession, such as Cartier's raising of a cross or LaSalle's mass on the Mississippi, meant something quite different to Europeans than to indigenous North Americans.[29] As a result of such gaps in understanding, Native people mistakenly identified by Europeans as 'kings' would be happy to 'sell' to newcomers land that neither they nor their people 'owned' in the European sense.

With little interest in creating or expanding hierarchical political organizations, Aboriginal peoples made war for different reasons than Europeans. Raids might be conducted for purposes of revenge, or to take women and children captive as replacements for lost band members, but also in part to demonstrate the warriors' individual prowess: success in battle was an important test of manhood. In the seventeenth century, when various European and Aboriginal nations formed alliances, the Europeans often failed to recognize that the latter had their own military agendas, with the result that from the European perspective, they often appeared capricious and untrustworthy.[30]

Several of the most striking differences between Aboriginal and European cultures were evident in their respective approaches to childrearing. Europeans believed that essential habits—hard work, obedience, self-control, deferral of rewards in the pursuit of long-term objectives—had to be instilled and reinforced from the earliest age, usually by means of corporal punishment. Native people, on the other hand, treated their children with affectionate indulgence, seldom expressing disapproval, let alone inflicting punishment. Despite this gentle approach—or perhaps because of it— children learned quickly and thoroughly from their elders. As young warriors grew, their schooling became more intensive, aimed at developing self-control and the ability to endure hardship and physical pain.

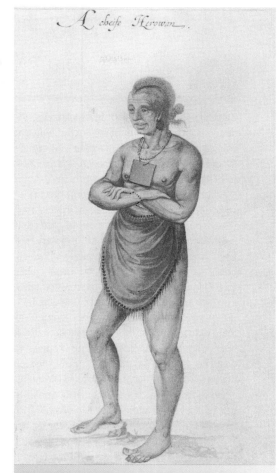

■ 'A cheife Herowan'. © Copyright The British Museum.

The same Europeans who commented on the freedom that Aboriginal children were allowed often remarked on what they saw as excessive exploitation of Aboriginal women. Although European society at the time could scarcely be called liberal in its attitudes towards women, European men performed work that any Native man would have found demeaning. In most cases, what the newcomers saw as exploitation simply reflected the standard divisions of labour within a warrior society: men hunted and

EUNICE WILLIAMS

(A.K.A. MARGUERITE GANNENSTENHAWI OR AONGOTE)

Born in 1696 in Deerfield, Massachusetts, the daughter of a Puritan minister and his wife, she was captured with other members of her family by a raiding party of French and Iroquois (mostly Mohawk) from Sault-Saint-Louis (Caughnawaga, Quebec), in February 1703/4.[31] Over 100 prisoners were taken in this raid, which became one of the most notorious episodes in the border warfare between New England and its French and Aboriginal neighbours. Captives of the latter were usually taken to Canada, where many of them were taken into the households of French families, and others—including Eunice—were adopted by their Native captors. In his famous account of his experiences in captivity, *The Redeemed Captive returning to Zion* (published in Boston in 1705) her father, John Williams, lamented her loss. He subsequently spoke to her, and several leading officials of New France and New York made strenuous efforts for her release. Johannes Schuyler of New York reported in early 1706/7 that Eunice was in good health, 'but seemed unwilling to returne,

and the Indian not very willing to part with her'. Continuing efforts to repatriate the girl were all unsuccessful. In 1713 Schuyler learned that she had been baptized, had married a Mohawk, and had become totally assimilated into the Mohawk community, even to the point of claiming that she had forgotten how to speak English. In 1714 her father travelled to Canada to beg her to return, without success. Eunice and her husband did visit Longmeadow, Massachusetts, where her brother Stephen was a minister, at least twice in later years, during periods of peace between New England and New France, in 1740 and 1761. But although she acknowledged her past life, Eunice resolutely refused to return to New England to reside. She died at Caughnawaga, Quebec, in 1785. Because of Mohawk naming practices, which followed the maternal line, her children all carried the surname of Williams. Over the years, Eunice Williams has become the most famous example of the young captives who, having become assimilated into Native society, preferred to remain there.

---

fought, while women did everything else. Interestingly enough, in the colonial period, when European women were occasionally captured by raiding parties and integrated into their captors' communities, many chose to remain there rather than return to their own people.[32] Those who did go home often remarked on the sense of love and community that Aboriginal societies offered; one set of repatriates remarked on 'The most perfect freedom, the ease of living,

[and] the absence of those cares and corroding solicitudes which so often prevail with us.'[33]

As for sexual mores, the newcomers often remarked on the 'generosity' of the men in societies where it was permitted for women to bestow sexual favours on visitors. On the other hand, returned captives maintained that few if any woman prisoners were ever assaulted sexually, and once a woman had been adopted into the tribe she was protected by the same incest taboos

■ 'One of the wyves of Wyngyno'.
© Copyright The British Museum.

■ 'The flyer'. © Copyright The British Museum.

that governed all members of the society.[34] Furthermore, in many groups rape was the only offence punishable by death. While some observers remarked on Native promiscuity, a few had the decency to acknowledge that Europeans were hardly blameless in this regard. Over the centuries of European exploration and invasion around the world, the first on the scene were always men, and it would be a long time before any European women arrived. In Canada, as elsewhere, relationships—many of them enduring—

between European men and local women eventually produced a distinctive mixed-blood society.

SPIRITUALITY

Nowhere was the gulf between First Nations and Europeans greater than in the spiritual realm. Centred on a complex religio-magical world that humans shared with the flora and fauna, Aboriginal spirituality was often not readily apparent to the newcomers. Everything in the natural world—from the animals on which hunting societies depended to the rocks, trees, and water—had its own spiritual significance, and rituals associated with everyday activities, including the consumption of food, constituted a form of worship.[35]

All groups had their legends about the origins of the world, and a few may have believed in a single Creator—although it is unclear to what extent the missionaries' accounts of these legends may have been influenced by their own desire to find parallels between Aboriginal and Christian beliefs.[36] After four centuries, the merging of authentic Aboriginal lore with European ideas has made it difficult—perhaps impossible—to separate one from the other.[37] The legends and myths reprinted in the previous chapter suggest some of the elements of European intrusion. And what are we to make of the dream of an Ojibwa that speaks of white men, large canoes with white wings, and long tubes that produce smoke and kill birds and beasts?[38] In any event, most groups distinguished between what had happened before the world assumed its present form (mythology) and what had happened subsequently (history). Certain features of the tales are common to many groups from coast to coast; others are specific to particular regions. One of the most common features is the theme of the trickster, which is found in most indigenous North American cultures, although the character of the trickster varies from place to place. Such myths and legends, often recounted around the fire as folktales, anchored the group's world view, articulated its values, and transmitted its history.

Shamans claimed supernatural powers and practised various kinds of folk medicine, from herbal treatments to exorcism. Europeans tended to see their activities as central to Native religion, but in fact shamans were no more priests than Native leaders were kings. That Native religion had no institutional presence, no buildings, no hierarchy, must have been deeply disorienting for many Europeans. But toleration of difference in matters of religion was rare in the period when Europeans first arrived in North America. At a time when Europe was torn between proponents of the Protestant Reformation and the Catholic Counter-Reformation, both sides were prepared to take fierce action against any deviation from official belief and practice. In North America, it was clear to Catholic and Protestant alike that 'pagan superstition' must be uprooted and replaced with the 'true faith'.

CONCLUSION

From beginning to end, the first encounters between Europeans and Native North Americans were marred by cultural misunderstanding. But these meetings were not necessarily as unequal as has often been suggested. Each party assumed its own superiority. The First Nations initially greeted the intruders as friends whose technology could enhance their lives. Only gradually did they realize that the Europeans sought to dominate the relationship, and by then it was too late to prevent either the ongoing encroachment on their territory or the gradual undermining of the social and spiritual foundations of their way of life.

SHORT BIBLIOGRAPHY

Axtell, James. *Natives and Newcomers: The Cultural Origins of North America.* New York, 2001. An important collection of essays on various aspects of early contact.

Bailey, A.G. *The Conflict of European and Eastern Algonkian Culture 1504–1700: A Study in Civilization,* 2nd edn. Toronto, 1969. The pioneering piece of Canadian ethnohistory, still useful today.

Bitterli, Urs. *Cultures in Conflict: Encounters between European and Non-European Cultures, 1492–1800,* trans. Ritchie Robertson. London, 1997. Puts the conflict of cultures between Europe and Native peoples in an international context.

Cummings, W.P., et al. *The Exploration of North America 1630–1775*. New York, 1974. A useful survey, copiously illustrated.

Delâge, Denys. *Bitter Harvest: Amerindians and Europeans in Northeastern North America, 1600–1664*, trans. June Brierly. Vancouver, 1993. A French-Canadian perspective on early contact.

Fisher, Robin. *Culture and Conflict: Indian–European Relations in British Columbia 1774–1890*, 2nd edn. Vancouver, 1992. One of the first of the modern ethnohistories for Canada, still extremely judicious and useful.

Gaudio, Michael, *Engraving the Savage: The New World and Techniques of Civilization*. Minneapolis, 2008. A study of the early engravings published in Europe of Aboriginal peoples.

Greenblatt, Stephen J. *Marvellous Possessions: The Wonder of the New World*. Chicago, 1991. A collection of essays on cultural contact in America, focusing on the problem of communication.

Jaenen, Cornelius. *Friend or Foe: Aspects of French–Amerindian Culture Contact in the Sixteenth and Seventeenth Centuries*. Toronto, 1976. One of the first books to re-examine the subject of cultural contact in early French Canada.

Paul, Daniel N. *We Were Not the Savages: A Mi'kmaq Perspective on the Collision of European and Aboriginal Civilization*. Halifax, 1993. As the title suggests, the story of cultural contact from the Aboriginal perspective.

Trigger, Bruce. *Natives and Newcomers: Canada's 'Heroic' Age Reconsidered*. Montreal and Kingston, 1986. The standard revisionist account by one of Canada's leading anthropologists.

STUDY QUESTIONS

1. How did the First Nations resist European intrusion?

2. Suggest some arguments for and against Christian missionary activity in early North America.

3. Imagine you are advising a European monarch in the sixteenth century on how to deal with North America and its Aboriginal population. What course of action would you recommend?

4. Imagine you are advising a modern nation-state that has been contacted by an alien civilization. What response would you recommend in this situation?

5. What does the excerpt from La Vérendrye tell us about early exploration in the interior of North America?

CHAPTER THREE

Early European Approaches

Generations of Canadian schoolchildren could be forgiven if they thought that the early European exploration of North America was carried out singlehandedly by a few extraordinary 'great men'. Perhaps more than most eras, the exploration period seems to lend itself to the biographical approach. Biographers today do not necessarily treat their subjects as larger-than-life heroes, but the focus is still on the individual. We learn almost nothing about the men who sailed the 'great' captains' ships, nor about the Aboriginal guides and French voyageurs who not only did the hard physical work but provided the knowledge that made it possible to move inland.

It could certainly be argued that the early discoverers have been overrated. They were almost without exception credulous men motivated chiefly by greed, eager to believe any story that suggested riches available for the taking. When they succeeded in finding something of interest, in many cases it was only because they stumbled across it. Nevertheless, most of them did leave behind substantial written records of their activities. This chapter investigates what we know of the earliest explorers in the Atlantic region.

THE NORSE EXPLORERS

Although legends of American landfalls abound—originating with the ancients and continuing through the Middle Ages—the first documented European visitations to North America were made around the year 1000 by Norse sailors, or as they are often called today, the 'Vikings'.[1] Contemporary evidence in the form of Iceland's epic sagas was confirmed in the 1960s by archaeological excavations near L'Anse aux Meadows, at the northern tip of Newfoundland.[2] The two great sagas describing the Norse expeditions are the *Saga of Eric the Red* and the *Saga of the Greenlanders*. Important additional material has been found in the *Islendingabók* ('Book of the Icelanders'). Scholars have debated the dates of composition of these sagas, but the most widely accepted view is that they were transcribed from oral tradition in the thirteenth century.[3]

Originating in Scandinavia, the Vikings were intrepid sailors, travelling both east into what is now Russia and west to the coasts of North America. They were experts at latitude sailing, using stellar sightings, knowledge of natural phenomena, and probably a workable bearing dial or compass to make their way unerringly across the

TIMELINE

985
Norse under Eric the Red settle Greenland.

1000
Eric's son Leif leads Norse expedition to the west; names Helluland, Markland, and Vinland.

1497
John Cabot makes landfall on 'newfoundland'.

1498
Cabot and his fleet are lost at sea on his second voyage to North America.

1500
Gaspar Corté-Real takes Beothuk captives from Newfoundland to Portugal.

1520
João Alvares Fagundes visits Penguin Island off coast of Newfoundland.

1527
John Rut sails along the coast of Nova Scotia.

1534
First voyage of Jacques Cartier to the St Lawrence.

1536
Richard Hore brings two vessels of English 'tourists' to Newfoundland.

1576
First voyage of Martin Frobisher to Baffin Island.

1577
Francis Drake embarks on voyage around the world.

1583
Humphrey Gilbert takes possession of Newfoundland for England.

1585
John Davis enters Davis Strait.

1589
Henry III, King of France, assassinated.

1610–11
Henry Hudson explores Hudson Bay.

1616
Robert Bylot (captain) and William Baffin (pilot) sail through Davis Strait and discover both Baffin Bay and Lancaster Sound to the north of it.

high seas in small open ships called *knarrs*.[4] Constructed of overlapping wooden planks fastened with iron rivets, powered by a single square sail and auxiliary oars and steered with a narrow side-hung rudder, these ships were quite fast and tacked well against the wind. By the ninth century they had reached Iceland and the Faeroe Islands. Faced with increasing population pressure in Scandinavia, where the rocky terrain provided only limited possibilities for agriculture, the Norse decided to begin colonizing these places.

According to the sagas, in the tenth century Eric the Red left Norway for the Iceland colony, and from 982 to 985 explored Greenland, which he colonized over the next two or three decades with his second son, Leif. About the year 1000 Leif, pursuing stories about land to the west of Greenland, set sail into the western unknown.

L'ANSE AUX MEADOWS

❖

In 1961 the Norwegian explorer Helge Ingstad announced that he had found Norse buildings in northern Newfoundland. Many were skeptical, but in excavations executed between 1961 and 1968 by Ingstad and his wife Anne (and continued by Parks Canada in the 1970s), eight ruined buildings were uncovered in a grassy cove overlooking the Strait of Belle Isle. Seven of the buildings are grouped into three complexes located on a north–south axis. Each complex includes a hall of several rooms and a smaller one-room hut. Each of the huts may represent housing for a different vessel. Radiocarbon dating indicates an occupation between 980 and 1020. The buildings are substantial, with sod walls and permanent roofs. They were obviously constructed to be lived in year-round by up to 100 people. Each hall had a workshop: the southernmost one a smithy, the middle one a carpentry shop, and the northern one a boat-building lean-to. This was not a typical Norse arrangement, for there were no signs of livestock or domestic animals. The settlement apparently was not intended for farming, but probably as a base for further exploration of the region. The short duration of the season of navigation in these northern waters demanded that the Norse winter over in Vinland in order to scout out the region. The settlement was abandoned fairly swiftly in an orderly manner, leaving behind little equipment and no burial site.

The archaeologists speculate that the site was the headquarters of Leif Eriksson himself, for the population here represented as much

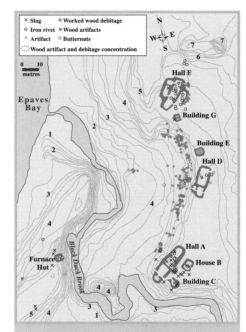

SOURCE: William Fitzhugh and Elisabeth I. Ward, eds, *Vikings: The North Atlantic Saga* (Washington and London: Smithsonian Institution Press, 2000). Reprinted by permission of Smithsonian Books.

as 10 per cent of the Greenland Norse colony, mainly comprising workmen. Apparently this location (and the region surrounding it) was not sufficiently attractive to produce a permanent colony, both because of the climate and because of the unfriendly local inhabitants. But it co-ordinates well with what is known of the Norse experience in Vinland as reported in the Vinland sagas.

Most scholars now agree that his party landed on Baffin Island (Leif called it Helluland, 'rocky land') and on the southern coast of Labrador (Markland, or 'wooded land'), and then headed south to another region—still not positively identified—which they called Vinland, after the wild grapes and vines they found growing there. They wintered in the south, perhaps at the Anse aux Meadows site, which has been dated about 1000 and is the only confirmed Norse settlement in North America. The archaeological excavations done there have disclosed a small year-round settlement consisting of eight buildings with thick sod walls and roofs over wooden frames. Numbering perhaps as many as 75 to 90 people—the Greenland colony itself probably had no more than 500 inhabitants—the settlement was likely intended as a staging point for further exploration and colonization.

The need for an interim base reflected the short navigational season in the north, which meant that it was essential for anyone hoping properly to investigate the region to winter in Newfoundland. The site was inhabited for no more than a few years, and it was abandoned in orderly fashion. Between 1003 and 1015 Thorfinn Karlsefni led some 160 colonists in search of a warmer location. Although the Icelanders found the climate of Vinland more hospitable than that of Iceland, they were intimidated by the hostile Native people (whom they called 'Skraelings', in reference to their small stature), and soon left. Why these Vikings, generally considered to be a warlike and militant people, were so easily driven off by the inhabitants—probably ancestors of modern Inuit—is a question that has never been answered. In any event, with their departure Vinland virtually disappeared from the record.

Later Greenlanders may have cut timber on Baffin Island and even intermarried with local people; attempts have been made to trace the Thule culture to such relationships.[5] But Greenland itself gradually lost most contact with Europe, and the Norse settlements there were

■ The Oseberg ship, built c. 815–820 CE and used as a burial ship for a prominent woman who died in 834. Constructed of oak, 22 metres long and 5 metres wide, it was designed for rowing as well as sailing and could reach speeds of over 10 knots. Photo by Eirik Irgens Johnsen. © University Museum of Cultural Heritage–University of Oslo, Norway.

abandoned, perhaps because of climatic changes, in the fifteenth century. In the 1960s a world map came to light that was supposedly made in the mid-fifteenth century, showing a realistic

Greenland and islands to the west, and including inscriptions referring to Vinland. While it encouraged speculation about Europe's geographical knowledge before Columbus, this 'Vinland Map' was never fully authenticated; indeed, later tests suggested that the ink was modern,[6] though no one knows who might have been responsible for the forgery.[7] More recently, the possibility that the map was genuine has been revived, since the scientific tests have proved inconclusive.

■ An astrolabe. By turning the sighting rod to point at the sun or a bright star, a mariner could estimate its altitude above the horizon and use that information as an aid to navigation. © Canadian Museum of Civilization, image no. S94-37602.

THE EUROPEAN 'DISCOVERY' OF THE AMERICAS

The idea of 'discovering' a part of the world already inhabited by millions of people was, of course, profoundly Eurocentric. Nevertheless, it was in keeping with the explosion of knowledge and the surge of intellectual confidence associated with the Renaissance. By the last quarter of the fifteenth century, geographers such as Paolo dal Pozzo Toscanelli, an Italian cosmographer in Portuguese service, were arguing that Europe and Asia were closer than the ancients had imagined. Thus the mariners who were to accomplish the great 'discoveries' did not merely set sail into the unknown; decades of geographical speculation had laid the groundwork for their seemingly fanciful quests.

Advances in ship design and navigational aids also encouraged transatlantic voyages. The Germans had developed the *cog*, a single-masted ship decked over and fitted with rudder and tiller, sometime in the twelfth century. In the early fifteenth century the hull was lengthened and the *cog* was given two additional masts, becoming the carvel (or caravel or *nef*)—a relatively small vessel that many mariners found more manoeuvrable than larger ones, and came to prefer on transatlantic voyages. Rigging also improved, particularly with the addition of the square sail to the earlier lateen (triangular) variety. The art of navigation advanced in parallel fashion, a gradual product of trial and error by countless mariners. The greatest advance was in written sailing directions based on the taking of latitudes in relation to Polaris and the sun (accurate calculation of longitude would not become possible until the late 1700s). In addition to the compass, seamen used quadrants and astrolabes to determine latitude, and were familiar with the need to transfer their data on latitude and longitude onto charts ruled for these variables. *Routiers*—coastal pilot charts of European waters—were readily available. But none of the early visitors to North America had the faintest idea of the hazards of its coasts. Perhaps the most remarkable feature of the first known voyages was the infrequency with which mariners ran into serious problems with rocks, shoals, and tides. Master mariners, with an instinctive 'feel' for the sea, were able to read and deduce a great deal from its colour and surface patterns.

The great voyages of the sixteenth century took place against a complex background of dynastic manoeuvring, the rise of the modern nation-state, religious conflict (the Protestant Reformation and the Catholic Counter-Reformation), and the growth of capitalistic enterprise fuelled by the infusion of new wealth in the form of gold and silver bullion from the Indies. From the late fifteenth through the sixteenth century Henry VII of England, François I of France, and Henry's granddaughter, Elizabeth I, all hoped to gain national advantage by sponsoring voyages of exploration to the west. The dissolution of an earlier alliance between Spain and England in the wake of the latter's becoming Protestant, and the complex relationships between the ruling houses of the two countries, encouraged Elizabeth to turn her 'sea dogs' loose on the Spanish Empire. English exploration was inextricably bound up with 'singeing the Spanish beard', and at a time when political hostility to Spain was heightened by religious sentiments, English adventurers often combined the activities of explorer, pirate, and even colonizer. France—after Jacques Cartier's pioneering voyages of 1534, 1535–6, and 1541–2—became more involved in its internal dynastic struggles than in overseas adventuring and did not show much state interest in North America until the end of the century. In both France and England, overseas investment by an emerging mercantile class took over from the earlier thrusts of discovery by intrepid mariners backed by the Crown. Cartier's third voyage marked for France the transition from public to private enterprise, and the 1576 voyage of Martin Frobisher in search of a Northwest Passage to the Orient demonstrated the new importance to the English of mercantile

investment. The Netherlands was always motivated by its merchants.

JOHN CABOT AND THE PORTUGUESE MARINERS

As with most of the early master mariners who sailed to North America, the early years of the man who came to be called John Cabot are shrouded in mystery. Giovanni Caboto (*c.* 1449/50–1498/9; *caboto* in Italian means 'coasting seaman') was probably an Italian, perhaps even a Genoese like Columbus himself, although he became a citizen of Venice in 1476.[8] As a merchant sailor employed in the Mediterranean trade, Caboto—like many another fifteenth-century Italian of humble origins who displayed ambition and talent—was prepared to go wherever employment beckoned. In the 1490s he was in Spain, involved in plans for the construction of a new harbour at Valencia, but the success of Columbus meant that Caboto would have little chance of gaining the Spanish Crown's support for any plans he might have had to sail west to Asia. He would need to find another patron, perhaps in a more northerly nation. Caboto decided to try his luck in Bristol, an English port long associated with Atlantic seafaring; Bristol traded more dutiable goods than any other provincial port in the kingdom, and was known for its aggressive merchants, always seeking new trade.[9]

In 1497, an anglicized John Cabot obtained the support of Henry VII for a voyage in search of a short route to Asia, in a small caravel with a crew of 18. Although there is little contemporary evidence to go on, the *Matthew* is known to have had a displacement of 50 tuns and to have been a quick sailor. Modern scholars planning a reconstruction of the vessel for the 500th anniversary celebrations in 1997 worked out a design featuring a rounded hull, a pointed stern, and a square rig.[10] The reconstructed ship was just over 24 metres long at its outer extremities. Bristol had long been involved in the Icelandic trade, and its seamen were familiar with the prevailing winds,

which blew easterly in the spring. Cabot therefore set sail in mid-May, and on 24 June 1497—
as a later chronicle put it—'was newfoundland
fowend by Bristol men in a ship called the
Mathew'. Except for the date (supplied by Cabot's
son Sebastian half a century later), no details survive for the 1497 landfall. We cannot even be
certain that the place Cabot arrived at was present-day Newfoundland; a number of other candidates, including Cape Breton Island, have been
suggested over the years.[11] Wherever his landfall
actually was, Cabot apparently believed he had
reached Asia. He went ashore briefly, declared
possession for England by raising a flag, and then
sailed along the coast, observing the land and
great schools of fish. In early August 1497, after
a voyage of only 15 days, he returned to Bristol
and hastened to London to inform the king of his
discoveries and collect his reward.

Cabot had little enough to tell, let alone to
show. He had not even seen any of the indigenous inhabitants up close, although he probably
did find signs of human habitation. He emphasized that the land he had found was an island—
possibly reflecting what he had been expecting to
find—although he had not coasted around it
completely. So Henry's reward of ten pounds (a
substantial amount of money at the time) 'to hym
that founde the new Isle' was quite generous.
Cabot also received royal support for a follow-up
voyage, the king and various London merchants
fitting out one ship and Bristol merchants adding
four more carrying 'course cloth, Caps, Laces,
points and other trifles' to trade with the 'Asian'
inhabitants that Cabot had not yet really seen.
The little fleet left Bristol in May 1498. One ship
put into Ireland in distress and the remaining
four, along with Cabot himself, were lost at sea.
In the long run, the codfish that Cabot discovered would prove to be of enormous significance.
But England would not follow up on the fishery
until after 1570, and codfish could hardly compete with the silver, gold, and pearls that men
like Cortés and Pizarro were to find in Mexico
(1519) and Peru (1532).

In 1502 three Native men were captured by
sailors from the 'Newe Found Ileland'—where
exactly that was is not known—and taken to
England. Initially 'clothid in beastys skinnys' and
behaving like 'Bruyt bestis', they were later
attired in fancy courtiers' dress and kept at the
royal court as living specimens of the wonders of
America. Even after several years in London, they
did not speak a single word of English.[12]

Maps from the early sixteenth century
located the discoveries of Cabot and Gaspar
Corté-Real at the eastern extremities of Asia. John
Cabot's son Sebastian was subsequently reported
to have sailed to America in 1508–9, returning
with questionable accounts of the coasts of the
Atlantic region and claims that another great continent existed to the west of the new-found
islands. In 1521 he attempted to organize an
expedition to Newfoundland, but two London
guilds advised Henry VIII against the project, on
the grounds that Sebastian had never been there
himself. The maps of the first quarter of the sixteenth century began to show a more clearly
defined Newfoundland, but most of the place
names were Portuguese rather than English.
Portugal may have attempted to settle a colony on
the Newfoundland coast under the leadership of
Juan Fagundes, who had earlier sailed as far as the
Gulf of St Lawrence. Fagundes reportedly ended
up on Cape Breton Island, where his little settlement was destroyed by Native people who 'killed
all those who came there'.

By the later 1520s, Europe clearly understood that North America was a new continent.
To get to Asia, therefore, it would be necessary to
sail either around North America or through it.
In 1527 Henry VIII commissioned John Rut to
lead the attempt. Rut reached the harbour at
what is now St John's, Newfoundland, reporting
to the king on 3 August that he found 14 French
and Portuguese fishing vessels anchored there.
He subsequently sailed along the coast of North
America, but found no 'indrawn sea'. Nevertheless, the English were fascinated by the possibility. In 1527 a London merchant named Robert

Thorne, whose father had been involved with the Cabots, sent a document entitled 'A Declaration of the Indies' to Henry VIII in which he argued that 'There is left one way to discover, which is into the North; for that of the foure partes of the worlde, it seemeth three parts are discovered by other Princes.'[13] Thorne further argued that the best route to Asia would be over the North Pole, for according to geometry this was the direct route and there was 'no sea unnavigable'. Henry VIII did not follow up on this argument, but the English remained attracted by the northern possibilities. In 1536, the London merchant Richard Hore signed up 120 passengers, 'whereof thirty were gentlemen', for a 'voyage of discoverie upon the Northwest parts of America'. When provisions ran short on the Newfoundland coast, some participants allegedly resorted to eating their compatriots. The survivors were understandably pleased to get home.[14]

JACQUES CARTIER

It was at roughly this point that France entered the picture. France was not a maritime nation in the way that England and Portugal were, since it had a large agricultural hinterland and was not so dependent on overseas trade. But the coastal provinces of Normandy, Brittany, Saintonge, and Guyenne (or Guienne) had long seafaring traditions. The Norman seaports of Dieppe, Rouen (situated on the Seine, near its mouth on the English Channel), and Le Havre by the sixteenth century had many mercantile families and a considerable international reputation for shipbuilding and commerce. Brittany, home to small fishermen and coastal traders, was famed for its pilots and sailing skills. And farther south, on the exposed Atlantic coast, was the great trading port of La Rochelle, whose mariners specialized in fishing and the wine trade.

France first became involved in North America through the activities of another Italian master mariner, Giovanni da Verrazzano. Unlike most of his colleagues, Verrazzano was well born,

■ The frontispiece to *The Voyages of Jacques Cartier,* edited by H.P. Biggar. This 'portrait' of Cartier—if such it is—is imaginary, since we do not have a likeness of him. Thomas Fisher Rare Book Library.

a gentleman comfortable at the French court. Yet like Columbus and Cabot, he was also an experienced and highly skilled seaman. In 1523 he persuaded François I to sponsor a voyage of exploration to North America, getting one ship on loan from the French navy and another from private backers in Lyons and Rouen. Verrazzano wrote that his intention 'was to reach Cathay and the extreme eastern coast of Asia, but I did not expect to find such an obstacle of new land as I have found; and if for some reason I did expect to find it, I estimated there would be some strait to get through to the Eastern Ocean.'[15] In coasting from North Carolina to Newfoundland, however, he missed every important opportunity to penetrate into the interior of the continent. By the end of his voyage Verrazzano was convinced that what he had visited was not part of Asia, but a totally new continent. His North American ventures prepared the way for Jacques Cartier.

Born in Saint-Malo, a small port on the northern Brittany coast, in 1491, Cartier went to sea as a young man and was said to have travelled to both Brazil and Newfoundland. In 1532 he was recommended to the king as a suitable leader for an expedition to North America, and two years later he was ordered to embark on a search for new lands 'where it is said that a great quantity of gold, and other precious things, are to be found'.[16] Over the next nine years Cartier would make three voyages to what became known as New France.

On the morning of 24 July 1534, at the entrance to Gaspé Harbour, Cartier and his men erected a wooden cross nine metres high. Below the crossbar they had placed a shield bearing three fleur-de-lys and above it a board carved in large Gothic letters: VIVE LE ROY DE FRANCE. Observing this activity were a large group of Native people who had arrived a few days earlier to fish for mackerel and had already received gifts of trinkets.

After the sailors had returned to their ships, a man they took to be a local chief arrived in a canoe with four others. They would later learn that his name was Donnacona. According to Cartier's journal:

> pointing to the cross he made us a long harangue, making the sign of the cross with two of his fin-

gers; and then he pointed to the land all around about, as if he wished to say that all this region belonged to him, and that we ought not to have set up this cross without his permission.[17]

The Frenchmen beckoned to the visitors to come closer, then forced them to board the ship. They indicated that they wanted to take away two of the young men—Cartier calls them 'ses filz', the chief's sons—promising to return them eventually to the harbour. The young men were dressed in shirts and red caps and given brass chains to wear around their necks. Their 'old rags' of fur were given to their companions, who were then sent away with presents of hatchets and knives. Later that day more canoes arrived filled with people wanting to say goodbye to the captives and give them gifts of fish. 'These made signs to us that they would not pull down the cross, delivering at the same time several harangues which we did not understand.' The next day the Frenchmen weighed anchor and sailed back to France.

Like many accounts of early contact episodes, this one raises more questions than it answers. Why did the local indigenous people allow the French sailors to raise their cross? Why did they trust the French to the extent of boarding their ships? Did the two young men realize they had been taken captive? Did they have any idea of the voyage they were about to make? What led the chronicler to think that he understood any of what the local people were saying? Or did he simply invent the 'promise' not to pull down the cross? We may never be able to answer questions like these, but we can (and should) remember to pose them.

In any event, on his return Cartier presented his captives (only in the account of his second voyage do we learn that their names were Taignoagny and Domagaya), drew a map of the Gulf of St Lawrence, and persuaded the king that there was much more to be seen inland from its shores. The principal evidence of Cartier's success, the captives helped to stir the imagination

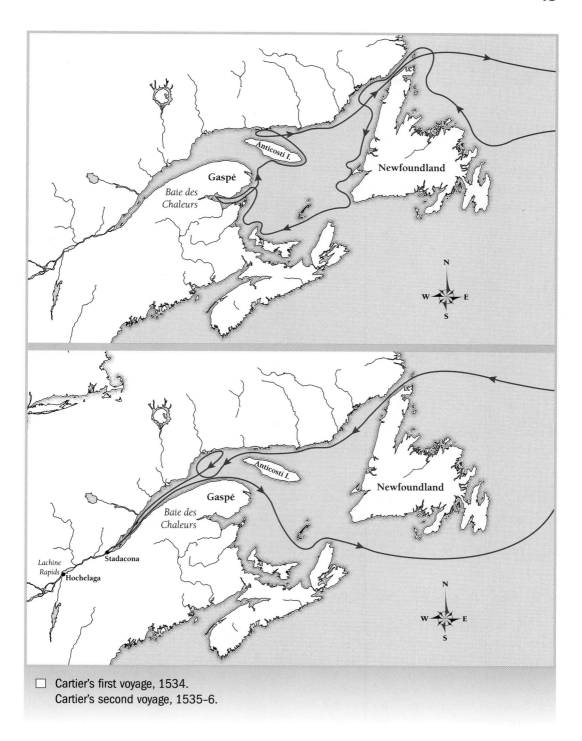

Cartier's first voyage, 1534.
Cartier's second voyage, 1535–6.

❧Brief recit, &

fuccinĉte narration, de la nauiga-
tion faiĉte es yfles de Canada, Ho-
chelage & Saguenay & autres, auec
particulieres meurs, langaige, & ce-
rimonies des habitans d'icelles: fort
deleĉtable à veoir.

Auec priuilege.

On les uend à Paris au fecond pillier en la grand
falle du Palais, ⁊ en la rue neufue noftredame à
l'enfeigne de lefcu de fràce, par Ponce Roffet diĉt
Faucheur, ⁊ Anthoine le Clerc freres.

1545.

■ The title page of Cartier's account of his
travels in Canada, from the volume published in 1545. Metropolitan Toronto
Reference Library.

of the king, who provided 3,000 livres for a follow-up voyage the next year.

On 19 May 1535 Cartier departed from
Saint-Malo with three ships, several 'gentlemen'
passengers, and the two captives, who would be
invaluable as interpreters. On 15 August the little fleet entered the St Lawrence River, guided by
Domagaya and Taignoagny, who said that here
was 'the beginning of the Saguenay and of the

inhabited region'. In addition they spoke of copper, adding that up the river was 'the route
towards Canada, and that the river grew nar-
rower as one approached Canada; and also that
farther up, the water became fresh, and that one
could make one's way so far up the river that they
had never heard of anyone reaching the head of
it. Furthermore that one could only proceed
along it in small boats.'[18] The farther inland he
went, the more Cartier depended on his
Aboriginal guides for geographical information.
In early September the French anchored off the
Île d'Orléans and landed on the north shore of
the river. The party were met by Iroquoian-
speakers living nearby in a small fortified village
called Stadacona, who welcomed Taignoagny
and Domagaya with dancing and ceremonies.

Cartier found a place to lay up his two
largest ships for the winter and in the *Émirillon*
sailed upriver to find a village he had heard of
called Hochelaga. He reached it on 2 October,
met by 'great numbers' of friendly Iroquoians
who conducted the party (including the 'gentlemen') to the clearing (or 'square') in the centre of
the village. There they were invited to sit down,
on a mat the women provided, to receive the
chief. Agona was carried in seated in a deerskin.
Though only about 50 years old, he was para-
lyzed and hoped to be cured by the visitor; many
other sick people also came forward. 'Seeing the
suffering of these people and their faith, the
Captain read aloud the Gospel of St John, namely
"In the beginning, etc.", and [made] the sign of
the Cross. . . .' Hochelaga was a circular pal-
isaded village of some 50 longhouses made of
wooden frames covered with bark slabs, each
about 50 paces long and 15 paces wide. Behind
it was a high hill, which Cartier climbed and
named Mont Royal. From there he viewed 'the
most violent rapid it is possible to see, which we
were unable to pass'. After mentioning another
large river that came from the north (the
Ottawa), the Iroquoians 'seized the chain of the
Captain's whistle, which was made of silver, and
a dagger-handle of yellow copper-gilt like gold,

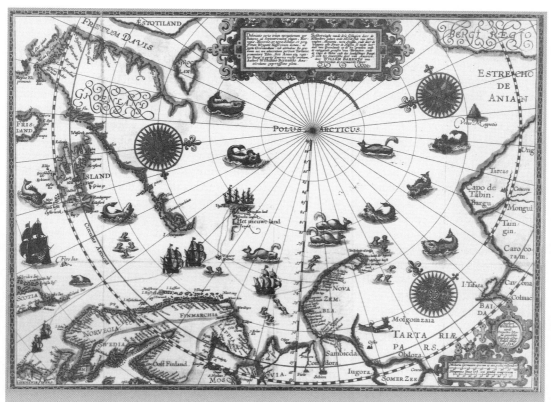

A map by Willem Barents, 1598, showing European explorations into the Arctic Circle. LAC, NMC-21063.

that hung at the side of one of the sailors, and gave us to understand that these came from up that river.'[19]

The winter at Stadacona was difficult. It lasted much longer than the Europeans expected—from November to April. The river froze. Twenty-five men died and most of the others took sick from scurvy. The cure, provided by Domagaya, was an important gift: a drink made from the juice (filled with vitamin C) from the leaves of the white cedar. During the long nights the French heard much more about the Saguenay, mainly from Chief Donnacona. The inhabitants were white men, fabulously wealthy in gold, silver, and rubies. A neighbouring region was the home of people who, 'possessing no

anus, never eat nor digest, but simply make water through the penis'. (It is tempting to imagine that the chief enjoyed acting out this description himself.) Cartier determined to sail for France as soon as possible in the spring, taking Donnacona with his two sons, as well as a number of others. He also had some pieces of 'gold'.

Cartier had more to report from this second voyage than from the first. Having found a water route into the interior of the continent, he and his crew had become the first Europeans to penetrate into the heart of North America. This would not have been possible without the assistance of the Native people who shared both their survival skills and their geographical expertise. Cartier had become more or less familiar with the region's people and had apparently reached the margins of some fabulously wealthy civilization. Perhaps the tales of the Saguenay in fact reflected distant echoes of Native information about the peoples of Peru and Mexico; but this has never been proved. Certainly the French court listened attentively, and believed, even when Donnacona elaborated: in the great kingdom of Saguenay there were gold and silver mines, as well as rich spice crops and some inhabitants who flew like bats from one tree to another. François I was convinced; after all—as he told the pope's ambassador—the Aboriginal informants had never been caught in error before, and all their testimony had been sworn before a notary. Belief would have been facilitated by the knowledge that the Spaniards had indeed found great cities—and quantities of gold—in Mexico and Peru, and no doubt the French stimulated Donnacona's imagination with accounts of the wonders observed by the Spanish to the south.[20]

Inevitably, a third expedition followed in 1541. It was a disaster. At first Cartier was to lead it, but then the king—determined not to give a mere sailor a monopoly over his discoveries (as Ferdinand and Isabella of Spain had done with Columbus)—appointed a nobleman, the Sieur de Roberval, Viceroy of the Saguenay and put him in charge, demoting Cartier to pilot. Roberval's commission included explicit commands not only to colonize the region but to Christianize the Native inhabitants (interestingly, Roberval himself was a Protestant); a missionary gesture was deemed necessary to placate the Church, since the French were defying an earlier papal bull that had divided the New World between Spain and Portugal. (When one Spaniard complained of France's plans, the king replied 'that the sun shone for him as for others, and he would like very much to see Adam's will to learn how he divided up the world!'[21])

By the time the expedition sailed from Saint-Malo, with five ships, in late May 1541, Cartier was nevertheless the effective leader:

Roberval stayed behind to raise more money to support the expedition. This time none of the Aboriginal captives returned to their home: after five years in France, all of them were dead. Under Cartier's command, the French built two forts upriver from Stadacona. Cartier then made his way as far as Hochelaga and the Lachine Rapids, but without the assistance of Native informants he was soon forced to turn back. Spending the winter at one of the new forts, Charlesbourg-Royal, the French faced both scurvy and hostile Iroquoians. The first problem was more easily handled than the second. In June 1542 Cartier peremptorily broke camp and set sail for home. Meeting Roberval's three ships anchored in the harbour of St John's, Newfoundland, he told the viceroy that he had with him 'certaine Diamonts, and a quantitie of Golde ore, which was found in the Countrey', and said that he had left because his small company could not withstand the Natives, who 'went about dayly to annoy him'. Although he 'commended the Countrey to bee very rich and fruitful', he refused to return. According to the French account reprinted in Richard Hakluyt's *Voyages and Discoveries* (1600), 'he and his company, moved as it seemeth with ambition, because they would have all the glory of the discoverie of those partes themselves, stoll privily away the next night from us, and without taking their leaves, departed home for Bretaigne [Brittany].'[22]

Roberval carried on, establishing his party at Cartier's Charlesbourg-Royal, which he renamed 'France-Roy'. Most of the 200 colonists had come from French prisons, and perhaps they needed a firm hand, but Roberval soon proved a harsh, even cruel, leader. The men were forced to work, and were often deprived of food and drink. A petty theft involving no more than five *sous* might be punished one day by flogging, another day by banishment to an island, in leg irons, or even hanging.[23] In June 1543 Roberval travelled up the St Lawrence towards Hochelaga in search of the Kingdom of Saguenay. But without Native

THE STORY OF MARGUERITE DE ROBERVAL

The story of Marguerite de Roberval was recounted by both Queen Marguerite of Navarre, in her *Heptaméron des nouvelles* (Paris, 1559), and Father André Thevet, the first French historian to visit America, in his *Cosmographie universelle* (Paris, 1558). Based on an interview with the victim herself, this account cannot be verified; however, Thevet's information on many other subjects has proved accurate.

Roberval . . . took with him a good company of gentlemen and artisans of all kinds and several women: among others a Damoiselle who was a rather close relative of his, named Marguerite. . . . Among the gentlemen of good birth who accompanied him there was one who went along more for the love of the said Damoiselle than for the service of the king or respect for the captain, as became evident a short time afterwards. Once upon the sea, this gentleman wasted no time in paying such private attentions to the said Damoiselle that despite the perils and dangers which are common to those who expose themselves to the mercy of the winds, they played their roles together so well that they passed beyond promises and mere words. Now all this was prompted by an old servant-woman of the said Damoiselle named Damienne, a native of Normandy and a very clever bawd, who played the sentinel while the two lovers were about their business. . . . When he [Roberval] reached [the]. . . Isle of Demons, he made his relative land there and the old woman her servant, telling her this was the place he had ordained for the penitence of her crime and of the scandal she had done him. He had four arquebuses given her and ammunition for her defense against the animals.

The poor woman, having returned to France after living two years five months in that place, and having come to city of Nautron in the country of Perigord when I was there, gave me an account of her past adventures and told me among other things that the gentleman, seeing this cruelty and fearing lest they do the same to him in some other isle, was so beside himself that forgetting the peril of death into which he was hurling himself and fearful tales he had been told about this land, took his arquebus and clothing, with a fire-steel and a few other commodities, some measures of biscuit, cider, linen, iron tools, and a few other things necessary for their use, and precipitated himself onto the isle to accompany his mistress. There Roberval left them, angry at the wrong his relative had done them and joyous at having punished them without soiling his hands with their blood. . . .

During this time the woman became pregnant, . . . and when she was near her time the poor gentleman died of sadness and disappointment: [and] in the eight months he had been there no vessel had passed which might afford them help, succor, and liberty. This death was distressing to the woman, but somehow making of necessity virtue, the mistress as well as the servant, they defended themselves very valiantly against the fierce beasts with their arquebuses and the sword of the dead man. . . . Having given birth to her child and baptized it in her own way in the name of God, without ceremonies, fortune is about to give her another shock. It was her servant who followed the path of the gentle lover, the sixteenth or seventeenth month that they were on the island, and shortly afterwards the child went following the road of the two others. . . . Finally, having, as I said, for the space of two years five months remained in that place, as some ships from lower Brittany passed by there fishing for cod, she was on the edge of the water shouting for help and signalling with smoke and fire. . . . Finally they drew near and realizing what she was, took her into the vessel and brought her back to France.

SOURCE: Roger Schlesinger and Arthur P. Stabler, editors and translators, *André Thevet's North America: A Sixteenth-Century View* (Montreal and Kingston: McGill-Queen's University Press, 1986), 63–7.

assistance this venture inland led to nothing. The following month the entire expedition packed up and returned to France. The aftermath was predictable, including recriminations and a royal commission to examine the accounts. Financially ruined, Roberval was eventually assassinated leaving a Calvinist meeting in Paris.

As for Cartier, his 'gold and diamonds' turned out to be iron pyrites and quartz; 'false as Canadian diamonds' became a catchphrase in France. Although the king's decision to put Roberval in charge meant that Cartier did not become the chief scapegoat, he was never given another major command; he spent the remaining 16 years of his life in retirement as a *noble homme* at his estate near Saint-Malo. Together, the disastrous third voyage and internal political problems arising after the king's death in 1547 put the French off any further colonization ventures until early in the next century.

MARTIN FROBISHER
(C. 1539–94)

Martin Frobisher (or Furbusher, as his name was often spelled) was born near Wakefield, Yorkshire, around 1539. His widowed mother sent him to an uncle in London to be educated, and in 1553 his uncle sent him to sea with a trading expedition to the Guinea coast of Africa. On a second venture to Guinea, the following year, he was held hostage for some months before being released. Endowed with 'great spirit and bould courage, and naturall hardnes of body', by 1564 he was one of England's leading 'sea dogs', a master mariner renowned for his exploits both in legitimate trade and in privateering. He was charged with piracy at least three times, though never brought to trial, and even English merchants complained of his depredations against their vessels, commenting that 'no six of their ships were fit to cope with Frobisher'. Following his Arctic adventures, Frobisher returned to a successful career as a buccaneer, serving as Francis Drake's second-in-command in a 1585 privateering expedition against Spain and as a principal commander in the English defence against the Spanish Armada in 1588, for which he was knighted. He died in 1594 from a wound incurred in the siege of a Spanish-held fortress in France.

Nevertheless, Cartier had established a firm French claim to the St Lawrence region, and the French would ultimately return there.

LATER ENGLISH ACTIVITIES

For the following half-century the exploration spotlight was turned on the English. Despite Cabot, the English had not made any particular effort to exploit the Newfoundland cod fishery, and now hundreds of French, Spanish, Basque, and Portuguese vessels were congregating there in the summer. The fishery expanded considerably thereafter.[24]

Instead of competing for fish, however, England in the second half of the sixteenth century concentrated on expanding legitimate markets for trade in other commodities and mounting highly successful raiding forays against the overseas trade of other nations, particularly Spain. Together, the quests for markets and booty inspired a new kind of English adventurer typified by Martin Frobisher.[25]

Like others of his generation, Frobisher had long been fascinated by the idea of a short route to Cathay through North America. The potential returns from such a route would dwarf even the rich profits available in the slave trade or privateering. Frobisher spent many years attempting to find investors willing to support an expedition to find such a passage. The English monopoly on such ventures was held by merchants trading to Russia as the Muscovy Company. It had sent several parties to seek a passage to the East in the 1550s, and eventually Frobisher succeeded in persuading it to license an expedition. With the assistance of Michael Lok, the Company's director, he raised funds for three small vessels. The largest, a 30-tonne bark named the *Gabriel*, was built especially for the venture by the royal master shipwrights.[26] Easier to manoeuvre than larger ships, such small vessels also represented a less grievous expense when they were lost at sea.

Dr John Dee—a curious figure of Elizabethan science who combined skills as a mathe-

■ Martin Frobisher, plate to *Heriologia Anglica* by H[enry] H[olland] (1620). LAC, C-011413.

matician and hydrographer with an interest in astrology and the occult—helped to instruct the Frobisher party in the latest navigational aids. The little fleet lost one vessel near Greenland, and another turned back from fear of the ice. But Frobisher, aboard the *Gabriel*, carried on, 'knowing that the Sea at length must needs have an endyng, and that some lande should have a beginning that way'. On 28 July 1576 he sighted land, to the north of which was a 'great gutte, bay or passage', into which the little bark sailed.[27] Nearly a month later Frobisher climbed a hill on the coast of the narrow 'strait' he was sailing. Looking west, he:

> saw far the two head lands at the furthest end of the straits, and no likelyhood of land to the north-weards of them and the great open betwene them

which by reason of the great tydes of flood which they found comming owt of the same, land for many other reasons they judged to be the West Sea, whereby to pass to Cathay and to the East India.[28]

In fact, Frobisher took his sighting not from the coast of Asia but from Baffin Island, and the 'strait' he was navigating (which would be named for him) was actually a deep bay. Worse, a hostile reception from the local Inuit—who may have remembered the kidnapping of a family of three by Basque whalers 10 years earlier[29]—ended in the loss of five crewmen. The English captured one man with his kayak and sailed home. As Frobisher had hoped, his return to London with this 'strange man and his bote' created 'a wonder onto the whole city and to the rest of the realm that heard of yt'[30]—although the captive soon died of a cold caught at sea.

When the rocks brought from Baffin Island were assessed by four experts, three were unimpressed; only one—who by his own account knew 'how to flatter nature'—pronounced it gold-bearing.[31] Nevertheless, Frobisher's backers, led by Michael Lok, used this dubious assessment to encourage investment in a follow-up voyage.[32] Instructed to concentrate on 'the Gold Ore, and to deferre the further discoverie of the passage until another tyme', Frobisher set out in May 1577 with three ships and 120 men. Among them were George Best, whose reports of the second and third voyages remain his principal legacy, and John White, the artist who was to produce the first pictorial representations of Native North Americans in their home environment, including a sketch of an armed confrontation between the English and Inuit at Frobisher Bay. The expedition clearly had posterity on its mind.

To Frobisher's credit, he spent much of the summer of 1577 searching for the lost sailors. He returned to England with another 200 tonnes of rock and three more Inuit, all of whom died shortly after arriving. In 1578, a third expedition consisting of perhaps 10 per cent of all England's larger ocean-going vessels returned with huge quantities of ore. For the next five years the expedition's sponsors tried to find evidence of value in this cargo, but it proved to be nothing more than sandstone flecked with mica. At last, everyone involved admitted failure. The rock itself was eventually used in Elizabethan road construction.

THE QUEST FOR THE NORTHWEST PASSAGE

Fascination with the possibility of a Northwest Passage would continue for centuries to lure mariners into the icy Arctic waters. Over the next 50 years a series of explorers—mainly Englishmen, backed by English capital—greatly expanded Europe's knowledge of these northern regions. In three voyages from 1585 to 1587, John Davis entered and named Davis Strait (1585), the first link in the Passage, and crossed Hudson Strait (1587) without entering it. His log books were shown to Henry Hudson, who used them for his last voyage, under Dutch auspices. Hudson sailed into the Strait, entered Hudson Bay, and navigated its eastern coastal waters southward into James Bay (named by Thomas James, who visited it 20 years later), where he wintered. In the spring of 1611 Hudson's crew, rebellious after too long at sea, cast their captain adrift in a small boat, along with his son and six others. His ship *Discovery* was sailed back to England by Robert Bylot. Tried (with eight other crewmen) for Hudson's murder and pardoned, Bylot commanded two voyages on the *Discovery* with William Baffin as his pilot. On the second, in 1616, they sailed through Davis Strait and discovered both Baffin Bay and Lancaster Sound to the north of it—without realizing that the latter was the entrance to the passage for which so many had searched.[33] This fact would not be discovered for another two centuries. Geographical information aside, the only result of these daring feats of seamanship was to anticipate and partially justify an English claim of discovery to Hudson Bay and James Bay.

CONCLUSION

The seaborne exploration of the sixteenth century had taught Europe virtually nothing about the vast interior of North America. Nevertheless, accounts of the voyages did serve to publicize the New World and catch the imaginations of many more Europeans. Because of the early failure to find anything—besides fish—worth exploiting in the northern reaches of North America, European countries were slow to begin asserting their sovereignty in the region. By the end of the sixteenth century, however, some people had begun to see the region as a place not merely to visit but to live.

SHORT BIBLIOGRAPHY

Braudel, Fernand, et al. *Le Monde de Jacques Cartier*. Montreal and Paris, 1984. A useful background work, profusely illustrated.

Cook, Ramsay, ed. *The Voyages of Jacques Cartier*. Toronto, 1993. The latest edition of the Cartier journals.

Fitzhugh, William, and Elizabeth Ward. *Vikings: The North Atlantic Saga*. Washington and London, 2000. A summary of current knowledge, copiously illustrated.

Harris, R. Cole, ed. *Historical Atlas of Canada. Volume One: From the Beginning to 1800*. Toronto, 1987. A brilliant depiction of early Canadian history in cartographic form.

McGhee, Robert. *The Arctic Voyages of Martin Frobisher: An Elizabethan Adventure*. Montreal and Kingston, 2001. A recent study, well illustrated, by a Canadian scholar.

Oleson, Tryggvi. *Early Voyages and Northern Approaches 1000–1632*. Toronto, 1963. A controversial study arguing that the Thule were the descendants of Vikings and Native people.

Pope, Peter. *The Many Landfalls of John Cabot*. Toronto, 1997. One of the many recent books on Cabot published to mark the five hundredth anniversary.

Quinn, D.B. *North America from Earliest Discovery to First Settlement: The Norse Voyages to 1612*. New York, 1977. An authoritative account of early maritime discovery.

Savours, Ann. *The Search for the Northwest Passage*. New York, 1999. A recent account of the search for the fabled passage.

Wilson, Ian. *John Cabot and the Matthew*. St John's, 1996. A brief study of the first Cabot voyage.

STUDY QUESTIONS

1. Why did the Viking experience in North America not play a more significant part in the later expansion of Europe overseas?

2. What might account for the Skraelings' success in driving off the Norse settlers? Would a similar action by the people of the Gaspé region have driven off Cartier and his men?

3. How had Europe changed between the Norse landfalls and the 'discovery' of America at the end of the fifteenth century?

4. What was most significant about John Cabot's landfall in 1497?

5. From the perspective of geographical knowledge in the sixteenth century, argue in favour of a northwest passage to Asia.

6. What are the strengths and weaknesses of the biographical approach in historical study?

7. Why did many of the early discoverers make three voyages?

8. The terms 'discovery' and 'exploration' are often used interchangeably. Is there any difference between them?

CHAPTER FOUR

The Atlantic Region to 1670

The first would-be colonizers of northern North America were profoundly ignorant of the land they proposed to inhabit. Europeans were accustomed to great dynastic struggles over territory, and for them the vast expanses of land on the 'new' continent—claimed only by an apparent handful of Aboriginal people—must have seemed easy pickings. At a time when hardly any Europeans had attempted to live there year-round, little thought was given to the possibility that one might possess vast tracts of land and still not be able to eke out a living. Ignorance bred optimism, not least among those who had no intention of becoming settlers themselves. This chapter will explore some of the early efforts at planting colonies, the motives behind them, and the conflicts they produced.

The history of the early colonization period is usually told from the perspective of the founding of the United States. Yet both the French and the English were planting colonies to the north in the early years of the seventeenth century, not long after the permanent establishment of Virginia and before the founding of New England. Although most of these early settlements, French and English, were little more than trading posts ('factories'), in an era of intense imperial rivalry they also represented outposts of the competing European powers. Moreover, they

were small and isolated, without any institutional presence to protect them. Almost every one of these communities therefore lived under constant threat of physical harassment and siege, sometimes by the local First Nations, sometimes by European rivals acting in the names of their respective sovereigns. As a result, the history of the early colonial period can sometimes seem to consist of little more than a bewildering succession of raids and counter-raids. But out of incidents like these would emerge the subsequent territorial claims for which France and England would battle in North America.

THE MOTIVES FOR COLONIZATION

The most enthusiastic promoters of North American settlement were mainly absentee colonizers. The few promoters who came to the New World themselves soon discovered how empty their rhetoric had been. Lord Baltimore, who resided in Newfoundland for a year and a half, wrote to his sovereign on 19 August 1629:

> I [have] met with greater difficultyes and encumbrances here which in this place are no longer to be resisted, but enforce me presently to quitt my residence; and to shift to some other warmer climate of this new worlde, where the wynters be

TIMELINE

1597
English religious dissenters granted permission to establish colony of Ramea in Gulf of St Lawrence.

1598
Marquis de la Roche de Mesgouez establishes colony on Sable Island.

1603
Pierre Du Gua de Monts granted a monopoly 'of the coasts, lands and confines of Acadia, Canada, and other places in New France' and hires Samuel de Champlain.

1604
De Monts settlement established at Dochet Island.

1605
De Monts settlement moves to Port-Royal.

1606
Virginia Company of London sends three ships with 105 settlers to North America.

1607
Port-Royal abandoned.

1610
First Newfoundland settlement at Cupid's Cove. Port-Royal re-established.

1611
The first French priests arrive in Acadia.

1613
Samuel Argall sacks French settlements at Mount Desert Island on the Maine coast and at Port-Royal.

1620
Whitbourne writes 'Discourse and Discovery of New-Found-Land'.

1623
George Calvert, Lord Baltimore, receives his charter for Avalon.

1624
Sir William Alexander receives grant for New Scotland. Cardinal Richelieu becomes Louis XIII's chief minister.

1628
Robert Hayman publishes *Quodlibets* in London.

1629
Scots expedition to Port-Royal. The Kirke brothers capture Quebec.

1642
Charles de la Tour ordered home to answer treason charges.

1645
Defence of Fort La Tour by Madame La Tour.

1650
Charles d'Aulnay dies.

1654
La Tour surrenders his garrison to the English.

shorter and less rigorous. For here, your Majesty, may please to understand, that I have found by too dear bought experience, which other men for their own private interests always concealed from me that from the middest of October, to the middest of May there is a sadd face of wynter upon all this land, both sea and land so frozen for the greatest part of the tyme that they are not penetrable, no plant or vegetable thing appearing out of the earth untill it be about the beginning of May nor fish in the sea besides the ayre so intolerable cold, as it is hardly to be endured.[1]

The motives behind their grand projects were complex, some laudable and some despicable. National advantage, religion, humanitarianism, greed, and ambition all played a part. The Crown—English, Scottish,[2] or French—was the source of the charters and grants on which settlement projects depended, but the sovereigns themselves invested virtually nothing in the first colonies established under their auspices. The documents of territorial title and trade monopoly they bestowed on their subjects usually contained performance clauses that could be used to justify revocation when another prospective promoter came along.

Given that such settlement projects were rarely subject to serious planning, and that the (largely uncharted) territories involved appeared to offer virtually unlimited space, it is hardly surprising if monarchs did not worry too much about duplication, particularly in the earliest period. For example, in January 1598 Henri IV of France granted the Marquis de La Roche de Mesgouez title to the territories of Canada, Newfoundland, Labrador, and Norumbega (the Penobscot region of Maine), as well as a monopoly of the fur trade in these regions; the following year he made an almost identical grant to Pierre de Chauvin de Tonnetuit. Competing claims were common even between subjects of the same European monarch, and when the claimants came from different countries, they often settled their disputes by force.

If European monarchs and their advisers were happy to leave the establishment of a national presence in North America in the hands of private enterprise, at the same time they liked to think that in encouraging such activity they were assisting in God's work. But in reality, saving

the souls of indigenous North Americans was not a priority. Richard Whitbourne, who led a party of colonists to Newfoundland in 1617, did write about the possibility of missionary work among the indigenous people, but John Mason, author of *A Brief Discourse of the New-Found-Land* (1620), obviously did not think that there were many potential converts on the island in the first place: he argued that one of its advantages was its 'securitie from foraigne and domesticke enemies, there being but few Savages in the north, and none in the south parts of the Countrie'.[3] None of the English ventures to Newfoundland before 1625 included a clergyman; nor did the first French expeditions before 1611 include any priests.

Nevertheless, religion did play a part in some early ventures. The first English attempt at settlement in what is now Canada—an ill-fated colony called Ramea on one of the Îles de la Madeleine, in the Gulf of St Lawrence—was begun in 1597 by a group of dissenters who had broken with the Church of England and asked permission to go 'to a foreign and far country which . . . lieth to the west from hence in the Province of Canada' in order 'to worship God as we are in conscience persuaded by his Word'.[4] The Crown authorized these sectaries 'to plant themselves in an Island called Ramea or thereabouts' as an alternative to conforming in religion at home. But part of an advance party, including George Johnson,[5] was inadvertently shipwrecked on one of the Magdalen Islands and was driven off the island by Basque and Breton fishermen, assisted by Mi'kmaq allies. These early settlers squabbled continually among themselves, and, after returning to London, they led their fellow dissenters to Amsterdam (some of them would finally travel to America in 1620, aboard the *Mayflower*). Lord Baltimore's conversion to Roman Catholicism and his ambition to turn 'Avalon'—the name he gave to his struggling plantation on the Avalon Peninsula of Newfoundland—into a religious refuge were well known at both the English court and the Vatican in the 1620s.[6] France was far more circumspect than Britain about encouraging

☐ The Descelliers map, 1546. Here the usual perspective is reversed: 'La Mexique' is at the upper right, 'La Terre du Laboureur' (Labrador) at the lower left. In this period Newfoundland was often drawn as an archipelago. LAC, NMC-40461; original in the University of Manchester.

dissenters to become colonizers and colonists. Nevertheless, several early recipients of royal support for North American ventures were prominent Calvinists, among them Chauvin de Tonnetuit and Pierre Du Gua de Monts—although there is little evidence that their own motives were particularly religious.

The possibility of using North America as a place to send people unwanted at home was of interest to many colonial promoters. Undesirables made ideal colonists precisely because they were expendable. The Marquis de la Roche de Mesgouez, who established the first French colony in what is now Canada, on Île de Sable (Sable Island, off the Nova Scotia coast), had attempted to recruit criminals by offering those of 'considerable means' their freedom in return for a substantial sum of money, but the French courts refused to release any prisoners to him under such conditions.[7] Accordingly, in 1598 he selected his settlers from among 250 'vagabonds and beggars' turned over to him by the

Parlement of Rouen. On the whole, however, the English seemed more interested than the French in the prospect of transplanting unwanted population to North America. No doubt one reason was that in this period England and Wales were thought to be dangerously overpopulated. Agricultural transformations were displacing many rural people and turning them into 'vagabonds'—or worse. In 1596, for example, a Somerset justice of the peace complained that, despite the execution of 40 felons in his county, many more had escaped, adding:

> And these that thus escape ynfect great numbers, ymboldenynge them by ther escapes. And they will change both name and habytt and commonly go ynto other sheeres [shires] so as no man shall know them. . . . I do not see how yt ys possible for the poore cuntrymean to beare the burthens dewly layde upon hym and the rapynes [plunderings] of the Infynyt numbers of the wicked wandrynge Idell people of the land.[8]

The Welshman Sir William Vaughan in *The Golden Fleece* (1626) saw in Newfoundland— 'neer unto Great Britane, the next *Land* beyond *Ireland*, in a temperate Aire'—opportunities both for those driven from their farms and for younger sons who could not expect any inheritance. His colony of Cambriol, first proposed in 1616 and established in Newfoundland by Richard Whitbourne in 1617, was to be a new Wales, 'where the *Golden Fleece* flourisheth on the backes of *Neptunes sheepe*, continually to be shorn. . . . *Great Britaines Indies*, never to be exhausted dry'.[9] One contemporary described Vaughan's settlers as 'welch fools', and indeed they did not prosper; the settlement soon disappeared.[10]

More than one promoter recognized the opportunity for upward mobility available to those who got in on a colonization scheme at the beginning. None pressed this insight further than Sir William Alexander, Earl of Stirling. Alexander was of obscure origins but established a reputation as a poet and scholar at the Scottish court.

In 1624 he produced a 47-page pamphlet entitled *An Encouragement to Colonies*, dedicated to Prince Charles. For modern readers, its most interesting feature may be the map, loosely based on a French model, showing Alexander's plans for a colony in 'New Scotland', a region extending from the St Croix River to the St Lawrence, and the names he planned to give these rivers. There were two districts, named Caledonia and Alexandria; the river separating 'New England' from 'New Scotland' (now the St Croix) was to be called the Tweed, and the Saint John River the Clyde. Among other arguments for such a colony, Alexander pointed to the need for missionary activity among the indigenous people, and the refuge that North America could offer those seeking a 'retreate' into the contemplative life without joining a monastery.

Attracted by the pamphlet, the king instructed the Privy Council of Scotland to offer a barony and title ('Baronet of Nova Scotia') to any Scot who would undertake to finance six settlers for two years in Alexander's colony. When no takers came forward under this scheme, the Crown offered to grant a barony to anyone paying 3,000 marks (about 150 English pounds—a substantial sum) directly to Alexander, who would transport and provision the settlers himself. Even after Charles I made it possible for canny Scots to take up baronies 3 by 6 miles (5 by 10 km) in extent without actually travelling to America—by incorporating Nova Scotia into the Scottish Kingdom and instituting a ceremony on 'Nova Scotian' soil at Edinburgh Castle—not enough buyers came forward to provide adequate financing. Nevertheless, in 1629 Alexander did send an expedition to the Port-Royal area, on the northwestern shore of the Bay of Fundy, which managed to survive for several years. He also intended a spinoff settlement on Cape Breton Island. In 1631 New Scotland was turned over to the French with only 85 baronies sold, but an additional 25 titles were conveyed between 1633 and 1637. By this time the scheme was little more than a way of raising money for a beleaguered monarch unwilling to summon Parliament. Although the 'New Scotland' titles were regarded with suspicion, they remained part of the estates of those who had invested in them, and some Scots today are still baronets of Nova Scotia.[11]

Behind all the early colonization schemes, including those inspired in part by religious and humanitarian motives, was the expectation that great profits were to be made in North America. In the sixteenth century, fishermen from many nations sailed annually for the Grand Banks off Newfoundland and for the Gulf of St Lawrence. In 1591 an English privateer captured a French–Basque vessel, the *Catherine de St Vincent*, returning from northern Atlantic waters with a cargo of oil, salmon, fish, and 'a great store of rich furs, as beaver, martenes, otters and many other sorts'.[12] Obviously more than fish was involved in this lucrative trade. Many of the early French 'colonizers' were merchants who had been active in the region as fishermen and traders, and who hoped to use new settlements as trading bases.

THE SETTLEMENT OF NEWFOUNDLAND

While the French dominated the trading activity on the northern mainland coasts of North America in the late sixteenth century, the English were the most knowledgeable about Newfoundland and they turned their efforts in that direction. Of all the early colonization ventures in what would become Canada, the one launched by the London and Bristol Company for the Colonization of Newfoundland (founded in 1610) was the best conceived and financed. At its heart was a shrewd economic plan. Newfoundland clearly had a marketable commodity in codfish, caught on the Grand Banks and dried by fishermen on shore, along the coast of the Avalon Peninsula. Europe was desperately short of a protein food within the means of the poor, and dried cod found ready markets, especially in countries

where the Catholic Church forbade the faithful to eat meat on Fridays. The 48 subscribers of £25 each who organized the Newfoundland Company expected that permanent settlers would have some advantage in the fishery over the English Westcountrymen who came out to fish every spring and returned home in the fall. The Company's first settlement was established on a strict business-like basis by John Guy, who led 40 colonists from Bristol to Cupid's Cove on Conception Bay in July 1610, only months after the Company had been granted the whole island and the venture had been funded by sale of stock. Benefiting from experience acquired in earlier colonization ventures to the south, particularly through the Virginia Company, this Newfoundland settlement was well provisioned and directed by a shrewd merchant who understood the importance of diversifying the contents of the cargoes returning to England. Fish, of course, would have an assured market.

Two methods of fishing were common by the seventeenth century. One was more popular among the French, the other among the English. The 'wet' or 'green' fishery of the French centred on large vessels working the relatively shallow offshore waters (the 'banks'). Codfish were caught on lines, cleaned, and filleted, then stacked in the hull with copious quantities of salt. When the hull was full, the fishing vessel would head for market in Europe. These 'wet' fish did not attract premium prices. In the 'dry' fishery preferred by the English, smaller boats worked quite near the shore, then took their catch on land for processing. The fish were cleaned and filleted, and then set out on wooden 'stages' to be dried by the sun and wind using a minimal amount of salt. This method brought better prices, but unlike the French method it required onshore establishments for processing. The need for such bases made Newfoundland particularly attractive to would-be colonizers.

More settlements soon followed the one at Cupid's Cove. Around 1618 another syndicate of merchants applied for a land grant around

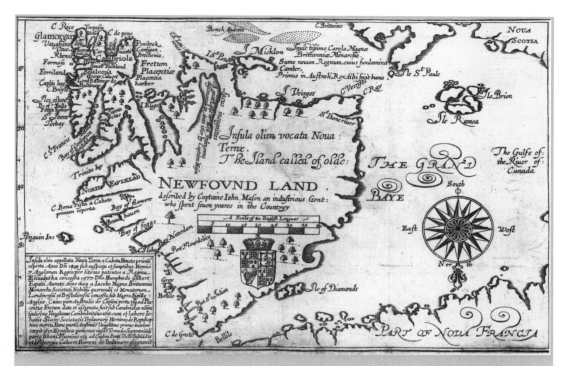

■ 'The Iland called of olde: Newfoundland described by Captaine John Mason, an industrious gent: who spent seven yeares in the countrey', 1617. This was the first English map of the island. LAC, NMC-21046.

Conception Bay and established Bristol's Hope. An early governor of Bristol's Hope was Robert Hayman, who had enough time on his hands to write poetry and dabble in translation.[13] The result was the publication in London in 1628 of the first collection of English verse written in North America, a miscellany entitled *Quodlibets, lately come over from New Britaniola, Old Newfound-land.*

Despite its advance planning, the Newfoundland Company soon had to face the fact that achieving self-sufficiency would take the colonists much longer than expected. The soil was neither fertile nor extensive, the climate was unsuited to European seed, and it was difficult to keep settlers as landless employees labouring under difficult conditions solely for the profit of

their employers. Continual injections of new manpower and provisions would be required, as would the patience to wait some time before turning a profit. Unfortunately, the Newfoundland Company, like most commercial ventures in early North America, expected rapid returns on investment, not constant capital outlays. As relations worsened between those on the spot and those at home, the former demanding more financial assistance and the latter insisting on immediate profits, the settlers lived in fear of armed attack from 'pirates'—many of them summering fishermen of various nationalities who were becoming increasingly concerned about competition. The truth was that the Newfoundland fishery did not really require permanent settlement. Colonization might eventually produce some marginal economic advantages, but the cost of establishing settlements was higher than investors were willing to pay.

Neither John Guy's settlement nor any of the successors sponsored either by the Newfoundland Company or by private promoters was spectacularly successful. Even so, by the 1660s a series of year-round settlements numbering some 1,500 inhabitants in all had taken hold along the rocky 'English Shore'. These settler societies were considerably more complex than historians once assumed, consisting of servants, planter employers, and a planter gentry of literate merchants.[14] Fishermen's incomes were reasonably good, and the local communities were no less stable than comparable ones in New England. The elite was dominated by the Kirke family, which was active in trading with Canada (and buccaneering in the 1620s), in the Newfoundland sack (sherry) trade of the 1630s and 1640s, and later was among the original investors in the Hudson's Bay Company. In 1675 the widow of Sir David Kirke and her son operated 10 fishing boats, and the Kirke family as a whole in that year had 17 boats, employing 81 crew members. Indeed, on the English Shore of Newfoundland as in many other early communities of North America, widows found opportunities for autonomy in business enterprise that they would not have enjoyed at home. Although Newfoundland had been one of the earliest sites in the New World for English colonization, the focus had quickly shifted south, where the English by 1650 had developed a number of successful colonies with a total population in excess of 100,000. The 'new-found' land continued to provide enormous wealth to the British Empire in the form of fish, and remained an important area of English (and later Irish) settlement.

ACADIA

Operating anything more than small trading factories in the North Atlantic region of the New World was no easier for the French than for the English. French efforts focused first on the exposed Atlantic seaboard, then moved to the more sheltered Bay of Fundy, and finally to the shores of the St Lawrence. In time, France would concentrate on the idea of a permanent settlement on the St Lawrence; but that shift in thinking did not occur until well into the seventeenth century. For most of the period before the 1650s, the maritime region that the French called 'Acadia'—vaguely bounded by the St Lawrence to the north, the Atlantic Ocean to the east and the south, and the St Croix River to the west—was almost as important to France as the St Lawrence Valley colony known as 'Canada'.[15]

Few settlements had a more violent internal history than the one established by La Roche de Mesgouez on Sable Island. The initial 250 colonists had been beggars in France, and at first they flourished in their new environment, living on the local fish and game, and trading for furs on the mainland. In 1602, however, La Roche failed to send the annual shipment of supplies, and over the winter of 1602–3 the settlers murdered not only their leaders but several of their own number. By the time relief arrived in 1603, only 11 colonists remained. On their return to France with their furs, they were rewarded by the King, although La Roche himself thought they should have been hanged.[16] Winter had also wreaked havoc on Chauvin de Tonnetuit's settlement of Tadoussac, at the mouth of the Saguenay River. The 16 men left there in 1600–1 found 'what difference there was between France & Tadoussac' when, having quickly run out of food, they took to quarrelling with one another.[17] Reduced to dire straits by lethargy and sickness, they took refuge with the local Aboriginal people. Five of them managed to survive.

In 1603 Pierre Du Gua de Monts, a Calvinist supporter of Henri IV who had been at Tadoussac in 1600, was granted a trading monopoly 'of the coasts, lands and confines of Acadia, Canada, and other places in New France'. In return he was obliged to settle 60 colonists there each year and to establish missions among the Native people. De Monts organized a trading company in the French coastal cities, and among his first recruits was a young draftsman, Samuel de Champlain (*c.* 1570–1635), who had been to Tadoussac in 1603 and would serve as geographer and cartographer for the expedition. Arriving on the Nova Scotia coast in May 1604, de Monts and Champlain searched the shores of the Bay of Fundy for a suitable site. They were impressed with the Annapolis Basin, but decided on Île Sainte-Croix (Dochet Island, Maine), in the mouth of the St Croix River. The 80 colonists constructed buildings (of imported French lumber!), and planted gardens and wheat. But 35 of them died, mainly of scurvy, in the harsh winter of 1604–5, and the crops were severely damaged. In the spring de Monts moved the remaining colonists to Port-Royal, in the Annapolis Basin, and built a 'habitation' there, while continuing to search the eastern seaboard for a location that offered a milder climate, fertile soil, exploitable mineral wealth, and co-operative Native people. Such a combination was hard to find. Champlain sailed along the New England coast as far as Cape Cod with Mi'kmaq guides, but his report was not enthusiastic.

In September 1605 De Monts returned to France to raise more money, leaving his deputy, François Gravé Du Pont, to administer the settlement in his absence; Champlain remained merely an observer. Having received more backing, de Monts arrived back in the summer of 1606 with a nobleman, Jean de Biencourt de Poutrincourt, Poutrincourt's young son Charles de Biencourt, and Marc Lescarbot, a Paris lawyer who wanted a taste of life in the New World and soon became a sort of resident historian and poet. The festive atmosphere that Lescarbot described shortly after their arrival—'All this month [August] we made merry. Monsieur de Poutrincourt . . . opened a hogshead of wine, one of them that was given for his own drinking, giving leave to all comers to drink as long as it should hold, so that some of them drunk until their caps turned round'—continued into the

next year, particularly when Champlain instituted the Ordre du Bon Temps (Order of Good Cheer)—a kind of dining club with extemporaneous entertainment—to boost morale. To celebrate Poutrincourt's return to Port-Royal after an extended trip of exploration, Lescarbot wrote a masque that was the first play composed and performed in North America:

> After many perils . . . Monsieur de Poutrincourt arrived in Port Royal the 14th day of November, where we received him joyfully, and with a solemnity altogether new in that part. For about that time that we expected his return (with great desire, and that so much more that, if any harm had happened him, we had been in danger to have confusion among ourselves) I advised myself to show some jollity going to meet him, as we did. And forasmuch as it was in French verse made in haste, I have placed them with the Muses of New France by the title of Neptune's Theatre, whereunto I refer the reader. Moreover, to give great honour to the return and to our action, we did place over the gate of our fort the arms of France, environed with laurel crowns (whereof there is great store along the woods' sides).[18]

At the end of July 1607, however, de Monts, unable to prevent illicit trade in furs by Basques, was forced by his backers to relinquish his monopoly, and the colonists were obliged to leave Port-Royal for either France or Canada. Lescarbot's narrative, *Histoire de la Nouvelle France* (1609), contains a sympathetic and informative account of de Monts's ill-starred venture in Acadia.[19]

Three years later, in 1610, Poutrincourt and his son Biencourt re-established a post and settlement at Port-Royal. They were accompanied by Claude de Saint-Étienne de La Tour, his son Charles, and a priest named Jessé Fléché, provided by the Jesuits at the request of Poutrincourt. Not understanding the local people's language, Father Fléché did not make much headway in his mission to them, although he did bap-

☐ Champlain's map of New France, 1632. LAC, NMC-15661.

■ Champlain's drawing of the habitation at Port-Royal, built in 1605 on the north shore of the Annapolis Basin. The parts of the complex are identified in an accompanying key. For example, building 'A' was the artisans' quarters, and 'B' was a platform for cannon. Champlain's own quarters were in building D. LAC, C-7033.

tize chief Membertou. The next year Antoinette de Pons, Marquise de Guercheville, began raising money in France for missionary work in Acadia, intending that some of the profits from the fur trade be used to support the Jesuits' efforts with the Native inhabitants. Guercheville was one of a growing number of devout women in France who directed their piety towards the New World. The missionaries she sponsored, Fathers Pierre Biard and Enemond Massé, found themselves opposed by Biencourt and engaged in unseemly disputes with him. In May 1613 the Jesuits joined a small colonizing expedition, ordered by Madame de Guercheville, that settled at Saint-Sauveur opposite Mount Desert Island (now in Maine). In July it was attacked by Captain Samuel Argall, admiral of Virginia, acting under instructions from the Virginia authorities to expel the French from all territory claimed by England.

Argall was a typical seventeenth-century thug who, before his attack on Saint-Sauveur, had journeyed up the Potomac River and abducted Pocahontas, the daughter of Powhaten, to exchange her for English prisoners taken by her father. The tiny French establishment at Saint-Sauveur was easily surprised and overcome, but not without a brief battle in which several Frenchmen were killed. On a second expedition,

LE THEATRE
DE NEPTVNE EN LA
NOVVELLE-FRANCE

Repréfenté fur les flots du Port Royal le quator-
ziéme de Novembre mille fix cens fix, au retour
du Sieur de Poutrincourt du pais des Armou-
chiquois.

Neptune commence revétu d'vn voile de couleur
bleuë, & de brodequins, ayant la chevelure & la barbe
longues & chenuës, tenant fon Trident en main,
affis fur fon chariot paré de fes couleurs : ledit chariot traîné fur les ondes par fix Tritons jufques à
l'abord de la chaloupe où s'eftoit mis ledit Sieur de
Poutrincourt & fes gens fortant de la barque pour
venir à terre. Lors ladite chaloupe accrochée, Neptune commence ainfi.

NEPTVNE.

A RRETE, Sagamos, * arréte toy ici,   *C'eft vn*
    Et écoutes vn Dieu qui a de roy fouci.   *mot de*
    Si tu ne me conois, Saturne fut mon pere, *Sauvage,*
Ie fuis de Iupiter & de Pluton le frere.   *qui figni-*
                                                fie Capi-
                                                taine.

DEVXIEME SAVVAGE.

Le deuziéme Sauvage tenant fon arc & fa
fleche en main, donne pour fon prefent des
peaux de Caftors, difant:
    Voici la main, l'arc, & la fleche
    Qui ont fait la mortele breche
    En l'animal de qui la peau
    Pourra fervir d'vn bon manteau
    (Grand Sagamos) à ta hauteffe.
    Reçoy donc de ma petiteffe
    Cette offrande qu'à ta grandeur
    I'offre du meilleur de mon cœur.

■ Lescarbot's masque, 'Le Théâtre de
Neptune en la Nouvelle-France'.
Bibliothèque de la ville de Montréal.

Argall destroyed what was left of Saint-Sauveur
and then looted Port-Royal, devastating the crops
and burning most of the buildings to the ground.
So began the Anglo–French struggle for control
of the continent that would end only with the
conquest of Canada in 1760.

Biencourt nevertheless rebuilt and continued to operate Port-Royal as a fur-trading headquarters. His close friend and lieutenant, Charles
de Saint-Étienne de La Tour, who inherited
Biencourt's claim as governor when the latter

died in 1624, wanted to establish a trading post
at Cap de Sable, on the southeastern tip of present-day Nova Scotia, and built Fort Lomeron
there. According to La Tour, he trained and led
an armed French–Native party in an effort to
enforce French fishing and trading rights against
English encroachments, thus responding in kind
to bullying tactics like those of Argall.

The confusing history of Acadia after 1624 is
inextricably bound up with the exploits of the La
Tour family, who could well have served as the
models for a swashbuckling novel.[20] In 1626,
Charles's father Claude, who had remained in
Acadia, returned to France. On his return voyage
to Acadia his vessel was captured by a squadron
led by Sir David Kirke and he was taken to
England. Quickly making himself at home, he
was accepted at court and married one of Queen
Henrietta Maria's ladies-in-waiting. He also managed to impress Sir William Alexander with his
knowledge of Acadia, accepted Nova Scotia
baronetcies for himself and his son, and in 1629
accompanied Alexander's son William to Acadia,
where they built Charles Fort near the remains of
the habitation at Port-Royal. For a time, following the capture of Quebec by the Kirkes, Charles
de La Tour's tiny trading post would be all that
was left of a French presence in North America.

Thanks to the recent discovery of the manuscript by Richard Guthry, one of those who
accompanied Alexander and Lord Ochiltree,
holder of another patent from the Scottish
Crown for North American settlement, we have a
much clearer notion of the establishment of 'New
Scotland'.[21] At 'Port Anglois' (later Louisbourg),
the Scots took possession of the harbour and
built a small fort. To the surprise of the leaders, a
number of the colonists brought out by Lord
Ochiltree turned out to be Puritan reformers,
who refused to co-operate with the larger body of
his settlers and apparently attempted to set up a
small settlement of their own; we do not know
what happened to them. Guthry's account shows
that he was familiar with the difficulties experienced by Lord Baltimore, writing of Newfound-

SIR DAVID KIRKE

(C. 1597–1654)

If Canadians remember David Kirke at all, it is probably in connection with the notorious Kirke brothers' capture of Quebec in 1629 (see p. 82). But his life and his North American career were considerably more complex than one buccaneering expedition. Kirke was the son of an English merchant who worked out of the French port of Dieppe, where it is thought he was born around 1597. In 1627 his father was one of a consortium of English merchants who financed an expedition, led by David, to drive the French from Canada. David commanded a fleet of three vessels and was accompanied by several of his brothers. In 1627 Champlain refused to surrender and Kirke did not press the issue. But in the Gulf of St Lawrence his ships met and defeated a French fleet, and Kirke returned to Europe with considerable booty. Kirke was rewarded by Charles I with the exclusive right to trade and settle in Canada, to which Sir William Alexander objected. Kirke and Alexander negotiated a compromise to establish an Anglo–Scots colony at Tadoussac. In 1629 he apparently sailed in command of a second fleet accompanying a fleet carrying Scottish settlers to Nova Scotia (see the document with this chapter). When Kirke learned from a French deserter that the French garrison at Quebec was in a parlous state, he returned there in July 1629—and this time Champlain surrendered. The

Kirkes evacuated the colony (the inhabitants were taken to England), seized all the furs, and attempted to work the fur trade with the assistance of a number of bushlopers, including Étienne Brulé.

Quebec was returned to the French by the Treaty of Saint-Germain-en-Laye in 1632, but a year later Kirke was knighted for his services to the English Crown. By 1637 he was part of the consortium (the Company of Adventurers to Newfoundland) that was given proprietorship of the island, and in 1639 he was appointed its first governor. The four Kirke brothers were made English citizens at about the same time. In time, David Kirke became one of the principal Planters on the island, although his political actions were always controversial. In 1651 he was called home and charged with withholding taxes. He remained under a cloud until his death in 1654, probably in prison in the Clink in Southwark. His family, led by his widow, fought a number of legal battles seeking compensation for losses (including the loss of Quebec when it was returned to France) and stayed on as merchants in Newfoundland until 1673, when the Dutch burned their settlement at Ferryland. Kirke's career—including his flexible loyalties—exemplified the fluidity of affairs in northern North America in the first half of the seventeenth century.

land that 'the land in respect of barrennesse being bare, rocky, montaneous, and in respect of long bitter winters be almost inhabitable fitter for

beasts then men; as some that planted there found true by miserable experience [for my Lord Baltamore is removing for New England]'. But he

THE ESTABLISHMENT
OF NEW SCOTLAND

Very little was known of the details of Scottish colonization in the Atlantic region in the seventeenth century until the recent serendipitous discovery, in the National Archives of Scotland, of the 13-page manuscript by Richard Guthry written to Sir William Alexander and excerpted here.

A Relation of the Voyage and plantation of the Scotts Colony in New Scotland under the conduct of Sr Wm Alex'r Younger 1629

It pleased your honour at my depairtur from England to lay a charge upon me, to writt a particular relation of our Voyage at Sea and of the nature and condition both of people and Country where now by the mercy of God we are planted, and setled in to the glory of God to the honour of our gracious Soveraigne and benefite of Great Britane to the eternal and famous memorie of your honor, and our gratious and religious General, whom the Lord long prosper in health over us, to the good of all these that are undertakers, and us that are employed in the busines by him, which in candore et virtute, according to my weake Judgment, I shall faithfully relate. . . .

The first day of Agust we came in sight of Cap-Brittan. The second day we coasted for the Cape, and for Porte Anglois, and seing some fishermen at sea afishing in there boats, we sent our Shallope to Speake with them they leaving there boats fled to the woods. We drew toward the Shoare, and espied ane harbor called Port Ballance tuo leagues from Port Anglois [English Harbour, later Louisbourg Harbour] where we found three Ships, fishermen, tuo of Rochell of the religion the third a Biscaigne, we entered the harbour, and upon deliberat tryall found her prise to the General's use. My Lord Uchiltrie determined to plant there, and by ye advise of Capt Ogilvy, built upon a small rocke a fort with three small pieces of Ordinance, a place strong enough, furnished with ordinance, to command the sea and land. The fort was named by our Generale Rosemarine.

As there is no action of what goodness one moment soever, but is subject to hinderences and inconveniences, and that in ovo: [before its birth] so fell it out with some of my Lord Uchiltreis plantation, to his great grief, for eight housholds of his company hiding fire under ashes for a time, at last it burst forth shewing there ingratitude to my Lord, having been at great charge with them and the rottennes of there hearts, a thing verry common among all factionists and schismaticks: for in plain tearms they refused to joyne stocks with my Lord, and did separat themselves from their company they will admitt none to their society without publick confession, they allow no pastorall function, censorious above measure, holding all papists damned, raylors against superiours, refractory to powers especially to Bishops, and the Setled State of England's church, great Seducers: they glory in the name of Brownists: good Lord deliver all plantations from such people, and root them out, or convert them where they live. . . .

The 28 day we anchored before Port Royall in the night we came in, our fleet being parted from us, partly by storms but principally by fogg and mists, weel may it be termed Port Royall, a royall entrie a river navigable twenty leagues by ships of the burden of tuo or three hundereth tunns, fortifyed on both sids with hills; and fruitfall vallies adorned and enriched with trees of all sorts, as goodly oakes, high firres, tale beich, and birch of incredible bignes, plaine trees, Elme, the woods are full of laurall store of ewe, and great variety of fruit trees, chesnuts, pears, apples, cherries plumes and all other fruits, willow hasell, sallow, we eat apples like in tast to bitter sweitings in England and of Shrubish fruit. . . . The 10 day came tuo Salvages in a canow, the ribbs of it of small firre knit in with wicker, curiously wrought, and lyned with the barke of trees, tuo oares, like two peeles for pasties. . . . There language not copious, long words, marred with the Basques language, subtill in their truckings, and nimble fingered, fair cariaged a people among whom people may live verry weel. continuall eaters and drinkers of the best if they have it. . . .

SOURCE: John Reid and Naomi Griffiths, eds, 'New Evidence on New Scotland', *William and Mary Quarterly* 3rd ser., 48 (1991): 502–7.

found much richer vegetation around 'Port Royall', including apples ('like in tast to bitter sweitings in England') and many berries. He also reported that the land was fertile, for the root vegetables sowed in a garden plot germinated in only a few days. The account, dated 13 August 1629, ends with the settlers 'about our husbandry, digging the ground for corne, which will yeelde it plentifully, as all store of fruits whatsoever'. Sublimely ignorant of the Bay of Fundy climate, Guthry obviously expected the growing season to be far longer than it was.

The following year Claude de la Tour returned to Acadia with his bride as part of another Anglo–Scots expedition. Hoping to persuade his son to join him, he stopped at Cap de Sable, but Charles replied that 'he would rather have died than consent to such baseness as to betray his King.' In response, Claude declared his son an enemy and led an attack on the fort at Cap de Sable. 'The ensuing battle between father and son', one historian has written, 'lasted two days and a night and has no parallel in the history of the New World.'[22] Charles put up a successful resistance and his father retreated to Port-Royal, only to discover that the Scots planned to abandon it. Seeing his prospects in 'Nova Scotia' disappearing, the elder La Tour:

did not dare to return to England for fear lest he should be made to suffer. His wife was also a great embarrassment to him; to her he did not dare confess, though in the end he was obliged to do so, telling her that he could find nothing better, nor any other course to take, than to remain with his son, for there was no more safety for him in France than in England after the attempts he had hazarded.[23]

Claude came to terms with his son, who by now had received a formal governor's commission from the French Crown. The elder La Tour was permitted to live at Cap de Sable in a house outside the fort. Re-establishing his position with the French, he remained there, 'very amply provided', with his English wife until his death in 1636.

Although the conflict with his father had ended, Charles de La Tour continued to lead an embattled life. The chief bone of contention was not settlement—Charles never displayed any real interest in transplanting colonists into the territories he claimed—but trade. In 1631 he built Fort La Tour (also known as Fort Sainte-Marie, at the mouth of the Saint John River), but after Acadia (and Canada) were returned to France by the Treaty of Saint-Germain-en-Laye in 1632, Isaac de Razilly was appointed the new governor instead of La Tour. Charles, who got on well with Razilly, returned to France and managed to get their respective spheres of authority regularized by the Compagnie des Cent-Associés (Company of One Hundred Associates, also known as the Compagnie de la Nouvelle France), which controlled French North America at the time. But

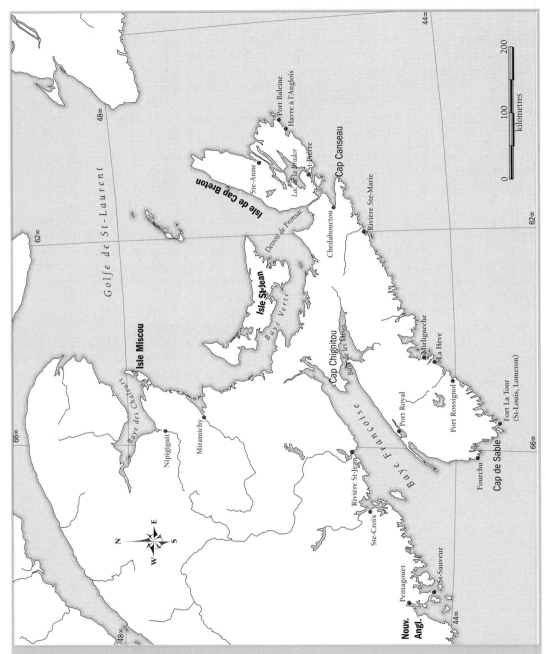

☐ Acadia and environs to 1670. Adapted from A.H. Clark, *Acadia: The Geography of Early Nova Scotia to 1760* (Madison: University of Wisconsin Press, 1968), 76.

CHARLES DE MENOU D'AULNAY
(C. 1604–50)

Early Acadia was a classic example of a territory governed by the militarily strong, as had been the norm in Europe during the Middle Ages. Throughout much of the first half of the seventeenth century, it was contested by two families of nobility, one originally headed by Isaac de Razilly, who had the support of Cardinal Richelieu, and the other by Claude de la Tour. Charles de Menou d'Aulnay was a cousin of Razilly, serving as his naval lieutenant after 1632. Given the nature of the terrain, with hundreds of miles of seacoast and virtually no settled population, it was hardly surprising that the contestants should operate by sea rather than by land. Lacking any established authority, the region fell prey to conflicting claims based on directions from the French court. After Razilly's death in 1635, d'Aulnay in 1638 received a letter from the King granting him the title of lieutenant-general of Acadia. Charles de La Tour defied this authority and in 1640 opened fire on d'Aulnay's ships. This action was resulted in his being taken prisoner along with his crew. He was subsequently released. At the outset, d'Aulnay had the advantages of the support of the Compagnie de la Nouvelle France, the financial backing of a leading merchant of La Rochelle, and allies at court as well. After several years of minor scuffling, in early 1645 d'Aulnay attacked La Tour's stronghold at Saint John. Defended by La Tour's wife, the fortress was stormed by d'Aulnay's forces and Madame de La Tour surrendered on a promise of mercy for herself and her men. For whatever rea-

sons, d'Aulnay did not honour this promise and had the defenders executed, forcing Madame de La Tour to watch the proceedings.

This harsh action, along with others, has led many (though not all) of the early historians to favour the La Tour interests in their accounts of the long struggle between the families, although there is considerable evidence that d'Aulnay had a considerable and superior claim to legitimacy and to constructive colonizing activity. Certainly, in 1647 his power as governor of Acadia was confirmed by the French court, and he was given a monopoly of the fur trade. D'Aulnay for years had been asserting political and economic power in the region, and he made many attempts to prevent interlopers from entering the territory. What he could not do was pay back the money he had borrowed in order to maintain his position, and when he died in 1650 in a boating accident, he left an estate mortgaged to the hilt. He had accomplished much in Acadia on his own initiative—building forts, clearing farms, importing settlers, establishing mills, and even establishing schools. Far more of the population of the region owed their presence in Acadia to d'Aulnay than to the La Tours. Ironically, his wife, Jeanne Motin, subsequently married Charles de La Tour, who raised his children. Almost all that we know about Charles de Menou d'Aulnay comes from second- and third-hand sources, and his own personality never comes to light in the narratives, apart from his occasional acts of cruelty to his enemies.

Razilly died in 1635, and his interests passed to his cousin and lieutenant, Charles de Menou d'Aulnay, who almost immediately came into conflict with La Tour.

The situation was exacerbated in 1638 when an attempt by the French Crown to divide Acadian territory between the two men put the central base of each on the land of the other. There ensued one of several intricate La Tour episodes, in which d'Aulnay, resenting a visit Charles de La Tour made in 1640 to check the furs at Port-Royal—the profits from which, it had been understood, he would share with Razilly—looked upon this visit as an act of aggression, convinced the King of Charles's disloyalty, and took command of Fort Lomeron at Cap de Sable. When Charles responded by sending an emissary to Boston to negotiate rights to trade and to recruit mercenaries, d'Aulnay rushed to France to report further complaints about Charles. In August 1642 d'Aulnay returned to Acadia with the official order that La Tour appear before the King to answer charges of treason.

La Tour decided to send his wife, Françoise-Marie Jacquelin, to represent him at the royal court. A member of the lesser French nobility, she had been wooed by La Tour in absentia, and came out to marry him in 1640.[24] She successfully argued her husband's case in 1642, then returned in a French warship, carrying supplies for La Tour. In 1644 she went again to France, but this time was unable to protect her husband's interests. Escaping to England with borrowed money, Françoise chartered an English ship to carry her and supplies back to her husband. Off Cap de Sable the ship was detained and searched by d'Aulnay, but she hid in the hold. In Boston she successfully sued the ship's captain for unwarranted delay, and used the money to hire ships to reinforce her husband's position at Fort La Tour. Early in 1645, with Charles again off in Boston seeking assistance, she commanded the defence of Fort La Tour against an attack by d'Aulnay. Her 45 defenders held out for four days against an invading force of 200, but she eventu-

ally surrendered on the understanding that d'Aulnay would 'give quarter to all'. But the victor went back on his word. All the captives were hanged. Madame de La Tour, who was forced to witness the executions with a rope around her own neck, died scant weeks later. After his wife's death, Charles de La Tour retreated to Quebec, where he was warmly welcomed. He remained there until 1650.

With La Tour out of the picture, d'Aulnay took over Fort La Tour, trading 3,000 moose skins there in one year. He also took over La Tour's connections with New England, signing a peace treaty and eventually receiving symbolic reparation—in the form of a sedan-chair captured by a pirate in Mexico—for the Yankee assistance to his rival. Keeping up his connections at the court, d'Aulnay was made governor of all Acadia in 1646 and given a monopoly of the fur trade—a privilege he was already forcefully asserting against the protests of the rival Compagnie des Cent-Associés. Upon d'Aulnay's death in 1650 at Port-Royal, his wife, Jeanne Motin, remained there, assuming the direction of her late husband's empire, as well as his enormous debt of more than 300,000 livres and guardianship of their eight children.[25]

As for Charles de La Tour, he returned to France to demand an inquiry into his case. With the support of the Compagnie des Cent-Associés, he was vindicated and received again into royal favour. Returning to Port-Royal with a few new colonists in 1653, he successfully courted d'Aulnay's widow, ending their rivalry by merging their interests (and their debts); the couple eventually had five children together. But La Tour's troubles were hardly over. Pursued by his debts, he was forced in 1654 to surrender his garrison of 70 at Fort La Tour to an invading English expedition of 500 men. La Tour was taken to England, where Oliver Cromwell refused to restore his property in Acadia but did agree to recognize the long-dormant baronetcy of Nova Scotia—earlier negotiated by Claude—if Charles would accept English allegiance and pay his English debts. Twenty-five years after denying his father and asserting his loyalty to the French Crown, Charles de La Tour felt compelled to accept Cromwell's terms. He sold out his rights in Acadia to English partners and retired to Cap de Sable with his wife and family. The French Crown belatedly (in 1700) recognized the Acadian rights of La Tour's children, suggesting some sympathy with his tribulations.

CONCLUSION

For more than 40 years La Tour and his family had kept French interests alive in Acadia. But he was a trader, not a colonizer. The few settlers he brought to the New World were only incidental to his economic and military activities. Unlike Champlain in New France, La Tour had no particular vision of a French agricultural presence in Acadia, and after his surrender to the English in 1654 the scattered Acadian set-

tlers were very much on their own until formal French occupation was restored by the Treaty of Breda in 1667.

While the period of English control from 1654 to 1667 left little internal mark on the region, it did remove Acadia from official French consideration when, in the early 1660s, the Crown decided to take a more active interest in its North American colonies. The region continued to be a hostage of empire, however, and part of it was temporarily occupied by a Dutch naval force in 1674 and renamed 'New Holland'. As a result of Acadia's isolation and various foreign occupations, its subsequent status was never properly clarified, and in the absence of any firm external control, the Acadian people developed a somewhat autonomous outlook. French attention was always attracted to the St Lawrence, and Acadia, despite its obvious strategic importance, would remain a backwater until well into the eighteenth century.

SHORT BIBLIOGRAPHY

Brebner, J. Bartlet. *New England's Outpost: Acadia before the Conquest of Canada.* New York, 1927. The classic study of Acadia: still useful.

Cell, Gillian. *English Enterprise in Newfoundland 1577–1660.* Toronto, 1969. The best survey of early settlement in Newfoundland.

Codignola, Luca. *The Coldest Harbour of the Land: Simon Stock and Lord Baltimore's Colony in Newfoundland, 1621–1649.* Montreal, 1988. A fascinating part of the Newfoundland story, based on documents in the Vatican Archives.

Davis, Ralph. *The Rise of the Atlantic Fisheries.* Ithaca, NY, 1973. The best general account of the fishery.

Handcock, W. Gordon. *'Soe longe as there comes noe women': Origins of English Settlement in Newfoundland.* St John's, 1989. A rich analysis of early settlement in Newfoundland.

Humphreys, John. *Plaisance: Problems of Settlement at this Newfoundland Outpost of New France, 1660–1690.* Ottawa, 1970. The story of the French

settlement in Newfoundland.

MacDonald, M.A. *Fortune and La Tour: The Civil War in Acadia.* Toronto, 1983. A stirring account of the La Tour family and its enemies.

Pope, Peter. 'The South Avalon Planters, 1630 to 1700: Residence, Labour, Demand and Exchange in Seventeenth-Century Newfoundland'. Ph.D. dissertation, Memorial University of Newfoundland, 1992. A revisionist account of the fate of the English settlements in Newfoundland after the early years.

Rawlyk, George. *Nova Scotia's Massachusetts: A Study of Massachusetts–Nova Scotia Relations 1630–1789.* Montreal, 1973. An important study focusing on the interaction between Nova Scotia and New England.

Reid, John. *Acadia, Maine and New Scotland: Marginal Colonies in the Seventeenth Century.* Toronto, 1981. An award-winning analysis of the early colonization of the Acadian region.

STUDY QUESTIONS

1. Why did many in the early colonization period believe that England was overpopulated?

2. Why did the English begin establishing settlements in Newfoundland?

3. Many residents of the Atlantic region in the seventeenth century appear to have held national loyalty lightly. Why?

4. What does the Guthry manuscript tell us about New Scotland?

5. The early history of the Atlantic region was unusually complex and characterized by international conflict. Why was this the case?

6. What was Madame de La Tour's role in the family wars?

7. Why did France lose interest in the Atlantic region after the middle of the seventeenth century?

CHAPTER FIVE

Canada to 1663

■ The European settlement of Canada began in 1608, when Samuel de Champlain established a small trading post at Quebec financed by a private company. Not until 1663 would the French Crown take over the administration of the colony. Nevertheless, France had become involved with Canada in a variety of ways over the intervening years. For the first few decades, activities revolved around the fur trade as the French worked to develop trading relationships with the First Nations north of the St Lawrence, defend themselves against those to the south, and find new sources of furs. In the 1620s Champlain persuaded the French Crown to assist in a major settlement effort, but this project was still chiefly a private enterprise. The nature of French involvement in Canada did not seriously begin to change until the 1630s, with the beginning of the first great missionary thrust. Although the earliest missionaries were members of the Récollet and Jesuit orders, much of their funding came from devout women in France, a number of whom soon made their own way to Canada to assist in the good work. In addition, by the 1640s a few families were starting to farm along the St Lawrence.

The presence of family-based agricultural settlers marked a significant difference between the St Lawrence colony and the Atlantic region, where the settlers consisted almost exclusively of men living in small, isolated communities along the seacoast. Another difference was that in Canada the main economic activity, the fur trade, was increasingly conducted in the interior of the continent, away from the St Lawrence settlements, whereas on the coast the settlements existed to serve the needs of trading and fishing interests. In both regions the early communities were constantly at risk of attack, but in Canada the threat came from the First Nations (the Iroquois in particular), while in the Atlantic region it came from European thugs taking advantage of the period's ongoing imperial rivalries. In Canada, the presence of missionaries and settlers would ultimately lead the French Crown to assume responsibility for the colony. By contrast, both the French settlements in Acadia and the English ones in Newfoundland would fall between the cracks of their respective mother country's imperial policy; in the latter years of the seventeenth century, they would essentially be left to their own devices.

CHAMPLAIN AND THE FOUNDING OF QUEBEC

In 1607 Pierre de Monts received a one-year extension of his fur-trading monopoly on the

TIMELINE

1603
Champlain travels up the St Lawrence River.

1607
Pierre de Monts receives an extension of his monopoly, conditional on founding a colony on the St Lawrence. Founding of Jamestown, Virginia.

1608
Champlain builds the 'habitation' at Quebec.

1609
Champlain's first armed encounter with Iroquois.

1618
Champlain appeals to the Crown for financial assistance.

1627
Cardinal Richelieu creates the Compagnie des Cent-Associés.

1629
The Kirke brothers capture Quebec.

1632
Quebec restored to France by Treaty of Saint-Germain-en-Laye. Champlain returns and Father Paul Le Jeune arrives. Jesuits are given a monopoly of religious service in Canada. Le Jeune begins the *Jesuit Relations*.

1634
Champlain founds Trois-Rivières.

1635
Champlain dies.

1639
Jesuits build Sainte-Marie-aux-Hurons. Marie de l'Incarnation arrives.

1640
Iroquois wars begin in earnest.

1641
Paul de Chomedey de Maisonneuve embarks for Montreal with a party of settlers including Jeanne Mance.

1642
Montreal founded. St Lawrence floods at Montreal.

1645
Compagnie des Cent-Associés gives its monopoly to local merchants and withdraws from Canada.

1649
Fathers Jean de Brébeuf and Gabriel Lalemant are killed by Iroquois. Sainte-Marie-aux-Hurons is abandoned.

1653
Marguerite Bourgeoys arrives at Quebec.

1659
François de Laval appointed vicar-general of Quebec.

1661
Witchcraft incident in colony.

1663
Earthquake strikes Quebec. Royal takeover.

■ Champlain's drawing of the battle of 31 July 1609, in which he led a party of Algonquins, Hurons, and Montagnais against 'nearly two hundred' Iroquois. The First Nations allies of the French were eager for the battle, and 'dispatched two canoes by themselves to the enemy to inquire if they wished to fight, to which the latter replied that they wanted nothing else'. LAC, B-198.

condition that he establish a post on the St Lawrence River. His cartographer, Samuel de Champlain, had already explored the river in 1603 as far as the Lachine Rapids, west of Montreal; accordingly, in 1608 de Monts entrusted Champlain with this initiative. Leaving the Île d'Orléans at the beginning of July, Champlain reported:

> I searched for a place suitable for our settlement, but I could find none more convenient or better situated than the point of Quebec . . . which was covered with nut-trees. I at once employed a portion of our workmen in cutting them down that we might construct our habitation there: one I set to sawing boards, another to making a cellar and digging ditches, another I sent to Tadoussac with the barque to get supplies. The first thing we made was

> the storehouse for keeping under cover our supplies, which was promptly accomplished through the zeal of all, and my attention to the work.[1]

At the base of a high cliff Champlain's men toiled into the fall, erecting three two-storey buildings connected by a gallery around the outside ('which proved most convenient') and surrounded by a moat and palisades.

Soon after their arrival at Quebec[2] a conspiracy was discovered, led by the locksmith Jean Duval, who had earlier accompanied Champlain south to Cape Cod and been wounded by a Native arrow. The plan was to murder Champlain and deliver the establishment at Quebec to the Spaniards or the Basques in return for a large payment. Duval was tried, convicted, and then 'strangled and hanged at Quebec; and his head

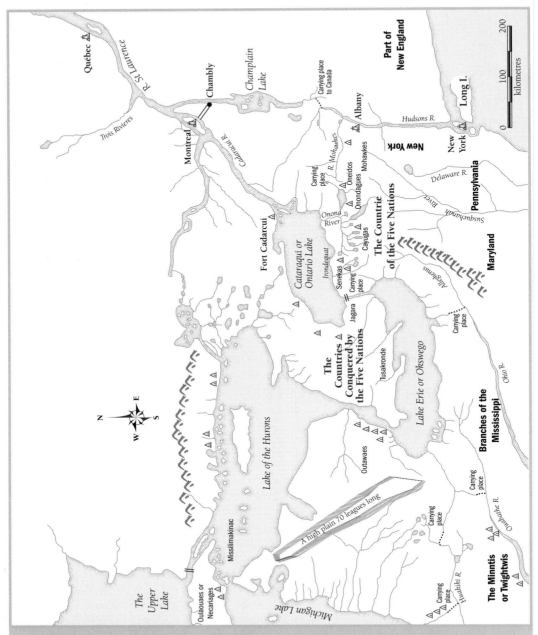

☐ 'The country of the Five Nations', based on the frontispiece to vol. II of *The History of the Five Indian Nations of Canada* (New York, 1902) by Cadwallader Colden (1688–1766), surveyor-general (1720) and lieutenant-governor (1761) of colonial New York.

was put on the end of a pike, to be set up in the most conspicuous place on our fort'.[3] The remaining conspirators were sent back to France. In February of 1609 scurvy broke out. When spring arrived, only nine of 25 had survived. It had not been an auspicious beginning.

For a century the First Nations living north and south of the St Lawrence had been part of a network trading furs to fishermen and traders for European goods. Both groups were determined to gain control of this trade, for which the St Lawrence was the crucial channel. The southern group was the Iroquois Confederacy of five nations—Mohawk, Oneida, Seneca, Onondaga, and Cayuga—all living in present-day upstate New York. The northerners included the Iroquoian-speaking Huron, who lived in semi-permanent agricultural communities east of Lake Huron's Georgian Bay, as well as the hunting societies of the Algonquin and Montagnais, who ranged as far northeast as the Gulf of St Lawrence. These northern peoples were the allies that Champlain sought to cultivate in order to ensure the success of his fur-trading establishment. In the spring of 1609 he wanted to explore 'the country of the Iroquois', but the Montagnais were determined to make war on them. Champlain co-operated, accompanying his allies up the Rivière des Iroquois (the Richelieu River) to the lake that he named after himself. At Ticonderoga (Crown Point, NY) a miniature battle took place. 'When I saw them [the Iroquois] making a move to fire [arrows] at us, I rested my musket against my cheek and aimed directly at one of the three chiefs. With the same shot two fell to the ground; and one of their men was so wounded that he died some time after.'[4] The Iroquois fled into the woods, 'whither I pursued them, killing still more of them'. Thus ended the first armed conflict between Native people and Europeans in New France.

By 1615 some 50 Frenchmen were living on the St Lawrence. Among the early arrivals, the only one to set about farming the land was Louis Hébert, who had moved to Quebec in 1617 after long service at Port-Royal as a surgeon. The company, however, had no interest in agricultural settlement; they wanted to make use of Hébert's medical skills, and actually tried to discourage him from farming.[5] Not until 1618—when Champlain outlined a grand colonization scheme for the King and the French *chambre de commerce*—did France entertain anything approaching the plans for settlement proposed by the Newfoundland Company.

THE COMPAGNIE DES CENT-ASSOCIÉS

Until 1618 Champlain had served as an agent for others rather than as a colonial promoter in his own right. In that year he presented a proposal combining commercial arguments designed to appeal to investors with a settlement scheme designed to appeal to the imperial pretensions of the Crown. New France and the St Lawrence offered the possibility not only of a short route to Asia but of 'a great and permanent trade' in a wide variety of goods besides furs, including fish, timber, and whale oil. The annual income was projected at 5,400,000 livres, virtually none of it to come from agriculture and less than 10 per cent from furs. Champlain requested that 300 families of four persons each, and 300 soldiers, along with several priests to minister to them, be sent to his base on the St Lawrence. The French response was enthusiastic, and Louis XIV instructed the syndicate employing Champlain to expedite his plans. But the syndicate was unable to agree on terms with Champlain. Not until 1627, when Cardinal Richelieu assumed supervision of New France and established the Compagnie des Cent-Associés, did Champlain's grandiose scheme receive substantial backing.

Richelieu's company—unlike the Newfoundland Company or the Virginia Company—was a top-down venture, organized by the government, rather than a grassroots operation inspired by interest in the profits of colonization. It was to be capitalized at 300,000 livres, each participant contributing 3,000, and initially the profits were to be ploughed back into the company. Of the 107 members listed in May 1629, only 26 were merchants or businessmen, mainly from Paris; the rest were courtiers and state officials. In 1628 the company dispatched to Quebec four ships carrying 400 crewmen and passengers, together with 'all necessary commodities & quantities of workmen & families coming to inhabit & clear the land and to build & prepare the necessary lodging', at a cost of 164,270 livres.[6] Unfortunately, war had broken out between England and France the previous year, and the ships were captured off Gaspé by an armed Anglo–Scottish expedition led by the brothers Kirke. A year later, in July 1629, the Kirkes forced Champlain's starving outpost to surrender. The brothers' occupation of the St Lawrence was extremely profitable; they left taking not only Champlain and most of the settlers but booty ranging from furs to a fleet of 19 fishing boats.

Champlain was exiled from New France for the next four years. In 1629 the Cent-Associés spent another 103,796 livres in an effort to retake Quebec, but it was defeated by shipwrecks and pirates. By now the company had spent virtually all of its original capital without having planted a single colonist, and the only ones who had made any profits were the freebooters. For the next 33 years colonization was subcontracted to undercapitalized private companies, none of which was able to match the ambitions of the Cent-Associés.

THE COLONY RESTORED AS A MISSIONARY BASE

Quebec was restored to France in 1632, under the Treaty of Saint-Germain-en-Laye. One of the first Frenchmen to arrive thereafter, in July of the same year, was Father Paul Le Jeune, recently appointed superior-general of the Jesuit missions in Canada. Le Jeune's arrival marked the beginning of a new direction for the colony as a centre for missionary activity among the Aboriginal

people—financed chiefly by the contributions of devout laypersons in France. He describes the welcome he received:

> We celebrated the holy Mass in the oldest house in the country, the home of Madame Hébert, who had settled near the fort during the lifetime of her husband. She has a fine family, and her daughter is married here to an honest Frenchman. God is blessing them every day; he has given them very beautiful children, their cattle are in fine condition, and their land produces good grain. This is the only French family settled in Canada. They were seeking some way of returning to France; but having learned that the French were coming back to Quebec, they began to regain courage. When they saw our ships coming in with the white flags upon the masts, they knew not how to express their joy. But when they saw us in their home, to celebrate the holy Mass, which they had not heard for three years, good God, what joy![7]

In 1632 Father Le Jeune sent to the Provincial Father of the Society of Jesus in Paris the first in a series of annual reports that would continue until 1791 and become famous as the *Jesuit Relations*. His first letter was intended as nothing more than an account of his experiences. But his superiors recognized its value, and immediately ordered that it be published.

Le Jeune had not sought to become a missionary. But he had accepted his assignment as superior-general of the Jesuits in Canada with joy and enthusiasm, for the extension of his Church's mission was a central feature of the Catholic Counter-Reformation in which he had been nurtured. The 'Relations' soon became public documents, consciously tailored for consumption in France, to explain and promote the missionaries' efforts. They combined a wealth of detail about life in New France, the local Native peoples, exploration, and travel, with accounts of the priests' missionary activities and instances of what they believed to be miraculous conversions among the Aboriginal population. These writings

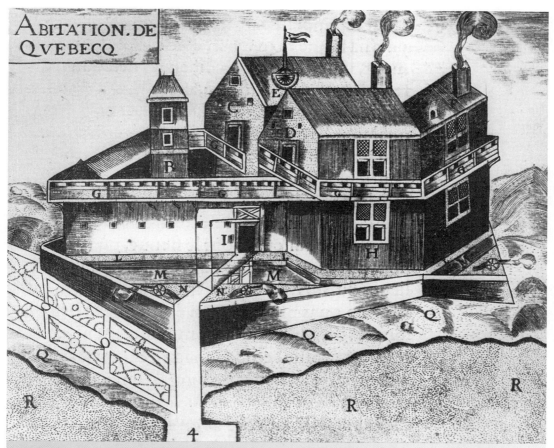

ABITATION. DE
QVEBECQ

- The habitation at Quebec, 1608, from Champlain's *Voyages* (1613). The accompanying key identifies, among other things, the garden (O) in the lower left—above the R for St Lawrence River; a dovecote (B); a sun-dial (E); and the gallery (G) 'made all round our buildings on the outside, at the second story'. Rare Book Collection, LAC, neg. 875920.

did more than colour the telling of the history of New France and especially of the interaction between the Jesuits and the Aboriginal people. For many generations they provided the basic structure for that history, including such fundamental elements as the standard Jesuit characterizations of the Native people as savages, of the colony as a missionary centre, and of the European mission in North America as a desperate war against heathenism and the devil.

CHAMPLAIN'S ACHIEVEMENT

When Champlain himself returned to Quebec, in May 1633, he found that the palisade of Fort St Louis, erected on the cliff 170 feet above the habitation in 1620, was still standing, but the habitation itself had been destroyed. In August 1634 he reported to Cardinal Richelieu on the reconstruction of the colony. He had been given great confidence by the support of the Cent-

Associés, he wrote: 'it gives me fresh courage to see the many craftsmen and families they have sent out this year and intend to send later . . . , with plentiful supplies of munitions and food.'[8]

But the Compagnie des Cent-Associés was unable to maintain its trading monopoly, and although it remained the titular owner of the territory of New France, over the long haul it did not play an active part in the colony's development. It did, however, in 1634 grant to Robert Giffard de Moncel one of the first seigneuries in New France, 'a league of ground to be taken up along the shore of the St Lawrence River for a depth of a league and a half inland, at a place where the River called Notre Dame de Beauport flows into the said St Lawrence River'.[9] Giffard, his wife, and their two children were among 30-odd other colonists, all from the Perche region of Normandy, who arrived in that year.

While settlement was painfully slow, the fur trade prospered. In 1634 Champlain sent Jean Nicollet, an interpreter and clerk of the Cent-Associés, to establish relations with the western Indians and to look into the possibility of reaching the China Sea. Travelling as far as Lake Michigan—the first European to see it—Nicollet carried with him a 'great robe of Chinese damask, with flowers over all & birds of various colours'.[10] Though the robe never was returned to China, it apparently did help to persuade the Winnebagoes of Green Bay to smoke the pipes of peace with Nicollet. He returned to Quebec in the autumn of 1635 to find that Champlain had suffered a paralytic stroke shortly before his arrival. But the west had now been opened.

Champlain died on Christmas Day 1635. Circumstances had dictated that, instead of leading a prospering colony through its initial growth and the establishment of colonial institutions, he had spent much of his career dealing with the preliminaries of settlement. Despite years of tireless effort—including nine voyages to France—by the time of his death there were still only 150 settlers on the St Lawrence. Nevertheless, Champlain had laid the foundation on which Canada would be built. He had also written a number of volumes of *Voyages*—published in Paris in 1613, 1619, and 1632—that are the source for much of what we know about Canada under his leadership.[11] Champlain's latest biographer—and he has many more than any other figure in early Canadian history—argues that his dream was for a New World in which Aboriginals and Europeans shared mutual respect and dignity.[12]

EVANGELIZATION

More effective in attracting settlers to the colony than either the emerging French state or private enterprise was Catholic zeal for evangelization. The missionary enterprise in Canada had two basic wings, often only loosely connected: that of the Jesuits and that of the lay missionaries.

The Society of Jesus had been founded by Ignatius Loyola in 1540 as a militant (and militarily organized) order devoted largely to missionary activity. The Jesuits travelled the globe, especially in the period 1550–1650, preaching and teaching among indigenous peoples ranging from the Aztecs to the Japanese. They developed a reputation for adapting Christianity to the customs of the people with whom they came into contact, and they were probably less rigid than other missionaries in their view of what constituted true conversion. As soldiers of Christ, they expected their mission to require bloodshed, even martyrdom—although they were not supposed to go out of their way to seek it. In the *Relation* of 1639–40, Le Jeune wrote:

> We have sometimes wondered whether we could hope for the conversion of this country without the shedding of blood; the principle received, it seems in the Church of God, that the blood of martyrs is the seed of Christians, made me at one time conclude that this was not to be expected,—yea, that it was not even to be desired; considering the glory that redounds to God from the constancy of the Martyrs, with whose blood all the rest of the earth has been so lately drenched, it would be a

sort of curse if this quarter of the world should not participate in the happiness of having contributed to the splendour of this glory.[13]

In France the Jesuits were respected for their obvious commitment and discipline; however, in addition to the usual vows of poverty, chastity, and obedience they took a vow of loyalty to the pope, and this made them suspect in the eyes of many secular authorities, including the French Crown. Despite the suspicions, they were given a monopoly of religious service in Canada in 1632. In 1634, three priests led by Father Jean de Brébeuf established a base in Huronia, and five years later construction began on an elaborate fortified headquarters, Sainte-Marie-aux-Hurons, on the Wye River. It eventually comprised 20 buildings, including a residence for priests, a church, a hospital, outbuildings for farming, and residences for lay workers and Native converts, as well as a canal with three locks. The first substantial religious settlement north of Mexico, by 1649 it housed 18 priests, 4 lay brothers, 29 workers and servants (donnés), 11 domestics, 4 boys, and 6 soldiers.

Historians over the centuries have found it difficult to deal with the record of the Jesuits in North America. The nineteenth-century American historian Francis Parkman, a Protestant, conceded that their sincerity was unquestionable, but wondered whether sincerity was enough to justify their efforts to overturn entire civilizations of 'pagan' peoples (in fact, evangelization among 'alien' people had always been central to Christianity, so in that respect the Jesuits were hardly unique). In any event, the Jesuits were a powerful force in the post-1632 life of the colony, not least because of their cultural assumptions. The Jesuits had no doubt that the indigenous North Americans were human beings, separated from Europeans only by their lack of 'gentleness, grace, and education'.[14] But they also believed that the Native people were deeply misguided, not only in their spirituality but in their permissive attitudes towards marriage and children. The

Jesuits were able to fit the Native people into their demonology as well as into their humanism.[15]

The Jesuits actively sought financial assistance for their Canadian mission from the laity in France, and their efforts inspired some to undertake their own missionary projects. For example, when the young widow Marie-Madeleine de Chauvigny de la Peltrie recovered from a serious illness in 1635, she took a vow to establish a school for 'sauvagesses' in New France. She persuaded an Ursuline teacher named Marie de l'Incarnation to join her, put much of her fortune in trust for the school, and even financed a ship for the voyage. Soon after their arrival they founded the Ursuline convent in Quebec. Another noblewoman sponsored three nursing sisters of the order of Augustinian Hospitalières, who arrived on the same ship as the Ursulines and founded a hospital at Sillery to care for Aboriginal patients—Huron, Montagnais, Algonquin, and Abenaki.

In 1639, the Société Notre-Dame de Montréal pour la Conversion des Sauvages de la Nouvelle-France—financed by private donations from wealthy Frenchmen and Frenchwomen—launched a major project to establish a missionary colony at Montreal. Of its 46 members, 34 were lay people, and 12 were women.[16] Led by Paul de Chomedy de Maisonneuve, a small group of 40 settlers left La Rochelle in two ships in May 1641. The ship carrying Jeanne Mance, who would later found the Hôtel-Dieu at Montreal, reached Quebec in early August. But Maisonneuve's vessel did not arrive at Tadoussac until late September, and he and his companions were forced to winter at Sillery, near Quebec. The party arrived at Ville-Marie (Montreal) on 17 May 1642. The next day, Sunday, Father Barthélemy Vimont celebrated the new colony's first mass. His sermon predicted great things:

> . . . what you see is but a grain of mustard seed, but it is sown by hands so pious and so moved by the spirit of faith and piety that Heaven must doubtless have vast designs since it uses such

PAUL DE CHOMEDEY DE MAISONNEUVE

(1612–76)

Paul de Chomedey de Maisonneuve was a member of a distinguished French seigneurial family. He spent his early years in military service in Holland, and at some point he became quite devout. In the late 1630s, while seeking a new vocation, he came upon the *Jesuit Relations* and was impressed by the activities of Father Charles Lalemant, the first superior of the Jesuit mission at Quebec. He went to visit Lalemant, who recognized in him a potential leader for a new colony planned for Montreal under the auspices of several private lay societies in France, including the Compagnie du Saint-Sacrement. Lalemant recommended M. de Maisonneuve as a gentleman who would meet all the requirements, and Jérôme Le Royer de La Dauversière, the layman who was the guiding genius behind the Montreal initiative, quickly agreed. Maisonneuve was given the power to choose the colonists and organize the expedition, and on 6 May 1641 he set off for Canada. Exactly when he arrived is unknown, but in September of that year he served as godfather (with Jeanne Mance as godmother) at the baptism of an Aboriginal girl.

Forced to spend the winter at Quebec, he discovered that the settlers there were opposed to the new colony, chiefly because of Montreal's exposed position in relation to the increasingly hostile Iroquois. But when he was offered a site on the Île d'Orleans instead, he replied, 'Sir, what you are saying to me would be good if I had been sent to deliberate and choose a post; but having been instructed to go to Montreal by the Company that sends me, my honour is at stake, and you will agree that I must go up there to start a colony, even if all the trees on that island were to change into so many Iroquois.' His inflexible stance won that argument, although there were continual struggles with the Canadien administration over other issues (such as the use of firearms). Finally, in August 1642, Maisonneuve and a second party celebrated their arrival at Montreal.

In the years that followed, there would not be many occasions to celebrate. When the Iroquois began their attacks, in 1643, Maisonneuve initially prohibited his people from leaving the fort, but in March 1644 he led a party against the Iroquois attackers, ultimately engaging in hand-to-hand combat with the leader of the Iroquois force. Making several journeys back to France to deal with administrative and financial affairs relating to the settlement, in 1651 he vowed not to return without at least 100 soldiers, and two years later he was able to sail for Canada with 120 new recruits, privately funded by Madame de Bullion, and accompanied by Marguerite Bourgeoys. The newcomers helped the settlement to survive through the 1650s. In 1665, Maisonneuve—who was not popular with the new royal administration in New France—was recalled to Paris. His departure symbolized the close of an era in the history of New France, as private benevolence was succeeded by state initiative as the determining force in the colony.

workmen, and I have no doubt that this seed will grow into a great tree, one day to achieve wonders, to be multiplied and to spread to all parts.[17]

A second contingent of settlers arrived in August, and the feast of the Assumption was celebrated with the thunder of cannon. Later that year the island of Montreal was nearly inundated by flood waters from the St Lawrence. The following June, the Iroquois made their first raid on the settlement.

THE IROQUOIS WARS AND THE DESTRUCTION OF HURONIA

The 1643 raid marked the beginning of a new stage in the long rivalry between the Iroquois and the northern peoples allied with the French. The struggle for control of the fur trade would rage for the next two decades, with disastrous consequences for the Huron in particular.

The Huron were crucial to the fur trade in the first half of the seventeenth century, serving as middlemen between the northwestern peoples who supplied the furs and the French traders in Montreal and Quebec. They had once numbered twice as many as the Iroquois—30,000 to 15,000—but in the 1630s their numbers were reduced to perhaps 12,000; no doubt a major reason was disease contracted from the French, including an epidemic of measles that swept Huronia in 1634, the same year the Jesuits set up their first missions there.

The Iroquois, for their part, were just as determined as the Europeans to control the flow of furs. Supplied by the Dutch with firearms—which the French were reluctant to give to their Native allies—they ambushed the Huron fur-fleets on the Ottawa River, and in the early 1640s began blockading the river and attacking the French settlements on the St Lawrence. 'In former years', wrote Father Vimont in 1643:

the Iroquois came in rather large bands at certain times in the Summer, and afterwards left the River free; but this present year, they have changed their plan, and have separated themselves into small bands of twenty, thirty, fifty, or a hundred at the most, along all the passages and places of the River, and when one band goes away, another succeeds it. They are merely small troops well armed, which set out incessantly, one after the other, from the country of the Iroquois, in order to occupy the whole great River, and to lay ambushes along it everywhere; from these they issue unexpectedly, and fall indifferently upon the Montagnais, Algonquins, Huron, and French.[18]

Sporadic attacks continued over several years.

Meanwhile, the Compagnie des Cent-Associés withdrew from New France in 1645, when it gave its fur-trading monopoly to the Communauté des Habitants, an organization of Canadien merchants who agreed to pay for the administration of the colony. This shift in control of the fur trade, from the metropolis to the local level, was a positive step for the colony, but Iroquois hostilities would continue to hamper the fur trade for the next two decades.

In 1648 the Iroquois turned their attention to Huronia. Seneca warriors destroyed the mission of Saint-Joseph and killed 700 Huron in July of that year, and the following March a party of 1,200 Iroquois destroyed Saint-Louis and Saint-Ignace, where Fathers Jean de Brébeuf and Gabriel Lalement were tortured to death. Already weakened, those Huron who were not killed either surrendered or fled. Before the Iroquois could reach Sainte-Marie, the Jesuits there 'applied the torch to the work of our own hands' and fled with some 300 Huron families to Christian Island in Georgian Bay. Over the next few months, wrote Father Paul Ragueneau, the missionaries were 'compelled to behold dying skeletons eking out a miserable life, feeding even on the excrements and refuse of nature'.[19] The next year the missionaries returned to Quebec with a few hundred survivors—the pathetic remnant of a once-powerful nation—and by 1651, according to the Sulpician priest François Dollier

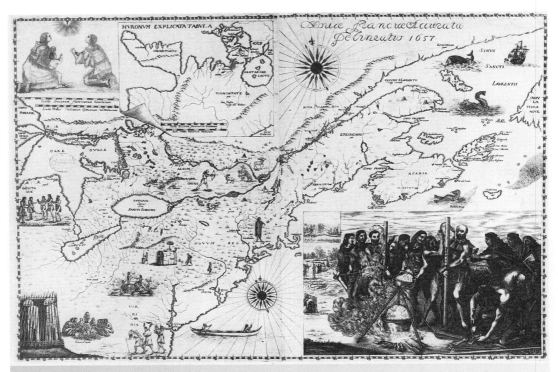

■ 'Novae Franciae Accurata Delineatio, 1657'. Among the vignettes included on this map are Huron converts at prayer and the martyrdom of the Jesuits Brébeuf and Lalemant. LAC, C-116786.

de Casson, 'there were no more Huron left to destroy'. Now the Iroquois:

> turned their faces towards the Island of Montreal, which they looked on as the first object of attack in descending the river. Therefore, when the winter was over, they began to attack us in good earnest, and with such obstinacy that they scarce left us a day without an alarm. We had them on our hands incessantly; not a month of the summer passed without our roll of slain being marked in red at the hands of the Iroquois.[20]

Today it is generally accepted that the missionaries contributed, however inadvertently, to the destruction of Huronia both by exposing the people to new diseases and by undermining their culture in the effort to impose alien beliefs and practices on them.[21] The Huron themselves may not have known germ theory, but they could easily see a connection between the presence of missionaries and disease. In 1640 a Huron woman addressed a meeting of her people:

> It is the black robes who make us die by their spells; listen to me and I'll give you incontrovertible proof. They arrive in a certain village where everyone is healthy. As soon as they are established there, everyone dies, except for three or four people. Then they change places, and the same thing happens again. They have only to enter a cabin to bring sickness and death with them. Don't you see that when they move their lips, which they call praying, they are really casting spells. It's the same thing when they read their books. Moreover, they have big wood [firearms]

■ 'Mort Héroique de Quelques Pères de la Compagnie de Jésus dans la Nouvelle France', lithograph by Et. David, 1844. This composition appears to be modelled after the scene on the map on page 90, but includes several more of the Jesuits who were killed in New France. LAC, C-4462.

in their cabins and they use these to make noise and send their magic everywhere. If we don't put them to death immediately, they will ruin the country and leave no one alive.[22]

The Jesuits themselves were well aware of strong feelings against them. As Le Jeune wrote in 1636:

> our lives depend upon a single thread; and if, wherever we are in the world, we are to expect death every hour, and to be prepared for it, this is particularly the case here. For not to mention that your Cabin is only, as it were, chaff, and that it might be burned at any moment, despite all your care to prevent accidents, the malice of the Savages

gives especial cause for almost perpetual fear; a malcontent may burn you down or cleave your head open in some lonely spot. And then you are responsible for the sterility or fecundity of the earth, under penalty of your life; you are the cause of droughts; if you cannot make rain, they speak of nothing less than making away with you.[23]

Yet relatively few missionaries in New France came to harm at the hands of the people among whom they lived. Similarly among French residents in general, relatively few actually lost their lives to the Iroquois; most of the Five Nations' victims were other Aboriginal people, above all the Huron. Of the 200-odd French who were killed in the wars of the seventeenth century, many were recent arrivals in Canada, unfamiliar with Aboriginal warfare. In 1652, for example, Guillaume Guillemot (also known as Du Plessis-Kerbodot), governor of Trois-Rivières, insisted on leading an expedition against the Iroquois himself, even though he was not a soldier and knew nothing about Native warfare. He had only arrived in the colony in late 1651, a few months before his misadventure. Against advice from more experienced hands, he led his forces into a swamp where they were ambushed and 22 of them, including Guillemot himself, were killed.[24] Eight years later, Adam Dollard des Ormeaux—who had come to Canada in 1658— led 15 companions and a party of Huron and Algonquin in search of Iroquois to ambush. Instead he met a much larger party of Iroquois, and his force became trapped in an indefensible fort without any water. When he allowed his men to break a truce by opening fire on the enemy, the latter rushed the barricades and all the French inside were killed.[25] The worst years for attacks on the settlements were 1650–3 and 1660–1. Although Montreal was under more frequent threat than the other Canadien communities, the dangers doubtless seemed worse than they really were.

THE WOMEN OF THE MISSIONARY MOVEMENT

In the early years, virtually the only French women in Canada were there for religious reasons, whether as members of holy orders or as devout lay workers. In 1635 Father Le Jeune wrote in the *Jesuit Relations*:

> What amazes me is that a great number of nuns, consecrated to our Lord, want to join the fight, surmounting the fear natural to their sex to come to the aid of the poor daughters and poor wives of the savages. There are so many of them who write to us, and from so many monasteries . . . that you would say they are competing to see who can be the first to mock the difficulties of the

sea, the mutinies of the ocean, and the barbarity of these lands.[26]

In the colony, women's right to catechize was taken for granted, and women's orders enjoyed considerably more freedom than they did in France. Three women in particular played extremely important roles in the years after 1640. While the Jesuits constituted a highly disciplined army of missionary soldiers, these women may have represented a less militant approach.

MARIE DE L'INCARNATION

The Ursuline teacher who travelled to Quebec with Mme de la Peltrie in 1639, Marie de l'Incarnation (1599–1672) was a towering figure of the generation that succeeded Champlain in New France, but she has rarely received the attention she deserves from secular historians. Born in Tours, the daughter of a master baker, Marie Guyart was a devout child who married at the age of 17. Her husband died two years later, leaving her with a son. Soon afterwards she experienced a mystical conversion. Having taken vows of chastity, poverty, and obedience, she lived for some years with her sister and brother-in-law and worked with them in their transport business. But at 27 she had another experience of the 'inner paradise' and, leaving her son with her sister, joined the Ursuline order of nuns. After taking her vows in 1633, Marie had a dream in which God took her to a land resembling Canada. Six years later she arrived at Quebec, where she established the Ursuline school.

In the early years, most of the school's pupils were Aboriginal, from several different communities. Including boys as well as girls, they represented a range of ages, and no doubt many were attracted to the school by the promise of food. The curriculum—prayers, hymns, and catechism—was taught in the students' own languages, and some nuns became quite proficient in several tongues. The boarders were instructed in household arts, such as needlework. The goal

MARIE DE L'INCARNATION TO HER SON, 17 MARCH 1650

Marie de l'Incarnation wrote over 13,000 letters, many to her son Claude Martin. After her death, he edited 221 of the letters—polishing hastily written prose—and published them. Then he gave the originals away; since then most of them have disappeared. The following translation, from his 1681 edition, is by Joyce Marshall.

As for us, as I have said, we have been at peace. But a fortnight ago the Iroquois appeared. Some of them were captured and the others put to flight. Some of them, nevertheless, have done what they have never dared do till now. They have never approached nearer than forty leagues of us but on this occasion they came to within three leagues of Quebec, where they attacked the habitation of one of our habitants, killed two of his domestics, put his whole family to flight, and pillaged his house and his goods. . . .

The Reverend Father Bressani, who set out to go on mission in the month of September, retraced his steps when he had not yet made fifty leagues of the journey. He spent the winter here with a group of Hurons that he was instructing. Our three religious houses, and some charitable persons, joined together to nourish these poor exiles, who have just departed to fetch the other members of their families from their country so as to settle close to us. These new habitants oblige us to study the Huron tongue, to which I had not previously applied myself, having contented myself with knowing only that of the Algonkins and Montagnais who are always with us. You will perhaps laugh that at the age of fifty years I am beginning to study a new tongue, but one must undertake all things for the service of God and the salvation of one's neighbour. I commenced this study a week after the octave of All Saints, and the Reverend Father Bressani has been my master till the present with an entire charity. As we can only study tongues in winter, I hope that someone else will come down this autumn who will render us the same assistance. Pray to Our Lord that it may please him to open my mind for his glory that it may render him some little service. . . .

As I finish this letter, I learn that the young men are being gathered together to go against the Iroquois, who are quite close. Everyone fears them, because they hide in the underbrush and pounce upon people when no-one is thinking of them. They are real assassins that cannot be extinguished and laugh at the most skilful.

SOURCE: Joyce Marshall, ed., *Word from New France: The Selected Letters of Marie de l'Incarnation* (Toronto: Oxford University Press, 1967), 179–81.

was assimilation, and eventually a few former students would marry Frenchmen. The majority, however, returned to their traditional ways of life; by 1668, after nearly 30 years of effort, Marie admitted to her son that 'Of a hundred that have passed through our hands we have scarcely civilized one.'[27] In addition, the Ursulines provided a different sort of education for the daughters of the French colonists—girls whom the nuns found to be quite undisciplined and more advanced 'in several dangerous matters' than their counterparts in France. Much of their curriculum consisted of French grammar and decorative arts.

Marie de l'Incarnation combined a fervent spiritual life and devotion to the care of souls

■ Marie de l'Incarnation, oil portrait attributed
to Abbé Hugues Pommier (1637–86).
Archives des Ursulines de Québec.

the love which possessed me. Finally I lost my
voice, as if the Spirit of my Jesus had wanted the
rest for Himself. I could not restrain myself on this
occasion, which subsequently caused me much
confusion, something which has since happened
to me unexpectedly on other occasions.[28]

Fortunately for modern historians, Marie's correspondence also included detailed descriptions of
daily life in the colony.

JEANNE MANCE

The daughter of a middle-class family in east-
central France, Jeanne Mance (1606–73) was
educated by the Ursulines. Instead of joining the
order, however, she began working as a nurse in
nearby hospitals during the Thirty Years War
(1618–48). In 1640 she learned of the missionaries at work in New France and soon determined to join them. Travelling to Paris, she lobbied not only with the Jesuits but with ladies of
the court, including the queen herself. Eventually she was introduced to Angélique Faure, a
rich and well-placed widow who supported a
number of charitable works. Impressed with
Mance's sincerity, she asked her to take charge of
a hospital in Quebec, the money for which Faure
had already pledged, but she made Mance promise to keep the source of the funding a secret. The
need for secrecy in early missionary financing
suggests a fear of the authorities in both Church
and state, who tended to associate lay evangelism
with Protestantism. Mance subsequently suggested to the Jesuits that a society be established
to collect contributions from the devout women
of Paris for use in North America.

Within months of her arrival in 1642, Mance
responded to pleas from the founders of Montreal
and had established 'a little Hospital' in Montreal.
Three years later she supervised the construction
of the Hôtel-Dieu, and she returned to France
several times to raise money in support of both
the hospital and the colony at large. As a layper-
son of undoubted piety, she served as a bridge

with skills both as an administrator and as an
observer of the secular life around her. In addition to teaching her pupils, she taught catechism
to local Native people, studied their languages,
and prepared not only an Iroquois catechism but
two   dictionaries,   (French–Algonquin   and
French–Iroquois). She also wrote extensively:
spiritual autobiographies, lectures on faith, notes
on prayer—and more than 13,000 letters, most
of them to her son.

Marie's letters bear witness to the mystical
nature of her faith. On one occasion she was asked
to explain a line in the Song of Solomon (1:2):

Without further ado I began with these words: Let
him kiss me with the kisses of his mouth: this led
me to an address, so that, starting from this quo-
tation, no longer being in control of myself, I
spoke for a very long time, under the influence of

between the mission-oriented colony and the lay communities in France that provided much of the financing for its activities in the early years.

MARGUERITE BOURGEOYS

Marguerite Bourgeoys (1620–1700) was the daughter of a master candle-maker in Troyes, near Paris. Although we know very little of her early life, it seems that she tried and failed to find a satisfactory home in a number of religious communities before obtaining her confessor's permission to take private vows while remaining in the secular world. This was an unusual concession at a time when most religious women were cloistered (partly to preserve their chastity). Some women may have welcomed the protection of the convent, but for others like Bourgeoys, who sought to express their faith through activity in the world, it apparently was a real hardship. Having joined a group of secular teachers attached to the Congrégation de Notre-Dame in Troyes, she arrived in Montreal in 1653 and five years later opened her first school. At the same time she began working to form a non-cloistered spiritual community that would offer a third way of life for consecrated women like herself. It took more than four decades to persuade the Church hierarchy to grant formal authorization, but in 1698 the Congrégation de Notre-Dame was canonically constituted and Marguerite Bourgeoys was at last able to take simple vows.[29]

■ Marguerite Bourgeoys, 'Le Vrai Portrait', painted the day after her death in January 1700 by Pierre Le Ber. This work was not discovered until the mid-twentieth century, when a work previously believed to be an authentic likeness was x-rayed, revealing the 'true portrait' under several layers of paint. Musée Marguerite-Bourgeoys.

LAY MOVEMENTS AND THE CHURCH

For its first two decades New France developed without any formal ecclesiastical hierarchy. One important consequence was that devout women like Marie de l'Incarnation, Jeanne Mance, and Marguerite Bourgeoys were not continually under the scrutiny of a bishop empowered to govern virtually their every move.[30] The freedom that they enjoyed was particularly significant at a time when the Roman Catholic hierarchy was attempting to reassert its control over the lay movements that had proliferated with the Counter-Reformation, many of which Rome suspected of 'Jansenism'. Regarded by the orthodox Church as Protestants in Catholic clothing, Jansenists believed in an uncompromising Christianity, emphasizing the importance of personal piety and individual conscience over the sacraments, and offering an interpretation of grace (derived from St Augustine) that came dangerously close to the Calvinist doctrine of election.[31]

There was no heresy per se in early Canada; but from the point of view of the authorities—in

Church and state alike—lay movements could come dangerously close. Even the Société Notre-Dame de Montréal was not entirely free of suspicion: the organization most responsible for its creation, the Compagnie du Saint-Sacrement, was itself a secret society of secular priests and laymen dedicated to missionary and other good works, and was eventually suppressed by Cardinal Mazarin. It was one thing for members of a religious order such as the Jesuits to devote themselves to missionary activity on the orders of their superiors and under their direction. For unsupervised lay people voluntarily to undertake such work was quite another thing—and all the more dangerous when those people were women. From the standpoint of an orthodox ecclesiastical hierarchy, people like Jeanne Mance and Marguerite Bourgeoys were to some extent threats to the natural—male—order of things.

THE COUREURS DE BOIS AND THE MISSIONARIES

The geographical shakedown of European colonization in the late sixteenth and early seventeenth centuries determined that the French would take the lead in overland exploration. While the English, Scots, Dutch, and Swedes established settlements along the eastern seaboard, the French—belatedly following up on Cartier's discoveries—founded their colony on the St Lawrence River. Providing access to the Great Lakes as well as most of the major river systems of the continent, the St Lawrence would confer enormous power and influence on the nation that controlled it. It directed the French inland in their search for new sources of furs to supply the major export commodity of New France, and encouraged young Frenchmen to adopt and take advantage of both the First Nations' technology and their knowledge of the country.

The first major French overland adventurer after Champlain was Étienne Brûlé, who lived with the Hurons near Georgian Bay, Lake Huron, in 1612, and may have been the first European to see Lakes Superior and Erie. Like so many early explorers, Brûlé was an elusive figure who left no written accounts of his life, but it is likely that he had volunteered in 1610 to live with the Hurons and learn their language; he was probably the young man mentioned by Champlain in 1611 as accompanying a Huron party to a meeting with the French: 'I also saw my French boy who came dressed like an Indian. He was well pleased with the treatment received from the Indians, according to the customs of the country, and explained to me all that he had seen during the winter, and what he had learned from the Indians. . . . [He] had learned their language very well.'[32] In 1615 Brûlé travelled with a Huron party into the territory of the Susquehannah, south of the Iroquois in what is now southwestern New York State. He took advantage of the opportunity to investigate the neighbouring regions, including modern Pennsylvania, and may have reached as far as Chesapeake Bay. Brûlé subsequently journeyed to the north shore of Georgian Bay, and then in the early 1620s along the St Marys River to Lake Superior.

Like many Europeans who 'went native', Brûlé was respected for his skills as an interpreter. Yet his compatriots were intensely suspicious of his new persona. Brûlé's final 'treachery' came in 1629, when he entered the employment of the Scottish Kirke brothers following their capture of Quebec, but Champlain had already found occasion to criticize his moral character and behaviour. Brûlé would not be the only European in the early period to put his own agenda ahead of the abstract national loyalties dear to European hearts. By 1633 he was dead, reportedly killed and eaten by Hurons.

Among Brûlé's successors was François Marguerie de la Haye. Born in Rouen, Marguerie worked as a guide and interpreter for the Jesuits in the mid-1630s, before he was captured by Iroquois. While in captivity he adapted so well that the Iroquois called him the 'double man'. Eventually, when his captors were planning an attack on Trois-Rivières, he was sent to negotiate the town's capitulation, having given his word of honour that he would return to captivity if unsuccessful. Instead of negotiating, he warned the town against the Iroquois; but he did return, and was later released by his captors. He died in a canoe accident on the St Lawrence.

Over the course of the seventeenth century, interpreters like Brûlé and Marguerie were transformed into coureurs de bois—'runners of the woods' or 'bushlopers', as the English called them. In their rough and often ruthless ways, such men offered a sharp contrast to the lay missionaries, especially the women. As conduits for Aboriginal knowledge, they were responsible for much of the Europeans' constantly broadening geographical knowledge of the North American continent. Their motives, however, had less to do with improving cartography than with exploiting new sources of wealth, particularly furs, and above all enjoying a free and adventurous life in the woods. Whether or not these wilderness braves became completely assimilated into Native society and culture—and some did—they all gained skills and knowledge that made them crucial figures in the economy of New France: how to live off the land, paddle a canoe for long distances with few breaks, hunt animals for food, and, of course, communicate with local populations, not merely in terms of language but at a level of genuine cultural understanding. Travelling in small parties, exposed to every danger, they lived by their wits and had to be constantly adaptable. They made splendid guerrilla warriors—as the English would discover to their dismay in the subsequent wars for control of the continent.

On some of their travels the coureurs de bois were accompanied by missionaries, who were constantly seeking new mission fields, especially after the destruction of Huronia. The missionaries were not necessarily skilled woodsmen, but they were often adept at learning Aboriginal languages. They were also quite fearless and energetic. By 1661 a number of missionaries had established themselves at stations or posts virtually ringing the northern approaches to the

Mississippi River: Green Bay, Michilimackinac, Black River (Wisconsin), and Sault Ste Marie. Father Charles Lalemant, in the *Jesuit Relation* of 1659/60, was able to describe the great river as part of a waterway system stretching from the Gulf of Mexico to Hudson Bay. Only the hostility of the Iroquois prevented the missionaries from pressing directly into the upper Mississippi basin.

Few coureurs de bois kept detailed records of their adventures or even their personal lives. But one of the greatest, Pierre-Esprit Radisson, has left accounts of six of his 'voyages' into the interior in the form of a series of autobiographical narratives, the first four of which he dictated in imperfect but vivid English.[33] They constitute some of the most fascinating documents of the early period of European settlement and expansion across the continent, providing a window onto a world where life was lived according to rules quite different from those governing 'civilization'.

Radisson was born in France sometime between 1636 and 1640, and moved to Canada as a child. In 1651 he was living in Trois-Rivières when he was captured by a Mohawk raiding party. Adopted into a prominent family, he rapidly acquired Mohawk ways, but when he met another young Frenchman, in similar circumstances, on a hunting trip, the two young men murdered their Native comrades and escaped. They were soon recaptured. Radisson was tortured—in ways meticulously described in his account—but was saved by his adoptive parents. Later, as a member of a raiding party into the country controlled by the Dutch, he initially rejected an offer of repatriation from a Dutch trader, but when he returned to his village he changed his mind and determined to escape while he was still trusted. As he put it, 'I repented of a good occasion I let slip, finding myself in the place with offers of many to assist me, but he that is of a good resolution must be of strong hopes of what he undertakes, and if the dangers were considered which may be found in things of importancy, you ingenious men would become cooks.'[34] Radisson had no intention of becoming a cook.

■ Pierre-Esprit Radisson, 're-drawn from a rare old Paris print'. LAC, B-70.

He escaped and by 1654 was back in Trois-Rivières, where he found that his widowed half-sister had married Médard Chouart Des Groseilliers, who would become his associate in a series of wilderness expeditions and adventures.

In 1657 Radisson accompanied some Jesuit missionaries to the Iroquois village at Onondaga in present-day New York State. Relations between the visitors and the local people were tense over the ensuing winter, so Radisson used his knowledge of Iroquois ways to plan an escape. In the spring, the French invited the Iroquois to a great feast, knowing that their guests would not sleep until all the food and drink that was provided had been consumed. Eventually, according to Radisson, the Iroquois could 'hold out no longer; they must sleep. They cry out, "Skenon"!—enough. "We can bear no more." . . . They are told the French are weary and will sleep awhile. They say, "Be it so." We come away. All is quiet. Nobody makes a noise after such a hurly-burly. The fort is shut up as if we had been in it. We leave a hog at the door for sentry, with a rope tied to his foot.'[35] The Jesuits prevented their secular companions from slaughtering the sated (perhaps drugged) Iroquois and their families—a possibility that Radisson had considered without qualms. He wrote simply, 'It was no great matter to deal with five or six hundred women and maybe a thousand children.' But instead the French stole silently away.

Radisson began his partnership with Groseilliers, his brother-in-law, in 1659 on a journey to Lake Superior that excited their interest in exploiting the fur-bearing regions they knew extended as far north as Hudson Bay. Departing with a mixed group of Huron, Chippewa, and Odawa, at one point their little fleet numbered 14 canoes carrying 40 men. Everywhere they went they were welcomed and entertained by the local people. The pair returned to Montreal in August 1660 with a vast haul of beaver skins that was seen as the colony's salvation. But the traders themselves were not so warmly received. The skins were confiscated by the authorities and both men were prosecuted for trading without official permission. By 1664 the partners had decided to seek support for their plans elsewhere. Travelling first to Boston and then to London, they found the English far more enthusiastic than the French about Hudson Bay, which had been discovered half a century earlier by Henry Hudson but at the time had offered no economic incentive for further exploitation. Now, however, its fur-trading potential was clear.

THE COLONY IN TRANSITION

In 1659 François de Laval arrived in Canada as the pope's vicar-general (he would not become bishop until 1674, when the pope created the diocese of Quebec). Laval's appointment is often discussed in the context of the ongoing struggle for control of the Church between the pope in

Rome and the Gallican Church of France.[36] At least as important, however, were the contemporary struggles between private, individual piety and public ecclesiastical authority. Under Laval, the religious atmosphere in the colony became much less free. Jeanne Mance was quickly marginalized; as her *DCB* biographer diplomatically puts it, she 'encountered the inability of authorities whom she revered to understand her deeds of deliverance in earlier days'.[37] By 1665 Maisonneuve had been ordered back to Paris. Although Marguerite Bourgeoys managed to gain the support not only of secular authorities but of the King himself (in 1671), a series of bishops refused to formalize her lay teaching community for another quarter-century. And even Marie de l'Incarnation came into conflict with Laval when he tried to intervene in the running of her convent, writing: 'we are dealing with a Prelate who, being of a very exalted piety, will never give up if once he is persuaded that God's glory is in question.'[38] By the early 1660s, the age of both lay and female piety in New France was for all intents and purposes over.

By now the colony as a whole was experiencing tensions that expressed themselves in various ways. Witchcraft was alleged in 1661, when a recently arrived Protestant miller was accused of using his 'diabolic art' to cast a spell over a young girl whose parents refused him permission to marry her. An epidemic of whooping cough at the same time was attributed to 'sorcerers'.[39] The miller was tried in an ecclesiastical court, found guilty of witchcraft, and shot. The atmosphere of unease and apprehension increased when in February 1663, in the midst of carnival season, the colony was struck by an earthquake. Marie de l'Incarnation described it vividly:

> Thick dust flew from all sides. Doors opened of themselves. Others, which were open, closed. The bells of all our churches and the chimes of our clocks peeled quite alone, and steeples' and houses shook like trees in the wind—all this in a horrible confusion of overturning furniture,

> falling stones, parting floors, and splitting walls. Amidst all this the domestic animals were heard howling. Some ran out of their houses; others ran in. In a word, we were all so frightened we believed it was the eve of Judgement, since all the portents were to be seen.[40]

The tremors continued for many months.

About this time the French Crown withdrew trading privileges and land ownership from the Compagnie des Cent-Associés and made New France a Crown colony. Since 1647 Canada had been governed by a central Council, in consultation with elected representatives of the districts of Quebec, Trois-Rivières, and Montreal. That arrangement had worked fairly well, giving the government the independence from France that it needed to respond to the wishes of the inhabitants, but it was not so much a positive reform as an effort to avert an emergency at a time when many feared that the colonists were ready to abandon Canada altogether. By 1663 most of the colony was probably happy to trade autonomy for the security of French financial and military assistance. As for the Crown, it had little choice but to assume responsibility for the colony if it wanted to maintain a French presence in North America.

In June 1665 four companies of the Carignan-Salières regiment arrived from France with orders to quell the Iroquois. They were followed in September of that year by a chief civil administrative officer, Intendant Jean Talon. One of Talon's first aims was to increase the population, and to this end a contingent of 'filles du roi'—orphan girls who had been raised at the King's expense—were dispatched to the colony.[41] 'The hundred girls the King sent this year', Marie de l'Incarnation wrote in October 1665:

> have just arrived and already almost all of them are married. He will send two hundred more next year and still others in proportion in the years to come. He is also sending men to supply the needs of the marriages, and this year full five hundred have come, not to speak of the men that make up

TABLE 5.1
CENSUS OF 1665–1666

New France

Table IV–Professions and Trades

Professions and Trades	Localities					
	Québec	Côtes nord	Orléans & Côtes sud	Trois-Rivières	Montréal	Total
Armourers	2	0	2	0	0	4
Gunsmiths	2	0	0	2	3	7
Gentlemen of means	15	1	0	0	0	16
Bakers	1	3	4	0	3	11
Butchers	0	3	2	0	2	7
Button makers	0	1	0	0	0	1
Brewers	1	0	0	0	0	1
Brick makers	0	1	0	0	0	1
Hatters	0	4	1	0	2	7
Wheelwrights	0	2	0	0	0	2
Surgeons	2	2	0	0	1	5
Carpenters	3	21	4	1	7	36
Charcoal Burners	0	1	0	0	0	1
Braziers	0	2	0	0	1	3
Chandlers	1	2	0	0	0	3
Rope makers	1	3	1	0	1	6
Shoe makers	6	7	3	0	4	20
Curriers	0	1	4	0	3	8
Nailers	3	0	1	0	0	4
Cutlers	0	1	0	0	0	1
Slaters or Roofers	0	1	0	0	0	1
Drapers	0	1	3	0	0	4
Servants	93	115	47	72	74	401

TABLE 5.1 (CONTINUED)

Professions and Trades	Québec	Côtes nord	Côtes sud	Rivières	Montréal	Total
Tinsmiths	1	0	0	0	0	1
Foundrymen	1	0	0	0	0	1
Sword grinders	1	0	0	0	0	1
Bailiffs	3	1	0	0	0	4
Printers	0	0	1	0	0	1
Teachers	2	0	0	1	0	3
Gardeners	2	1	0	0	0	3
Masons	7	12	5	0	8	32
Ship captains	1	0	0	0	0	1
Merchants	13	1	0	1	3	18
Joiners	9	8	3	2	5	27
Millers	0	5	2	1	1	9
Sailors	4	9	6	0	3	22
Notaries	2	1	0	0	0	3
Jewellers	0	0	1	0	0	1
Confectioners	3	1	0	0	1	5
Furriers	1	0	0	0	0	1
Wooden shoe makers	0	1	0	0	0	1
Stone cutters	1	0	0	0	0	1
Saddlers	0	1	1	0	1	3
Locksmiths	0	1	0	1	1	3
Edge tool makers	8	1	2	1	2	14
Tailors	8	9	4	2	7	30
Carpet weavers	0	2	1	0	0	3
Weavers	1	11	3	0	1	16
Coopers	4	1	0	1	2	8
Turners	0	0	0	0	1	1
Total	202	238	101	85	137	763

the army. In consequence it is an astonishing thing to see how the country becomes peopled and multiplies. It is said that His Majesty intends to spare nothing.[42]

How long the Crown's support would continue was uncertain, but the effect on the colony was dramatic. The first nominal census of the colony would be taken in 1665–6, before the arrival of the soldiers. It disclosed an intriguing society in the process of becoming (see Table 5.1).

CONCLUSION

In some respects the first half-century of the St Lawrence colony did not look promising. In 1661, just before the royal takeover, the colonists numbered barely 3,000, nearly two-thirds of them in the Quebec area. Europe appeared to be losing a war of attrition to the Iroquois, who boasted that the French 'were not able to goe over a door [a threshold] to pisse' in safety',[43] and the missionary activities of the Jesuits had been virtually brought to a halt by the conflict. On the other hand, almost all the colonists had been planted through the efforts of private enterprise, rather than the state, and on most of them government sat fairly lightly. As long as the situation with respect to governance—Church and state alike—had remained fluid, women were able to make autonomous lives. The royal takeover would 'reform' both the administrative and the economic structure of New France. The change would prove both beneficial and stultifying.

SHORT BIBLIOGRAPHY

Anderson, Karen. *Chain Her By One Foot: The Subjugation of Women in Seventeenth-century New France*. London and New York, 1991. A feminist account that tends to blame most European abuses of the First Nations on patriarchal attitudes.

Armstrong, Joe C.W. *Champlain*. Toronto, 1987. A readable biography, with a Canadian perspective.

Blackburn, Carole. *The Jesuit Missions and Colonialism in North America, 1632–1650*. Montreal and Kingston, 2000. A recent deconstruction of the Jesuit texts, arguing their imperialist masculine attitudes.

Choquette, Leslie. '"Les Amazones du Grand Dieu": Women and Mission in Seventeenth-Century Canada', *French Historical Studies* 17, 3 (1992): 627–55. A splendid brief overview of the subject.

Fischer, David Hackett. *Champlain's Dream*. New York, 2008. A massive study by a leading American historian.

Kennedy, J.H. *Jesuit and Savage in New France*. New Haven, 1950 (reprinted 1971). The standard case for the Jesuit missions.

Moogk, Peter. *La Nouvelle France: The Making of French Canada—A Cultural History*. East Lansing, Mich., 2000. A revisionist work emphasizing cultural studies.

Rapley, Elizabeth. *The Dévotes: Women and Church in Seventeenth-Century France*. Kingston, 1990. A study of the French background of the lay missionary movement.

Simpson, Patricia. *Marguerite Bourgeoys and Montreal, 1640–1665*. Montreal and Kingston, 1997. A sympathetic biography of a major figure.

Trudel, Marcel. *The Beginnings of New France, 1524–1663*, trans. Patricia Claxton. Toronto, 1973. The classic study, detailed and exhaustive in nature.

STUDY QUESTIONS

1. Why were the *Jesuit Relations* so important to Canada?

2. Why was Champlain not more successful as a colonizer?

3. Why were the missionaries so dedicated to their work? What were the differences between male and female missionaries?

4. In what ways was the Iroquois military menace important to the colony?

5. What factors together destroyed the Huron?

6. Why did Marie de l'Incarnation, Jeanne Mance, and Marguerite Bourgeoys come to Canada?

7. Why was the appointment of Bishop Laval so important to Canada?

8. Imagine a debate between a Jesuit missionary and an Aboriginal leader on the subject of evangelization. What sorts of arguments would each side present?

9. What do the occupational listings of the census of 1665–6 tell us about Canada at this stage of its development?

CHAPTER SIX

Canada 1663–1763: Government, Military, Economy

Canada under the French Crown was subject to continual tension between the colonists' European roots and the realities of a world in which almost everything was new, even alien—from the long, bitter winters to the vast, unpopulated forests to the unfamiliar, hence threatening, culture of the Aboriginal people. The mother country provided a set of governing principles based on assumptions about how the society should be organized and how it ought to operate: as a hierarchy in which the various social orders stayed in their places and subordinated their interests to the good of the whole as defined by the Crown. It also provided the institutions required to implement those principles, and to some extent they succeeded, particularly when the French colony was compared with its British counterparts to the south. 'The difference between the manners and customs of the French and Montreal and Canada,' wrote the Swedish naturalist Peter Kalm in 1753, 'and those of the English in the American colonies, is as great as that between the manners of those two nations in Europe.'[1] Nevertheless, the daily realities of the North American context constantly undermined the colony's efforts to emulate its parent. A further complication was that the French Crown itself did not want simply to replicate the familiar insti-

tutions of the Old World in North America: it wanted to purify them, specifically by turning back the clock on a centuries-old French trend towards decentralization of power and limitation of royal authority following the consolidation of royal power in the thirteenth century. The result was that the conflict between Crown and nobles that characterized the *ancien régime* in France never had the same strength in North America.[2]

Over the centuries, commentators have usually assessed early Canada by comparison with either France or the English colonies. Although European observers often remarked on the familiarity of the colony's institutional arrangements, beneath the surface new pressures were creating quite different relationships and patterns of operation. Thus, Canada had an autocratic form of government, but one that was responsive to the wishes of the people and emphasized the availability of justice to all inhabitants. Its Church was under the thumb of the state, but the people themselves were extremely devout Catholics. It depended on French members of the regular army for defence, but most of its military successes were achieved by local militia troops and guerrilla tactics. It had a seigneurial system that wasn't really feudal. And it had a major economic enterprise—the fur

TIMELINE

1663
Royal takeover and reorganization of New France.

1665
Arrival of Jean Talon, Carignan-Salières regiment, and first contingent of '*filles du roi*'.

1666
Regiment marches into New York against the Mohawk. First census taken.

1669
Colonial militia established.

1671
French fur traders and missionaries begin penetrating Great Lakes and Mississippi River regions.

1673
Marquette and Jolliet travel down the Mississippi to the 33rd parallel.

1674
Second royal government established.

1682
La Salle reaches mouth of Mississippi.

1683
Death of Colbert.

1701
Peace treaty with Iroquois.

1703
Conseil Souverain renamed Conseil Supérieur and number of councillors increased to 12.

1711
Edict of Marly.

1712
Founding of colony at Louisiana.

1713
Treaty of Utrecht gives Acadia to Britain.

1719
Judicial organization of colony completed with establishment of admiralty court in Quebec.

1733
Iron forges at St Maurice in operation.

1743
Four 'assessors' added to Council as advisors, especially on appeals.

1748
Bigot appointed intendant.

trade—on which its government persistently tried to impose limits. This chapter will examine these contradictions in the contexts of the colonial government, the Church, military affairs, and economic activity. The following chapter will address immigration and demography, society, and culture in the same period.

THE ROYAL TAKEOVER

The royal takeover of 1663 put the development and execution of French administrative policy for the colonies in the hands of two men, Jean-Baptiste Colbert and Jean Talon. Colbert was Louis XIV's chief bureaucrat, a highly experi-

JEAN TALON
(1626–94)

■ Jean Talon, intendant of New France. This portrait is a nineteenth-century copy, attributed to Théophile Hamel, of a seventeenth-century painting by Frère Luc (see p. 133). LAC, C-7100.

Jean Talon was born in Champagne into a family of jurists. He was educated in Paris at the Jesuit Collège de Clermont and then entered the French administrative services for the military. Coming to the eye of Cardinal Mazarin, he became intendant of the French province of Hainault in 1655. Ten years later he was appointed the first intendant of Canada, his mission to complete the reorganization of the colony and to reduce the authority of the governor who had administered the colony under the Compagnie des Cent-Associés. Talon was in charge of justice, police, and finances in New France in two periods, 1665–8 and 1670–2. Given his subsequent reputation as the founding genius of the colonial administration, it is worth noting how brief Talon's tenure actually was. In two whirlwinds of activity he drafted legal regulations for the administration of justice and submitted them to a Sovereign Council, introduced coherent legislation, and planned the colony's early policy. He sought to increase the population both through subsidized immigration and through police regulations, such as one that obliged bachelors to marry the '*filles du roi*' arriving in the colony on pain of losing the right to fish and hunt. He also established three farming villages in 1665–6 as models for the colony, based on centralized houses grouped around a church, and distributed over 60 fiefs to new seigneurs. Besides encouraging manufacturing (through the introduction of looms and the establishment of a brewery, for example), he also sought to improve the breeding stock by importing new animals. In his second administration he attempted (without much success) to forbid young men from disappearing into the woods either to enter the fur trade or simply to live like the Native people. He also tried to make better use of the forests by setting up a lumber industry to provide masts for the French navy and wood for the West Indies. Although he was wary of relying too much on the fur trade, he allowed it to expand during his second period of office, searching for natural geographical limits to the colony.

Unfortunately, most of Talon's ambitious schemes did not survive his two administrations—perhaps in part because none of his successors enjoyed either the King's confidence or his financial support to the extent that Talon had. Even during his heyday, his power and policies were widely criticized, especially by the colony's established merchants and its clergy. After his return to France in 1672, royal funds were no longer available to the colony. While the colony languished, Talon became an important figure at the royal court, living in luxury in Paris until his death.

enced civil servant whose major tasks both at home and abroad were to strengthen royal control of government and to expand the French economy. As *ministre de la marine*, responsible for the navy, the colonies, and overseas trade, he served as the seventeenth-century equivalent of colonial secretary, amid a myriad of other responsibilities. To implement policy in the colony, Colbert decided to rely not on the governor but on the intendant: a civil service position recently created in France to counteract the devolution of royal power and act directly on behalf of the state. Appointed intendant in 1665, Talon immediately set about reorganizing and centralizing the colony's administration. The governor was still the titular head, with responsibility for the military, external affairs, and the colony's relations with the Church (which included education); over the years the governors would invariably be members of the French nobility and experienced soldiers. But routine administration was placed in the hands of the intendant, a career civil servant. There would be some classic confrontations between the two positions, particularly during the governorships of Louis Buade de Frontenac (1672–82 and 1698–90). But the Crown always backed the intendant.

Together, Colbert and Talon managed not only to put the colony of Canada back on its feet but to establish the administrative and institutional framework for the entire century during which France would control large portions of North America. Although the term 'New France' is often applied to the colony along the St Lawrence, in fact it encompasses all the French territory in North America, which would ultimately consist of two major colonies ('Canada' on the St Lawrence and, later, Louisiana) and two smaller ones enjoying less stable administrative relationships with the metropolis (Acadia and the Ohio River Valley).

The project undertaken by Colbert and Talon was not easy, and they understandably tended to concentrate on Canada, to the neglect of the peripheries. For Canada, political institutions had to be established that would be at once responsive to the royal will and satisfactory to the inhabitants; external threats had to be confronted; population growth had to be encouraged through both immigration and natural increase; and a viable economic structure had to be created that would not pose any threat to the mother country. From the interaction of these factors would emerge a set of societies and cultures of enormous tenacity, possessing many resources for regeneration and change.

GOVERNMENT

THE POLITICAL SYSTEM

Traditionally, English-speaking chroniclers of New France and post-Conquest Quebec have pointed to the absence of representative government under the French regime and emphasized the fact that it was introduced under the British. But the political system that developed in seventeenth-century Canada, while centralized and autocratic, was not totally insulated from the popular will. What had been the governor's council was reorganized by Colbert in 1663 as the Conseil Souverain, with membership made up of the governor, the bishop, the intendant, several legal officials, and five (later 12) councillors, drawn from the colony's elite (usually seigneurs and merchants). After 1675 the councillors served at the King's pleasure, and the intendant (rather than the governor) presided at meetings. The council had both legislative and judicial responsibilities, but over time it generally concentrated on the judicial side. In its functions and membership this council was typical of every colonial government in America; but its control by the intendant rather than the governor was unique to Canada.

It is true that Canada did not have a regularly elected political body representing the inhabitants. But the absence of such an institution did not mean that those who governed New France did so in anti-democratic defiance of public opinion. Nor did the fact that, in the English colonies, the men who made up the equivalent of the Sovereign Council were elected by adult male property-owners (rather than appointed by the Crown) in itself guarantee democratic representation of the popular will. Indeed, the very absence of representative institutions forced the government of Canada to develop alternative ways of testing public opinion. Public gatherings were summoned on a number of critical occasions to comment on current affairs. The merchants of Quebec and Montreal had institutionalized access to the government through their *chambres de commerce*, and the habitants (ordinary people, not necessarily 'peasants') were encouraged to meet frequently on local matters, often under the leadership of the local militia captains, who were employed by the intendant as his community deputies.

When those arrangements did not suffice to express their grievances, the common people could always resort to public protest: 'riots' were a common feature of life in both Europe and America at the time. Public demonstrations in early French Canada, as elsewhere, were generally touched off by immediate problems, and did not necessarily reflect deep-rooted political discontent. In Europe protests were most often triggered by oppressive taxation, but this was not an issue in Canada because no taxes were levied. Rather, most protests were sparked by food shortages—and the demonstrators were usually women. In December 1757, for example, a move by the colonial authorities to eliminate the regulated distribution of bread in Montreal and to sell half the price-regulated meat supply in the form of horse-meat led to a demonstration at the residence of Governor Pierre de Vaudreuil. He attempted to reason with the women, then sent them away with threats of jail and even hanging if they rioted again. But he did not follow through on the threat: the women staged two more demonstrations in the next year, without repercussions. The government had the right and the power to meet such actions with force, and even to punish the ringleaders, but by convention it was lenient unless violence or property damage ensued. That French Canada under the *ancien régime* experienced only about a dozen serious protests over 100 years, mainly in the last years of French control, suggests that the government was largely successful in responding to public opinion and meeting the needs of the population as a whole.[3]

THE CHURCH

Governance in the colony did not depend solely on secular authorities. In Canada as in France, the Roman Catholic Church had an indirect political role in addition to its direct spiritual role in society. Among its political tasks was to encourage due subordination to secular as well as spiritual authority—a job that was frequently

■ The Jesuit Church and College, Quebec City, 1 Sept. 1761, by Richard Short. LAC, C-354.

beyond its capabilities. Most of the Canadian Church's injunctions against public misbehaviour and immorality suggest that it was fighting a losing battle. Thus, when we read of Bishop Jean St Vallier thundering in 1719 against 'the Bad Habit . . . of appearing in underwear without bottoms during the summer to avoid the Great Heat' and threatening 'the damnation of a large number of heads of families as well as of children, if you do not have regard for our remonstrance and paternal Exhortations', we may assume that obedience could not be taken for granted.[4] Similar injunctions against immodest dress among young women, or the racing of horses outside churches during mass, suggest that the Church was largely impotent when it came to controlling public behaviour. It did succeed in limiting the number of theatrical performances for many years, but it was certainly

not able to prevent the use of liquor in the fur trade. Despite the Church's assertions of the grave evils of the traffic and its harmful effects on the Native people, the Crown found alcohol essential to trade, and so it remained.

In addition, the Church was responsible for education and health care in the colony. Hospitals were staffed mainly by nuns. Priests living with Aboriginal groups often acted as agents of the government, and some were sent to the English colonies for diplomatic purposes, occasionally even as spies. Yet despite the multiplicity of functions performed by the Church, the colony was certainly not priest-ridden. In 1730 one ecclesiastical administrator reported that 'among about a hundred parishes in the diocese of Quebec, there are now only about twenty with titular curés; all the others, many of which are not even erected as parishes, are ministered to by simple missionaries.'[5] Although there were over 200 women in religious orders in Canada at mid-century, ordained priests who could celebrate the sacraments were typically in short supply. In 1759 fewer than 200 clergymen served a population of between 75,000 and 80,000: such a small number could scarcely have much contact with the people, let alone authority over them. Moreover, only 73 of those clergymen were actually parish priests—hardly enough to minister to everyone in the colony, especially outside the towns. The average habitant simply did not have regular access to mass and confession.

In the symbiotic relationship between Church and state that characterized Canada after 1663, the state was clearly the dominant partner. It appointed bishops, granted seigneuries, and thus provided much of the Church's revenue— up to 40 per cent. But the fact that the Church was subordinate to the state did not in any way diminish the religious devotion of the colony's inhabitants. The closest Canada had come to overstepping the bounds of orthodoxy was in the extent of its lay piety, especially among women, and that was quickly suppressed once an ecclesiastical hierarchy was established. Canada had been born in deep Catholic piety, and Catholic orthodoxy remained the norm.[6]

THE ROLE OF THE MILITARY

Almost from its inception, the colony existed in a state of siege. The immediate threat in 1663 was the Iroquois. A show of force was provided by the initial assignment of troops, consisting of 1,100 veteran soldiers of the Carignan-Salières regiment.[7] By 1666 the soldiers still had not engaged a single Iroquois warrior in battle—but they razed four Mohawk villages in New York to the ground. Conscious of a new resolve among the French, and under pressure from Algonquian nations to the west, the Iroquois agreed to peace in 1667. But they were never entirely removed as a threat, since they retained close links with the English, who remained at war with France throughout much of the colonial period. Even after 1667, therefore, the French kept up a military posture.

In the mid-1660s a colony with a population of little more than 3,000 was supporting a defence force of 1,300 regular soldiers. Although the military presence became proportionally smaller over time, it remained an important influence. As has so often been the case in the history of nations, France was willing to accept expenditures on the military that it would not have countenanced for civilian purposes. Colbert had set the civil budget of New France at a mere 36,000 livres, for example, but allocated another 150,000 livres to feed and maintain the regular troops. If the army received the lion's share of the financial support, however, the soldiers' pay was an important source of cash for the Canadian economy, and the army was the best local customer for Canadian merchants. As early as 1665, Marie de l'Incarnation noted that 'money, which was rare in the country, is now very common, these gentlemen having brought a great deal with them. They pay for everything they buy with money, both their food and their other necessities, which suits our habitants very well.'[8] Colonel Louis-Antoine Bougainville echoed these comments towards the end of the French period, when he remarked that '*La guerre enrichit le Canada.*'

In addition to defending the colony and attracting frequent infusions of money from France, regular soldiers served as a source of labour for the habitants, with whom the majority of them were normally billeted every year from October to May: 'the habitant who provided only the tools to his soldier employs him ordinarily for felling trees, uprooting stumps, clearing land, or wheat-threshing in the barn during that period, at a salary of ten *sols* daily plus food.'[9] Whenever funds to support the troops were temporarily exhausted—as they often were, owing to the period's primitive accounting and budgeting practices—the soldiers were sent off again for billeting. An ordinance of 1685, wrote one officer, gave:

the soldiers . . . the freedom to work and to live with the said habitants to earn thus their board and lodging, whilst waiting that His Majesty send us the wherewithals to pay their salary as usual. This obliges us to inform all the habitants of this Colony that they may hire such soldiers as they wish to work with them according to what they consider reasonable, prohibiting them to pay each of the soldiers more than 10 or 12 livres per month.[10]

The soldiers not only mixed freely with the civilian population, but were from the beginning encouraged to join it when their terms of enlistment expired. In some cases it was even possible to be released from military service in order to settle in the colony. In 1698, for example, the King (through his intendant) ordered that:

those who find it possible to establish themselves through marriage to women or widows born or settled in the . . . colony be discharged from [their] companies at their first request, and that they keep the clothing which they have without the officers using any pretext to withhold it.

In addition, to tide them over while they established their farms, such men were granted a full year's salary.[11]

In the years after 1663, French North America regularly found itself at war with the English and their Iroquois allies; between the royal takeover and the English Conquest there were only forty years of peace. Only between the Treaty of Utrecht, signed in 1713, and the opening of a new round of warfare in the 1740s did the French colonies experience an extended period free from threats of foreign invasion—and even in those years there was constant skirmishing with Native groups on the frontiers. Regular troops were not regarded as a sufficient military force, and from 1669 every male resident of Canada between the ages of 16 and 60 was required to serve in the militia under the local command of captains chosen from their ranks.

Not until 1684 was the militia actually called into action, but from then until 1760 it was used regularly, and virtually every able-bodied Canadian male served in at least one campaign, whether against the Iroquois or the English. A general peace with the First Nations in 1701 reduced the threat from the Iroquois, but this did not have any effect on the English colonies to the south, who continued to attack Canada until 1713.

There were never enough professional soldiers. Moreover, throughout the seventeenth century the troops sent to Canada tended to be poor specimens, best suited for garrison work. The Canadian militiamen did the bulk of the fighting and suffered the heaviest casualties. The large number of independent widows in Canada throughout the period of the royal regime reflected the heavy losses suffered by the militia—and not always in active fighting. In the first conflict involving the militia on a large scale, Governor Le Febvre de La Barre in 1684 mustered nearly 800 men at Montreal and led them against the Iroquois cantons in New York. But the troops were laid low by a virulent influenza epidemic, and the governor was forced to negotiate a humiliating peace. Nor were expeditions against the Iroquois the only occasions for summoning the militia. Guerrilla raids involving joint parties of Canadiens and their Native allies were a feature of every Anglo–French war, intended chiefly to keep the English colonies off balance and prevent them from using their superior numbers to invade the St Lawrence.

Foreign observers were always impressed with the martial spirit and skill of the Canadiens. As one British officer in the mid-1700s complained, 'Our men are nothing but a set of farmers and planters, used only to the axe and hoe. Theirs are not only well trained and disciplined, but they are used to arms from their infancy among the Indians; and are reckoned equal, if not superior in that part of the world to veteran troops.'[12] As is often the case, this reputation persisted well past the time when it was deserved. While the militiamen were a powerful aid to the

THE GREAT PEACE OF 1701

❖

By the end of the seventeenth century, the various warring parties in the backcountry of North America were worn out. The wars were mainly ones of capture. The Iroquois especially used war for population replacement, aided by the matrilineal arrangement of their society, in which descent was transmitted through the female line and adoption was common. As one French observer put it, 'Strangers are adopted as children of the house, as brothers, sons-in-law, or other relatives.' The Iroquois were also increasingly bound to the British by Covenant Chain, an alliance of peace and friendship that was renewed at Albany in most years from 1677 to the late 1700s, and the French were increasingly active in forming alliances with other western tribes in opposition to the Iroquois and in seeking for general peace agreements that would include the Iroquois. French alliances with the tribes to the west insisted that a French peace with the Iroquois would include the western allies, while the Iroquois before 1700 refused to include the western nations in any peace treaty with the French.

The negotiations leading to the Great Peace of 1701 included the French, the New York English, the Iroquois, and the several western allies of New France. To a considerable extent these negotiations occurred independently of the formal international conflict between the English and the French. From the Iroquois perspective they were propelled by demography.

The number of Iroquois warriors in the Confederacy dropped by more than half (from 2,550 in 1689 to 1,230 in 1698). This decline was caused mainly by war, disease (including perhaps alcoholic consumption), and migration from the geographical heartland of the Confederacy, and it meant that the Five Nations no longer had the numbers to raid successfully in the west to replenish its population. A distinct obstacle to peace was the refusal of all parties to surrender their captives, who had been adopted to various tribes. By the summer of 1701 a long round of negotiations had ended in Montreal, where representatives of 40 separate nations signed the Treaty of Montreal.

The grand council was a spectacle never before seen in North America. A large plain was turned into a rectangular arena, 43 metres by 24 metres. More than 2,000 people attended in a theatre made of boughs at one end of the arena, both colonists and 1,300 Aboriginal representatives, all parties dressed in their ceremonial costumes. The Aboriginal nations sent their finest orators to state their positions, and the speeches were carefully translated. The main points of the peace were the sharing of hunting grounds and the exchange of prisoners. While many participants probably saw the agreement as a mere truce, it lasted throughout the period before 1760, especially in committing the Iroquois to relative neutrality in the subsequent European wars of the century.

French authorities in the earlier period, especially in guerrilla warfare, by the middle of the eighteenth century the French officers who were trying to introduce tactical warfare regarded

them as more of a liability than an asset. In 1758 Colonel Bougainville, the aide-de-camp to the Marquis de Montcalm, reported that they were becoming 'disgusted; they wish to return home, to sow and to harvest; soon they declare them-selves sick. Either they must be sent home or they become deserters.' Furthermore, he said, the militiamen lacked the habits both of order and of submission to their officers.[13]

In a colony where the defence industry over-shadowed agriculture and even the fur trade in economic importance, the able and ambitious sons of the Canadian elite were generally expected to pursue a military career. In its pref-erence for military service—in an officer class—over commerce and industry, the colony resem-bled its mother country. The English colonies, which had less of a military tradition, did not encourage the development of a class of profes-sional soldiers, but the Canadiens lionized their native-born officers. Young boys began their training early, and there were constant pressures to reduce the age of entrance to the military; after 1729 it was set at 15. For several decades in the eighteenth century there existed an *expectative* or waiting list behind every rank from cadet to lieu-tenant, which enabled the young sons of leading families to fill the first vacancies. By the eigh-teenth century the Canadien elite provided most of the officers for the regular army, and even expected commissions to be reserved for the sons of serving officers.

ECONOMIC DEVELOPMENT

Recognizing the colony's heavy dependence on the fur trade, after 1663 France emphasized the importance of economic diversification. Colbert and Talon had no wish to put an end to the fur trade; but they did hope to encourage agriculture and timbering to the point where the colony would be able to supply the West Indies with goods currently supplied by the English. Indeed, from Colbert's perspective the fur trade was a positive menace, enabling 'the habitants [to] remain idle a good part of the year . . . ; if they were not allowed to engage in it they would be obliged to apply themselves to cultivating their land.'[14] But progress towards diversification was

slow. French success in penetrating the interior (which came to be known as the *pays d'en haut*), establishing good relations with the Aboriginal people who provided the furs there, and setting fixed prices encouraged expansion of the terri-tory involved in the trade. Colbert recognized the danger of embracing 'too vast an area' and perhaps being forced to abandon certain trading partners 'with some reduction of the prestige of His Majesty and of the State'.[15] But the constant westward press of the coureurs de bois contin-ued unabated, contributing to a circular effect in which the successful French quest for furs brought the colony into conflict with the English to the south, and the ensuing struggle made it virtually impossible to limit the fur traders, since they were the ideal shock troops for dealing mil-itarily with the enemy. Furthermore, investment in the trade by royal officials, including Governor Frontenac, prevented any serious effort at restraining it.

THE SEIGNEURIAL SYSTEM

Agricultural settlement in New France was organ-ized on the basis of the seigneurial system, first extended from France to the St Lawrence Valley in 1627. Although seigneurialism is often associ-ated with the physical layout of French-Canadian farms as long, narrow strips extending back from a small river frontage, in fact this arrangement owed more to the importance of the rivers than to seigneurialism in itself. In Europe the seigneurial system provided the framework for both the social hierarchy and the economic relationship between landlords and tenants, many of whom were still feudal serfs in the 1600s. Whether it ever operated that way in Canada, however, has long been a subject of dispute among historians. In North America it seems to have functioned not as a feudal structure but mainly as a system for allocating land and organizing settlement. As was often the case in the European colonies of North America—English as well as French—the state distributed land to landlords, who would then

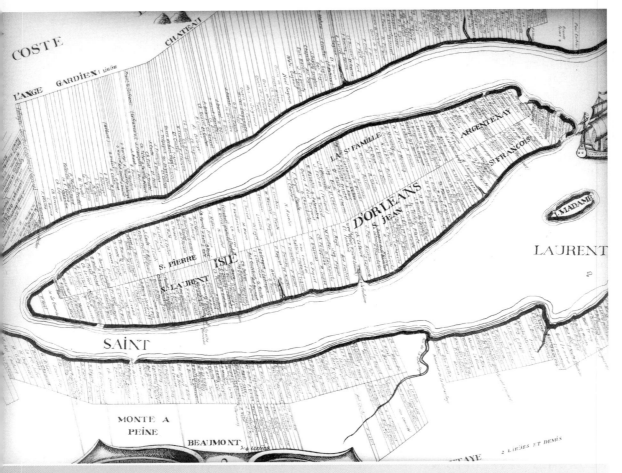

■ The Île d'Orléans and north and south shores of the St Lawrence, showing the boundaries of the land grants with the names of the seigneurial families in 1709, mapped by Gédéon Catalogne and drawn by Jean-Baptiste de Couagne; detail from a larger map of the Quebec region. LAC, NMC-0048248.

find settlers to work the land as their tenants. In Canada, 70 seigneuries were granted before 1663, and over 150 more between that year and 1740. The most successful seigneuries were those located along the banks of the rivers, particularly the St Lawrence. Roughly one-quarter of the seigneurial land was in the hands of the Catholic Church, which was more assiduous in its management than individual owners, especially in the seventeenth century.

As to the feudal aspects of seigneurialism in Canada, many scholars think that, on balance, the system of mutual obligations worked to the advantage of the tenants, or *censitaires*. It is true that the latter owed various rents and feudal dues to their seigneurs, but these appear to have amounted to very little, except on the best land in the most prosperous years. Furthermore, seigneurs were obliged to provide certain community goods and services, such as ovens and mills, and tenants were entitled to insist that they do so regardless of whether these capital-intensive fixtures would be immediately profitable.[16] Until 1711, seigneurs could withhold land from settlement in anticipation of a rise in prices, but in that year the Edict of Marly obliged them to settle their property if there were prospective *censitaires* looking for land to farm. This royal attempt to prevent land speculation and encourage orderly settlement was not unusual in North America, but neither was it very successful. And although in principle it interfered with the autonomous power of the seigneurs, in practice the seigneurs had very little independent authority over their *censitaires* in any case, as the intendant usually stepped in to settle any disputes.[17]

In economic terms, the tenants obviously did not own the means of production; nevertheless, most of them were probably more than subsistence farmers. They may still have been more like French peasants than American petty capitalists (of the New England or Virginia farmer variety), but their European qualities were probably what led Peter Kalm to prefer them to the Americans, whom he regarded as bumptious and acquisitive. Nor did the seigneurs themselves realize significant economic benefits from their lands: not until the very end of the French period, when the colony's population had grown to over 70,000, were the seigneurs able to find buyers for their lands.[18] Their economic position would become far stronger under the British than under the French royal regime. What the seigneurs did unquestionably possess during the French period was social status, for although most of those who became seigneurs were already members of the elite, the holding of land raised them to the ranks of the colonial upper class, above mere merchants.

In short, the seigneurial system seems to have been neither very onerous for the tenant nor very profitable to the landlord. Its effects on agricultural production were another matter. Plainly, it did not encourage the large-scale staple-crop farming that was practised in many of the English colonies to the south. Nor did it encourage adoption of the improved techniques—such as crop rotation and use of manure as a fertilizer—developed as agriculture in Europe became more intensive. The availability of land made it easier to move than to improve. The habitants have often been criticized for their low yields and generally slovenly agricultural practices, but these may be attributed as much to the sheer quantities of land available as to the fact that those who worked the land did not own it. In a situation where land was abundant compared to labour, farming practices naturally tended to be extensive rather than intensive, and slash-and-burn agriculture was common. Wheat was the preferred crop, although other grains and legumes were also grown, and every habitant kept livestock as well. Markets for this produce (especially outside the colony) were limited partly by transportation costs and partly by the constant disruption of overseas trade in times of war. Not until the 1720s was there enough land under cultivation to produce a dependable surplus, and bad harvests were always a threat, particularly at a time before the development of seed strains capable of withstanding difficult growing conditions.

The seigneurial system obviously did not produce the sort of small agrarian capitalist who pressed for maximum production and speculated eagerly in land. On the other hand, the seigneurs did seek to speculate, and did so increasingly in the eighteenth century. Few seigneurs had ever lived on their lands, for the system did not produce enough revenue to permit the emergence of a proper landed aristocracy that could flourish without government patronage. By the eighteenth century, the typical seigneur was an absentee landlord who lived in one of the towns and was involved in a variety of economic and political activities.[19] A seigneury was part of a diversified portfolio of investment for an elite in whose ranks specialization of economic activity had yet to develop.

One seigneurial type was represented by Nicholas-Gaspard Boucault (*c.* 1689–1755), who was royal attorney, merchant, and seigneur rolled into one. Boucault arrived in Quebec from France in 1719 and rose rapidly in the colony's legal service, collecting a number of remunerative offices along the way to appointment as lieutenant of the provost court and lieutenant-general of the admiralty court. His success was based on his professional status. He was equally active in commercial matters, helping to sponsor seal-hunting expeditions and becoming a major fixture in the Louisbourg trade. In 1723 he bought a seigneury on the Chambly River, which he saw as part of a general investment strategy, although he does not appear to have made much money from it, and a decade later he built a large stone house on Quebec City's rue Saint-Paul. Boucault retired to France in 1754.

Another familiar seigneurial type was represented by Louis Charly Saint-Ange (1703–67), one of the heirs to a Canadian fur-trading business. His success was a result of his access to capital. Charly invested heavily in an unsuccessful western copper-mining enterprise and continued to be active in the western fur trade. The owner of a house in Montreal, he acquired the small seigneury of Îles Bourdon in 1751. In 1764 he sold his Canadian estate to an incoming Englishman and retired to France.[20]

Not all seigneurs were either as diversified or as mobile at Boucault and Charly, but most engaged in a variety of business and administrative activities. Diversification was a necessary economic strategy in most colonial situations, and would continue to be a common characteristic of North American elites—French or English—until well into the nineteenth century.

COMMERCE

In the past, the image of early Canada as a rural, agricultural society prevented recognition of the extent of commercial and small-scale (mainly artisanal) industrial activity under the French regime. Such activities entailed enormous amounts of both effort and risk. Nevertheless, most members of the colony's elite engaged in some form of entrepreneurship. In the period when war constituted the colony's principal industry, a small merchant class specialized in supplying the troops. In both war and peace, imports far exceeded exports, so that the overseas trade of the colony, within the French mercantile system, showed an unfavourable balance of payments. There was a substantial and constantly increasing volume of transatlantic shipping, and considerable traffic between Canada, Louisbourg, and the French West Indies. Overseas trade was particularly complex and risky because of the distances involved. To compensate for their lack of up-to-date information about markets and prices, merchants tried as much as possible to diversify their cargoes and enterprises; to manage their overseas operations, they preferred to rely on family and clan connections rather than strangers; marriage alliances established new branches of family firms in distant ports; and after the deaths of their husbands, widows often took over local enterprises. In imperial terms the Canadien merchants were small fry—petty entrepreneurs rather than major capitalists.[21]

The economy over which the merchants presided was relatively fragile. Although it expanded steadily throughout the French regime, it required peace and stability to perform best. Even by the 1740s, only a dozen ships a year were sailing from France to Canada. Smaller vessels plied the St Lawrence, and the Atlantic from Louisbourg to the West Indies, picking up cargoes wherever they could be found and depositing them wherever they could be sold, and this relatively local 'coasting' trade was of greater consequence for the colony than its trade with Europe. The trade deficit with the mother country was endemic. It decreased substantially in the latter years of the peace between 1713 and the 1740s, but in wartime, when government spending increased enormously, it skyrocketed.

Like most colonial economies, that of New France suffered not only from chronic deficits in the international balance-of-payments equation,

INTENDANT RAUDOT ON THE CARD MONEY, 1706

Beginning in 1685, New France dealt with its shortage of metallic coins by issuing decks of cards signed by the intendant and inscribed in various denominations. The French government was not keen on the practice. In 1706 Jacques Raudot, intendant of New France 1705–11, wrote a memorandum to the Crown justifying the practice. It offers a little lesson in monetary policy.

Memorandum on the Cards of Canada, Quebec, September 30, 1706

The cards which are issued in Canada serve as money just as coin does in France.

The Kingdom of France derives a certain utility from these cards, since, by this means, the King is not obliged to send funds in coined money for the expenditures which he has the goodness to incur. If it were necessary to send this, it would withdraw from the Kingdom annually 100,000 écus. Consequently this currency leaving the country would render money scarcer. It is true one would not appreciate this disadvantage during the abundance of money, nevertheless it is certain that it would effect a diminution. Moreover, France, by this device, not sending coined money, runs no risk as to it either from the sea or from enemies.

If coined money were sent to Canada, it would afterwards leave the country by two avenues, one part would return to France, the other would go to New England to purchase certain merchandise, which may be had cheaper there than from France. The part of this money returning to France would run the risks of the sea and enemies. The vessels may be taken or lost, and consequently the money they carry is lost to France, and there can be no greater injury to the Kingdom than the loss of its money.

The other part of this money being carried to New England for the purchase of merchandise, results in a considerable injury to France in the loss of its coinage and the advantage which it would produce among her enemies. . . .

Furthermore, there is no fear that money may be carried to New England, which would be very difficult to prevent if there were any in the colony, there being as in France persons who to gain something would risk much.

It is even a matter of policy for kings to attach the prosperity of their subjects to their own persons, in order to render the former more submissive and to take care that all the means which the colonies may have in money are always in the kingdom on which they are dependent. Canada, having nothing but cards, which are secured only on the word of the King, and seeing no other resource except in the good faith of the sovereign, will be still more submissive to him and still more attached to France for the reason that all the supply it can have in money depends on it. Hence, it appears to me that one cannot do better than to permit the continuation of the card money in Canada.

There may arise great abuses regarding these cards; they may be counterfeited in the country; this, however, can be prevented by a close attention, the easier bestowed as the resources of every person are known. Counterfeits may also be sent from France and so exactly imitated that one cannot distinguish the true from the false. That is almost impossible to do here, there not being clever people enough of that type. But even if there were some counterfeits they could not remain long without being recognised. To prevent this abuse one has only to change the dies, and shape of the cards every year after the departure of the vessels for France.

It is true that the colony of Canada will suffer somewhat by these cards, it being quite certain that it will buy French merchandise cheaper if it pays for them in coined money and not in cards, for which the merchants receive only bills of exchange which for the most part are not met at maturity. But it is proper that the colony of Canada suffer for the sake of the kingdom from which it receives its benefits, and it is only fair that this kingdom should run no risk of losing its money by the possible loss of its vessels bound for it. . . .

SOURCE: Adam Shortt, ed., *Documents Relating to Canadian Currency, Exchange and Finance during the French Period* (Ottawa: King's Printer, 1925), I, 157–8.

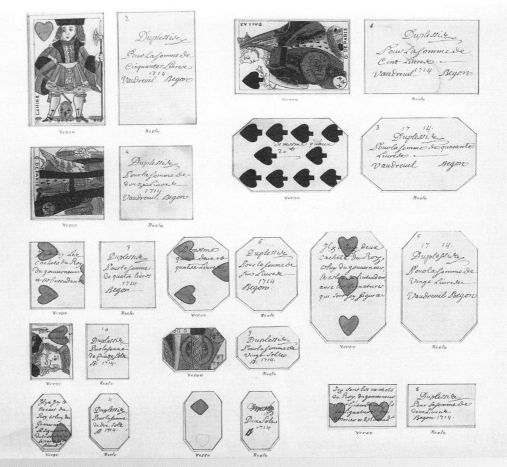

■ 'Playing Card Money', pen with black ink with watercolour by Henri Beau (1863–1949), an employee of the Public Archives of Canada who was employed in the Paris office specifically to copy views, portraits, etc., and to carry out iconographic research. LAC, C-17059.

FRANÇOIS BIGOT
(1703–78)

François Bigot was the grandson of an important and wealthy citizen of Bordeaux; his father was a lawyer and court clerk, a member of the French *noblesse de robe* (a 'law lord'). François was educated as a lawyer, and after several minor postings set sail in 1739 for the fortress of Louisbourg, on Île Royale, as financial commissary. Having achieved considerable success, in 1748 he was transferred to Quebec and promoted to intendant. His career there demonstrated an insatiable appetite for personal gain, but his eventual downfall needs to be placed in the context of the later years of the French regime. Bigot operated mainly in wartime, which lasted from 1744 to 1748 and again from 1756 to 1760, when both the opportunities for corruption and the problems of financial administration were most evident. He got things done, managing to supply the troops and the civil population throughout most of the years of war. His behaviour was often venal, as when he outfitted corsaires himself in order to capture British ships to be sold on his own account in France. His policies were often inflationary, as he issued *ordan-nances* for payments when the funds were not available to meet the demands of the holders. But they were also creative and necessary, given the mother country's failure to provide adequately for the colony. Furthermore, it is important to recognize that eighteenth-century accounting practices were not always capable of distinguishing between the personal and the public transactions of an official whose job it was to manipulate money.

In the end, France made Bigot the scapegoat for the loss of Canada, although others, including the Marquis de Montcalm, had a much more direct role in the debacle. The government in France connected Bigot's corruption with an inflationary spiral that was quite independent of his operations, and then added charges for the colony's military defeat that ought to have been levied against the army. Found guilty of many charges of corruption, Bigot was banished from France forever and all his property was confiscated. He spent his last years in Switzerland in disgrace. His corruption was substantial, but so were his administrative achievements. He was blamed for far too much.

but from the consequence of those deficits: the stripping-off of all available hard money (i.e., gold and silver) to service the deficit. The result was a constant shortage of a circulating medium of exchange. The colony's efforts to deal with this shortage are the stuff of legend. It was typical of colonial monetary policy that European currency was greatly overvalued. Beginning in 1685, the colony in effect created its own currency by using as paper money decks of playing cards inscribed in various denominations and signed by the intendant. Officially, the cards at first represented public promissory notes, to be redeemed when the mother country eventually sent the cash. But by the early eighteenth century the supply of card money greatly exceeded the amount capable of swift redemption, and the problem was compounded after 1735, when the playing cards were supplemented by military *ordonnances* (orders) that also circulated as legal tender.[22] The inflation that

THE   FORGES,   RIVER   ST   MAURICE

■ The iron forges on the St-Maurice, coloured lithograph by Joseph Bouchette, Jr from his book *The British Dominion in North America* (London, 1832). LAC, C-4356.

followed was perceived as directly related to the supposedly corrupt administration of Intendant François Bigot, which was long held to be partly responsible for the ultimate fall of New France.

INDUSTRY

From time to time both government and private entrepreneurs during the French regime attempted to create large-scale industrial operations. In the 1730s, two major efforts were encouraged by Intendant Gilles Hocquart: an ironworks near Trois-Rivières (the famous 'forges du Saint-Maurice') and a shipyard at Quebec. The former was a private enterprise, the latter state-supported. Both 'succeeded' in that they did produce iron and ships respectively, and each employed several hundred workmen—a substantial portion of the labour force in a colony of barely 50,000 people. However, neither business proved profitable: both

required large state subsidies to keep going, and the shipyard may actually have smothered private shipbuilding in the colony.[23]

Far more successful than large industrial producers were the small, local operations of skilled artisans. At the apex of the pyramid were those master craftsmen whose work, mainly for the Church, consciously aspired to high aesthetic standards. One such was the master woodcarver François-Noël Levasseur, who, beginning in 1740, turned out religious furniture and sculpture from his shop in Quebec with the assistance of his brother, Jean-Baptiste-Antoine. Their shop would continue producing crucifixes, statues, reliquaries, church pews, and communion tables until 1782.[24]

THE FUR TRADE

The numbers engaged in the fur trade— voyageurs and *engagés* (literally, contract workers)—also grew substantially, from perhaps 200 at the end of the seventeenth century to nearly 1,000 in the 1740s and 1750s. The work was both physically and emotionally demanding. Perhaps as many as a quarter of able-bodied Canadien males were involved in the western fur trade at some point in their lives, before they settled down with a wife and family in sedentary occupations along the St Lawrence.[25] A few rose to be specialists in the trade, some (as we shall see) remaining in the fur country throughout their lives, and about 20 becoming *marchands équipeurs* (outfitters), who organized the trading parties and provided the credit they needed to operate. Unlike the transatlantic merchants, the fur-trade merchants were almost exclusively Canadian-born. Given limited access to credit and the fact that it took many years to realize returns from a western 'outfit', even substantial markups on trade goods were not enough to alter two basic realities: partnerships were essential, and profit margins were small.[26]

CONCLUSION

French political, military, religious, and economic institutions were carefully transplanted to Canada after the French Crown took over the colony's administration in 1663. Yet Canada was never merely a colonial replica of the mother country. Rather, French models were adapted to North American realities and their implications.

SHORT BIBLIOGRAPHY

Bosher, J.F. *The Canada Merchants, 1713–1763*. Oxford, 1987. The best account of the colony's merchant class in the eighteenth century.

Dechêne, Louise. *Habitants et marchands de Montréal au XVIIe siècle*. Paris, 1974. Translated by Liana Vardi as *Habitants and Merchants in Seventeenth-Century Montreal* (Montreal and Kingston, 1992), this award-winning urban history covers a wide swath of the colony's life in the seventeenth century.

Eccles, W.J. *France in America*. Markham, Ont., 1990. The best survey of the entire French Empire in North America, by the dean of anglophone historians of New France.

———. *Canada under Louis XIV, 1663–1701*. Toronto, 1964. A still reliable volume in the Canadian Centenary Series, although the bibliographies are out of date.

———. *Essays on New France*. Toronto, 1987. Useful interpretive essays.

Harris, R.C. *The Seigneurial System in Early Canada: A Geographical Study*. Madison, Wis., 1966. The pioneering revisionist study.

Jaenen, Cornelius. *The Role of the Church in New France*. Toronto, 1966. A judicious account.

Miquelon, Dale. *New France, 1701–1744: A Supplement to Europe*. Toronto, 1987. A volume in the Canadian Centenary Series, strong on the mercantile side but weak on social and cultural history.

Pritchard, James. *In Search of Empire: The French in the Americas, 1670–1730*. Cambridge, 2004. A new, sweeping synthesis of the French presence in America.

Stanley, G.F.G. *New France: The Last Phase, 1744–1760*. Toronto, 1968. A Canadian Centenary Series volume focusing almost exclusively on military history.

Trudel, Marcel. *Introduction to New France*. Toronto, 1968. Dated, but still the best introduction to the colony.

Zoltvany, Yves, ed. *The Government of New France: Royal, Clerical, or Class Rule*. Toronto, 1971. A useful collection of readings and interpretations.

STUDY QUESTIONS

1. Describe some of the discrepancies between theory and institutional practice in colonial Canada. What factors might account for these discrepancies?

2. Was Canada a despotism?

3. What was the role of the Roman Catholic Church in Canada under the French regime?

4. Could Canada have survived without the military? What were the military's non-military functions?

5. What were the main characteristics of Canadian commerce under the French regime?

6. Why was Jean Talon such a successful administrator?

7. What was the financial theory behind the use of 'card money' in Canada?

CHAPTER SEVEN

Canada 1663–1763: Population, Society, Culture

■ From the beginning, the French colony on the St Lawrence had difficulty attracting European settlers. Unlike the English colonies to the south, which welcomed hundreds of thousands of immigrants from the British Isles, Canada never experienced a long-term, large-scale influx of settlers. The majority came to Canada between 1630 and 1680, and only a few of them paid their own way—perhaps only 5 per cent of the total (compared to roughly 50 per cent in the English colonies). The rest arrived as soldiers, contract labourers, servants, or slaves, or were subsidized by the Crown. Moreover, many of them eventually returned to their mother country. The colony's inability to attract—and keep—substantial numbers of immigrants limited its capacity for growth and put its future at risk.

Like the institutions discussed in the last chapter, Canadien society and culture under the French regime reflected both their European origins and the pressures exerted by North American realities. No doubt the most obvious of those realities was the physical environment; the climate alone may well have discouraged some potential immigrants. In any event, the very small population base prevented the colony from moving out of the pioneering stage during the French period, and was in itself a significant limiting factor.

THE DEMOGRAPHIC PROBLEM

In 1706 an anonymous French writer observed of the French Empire in America:

> If anyone gives considered attention to the progress the English have made in the case of their New England colonies, he will have good reason to tremble for our colonies in Canada. There is no single year but sees more children born in New England than there are men in the whole of Canada. In a few years we shall be facing a redoubtable people, one to be feared. As for Canada, her people will not number many more than they do today. Whether we must seek the reason in that mildness of climate which is so favourable to agriculture, stock-raising and all-year-round navigation, or whether we must seek it in the demesne of specialized industry, this is certain: on those shores the colonies of England have become as solidly established as England herself.[1]

The demographic problem had its origins in the first half of the seventeenth century, when France was unable to provide a population base for its continental American colonies in any way approximating that provided by the English. Private enterprise was able to transplant only a few thousand Frenchmen to the New World,

TIMELINE

1660
First pipe organ arrives in Canada.

1662
Carnival at Quebec.

1666
Construction begins on Jesuit church in Quebec City.

1668
Bishop Laval founds the Petit Séminaire in Quebec City.

1670
La France apportant la foi aux Hurons painted.

1672
End of most state-subsidized immigration.

1676
Aboriginal choirs established at Sillery; new church built at Sainte-Anne-de-Beaupré to accommodate pilgrims seeking miraculous cures.

1683
Clerical reaction against a charivari; construction of Séminaire de Saint-Sulpice in Montreal begins.

1685
'Code Noir' defines legal status of slaves.

1692
Conversion of Récollet monastery at Quebec into Hôpital-Général.

1718
Construction of Ursuline Chapel begins at Quebec.

1739
Construction of church of Saint François de Sales begins on Île d'Orléans.

1740
Duplessis case confirms Aboriginal slavery.

while the English migration had already turned into a flood. By 1663, when the French enumerated 3,215 people in Canada, the English could have counted several hundred thousand inhabitants in their mainland colonies. Whereas only some 5 per cent of French immigrants arrived without public subsidy, at least half of the British colonists had financed their own transatlantic voyages. The New England colonies were established without a penny of public funding.[2] Between 1608 and 1760 the total immigration to New France did not exceed 67,000 (this estimate itself, by Leslie Choquette, represents a radical upward revision), whereas immigration to British

North America during the same period came close to one million.[3] In the past, historians tended to assume that the French failed to immigrate because they were happier at home, or too indolent to leave, but a more modern analysis suggests that Canada simply was not a very attractive place.[4] 'Canada has always been regarded as a country at the end of the world,' explained one official, 'and as an exile that might pass for a [sentence] of civil death.'[5]

After 1663 French Canada matched the British colonies in its rate of increase, doubling its population every 25 years, but natural increase, however rapid, could never close the numerical gap. By 1715 the European population of New France was 20,000, but that of the English colonies was 434,000. In 1754 the gap had grown wider still, with 70,000 in New France and 1,485,000 in the American colonies.[6] Between 1663 and 1672 the French Crown did send as many as 500 men to Canada each year; it also sent up to 150 *filles du roi* to help make up the severe shortage of marriageable women.[7] But after 1672 the numbers of immigrants, publicly sponsored or privately motivated, began to fall; most women—nearly 70 per cent of the total female immigration—arrived in the 50 years between 1630 and 1680. The flow—male and female—averaged about 160 immigrants per year and represented only a minuscule percentage of the population of the mother country. Over two-thirds either returned to France or died in the colony unmarried.

Nevertheless, nearly 4,000 immigrants—almost all young single individuals born in France west of a north–south Bordeaux–Paris line and travelling alone—did settle in the St Lawrence Valley between 1665 and 1680, becoming the foundation of the French-Canadian population. The women tended to be considerably younger than the men they married. The fact that a disproportionate number of the younger women, especially the *filles du roi*, came from the Paris region helps to account for the eventual dominance of the Parisian dialect in Canada. Despite the harsh climate and difficult physical environment, the people of New France were considerably longer-lived than their counterparts in France, in part because most immigrants were healthier to begin with, and in part because the environment was relatively free of disease.

The French government never wholeheartedly encouraged a mass movement to North America, partly because it wanted its male population at home to serve in the military. As Colbert wrote in 1666, 'It would not be prudent [for the King] to depopulate his Kingdom as would be necessary in order to populate Canada.'[8] For their part, the ordinary people of France saw Canada as a frigid, isolated wasteland inhabited by fierce Aboriginal tribes, a place to be avoided at all costs. Thus, despite famine, unemployment, and general oppression at home, the French were reluctant to immigrate.

Although our anonymous Frenchman of 1706 offered some thoughts on why the British colonies were so much more attractive for newcomers—the so-called 'pull factors' of immigration, headed by the differences in climate—he failed to address the other key part of the equation, the 'push factors'. From the sixteenth century onward, the British Isles were subject to a continuing dislocation of population, both urban and rural, as they shifted gradually but inexorably into a new capitalistic economic phase of individual initiative and entrepreneurialism in which the paternalistic relationships characteristic of the medieval period were broken down, agricultural land was enclosed, and the age of communal agriculture ended. In France, no such discontented and displaced population was available for colonial migration on a massive level. Together, 'push' and 'pull' factors persuaded many British settlers to cross the Atlantic on their own, without subsidies, even if they had to contract their labour to pay for their passage. By contrast, because Canada was regarded as undesirable, deliberate government policy and public assistance were required to attract settlers, and France usually had other priorities. Moreover, although there were more Protestants and Jews in Canada than one might have expected, deliberate French exclusionary policies denied access to many people who might otherwise have been willing to settle in the New World.

More controversially, it has been suggested that the British transferred to America an ethos of individual enterprise that made those colonies more attractive both to immigrants outside the British Isles and to entrepreneurs within them. In most of Britain's American colonies, agricultural demand encouraged the importation of large numbers of workers, some of them under long-term labour contracts, others in permanent

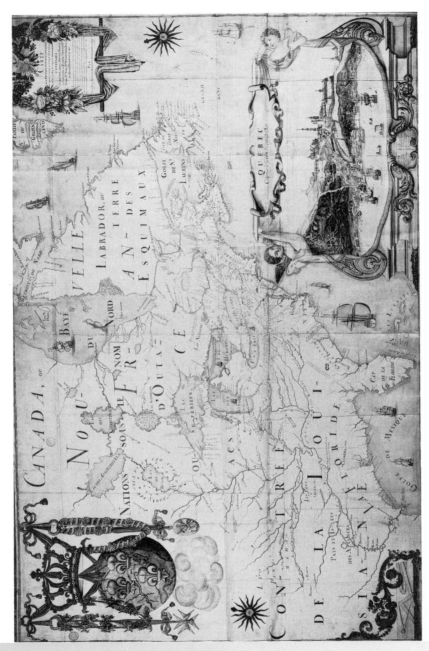

■ New France in 1688. The cartographer, Jean-Baptiste-Louis Franquelin, worked at Quebec from 1671 to 1692 as both geographer and hydrographer to the King. LAC, Cartographic and Architectural Archives Division PH/1000/1688.

bondage. The French were not opposed to slavery per se: they sent large numbers of Africans to the West Indies, and they accepted the enslavement of captives by the Aboriginal people. But only 540 black people—enslaved or free—ever lived in New France,[9] whereas the numbers in the British colonies had reached nearly half a million by the 1750s. The main reason for the discrepancy lay in the huge difference in agricultural organization. The British needed large labour forces to work their vast plantations growing tobacco and rice, but in Canada farming remained at a level not far above subsistence. In short, the entire economic and institutional structures of Britain and her American colonies encouraged massive immigration, but this was not the case for France and her colony in Canada.

On the other hand, to compare the French colonial experience with the British is in some senses unfair and misleading. Compared with most of the European nations that were establishing colonies in the Americas—Spain, Portugal, the Netherlands, Sweden, and Scotland—France did quite well, and as a settlement colony Canada was fairly typical. It was the British colonies that were different: in their numbers, their population size, and their dynamism. Not only were there more people in the British Isles who were willing to go to America, but the colonies offered many more situations in which to plant them. Whatever the administrative boundaries, France had four distinct colonial regions in North America—Acadia, Canada, the western interior, and Louisiana—while Britain had 13, all economically vibrant and located on the exposed flanks of New France. In the imperial rivalries that inevitably ensued, the French were at a large disadvantage from the start.

SOCIETY

THE CONTINUOUS VILLAGE

In the mid-eighteenth century Peter Kalm was able to describe the heartland of French Canada along the St Lawrence as 'a village beginning at Montreal and ending at Quebec'—a distance of roughly 270 kilometres—'for the farmhouses are never above five arpents [293 metres] and sometimes but three apart'.[10] Here and there a tiny village might develop around a church, but otherwise each small stone-and-timber farmhouse stood alone, and the only town between Quebec and Montreal was Trois-Rivières. Quebec and Montreal especially contained some impressive buildings, public and private, but by our standards both towns were quite small in population and area. The Aboriginal communities immediately outside the towns probably had larger populations than the towns themselves well into the eighteenth century. Thus the landscape of French Canada replicated neither the medieval villages from which many of its rural settlers had come, nor the English colonial pattern in which farmhouses tended to be isolated in the middle of their lots, separated from their neighbours by large expanses of fields. The typical Canadian holding was long and narrow, fronting on a river (for most settlers, the St Lawrence). This residential arrangement meant that it was as difficult in Canada as in the American colonies to mobilize the population for military or religious purposes. The most important local unit was the parish, which became the focus of local society. Parishes with permanent curates were usually better organized than those served by occasional missionaries.

Though not large, Quebec and Montreal were the centres of government, of economic decision-making, and of the Church and the social services it provided, such as health care and education. Inevitably, their populations included heavy concentrations of the colonial elite—royal officials, religious men and women, military officers, merchants, and seigneurs—who favourably impressed visitors like Peter Kalm. But these towns, which had grown rapidly in the seventeenth century, were not so dynamic in the eighteenth; their population growth rates remained well behind that of the colony as a whole. Construction of public buildings such as

■ The village of Château-Richer (on the north shore of the St Lawrence northeast of Quebec City), 1787, watercolour by Thomas Davies. Included in this pastoral scene are whitewashed stone farmhouses, wooden barns, and eel traps in the river. National Gallery of Canada, Ottawa, 6275. Purchased 1954.

churches and hospitals was the most important source of employment. The construction trades employed the largest numbers of workers and were the largest single element of local economies—as would be the case in Canadian towns until well into the nineteenth century.

WOMEN

As far as women were concerned, the fresh air of the New World did not bring about any remarkable transformations. The organization of Canadien society remained fundamentally patriarchal, with farms and businesses passing from fathers to sons. Nevertheless, women's traditional roles as helpmates and child-bearers were moderated by several factors. One was the frequent absence of husbands and fathers, whether in the fur trade or in the military, which meant that women had to be prepared to do heavy work while the men were away. The legal code of the colony, the Coutume de Paris, provided some limited protection for the property rights of married women, particularly by denying to husbands the sole right to dispose of the family estate. And the autonomous rights of widows were well protected by law as well as custom; many women ran successful businesses, inns and taverns or farming operations after the deaths of their husbands. The Coutume de Paris did, however, require the consent of the male head of the family for all property transactions and legal activities by his dependants. In theory, women ought to have been at least slightly better off in New France than in the mother country, not only because the unspecialized, family-oriented nature of much of the colonial economy prevented them from being shunted to one side, but also because they were in such short supply and so badly needed to bear children. What evidence we have supports the theory, but in truth historians do not have very much detailed knowledge about women in New France. The documents are more concerned with masculine than with feminine activities. Nevertheless, women were on the whole healthier than in France and less likely to die in childbirth, and some lived very long lives.[11]

While early Canada always had a substantial number of women in holy orders, most women in the colony did marry, and at an earlier age than in France (the average age in Canada during the colonial period was 22). Early marriage was encouraged by economic and social factors, including the absence of a recognized role for single women outside the church. If marriage (and remarriage) rates were high, so, too, were birth rates. Throughout the eighteenth century, annual raw birth rates ran over 50 per 1,000 inhabitants, and although childbirth was difficult and dangerous, women on average bore seven children, of which an average of 5.65 survived to adulthood (in France the latter figure was just 4.5). These demographic characteristics were typical of all colonial societies, not just French Canada.[12] Although nearly half of the males who immigrated to the colony ultimately left it, more than 90 per cent of the *filles du roi* remained in Canada. No doubt one reason for the difference was that the contracts binding male immigrants were legally limited, whereas marriage was a contract for life. Except perhaps among a few members of the elite, marriage for love was virtually unknown in New France.

CHILDREN

As in so many other areas of life, the situation of children in Canada reflected the comparable experience in France on a slightly different plane. Like France, Canada was a patriarchal society in which—by law, at least—children were subordinated to their parents well into adulthood; an unmarried child, male or female, was a legal dependant until the age of 25. Until then, according to the later Civil Code of Quebec, an unmarried minor was subject to 'reasonable and moderate correction'. Parents also had a legal right to approve of their minor child's choice of marriage partner.

Infants were bound in swaddling clothes as they were in peasant France. In addition, according to one seventeenth-century account, the infant's head was bound with a linen rag and covered with a cap, both for warmth and to protect the soft spot on the top of the head. Rates of infant mortality were extremely high. Children were supposed to be baptized by a priest within a week of birth, but the shortage of clergy meant that many were given lay baptism at home; in a period when life was precarious, it was essential to ensure that godparents and guardians were in place to care for children should anything happen to their parents. Illegitimate children were often adopted by Aboriginal families. Children without families were usually indentured by the state at age six or seven (when infancy was regarded as over) and apprenticed around the age of 12.

Surviving documents and material evidence indicate that, although childhood did not last nearly as long then as it does today, young children did have a variety of simple toys. But most were probably at work long before puberty, boys in the fields or the shop, and girls in the house. The majority of children received some religious instruction in the form of catechism, and boys got occupational training as apprentices, but instruction in reading, writing, and mathematics was extremely limited except among the families of the elite. More teaching took place in the home than in schools; in rural areas literacy rates declined rapidly in the eighteenth century, but even in Montreal, over half of householders could not write their names. In urban areas, where the Church ran relatively sophisticated educational institutions for both sexes, girls probably had more formal schooling than boys, but vocational instruction was generally restricted to sewing. Although there was no university in the colony, boys could obtain a classical education in both Quebec and Montreal.

Contemporaries complained constantly about the unruliness and independence of children in Canada. Governor Denonville in 1685 complained of the disorders that resulted from the 'light control that fathers and mothers and Governors have exercised over youth', adding that 'as soon as the children can shoulder a rifle the fathers can no longer restrain them and do not dare to make them angry.'[13] Such children apparently were outspoken and precocious, especially in sexual matters. Most children remained closely bound to their families, for whom they represented valuable economic assets.

ABORIGINAL PEOPLE

Most Native people continued to live in their traditional hunting areas throughout the colonial period. However, some did settle at or near missions, especially around the colony's two principal towns: the Hurons who had survived the destruction of their former home to the west had gathered at La Montagne, near Montreal (supervised by the Sulpicians), and Lorette, near Quebec, and these settlements actually expanded in population after 1663. The Iroquois resided at Caughnawaga (Kahnawake) and Oka (Kanesatake) close to Montreal. These communities were formally run by the missionaries, but the residents—known as *domiciliés* or *habitués*—were able to maintain a fair degree of autonomy, even refusing to accept the sovereignty of the French Crown. One reason was that the missionaries

(mainly the Jesuits) actively sought to protect them from the corrupting influence of European colonists. Another was that they were essential to the military posture of the colony, and a powerful military force in their own right; both the missionaries and the government realized that they had to tread carefully if they wanted to maintain good relations. Although the *domiciliés* were officially subject to the same laws as the settlers, in practice the authorities accepted some aspects of Native justice. The French never intruded in the Aboriginal communities themselves, and when Native people got in trouble with the law outside their own communities, they were treated leniently; the conviction rate for Aboriginal people was very low.[14]

Slavery. Without large plantations to work, New France never employed a large slave labour force, but slavery did exist in the colony. Most slaves were domestic servants. Not all were African; Aboriginal prisoners sold to the French were also kept in bondage. The colonial New Englander John Gyles was technically a slave when he was transferred from his Aboriginal captor to a French merchant on the Saint John River at the beginning of the eighteenth century. As Allan Greer has pointed out, the image of plantation slavery in the American South bears no relationship to the slave situation in French America, where many levels of bondage were possible, involving people from many different backgrounds—African, Aboriginal, and European.[15]

SOCIAL STRUCTURE

Canadien society was divided between two fundamental orders: those with access to government largesse and those without. The law was available to all, and in a society without trained lawyers, it was administered with a fair degree of equity. But only some Canadiens could expect public appointments (particularly in the military), government contracts, and seigneurial status. On the other hand, there was a certain degree of social mobility: the availability of land and economic opportunity meant that people of humble origin could move up the social ladder much more easily than in France. However, it seems that not many had the single-minded determination required to take advantage of those opportunities. Most contemporary observers were of the opinion that most habitants worked no harder than necessary. Both the aristocratic presumptions of the upper orders in the military and through the seigneurial system, and the non-acquisitive behaviour of the lower orders, suggest that some of the central values of the mother country had been transferred to North America.

Observers agreed that the habitants were typically more prosperous, and enjoyed considerably more personal liberty, than their European counterparts. As one royal official noted towards the close of the French regime:

> The ordinary habitant would be scandalized were he called a peasant. In fact, they are of a better cloth, have more spirit and more education than those in France. The reason for this is that they pay no taxes, have the right to hunt and fish, and that they live a sort of independence. . . . The Canadien is haughty, self-seeking, mendacious, obliging, affable, honest, untiring for the hunt, trips and voyages that they make to the upper country, [and] lazy in agriculture.[16]

According to another commentator, the independent behaviour of Canadiens reflected 'the fact that they were born in a country with a good climate, fed on good and abundant food and that they have the liberty, from childhood, to exercise in fishing, in hunting and in canoe trips'.[17]

CULTURE

Given the high rates of illiteracy in the early period, especially among ordinary people, it is hardly surprising that the colony's culture was primarily oral and visual.

LANGUAGE

The most striking cultural characteristic of French Canada has always been its language. In New France, the dominant dialect was that of the Paris region, and it was apparently spoken extremely well. 'All are of the opinion', wrote Peter Kalm in 1753, 'that in Canada the ordinary man speaks a purer French than in any province in France, yes, that in this respect it can vie with Paris itself.'[18] Yet, it was not until well into the eighteenth century that Parisian French established itself as the national language of France itself. In the seventeenth century, dialects varied widely between regions of France, and some regions, such as Brittany, had their own distinct languages. Given that most of the early settlers came from rural districts of the north and west of France, where regional differences were most marked,[19] the linguistic variety must have been quite striking before the *filles du roi* raised their children to speak the Parisian dialect that was their own mother tongue.[20]

A PROVINCIAL CULTURE

If French Canada was unmistakably Parisian in language, it did not resemble Paris in other aspects of its culture. In the past, generations of Anglo-Canadians assumed—some may even have been taught—that French Canada was culturally backward. A key piece of evidence used to support this charge was the fact that under the *ancien régime* the colony did not have even one printing press. To focus on that single emblem of 'progress', however, is both unfair and anachronistic. Members of the elite were no less interested than educated people anywhere in science and literature.[21] But Canada was numerically a small colony, and its needs for reading material could easily be met by France itself. True, it did not have a newspaper, but the English colonies to the south did not begin printing their own papers until the eighteenth century, as part of a communications revolution within the British Empire.[22] More to the point, to

MARGUERITE DUPLESSIS

Marguerite Duplessis was a Pawnee, born into slavery in 1718, somewhere around Green Bay. As with most Aboriginal women in early French Canada, the only reason we know anything about her is that she was taken to court. Marguerite's ownership had been transferred in 1726, when she still was a young child, from a fur trader in Green Bay to the wife of a merchant in Montreal. Like most Aboriginal slaves in Canada, she worked as a domestic servant rather than a field hand. After the merchant died in 1735, she was sold several times in rapid succession. Then in 1740 her last owner, one Marc-Antoine Huart Dormicourt, accused her of vice, libertinage, and theft, and determined to send her to the West Indies, where she would be sold once again, this time quite possibly as a field slave. While she was incarcerated in the Quebec prison awaiting transportation, Marguerite somehow managed to meet some humanitarians who took up her case. Maintaining that she was the mixed-blood daughter of the Green Bay fur trader who had sold her, she argued that since she had been a resident in the lands of the French King since birth, and had been baptized, she should be regarded as a free woman and not a slave.

Her argument was not particularly strong. Although the 'Code Noir' legislation of 1685, regulating slavery, had not mentioned Aboriginal slaves, in 1709 the intendant Jacques Raudot had enacted an ordinance extending the Code to them. Neither of these documents treated religious status or place of birth as a relevant issue. Furthermore, a legal challenge to the slavery law mounted a few years earlier had not succeeded. In 1732 a Native slave named Pierre had been the subject of a complex lawsuit when he was seized as a piece of property to be sold to repay a debt incurred by his owner. On appeal, his owner had argued that the sale should not be allowed and that Pierre should be freed because he was a Christian. The Sovereign Council had referred the case to the intendant, who decided against Pierre and his owner. (The case was an opportunity for the Crown to make further regulations regarding slavery in general or Aboriginal slavery, but it refused to intervene.) Marguerite's case was somewhat different from Pierre's, but it was no more successful, in part because she could not produce proof of either paternity or baptism. In the end, Dormicourt offered to free her if her supporters recompensed him, but her appeal was rejected (she was ordered to pay the court costs), and at that point she disappears from the historical record. It seems likely that she was sent to the West Indies with the autumn sailing of 1740.

concentrate on the written word as the mark of literary culture is to ignore the fact that early Canada did have an oral equivalent to literature in its folktales and songs. Moreover, it had a very rich artistic life associated with the ritualistic requirements of the church.

CULTURE AND THE CHURCH

Music. Given the religious impulse behind much of the early settlement of Canada, and the central roles played by priests and nuns in education, it was inevitable that the Catholic Church would contribute a great deal to artistic life in the colony. Music, for example, became a central feature in the missionaries' efforts to convert Aboriginal people. Thus, Father Jean Enjalran reported from the Huron seminary at Sillery in 1676: 'One is charmed to hear the various choirs, which the men and women form in order to sing during mass and at vespers. The nuns of France do not sing more agreeably than some savage women here; and as a class, all the savages have much aptitude and inclination for singing the hymns of the church, which have been rendered into their language.'[23] One enduring product of that period was the 'Huron Carol' ('In the moon of winter-time'), written by Father Jean de Brébeuf to a traditional French melody. The colony's first pipe organ was installed at the cathedral of Notre-Dame de la Paix in Quebec City in 1660, and as early as 1664 Bishop Laval was able to report that divine service was celebrated:

> according to the ceremony of bishops; our priests, our seminarists, as well as ten or twelve choir boys, are regularly present there. On the more important festivals, the mass, the vespers, and the eventide Salve are sung with instrumental accompaniment in counterpoint with viols, and each are arranged according to its own style; blending sweetly with the singers' voices, the organ wondrously embellishes this harmony of musical sound.[24]

Scholars are only beginning to uncover some of the richness of the early musical life in Canada. Of course part of the reason that life went unrecognized for so long was that records of it either disappeared or were confined to manuscripts buried in archives; but a colonial mentality was also a factor. If we assume that no important cultural production could have occurred in the past, then we will not look to find any evidence for it.

Visual Art. As with music, the Church played a central role in the visual arts. For the seventeenth century, all the artists we know of were clerics,

■ *La France apportant la foi aux Hurons de la Nouvelle France*, c. 1670, oil on canvas, attributed to Frère Luc. As was common in this period, there are several images within the picture. The two figures hold a painting showing the Trinity surrounded by the Holy Family, and in the heavens is another scene of the Holy Family itself. Monastère des Ursulines, Quebec.

mostly trained in France, and most of their work was intended for use in churches. Very little of it has survived—largely because, over the centuries, most of the oldest churches have been damaged if not destroyed by fire. But an anonymous canvas in the Monastère des Ursulines in Quebec entitled *La France apportant la foi aux Hurons de la Nouvelle-France*, dated around 1670, remains. This large canvas, over two metres square, shows a Huron kneeling in front of a female figure of France. It is usually attributed to Frère Luc (Claude François), a Récollet friar who was trained in Italy and came to Canada briefly in 1670.

■ 'Plan général d'église', by Jean Maillou, c. 1715. Musée de la civilisation, fond d'archives du Séminaire Québec, Polygraphie 2, no. 77.

By the end of the seventeenth century, art instruction was often a part of formal education in the colony and some indigenous painters were emerging. Pierre Le Ber came from a merchant family and was probably self-taught. His best-known work is the portrait of Marguerite Bourgeoys (p. 95 above), which has been described as the 'single most moving image to survive from the French period'.[25] In the eighteenth century, ex-voto paintings were becoming increasingly common, commissioned in gratitude for miraculous assistance, often from untrained (or 'naive') artists. The best-known ex-voto painter is Paul Mallepart de Grand Maison *dit* Beaucour, who was born in Paris in 1700, came to Canada as a soldier, and worked mainly in Quebec. Unfortunately, biographical information about artists of the early period is even rarer than their work.

Many of the most impressive buildings in New France were churches. Not surprisingly, there were two traditions. In the towns, churches and buildings associated with them were built of stone, based on plans or concepts imported from France. Peter Kalm described the Jesuit College in Quebec City: 'It consists of stone, is three stories high, exclusive of the garret, is covered with slate and built in the square form like the new palace at Stockholm, including a large court.'[26] It was said that the stone for the fine trim had been prepared in France and imported to Quebec as ballast.[27] These buildings influenced design in the rural regions, although local craftsmen tended to simplify the lines. One common plan, found in the archives of the Séminaire de Québec, was reproduced frequently in the early eighteenth century.[28] It called for a church three bays long, a nave with a semicircular apse, and an elaborate façade. Above the entrance rose a '*clocher*' or bell tower, which in the eighteenth century became the most distinctive feature of rural churches in French Canada. Whereas the earliest church buildings were built of wood, by the eighteenth century almost all churches were built of stone. The more impressive church structures were usually works in progress, never finished and continually evolving over the years.

POPULAR CULTURE

Probably the most vibrant cultural activity could be found among the ordinary habitants, who

A FOLKSONG OF EARLY CANADA

Most of the earliest folksongs in the colony can be traced back to France, but the following is obviously of Canadian composition. According to Marius Barbeau, the great expert on early Canadian folk culture who included this text in his *Folk-songs of Old Quebec*, it dates to the early colonial period.

LA PLAINTE DU COUREUR DES BOIS

Le six de mai, l'année dernier',
Là haut je me suis engagé;
Là-haut je me suis engagé
Pour y faire un long voyage.
Aller aux pays hauts,
Parmi tous les sauvages.

    Ah! que l'hiver est long,
    Que ce temps est ennuyant!
    Nuit et jour mon coeur soupire
    De voir venir le doux printemps,
    Le beau et doux printemps.
    Car c'est lui qui console
    Les malheureux amants
    Avec leurs amours folles.

Quand le printemps est arrivé
Les vents d'avril soufflent dans nos voiles
Pour revenir dans mon pays.
Au coin de Saint-Sulpice,
J'irai saluer m'amie,
Qui est la plus jolie.

    Qui en a fait la chanson?
    C'est un jeune garçon,
    S'en allant à la voile,
    La chantant tout au long.
    Elle est bien véritable.
    Adieu, tous les sauvages,
    Adieu, les pays hauts,
    Adieu, les grand's misères!

THE PLAINT OF THE COUREUR DE BOIS

The Sixth of May, a year ago,
It was that day that I went away;
It was that day that I went away
On a long and distant voyage,
To lands beyond the bay
Where the woodland people stay.

    O how long is the Winter!
    O how slowly time passes by!
    Night and day my heart does sigh,
    Longing for the Sweet Spring-time,
    The sweet and lovely Spring!
    For 'tis the Spring who will bring
    Joy to fond lovers pining
    For tenderness and cherishing.

When Spring at last has come to stay,
The winds in our sails are gay.
Now I shall see my country-side
At Saint-Sulpice far away.
There I shall greet my bride,
Who is the loveliest maid.

    Who sings this plaintive song?
    'Tis a lad that is young,
    Far away from his home land,
    Singing it as he walks along,
    Chanting the gay refrain:
    Farewell, all you savage people!
    Farewell, you rocky shores!
    Farewell, all misery, all pain!

SOURCE: Marius Barbeau, *Folk-Songs of Old Quebec* (Ottawa: National Museum Bulletin, no. 75, Anthropological Series, No. 16, rev. ed.), 29–30.

■ Two views of habitant dress, c. 1806. Fashion might change among the urban elite, but ordinary people would continue to dress in much the same way throughout the eighteenth century and even beyond. By John Lambert from his *Travels Through Lower Canada and the United States in the Years 1806, 1807, 1808* (London, 1810). LAC, C-113669 and C-1703.

brought with them to Canada a rich and varied heritage of songs, dances, folktales, games, and other amusements. Canadiens were said to be extremely fond of dancing, but singing and tale-telling around the fire must also have been hugely popular, especially in the long winter months. Most of the Quebec folksongs collected in recent years have their origins in the period before 1673. Continually revised and adapted as part of an ongoing oral tradition, some have

more than a hundred different local variants. A folksong like 'La Bergère muette' ('The Mute Shepherdess') exists in many more versions in North America than in France itself. While the form of the folksong (and even the melody) may hark back to the Old World, the words often describe Canadian events.[29] The 'complaint' or 'lament'—usually a story of a tragedy or disas-ter—was often adapted to include local colour. Stories and legends were particularly likely to have Canadian content, and many combined French and Aboriginal traditions.

Among the European customs brought to North America were the carnival and the charivari. The carnival during which the 1662 earthquake occurred was the 'mardi gras' festival preceding the beginning of Lent, when people flocked outdoors to celebrate with costumes, music, and street theatre. The charivari was a different sort of public event, a noisy demonstration involving lots of banging on pots and pans, usually intended to express disapproval of marriages considered unsuitable; one charivari in 1683, in protest against a young widow who had remarried just three weeks after burying her husband, lasted for six nights and ended only when the bishop issued a pastoral letter.

Clothing. The inventory of Jeanne Mance's wardrobe at her death in 1673 consisted of 33 hats and caps, 30 blouses, 5 jackets, 7 skirts, 1 gown, 5 pairs of stockings, and 3 pairs of shoes. Members of the urban elite did their best to keep up with the Paris fashions; visitors were impressed by the quantities of fine linen, damask, velvet, and silk imported from France.[30] By the eighteenth century, women especially were extremely conscious of fashion and hairstyles, and were fond of ornamentation in the form of ribbons and lace. But at a time when *'paniers'*—basket-like frames supporting overskirts looped up around the hips—were all the rage in Paris, such voluminous garments were not common in Canada; certainly they would not have been practical for trudging through deep snow.

The habitants dressed much as their counterparts did in Europe—women in skirts and hip-length jackets over loose shifts, men in shirts and doublets with breeches or trousers. Colours were muted, mostly browns and greys; underwear was generally woollen, even in summer; and outerwear consisted mainly of cloaks and capes, with generous use of fur. In addition, however, men in particular incorporated a few Aboriginal influences. Fur traders imitated their Native guides, wrapping their legs in strips of cloth,[31] and by the end of the French regime typical costume for the male habitant—a woollen jacket (*capote*), loose breeches tucked into heavy stockings, and a tuque—was not complete without moccasins. At the same time, more than one witness commented on the extent to which Native people had taken to mixing European items, often originating in the English colonies, into their traditional dress.

HOUSING

Domestic architecture in rural Canada had evolved its own distinctive style by the end of the seventeenth century.[32] Although there were regional variations, the typical house was rectangular with a steep roof (possibly with curved 'bellcast' eaves) and a heavy chimney. An observer from Europe described how this style had evolved by the mid-eighteenth century:

> The greater part of the houses in the country are built of wood, and sometimes plastered over on the outside. The chinks in the walls are filled with clay instead of moss. The houses are seldom above one story high. The windows are always set in the inner part of the wall, never in the outer, unless double windows are used. The panes are set with putty and not lead. In the city glass is used for the windows for the most part, but further inland they use paper. . . . In every room is either a chimney or a stove, or both. . . . The smoke from the stoves is conveyed up the chimney by an iron pipe in which there are no dampers, so that a good deal of their heat is lost. In summer the stoves are removed. The roofs are always very steep, either of the Italian type or with gables. They are made of long boards, laid horizontally, the upper overlapping the lower. Wooden shingles are not used since they are too liable to catch fire, for which reason they are forbidden in Quebec. Barns have thatched roofs, very high and steep. The dwelling houses generally have three rooms. The baking oven is built separately outside the house, either of brick or stone, and covered with clay.[33]

■ The hearth in the ancestral home of Philippe Aubert de Gaspé (1786–1871), author of *Les Anciens Canadiens* (1863), at St-Jean-Port-Joli, Quebec. LAC, PA-51704.

Furnishings were simple and made of wood; the few examples that have survived are much admired today for their elegant, functional lines.[34] By the mid-eighteenth century, the introduction of the iron stove made it possible for Canadiens to begin to overheat their houses during the winter months. But during the French regime most made do with fireplaces for cooking as well as heat.

Wood was the most common building material, for several reasons: it didn't conduct the cold the way stone (common in France) did; it was capable of adjusting as the ground shifted with the spring thaw; and it was widely available. Houses were small by modern standards: a typical farmhouse in the seventeenth century measured no more than eight by ten metres and had at best two rooms. Rooms did not have separate functions. Sleeping areas with straw mattresses might be partitioned off, but family members tended to stay close together for warmth. Meals consisted mainly of soups and stews, cooked in a single pot over the open fire, with bread. A variety of meat was available for the hunting much of the year. The Canadiens were fond of most root vegetables, except potatoes, and consumed large quantities of bread.[35] The core diet was made up of buckwheat, peas, pork, fish, apples, and milk.[36] According to Peter Kalm, 'The French have a strong taste for milk and great quantities of it are consumed, especially by the young. . . . Generally they boiled it, then threw into it chunks of bread and much [maple] sugar.'[37]

Together, the aromas of cooking, wood smoke, and human bodies must have made the habitant house a richly fragrant place, all the more so in the coldest months, when farm animals might be brought indoors as well. Whereas in France people would have been able to work outside virtually year-round, the severe Canadian winters meant long periods of forced togetherness indoors. No doubt the lack of privacy called for considerable social discipline; it is tempting to think that, by forcing people to work out ways of resolving disputes and getting along with one another, the Canadian winter might have been the most important influence on social behaviour.

CONCLUSION

Canada remained a colony with a very small population, thinly spread over the landscape, and responsible for a vast amount of territory, especially in the west. It had never been attractive to the French people, and there was never enough immigration to move out of the pioneering stage of settlement. In social and cultural terms, Canada was a distant province of France, with equal emphasis on both 'distant' and 'province'. Most institutions were strongly influenced by French origins—often replicated as folk memories—and the primitiveness born of underpopulation. Left to its own devices, such a society had much unfulfilled promise, and by itself, Canada was probably not much threatened by the British. But the future had been mortgaged through Canada's assumption of the role of defender of an expanding New France. The colony would eventually be overwhelmed by the exigencies of imperial rivalry.

SHORT BIBLIOGRAPHY

Charbonneau, Hubert, et al. *The First French-Canadians: Pioneers in the St. Lawrence Valley.* Newark, Del., 1993. Discusses the process by which immigrants founded families in the seventeenth century.

Choquette, Leslie. *Frenchmen into Peasants: Modernity and Tradition in the Peopling of French Canada.* Cambridge, Mass., 1997. A thorough analysis of the immigration process in Canada.

Douville, Raymond, and Jacques Casanova. *Daily Life in Early Canada.* New York, 1967. Still the best survey in English on everyday life in the colony.

Greer, Allan. *Peasant, Lord, and Merchant: Rural Society in Three Quebec Parishes 1740–1840.* Toronto, 1985. Offers an interpretation of rural society in the eighteenth century.

Kalman, Harold. *A History of Canadian Architecture*, vol. 1 (Toronto, 1994), 27–87. The best brief survey in English of architecture in New France.

Landry, Yves. *Orphelines en France, pionnières au Canada: Les Filles du roi au XVIIe siècle.* Montreal, 1992. The most detailed work on the topic, full of tables and statistical data.

Moogk, Peter. *Building a House in New France: An Account of the Perplexities of Client and Craftsmen in Early Canada.* Toronto, 1977. A fascinating account of the life and work of artisans in the colony.

———. *La Nouvelle France: The Making of French Canada—A Cultural History.* Vancouver, 2000. An important study, even though its definition of 'culture' is very broad.

Nish, Cameron. *Les Bourgeois-gentilshommes de la Nouvelle-France, 1729–1748.* Montreal, 1968. A useful account of the non-political elite in the colony in the eighteenth century.

Séguin, Robert-Lionel. *La Civilisation traditionnelle de l'habitant aux 17e et 18e siècles.* Montreal and Paris, 1967. An important source of material on everyday life in Canada.

———. *Le Costume civil en Nouvelle-France.* Ottawa, 1967. A detailed compendium on dress in the French colonies.

STUDY QUESTIONS

1. Why was the population of Canada so much smaller than that of the English colonies?
2. What does the story of Marguerite Duplessis tell us about Canada in the eighteenth century?
3. In what ways did the First Nations influence Canadien culture in the early period?
4. How would you characterize Canadien popular culture before 1763?
5. Why was the Roman Catholic Church such an important factor in high culture within the colony?
6. Were women in Canada appreciably advantaged over their French counterparts?

CHAPTER EIGHT

The Peripheries of the Empires, 1670–1760

■ Before 1763, both the French and English (later British) empires in North America were sprawling and decentralized operations, their boundaries constantly shifting and altering. 'New France' had never been a single, homogeneous entity. Within a few years of reaching its greatest geographic extent—with the addition of Louisiana in 1700—it was obliged by the Treaty of Utrecht (1713) to give up its claims to Hudson Bay, Newfoundland, and much of Acadia. Thereafter, New France consisted of four colonial regions (not all of them formal colonies). In the east, Acadia had been reduced to Île Saint-Jean (Prince Edward Island) and Île Royale (Cape Breton Island, site of the great fortress of Louisbourg). Along the St Lawrence River was Canada, the largest colony; to its west, the back-country fur-trade region known as the *pays d'en haut*, inhabited chiefly by Aboriginal people (although the mixed-blood population was beginning to grow), stretching south from Detroit along the Mississippi River; and finally, in the lower reaches of the Mississippi, Louisiana.

For the English, the northern colonies of Newfoundland and (after 1713) Nova Scotia were the outermost fringes of a colonial base along the eastern seaboard that stretched from present-day Maine to Georgia. As such, they were left largely to their own devices. Newfoundland would remain without formal colonial standing or government until well into the nineteenth century, and Nova Scotia, acquired from France in the Treaty of Utrecht, did not begin to receive serious attention until the late 1740s, when England decided that settlement was necessary to provide a counterweight to Louisbourg and signal a new emphasis on eliminating the French from North America. In the West, the vast territory of the Hudson Bay drainage basin was administered by a privately owned British trading company, the Hudson's Bay Company, whose monopoly—granted by the British Crown in 1670—had been recognized by the French in the peace treaty of 1713. Beyond those territories considered European imperial possessions lay lands inhabited by First Nations that Europeans had first begun to visit in 1690, and where they had developed a substantial trade in furs by the 1730s.

However marginal some of these regions might have appeared, they were nevertheless critical to European pretensions. Bouts of imperial arm-wrestling could erupt anywhere on the frontier, and resident populations like the Acadians and the First Nations often became victims of the ongoing struggles.

TIMELINE

1667
Treaty of Breda returns Acadia to France.

1670
Acadia actually restored to France.

1671
New settlers brought to Acadia by Governor Grandfontaine. Sieur de Saint-Lusson takes possession of Lake Superior/Great Lakes region for France.

1674
Dutch attack Acadia.

1675
Newfoundland census lists 30 settlements.

1686
The intendant of New France and the Bishop of Quebec visit Acadia.

1696
New France attempts to close western posts and withdraw to Canada.

1699
Act to Encourage the Trade of Newfoundland.

1701
Louisiana established. Grand Peace of 1701 with Iroquois.

1703
Jesuit mission established at Kaskaskia.

1713
Acadia and Plaisance ceded to Britain by Treaty of Utrecht. French retain Île Royale and Île Saint-Jean. Shift from inshore fishery to Grand Banks fishery in Newfoundland. Construction of Louisbourg begins.

1717
Illinois country annexed to Louisiana.

1719
French assign Île Saint-Jean to the Comte de Saint-Pierre.

1720
Negotiations held at Paris over Acadia's 'ancient boundaries' are inconclusive. Port La Joie established on Île Saint-Jean.

1729
Governor Philipps administers oath of allegiance to Acadians.

1730
Company of the East sends Jean-Pierre Roma to Île Saint-Jean.

1744
French attempt to cut back on expenses in *pays d'en haut*.

1745
Joint Yankee–British expedition captures Louisbourg.

1749
Founding of Halifax.

1751
'Foreign Protestants' dispatched to Nova Scotia.

1752
French resettle Acadians on Chignecto Peninsula.

1753
Foreign Protestants moved from Halifax to Lunenburg.

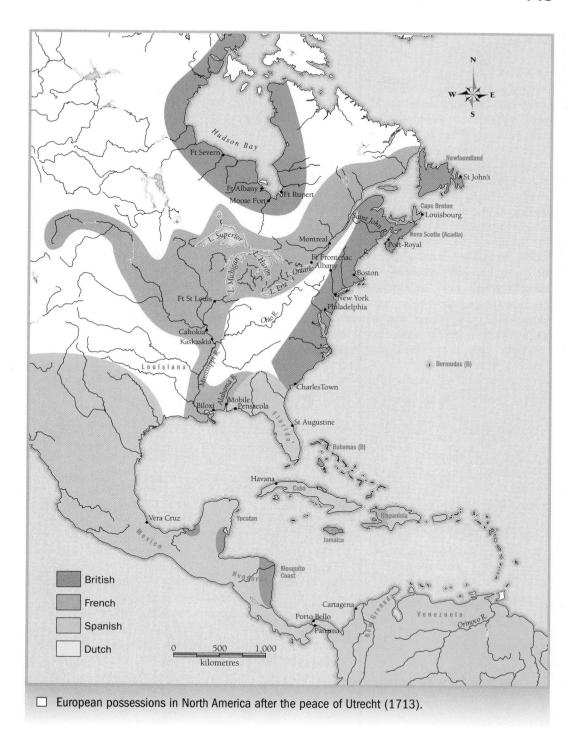

European possessions in North America after the peace of Utrecht (1713).

ACADIA

1670–1713

Acadia expanded considerably between 1670 and 1713, both in population and in territory cultivated. A census in 1671 counted 400 heads in the colony, mainly in the Port-Royal area of the Annapolis Basin, where there were 67 families (65 men, 67 wives or widows, 125 sons, and 91 daughters) cultivating 400 arpents (acres) and holding 650 cattle and 430 sheep. Perhaps another 100 souls were scattered thinly across the remainder of the Nova Scotia peninsula, mainly along the southwestern coast. By 1710 there were between 1,500 and 2,000 Acadians in the colony, with new concentrations developing around the Minas Basin, Cobequid, and Chignecto Bay. Although some new immigrants, mainly soldiers and artisans, had arrived since 1670, the bulk of the population increase was natural. At least two-thirds of the Acadian population in the mid-eighteenth century were descended from families that had arrived in the colony before 1670.

As would be typical of agricultural expansion in Canada until the twentieth century, most of the settlers moving to new territories in the seventeenth century had been members of a younger generation whose growing numbers were straining the resources of older communities. In Acadia as in Canada, land tenure was formally based on the seigneurial system, but—unlike their Canadien counterparts—Acadian *censitaires* operated as if they held their land in freehold. As elsewhere, landholding patterns were influenced by the topography. In the Bay of Fundy region, where high tides regularly inundated low-lying ground, dykes had to be built and marshlands drained to permit 'meadowland cultivation'. As the Sieur de Dièreville explained the process in 1608:

ACADIAN CENSUS, 1707

ACADIAN CENSUS OF PEOPLE, LAND, AND LIVESTOCK, 1707

	Port-Royal	Beaubassin	Minas	Cobequid
Total Population	570	271	585	82
Number heads of families	104	45	88	17
Families 2 or more people	96	45	86	15
Heads of families with cultivated land	83	41	73	17
Arpents of cultivated land	398	286	315	101
Number of Cattle	952	510	777	180
Number of sheep	1,237	476	732	124
Number of swine	855	334	643	114

SOURCE: Derived from Andrew Hill Clark, *Acadia: The Geography of Early Nova Scotia* (Madison: University of Wisconsin Press, 1968), Table 6.0, 234.

five or six rows of large logs are driven whole into the ground at the points where the tide enters the Marsh, & between each row, other logs are laid, one on top of the other, & all the spaces between them are so carefully filled with well-pounded clay, that the water can no longer get through. In the center of this construction, A Sluice is contrived in such a manner that the water on the Marshes flows out of its own accord, while that of the Sea is prevented from Coming in. An undertaking of this nature, which can only be carried on at Certain Seasons when the Tides do not rise so high, costs a great deal, & takes Many days, but the abundant crop that is harvested in the second year, after the Soil has been washed by Rain water compensates, for all the expense.[1]

Farms were relatively small in size, averaging 20 arpents each. Wheat and peas were the main crops, but other vegetables and especially fruits were commonly grown as well. At Port-Royal in 1698, the census counted 1,766 fruit trees on 54 of the 73 farms in the community. It was, claimed one visitor, 'as well planted with Apple trees as they would have been in Normandy.'[2] Even without dyking, tidal marshland provided large quantities of hay and grazing for livestock, the mainstay of the Acadian economy. Meat was the chief commodity traded by the Acadians. Trade with Canada, to which they supplied salted beef, was legal; but much of Acadia's meat was clandestinely traded to the New England in exchange for goods such as tools and hardware. Whatever the situation in Canada, farming in Acadia was not limited to the subsistence level and could be highly market-oriented. Specialized agricultural activity was pursued, and grain and livestock were also traded illegally with New England fishermen and coastal traders; a good deal of Acadian produce ultimately found its way through Yankee hands to the French Antilles. Most of the illegal trade with New England was conducted on a barter basis, for currency was always in short supply in North America. Royal officials, convinced that the

Acadians hoarded any gold and silver they obtained, were anxious to find a remedy. In 1710, one French official made it clear that this situation was not acceptable, writing the local governor: 'as you inform me that there is plenty of money in Acadia, but that the inhabitants do not put it in circulation, it is your business to discover the means of getting it into circulation.'[3]

On the outskirts of the tidal settlements, especially around Cap de Sable and on the southwest coast of Nova Scotia, were a number of fishing communities exposed both to the elements and to privateers. Residents of these outports engaged not only in fishing but also in hunting, fur-trading, and occasionally timbering; some even became privateers themselves. Minimal effort was made to settle on either Île Royale (Cape Breton Island) or the north shore of the Bay of Fundy before 1710. As would be the case in the Atlantic region until well into the nineteenth century, there were few roads and therefore no overland transportation links between settlements. Canoes and small boats (shallops) were the basic means of travel.

Government sat fairly lightly on the people of Acadia. Between 1670 and 1710, a continual flow of census data was produced as at least eight governors and administrators tried to establish control over the colony, and although the records were never complete, the fact that they exist at all indicates that the inhabitants did recognize authority when it was exercised. The seat of government was usually at Port-Royal, but even there no authorities were in residence for very long, particularly during the last 10 years of the seventeenth century. Before 1710 some 40 to 50 priests and missionaries were in service at various times; parish priests worked at Port-Royal after 1676 and at Grand Pré and Beaubassin from the mid-1680s. Sent to Acadia from Canada, the priests served as informal agents of royal authority; in fact, almost all the military activity carried out from Acadia—chiefly border raids against New England—was directed from Canada, often through missionaries who transmitted orders from Quebec to Aboriginal Catholics in the east. With Acadia's surrender to the British in 1713, however, these activities came to an abrupt end.[4]

THE BEGINNINGS OF ÎLE SAINT-JEAN

In 1719 the French government assigned Île Saint-Jean (the future Prince Edward Island) to the Comte de Saint-Pierre, making him a semi-feudal landlord with responsibility for colonization. Accordingly, he organized a company that sent three ships to the island in 1720 and quickly established a settlement at Port La Joie. The official settlement soon failed, but some families remained. A census in 1728 showed 297 people resident on the island. In 1730 a new company took over from Saint-Pierre, and one of its partners, Jean-Pierre Roma, actually took up residence on the eastern tip of the island. A man with 'so much causticity' in his character, wrote one contemporary, 'that it is to be feared he could not reconcile himself to anyone',[5] Roma fought valiantly against isolation and natural calamity, but his settlement was destroyed in the course of the Yankee invasion and capture of Louisbourg in 1745 (see Chapter 9). By now Acadian families had begun to immigrate to the island from the mainland; three years later the Acadian population had grown to 735, and the French government began actively encouraging those still in Nova Scotia to move to the island. By 1752 the island had more than 2,200 residents, mainly clustered in the Port La Joie area, on the Northeast River, and in the Pownal–Orwell area on the south coast. A census in that year showed 368 heads of families, possessing 98 horses, 1,259 cattle, 799 oxen, 1,230 sheep, 1,295 pigs, 2,393 hens, 394 geese, 90 turkeys, and 12 ducks. The community had seeded nearly 1,500 bushels of wheat, and had cleared land for another 1,500. Despite suffering caused by shortages of seed and grain, the settlement received another substantial influx of population in 1755–6 as Acadians who had escaped from

the British retreated there.[6] Replicating on the marshes along the island's coastal rivers the 'meadowland cultivation' they had practised on the mainland, they began to take hold.[7] A population of 6,000—well in excess of available food resources—would be discovered there by the British navy in 1758 when it sought to clear the region of Acadian inhabitants.

THE FOUNDING OF LOUISBOURG

Unfortunately for the French population in British Nova Scotia, their ancient loyalties were constantly being tested by France, which was still active in the region and still expected occasional assistance from its former citizens. After 1713 the French had turned their attention to Île Royale, and particularly to building a large fortress at Louisbourg on the southeastern coast. In 1716 Louisbourg contained about 600 people, mainly French fishermen evacuated there when Britain took over Plaisance (see p. 157). After 1720 it grew rapidly as the French government fortified the town, stationed a garrison there, and set about making it the military and economic nerve-centre of the Atlantic region. By 1734 the townsite—four east–west streets on about 100 acres—was surrounded by walls on three sides, with impressive gates. Inside the walls were the huge and stately King's Bastion and barracks (the largest building in New France), and numerous stone dwellings and other structures.

In the 1740s Louisbourg's population consisted of 600 soldiers (increased to 3,500 in the 1750s) and some 2,000 administrators, clerks, innkeepers, artisans, fishermen, and their families. We know much more about Louisbourg than we do about Acadia, partly because as a fortress it generated a considerable volume of records and partly because its reconstruction as a National Historic Site in the 1960s gave rise to a minor boom in publicly assisted historical research. Its complex urban society, heavily subsidized by the Crown, included a wide variety of tradesmen and a substantial servant-keeping

■ The Porte Dauphine, the entrance to the reconstructed fortress of Louisbourg, with the clocktower of the King's Bastion and barracks in the distance. Parks Canada, Fortress of Louisbourg National Historic Site of Canada, 01 A 339.

class, headed by 20 *marchands*. Always a major fishing port, serving as the centre of the French fishery after the surrender of Plaisance to Britain in 1713, Louisbourg in its prime was also an important naval station harbouring French warships as well as fishing vessels. Since its hinterland was completely undeveloped, supplies had to be imported from afar: not just from Canada, France, and Acadia, but even from New England (the Yankees actually supplied much of the building material for its fortifications). By the time open warfare resumed between Great Britain and France on 27 April 1744, Louisbourg

had become a major military and commercial entrepôt.[8] Its fate in the Anglo–French wars will be discussed in the next chapter.

THE BRITISH AND THE ACADIAN PROBLEM

When the Treaty of Utrecht gave Acadia to the British in 1713, it referred to the region's '*anciennes limites*' but did not define them. By 1720 the French came to insist that the 'Acadia' surrendered did not include what are now New Brunswick and northern Maine. As for the territory ceded to the British and henceforth called Nova Scotia—as a reminder of Britain's historic claims to the region—the treaty specified that its French inhabitants had one year to remove to French territory before they would become British subjects. But the year had expired with little change. The Acadians themselves did not want to leave their homes, and the British Board of Trade (which feared that a massive exodus would only strengthen the French at Île Royale) did not want to see them leave. As a result, the British tacitly allowed the Acadians to remain in Nova Scotia without insisting that they become full British citizens—but also without resolving any of the questions regarding land titles, language, religious rights, or the Acadians' political and military obligations to their new rulers. Left to deal with these questions on an ad hoc basis, the government of Nova Scotia accepted the Acadians' insistence on being treated as political neutrals and made no attempt to exercise much authority within the Acadian community, which informally chose its own deputies to deal with the British on its behalf.

With neither direction from London nor the manpower to exert military pressure on the Acadian population, the Nova Scotia government permitted the situation to drift, and the Acadians translated this unofficial tolerance, born of irresolution, into enshrined 'rights'. Of the many problems created by this situation, the most serious concerned Article XIV of the Treaty of Utrecht, which permitted former French subjects in the ceded territory 'the exercise of the Catholic and Roman religion, conformably to the laws of Great Britain'. Not only did this provision contravene British law, which proscribed Roman Catholicism, but the French insisted that it gave the Bishop of Quebec the right to appoint priests to serve the Acadian and Aboriginal Catholics of Nova Scotia. The British complained that the missionaries were mixing in politics, particularly in the disputed lands west and north of the Bay of Fundy.

The free pursuit of their religion and the question of political loyalty were the key issues over which the Acadians and their British masters conflicted. These matters had not been clearly resolved. In the mid-1720s, Lieutenant-Governor Major Lawrence Armstrong provoked a confrontation with the priests when he demanded that the Acadians take an oath of allegiance (composed by himself) enjoining them 'with all submission and obedience to behave ourselves as Subjects of so good and great a King and Crown of Great Britain Which we swear ever to be faithfull to'. When, in 1726, Armstrong attempted to administer this oath to residents of Annapolis, the Acadians insisted that it be read to them in French. They then asked for the insertion of 'a Clause whereby they might not be Obliged to carry Arms', and Armstrong, on the advice of his council, agreed to the inclusion of such a clause 'upon ye Margent [margin] of the French translations in order to gett them over by Degrees'.[9] This concession, however, was not communicated to the British authorities in London. Subsequent efforts to administer similar oaths met with similar responses and were dealt with in similar ways. After 1730 the Acadians had every reason for believing that the questions of religion and loyalty had both been resolved to their satisfaction.

Yet warnings concerning the Acadians continued to reach the British authorities from many quarters, and after 1748 they were finally heeded. As early as 1720, one British officer in Nova Scotia had argued that the Acadians 'have been always enemies to the English Government' and that 'what orders are or may be given out by the Governor of this Province, without they are backed by a sufficient force, will always be slighted and rendered of no effect.' Similarly in 1745, the Nova Scotia Council argued that, even if they were not 'absolutely to be regarded as utter Enemies to His Majesty's Government', still 'their conditional Oath of Allegiance will not entitle them to the Confidence and Privileges of Natural British Subjects nor can it even be expected in several generations whilst they have French priests among them.'[10] Beginning in

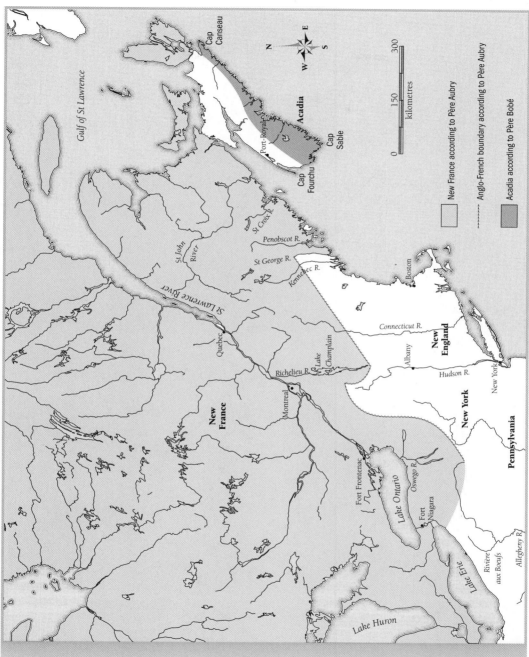

French territorial claims in Acadia, c. 1720. Adapted from M. Savelle, *The Origins of American Diplomacy* (New York: Macmillan, 1967).

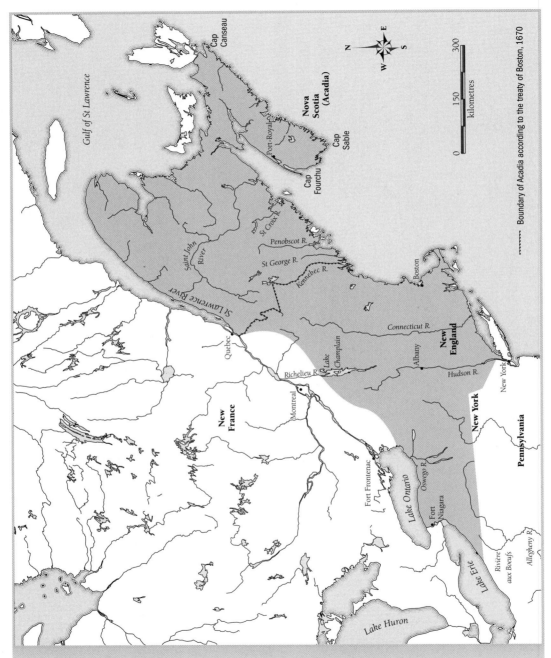

☐ British territorial claims in Acadia, c. 1720. Adapted from M. Savelle, *The Origins of American Diplomacy* (New York: Macmillan, 1967).

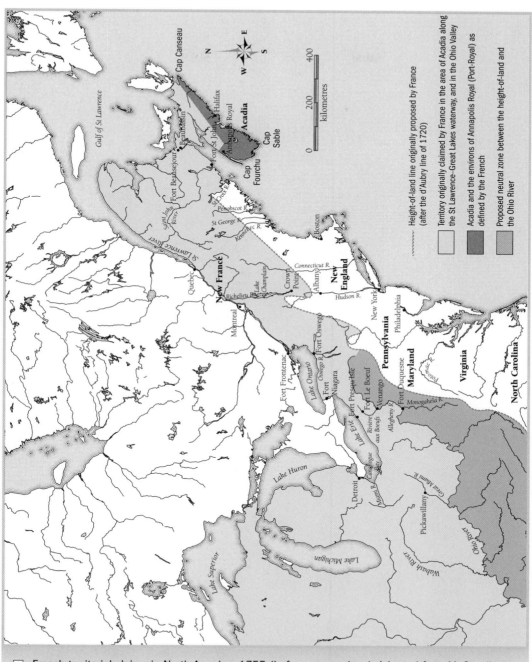

☐ French territorial claims in North America, 1755 (before concessions). Adapted from M. Savelle, *The Origins of American Diplomacy* (New York: Macmillan, 1967), 396.

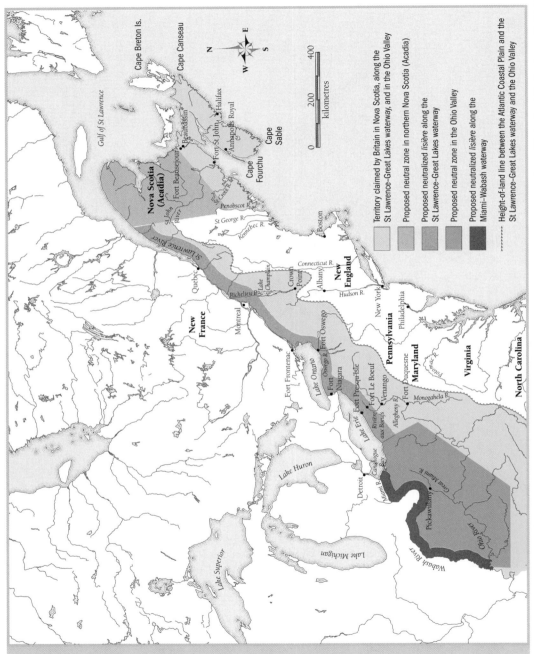

□ British territorial claims in North America, 1755. Adapted from M. Savelle, *The Origins of American Diplomacy* (New York: Macmillan, 1967), 397.

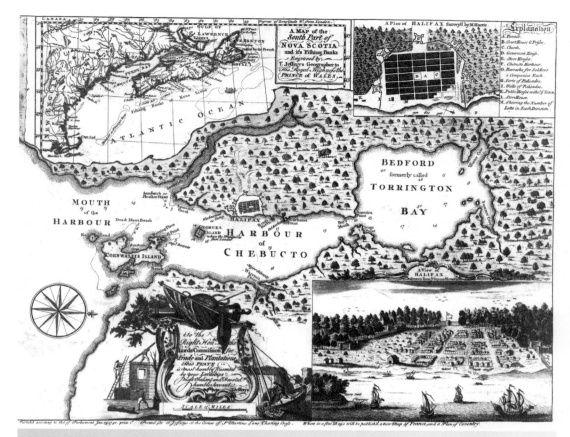

■ 'A Map of the South Part of Nova Scotia and its Fishing Banks', by Thomas Jefferys, 1750. Inset at the upper right is 'A Plan of the new town of Halifax Surveyed by M. Harris'; at the lower right, 'A View of Halifax drawn from ye top masthead'. LAC, NMC 1012.

1745, therefore, British settlement and Acadian removal were commonly coupled in the minds of British governments on both sides of the Atlantic, and with the founding of Halifax an almost inexorable sequence of events was set in motion, which would culminate in the '*grand dérangement*' (see Chapter 9).

THE FOUNDING OF HALIFAX

Because of the Acadian problem, Nova Scotia had not managed to attract many English-speak-

ing settlers. After the Treaty of Aix-la-Chapelle of 1748, however, during one of those pauses for breath in the ongoing wars for the empire in North America, a key faction in the British government pressed for a new commitment to North America. The Duke of Bedford, for example, recommended that disbanded British troops be encouraged to settle in Nova Scotia, to serve as the basis for a population 'inured to the use of arms, and able to endure the northern climate'. In December 1748 the Board of Trade and Plantations drew up a plan for a new settlement of 'Chebucto' to be established as a counter-weight to Louisbourg. Supplied with settlers the next year, it was renamed Halifax in honour of the board's president, the Earl of Halifax, who oversaw the settlement from England. With the founding of Halifax, the process of redistributing power in Nova Scotia had begun. Between 1749 and 1764, Britain would invest more than £600,000 in establishing a non-French population in Nova Scotia.

The decision to settle Nova Scotia at public expense marked a turning point: the first use of the public purse, rather than private capital, to people a British colony. It also marked Britain's first show of serious attention to the Atlantic region since the previous century. In importing a preferred population to contend with the Acadians for control of land and resources, along with a military force that could be swung into action whenever necessary, the mother country also stiffened the backbone of the Nova Scotia administration.

THE FIRST WAVE OF SETTLERS

Potential settlers for Halifax were hastily recruited among recently disbanded soldiers and sailors and also among London's artisans. Over 2,500 people left England with the first fleet in 1749—many of them from Ireland, giving Halifax an Irish tinge that would be enhanced over time by further immigration both from Ireland itself and from Newfoundland. A number of New England merchants, several of whom were already active in the Louisbourg trade, also arrived in Halifax, and would help to establish the town as a northern subsidiary of Yankee commercial enterprise. The New Englanders were not universally admired; one British settler in the early 1750s remarked: 'of all the people upon earth I never heard any bear so bad a character for Cheating designing people & all under the Cloack of religion.'[11]

Among the settlers who left England in May 1749 were 1,174 heads of families, only 509 of

whom were accompanied by their spouses. There were 414 children under the age of 16, and 420 servants, most of them male. Soldiers and sailors accounted for 654 of the heads of families; among civilian occupations the most frequently listed was farmer (161 names); 107 were in the building trades, and a wide variety of other occupations were also included.[12] As laid out by the surveyors and described in a contemporary English magazine, Halifax was to be a 'city . . . of 2,000 houses, disposed into fifty streets of different magnitudes', in its centre 'a spacious square with an equestrian statue of His Majesty'. The reality into which the settlers arrived was a primitive assortment of huts and tents. According to the new governor, Lord Edward Cornwallis, among the settlers 'the number of industrious active men proper to undertake and carry on a new settlement is very small—of soldiers there are only 100, of tradesmen, Sailors and others able to work, not above 200'; the rest 'were poor idle worthless vagabonds that embraced the opportunity to get provisions for one year without labour, or sailors that only wanted a passage to New England. Many have come as into a hospital to be cured, some of Venereal Disorders, some even Incurables.'[13]

Many settlers died over the first winter, and hundreds more left for New England. Anyone who refused to assist in burying corpses in St Paul's Cemetery was struck off the ration list. Disbanded soldiers here, as elsewhere, proved unsatisfactory settlers. While Governor Charles Lawrence may have exaggerated when he wrote, in 1760, that 'every soldier that has come into the Province, since the establishment of Halifax, has either quitted it or become a dramseller [gone into the liquor trade]', there likely was some truth to the claim.[14]

THE FOREIGN PROTESTANTS

Anxious to find a new source of settlers, the British government turned to a long mooted project of recruiting 'Foreign Protestants'—

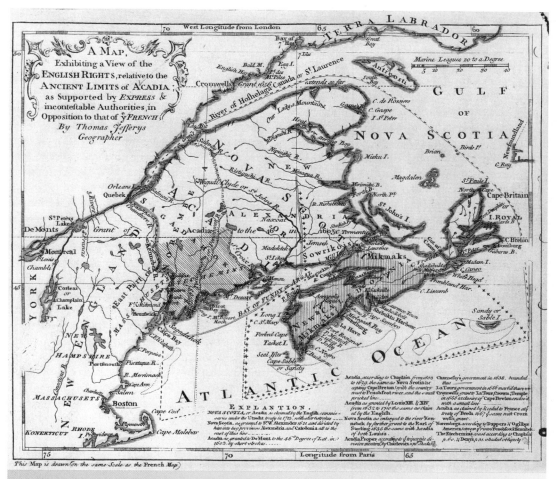

■ A map by Thomas Jefferys showing the British claims to Acadia. Library of Congress, Prints and Photographs Division, 705008.

chiefly Swiss, French Huguenots, and Germans. Its recruiting agent was a young Scotsman named John Dick, who was plainly one of those men who sailed close to the wind (his colourful later career would include involvement in a Russian adventurer's scheme to carry off a purported illegitimate daughter of the Empress Elizabeth of Russia in a sham marriage). Over the winter of 1749–50, while working as a merchant in Rotterdam, Dick was empowered by the Board of Trade to recruit up to 1,500 European

Protestants willing to pay their own passage in return for a parcel of land and a year's subsistence, together with weapons and tools. Dick thought that free passage would be a more effective inducement, but in 1750 he nevertheless managed to dispatch to Halifax one ship with 322 passengers, all of whom financed the voyage by contracting their labour to the government.[15]

One in a long line of recruiting agents whose tactics would provoke complaints, Dick was severely criticized for collecting 'in general old miserable wretches', misleading them about conditions in the colonies, sending them there in overcrowded vessels, and exploiting their labour. Such censure would become a familiar part of the immigration process, and was especially common when the agents themselves had no stake in the settlement. In 1751, Dick dispatched 1,000 passengers in four vessels, and another 1,135 in 1752, while other agents found additional young male candidates in Switzerland. The total came to over 2,700 'Germans and Swiss', although many of the latter were actually French Huguenots from Lorraine.

Of these immigrants, 40 per cent were adult men, 25 per cent adult women, and 35 per cent children; most of the adults were under the age of 40. As was typical of European immigrants to Canada throughout its history, those in family groups settled more easily than single individuals, especially males. The largest single occupational component—well over 60 per cent—described themselves as farmers; but more than 50 other trades and professions were also represented, including carpenters, surgeons, watchmakers, schoolmasters, and clergymen; few unskilled labourers appeared on the passenger rolls. The government intended to settle these newcomers in agricultural communities, chiefly on the Bay of Fundy. But most remained in Halifax because of the uncertainty over title to Acadian lands, and they did not like their new shantytown home.

One petition of 1752 complained of the difficulty of obtaining land and building materials, of high rents and exorbitant prices. Assistance with victualling was only reluctantly granted by the Nova Scotia (and British) authorities. Because of the many problems caused by these 'Foreign Protestants', the British ceased actively recruiting them in 1752 and never tried again for any other North American colony (although settlement of 'Foreign Protestants' was one of the requirements for a land grant on the Island of Saint John in the 1760s). Apparently the Board of Trade never understood that many of the problems in Nova Scotia could be traced to the fact that the cleared land promised to the newcomers was still occupied by Acadians. The Nova Scotia government had a better grasp of the occupancy situation.

Desperate for a solution to the 'foreigner' problem, Governor Hopson and his council, in the spring of 1753, determined to move the Protestants about 80 kilometres west of Halifax, to a place where there were ostensibly several hundred acres of cleared land and decent soil. The first contingent of settlers left Halifax for their new home—now renamed Lunenburg—in a flotilla of small vessels under the direction of Charles Lawrence. On 19 June 1753 they were given land, and two months later Lawrence reported that 'Most of them are well under cover. All of them have gardens and many of them good Framed Houses.'[16] Even so, he added, they were 'inconceivably turbulent, I might have said mutinous'. Given the treatment they had received, turbulence could have been expected. In mid-December of that first year the settlers rose in armed rebellion, apparently touched off by rumours that the people were not receiving all the support authorized by the British Parliament. The Nova Scotia government moved quickly to quell the uprising, but it never did manage to grapple with its underlying causes. The Lunenburg rebellion came to be counted as yet another black mark against the Acadians, who continued to farm the lands that the authorities wanted to give the newcomers while still claiming neutrality and refusing to become British subjects.

NEWFOUNDLAND, 1670–1760

Before 1749 Britain had been largely indifferent to Newfoundland as well as Nova Scotia, especially as a settlement colony. But after that year it did begin to take an interest, and before long the island's 7,000 permanent residents—who had settled there without any help from the British government—would be substantially augmented by additional colonists, this time subsidized by the state.

Newfoundland had been one of the earliest centres of English colonization activity, but over time the settlements had not flourished, and attention had shifted farther south. Nevertheless, many of the early sites were still inhabited year-round. The French continued after 1670 to be active on the south coast, particularly at Plaisance, which in 1684 was home to 256 of the island's 640 French inhabitants, including a small garrison. At the time of the Treaty of Utrecht in 1713 the French had nearly as many permanent residents as the British in Newfoundland, and French naval raids led by Pierre Le Moyne d'Iberville (see Chapter 9) had done great damage to the English settlements around the island in the 1690s. But the overall French position internationally in 1713 was not good, and as a result Louis XIV was forced to surrender any claim to the island in the Treaty of Utrecht. In return for guaranteed fishing rights, the French agreed to evacuate their inhabitants and to maintain neither permanent residences nor fortifications. The French fishers were removed to Île Royale (mainly to Louisbourg), and the British had unchallenged territorial control of Newfoundland, including the former Plaisance, which they renamed Placentia.

Yet even with exclusive sovereignty over the island, Britain had no interest in treating it as a colony or encouraging settlement there. The dispute between English West Country interests, which sent fishing parties to Newfoundland each summer, and those who favoured full-scale colonization, which would put in place a permanent population in direct competition with the summer visitors, continued throughout most of the eighteenth century. The British authorities allowed settlement to proceed, but deferred to the West Country by refusing to establish a year-round government. As a result, the island's permanent population—largely made up of fishers (including women and children) who decided to stay behind rather than return home with their vessels—continued to grow without any government supervision. As the summer population

increased, to 3,500 by 1730 and 7,300 by the 1750s, permanent residents came to make up ever greater proportions of the total: from 15 per cent in the 1670s to 30 per cent in the 1730s to at least 50 per cent by 1753. And increasingly they came from Ireland rather than England.[17]

In the seventeenth century, almost all the year-round residents had been of English origin, chiefly from the West Country counties of Cornwall, Devon, and Dorset. As late as 1732, 90 per cent of the permanent population was still English; but most of the eighteenth-century additions came from southern Ireland, through the increasing links between Newfoundland and the Irish ports of Waterford and Cork. One census of wintering inhabitants in 1753 showed 2,668 Irish and 1,916 English. The Irish were being pushed out of Ireland by famine and unemployment, and were attracted to Newfoundland by the prospect of work and the availability of affordable transportation,[18] though not all who jumped ship on the island remained there: by 1750 Newfoundland had become a conduit for Irish Catholics on their way to mainland North America.

With the increase in population, Newfoundland began to develop a deep schism in its population that was simultaneously ethnic, religious, and economic. The chief economic division was between those who owned the boats and those who laboured on them. Not all Protestant West Countrymen were boat-owners, but very few of the Catholic Irish were.

Fishing practice, too, changed in this period. Throughout the seventeenth century the quest for cod, the mainstay of the Newfoundland fishery, was conducted entirely from shore, either by year-round residents or by summering fishers, in small boats called shallops, manned by crews of between three and five and venturing no farther than 'a Cannon shott' from shore. By 1714, however, the fishing vessels from England had begun fishing directly from the offshore banks. The 'bankers' salted their catch far more heavily than did the traditional inshore fishers, who salted lightly and then dried the fish on wooden platforms called flakes. Although the quality of the bankers' fish was lower, so, too, were their expenses: the cost of one banker with 10 hands (plus staff on shore) was calculated to be £70 per season, whereas catching a smaller quantity of fish near shore and preserving the catch on dry land would require seven shallops employing 35 men at a cost of £400. Until 1750 the inshore fish stocks held up fairly well, but after that date diminishing catches further encouraged labour-saving offshore techniques. Inshore fishermen were forced to expand onto the north of the island, and to diversify into salmon, furs, and especially seals. Sealing was carried out in December, using nets,[19] and the seal oil resulting from this dangerous work was highly prized. Further diversification, however, was hard to achieve. Newfoundland's economy remained almost totally dependent on the sea.

THE WESTERN COUNTRY

While the French and the English shared uneasily in the Atlantic region, their rivalry did not extend any farther: west of the Gulf of St Lawrence, only the French were active. Canadian historians have generally been reluctant to discuss the vast French territory beyond Canada except in relation to the fur trade—largely because most of it would eventually become part of the United States and pass into American history. To ignore this region during the French period, however, would be an anachronism, and to treat it merely as a fur-trading area would also be a mistake.

THE FRENCH EXPLORERS

Not long after Radisson and Groseilliers had opened up the Hudson Bay basin in the late 1650s (see Chapter 5), Father Jacques Marquette and Louis Jolliet began investigating the Mississippi River system to the south. Until the mid-1600s the Iroquois had stood in the way of any

such expansion, but now that they had been (temporarily) cowed by Carignan-Salières regiment, the southern Great Lakes were open to both the coureurs de bois and the Jesuits. For the fur traders, wrote Nicholas Perrot—who was one of them—'it was a Peru.'[20] The French, quickly losing interest in Hudson Bay and Lake Superior, shifted their attention to 'the Sea of the South'. By the early 1670s the First Nations had provided enough information that the French were able to construct a fairly accurate map of the region, but they still did not know the ultimate destination of the river. Early in 1672 Jolliet was chosen by Intendant Talon to answer this question, and he headed west with orders for Father Marquette to join his expedition 'to seek . . . new nations that are unknown to us, to teach them to know our great God'.[21] The two men set out in May 1673 from Michilimackinac, asking directions of local Aboriginal peoples as they went. When they finally found themselves unable to communicate with the local people—somewhere around the present boundary of Arkansas and Louisiana—the Frenchmen decided that they had seen enough. Having ascertained that the river flowed into the Gulf of Mexico, which they thought was close by (in fact, it was still some 1,100 kilometres away), they turned back.

The follow-up to this expedition was led by René-Robert Cavelier de La Salle, a scapegrace son of a wealthy Rouen family who, although he had little wilderness experience, had received an authorization from Louis XIV himself (in 1677) to explore the interior. Finally reaching the mouth of the Mississippi River early in 1682, La Salle took possession of the country in a splendid ceremony on 9 April of that year. According to its chronicler, 'the whole party, under arms, chanted the *Te Deum*, the *Exaudiat*, the *Domine salvum fac Regem*; and then, after a salute of firearms and cries of *Vive le Roi*, . . . with a loud voice in French' made his proclamation, to which the whole assembly responded with shouts of '*Vive le roi*' and salutes of firearms.[22] La Salle went on to establish a French colony in Louisiana, but he was a terrible organizer and leader, and in 1687 he was murdered by a colleague with a personal grudge against him. Although his contemporaries saw him as a man who mixed 'great defects and great virtues',[23] nineteenth-century historians in both the United States and Canada, headed by Francis Parkman of Boston, turned him into the quintessential western explorer.[24] His overblown reputation has been systematically debunked in more recent times.

LOUISIANA

In 1699, 17 years after La Salle had claimed Louisiana for France, Pierre LeMoyne d'Iberville established a settlement at Fort Biloxi composed largely of Canadien traders. In 1701 a settlement was founded on the west side of the Mobile River. A decade later it moved to the river mouth; and, as Mobile, it served as the capital of the region until 1722, when it was displaced in that role by New Orleans. A handful of Frenchmen headed by Jean-Baptiste le Moyne de Bienville traded with the local Aboriginal people in the early years. In 1712 the Crown turned Louisiana over to the financier Antoine Crozat, giving him a 15-year monopoly on its trade. In return, Crozat was responsible for settlement, although the Crown appointed the governor and the *'commissaire ordonnateur'* (a sort of intendant), who in theory were subject to the governor general and intendant in Quebec. By 1717, however, Crozat had spent 700,000 livres in a fruitless search for mineral wealth in the region, and he surrendered his privileges. France then transferred Crozat's monopoly to the Scotsman John Law, who quickly organized a substantial program to recruit settlers. Shipped to the colony in substantial numbers between 1717 and 1720, the settlers in turn began importing African slaves as a labour force. In 1731, Louisiana reverted to the Crown, and by 1739—thanks to the labours of 4,000 slaves—it had a considerable plantation economy. Yet it was still draining the French treasury of as much as 800,000 livres per annum. Corruption

and infighting among the French officials in Louisiana also represented a serious drain on the mother country. Nevertheless, as the southern anchor of the great crescent of French territory that encircled the English colonies to the east, Louisiana was a valuable asset for France.

THE PAYS D'EN HAUT

The 'upper country' was the territory upriver from Montreal, beginning somewhere beyond Huronia and stretching down past the Great Lakes and then on to Louisiana. Claimed by the French by right of exploration and usage, it was originally inhabited almost exclusively by Algonquian peoples, but the seventeenth century had brought an influx of other groups fleeing westward from the Iroquois. These refugees reestablished themselves in the country between the Ohio River and the Great Lakes to the west of Lake Michigan, where local populations themselves had been reduced by the Iroquois. Gradually some of the fur traders, especially those who had married Native women and started families, began to establish themselves in settlements along the river systems. A series of forts and towns, the former the product of deliberate French policy, the latter mostly unplanned, grew up in the region; the most prominent were Detroit, Michilimackinac, Green Bay, Cahokia, and Kaskaskia. Until 1815, however, the Great Lakes region remained almost exclusively under Aboriginal control.

THE FRENCH–FIRST NATIONS ALLIANCE

By the 1650s, traditional territories, communities, and relationships in the *pays d'en haut* had been radically disrupted, chiefly by the aggressive activities of the Iroquois.[25] Members of various Aboriginal nations fought frequently among themselves, and at the same time tried to reestablish some sort of stability, often through intermarriage and adoption. Gradually, however,

ORONTONY

Orontony, also known as Nicholas (d. 1750), was a member of one of the Huron–Petun bands that had retreated from Huronia in the mid-1600s and resettled around Detroit. When the Huron–Petun became involved in local warfare and provoked the wrath of the nearby Algonquian groups, especially the Ottawas, in the 1730s, they called on the French to allow them to settle around Montreal. Orontony first appeared in 1739 as one of the leaders of the Huron–Petun. When the French authorities at Detroit dithered, in 1740 Orontony personally visited Governor Charles de Beauharnois in Quebec to request that his people be moved. But the French were unable to decide on a policy, and negotiations dragged on for years.

One complicating factor was the French effort to cut costs by reducing expenditures on gifts and leasing out many trading posts. The lessees, of course, had to raise prices and also cut back on presents in order to recover their costs. As a consequence, leadership of the Huron–Petun shifted from the traditional chiefs who were associated with the French alliance and loyalty to 'Onontio' (the French King) towards several lesser chiefs. Among the latter was Orontony, who advocated moving to the margins of the Ohio country and trading with the British entering the region from Pennsylvania. Orontony thus sought simultaneously to supersede his people's former leaders and to break the French alliance that had dominated the *pays d'en haut* for several generations. Followers of Orontony and his colleague Angouriot began to call themselves 'Wyandot', resurrecting an old name for the Huron that had not been used for many years.

Orontony told the British in Pennsylvania that the French required constant military assistance and charged too much for their trade goods. George Croghan, a British trader from Pennsylvania, sought an alliance with the Wyandot, who in 1747 were accused of involvement in the killing of French traders in the Detroit region. When the French responded by sending military assistance, Orontony burned his village and led a party of 119 warriors farther west into the Ohio region. He and other dissident Indian leaders were more interested in ending the French hegemony in the *pays d'en haut* than in forming an alliance with the British, and the French themselves recognized the village rebellions of 1747 as a 'general conspiracy of the redskins against the white'. Nevertheless, the rebels appealed to Pennsylvania for assistance, and in so doing linked their local resistance to the French with the large-scale French–British conflict. Orontony was among the Aboriginal leaders who met with Conrad Weiser of Pennsylvania at Logstown in August 1748, prominently displaying a treaty belt earlier given at Albany; Orontony and his colleagues were admitted by the Six Nations to the council fire. Before he could complete his project of realignment, however, the war ended. Orontony died in the course of an epidemic that devastated his village in 1750.

the French came to serve as a kind of glue holding the various Native communities together. By the end of the seventeenth century, the French had negotiated treaties with 39 separate Aboriginal groups, and the resulting multi-party alliance had not only become the principal political reality in the region, but had finally triumphed over the Iroquois in a series of desperate wars during the 1690s. The outcome was the Great Peace of 1701, in which the Iroquois gave up their claims west of Detroit and promised to remain neutral in any future European war.[26]

Relationships between Native people and the French were carefully negotiated. Formerly casual liaisons between Native women and Frenchmen became formal marriages, and were perceived by the Native people as symbols of the larger alliance. Over time, the Jesuits came to accept such marriages, provided the women were Christian, but the colonial authorities continued to oppose them. According to Governor Vaudreuil in 1709, 'Our experience . . . in this country ought to prevent us from permitting marriages of this kind, for all the Frenchmen who have married savages have been licentious, lazy and intolerably independent; and their children have been characterized by as great a slothfulness as the savages themselves.' In fact, the French objected to anything that might lead to permanent settlement and interfere with the fur trade, and mixed marriages were especially dangerous in this context.

A central element in forging and maintaining alliances was the exchange of gifts.[27] Officials in Paris, anxious to control costs, demanded that traders in Canada insist on quid pro quo arrangements—no gift without something in return. But such instructions were impossible to follow: for the Aboriginal people, gift-giving had a symbolic value far beyond the material worth of the goods in question, and neither trade nor military alliances would have been possible without it. (In fact, gifts never amounted to more than 10 per cent of colonial spending.) Outlays increased substantially in later years—when the profits from the fur trade were in decline—because the French feared that, otherwise, their Native allies would defect to the British. Governor Beauharnois explained the necessity of careful management to

the Crown in 1741: 'The stratagems resorted to by the English to attract our Savages, compel me to use great circumspection toward them, and to Content them as much as I can'; '[they] would seize the first pretext to break the word they have given me were I to fail to keep mine.'[28] Over the next few years, military exigencies produced a new, enhanced alliance system binding 'Onontio' (the French King) to his Aboriginal 'children', not only by gifts but by rituals such as smoking the peace pipe as well as mediation.

Gifts were only the most obvious component in France's effort to keep its Native allies content. Another was the maintenance of the Jesuit missions. Finally, some changes in the conduct of the fur trade itself could also be seen in part as concessions to the Native partners in the business. For example, in order to trade at source, the French were prepared not only to employ voyageurs to travel deep into the fur-bearing region and meet the hunters on their own ground, but to establish trading posts and garrisoned forts not far from them. They also developed a licensing program, aimed in part at controlling the quantities of furs shipped east, in order to stabilize prices, but also at reducing competition—and hence friction—between the French and Aboriginal traders.

MIXED-BLOOD COMMUNITIES

After 1700 a number of permanent communities began to develop in the Great Lakes country. Some grew up around forts; the largest of these was Michilimackinac, where the permanent population of several hundred became much larger in the summer. The majority, however, were fur-trade settlements catering mainly to the local Aboriginal populations. Most residents were of mixed blood, though substantial numbers— many of them slaves—were Aboriginal or black. One such community was Kaskaskia, a town in what is now Illinois, adjacent to the rich bottom land of the Mississippi Valley where a handful of French traders and their wives settled after a

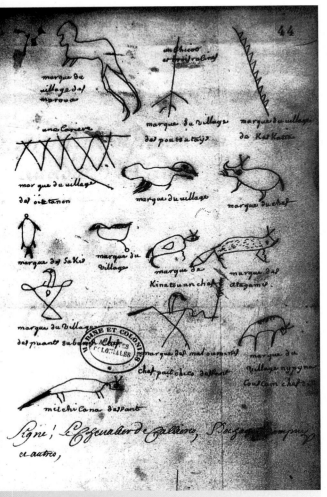

■ The treaty signed at Montreal in 1701, with the totemic marks of some of the First Nations signatories. LAC, C-137798.

and in 1718 a civil government for the region was established by decree from Paris. This arrangement was continued after Louisiana was returned to the Crown in 1731. Meanwhile, the village of Kaskaskia developed its own local government, with most business conducted in assemblies held in front of the church after mass. (Much the same system had grown up in Acadia, with which the Illinois country can usefully be compared; however, no such study has yet been undertaken.)

The village itself consisted of a central church surrounded by roughly 80 houses in the Canadien style but with the addition of a 'galerie' (porch) extending around several sides of the house. Most of the houses had three rooms and a stone fireplace. By 1752 a regional census showed a population of nearly 500 in the town, including close to 250 'Negroes' and 75 'savages'. The census also counted livestock, including more than 600 cows, bulls, and heifers and around 500 horses. Over 130 arpents of land were under cultivation.[29] Few households owned many slaves, but most had at least one. The male householders practised a variety of trades; there were toolmakers, joiners, carpenters, masons, gunsmiths, blacksmiths, and even a wig-maker. The community also served as a base for transient voyageurs who traded in the interior. The 1752 census showed a total population for the communities of Kaskaskia, Fort de Chartres, St Philippe, Port du Rocher, Cahokia, and Ste Genevieve of approximately 1,000 Europeans, more than 500 blacks, and several hundred Native people, not counting the 300 soldiers in garrison at Fort de Chartres, Cahokia, and Kaskaskia. Except for their more varied populations, in many ways the western communities seem quite similar to their counterparts in Acadia, particularly in their relative freedom from close imperial supervision.

By the 1740s the French administrators of the upper country were increasingly trapped in circumstances beyond their control. Much of their policy for the west was increasingly defensive and circular in nature: alliances with Native

Jesuit mission was established there in 1703. French and Native residents planted together in the fields, and the crops were abundant. Despite an epidemic in 1714, the French population in Kaskaskia continued to grow as fur traders and their Native wives settled there to raise their children. In 1717 the French government annexed Illinois to Louisiana under the Coutume de Paris, groups had to be maintained to preserve the fur trade; the fur trade had to be maintained to preserve the territory; and the territory had to be protected to keep the British out of it. But one of the main reasons the British wanted into the upper country was to break the French 'noose'

ILLINOIS CENSUS OF 1752

	Kaskaskia	Fort de Chartres	St Philippe	Port du Rocher	Cahokia	Ste Genevieve
Men	58	26	15	10	18	7
Women	50	24	12	0	13	4
Widows	8	7	2	2	1	0
Boys of military age	36	20	9	6	3	1
Boys over 12	64	20	6	6	16	–
Marriageable girls	11	10	8	1	6	–
Girls over 12	46	36	12	5	17	4
Negroes	102	34	20	19	11	3
Negresses	67	25	7	8	6	–
Negro boys	45	16	10	8	6	–
Negro girls	32	13	8	6	3	–
Males savages	31	13	11	4	11	–
Female savages	44	23	4	4	12	–
Oxen	320	172	96	87	84	18
Cows	331	131	63	80	90	19
Bull calves	147	80	51	54	53	23
Heifers	145	78	32	37	45	12
Horses	346	72	35	29	12	24
Mares	75	30	27	19	25	4
Pigs	841	198	184	174	100	185
Arpents of land under cultivation	131	62	74	74	33	33

SOURCE: Derived from N.M. Belting, *Kaskaskia under the French Regime* (Urbana, Ill., 1948), table, 39.

that was preventing their seaboard colonies from expanding. Such circularity was not unusual in the imperial confrontations between the French and the British.

BEYOND THE FORMAL EMPIRES: HUDSON BAY AND THE PRAIRIES

In 1667 Radisson and Groseilliers left Boston (see Chapter 5) for London, where they succeeded in persuading a group of English merchants to send two ships to Hudson Bay the following year. Radisson's ship turned back, but his brother-in-law carried on, returning in October 1669 with a superb cargo of furs. On 2 May 1670 the merchants founded by royal charter a formal trading company, 'The Governor and Company of Adventurers of England Trading into Hudson Bay', usually called the Hudson's Bay Company, which received title to the entire drainage basin of Hudson Bay—some 40 per cent of modern Canada. Later that month Radisson and Groseilliers again went to the Bay, Radisson to the mouth of the Nelson River, where the overseas governor of the new company, Charles Bayly, took possession of the land. (Bayly had accepted the posting as a condition of his release from the Tower of London, where he had been imprisoned for seditious practices associated with his Quaker beliefs.)[30]

Now England had established a direct route to the fur-bearing regions of the North that

THE JOURNAL OF HENRY KELSEY, 1690

Henry Kelsey's two exploratory journals, probably not in his handwriting, were part of a bound journal given to the Public Record Office of Northern Ireland in 1926 by a descendant of Arthur Dobbs, an eighteenth-century critic of the Hudson's Bay Company, and first published in 1929. In 1994 they were reprinted with a new introduction by John Warkentin.

Henry Kelsey his Book being ye Gift of James Hubbard in the year of our Lord 1693

1690
Now Reader Read for I am well assur'd
Thou dost not know the hardships I endur'd
In this same desert where Ever y't I have been
Nor wilt thou me believe without y't thou had seen
The Emynent Dangers that did often me attend
But still I loved in hopes y't once it would amend
And make me free from hunger & from Cold
Likewise many other things w'ch I cannot here
    unfold
For many times I have often been opprest
With fears & Cares y't I could not take my rest
Because I was alone & no friend could find
And once y't in my travels I was left behind
Which struck fear & terror into me

But still I was resolved this same Country for to see
Although through many dangers I did pass
Hoped still to undergo y'm, at the Last
Now Considering y't it was my dismal fate
For to repent I thought it now to late
Trusting still unto my masters Consideration
Hoping they will Except of this my small Relation
Which here I have pend & still will Justifie
Concerning of those Indians & their Country
If this wont do farewell to all as I may say
And so my living i'll seek some other way
In sixteen hundred & ninety'th year
I set forth as plainly may appear
Through Gods assistance for to understand
The natives language & so see their land . . . .

bypassed the interior channels into the continent controlled by New France. Concerned by this competition, in 1675 France made overtures to Radisson and Groseilliers, inviting them to return to its employ. For the next 10 years the partners attempted to play English against French to their own advantage, but they were very small players in the complex imperial intrigues of the day. Only in the wilderness was Radisson master. One of his exultant phrases about his life in the interior—'We were Caesars, there being none to contradict us'—captured perfectly the spirit of the seventeenth-century coureur de bois. But he was out of his depth on the international scene.

As we shall see in the next chapter, Hudson Bay would be a bone of contention between England and France from the 1680s to 1713,

when the latter conceded its claim in the Treaty of Utrecht. In 1714 the English reoccupied their posts on the southern edge of Hudson Bay, which had been neglected during the years of military conflict with the French. HBC governor James Knight was eager to establish a northern post, but virtually nothing was known of the Chipewyan people who inhabited the region. Most of the available information came from Chipewyan women held captive by the Cree. Of these, the leading informant was Thanadelthur (d. 1717), known as the 'Slave Woman', who had escaped from the Cree in the autumn of 1713. Having made her way to York Fort late in 1714, she was subsequently sent to accompany a large party of Cree, who were instructed to make peace with the Chipewyan. After a series of mishaps and fatal encounters, Thanadelthur left

■ 'A Hunter-family of Cree Indians at York Fort, drawn from nature, 1821', Peter Rindisbacher. LAC, C-1917.

what remained of the party to track down a large band of Chipewyan, whom she somehow persuaded to return with her and make peace with the Cree. The English were very impressed and employed her as an interpreter until her death early in 1717. James Knight described her as 'one of a Very high Spirit and of the Firmest Resolution that ever I see any Body in my Days and of great Courage & forecast'.[31] We know the names of very few Aboriginal women of the exploration period, but Thanadelthur's exploits illustrate how important their contributions could be.

The English had been trading furs from posts on the southern coast of Hudson Bay from 1670, but until the middle of the eighteenth century they showed little interest in moving much beyond their establishments. Instead, they encouraged the First Nations to bring their furs to the Bay for trading purposes. The local peoples quickly adapted to this situation and an elaborate trading network was soon established. The negotiations with the English were conducted by 'trading captains'. The importance of these individuals was recognized by the traders of the Hudson's Bay Company, and they were even given uniforms to distinguish them from their fellow traders.[32] Increasing competition from the French after the 1730s was accompanied at home by attacks on the company for its lack of activity. A parliamentary inquiry in 1749 was highly critical of the 'Sleep by the Frozen Sea', and the management of the HBC recognized the need for a more active pursuit of resources other than furs. But a reinvigorated company would not emerge until after the end of the French wars.

THE PRAIRIES

While the French and English were still jostling for control of the Bay, on 12 June 1690 a young Englishman named Henry Kelsey started from York Factory on Hudson Bay on an overland journey to the southwest, 'to discover and bring to a Commerce' the Gros Ventres of the Saskatchewan. An 'active Lad Delighting in Indians Company, never better pleased than when hee is Travelling amongst them', Kelsey was accompanied at various stages by people from several bands, depending on who was available. Throughout his journal of the trip, Kelsey used the pronoun 'we': not the 'royal we', but an accurate reflection of the collaborative nature of the expedition. From the Saskatchewan River he travelled into the country of the Assiniboine, where he became the first European to describe buffalo and grizzly bears. He returned to York Factory in the summer of 1692, having been away for two years. Although accounts of his journey were sent home to London and published in parliamentary papers without his name, they were not acted on by the company, which seems to have suppressed the information they contained.

Thus it was not Kelsey who would open the vast western prairies in the first half of the eighteenth century. Rather, the La Vérendrye family (Pierre and his four sons) laid claim to the region for France. Yet the prairies were never really counted as part of New France; indeed, much of the La Vérendryes' work was done in the face of passive and often active opposition from the government of Canada. The authorities dragged their feet partly because, as much as they needed new sources of furs, they clearly understood the dangers of territorial overexpansion, and partly because many felt the La Vérendryes were too interested in the furs.

Unlike many earlier 'explorers', the La Vérendryes made no secret of their total reliance on the geographical knowledge of the local First Nations. In the report on 'the discovery of the Western Sea' that Pierre Gaultier de Varennes de La Vérendrye attached to a letter of October 1730 (p. 28 above), he described in considerable detail the Native sources of his information, even naming the individuals he consulted. He had learned much from three members of a Cree band located around Lake Nipigon, and later learned more from a Cree chief named Tacchigis,

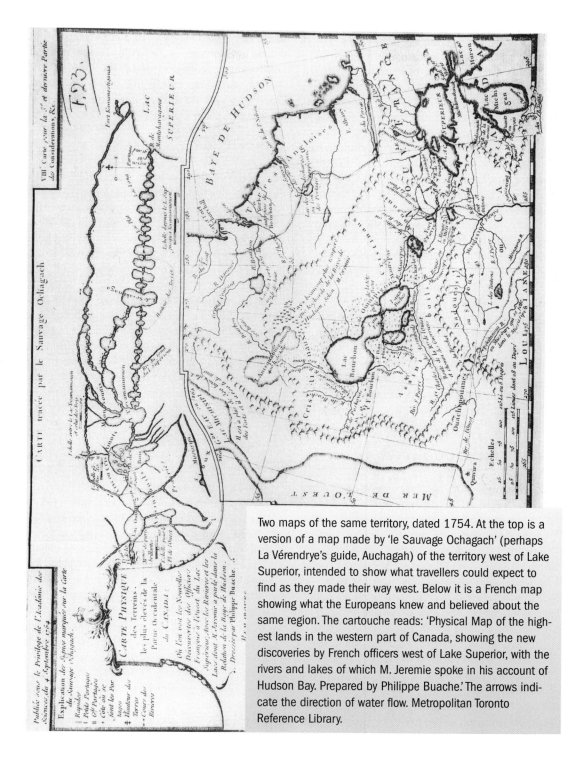

Two maps of the same territory, dated 1754. At the top is a version of a map made by 'le Sauvage Ochagach' (perhaps La Vérendrye's guide, Auchagah) of the territory west of Lake Superior, intended to show what travellers could expect to find as they made their way west. Below it is a French map showing what the Europeans knew and believed about the same region. The cartouche reads: 'Physical Map of the highest lands in the western part of Canada, showing the new discoveries by French officers west of Lake Superior, with the rivers and lakes of which M. Jeremie spoke in his account of Hudson Bay. Prepared by Philippe Buache.' The arrows indicate the direction of water flow. Metropolitan Toronto Reference Library.

who made a map of the western river system with a piece of charcoal. As guide for his journeys, La Vérendrye chose a man named Auchagah, who drew him a map showing not only the rivers but the 'lakes, rapids, portages, the side on which the portage must be made, and the heights of land'.[33] By comparing the different maps, the Frenchman was able to confirm the information he had been given. Another map made for La Vérendrye by a group of Cree living near Lake of the Woods was particularly useful as confirmation. By now, even administrators in Canada were sufficiently aware of the crucial role played by Native guides to insist that those 'who have no idea whatever of those regions nor the slightest knowledge of the languages spoken there' had no place in the canoes heading west to meet up with the fur traders.[34]

La Vérendrye was notorious for establishing new trading posts at the edges of the country he had travelled and then using them as bases for further exploration; his critics argued that the furs were far more important than new knowledge. Scholars disagree over the importance that La Vérendrye himself attached to the search for

the 'Sea of the West'.[35] Nevertheless, in the course of their western activities members of his family journeyed as far south as Pierre, South Dakota, and as far west as the Rocky Mountains. The fur trade did indeed take the French to remote and distant places.

CONCLUSION

The western and eastern extremities of the European empires in northern North America were remote and for the most part economically marginal to both the French and the English. Nevertheless, these regions took on considerable importance in the context of the imperial struggle for control of the continent, which continued on and off from the end of the sixteenth century to the middle of the eighteenth. Many of the policies that the European powers undertook in these regions were necessitated by larger imperial strategies and manoeuvres. Quite apart from the actual warfare, which will be discussed in the next chapter, imperial rivalry dominated the development of both east and west in the late seventeenth and early eighteenth centuries.

SHORT BIBLIOGRAPHY

Adams, Arthur T., ed. *The Explorations of Pierre Esprit Radisson from the Original Manuscript in the Bodleian Library and the British Museum*. Minneapolis, 1961. A modern edition of the only known autobiographical accounts by a coureur de bois.

Balcom, B.A. *The Cod Fishery of Isle Royale, 1713–1758*. Ottawa, 1984. A work demonstrating there was more to Île Royale than the fortress of Louisbourg.

Bell, Winthrop P. *The 'Foreign Protestants' and the Settlement of Nova Scotia: The History of a Piece of Arrested British Policy in the Eighteenth Century*. Toronto, 1961. Perhaps overly detailed, but essential for understanding the process of settlement in early Nova Scotia.

Belting, Natalia Maree. *Kaskaskia under the French Regime*. Urbana, Ill., 1948. Still the best microstudy

of a Great Lakes community.

Clark, Andrew Hill. *Acadia: The Geography of Early Nova Scotia*. Madison, Wis., 1968. A geographer's analysis, strong on land settlement and usage.

Eccles, W.J. *France in America*, rev. edn. Markham, Ont., 1990. An overview of the French Empire in America by the leading expert writing in English.

Griffiths, Naomi. *The Contexts of Acadian History 1587–1781*. Montreal, 1992. An overview of the history of early Acadia by the reigning academic expert.

Head, C. Grant. *Eighteenth-Century Newfoundland: A Geographer's Perspective*. Toronto, 1976. The standard modern account of the island in the eighteenth century.

Johnston, A.J.B. *The Summer of 1744: A Portrait of Life

in *Eighteenth-Century Louisbourg*. Ottawa, 1978. A fascinating social history.

Moore, Christopher. *Louisbourg Portrait: Life in an Eighteenth-Century Garrison Town*. Toronto, 1982. An award-winning book that shows what can be learned from court records.

Upton, L.F.S. *Micmacs and Colonists: Indian–White Relations in the Maritimes, 1713–1867*. Vancouver,

1979. This work perhaps focuses too exclusively on public relationships, but it is based on extensive research.

White, Richard. *The Middle Ground: Indians, Empires and Republics in the Great Lakes Region, 1650–1815*. Cambridge, 1991. A revisionist work that has transformed the early history of the region by putting the First Nations at its centre.

STUDY QUESTIONS

1. What sort of farming did the early Acadians do?
2. When Acadia was transferred to Britain in 1713, what loose ends were left hanging?
3. Why do we know so much about Louisbourg?
4. Why did Britain turn to 'Foreign Protestants' to settle Nova Scotia?
5. What was the most significant development in Newfoundland in the first half of the eighteenth century?
6. What were the characteristics of the *pays d'en haut*?
7. Compare Acadia and the *pays d'en haut*.
8. What do the census documents tell us about life in Acadia and Kaskaskia?

CHAPTER NINE

A Century of Conflict, 1660–1760

Warfare was endemic in colonial North America. The French lived under constant threat of attack by the Iroquois for 50 years, until the 'Great Peace' was negotiated in 1701. By then, the French and the English (with their various First Nations allies) had already fought one war in North America and were about to fight a second. The Treaty of Utrecht in 1713 initiated three decades of relative peace, but war erupted again in 1744, and thereafter continued almost unabated until 1760.

North America was only one front in the imperial wars, and from the European point of view it was by no means the most important one. Until the 1740s the bulk of the North American fighting took place between irregular armies of colonials, in collaboration with their respective Aboriginal allies, and was largely a hit and miss affair. Only at the end would regular armies and navies become involved in substantial numbers. Even if it was intermittent, however, the war that ended in the 'British Conquest' still represented a constant menace for all North Americans—French, British, and First Nations.

Few events in that century-long war brought suffering to quite so many innocent people as the expulsions of the Acadians in the 1750s. But fishing communities in Newfoundland were pillaged and burned by coastal raiders, fur-trading posts in Hudson Bay were destroyed, and several thousand captives were forcibly removed from their homes by guerrilla forces, often never to return. Thus, wartime misfortune—often wreaked suddenly on the unsuspecting—was a constant companion for all the inhabitants of the continent in these years.

THE WARS AGAINST THE IROQUOIS

Almost from its inception New France had existed in a state of siege. After the royal takeover in 1663 the immediate problem was with the Iroquois, and First Nations warfare remained the chief military danger for New France for most of the next 40 years. A show of force was provided by the 1,100 veteran soldiers of the Carignan-Salières regiment sent to the colony by Louis XIV in 1665. But the Iroquois threat was never entirely removed. Battles would continue in the *pays d'en haut* throughout the seventeenth century, and in the eighteenth century the Five (later Six) Nations[1] were always willing to join the British in military activities against the French. Nevertheless, the presence of the Carignan-Salières regiment served to encourage the colonists, demonstrating the competence of the French state and its commitment to North America.

TIMELINE

1686
Iberville campaigns in James Bay.

1689
Beginning of War of the League of Augsburg (King William's War).

1690
French raid on Schenectady, NY. Sir William Phips captures Port-Royal. Invasion of Quebec fails.

1696
Iberville devastates Newfoundland coast.

1697
Treaty of Ryswick leaves outstanding issues unresolved.

1701
French and Iroquois leaders sign 'Great Peace'.

1702
War of the Spanish Succession (Queen Anne's War) begins.

1704
French raid on Deerfield.

1707
Port-Royal expedition of Americans fails.

1710
Americans take Port-Royal.

1711
British attempt to invade Quebec, unsuccessfully.

1713
Treaty of Utrecht transfers Acadia and Plaisance from France to Britain.

1722
'Indian war' in New England begins.

1745
Yankees capture Louisbourg.

1746
French naval armada wrecked at sea and in Halifax harbour. English reject idea of invading Quebec.

1748
Treaty of Aix-la-Chapelle returns Louisbourg to France.

1755
Braddock expedition destroyed in Pennsylvania. British capture Fort Beauséjour, find many Acadians inside. First Acadian expulsion.

1756
French capture Fort Bull in New York, then Oswego.

1758
Louisbourg captured by British. Second Acadian expulsion.

1759
Battle of Plains of Abraham.

1760
Battle of Ste-Foy. French capitulate at Montreal in early September.

In 1682 Paris recalled Governor Frontenac, who despite warnings had continued to take an active role in the western fur trade. His replacement, Joseph-Antoine Le Febvre de La Barre, was a naval man with a considerable record of military accomplishment in the West Indies. The King advised him to use diplomatic means with the Iroquois and not to attack them unless he was sure to win. But La Barre, like Frontenac, was unable to keep his fingers out of the fur trade, and contemporaries whispered that it was to protect the trade that in 1684 he decided to attack the Iroquois cantons in what is now New York State. The first commander to employ Canadien militiamen on a large scale, La Barre mustered nearly 800 troops at Montreal, but as we have seen, they were defeated by influenza before the battle could begin. This fiasco, which ended in a humiliating peace treaty, led directly to La Barre's recall. His successor, the Marquis de Denonville, gathered an even larger force in 1687, including Native warriors as well as 930 Canadien militiamen, and marched them overland into the New York country of the Seneca. After a brief skirmish the Seneca fled into the woods, where Denonville's Native allies refused to pursue them. The Seneca villages and food supplies were thereupon destroyed, but the Five Nations' power was far from broken. Two years later the unsuspecting village of Lachine was devastated by 1,500 Iroquois, who disappeared into the bush when a relief expedition approached the area. In effect, the war to the southwest of Canada served to create small groups of tough guerrilla raiders, both French and Aboriginal, who would subsequently wreak havoc on exposed frontier communities in the English colonies. Not until 1701 would peace be achieved with the Iroquois.

THE WAR OF THE LEAGUE OF AUGSBURG (KING WILLIAM'S WAR)

After 1689, the troubles with the western Iroquois merged into a much more general conflict of continental and even international proportions. As was usually the case, the North American dimensions of the conflict were not closely related to the European. Most of the successful French activity of this period was associated with Pierre Le Moyne d'Iberville, who has been called the 'first truly Canadian hero'.[2] Iberville was hardly a typical soldier, even of the officer class, but his career was legendary in his own time. He has remained fascinating ever since—no native-born Canadien from the French period has been the subject of more biographical study—and for many he came to symbolize the spirit of martial heroism so characteristic of his time and place.[3]

Born in Montreal in 1661, Iberville began his career in the service of his father, one of Canada's leading military men. At some early stage in his life he acquired experience as a seaman. On the eve of his first campaign after his father's death, he was found guilty by the Sovereign Council of seducing a young woman and fathering an illegitimate child (he was made responsible for this daughter until she was 15). Similar charges of philandering would plague him throughout his life. Iberville flourished at the margins of Europe's American empires in an age when governments did not make tidy distinctions between public and private sectors, and when military adventurism was encouraged if it offered any advantage in the imperial context. He was, in short, a buccaneer or *filibustier*, rather than a professional soldier in the conventional sense of the term—closer in spirit to the Kirke brothers or the pirate Captain Kidd than to the Marquis de Montcalm.

In Iberville's first campaign he led a party of Canadien voyageurs to James Bay as part of a French expedition under the command of Pierre de Troyes. The expedition—launched in 1686 while England and France were trying to negotiate their differences in North America—followed the Ottawa River and connecting waterways all the way to the Bay, a perilous journey that lasted 85 days. At Moose Fort (Moose Factory),

Iberville single-handedly gained entrance to the fort, but once he was inside the palisade the 17 Englishmen there closed the gate; while his companions forced it open again, Iberville distracted the Englishmen with his bravado until his men entered and forced the fort to surrender. His reputation for intrepid heroism was born, and he was put in command not only of Moose Fort but of two other James Bay posts captured by the French, Rupert and Albany (renamed Saint-Jacques and Sainte-Anne). On the Albany River in 1688 he added to his reputation for bravery one of total ruthlessness towards the enemy. When scurvy struck the English, for example, he invited the English surgeon to join him in a hunt for fresh meat, and then took him captive. Iberville was soon made second-in-command of a French campaign to raid the English settlements in New York. Pouncing on the unguarded village of Corlaer (now Schenectady) in February 1690, the French killed 60 people in their beds before taking off with quantities of both prisoners and booty. This sort of guerrilla warfare, consciously emulating Aboriginal tactics, gained the French a fearsome reputation in the English colonies, and would be the secret of most French military successes in North America.

Early in the war the Americans made several attempts to invade New France. In 1690 an expedition under Sir William Phips succeeded in capturing Port-Royal, in Acadia. Phips attempted to follow up this small victory with another invasion, this time of Quebec. On this occasion, as on many others to come, two untrained armies faced one another. Thirty-two vessels brought 2,300 English volunteers, mostly ill-prepared, up the St Lawrence late in 1690. The flotilla arrived at Quebec in early October. Smallpox had hit the American troops, and the ice was closing in. Only a week earlier, Quebec's defence force had numbered scarcely 150 men, but now the militia swarmed to Quebec from their farms and even as far away as Montreal. Frontenac—now reinstated as governor—succeeded in persuading the invaders that the French were prepared to fight,

■ Pierre Le Moyne, Sieur d'Iberville, by Alfred Sandham, from G.D. Warburton, *The Conquest of Canada* (London, 1850). NLC, C-26026.

with his well-known rejoinder to an English officer who demanded his surrender: 'I have no reply to make to your general other than from the mouths of my cannon and muskets.' Phips's force made one attempt to land but quickly turned back. The untrained American volunteers proved useless in the brief battle, and the entire expedition came at a heavy cost of life and money; the Massachusetts government lost more than £40,000.

As for Iberville, he sailed with three vessels back to Hudson Bay in July 1690, but was driven off York Fort in late August. Two years later his naval squadron, complete with French frigates—unable to sail to the Bay before the onset of winter ice—was ordered to harass the English coastal colonies in Newfoundland, which he did. He returned to the Bay in 1694, this time under a formal buccaneering agreement with the French Crown, and captured York Fort (renamed Fort Bourbon), again provoking charges of ruthlessness for his violation of the rules of surrender. Returning to France as a hero, he was ordered to take his squadron to the Atlantic coast and Newfoundland, where in the winter of 1696–7 he led his Canadiens in devastating raids on 36 English settlements, as usual with heavy losses of life as well as prisoners and booty. (Some Newfoundland historians argue that these raids set the colony's development back for many years.[4]) Leaving Newfoundland for Hudson Bay before English reinforcements could arrive, his ship *Pélican* became separated from its companions and was forced to fight a naval battle with three English warships at the mouth of the Hayes River;

Iberville sank one and captured another, while the third fled the scene. This triumph over the European nation that now regarded itself as master of the sea was the crowning glory of his career.

Following the peace of Ryswick (1697), Iberville was sent on two voyages (1699 and 1701) to fortify and defend the mouth of the Mississippi River. By 1706 war was raging again and he was placed in command of a squadron of 12 vessels ordered to raid in the British West Indies. Leading a force of several thousand regulars, Canadien voyageurs, and buccaneers in an attack on the island of Nevis, he succeeded in taking it for the French Crown. This expedition had begun under a cloud of accusations of improper outfitting and preparations for illicit trade. A royal commission eventually found

■ 'Bombardement et Prise de Fort Nelson [York Factory]', 1697, from Bacqueville de la Potherie, *Histoire de l'Amérique Septentrionale* (1753). Although this image purports to show Iberville's second attack on the fort, written descriptions of that action suggest that the one depicted here was the first, in September 1694. LAC, C-21939.

THE 'INFAMOUS COMMERCE' OF THE FRENCH TROOPS

Many people in New France complained about the behaviour of the soldiers stationed there. The following letter, addressed to the Intendant of Champigny in August 1702, was written by Father Étienne de Carheil, a missionary at the mission of St-Ignace, near the Mackinac Straits. Fort Buade had been constructed near the mission in 1690.

If His Majesty desire to save our missions and to support the establishment of religion, as we have no doubt he does, we beg him most humbly to believe what is most true, namely, that there is no other means of doing so than to abolish the two infamous sorts of commerce which have brought the missions to the brink of destruction, and which will not long delay in destroying these if they are not abolished as soon as possible by his orders, and be prevented from ever being restored. The first is the commerce in brandy; the second is the commerce of the savage women with the French, which are both carried on in an equally public manner . . . . All the pretended service which is sought to make people believe that they [the soldiers] render to the King is reduced to four chief occupations of which we beg you to inform the King.

The first consists in keeping a public tavern for the sale of brandy, wherein they trade it continuously to the Savages, who do not cease to become intoxicated, notwithstanding our efforts to prevent it. . . .

The second occupation of the soldiers consists in being sent from one post to another by the Commandant in order to carry their goods and their brandy, after having made arrangements together, none of them having any other object than to help one another in their traffic. . . .

Their third occupation consists in making of their fort a place that I am ashamed to call by its proper name, where the women have found out that their bodies might serve in lieu of goods and would be still better received than beaver, so that it is now the most usual and most continual commerce, and that which is most in fashion. Whatever efforts all the missionaries may make to denounce and abolish it, this traffic increases, rather than diminishing, and grows daily more and more; all the soldiers hold open house for all the women of their acquaintance; from morning till night, the women spend full days, the ones after the others, sitting by their fires and often on their bed in talk and action fitted to their trade which ends ordinarily but at night, the crowd being too dense during the day for them to complete the transaction, although often they arrange to leave a house empty not to defer the completion till night.

The fourth occupation of the soldiers is gambling, which occurs when the traders assemble; it sometimes proceeds to such excess that they are not satisfied with passing the whole day, but they also spend the whole night in this pursuit; and it happens too often that, in the ardor of their application they forget, or if they remember, they fail to mount the guard of the posts. But what makes their misconduct even worse is that so persistent an attachment to the game hardly ever goes without a general intoxication of all the players, and that drunkenness is almost always followed by quarrels which arise among them and which, taking place publicly in front of the Indians, cause among the latter three great scandals: the first, of seeing them drunk; the second, of seeing them fighting among themselves so furiously as to take their rifles to kill one another; and the third, of witnessing the missionaries' inability to stop this. . . .

SOURCE: Letter of Father Étienne de Carheil, of the Company of Jesus, to the Intendant of Champigny, 30 August 1702, in Francis Parkman, *The Old Regime in Canada* (Toronto, 1899), II, 243–6.

Iberville guilty of many improper acts, including embezzlement of supplies, but Iberville himself did not have to face the charges: his health had been bad for years, and he died shortly after the Nevis expedition. Other accusations of financial malfeasance would surface later, and his widow spent much of his fortune attempting to avoid orders for financial restitution.

In many respects, Iberville's exploits were a dead end, for they achieved virtually nothing of lasting importance. The English colonies (except perhaps for Newfoundland) soon recovered from his depredations, and others would succeed in Louisiana where he had failed. But a dead end was almost preordained. Iberville's intrepid buccaneering worked well in the context of the imperial conflict, but it was still buccaneering. While he demonstrated the extent to which Canadiens could succeed in such enterprises, as well as their adaptability and bravery, the Atlantic world was changing and becoming less vulnerable to individual adventurers. The conditions of seventeenth-century Acadia no longer prevailed. Later success would come to others less daring.

The Treaty of Ryswick had brought the War of the League of Augsburg to a conclusion, but nothing had been resolved. Because France had lost on the international front, Newfoundland and Hudson Bay were restored to the English and Iberville's actions came largely to nought. The combatants took a deep breath and waited, knowing that international war would soon break out again.

THE WAR OF THE SPANISH SUCCESSION (QUEEN ANNE'S WAR)

As its name suggests, the War of the Spanish Succession began over dynastic manoeuvres in Europe. As in the earlier war, New France was again on the defensive, and relied on lightning strikes over the border to intimidate the Americans. Thus, the early period of the North American phase of this war was dominated by French and First Nations guerrilla raids on fron-

tier towns, mainly in New England. These included the most notorious of the colonial raids, on Deerfield, Massachusetts, which eventually became widely known through a book (one of more than 20 narratives of captivity printed in the American colonies between 1682 and 1763) entitled *The Redeemed Captive, Returning to Zion* by the Reverend John Williams.[5] Williams and his family were taken captive by a joint French–First Nations raiding party in February 1704. Mrs Williams, still weak from a recent childbirth, soon fell behind and became separated from her husband; unable to maintain the pace, she was killed with a tomahawk. At White River, Williams was separated from his five surviving children. Stephen went up the Connecticut River with one party, while Samuel, Eunice, and two other youngsters scattered in various directions. Williams himself was taken north to Canada.

As we saw in Chapter 2, Eunice remained with her captors, was adopted into their tribe, and refused to return to her father, who was eventually repatriated to Boston. As for Samuel, then 15, he was sent to school to learn French. When he wrote his father a letter describing how two American women had converted to Catholicism on their deathbeds, Williams insisted that the story must have been the work of his son's teacher. Then Samuel announced that he had embraced Roman Catholicism. Though his conversion proved to be only temporary, his father was deeply distressed. It would be simple enough—and obviously not inaccurate—to attribute such distress to differences of religion so apparent as to require no analysis. But in the end it may have been the success of both the French and the Native people in winning converts among the young that moved the writers of the captivity narratives to paroxysms of moral outrage and concern. Between 1689 and 1713, for example, about 600 captives were taken from mainly Puritan families on the borders of New England. Of those who survived, 174 returned to British North America, 90 became integrated into Aboriginal bands, and 146 remained in

Canada, converted to Catholicism, and became thoroughly assimilated into French-Canadian society.[6] Early in 1698, a mission from New York to Canada to redeem captives had found almost none who were willing to return. Children hid rather than be repatriated, and only after an agreement was reached that those under 12 were too young to decide their own fates were the envoys able to persuade Governor Frontenac to round them up and return them. The same patterns would recur in later wars. Meanwhile, the captivity narratives helped to keep up a spirit of hostility towards New France that in the end probably made the border raids counterproductive from the French standpoint, since they were intended to keep the Americans off balance.

The British did not immediately respond to the raids, but eventually they moved into action. In 1707, a force of 1,000 militiamen in 23 transports set out from New England to take Port-Royal. They failed, and on their return to Boston were greeted with jeers. According to Governor John Winthrop of Connecticut:

> They landed at Scarlett's wharfe, where they were met by severall women, who saluted them after this manner: 'Welcome souldiers?' and presented them with a great wooden sword, and said withall 'Fie, for Shame, pull off those iron spits wch hang by yor sides, for wooden ones is all the fashion now.' At wch one of the officers said, 'Peace, sille woman, etc.' which irritated the female tribe so much the more, that they cal'd out to one another as the past along the streets, 'is yor piss-pot charg'd [full], neighbor? Is yor piss-pot charged neighbor? So-ho, souse the cowards. Salute Port Royal.'[7]

Although the Yankees did succeed in capturing Port-Royal in 1710, the earlier humiliation stayed in the collective memory of New Englanders, merging with what they took to be the oppressive and cruel treatment meted out to captives.

Partly in response to the publicity about the Deerfield incident and other guerrilla raids, a series of large-scale expeditions to capture Quebec was mounted in 1711. The venture was carried out amid considerable disagreement between the colonials and the British navy. Nearly 6,500 men left Boston in an armada of 14 ships of the line and 31 transports, while another 2,300 marched overland along Lake Champlain. Again the Canadien militia turned out, and again the invaders retreated. The fleet lost nine vessels in a storm at the mouth of the St Lawrence, and a British council of war decided that it was too late in the year to try heading upriver again.[8]

Although New France had held its own in this war, internationally France had not done well. As a consequence, it lost a good deal of its North American territory and power in the Treaty of Utrecht of 1713. All of its claims to Newfoundland were surrendered, except for a few fishing rights and the islands of St Pierre and Miquelon off the south coast of Newfoundland, which were returned to France as a refuge for a number of exiled Acadians. At the same time, most of Acadia and all claims to the Hudson Bay territory were granted to the British. In addition, France agreed to Clause XV: 'The Subjects of France inhabiting Canada shall hereafter give no Hindrance or Molestation to the Five Nations or Cantons of Indians subject to the Dominion of Great Britain nor to the other natives of America who are Friends to the same.'[9] The same clause allowed all Aboriginal groups the right to trade with whichever power offered the best trade goods, providing a British entrance into the fur trade of the West.

THE WAR OF THE AUSTRIAN SUCCESSION (KING GEORGE'S WAR)

After the Treaty of Utrecht, the imperial combatants experienced more than a generation of peace. In North America this respite allowed both the British and the French colonies to grow and develop their economies. However, violence persisted on the northern frontier of New England

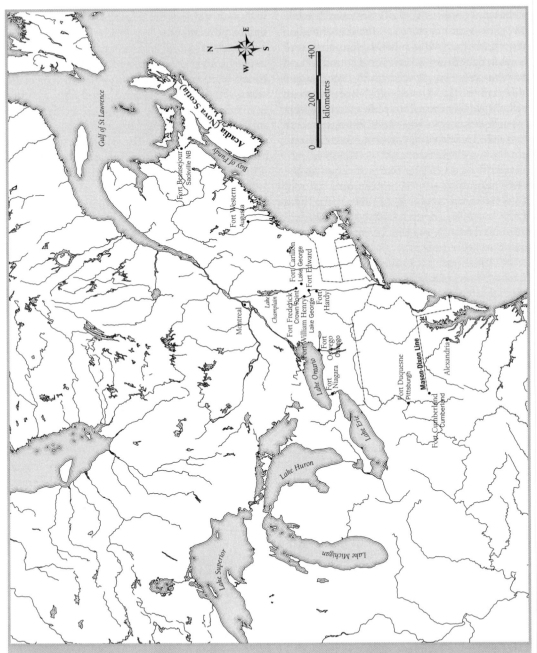

☐ The war in 1755. Adapted from Seymour Schwartz, *The French and Indian War 1754–1763: The Imperial Struggle for North America* (New York: Simon and Schuster, 1994), 37.

and in Nova Scotia, where insensitive treatment of the Aboriginal population led to a series of incidents, beginning in 1715, that eventually merged into a larger 'Indian war' fought mainly with New England from 1722 to 1725. Mi'kmaq, Maliseet, and Abenaki fought together to stem British incursions into their territories, and took a number of American captives. The Native warriors were never totally defeated, but they made a peace in Boston late in 1725 that was ratified in Nova Scotia a few months later. The British promised not to interfere in their territory and the Native people in turn acknowledged the British King as the 'rightful Possessor of the province'. Whether either party appreciated how the other understood these commitments is doubtful.

Not long after European dynastic squabbles led to a resumption of open warfare in 1744, the British mounted an expedition against the French stronghold of Louisbourg. Such action had been urged for some time in New England, and proponents became more insistent after French troops from Louisbourg attacked Canso, in May 1744, and—with the help of their Aboriginal allies—Annapolis Royal (formerly Port-Royal) in August. By the spring of 1745 the Massachusetts Assembly was ready to strike, perhaps encouraged by news that the garrison at the fortress had mutinied over the winter.

More than 3,000 troops hastily raised in Massachusetts were joined by recruits from Connecticut and Rhode Island. The expedition was under the command of William Pepperrell, with the assistance of a naval squadron commanded by Admiral Peter Warren. Assistance was not necessarily co-operation. 'So striking was the mutual independence of the land army and fleet', wrote one inhabitant of the fortress, 'that they were always represented to us as of different nations.'[10] As in many ways they were.

Until now, most Anglo-American expeditions against the French in North America had amounted to little more than wild goose chases, but in this case, as one Bostonian commented, 'we got the goose.'[11] Casualties were light—only

53 French and 101 American troops were killed, most of the latter in accidents resulting from inexperienced use of captured cannon—and after a two-month siege the fortress surrendered on 28 June 1745. For a change, Admiral Warren's naval commanders, and the leaders and soldiers of the American militia, were allowed the luxury of squabbling over the details of a victory rather than fixing the blame for the more customary debacle. Governor William Shirley of Massachusetts complained that Admiral Warren's assumption of command 'on shoar' was 'an unwarrantable usurpation', and one of the American soldiers protested, ''tis Galling . . . that the army should both fight for and afterwards Guard the City, and yet they have none of the Prizes which Cost the Men of War [ships of the Royal Navy] nothing more than to go and meet them. . . .'[12] The French found scapegoats for their loss in the leaders of the previous winter's mutiny; after the fall of Louisbourg, many French soldiers were court-martialled.

The capture of Louisbourg had implications for all the players in the long-standing imperial struggle in the Atlantic region. It demonstrated that when the British and Americans worked together, they could succeed militarily. It also gave the victors a toehold on a territory that was temptingly ripe for settlement and economic exploitation. The French, however, were not yet prepared to abandon Acadia. In 1746 they sent a great armada off to America, but a storm scattered the fleet; the troops that put temporarily ashore at Chiboucto (Chebucto, as Halifax harbour was then known) carried a variety of infectious diseases (mainly typhus and typhoid) that may have wiped out most of the local Aboriginal population.[13]

In May 1747 another French squadron conveying merchantmen to America was destroyed by the British, and a second, larger fleet sent to the West Indies that same year was devastated by Rear-Admiral Edward Hawke. The only consolation for France was the fact that the British and their allies were as unsuccessful on land in Europe as the French fleet was at sea.

THE FRENCH NAVAL EXPEDITION OF 1746

❖

In 1746 the French made a major effort to alter the balance of military power in North America by mounting a great armada to defend Canada. It represented the most ambitious French attempt at a combined army–navy operation abroad before 1775, and proved a total failure, achieving none of its objectives. It involved 45 troop transports (most of them leased from private merchants and carrying nearly 10,000 infantry troops), 10 ships of the line, and a variety of ancillary support vessels, including a hospital ship. The expedition foundered off the Nova Scotia coast, driven off course and badly damaged by heavy storms at sea. The failure was quickly buried by the French government and did not become well-known at the time. It was intended as a response to the Anglo-American capture of Louisbourg in 1745, but Louisbourg's recovery was not as high a priority for this military adventure as was the defence of Canada, an objective that was not in the slightest realized. The French naval ministry that hastily organized the armada was underfunded and lacking in both energetic officers and first-rate warships, and officials had difficulty finding sufficient experienced seamen and packed food, much of which was inedible. Bad food contributed to sickness before the fleet sailed into a serious Atlantic storm. Scurvy, typhus, and typhoid were the common culprits. Many vessels returned to France without reaching the immediate rendezvous point of Halifax harbour; the commander of the force, Jean Baptiste-Louis Frédéric de la Rochefoucauld de Roye—a cousin of Louis XV—died off the coast of Nova Scotia and was not replaced by anyone really prepared to take command. The ships of the expedition not destroyed by the weather returned to France without firing a shot, although one was destroyed by a British ship while scuttling into a French port. The failure of the armada is important for what it tells us about French military priorities in 1746 and France's inability to execute them successfully.

The British, for their part, saw the capture of Louisbourg as an embarrassment or even a setback, since it would prevent the French from sitting down to discuss peace until they had something to offer in exchange for its return. A proposed British invasion of Canada in 1746 was actually rejected on the grounds that it would exacerbate the difficulty of making peace, although its supporters began talking openly of the need to secure the American colonies through 'the entire expulsion of the French out of the Northern continent of America'.[14] In the end, Louisbourg was returned to France in exchange for the latter's agreement to vacate the Austrian Netherlands in the Treaty of Aix-la-Chapelle of 1748. Thus, a formal peace was achieved—but North American issues remained unsettled.[15]

THE FIRST EXPULSION OF THE ACADIANS

The British settlement policy for Nova Scotia that included the founding of Halifax in 1749 was only one in a series of new pressures now bearing down on the region's Acadian population. The French government had begun rebuilding the fortifications at Louisbourg and constructing new forts (Beauséjour and Gaspéreau) on the disputed Chignecto Peninsula. At the same time, it began encouraging Acadians in Nova Scotia to remove to French territory, particularly the previously neglected Île Saint-Jean. Although some did move, the majority stayed where they were in British Nova Scotia. Others succumbed to pressure from French authorities; for example, after 1748 France forced Acadians near Fort Beauséjour to bear arms under threat of deportation.[16] In 1749 the Acadians themselves induced Governor Cornwallis to back down from an attempt to administer an unconditional oath. By now it was plain that French 'neutrals' could not be turned into model British subjects, and it was equally apparent that new settlers could not (and would not) take up lands in areas of Acadian concentration while the question of titles remained unclarified. In 1754 the renewal of undeclared war in North America between France and Britain helped to convince the Nova Scotia authorities that the Acadian question must be resolved once and for all. When, in June 1755, the British captured Fort Beauséjour and discovered 300 armed Acadians inside the French lines, Lieutenant-Governor Charles Lawrence decided that the time had come. Accordingly, on 3 July he forced a confrontation between the Executive Council and informally elected representatives of the Acadians.

In early July 1755 the Executive Council of the British province of Nova Scotia met in the residence of Governor Sir Peregrine Hopson—one of the few public buildings in the young town of Halifax. The governor himself had left Nova Scotia in 1753 because of serious eye problems, and the meeting was called to order by the lieutenant-governor, Colonel Lawrence, a successful career officer who had spent some years after the return of the Louisbourg fortress to the French in 1748 preparing the defences of the Bay of Fundy region for the day when war would again break out. By the time of this meeting it

was clear that the temporary peace cobbled together at Aix-la-Chapelle in 1748 was rapidly disintegrating around the world. Britain and France—and their empires—would soon be fighting openly once again, as they had been doing sporadically for centuries.[17]

The meeting had been summoned as part of the process, already in motion, of dealing with the Acadian threat. Lawrence placed before the Council two petitions signed by the deputies and inhabitants of several Acadian communities in the Minas Basin. The signers declared that they had remained faithful to the British despite the efforts of 'another power' (France was not named), and promised that they would remain loyal provided they could continue to enjoy the same 'liberties' previously allowed them. The petition did not elaborate on those earlier liberties, but they included full acceptance of their rights as set out in the 1713 Treaty; de facto recognition of their property rights; and exemption from any obligation to bear arms (the same conditions worked out in the late 1720s in the context of the oaths of allegiance). One of the petitions went on to demand the return of arms seized in the spring of 1755: 'It is not the Gun the Inhabitant possesses which will lead him to Revolt, nor the depriving him of that Gun that will make him more faithfull, but his Conscience alone ought to engage him to maintain his Oath.' But this eloquent appeal to the right of conscience only raised the ire of the Council. The Acadian deputies were called into the meeting room and 'severely reprimanded for their Audacity in Subscribing and Presenting so impertinent a Paper'.[18]

The Acadians were asked to produce an example of hardships imposed on them by the government, and then to advance a single instance of their service to that government. To both questions there was no reply. They were then informed that conditional fealty was impossible: 'All His Majesty's Subjects are protected in the Enjoyment of every Liberty, while they continue Loyal and faithfull to the Crown, and when they become false and disloyal they forfeit that

Protection.' As for the guns, the laws of England forbade Roman Catholics to bear arms. What right had they to expound to the government on the 'nature of Fidelity, and to prescribe what would be the Security proper to be relied on by the Government for their Sincerity?'

The Council then told the Acadian deputies that they must immediately take the oath of allegiance in its common form. The deputies replied that they were not ready, and must return to consult the body of people on the question, for 'they could not do otherwise than the Generality of the

Inhabitants should determine.' The Council rejected this 'extraordinary' reply and sent the deputies away for an hour to consult among themselves. They returned to answer that they were prepared to take the oath they had always taken. This reply was deemed unacceptable, and the Acadians were sent away until ten o'clock the following morning.

The next day the Council informed the deputies that new representatives of the French inhabitants would be summoned, and that if they, too, refused to take the unconditional oath

■ Letter from Charles Lawrence regarding the expulsion of the Acadians, 11 August 1755. LAC, MG53, No. 71 2–4.

'effectual Measures [would] be taken to remove all such Recusants out of the Province'. At this point the Acadians from Minas offered to take the oath required. But the Council refused to administer it, on the grounds that, 'as there was no reason to hope their proposed Compliance proceeded from an honest Mind', their compliance 'could be esteemed only the Effect of Compulsion and Force'. The die was now cast, and Lieutenant-Governor Lawrence set in motion the process by which thousands of people would be summarily deported from the province.

As so often happens when people finally resolve in their own minds a dilemma that has persisted for some time—in this case for over 40 years—events moved quickly now. Charles Lawrence did not bother to consult the British government on the question of the Acadian removal. Although the Board of Trade had often mentioned the possibility, it had never actually recommended it. Nor did Lawrence inform the Acadian leaders of the result of the deputies' failure to take the unconditional oath. When, shortly after the meeting with the Acadians, news arrived of the defeat, in western Pennsylvania, of General Edward Braddock by a force of French and First Nations allies, Lawrence only stiffened his position. On 25 July a group of newly selected Acadian deputies were told by the Council that 'they must now resolve either to take the Oath without any Reserve or else quit their lands, for that Affairs were now at such a Crisis in America that no delay could be admitted.'[19] When they refused to take the oath, the Nova Scotia Council agreed unanimously that 'it would be most proper to send them [the Acadians] to be distributed amongst the several Colonies on the Continent, and that a sufficient number of Vessels should be hired with all possible Expedition for that purpose.'[20] The decision to distribute the Acadians among other English colonies reflected Britain's desire not to add strength to the remaining French settlements by permitting them simply to go where they wanted. It seemed the obvious strategy to adopt.

According to the formal plan prepared for the deportation, the Acadians were to be persuaded that they were being removed to French territory (any ruse was acceptable to prevent resistance), and their settlements in Nova Scotia were to be destroyed. Details concerning the actual process of removal are scanty, but the diary of Lieutenant-Colonel John Winslow, who supervised the removal at Grand Pré, indicates that it was carried out with firmness and met little resistance. On 5 September 1755 Winslow summoned the Acadian men to the parish church, and from a table in its centre (surrounded by armed officers) informed them of their fate. Families would be kept together on the same vessel and would be permitted to take their money and household goods, but would forfeit their 'lands and tenements, cattle of all kinds and live stock of all sorts' to the Crown. On 10 September Winslow placed another 230 Acadians aboard five transports, although they did not sail until a month later. By 3 November he had sent off 1,510 people, and followed subsequently with another 600.[21] Another 1,100 Acadians were removed from Piziquid, 1,664 from Annapolis Royal, and 1,100 from Fort Cumberland. The only serious resistance came at Chepody, where 300 Acadians and Aboriginal allies successfully drove the British forces back to the ship. In other cases, those who refused to sail simply abandoned their property and escaped to the woods, then made their way to French territory—as far away as Louisiana—or to uninhabited districts of the colony, mainly in what is now New Brunswick.

THE SEVEN YEARS' WAR

Informal warfare between France and Britain had broken out on the Virginia frontier in 1754, long before a state of war was formally declared in Europe. At the beginning, of course, nobody could have known that this conflict would end in the expulsion of France from North America. The North American combatants were in much the same relative positions they had been in for more than 50 years. New France was still vastly overextended, forming a great but tenuously defended arc around the more compactly organized English colonies. The *pays d'en haut*, where the French had only recently put down a First Nations conspiracy (see 'Orontony', p. 160) to drive them out of the region, was particularly vulnerable. The French population was still hugely outnumbered by the British, and even worse, a series of bad harvests in the mid-1750s had left Canada unable to feed itself. From the French standpoint, the saving grace was that the English colonies spent most of their time fighting among themselves, and were consistently incapable of mounting a major military campaign against Canada.[22]

Neither mother country had ever really focused its attention on its North American colonies, and the British ministry of the Duke of Newcastle at the start of the formal war in 1756 was still committed mainly to fighting the war in Europe. The French authorities in Canada had been told in 1754 that unless government expenses were significantly reduced, the colony would have to be abandoned. Most of the 6,600 regular French troops in America had been dispatched before the war actually began, and they were not reinforced. On the other hand, the British navy, with 130 ships of the line, was twice the size of the French one, which still had not recovered from its losses in the 1740s. So long as both France and Great Britain continued to treat North America as a sideshow to the main event in Europe, the military situation was unlikely to change much. Aboriginal allies remained important to both sides, and European commanders regularly lamented their refusal to play by European rules.[23]

THE CONQUEST OF LOUISBOURG AND THE SECOND ACADIAN EXPULSION

In this war, the numbers of British regulars sent to the New World rose constantly. By 1758 Major-General Jeffrey Amherst was able to lead an expedition against Louisbourg consisting of 15,000 soldiers (most of them regulars) and more than 150 ships. When at last the fortress surrendered, after a siege of nearly two months, James Wolfe—one of three brigade commanders—remarked that 'If it had been attacked by anybody but the English, it would have fallen long ago.' Following the conquest of Louisbourg, the British carried out a second expulsion of Acadians—one that has been virtually forgotten in Canadian history. This time the targets were the Acadians who had made their way to Île Royale and Île Saint-Jean. More than 6,000 were forcibly removed from the region, over 3,500 of them from Île Saint-Jean, and shipped to France. Tragically, the fleet carrying them was devastated by a storm at sea, and several thousand Acadians died in the course of the voyage, either by drowning or from disease. When the survivors arrived in France they were greeted with little sympathy.[24] The people who hid in the woods in 1755 and 1758 would become the foundation of the region's future Acadian population.

The 1758 expulsion has never received the attention that the expulsion of 1755 has, although its results were equally tragic. Perhaps part of the reason is that the legal situation of the Acadians had changed: by 1758, France was at war and the Acadians could be considered a legitimately defeated enemy, whereas this was not the case in 1755. Nevertheless, large resident populations are not routinely removed upon conquest, and the Acadians could have been allowed to remain where they were in 1758.

After the reconquest of Louisbourg in 1758, the government of Nova Scotia once again turned its attention to the problem of attracting settlers. This time the plan was to mount a recruiting drive in New England using public advertisements. Only a few days before the advertisements were published, a legislative assembly—the first widely elected governing body in what is now Canada—met in Halifax. Necessary to attract settlers, the assembly had also been insisted upon by the British authorities, who as early as 1719 had underlined to Governor Richard Phillips the need for 'such reasonable laws and statutes as hereafter shall be made and assented to by you by the advice and Consent of our Council and Assembly of the said Province hereafter to be appointed'.[25] The creation of an elected assembly had been delayed by the ongoing turmoil in the colony and in particular the difficulty of deciding what to do about the Acadians, who as Roman Catholics were ineligible to participate under British law; once the Acadians had been removed, however, there was no longer any reason not to move ahead. Furthermore, by 1757 members of the Halifax mercantile elite were so frustrated that they were denouncing the Nova Scotia government to London itself; as one put it, 'We are, the Shamefull and Contemptible By-Word of America; The Slaves of Nova Scotia; The Creatures of Military Gov'rs; Whose Will, is our Law, & whose Person, is our God.'[26] In early 1758 the Board of Trade virtually ordered Governor Lawrence to establish an assembly: 'We think it of indispensable necessity that it should be immediately carried into execution.' When the 20 legislators—almost all New Englanders resident in Halifax—did finally meet, in October, they voted to serve without remuneration and quickly settled down to the passage of legislation. One of their first acts established a court of divorce, with far more liberal rules than existed in the mother country.[27] Nova Scotia was now a full-fledged British colony.

THE BATTLE OF QUEBEC

Near dawn on 13 September 1759 a Canadien militiaman arrived at the outskirts of the French defences north of Quebec and the Plains of Abraham and reported that the enemy was scaling the heights. The location seemed so improb-

able, reported one French witness, that 'people did not believe a word of this man's story, thinking that fear had turned his head.'[28] But soon the sound of guns intensified, and the British troops were moving towards the heights. The French commander-in-chief, the Marquis de Montcalm, rode out just after 7 a.m. to survey the situation. He said nothing as he looked over the field of scarlet uniforms still forming on the plains: nearly 4,500 British regulars, mainly crack regiments of Highland Scots, Britain's best soldiers. Montcalm returned to his headquarters to organize his response, and at roughly 9:30 a.m. he told one of his officers: 'We cannot avoid giving action; the enemy is entrenching, he already has two pieces of cannon. If we give him time to establish himself, we shall never be able to attack him with the sort of troops we have.' Soon after, the officer to whom Montcalm had spoken saw the French force begin moving, 'M. de Montcalm at its head and on horseback.'[29] The military showdown for control of North America, which had been building for nearly a century, was about to begin.

The failure of three previous attempts to seize Quebec, the administrative capital of New France—in 1690, 1711, and 1746—had not prevented Britain from trying again. The largest and best-equipped military force that North America had ever known had assembled at Louisbourg over the winter of 1758–9, while the frozen ice of the St Lawrence kept the French isolated and immobilized at Quebec. It consisted of 8,600 troops, most of them regulars, and 13,500 sailors aboard 119 vessels, including 22 ships of the line and five frigates. So vast was this armada that when it left Louisbourg, in early June, it took six days just to clear the harbour. On 27 June General James Wolfe landed his army on the Île d'Orléans without serious French opposition. A flotilla of French fireships—old hulks set ablaze and costing Louis XV a million livres he could ill afford—was sent downriver a day later to wreak havoc among the British transports, but they were fired prema-

■ Louis-Joseph, Marquis de Montcalm, 1790, mezzotint by Antoine-Louis-François Sergent. LAC, C-14342.

■ General James Wolfe. This sketch is said to be a copy of one made at the Montmorency camp on 1 Sept. 1759, two weeks before his death. LAC.

turely and caused little damage. More than two months of skirmishes followed as Wolfe tried to find a place to land his army closer to the French forces and Montcalm worked to prevent such a move. Meanwhile, Wolfe and the British admiral, Sir Charles Saunders, were at constant loggerheads, and Montcalm saw evidence that his forces, mainly Canadien militiamen, would not stand up to offensive action.

Wolfe was becoming desperate. Never blessed with a strong constitution, for years he had had premonitions of an early death; he also longed to prove himself a hero. In the weeks before the battle, when a fever forced him to take to his bed, he remarked that he 'would cheerfully sacrifice a leg or an arm to be in possession of Quebec'. Major-General Montcalm, for his part, had suffered recurring bouts of depression over the 'miserable dissensions' and lack of preparedness of the colony he had defended since 1756. 'I should like as well as anybody to be Marshall of France,' he wrote to a friend after a victory at Ticonderoga in 1758, 'but to buy the honor with the life I am leading here would be too much.' He despaired of returning to his home: 'When shall I see my château of Candiac, my plantations, my chestnut grove, my old mill, my mulberry trees?'[30] Only a few days before the final showdown against Wolfe and the British, he complained to an aide that his 'health [was] going to pieces'.[31]

By the time Wolfe had begun to recover from his fever—the doctors had bled him profusely and fed him opiates, the standard treatment of the time—it was clear that a final effort would have to be made quickly, before the inevitable freeze-up of the St Lawrence. The British finally found a path up the cliffs to the plain above, and managed to pass the French sentries unmolested—apparently because the French had not prearranged a password. Beginning the climb at 4 a.m., they reached the top of the cliffs by 8 a.m. and proceeded to form their battle lines: only two deep instead of the normal three, but covering the plain.

■ Attack by French fire-ships on the British fleet at Quebec, 28 June 1759. From a copy in oils of the original painting by Dominic Serres, 1767. LAC, B-250.

Montcalm arranged his forces with a militia unit within each regular battalion, and at approximately 10 a.m. gave the order for the three columns to advance at a run, himself in the lead. Not until the French were at close range (some accounts say 40 yards, others 60) did the British fire. The French broke ranks and retreated back towards the city, pursued by the victors. Wolfe, who had recklessly exposed himself in the midst of his troops, was hit several times by musket fire; a ball in the chest was fatal. His last words were 'Now, God be praised, I will die in peace.' Soon after, Montcalm, too, was mortally wounded; he would die the next day. The battle was not over: the fighting continued for some time, with considerable loss of life. Nor was it the end of the war, for the bulk of the French army escaped and would fight valiantly on for the best part of a year. But the British possessed the fortress of Quebec.

For all that has been written about the Battle of the Plains of Abraham, tantalizing questions remain that may never be completely answered. Why did Montcalm attack without

■ The death of Wolfe, preparatory drawing for the engraved print by James Barry, watercolour over pen and ink, c. 1763. This romanticized image would be widely copied in the nineteenth century. LAC, P3253 (Peter Winkworth Collection of Canadiana).

waiting for the reinforcements that he knew were on their way? Why did he attack at all? Unopposed, the British would quickly have run out of food, and in the meantime the French could have put snipers to work reducing their forces. Did Wolfe deliberately expose himself to a hero's death? In the event, the battle came out much as could have been predicted. It was probably the first engagement in North America that was fought almost entirely on European, rather than American, terms, the first occasion when a fully professional army, well disciplined and—on the day—well led, defeated a partly untrained one. Fully backed by a government at home with regular troops and naval support, the British finally breached the defensive position that the French had enjoyed for nearly a century.

COMPLETING THE VICTORY

Montcalm's successor, the Duc de Lévis, rallied the French forces, marshalling an army of 7,000 men, half of them regulars, the rest militia and Native allies. He led them from Montreal to Quebec, hoping to retake the town before General James Murray could receive reinforcements after the spring breakup of the St Lawrence.

On 28 April 1760 Murray was forced to return the British troops to the Plains of Abraham, where—in the Battle of Ste-Foy—he proceeded to repeat Montcalm's mistakes, attacking the enemy and seeing his men retreat in disarray. But this time the outcome was not clear-cut, and both sides waited to see which would first receive reinforcement. In the meantime, Lévis subjected the devas-

■ Quebec: 'View of the Bishop's house with the ruins as they appear in going down the Hill from the Upper to the Lower Town', by B. Short from a drawing made at the siege in 1759. LAC, C352.

FRANÇOIS LÉVIS, DUC DE LÉVIS
(1719–87)

Many more Canadians, especially in English-speaking Canada, would recognize the name of Montcalm than that of François Lévis. Born near Limoux, France, to an impoverished noble family, he entered the army as a second lieutenant in the Régiment de la Marine in 1735. Thereafter he served in several European campaigns and developed a reputation as a good officer, but he had no money to raise his own regiment. Offered the chance to become second-in-command in Canada, with the rank of brigadier, Lévis accepted with alacrity, and arrived in Quebec on 31 May 1756. General Montcalm soon ordered him to Lake George, where he spent the summer orchestrating guerrilla raids against New England settlements. Anxious to advance his career, he did his best to avoid becoming embroiled in an ongoing quarrel between Montcalm and Governor Vaudreuil. For his part, Vaudreuil decided that the brigadier should be encouraged. In 1758 he ordered Lévis to take 3,000 men to the Mohawk cantons and somehow bring the Mohawks into the war on the side of the French. The orders were soon changed, however, and Lévis was sent instead to reinforce the garrison at Fort Carillon. When Lévis won a great victory there against more numerous British and American forces in 1758, Vaudreuil decided that he could replace Montcalm (who wished to be recalled). Although this plan did not succeed, Lévis did develop an overall defensive strategy—not to pin down all the French forces in fortifications—which the French authorities adopted in 1759.

At the time of the disaster at the Plains of Abraham, Lévis was in Montreal, but when he heard of Montcalm's death he opened his secret contingency orders and rushed to Quebec to take command. He restored some order to the demoralized troops, but was unable to prevent the city's surrender. (In his dispatches to the minister of war, he emphasized that he was not responsible for the debacle.) He spent the winter organizing what was left of the troops, and on 20 April 1760 marched them overland to Quebec. Ironically, General James Murray, inside the city, chose to meet the oncoming French on the Plains of Abraham. Lévis was more successful than Montcalm had been. The British withdrew inside the city's fortifications and the French began a siege that was brought to an end in May 1760 by the arrival of British reinforcements. Nevertheless, Lévis insisted that honour required that the French army fight on. When Vaudreuil decided, in September, to surrender the colony rather than put Montreal to the torch, Lévis refused to meet with General Amherst to exchange the customary courtesies. Instead, he ordered the regimental colours burned and rushed off for Europe to see that he was promoted, properly paid, and released from the article of capitulation stipulating that he not serve further in the war. He returned to service in Germany, where he distinguished himself.

After the war Lévis was appointed governor of Artois, and in later years he carried on an amiable correspondence with James Murray. He became a marshal of France in 1783 and a duke in 1784, three years before his death. (Many of his family were guillotined in 1794.) Lévis had been about as successful as was possible under the *ancien régime*, parlaying military competence and avoidance of political factionalism to good advantage.

tated town to yet another bombardment, and Murray answered with superior firepower. On 9 May a vessel was sighted rounding the final point in the river before Quebec. At first the French were hopeful, but the flag she flew was British. The frigate *Lowestoft* was soon followed by other warships, and the French conceded defeat. In early September 1760 a traditional three-point attack—anchored by a large army under General Jeffery Amherst from New York—forced the surrender of Montreal, the final French stronghold. The 55 articles of capitulation would govern the British occupation of Canada until the governments in Europe negotiated the Treaty of Paris in 1763. But in the autumn of 1760, no one knew how long it would be before a final peace would be made.

CONCLUSION

What was surprising was not that the British had won, but that it had taken them more than half a century to do so. When it was all over, the face of North America would be completely transformed. Less than a generation after driving France from the continent, the British themselves would be under attack and struggling to retain control of any part of it. Indeed, insurgents in the 13 colonies to the south were beginning the countdown to rebellion almost before the ink was dry on the peace treaty. In that countdown, the provinces that would ultimately become Canada were to play an important role.

SHORT BIBLIOGRAPHY

Frégault, Guy. *La Guerre de la Conquête*. Montreal, 1966. The story told from the French-Canadian point of view.

Gipson, L.H. *The British Empire before the American Revolution*, 15 vols. New York, 1936–70. The magisterial American study of the British Empire, several volumes of which focus on the wars.

Griffiths, Naomi E.S., ed. *The Acadian Deportation: Deliberate Perfidy or Cruel Necessity*. Toronto, 1969. The best introduction to the problem.

Parkman, Francis. *Montcalm and Wolfe*. 1884; many editions. The classic account of the confrontation between the two generals.

Pritchard, J.S. *Anatomy of a Naval Disaster: The 1746 French Expedition to North America*. Montreal and Kingston, 1995. A study that demonstrates both the military incompetence of the French and the difficulties of co-ordinating large movements of men and equipment in the eighteenth century.

Rawlyk, G.A. *Yankees at Louisbourg*. Orono, Maine, 1967. The standard account of the siege and capture.

Savelle, Max. *The Origins of American Diplomacy: The International History of Anglo-America*. New York, 1967. Despite its nationalistic-sounding title, a balanced and judicious account of the conflict between France and England in America.

Stacey, C.P. *Quebec, 1759: The Siege and the Battle*. Toronto, 1959. The classic study, perhaps a bit dated today.

Steele, Ian. *Guerillas and Grenadiers: The Struggle for Canada, 1689–1760*. Toronto, 1969. A useful short analysis of the subject from a Canadian perspective.

————. *Betrayals: Fort William Henry and the 'Massacre'*. Toronto, 1993. A study of one incident (1757) in the murky world of eighteenth-century North American warfare.

STUDY QUESTIONS

1. Was Iberville a typical soldier of his time?

2. Write a brief essay commenting on Father Carheil's criticism of the soldiers in 1702.

3. How do the Iroquois wars fit into the colonial struggle between France and England?

4. What did readers in the 13 colonies learn from the captivity narratives?

5. How were the two captures of Louisbourg (1745 and 1758) important to the development of Nova Scotia?

6. Why did the British expel the Acadians?

7. Outline some criticisms that could be levied against both parties—the British government of Nova Scotia and the Acadians—in the course of the Acadian expulsions.

8. Leaving aside the question of the brutal way in which the expulsions were carried out, could the Acadians have expected anything else in 1755?

9. Why do we hear so much less about the second Acadian expulsion, in 1758, than the first, in 1755?

10. What were the lessons of the Battle of the Plains of Abraham?

Writing about Aboriginal Peoples' History

■ Until very recently, Aboriginal peoples were treated as mere supporting players in the story of Canada's historical development. Before the 1960s, the study of indigenous peoples in general was, with a few exceptions, the preserve of archaeologists for the pre-literate period and of anthropologists and folklorists for the post-literate period. For the most part, the archaeologists focused on material artifacts while the anthropologists and folklorists focused on Aboriginal cultures as examples of a 'primitive' stage of development that, in the modern world, was rapidly being swept away. For the folklorists particularly, the task was to preserve as much as possible of these 'vanishing' cultures.

Historians themselves seldom thought much about Native people, and the standard histories of Canada largely ignored them except as participants in the fur trade. For example, the two most influential history textbooks of the post-1945 period, Donald Creighton's *Dominion of the North* (originally published in 1944) and Arthur Lower's *Colony to Nation* (1946), were both silent on the historical development of the people who inhabited Canada in the 'prehistoric' period before the Europeans arrived. Lower's opening chapter was entitled 'The First Hundred Years of Europe in America', Creighton's 'The Founding of New France'. Although Lower did recognize that contact with Europeans was 'calamitous' for Native peoples—a subject he discussed briefly in the context of the fur trade—he was no more prepared than Creighton to see that contact as the central element in the story of Canada's beginnings.

A new attitude towards Aboriginal peoples first began to emerge in the 1960s. It was the product of many influences. One was a growing political recognition around the world of the oppression of minorities, a recognition spearheaded in North America by the civil rights and Black Power movements in the United States. 'Rights' and 'empowerment' became the watchwords of the day. In Canada, the federal government's 1969 White Paper on Indian policy, which proposed to jettison the Indian Act and take away 'special' status for Native peoples, brought a tremendous outcry from the Aboriginal community and was instrumental in developing a new and more confident leadership and a more self-conscious awareness among Aboriginal peoples of what they had contributed to the peopling and growth of Canada. By the 1970s, plans for massive development projects such as the Mackenzie Valley gas pipeline directed public attention towards the Native peoples of the North. In the same period, First Nations leaders increasingly turned to the courts to enforce their rights and began to insist that they, too, were founding peoples of Canada, no less than the French and the English. As often happens, independent developments also played into the Aboriginal renaissance. Taste in art, for example, began to favour simple, bold design and vibrant colour. Suddenly Native art—from Inuit sculpture to Haida totem poles—became fashionable and even commercially important.

Since 1970, studies in Aboriginal history have virtually exploded across Canada. Three factors are probably critical in accounting for the explosion. First, the new international awareness of Aboriginal peoples was reflected in a major scholarly endeavour, particularly in the United States. A significant spur to rethinking of the early contact period came in the early 1960s, when historians studying sixteenth-century Mexico found evidence of a demographic disaster (W.W. Borah and S.F. Cook, *The Aboriginal Population of Central Mexico on the Eve of the Spanish Conquest* [Berkeley, Calif., 1963]). The most influential extension of this insight to other regions followed in 1983, with the publication of *Their Number Become Thinned: Native American Population Dynamics in Eastern North America*, by Henry Dobyns, with William R. Swagerty (Knoxville, Tenn., 1983). The realization that previous notions of the numbers of people before European intrusion were grossly inadequate led scholars to appreciate that there were other discrepancies in the usual interpretations as well. Over the next few years, international revisionism was given an enormous boost by the approaching 500th anniversary of the arrival of Christopher Columbus. Instead of being a celebration of Columbus's achievement, the occasion prompted scholars in all fields to question the Eurocentric assumptions underlying the concept of 'discovery' as it had been accepted for five centuries. Virtually every scholarly journal in the field published a '1492' issue, almost invariably questioning the traditional interpretations of the early history of the Americas.

A second crucial development was the entry of historians into the field of ethnology—the study of different peoples and their similarities and differences—which until about 1970 had been the exclusive preserve of the anthropologists. The result was the new discipline of ethnohistory. The relationship between history and ethnohistory is extremely complex. A major problem for students of the pre-contact and early contact periods is the nature of the evidence available. Without the sort of documentation that historians are accustomed to, the standard historical methodologies simply do not work. Thus, scholars who wanted to understand developments in the early period had to work with the methodologies of the anthropologist, the archaeologist, and the linguist. With the arrival of the historians, one of the major conventions of the anthropologist, which was to extrapolate backwards in time from the evidence of the present, could be modified, enriched, and made more accurate by judicious use of existent documentation. By and large, historians tend to be more cautious than anthropologists both in extrapolating from the present and in accepting at face value orally transmitted accounts of events from the distant past.

A third factor was specific to Canada. Aboriginal history—and its interpretation by various scholarly disciplines, notably history, anthropology, archaeology, and linguistics— has become a central issue in many court cases fought over land claims and Native rights. This was inevitable: legal cases of this kind have always hinged on documentation of the indigenous people's historical collective occupation of the land in the pre-contact period and their subsequent treatment by Europeans. The need to document Aboriginal claims has prompted detailed research into the early history of this country, and the courts have even played a role in validating the use of oral history as testimony in cases concerning peoples with an oral tradition. Many of the problems associated with the use of anthropological evidence in the courts are discussed by Antonia Mills in her book, *Eagle Down Is Our Law* (Vancouver, 1994). Mills had been one of the expert witnesses who testified in the famous Delgamuukw v. the Queen case, in which the judge rejected the anthropological testimony based on oral traditions and decided that the Wet'suwet'en and Gitksan people had no Aboriginal title. (The decision was overturned by the Supreme Court of Canada in 1997.)

Difficulties have not been confined to studies of the pre-contact period. Aboriginal peoples were never entirely neglected by historians of early Canada; studies of topics such as the fur trade and missionary activities necessarily included considerable material on them. But until recently most such discussions were full of negative stereotypes. James Walker in 1971 attributed the problem in large part to the biased nature of the sources on which such studies were based; the accounts of missionaries, explorers, and fur traders naturally reflected the ignorance and prejudice of their authors' own times (Walker, 'The Indian in Canadian Historical Writing', Canadian Historical Association, *Historical Papers* [1971]: 31 ff.). Walker also recognized that ignorance and prejudice continued long after the period of 'first contact' had ended, and that the fundamental issue went far deeper than the bias of the documentary sources. These sources could be quite revealing if 'scrutinized and sifted'. Later accounts, he pointed out, reflected a persistent prejudice among Canadian historians, who accepted characterizations of Native people as brutal, savage, superstitious, and duplicitous without making any attempt to look at the events described from the Native point of view. Canadian history was traditionally written from a Eurocentric perspective that reflected an unquestioned belief in the supe-

riority of European civilization. In short, Aboriginal people were forced into the European narrative and were not allowed a history of their own.

Although new material on the early history of Canada has emerged, chiefly through recovery of some Aboriginal oral traditions (especially important in the legal context), the biggest change that has occurred in recent years is a shift in perspective, which has enabled us to strip the historical accounts of their obvious (and less obvious) preconceptions and—perhaps equally important—to pose new questions of the old data, biased as it may be. The two processes often operate in tandem. The first breakthrough was probably the simple recognition that early contact was more complex than it first appeared, and that there was a Native point of view to be considered. Alfred Bailey's *The Conflict of European and Eastern Algonkian Cultures* (originally prepared as a thesis in 1934; 2nd edn, Toronto, 1969) not only recognized that a Native perspective existed, but pioneered in treating early contact as a matter of conflict between two quite different sets of cultures, and a topic worth exploring in its own right. Once historians began looking at interactions between Aboriginal and European cultures—rather than simply chronicling how the latter was imposed on the former—the study of Canada's early history was profoundly and irreversibly altered.

Bailey's work was not particularly influential when it was first published; not until the 1970s did revisionist interpretations of early Canadian (and early American) history begin to appear in large numbers. Most of these works were written either by ethnohistorians or by scholars in other disciplines (particularly history, anthropology, geography, and economics) who appreciated the importance of both ethnographic and interdisciplinary approaches. It became apparent that the old source materials were quite capable of answering new questions when they were examined carefully, and in retrospect many of the new findings have seemed transparently obvious once the appropriate question has been identified. To take one example, it turns out that the literature offers ample evidence of Native collaboration in the exploration process—it simply wasn't obvious until someone thought to look for it; there are also a good many more Aboriginal maps in archives, and in explorers' accounts, than anyone had imagined. To take another example, the literature by and about Europeans captured or held captive by First Nations yielded an entirely new insight into cultural contact when somebody finally thought to ask how many captives did not return, and what happened to them. The American scholar James Axtell has been particularly ingenious in finding fresh questions to pose, and he has been joined by a number of Canadian specialists whose works are listed in the bibliographies for Chapters 1 and 2. Some of the most rewarding new questions have come from scholars taking a fresh look at other areas of study, such as the role of women in Canadian history. In general, the new interpretations suggest that Native people operated with considerably more autonomy in their relationships with Europeans than was previously thought; at the same time, therefore, they render the ultimate dominance of the intruders far more problematic than it seemed in the past.

Finally, it should be emphasized that Canadian studies of the Aboriginal past are not conducted in isolation: similar studies of indigenous peoples around the world provide an essential context. Recovery of the pre-contact record and recognition of an Aboriginal history independent of European intruders is an international undertaking, with a mutually advantageous interchange of information and ideas. In recent years, one of the most interesting problems with respect to writing the history of cultural contact in Canada has been the extent to which the new interpretations have coincided not only with international developments in Aboriginal history but with recent trends in other areas of thought and action. In short, the history of early contact between Europeans and Aboriginal peoples is anything but dead and buried in the past: it is alive and important to us today. That importance is only highlighted by a succession of court cases dealing with Aboriginal rights and property. Most of those cases have advanced the cause of Aboriginal rights. One exception, however, is *Manitoba Métis Federation v. Canada and Manitoba*, heard in the Court of Queen's Bench in Manitoba with a decision rendered late in 2007, in which the judge denied that the Métis of Manitoba had any historic basis for a land claim. This decision has been appealed.

□ 'Lady Emily and Lady Mary Lambton', watercolour by Katherine Jane Ellice, 1838. All three women had travelled to Canada from England with Lord Durham's party, the Lambton sisters because the governor general was their father, and Jane Ellice because her husband was his secretary. LAC, C-013385.

PART TWO

■ 1760–1840

■ The years between 1760 and 1840 might well be labelled the colonial period for British North America. They began with Great Britain accepting the surrender of Canada and soon after, through the Treaty of Paris (1763), claiming sovereignty over virtually all of New France. The result was an enormously expanded British North America, consisting of more than 30 colonies on the continent and the adjacent Caribbean islands—some heavily populated and highly developed, others very lightly populated and relatively backward—as well as a vast expanse of western territory previously contested between France and Britain, and still inhabited mainly by First Nations. Yet, little more than a decade later this vast new British North American empire was torn apart by a cataclysmic revolution and civil war. The results were an independent republic to the south and a ragtag collection of colonies to the north that would now be reconstituted as the refuge for Loyalist exiles from the new United States.

The story from 1791 to 1840 focuses on the growth of those underpopulated, economically underdeveloped colonies into a British North America with continental pretensions to match those of its southern neighbour. An important stage in that development came with the War of 1812, when British North Americans, particularly in Upper and Lower Canada, defended their home against a series of American invasions. The issues that had created the conflict were not directly addressed in the Treaty of Ghent, which ended the war. Nevertheless, the boundary between the United States and British North America was largely settled—to the detriment of the First Nations in the territory south of the Great Lakes. Until then, the title to the region had been contested and the First Nations had been able to hope that they might retain some autonomy; but now the land was officially part of the republic, and the Aboriginal peoples' aspirations were definitively crushed.

The years after 1815 brought massive increases in the numbers of immigrants arriving from the British Isles, and the colonies prospered within the context of British paternalism. The mercantilist policies of the mother country encouraged the development of vibrant—if limited— resource-based economies, and the colonies gradually developed institutions of self-government, although some chafed under administrations that in many cases were kept in power with British assistance. Meanwhile, a colonial society was taking shape, and cultural institutions and practices of all kinds, imported and indigenous, were developing.

Throughout British North America, this colonial phase came to an end somewhere around 1840. Among the factors that im-pelled the colonies towards new maturity were the rebellions of 1837–8 in the Canadas, which threatened political stability and underlined the problems of the old politics, and a shift in British economic policy away from mercantilism and towards free trade. For many British Americans, the continent was becoming more important than the empire.

CHAPTER TEN

The Expansion and Contraction of British North America, 1760–1782

In 1763 Great Britain permanently acquired almost all of the French territories in North America that it had already conquered militarily—with very few commitments to the indigenous population of those territories. Indeed, the Acadians in the Maritimes had already been physically expelled from their homeland, and the British government could seriously contemplate overwhelming the French-speaking Roman Catholics of Quebec with English-speaking Protestants. The initial intention was to resettle most of those territories with loyal Britons and set aside the First Nations lands south of the Great Lakes and west of the Appalachian Mountains as an Aboriginal preserve. By 1783 some of those goals had been achieved, but others had not. Quebec was a thriving province being settled by large numbers of anglophones. However, some unknown number of Acadians had returned to the Maritimes to join thousands of American settlers resident there. As for the trans-Appalachian west, it was now in American hands.

In effect, the fears of those who had counselled the British against retaining Canada had come true. Freed of the threat posed by the French and allied First Nations on their northern and western frontiers, the colonial Americans had resisted British efforts to reform the North American empire. Instead, they had become further and further alienated by the mother country's clumsy efforts to retain its control. By 1775 the Americans were engaged in open warfare against the British government, and in 1776 they formally declared their independence. The military struggle quickly turned into the continent's first civil war as the Yankees tried—unsuccessfully—first to invade Quebec and make it the 'fourteenth colony' and then to liberate the Nova Scotia Yankees. For its part, after encouraging loyal Americans, First Nations, and former slaves to take up arms on its behalf, the mother country abandoned these allies for a hasty peace treaty with the Americans in 1783.

The Empire had been sundered, but the consequences were not quite as bad as they might have been. The loyal provinces of Quebec and Nova Scotia became destinations for thousands of American refugees who fled north for political reasons. Some of the new arrivals would move overland from Quebec into the northwestern part of the continent to trade in furs with the First Nations, while others would settle west of the St Lawrence. In time, the northernmost colonies would become part of a reconstituted British Empire.

TIMELINE

1759
Jesuits expelled from Canada.

1760
Arrival of first Planters in Nova Scotia.

1762
End of subsidies in Nova Scotia.

1763
Treaty of Paris. Proclamation of 1763.

1764
Beginning of Pontiac's rebellion. New judicial system for Quebec. Incident of Walker's Ear.

1766
Consecration of Bishop Briand. Governor Murray recalled and Guy Carleton appointed.

1767
Island of Saint John distributed to proprietors by lottery.

1769
Island of Saint John separated from Nova Scotia.

1773
First assembly meets on Island of Saint John.

1774
Quebec Act passed by British Parliament.

1775
Battles of Lexington and Concord. Capture of Fort Ticonderoga. Invasions of Quebec. Battle of Quebec and death of General Montgomery. British Parliament passes Palliser's Act for Newfoundland.

1776
Americans retreat from Quebec. Invasion of Nova Scotia and attack on Fort Cumberland.

1778
Surrender of Burgoyne's army at Saratoga. George Rogers Clark captures Fort Sackville in the Illinois territory. Peter Pond opens Athabasca region to fur-traders. James Cook visits Nootka Sound.

1779
Famine in Newfoundland. Capture of Col. Henry Hamilton by George Rogers Clark.

1781
Surrender of Lord Cornwallis at Yorktown, Virginia.

1782
French attack Hudson's Bay posts. Final peace treaty agreed between US and Britain at Paris.

1786
Lapérouse expedition visits Pacific coast.

BRITISH POLICY FOR NORTH AMERICA

RELATIONS WITH CANADA

Until the European powers could make a final decision on the future of Canada, Britain would have to treat the Canadiens with a fairly light hand. In the Articles of Capitulation, General Amherst had readily granted freedom of worship, security of property, and the right of the people to remain in their own homes (an important consideration, given recent events in Nova Scotia). His response to requests for neutrality and the continuation of customary laws was that the Canadiens had become 'subjects of the King'. But in the short term, such concessions were generally observed by the three military administrators of the colony, all of whom accepted French as the 'language of the country', especially in the military courts, which administered civil justice following local precedents. The military garrisons proved quite generous in providing informal assistance to the Canadiens.

The capitulation document forced French royal officials to abandon the country immediately; those held responsible for the debacle of 1759–60—notably François Bigot—returned to France in disgrace. Many of the colony's landed and commercial elite also left when it became clear that France had lost Canada, and the Jesuits had already been expelled by General Murray in 1759. Some of the Canadien elite, especially the merchants, stayed in the hope that they could adapt to the new order. However, the victorious armies brought in their wake—ominously—a new group of suppliers, mainly American colonials tied to British and American mercantile trade.

THE PEACE NEGOTIATIONS

Before 1761, the final outcome of the war was still uncertain and the possibility remained that Canada might be restored to France. Hopes in that regard were encouraged by discussion in the British press over the value of Canada, particularly in comparison with the West Indian sugar islands. This 'Canada versus Guadeloupe' debate, as it has been called, had little impact on the British government in its peace negotiations, which stalled in 1761—not because France balked at sacrificing North American territory, but because William Pitt had insisted on much more. When the French West Indies fell in 1762 and the British began their assault on Spanish Havana, the French and the Spanish found their backs against the wall. The French offered to sacrifice more continental American territory, giving

up Louisiana east of the Mississippi in return for Martinique and Guadeloupe. And, in exchange for surrendering all claims to territory in the northern part of the American continent, they were granted fishing rights in Newfoundland, as well as the islands of St Pierre and Miquelon. The Spanish proved no problem after the conquest of Havana. In a complicated transaction, Britain returned Havana and Puerto Rico but kept Florida, while France compensated Spain for its losses by ceding it the western half of Louisiana and the port of New Orleans. To sell the final arrangement to the British public, the new government of Lord Bute employed dozens of pamphleteers and newspaper editorialists to emphasize the great gains made in North America, while ignoring the absence of the other territorial acquisitions that might legitimately have been expected, given the totality of the international British victory.

SEARCHING FOR A POLICY

Having stressed the North American theatre, and the security that had been won for the American colonies as a result of the Seven Years' War—at tremendous expense to the British people in manpower and money—the government needed an American policy that would be popular at home. Finding one was not easy. The addition to the British Empire of a sizable number of French-speaking Roman Catholics in Canada, as well as the acquisition of complete responsibility for the Native peoples of the interior, meant that regular troops would have to be stationed in North America, and that the Americans themselves would have to contribute at least a token amount to their support. Over the winter of 1762–3 the government debated imposing a tax on the colonies to support the army, but paused to seek more information before proceeding.

George Grenville succeeded Lord Bute as chief minister in 1763. Proposals for an American policy came to him from all directions, many advocating an integrated approach that would combine solutions to all the outstanding imperial problems: administering the new territories; pacifying the First Nations; deploying the military; raising a colonial revenue; and reforming the administration of the North American colonies. One adviser argued: 'It might also be necessary to fix upon some Line for a Western Boundary to our ancient provinces, beyond which our People should not at present be permitted to settle, hence as their Numbers increased, they would emigrate to Nova Scotia, or to the provinces on the Southern Frontier, where they would be useful to their Mother Country.'[1] The British government wanted to honour its treaty obligations, and fortunately its commitments to the First Nations seemed to come together with other interests regarding both its old and its recently acquired colonies; as John Pownall, secretary to the Board of Trade, observed, Aboriginal policy and general policy 'do, in the present object, by a happy coincidence of circumstances, meet the same point, and form an exact union of system.'[2] The government put aside the far-reaching proposals for reorganization, however, probably because it could not rouse itself to such an effort, and the immediate result of all the advice and deliberations was the Proclamation of 1763: Great Britain's first attempt to produce a policy for its new territories and responsibilities.

THE PROCLAMATION OF 1763

Like most of the British policy developed for what is now Canada over the next few years, the Proclamation of 1763 was not directly intended to effect any fundamental changes in arrangements for Britain's older seaboard colonies. (The Stamp Act of 1765—requiring a tax stamp for publications and legal documents—was initially regarded as simply cosmetic tinkering.) For the moment, four new governments were carved out of the American acquisitions: Quebec (which was limited to the St Lawrence settlements previously called Canada), East and West Florida, and

Granada. The truncated Quebec was to be governed by British law and, as soon as possible, an elected assembly. The Island of Saint John (the future Prince Edward Island) and Cape Breton Island were attached to Nova Scotia. Land grants for retired officers and disbanded servicemen were to be made readily available in these regions. But in the West, beyond the river systems of the Atlantic coast, no land grants were to be made at all. This territory was to be reserved for the First Nations, and any traders in it were to be regulated by the imperial government. The Proclamation had ramifications beyond the territory ceded by the French, however. At the same time that it was issued, the Ohio Valley went up in flames in an uprising known as 'Pontiac's Rebellion', inspired at least in part by the prophetic teachings of some Aboriginal spiritual leaders. That insurgency would take two years and a major military effort to suppress. Together, the declaration of limits to American western settlement and the need to finance Britain's military responsibilities (especially in the West) enraged the British colonists in America. Within a dozen years, their provocative responses to British rule would escalate into an organized colonial 'revolution'. It would also become apparent that Great Britain could not implement its policy for its northernmost colonies in isolation from its policy for North America as a whole.

Although neither the Proclamation of 1763 nor any other British document ever laid out a fully articulated policy for what is now Canada, the outlines of that policy were perfectly clear. The British did not wish to populate their northernmost colonies with settlers from the mother country itself. Great Britain was at the beginning of a major economic explosion, usually called the Industrial Revolution, and it wanted to retain its own people, both as a labour force and for military purposes. It was, however, prepared to make land grants to disbanded professional soldiers, who would not represent any great economic loss to the mother country. Great Britain was also willing to accept 'foreign Protestants', although it hoped that colonial Americans already acclimated to the New World would make up the majority of the settlers. As a result of their experiences in Nova Scotia, the British had learned two lessons. First, the state could not afford to subsidize a large movement of people to a new colony (as it had in the case of Halifax). Second, the best way to deal with a population alien in language, religion, and customs was to outnumber it; forcible removal was neither humane nor effective. Their harsh treatment of the Acadians was to haunt the British for many years to come.

THE ATLANTIC REGION, 1759–1775

Even before the war had ended, the government of Nova Scotia began settling a third contingent of subsidized newcomers in the person of more than 8,000 New England 'Planters'. Starting in 1759, Governor Charles Lawrence took advantage of a substantial annual parliamentary grant for Nova Scotia to recruit these Yankees, providing them with land, transportation, and other assistance until 1762, when the financial tap was turned off. The New Englanders came mainly from land-hungry areas of Rhode Island, Connecticut, and southeastern Massachusetts, and saw migration to Nova Scotia as particularly attractive because it was being financed by the government rather than out of their own pockets. The migrants tended to move in kinship groups, often as entire communities. Most were farmers anxious for more or better land, although some were fishers looking for improved access to superior fishing grounds in Nova Scotia. The farmers settled on Acadian land in the Minas Basin, while the fishers moved to two south-shore outports, which they named Yarmouth and Barrington after their New England counterparts.

In addition to cheap land, the Planters had been promised liberty of conscience and a government 'like those of neighbouring colonies'. They took these promises to mean that, as in New England, land would be owned in freehold by the community's 'proprietors', and that a strong local democracy would develop around township government. The traditional concept of freehold tenure was respected, but the Planters soon found that the government of Nova Scotia had no intention of permitting strong local government. With political disillusionment added to disappointment over the quality of the new land and the harshness of the climate, perhaps half the new arrivals were gone within a few years of the termination of subsidies in 1762. The new townships were initially not very prosperous, particularly after the bottom fell out of the post-war economy. In their religious life the settlers often found themselves unable to afford the paid ministers to whom they were accustomed, and in many communities a vacuum developed into which lay preachers—and eventually a new kind of evangelist—would move. Population turnover in newly settled Planter districts was heavy, as was the land speculation that was endemic in Nova Scotia, from the top of society to the bottom.

Yankee proprietors in the recently established communities wheeled and dealt in small parcels of land, while members of the elite office-holding classes, both within the colony and outside, acquired large parcels of wilderness; three million acres were granted just in the last few days before the Stamp Act became effective in 1765, and in 1767 the entire Island of Saint John was distributed by lottery to large proprietors. Only a handful of the large-scale speculators became active in settlement ventures or commercial development, and those who did were a rather heterogeneous group. British proprietors like Captain William Owen on Campobello Island, Captain John MacDonald on the Island of Saint John, and J.F.W. DesBarres in Nova Scotia wanted to establish themselves as great European-style landowners, complete with peasant tenants—Welsh for Owen, Highland Scots for MacDonald, Acadians for DesBarres.

By 1767, when a detailed census was taken, the colony was well-populated, with 11,072 peo-

TABLE 10.1
POPULATION OF NOVA SCOTIA IN 1767 BY ETHNICITY

Place	English	Irish	Scots	Americans	Germans	Acadians
Nova Scotia	686	1,831	143	5,799	1,862	650
Cape Breton	70	169	6	170	21	271
North (NB)	25	53	17	874	60	147
Isl. of Saint John	130	112	7	70	3	197
Totals	912	2,165	173	6,913	1,936	1,265

ple in Nova Scotia proper, another 707 in Cape Breton, 1,196 in the northern section (now New Brunswick), and 519 on the Island of Saint John. The same census showed that the population was already quite diverse, with 2,246 Catholics to 11,228 Protestants, and several ethnic groups (see Table 10.1).

In addition, the returns showed a total of 95 'Negroes' and a scattering of 'Indians' (apparently no serious attempt was made to count them). Within a few years, substantial numbers of Scots would arrive from the Lowlands and especially the Highlands, adding Gaelic to the English, German, French, and Mi'kmaq already in use across the region.

QUEBEC, 1763–1775

After 1763, some English-speaking settlers did move to Quebec, where they tended to concentrate on commercial activity. But they were too few to resolve the outstanding problems facing the British administrators. The overall intention of the Proclamation of 1763 had been to remodel Canada as a British province. Until large numbers of British or Anglo-American settlers actually arrived in the colony, however, the Canadiens could not be expected to respond favourably to a wholesale reconstruction of their laws and religion. Accordingly, the colonial authorities temporized, introducing some British elements into the system while confirming many French ones. Thus, a British-style judicial system was proclaimed in 1764, introducing the laws of England and the principles of English justice (including the jury system), but an inferior court of common pleas was permitted to apply French law in cases involving Canadian-born residents. Initially, this court was to apply French law only in cases originating before 1 October 1764, but the principle was eventually extended to cases after that date.

That the vast majority of 'His Majesty's New Subjects' in Quebec were French-speaking Roman Catholics limited change and forced concessions where application of British rules would work hardship on them. (In what seemed to many a reversal of terminology, the newly arrived British were known as the 'Old Subjects'.) General Murray, who continued after the end of the military occupation as first civil governor of Quebec, refused to summon an elected assembly—that essential symbol of British government in the colonies—since the Catholic Canadiens would be ineligible either to vote for or to sit in such a body, which would therefore be dominated by a small group of English-speakers who chafed at the tolerance shown to the French.

■ Governor James Murray, 1783, published for *Universal Magazine*. LAC, C-26065.

Murray and his council were mainly sympathetic to the Canadiens (they would become known as the 'French party') and they waived the rule disqualifying Catholics from serving on juries, since it would have meant empowering a few Protestants to be 'perpetual judges of lives and property' for the impotent majority. The British authorities in London recognized the difficulty, and in the mid-1760s official legal opinions were offered according to which British laws against Catholics did not extend to Quebec, and respect for property rights implied the confirmation of French law in such matters. Finally, there was the problem of the Roman Catholic Church in Quebec, which had been drifting since the death of its last bishop in 1760. In the end, Grand Vicar Jean-Olivier Briand was chosen by his Canadien colleagues for 'presentation' at Rome. With Murray's support and the tacit agreement of the British government, he was consecrated bishop near Paris on 16 March 1766. In theory,

Briand would be only 'superintendent' of the Quebec Church, but in practice he was accepted as its bishop, and the traditional collection of tithes was officially permitted to continue.

Murray's concessions to the Canadiens were hardly radical. But an increasingly loud chorus of objections came from the English-speaking residents of the colony. The problem was not simply Murray's Canadien sympathies, but the hostility of the army he commanded to the new merchant class arriving in Quebec. Relations between the army and civilians reached a low point late in 1764, when intruders armed with 'swords Blodgeons and other weapons' entered the home of magistrate Thomas Walker, cut off his ear, and carried it to the Adjutant of the 28th Regiment 'for his supper'.[3] After a chorus of complaints about his policies, Murray was recalled in 1766. But his successor, Guy Carleton, was to prove even more conciliatory towards the Canadiens. Like Murray, Carleton was a professional soldier who had served under Wolfe. An Anglo-Irishman, he was also a member of the British gentry. He believed firmly in a landed aristocracy, the subordination of a tenant class, and the necessity of close connections between Church and state. Carleton quickly came to see that, with slight adjustments to circumstances, his overall vision for society was quite compatible with the active continuation and even the extension of Murray's policies. Moreover, Carleton came to see the Canadiens as ideal subjects when contrasted with the emerging 'mobocracy' that the British held to be behind the growing turmoil in the American colonies. It soon became Carleton's task to keep his province loyal and quiet in the face of the great movement of rebellion and potential separatism to the south. He was to find convenient allies in the Roman Catholic Church and the traditional seigneurs.

No policy documents or academic analyses were available to guide Carleton on how to rule an alien population in the imperial context. Nevertheless, building on the actions of his predecessor, he instinctively grasped the strategy that

■ Governor Guy Carleton painted in 1923 by Mabel B. Messer from a copy that hung in Rideau Hall; original artist unknown. LAC, C-2833.

would become standard within the British Empire for centuries afterwards. Essentially, the ruler's task was to find local collaborators among the 'alien population' and co-opt them into the governing process. In Quebec this strategy involved extending support for the remaining natural leaders among the Canadiens, chiefly the seigneurs and Catholic clergy, while protecting as many of the rights and privileges of the French inhabitants as was consistent with the colony's new situation. It also involved undoing some of the economic damage done by the geographical dismemberment of Quebec in the Proclamation of 1763.

Hence the Quebec Act of 1774. Most of the former territories of Quebec, to both the west

and the east (including those given to Newfoundland in 1763), were restored to the colony. His Majesty's subjects in Quebec 'professing the Religion of the Church of Rome' were granted free exercise of their religion and exempted from the traditional oaths of supremacy, which renounced Catholicism (a new oath was substituted), while the Catholic clergy were allowed 'their accustomed Dues and Rights, with respect to such Persons only as shall profess the said Religion'. Provision also was made for the support of a Protestant clergy. All matters relating to property and civil rights were to be decided by the traditional laws of Canada. In effect, this clause preserved the seigneurial system intact. English criminal law would continue in place, and the province was to be governed by a Legislative Council; no provision was made for an elected assembly.

Not surprisingly, debate in the British Parliament concentrated on the civil law and the absence of an assembly, although the issues of boundary provisions and the privileges extended to the Catholic Church were also raised. Lord North, the chief minister, argued for the Act: 'It has been the opinion of very many able lawyers, that the best way to establish the happiness of the inhabitants is to give them their own laws, as far as relates to their own possessions.'[4] Critics of the administration—mainly 'friends of the American colonies'—complained that the Act 'carries in its breast something that squints and looks dangerous to the inhabitants of our other colonies in that country.' Its most famous critic, Edmund Burke, added: 'When we are sowing the seeds of despotism in Canada, let us bear in mind, that it is a growth which may afterwards extend to other countries. By being made perpetual, it is evident that this constitution is meant to be both an instrument of tyranny in the Canadians, and an example to others of what they have to expect.'[5] Most of the attacks on the legislation assumed that it had some connection with the turmoil to the south, and while Burke was incorrect in his assertions that Britain intended to extend its

GUY CARLETON,
FIRST BARON DORCHESTER
(1724–1808)

Born in Strabane, Ireland, into an Anglo-Irish family, Carleton entered the army at an early age. He advanced rapidly, thanks partly to the patronage of James Wolfe (and later, Vice-Admiral Charles Saunders). He commanded the 2nd battalion of the Royal Americans at the Battle of the Plains of Abraham, sustaining a head wound. In subsequent campaigns in France and Cuba he was again seriously wounded, but recovered. His civil appointment as 'Lieutenant Governor and Administrator' of Quebec in 1766 was a bit surprising, since he had no civilian administrative experience, but powerful patrons meant more than paper credentials in the eighteenth-century British Empire. He was a highly successful soldier, however, a point that has been often overlooked. He replaced a highly unpopular governor, and quickly brought a fractious council into line.

From the outset, Carleton understood that one of his principal tasks was to defend Quebec, which meant coming to terms with the overwhelming Canadien majority. He made peace with the Roman Catholic hierarchy and generally halted the anglicizing thrust of the Proclamation of 1763. In 1770 he sailed to Britain, where he spent four years pressing for a new constitution that would preserve 'good Humour and a perfect Harmony in Quebec'. Carleton's understanding of the way to satisfy Quebec involved avoiding representative government, recognizing the Catholic Church, co-opting the seigneurial class, and accepting most of the French civil code—in effect, ruling

with the co-operation of the powerful elites of the colony. These policies were embodied in the Quebec Act of 1774. In the short run, they did not satisfy the ordinary habitants in Quebec, who supported the Americans in 1775–6 far more than he would have preferred. As for the Americans, on several military occasions he failed to act aggressively against them, probably because he still thought in terms of reconciling the rebels.

Carleton left Canada in July 1778, and two years later he became commander-in-chief of the British army in North America, in which capacity he was responsible for the British military evacuation. Carleton strongly supported the Loyalist refugees—black, white, and red—and helped them resettle in what remained of British America before returning to Britain in late 1783. In 1786 he returned to British America as Baron Dorchester, commander-in-chief of all its provinces but without direct overall control of the various parts as a proper governor general. His effectual power was limited to Quebec, and he played little role in the reforms that resulted in the Constitutional Act of 1791, since he had little further interest in placating the Canadiens. He resigned in 1794 in response to government chastisement over his support of Aboriginal rights in the western territory that had been ceded to America in 1783.

Carleton's two major achievements were the Quebec Act, based on principles of conciliating alien populations by co-opting their leadership, and the Loyalist migration in 1782–3, based on a vision of a powerful new British America. His dream of a united British America was not achieved in his lifetime. Nevertheless, he was easily the most powerful and influential colonial administrator in the eighteenth-century British Empire.

'despotism', he and others were quite right in appreciating that what Britain did in French Canada would not be without wider significance. If the British government intended the Quebec Act to assure the loyalty of the Canadiens, however, the strategy was not entirely successful.

BRITAIN AND THE GREAT LAKES REGION

Implementing British policy in the old *pays d'en haut* was, if anything, even more difficult than finding a modus vivendi for the old and new inhabitants of Quebec. The British army, which was responsible for administering this region, did not really appreciate the extent of the connections, through trade and marriage, that by now linked the French and the Aboriginal people in the West. One soldier commented of the French-speaking residents of the region (the British called them the 'interior French') that 'they have been in these upper Countrys for these twelve, twenty, or thirty years, [and] have adopted the very principles and ideas of Indians, and differ little from them only a little in colour.'[6] The return of British prisoners taken during the wars would not be easy, since many had become thoroughly integrated into their adoptive tribes. Part of the problem was that the British did not trust these people, many of whom had taken Aboriginal names, and thus did not treat them with the same consideration that the people of Canada received. Part of the problem was the British army's assumption that a heavy-handed imperialistic approach was the appropriate one for dealing with 'heathen savages'. The army simply did not understand the system by which the fur-trading country had long been governed. Thus, General Jeffrey Amherst, who was responsible for the West in the early 1760s, sought to eliminate the whole mediation process that had governed the 'middle ground' under the French, including the gift-giving relationship. 'Purchasing the good behaviour, either of Indians or any others is what I do not understand,' he wrote; 'when men of what race soever behave ill, they must be punished but not bribed.'[7] As British fur trader George Croghan observed, 'The British and French Colonies since the first Settling America . . . have adopted the Indian Customs and manners by indulging them in Treaties and renewing friendships making them large Presents which I fear won't be so easy to break them of as the General may imagine.'[8]

Further complicating matters for the British conquerors was the emergence of a movement of insurgency among the Aboriginal residents of the Great Lakes region. This movement had begun in the prophetic teachings of people like the Delaware leader Neolin. Sometime in 1761, Neolin sat in front of his fire and reflected on his people's situation, now that the French were gone and it would no longer be possible to play one European group off against the other. Only the British, with their alcohol and their seductive trade goods, were left in North America. The 'Master of Life' appeared to Neolin in a vision and 'told him these things he was thinking of were right'.

The path to happiness was blocked by 'the White people'. The First Nations must reject dependence on the white culture and set up on

FRANÇOIS BABY
(1733–1820)

François Baby was born in Montreal into a family long active in the fur trade. He fought bravely in the Seven Years' War and was taken to England as a prisoner of war. While in Europe, he transferred the family's business from French connections to London firms before returning to Montreal in 1763. Unlike most Canadien merchants, therefore, the Babys were able to survive within the new British commercial system. François spent the 1760s diversifying the family business and soon became a leader of the new Canadien bourgeoisie. In 1773, during the preparation of the Quebec Act, he delivered a petition to the British government calling for the retention of traditional laws and privileges and restoration of the old boundaries of New France; one opponent called the petition 'the foundation of the Quebec Act'. Baby was disappointed to receive no special reward for this service. Nevertheless, when the Americans invaded Quebec he played an active role in the Quebec militia, and in 1776 he was part of a commission that examined the performance of the militia in 50 parishes east of Montreal; most were found wanting in loyalty to the British Crown. He was subsequently appointed adjutant general of militia, and prepared the province's first militia law. In the mid-1770s Baby shifted his business efforts away from the Great Lakes into the Gaspé and Labrador, becoming part of a consortium that leased the 'King's Posts'—the fur-trading posts in eastern Quebec—and enjoyed a monopoly of the fur trade and fishery on the north shore of the lower St Lawrence.

By 1778 Baby was a lieutenant-colonel of militia, a member of the Legislative Council, and a part of the unofficial group that ruled the province under Governor Haldimand. His interests gradually shifted from commerce into government and politics, where, in association with the seigneurs, he remained a loyal supporter of Haldimand and a firm opponent of the demands of the mercantile community for an elected assembly and militia reform. In 1786 he married a 15-year-old heiress, acquiring a family association with the seigneurial class of the province. That same year he sold out his one-third interest in the King's Posts in return for a pension. Inheriting family properties of his wife, he finally became a seigneur in 1788. In the period after 1791, he opposed any signs of sentiment in favour of revolutionary France, and he received many rewards, including large grants of land, for his loyalty. His house was the centre of a social group that was acceptable to both the Quebec elite and the Catholic Church—no mean accomplishment. Few Canadiens from the *ancien régime* were so successful under the new one. Although, from the Canadien point of view, Baby could be seen as a collaborator, he helped to bridge the gap and paper over the cracks that the Conquest had produced in Quebec. He was a major transitional figure in the period 1763–1800.

their own. 'This land where you dwell I have made for you and not for others', the Master of Life told Neolin. 'Whence comes it that you permit the Whites upon your lands? Can you not live without them[?] . . . Send them back to the lands which I created for them and let them stay there. . . . Drive off your lands those dogs clothed in red who will do you nothing but harm.' Neolin left his village and took his message to the people of the region, drawing his vision on sheets of parchment paper and even selling the charts to his listeners. Salvation for the Aboriginal people depended on unification, purification, and restoration of the traditional life. The redcoats must be driven away. By 1762, British officials were hearing from all quarters about Neolin and other similar prophets, whose teachings would have to be taken into account in the process of reconstructing British North America after the elimination of the French.[9]

When the First Nations' resistance erupted in attacks on several forts, in the spring of 1763, Amherst had no compunction about suggesting that the troublemakers be given blankets infected with smallpox. But the uprising quickly burnt itself out. The ostensible leader, the Ottawa chief Pontiac, was unable to unite the many factions, and Amherst's successor, Thomas Gage, decided to try to mend some fences. Gage also determined to take advantage of Pontiac, and offered to treat him as if he really were a legitimate leader. In 1765 Pontiac accepted George III as his father and formally made peace. He would die in 1769 in the streets of the French village of Cahokia, clubbed from behind. Other Aboriginal leaders fought on, however, including Charlot Kaské, a Shawnee whose father was German and whose wife was a British captive adopted by Shawnees as a child. Kaské insisted that the British would strip the First Nations of their land: 'The English come there and say that the land is theirs and that the French have sold it to them. You know well our fathers have always told us that the land was ours, that we were free there. . . .'[10]

Despite the Royal Proclamation's ban, the British army administrators on the spot were prepared to tolerate European settlement, and the local First Nations knew it. Thus the region remained in a state of flux. When the British attempted to resurrect the old Aboriginal–

European alliance of the region, with themselves in place of the French, their chances of success were limited by London's refusal to provide the money for presents. At the same time, the British began to discourage their fur traders from moving into the lower Great Lakes. Instead, they used forts to distribute trade goods to the 'Interior French', who continued to dominate the trade. British traders would have far more success in the Northwest, where trading networks had not yet been established.

THE FIRST AMERICAN CIVIL WAR

In early April 1775 British troops attempting to seize illegal stockpiles of arms at Lexington and Concord, Massachusetts, were fired on by colonial militiamen, and a long-festering political crisis turned into a shooting war. From the vantage point of the American leaders, the ensuing conflict was a struggle to secure their rights against the arbitrary authority of the British Crown; from the perspective of the British government, it was a 'rebellion' against duly constituted authority. For many of the inhabitants of British North America, including those in the northernmost colonies, the conflict was a great 'Civil War' in which brother fought brother, friend opposed friend, and many were eventually pushed into exile. Indeed, the proportion of refugees from the new United States, relative to the total population, exceeded that from France after 1789, or from Russia after 1917.

One of the great challenges for Canadian historians is to determine the realities of public opinion in underdeveloped colonies, particularly on the part of those citizens who were not among the articulate elites. Even in our own time, accurate assessment of public opinion is difficult, but before opinion polls and regular elections it was virtually impossible. What the average Quebec habitant or Nova Scotia fisherman was thinking on the eve of the Anglo–American War remains a mystery. Only an occasional glimpse of sentiment can be obtained—sometimes from the written record, more frequently from patterns of behaviour. Clearly, few inhabitants of Britain's northern colonies had much experience with the issues that had led the southern colonies inexorably towards rebellion and war. But ignorance did not necessarily spare them from becoming involved.

THE INVASION OF CANADA

Conflict between the American colonists and Great Britain had been gradually escalating for some time, and the rebels were already organizing an alternative government through their Continental Congress when the shots were fired in Massachusetts. Meanwhile, two Connecticut hotheads, Ethan Allen and Benedict Arnold, both had the idea of attacking the British garrison at Fort Ticonderoga (New York), and raised small militias of their own to do so. The two joined forces and on the morning of 10 May 1775 they led some 100 men to the fort, while the garrison was still asleep. They took it without firing a shot. The second Continental Congress hastily began organizing an army under the command of George Washington of Virginia and—while that force was still in embryo—decided that an invasion of Quebec would deliver 'the *coup de grace* to the hellish junto' governing Great Britain.[11] Washington was somewhat more enthusiastic about this plan than he was about subsequent proposals to invade Nova Scotia. On 27 June, Major-General Philip Schuyler, commander of the troops in upper New York, was ordered to proceed to Quebec by way of Lake Champlain and the Richelieu River. Later in the summer Arnold received orders from General Washington to lead another army, by way of the Kennebec and Dead rivers in Maine and along the Chaudière to the St Lawrence. With over a thousand men, Arnold began his disastrous march to Quebec on 19 September.

The sudden turn of events threw the government of Quebec into shock and confusion. Governor Carleton, only recently returned from London the previous September with the Quebec Act in his dispatch case, transferred his troops from Quebec to Montreal and set up headquarters there. He surveyed the colony along the St Lawrence and informed Britain that he had 'not six hundred Rank and File fit for Duty upon the whole Extent of this great River, not an armed Vessel, no Place of Strength; the ancient Provincial Force enervated and broke to Pieces; all Subordination overset, and the Minds of the People poisoned by the same Hypocrisy and Lies practised with so much Success in the other Provinces.'[12] A public *mandement* from Bishop Briand, ordering the population to ignore American propaganda or be denied the sacraments, had little effect, and the seigneurs appointed to raise a militia found it difficult to do so. In short, Carleton's strategic alliance with Quebec's traditional leaders proved useless, largely because he had misunderstood their position under the *ancien régime*. The Church had seldom been able to exert much influence on public behaviour, and the seigneurs never did have much to do with the militia. The British merchants, whom Carleton never had tried to cultivate, proved singularly unco-operative. Nor were the Aboriginal peoples interested in fighting on Britain's behalf. Virtually the only military assistance the British received came when a Scottish-Canadian army officer, Colonel Allan Maclean, asked permission to raise two battalions of disbanded Highlanders, the Royal Highland Emigrants. The first—which took part in the defence of Canada that was soon to follow—was recruited in Canada and New York; the second was recruited in the Island of St John and Nova Scotia, and served in the latter.

Fortunately for the British, the Americans were neither as well organized nor as lucky as Wolfe's expedition had been in 1759, and the Québécois were less enthusiastic about liberation than the invaders had hoped. In September 1775 an unauthorized attack on Montreal, led by Ethan Allen, failed miserably, and Allen was sent back to Britain in chains, along with several of the town's American supporters. But after the

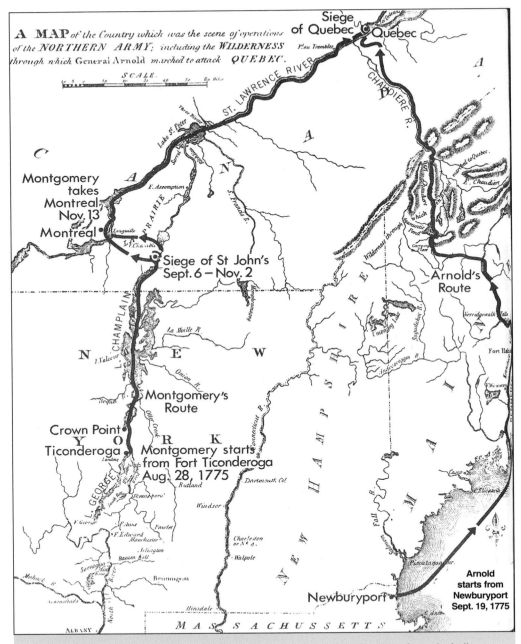

A MAP of the Country which was the scene of operations of the NORTHERN ARMY; including the WILDERNESS through which General Arnold marched to attack QUEBEC.

SCALE.

Siege of Quebec · Quebec

Siege of Quebec

ST. LAWRENCE RIVER

CHAUDIERE R.

Montgomery takes Montreal Nov. 13

Montreal

Siege of St John's Sept. 6 – Nov. 2

Arnold's Route

L. CHAMPLAIN

Montgomery's Route

Crown Point

Ticonderoga

Montgomery starts from Fort Ticonderoga Aug. 28, 1775

N E W   Y O R K

N E W   H A M P S H I R E

M A I N E

L. GEORGE

Newburyport

Arnold starts from Newburyport Sept. 19, 1775

M A S S A C H U S S E T T S

☐ 'A Map of the Country which was the scene of operations of the Northern Army; including the Wilderness through which General Arnold marched to attack Quebec'. Metropolitan Toronto Reference Library.

British surrendered Fort St-Jean, on the Richelieu River, to the invading Americans on 2 November, Carleton abandoned Montreal and left for Quebec. Meanwhile, General Richard Montgomery was struggling to bring an invading army up the Lake Champlain route; 'the privates are all generals', he wrote, complaining of his 'unstable authority over the troops of different colonies'.[13] He was concerned that the Canadiens had not turned out in greater numbers to support their liberation. Meanwhile, Benedict Arnold was bringing his army across what is now the state of Maine under horrendous late-autumn conditions, losing nearly half his troops in the process; he did not cross the St Lawrence until the night of 13 November. Two days earlier, on 11 November, Montgomery and his men arrived near Montreal—which was almost evenly divided between pro- and anti-Americans—and two weeks later they pressed on to Quebec, although Montgomery's soldiers were constantly deserting to return home as their enlistments expired. In Quebec, Col. Maclean had stiffened resistance by convincing the inhabitants that the Americans were 'the worst of Banditti', eager to loot and pillage; and Carleton, on his return, purged the city of 'useless, disloyal, and treacherous persons'. Montgomery joined Arnold at Pointe-aux-Trembles on 3 December and eventually determined that he lacked the force and supplies to lay siege to Quebec. Instead, he decided to storm the town. The assault on 31 December was a desperate move by the Americans, who were suffering from smallpox as well as problems of logistics and morale.

The garrison held, and the result was, as one British officer described it, 'A glorious day for us, as compleat a little victory as ever was gained.'[14] General Montgomery's frozen body was found not far from the barricade against which he had led the charge; General Arnold took a ball through the leg at the first battery; and more than 300 Americans were taken prisoner. Nevertheless, the American forces, now under Arnold's command, remained in military occupation of more than 50 parishes over the winter of 1775–6. In effect, this meant that the local people were forced to support them. 'The peasantry in general have been ill-used', one American officer reported in the spring. 'It is true, they have been promised payment, from time to time; yet they look upon such promises as vague, their labour and property lost, and the Congress and the United Colonies as bankrupts.'[15] According to one American, the use of paper currency cost the occupying army 'the affections of the people in general'. A commission from the Continental Congress (headed by Benjamin Franklin) wrote from Montreal to recommend that 'Till the arrival of money, it seems improper to propose the Federal union of this Province with the others.'[16] At St-Pierre-de-Montmagny, the early spring found rival military parties of Canadiens skirmishing with one another. But in May, British reinforcements arrived at Quebec, and by mid-June 1776 the Americans had completely retreated, never to return.

WARFARE IN THE ATLANTIC REGION

The Americans had desperately wanted Quebec, but they did not feel the same way about Nova Scotia—partly because it was protected by the British navy at Halifax, and partly because there was even less evidence that its residents were prepared to support an invading army. Some of the Yankee settlements on the Bay of Fundy had long chafed under Halifax's refusal to allow them their traditional New England forms of local government, and several American 'patriots' attempted to channel this discontent in more visible and specific directions. Legislation calling up a militia and imposing a tax for its support produced a petition of objection signed by 250 inhabitants of the Chignecto area, protesting against having to march 'into different parts in arms against their friends and relations'. The legislation was suspended, but discontent continued to simmer, local leaders complaining that some residents had 'a chaise and six horses, postillion and flag of liberty, and drove about the isthmus, proclaiming the news and blessings of liberty.'[17] Historians over the years have debated the extent of the unrest in Nova Scotia in 1775 and 1776, but the current view is that it was considerable, if unable to find a focus and firmly repressed by the authorities.[18]

For active American sympathizers like Jonathan Eddy and John Allan, the introduction of a few rebel troops would soon settle the question, and the two attempted to persuade the Continental Congress to mount a general invasion. Instead, they had to settle for a private army recruited chiefly from Machias (now in Maine) and Maugerville (now in New Brunswick). Consisting of 80 men, this contingent marched overland from the Saint John River towards the British outpost at Fort Cumberland in late October and early November 1776. This invasion was joined by some Chignecto residents, but was quickly suppressed by British reinforcements, leaving those Nova Scotians who had supported the Americans either to explain away their actions or to depart for American lines, leaving their wives and families behind them to be sworn at and 'often kicked when met in the street'. Not until 1779 were these refugee families exchanged for Loyalist prisoners. Rebel farms were seized for damages, and anonymous letters were written to legal officers threatening violence if more writs of seizure were executed.[19] Civil wars in this period could be truly nasty.

The Fort Cumberland business was more typical of this war than the full-scale invasion of Quebec had been, and such divisions among civilians were not to be treated lightly. Away from the armies, the opposing parties—rebel and loyalist—fought vicious little battles with one another for control of the 'neutral' population, often paying back old personal injuries along the way.

Privateers captured unarmed vessels on the high seas and attacked undefended settlements along the coasts. Between 1775 and 1781, they brought commerce to a halt in the Atlantic region for long periods of time, causing serious food shortages, particularly in Newfoundland and on the Island of Saint John, both of which went for years without receiving a single vessel from overseas. On the borders between loyal and rebel territory, guerrilla fighters (often including Native allies) raided farms and villages. Since most of the population of the northernmost colonies was located either on the coast or near a border with the Americans, everyone lived in constant fear of attack.

The need to make decisions about loyalties was largely confined to the earlier years of the rebellion and to the areas under military threat from the Americans, real or potential. The vast majority of people in the northernmost provinces who sided with the rebels left for the south in the first months after Lexington. Among those who remained, some found their commitment to their homes severely tested. This was certainly the case for the fishing communities of Newfoundland, which in addition to suffering food shortages came under pressure from the British recruiters who were extremely active on behalf of both army and navy. Between the press gangs and the privateers, the offshore fishery—particularly the bankers—was virtually wiped out for the duration. As late as 1781 a British official reported 'an amazing number of privateers when I arrived off the coast', and indeed in that year 16 privateering vessels were captured in Newfoundland waters.[20]

The offshore fishery was also the migratory fishery, and one of the major results of the American Revolution was that the resident population came to dominate the fishery. Local agriculture was encouraged, but in the short run could not fill the need for food. Prices skyrocketed, and one observer reported that Newfoundlanders were actually eating their own fish. In Conception Bay 'a raging Famine, Nakedness & Sickness' took hold over the winter of 1779–80. The local missionary wrote: 'None can express the heart felt woe of Women & Children mourning for want of Food.'[21] Many of the inhabitants of the outports removed to St John's, where they hoped to find work and sustenance. The population of the town grew considerably during the war, and some enlisted in the Newfoundland Volunteers, a militia group organized partly to provide government assistance for the unemployed and impoverished.

Whatever the attitude of the population in any northern region in 1775, by 1781 those sympathetic to the American cause had either left for the south or learned to keep quiet about their allegiance.

THE WEST AND THE AMERICAN REVOLUTION

Canadian students have only a hazy idea of developments in the backcountry during the period of the American Revolution. Often particularly difficult to comprehend is British policy in the region south of the Great Lakes, which is frequently neglected because it eventually ceased to be Canadian territory.

THE GREAT LAKES REGION

The revolutionary period was a complex one for the Great Lakes region. It saw the beginnings of serious European settlement in the backcountry regions of Virginia (now Kentucky). Many of the incoming settlers purported to be fleeing from the politics and warfare of the rebellion, and they could claim either American or British allegiance, depending on circumstances, while they took over vast tracts of Aboriginal land. The period also saw a continuing quest on the part of both the British and the American governments for a satisfactory 'Indian policy'. The British attempted to recruit the First Nations to their side for military purposes, while the Americans launched expeditions into the *pays d'en haut* in order to distract the local peoples from their alliances with the British. The most notorious expedition was led by George Rogers Clark in 1778. Clark was a pioneer settler of Kentucky who persuaded the Virginia government to sanction a punitive

invasion of the Ohio country ostensibly controlled by the British. In 1777–8 he led a small army of about 180 men west, capturing Kaskaskia, Vincennes, and eventually Fort Sackville after a series of difficult overland passages. Although he was unable to take Detroit, he also discovered that the Illinois country could easily be wrested from the British. His forces remained in control of the Illinois territory for the remainder of the war, establishing much of the basis for the American claim to this vast territory in the subsequent peace negotiations.

Having found that the region was ripe for the taking, Clark temporarily shifted his strategy from attacking the Native people to recruiting them, along with the 'interior French', to serve in his army. The British had some Native allies in the east, notably the Mohawk war chief Joseph Brant, but few Native leaders in the west had as clear a grasp of the future as Brant did. The Americans were also aided by the ham-handed approach of the British commander in the region, Colonel Henry Hamilton, who operated out of Detroit and was eventually captured by Clark at Vincennes in 1779.[22] The Americans demonized Hamilton as 'the Hair Buyer'—a reference to the bounties he offered for scalps—and both sides exchanged tales of brutalities and atrocities. Eventually the Americans' transparent hostility towards the First Nations would encourage the expansion of British influence in the region, but by then it was too late. The First Nations would soon discover that the British had turned the territory over to the United States in the peace treaty.

OPENING UP THE NORTHWEST

Unlike the territory south of the Great Lakes, the fur-trading lands of the northern peripheries, from Labrador to Hudson Bay, were virtually untouched by the war. The Proclamation of 1763 should have had a considerable impact on the fur trade in the traditional up-country region of the St Lawrence watershed, by setting it off as an Aboriginal reserve and requiring licences to

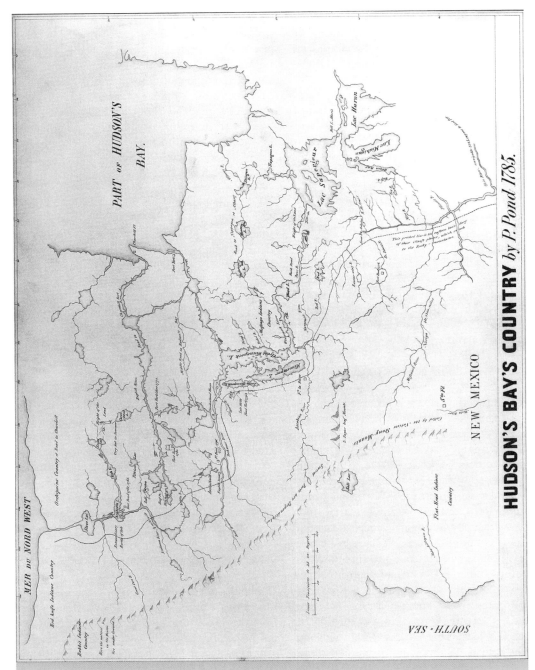

□   Peter Pond's map of the HBC Territory. Library of Congress, Geography and Map Division,
Kohl Collection #137.

■ Prince of Wales Fort (Churchill, Man.), c. 1777. This illustration accompanied Hearne's account of his travels, *A Journey from Prince of Wales's Fort in Hudson's Bay to the Northern Ocean* (1795). LAC, C-41292.

trade. Theoretically the licences were available to English and French alike, but Anglo-Americans who had arrived in Quebec with the army had better connections with the English market, and soon came to dominate the trade. Controlling the traders became increasingly difficult for the British government, since it required the co-operation of all the colonies—not easy to achieve even in better times. Gradually, Quebec increased its control of the northern trade, and in 1774 the Quebec Act returned the administrative responsibility for the northwestern territory to the colony.

The British traders were unable to make much headway south of the Great Lakes, for the Ohio and Illinois country were both controlled by 'interior French' traders. Not surprisingly, they turned their attention to the north, and began to employ Canadien voyageurs to travel towards Hudson Bay. Colonial Americans like Peter Pond seemed relatively unaffected by the American Revolution, continuing to ship their furs through Montreal regardless of the political

changes that had taken place. What mattered was that the northwestward movement of the Montreal-based fur traders had built up momentum. By the time of Lexington and Concord, they were pressing up the Saskatchewan River into the basin of the Churchill. In 1778 Pond made the breakthrough into the Athabasca region, the richest fur-trade country of North America. The competition of the 'Pedlars from Quebec', as one HBC man contemptuously referred to them, galvanized the English company into more aggressive action, and it began moving inland from the Bay to posts on the Saskatchewan. But the company was not able to compete on equal terms with the Quebecers, who were simply more ruthless and more ambitious.

Competition was always a mixed blessing for the First Nations, the primary labour force in the fur trade. On the one hand, rivalries among fur traders gave them a choice, and (as modern consumer organizations always insist) choice means control. On the other hand, the demand for trade goods among Aboriginal people was relatively inelastic, constrained by their limited needs and their itinerant way of life, which worked against the accumulation of possessions. Guns and ammunition, knives, cooking pots, and blankets were the sorts of practical goods that Aboriginal people could use, and the saturation point was easily reached. Competition meant higher prices and constant bidding for favour on the part of the fur traders, which inevitably led to increases in the quantities of non-material consumer goods—particularly tobacco and alcohol—introduced into the system. At the same time, competition also meant increasing intimidation of Native people by the fur traders, particularly the men from Montreal. The increasing incidence of both addictive commodities and violence in the trading system was a direct consequence of increasing competition.

THE PACIFIC SLOPE

Even more remote from the war were events on the Pacific coast. In 1776 the British Admiralty decided to send Captain James Cook on another quest for the Northwest Passage. The expedition was motivated in part by increasing European activity in the Pacific region, but especially by new information that led the British Parliament to offer a £20,000 reward for discovery of the fabled route to Asia. In 1771 Samuel Hearne of the HBC had trekked overland to the mouth of the Coppermine River, where he saw the Arctic sea; and although Hearne had seen no obvious passage, there might be one to the north. Hopes were further encouraged by the appearance in England of a Russian map, ostensibly based on first-hand information from Russian fur traders,

■ 'Inside of a House in Nootka Sound', March–April 1778. The drawing that was the basis for this engraving was made by John Webber, the draftsman on the Cook expedition. Metropolitan Toronto Reference Library.

showing Alaska to be an island separated from the mainland by a wide strait that might run into the Arctic Ocean.

James Cook had spent his early years as a hydrographer, surveying the coast of Newfoundland, and he had already made two important voyages to the South Pacific that had completely changed European perceptions of the region. Cook sailed again in July 1776 (the same month when the Americans signed their Declaration of Independence), rounding the Cape of Good Hope and crossing the Pacific Ocean to the northwest coast of America. He arrived off the Oregon coast in March 1778 and anchored later that month in Resolution Cove, Nootka Sound, off the western coast of Vancouver Island. Here he and his crew observed the local 'Nootka' (Nuu-chah-nulth) people who inhabited the shores of the cove. Cook and his crew were much impressed with their trading acumen and especially their principal trading commodity: the sleek, thick pelts of the sea otter. Cook left Nootka Sound on 26 April and continued north, but was unable to find any passage to the east. On the return voyage to England via the Pacific, Cook was killed by the usually peaceful people of the Sandwich Islands (now Hawaii). But his men carried on, and an impressive account of the voyage was published in England in 1784. Cook had worked out the outline of the northwest coast with some accuracy, and his officers provided much detail about the indigenous people of the region, including some wonderful drawings by the artists attached to the expedition. What most struck many readers of the official account, however, were the sea-otter pelts, and there was soon a rush to cash in on their obvious value, particularly in the difficult Chinese market. In 1786, a French scientific expedition commanded by the Comte de Lapérouse (who had earlier been involved in Hudson Bay) made its way down the western coast of America from Alaska to California before crossing the Pacific to China.[23] At about the same time, another expedition sponsored by the

Bombay Council of the East Indian Company, led by James Strange, arrived at Nootka Sound.[24] The Pacific slope had been discovered.

THE END OF THE WAR

Captain Cook's ships were still making their way home in 1781, when Britain conceded defeat in the War of the American Revolution. Most British statesmen, and most American loyalists, always held that a few hotheaded agitators had stirred up and misled the common people, whose deep-seated allegiance to the Crown would reassert itself as soon as the scheming politicians were removed. Throughout the war, the British had chased the chimera of the silent majority, apparently unaware that advancing armies, however well-intentioned, tended to make more enemies than friends. Military solutions to movements of national liberation worked no better in the eighteenth than in the twentieth century. Moreover, the Americans had found allies in Europe, particularly among the French, who signed a treaty with the United States in the wake of the abortive invasion from Canada led in 1778 by 'Gentleman Johnny' Burgoyne. The surrender of an entire British army at Saratoga encouraged the French to join the war themselves, but—fortunately for the British in Quebec—the Americans were suspicious of the intentions of their new-found allies, and various proposals to mount a joint invasion of Quebec came to nothing.

Unable to beat the Americans with regular troops, the British increasingly came to rely on provincial loyalist units to do the fighting for them—underlining the extent to which the conflict was in fact a civil war. On the New York and Carolina frontiers, loyalists and rebels fought fierce battles in which no quarter was asked or given, and in which the ostensible reasons for fighting were submerged in a host of other issues. In 1781, with the assistance of the French navy, the American army finally succeeded in trapping another British army under Lord Cornwallis in Virginia. Cornwallis's surrender

THE TREATY OF PARIS, 1783

On 3 September 1783, commissioners for the United States and for Great Britain signed the 'Definitive Treaty of Peace and Friendship between His Britannic Majesty and the United States of America'. As treaties go, this one was relatively brief. Some of the key clauses follow.

Art. I. His Britannic Majesty acknowledges the said United States . . . to be Free, Sovereign and Independent States; that he treats with them as such; and for himself, his Heirs and Successors, relinquishes all claims to the government, propriety and territorial rights of the same, and every part thereof.

V. It is agreed that the Congress shall earnestly recommend it to the Legislatures of the respective States, to provide for the restitution of all estates, rights, and properties which have been confiscated, belonging to real British Subjects: and also of the estates, rights, and properties of Persons resident in Districts in the possession of His Majesty's arms, and who have not borne arms against the said United States: and that Persons of any other description shall have free liberty to go to any part or parts of any of the 13 United States, and therein to remain 12 months unmolested in their endeavours to obtain the restitution of such of their estates, rights and properties as may have been confiscated; and that Congress shall also earnestly recommend to the several States, a reconsideration and revision of all Acts or Laws regarding the premises, so as to render the said Laws or Acts perfectly consistent, not only with justice and equity, but with that spirit of conciliation which, on the return of the blessings of Peace, should universally prevail. And that Congress shall also earnestly recommend to the several States, that the estates, rights, and properties of such last-

mentioned Persons shall be restored to them, they refunding to any Persons who may be now in possession the bona fide price (where any has been given) which such Persons may have paid on purchasing any of the said lands, rights or properties such the confiscation.

And it is agreed that all Persons who have any interest in confiscated lands, either by debts, marriage settlements, or otherwise, shall meet with no lawful impediment in the prosecution of their just rights.

VII. There shall be a firm and perpetual Peace between His Britannic Majesty and the said States, and between the Subjects of the one and the Citizens of the other, wherefore all hostilities both by sea and land shall from henceforth cease: all Prisoners on both sides shall be set at liberty, and His Britannic Majesty shall with all convenient speed, and without causing any destruction, or carrying away any Negroes or other property of the American Inhabitants, withdraw all his Armies, Garrisons, and Fleets from the said United States, and from every Port, Place, and Harbour within the same; leaving in all Fortifications the American Artillery that may be therein: and shall also order and cause all Archives, Deeds, and Papers belonging to any of the said States, or their Citizens, which in the course of the War may have fallen into the hands of his Officers, to be forthwith restored and delivered to the proper States and Persons to whom they belong.

SOURCE: Adam Shortt and Arthur G. Doughty, eds, *Documents Relating to the Constitutional History of Canada 1759-1791* (Ottawa: King's Printer, 1907), 491-3.

was the end of the line for the British ministry that had pursued the war. Having taken heavy criticism for years—mainly because of the costs and therefore the taxes necessitated by the war—the ministry could no longer pretend that victory was just around the corner. The British government fell, and its critics took office to negotiate the peace.

The peace-making process took more than a year, from mid-1781 to 30 November 1782, when provisional articles of peace were finally signed. British recognition of the independence of the United States was among the least contentious of the issues to be negotiated. More troublesome were the questions surrounding boundaries, fishing rights, Aboriginal rights and territory, blacks, and, of course, loyalists. While the emissaries from the two sides met in Paris, rumours were rampant across North America. British authorities in America were forced to address many matters before the final terms of the peace could be formally accepted and announced, and until then it was impossible to adopt an overall policy for what remained of Britain's American empire. The final terms were conditioned by two major factors: first, the British were more desperate than the Americans to end the fighting; and second, having decided to let the Americans go, the British did not want to make the final agreement a grievance. Thus the Americans got almost everything they demanded, and virtually no thought was given to the implications of the peace for what was left of British North America.

SHORT BIBLIOGRAPHY

Beaglehole, J.C. *The Life of Captain James Cook*. Stanford, Calif., 1974. The standard biography.

Brebner, John B. *The Neutral Yankees of Nova Scotia: A Marginal Colony during the Revolutionary Years*, 1937. Repr. Toronto, 1969. An old work, but its interpretation of the revolutionary period in Nova Scotia, emphasizing that the Yankees—like the Acadians earlier—attempted to remain neutral, still dominates the literature.

Clarke, Ernest. *The Siege of Fort Cumberland: An Episode in the American Revolution*. Montreal and Kingston, 1996. A more recent work emphasizing that not all Nova Scotians tried to remain neutral.

Conrad, Margaret, ed. *They Planted Well: New England Planters in Maritime Canada*. Fredericton, NB, 1988. A useful collection of essays from the first Planter Conference.

Dowd, Gregory Evans. *A Spirited Resistance: The North American Indian Struggle for Unity 1745–1815*. Baltimore and London, 1992. Explores the Amerindian agenda in the Ohio Valley.

Lanctôt, Gustave. *Canada and the American Revolution, 1774–1783*. Cambridge, 1967. The conventional wisdom from a Quebec perspective.

Lawson, Philip. *The Imperial Challenge: Quebec and Britain in the Age of the American Revolution*. Montreal and Kingston, 1989. Argues, on the basis of archival digging, that the Quebec Act represented a shift in British constitutional thinking.

Neatby, Hilda. *Quebec: The Revolutionary Age 1760–91*. Toronto, 1966. Older, but still the most comprehensive survey of the period, insisting on the inevitability of British policy concerning Quebec.

———, ed. *The Quebec Act: Protest and Policy*. Scarborough, Ont., 1972. A useful work that includes the Act itself and a selection of the historical writing about it.

Stanley, George F.G. *Canada Invaded 1775–1776*. Toronto, 1973. A solid account of the American invasion, by Canada's leading military historian of the early period.

Stewart, Gordon, and George Rawlyk. *A People Highly Favoured of God: The Nova Scotia Yankees and the American Revolution*. Toronto, 1972. A controversial work arguing that Yankee evangelicalism gave Nova Scotia a new and special identity.

STUDY QUESTIONS

1. What problems confronted the British government in the wake of the 1763 Treaty of Paris?

2. Why did the British issue the Proclamation of 1763?

3. What caused the disappointment of the new American settlers in Nova Scotia?

4. Why was the administration of Quebec so difficult in the years after 1763? How did Governor Carleton resolve the problems?

5. What was happening in the Great Lakes region after 1763?

6. What was the response of Quebec to the American invasions of 1775?

7. What did most supporters of the Americans in the northern colonies do during the war of the American Revolution?

8. Discuss the developments in the West during the American war.

9. How did the 1783 Treaty of Paris disadvantage Britain's loyal colonies?

CHAPTER ELEVEN

Loyalties and Loyalists, 1775–1791

■ The American Revolution was North America's first civil war. Britain's northernmost colonies did not play very active parts in the pre-war buildup. Quebec was inhabited chiefly by francophones who had their own agendas; Newfoundland and the Island of Saint John were too far removed from the agitation and too disorganized; and Nova Scotia's Yankees were probably too dependent on the mother country to mount much opposition to it. Nevertheless, the military activity on the part of the Americans, especially in Nova Scotia and Quebec, forced many people in those two colonies to make choices—often painful ones—early in the war. Most chose to remain loyal to the British Crown.

By the later 1770s the influx of Loyalist refugees north of the border and the British military commitment to those colonies would reinforce earlier decisions to remain part of the empire. In the years after 1781, when the Crown gave up trying to keep the Americans in its empire by force, the British authorities were compelled to do something about the thousands of allies and supporters left within the boundaries of the new United States. The result was a massive state-subsidized relocation of Loyalists to British territory: except for Newfoundland, every remaining British colony in northern North America received Loyalist refugees and disbanded soldiers. Blacks were resettled chiefly in Nova Scotia, First Nations principally in western Quebec.

The Loyalist refugees were a much more complex and multicultural group than was believed in the nineteenth century, and the impact of their arrival varied from place to place. But they remade the political map of British North America, and they greatly influenced its institutions.

THE RANGE OF RESPONSE

Loyalists arriving in British North America were likely to assume that the inhabitants of the northern colonies were untouched by the strife that had driven them from their homes. Nothing could have been further from the truth. For most people in British North America, survival was probably the foremost priority, even before the war had begun. When they were pressed to choose sides, survival no doubt continued to be uppermost in most minds. How one chose to survive, of course, depended largely on circumstances. The responses of inhabitants of the northern colonies—Nelly MacDonald of Tracadie, Island of Saint John; Simeon Perkins of Liverpool, Nova Scotia; Henry Alline of Falmouth, Nova Scotia; and Moses Hazen of St-Jean, Quebec—suggest the range of possible reactions to the complexities of the period.

TIMELINE

1776

Evacuation of Boston by the British. Term 'Loyalist' introduced into common parlance.

1778

Beginning of guerrilla raids from Canada into the Mohawk Valley, New York.

1779

British step up recruitment of blacks. Sir Henry Clinton issues Philipsburg Proclamation. Americans lay waste to Iroquois villages in New York, and Iroquois retreat to Fort Niagara.

1780

'Treason' of Benedict Arnold.

1783

Meetings over evacuation of black Loyalists from New York. Departure of British 'spring fleet' for Nova Scotia. Founding of Saint John, Shelburne, and Kingston. '55' petition for land in Nova Scotia. Loyalist Claims Commission established.

1784

New Brunswick and Cape Breton set off from Nova Scotia. Joseph Brant's Mohawks move to Grand River Valley.

1785

American Congress sets aside land for French-Canadian supporters.

1787

Charles Inglis consecrated first Anglican bishop of British North America.

1789

Proclamation of United Empire Loyalist designation by Lord Dorchester.

1791

Upper and Lower Canada established.

1792

Black Loyalists leave Nova Scotia for Sierra Leone.

1798

Cut-off date for arrival in Upper Canada of those to be designated United Empire Loyalists.

1880

Egerton Ryerson publishes *The Loyalists of America and their Times*.

1883

Loyalist Centennial celebrated in New Brunswick.

1900

Imperial Order of the Daughters of the Empire founded.

1914

United Empire Loyalist Association incorporated.

THE LOYAL WOMAN

Helen (Nelly) MacDonald (*c.* 1750–1803) was one of countless women everywhere in North America who were required to manage family affairs when the men went off to war. She had arrived on the Island of Saint John in 1772, and three years later, when her brothers John and Donald were commissioned in Colonel Maclean's Royal Highland Emigrants, she was left to supervise both the Highland settlement at Tracadie and the complex business interests of her family. John MacDonald—who was not simply a farmer but a self-conscious Highland laird responsible for a number of dependent tenants—did not return until 1792. Thus, for 17 years Nelly MacDonald was responsible not only for the family farm, with its 90 head of cattle, but for the estate and the rents to be collected from tenants—rents that were often paid in kind and therefore had to be marketed and sold. In addition, she oversaw the construction of a house for her brother, according to his specifications, and was expected to gather local political intelligence and send it to Halifax.

A constant flow of advice, orders, and remittances went from Halifax to Tracadie. 'You & the People should have dances & Merriment Among Yourselves', wrote John MacDonald in 1780, for 'it is very reasonable that You Should be innocently Merry, & make the Time pass Smoothly.' When Nelly contemplated marriage to a young officer she had met at one such gathering, however, her brother objected strenuously. The young man had no capital but his commission, and no family background: 'You had better not throw yourself away' and 'make yourself & me look silly in the Eyes of the world', he warned. As well as advice and orders, brother John sent 'care packages', which on one occasion included eight pairs of shoes and two pairs of galoshes. Although she had hoped to find a more congenial place to spend the war, Nelly MacDonald never left the island and suffered for years from its many privations.[1]

THE REBEL SOLDIER

Recommended early in 1775 for an army commission by Governor Guy Carleton, Massachusetts-born Moses Hazen (1733–1803) initially worked for the British. He was responsible for informing Carleton of the impending American invasion, and subsequently met with the American general, Philip Schuyler, to discourage the American advance. Attempting to play both sides, Hazen was arrested on succeeding days by the Americans and the British, and then spent 54 days in a Montreal jail refusing British offers for his loyalty. He was ultimately freed by the American army on its way to invade in November 1775. Sent as a messenger to the American Congress with the news of the failure of the attack and the death of General Richard Montgomery, Hazen was appointed by the Congress to command a regiment to be raised in Canada; he was promised indemnification for any loss of British pension he would sustain by entering American service.[2]

Returning to Canada, Hazen was initially successful in recruiting habitants for his regiment, and stopped at 250 men only because he ran out of money: the offer was for 40 livres in bonus plus a monthly stipend, recruits to supply their own clothing and equipment. But Hazen soon discovered the limits to Canadien enthusiasm. By April 1776 he was complaining that the habitants—resentful of having their goods looted and their property seized by an American army that was living off their land and paying only in worthless paper currency—were only 'waiting an opportunity to join our enemies'. In June 1776 Hazen retreated from Canada with the American forces and thereafter spent several years attempting—never quite successfully—to clear his name of charges of financial irregularities raised against him by, among others, Benedict Arnold. His regiment, in which the Canadiens were augmented by later American recruits, fought at the Battle of Brandywine in Pennsylvania in 1777, losing four officers and 73 men in what became an American rout; it never fought in a major engagement after October 1777, but served in a variety of non-combatant roles until it was disbanded at White Plains, NY, in November 1783.

Hazen spent the years after the war in ill health and in constant financial difficulties. He lost his lands in Canada to creditors (they were resettled, ironically enough, by incoming American Loyalists). As for the Canadiens who had served in his regiment, they and their families ended the war as stateless wards of the American Congress, which asked the state of New York to accept most of them as citizens. Not until well into the nineteenth century were the claims of Canadian and Nova Scotian refugees in the United States finally settled. Their experiences during and after the Revolution are a useful reminder that, in civil wars, questions of loyalty are never simple. Not all the refugees created by the American Revolution were United Empire Loyalists settling in British North America: the Loyalists had their counterparts in the United States.

THE LOYAL CIVILIAN

Like Moses Hazen, Simeon Perkins (1734/5–1812) was a native of New England, born in Norwich, Connecticut, to a prominent family. Perkins joined the pre-revolutionary Yankee migration to Nova Scotia, arriving in the fishing and lumbering town of Liverpool in May 1762 as one of the colony's 142 proprietors. There he engaged as a merchant in both trades, built a house (which has been preserved), and acquired positions of political importance that included a seat on the township committee (1770) and a commission as lieutenant-colonel of the militia (1772). As a merchant trading with both New England and the mother country, Perkins was more conscious of the developing conflict than most Nova Scotians. His response to the repressive measures adopted by Parliament in 1774 in the wake of the Boston Tea Party was to fear 'disagreeable consequences', and he was in New England in 1775 at the time of the Lexington affair that provoked open rebellion.

Despite his awareness of the implications, Perkins returned to Liverpool on 28 May 1775 and carried on with both his own business affairs and the local administrative duties ordered from Halifax. Nevertheless, his emotional confusion over loyalties is revealed in diary entries such as this one from 1776, about

American privateering depredations on his vessels: 'This is the fourth loss I have met with by my countrymen.'[3] Perkins mobilized the local militia, attended meetings of the Nova Scotia Assembly at Halifax to defend his community against charges of disloyalty, and carried on with his affairs. His position was perhaps best revealed in a diary entry from early 1777: 'I should be happy to be in a private station in these times of difficulty, but as I had been a Magistrate many years in times of tranquillity, it might be out of character to resign in times of difficulty.'[4] Despite conflicting allegiances, Simeon Perkins remained consistently loyal to his community, his colony, and his monarch. And as the war continued, the personal conflict lessened, for when American privateers raided both Liverpool itself and its vessels at sea, the United States was forcibly established as 'the enemy'. The Nova Scotia government was slow to provide Liverpool with adequate protection, and the town was forced to defend itself. Later in the war Liverpool even mounted its own privateers, and Perkins invested in some of these enterprises. By 1780 he was appointed a local marshal of the provincial court of admiralty, authorized to auction vessels and cargoes captured at sea by British privateers. Overcoming any personal feelings about his native land, Simeon Perkins eventually found his duty and his self-interest coinciding. The epitaph on his gravestone described him first as 'LOYAL to his KING', and only second—almost parenthetically—as 'A SINCERE CHRISTIAN'.

THE RADICAL DROPOUT

If Simeon Perkins placed political loyalty ahead of religious commitment in his hierarchy of values, Henry Alline (1748–84) of Falmouth reacted to the confusions of the revolutionary period almost entirely in spiritual terms. That response, of course, made an implicit political statement of its own. Born in Newport, Rhode Island, Alline had come to the Minas Basin area of the Annapolis Valley in 1760 with his parents, who received a land grant of 500 acres for themselves and their seven children.

While political turmoil swirled around him, Henry Alline was preoccupied with internal conflict over the state of his soul. Although he continued to be 'chief contriver and ringleader of the frolicks' of his contemporaries, he was actually uneasy and 'would act the hypocrite and feign a merry heart'. By the time the American revolutionary conflict began escalating he was still unmarried, though in his mid-twenties, and his chief concern was with 'carnal passion'. He had a series of visions and walked around for several years 'groaning under a load of guilt and darkness, praying and crying continually for mercy'. He found release through a religious experience on 26 March 1775, when 'redeeming love broke into my soul with repeated scriptures with such power, that my whole soul seemed to be melted down with love.' But this experience hardly resolved Alline's problems, for he had become extremely suspicious of the traditional teachings of the New England Puritanism in which he had been raised. Moreover, while Alline's experiences called for him to go forth to preach the gospel to others, his upbringing told him that only those with formal educational credentials could become ministers.

Alline's struggle with the inconsistencies between his vocation and traditional New England doctrine paralleled the confusion in Nova Scotia resulting from the outbreak of armed rebellion in New England. He noted about the call to preach, soon after his 1775 conversion, that 'the prejudices of education and the strong ties of tradition so chained me down, that I could not think myself qualified for it, without having a good deal of human learning.'[5] He tried unsuccessfully to find passage for Boston, and rejected the offer of a commission in the Nova Scotia militia, deciding that his only commission should be one 'from heaven to go forth, and enlist my fellow-mortals to fight under the banners of Jesus Christ'. On 18 April 1776, a day set aside by the Nova Scotia

government for 'fasting and prayer' over the current emergency—coincidentally the first anniversary of the Lexington battle—Henry Alline decided on a public preaching career. He had successfully rejected both New England and Nova Scotia, in favour of offering to others what he himself had found: a spiritual assurance that rejected and transcended the tribulations of the secular world. In the struggle to make sense of civil war, many routes were possible.

Few in official Nova Scotia appear to have paid much attention either to Alline or to the movement of Christian pietism and rejuvenation he began. Not until well after his death in 1784, which occurred while he was on a preaching tour to New England, did the authorities in Church and state begin to recognize the dangers of the levelling egalitarianism he had espoused, which rejected secular authority in favour of the self-government of the godly. Alline deliberately denied that 'earthly dignity, the esteem of man or a conspicuous station in the world' made a man of God, insisted that political leaders would have no special privileges on the day of judgement, and emphasized that Christ commanded his followers 'to salute no man by the way'. For those who shared his vision, Alline insisted on withdrawal from 'this ensnaring world' on the grounds that 'you have no continuing city here.' In his own way Henry Alline was a radical leveller, with populist overtones. He travelled the countryside composing and singing hymns, regarding music not only as a way to attract and hold an audience, but as a useful vehicle on the road to salvation. To the Atlantic region he left a legacy of evangelism and revivalism—his followers were called 'New Lights'—although his theological concepts found their greatest appeal among the Free Will Baptists of the United States. In a period of confusion in Nova Scotia, however, when the province was experiencing the fallout from the American Revolution, Alline—whose own life was a form of rebellion against society—offered an alternative to public declarations of political allegiance.

■ 'Portrait of Joseph Brant', c. 1807, by William Berczy, oil on canvas. This portrait was painted after Brant's death in November 1807, perhaps as a tribute, but Berczy had painted him from life at least once. In 1799 he wrote of Brant: '. . . he is near 6 feet high in stance, of a stout and durable texture able to undergo all the inconvenience of the hardships connected with the difficulties to carry on war through immense woods and wildernesses—His intellectual qualities compared with the phisical construction of his bodily frame—he professes in an eminent degree a sound and profound judgement. He hears patiently and with great attention before he replies and answers in general in a precise and laconic stile. But as soon as it is the question of some topic of great moment, especially relative to the interest of his nation he speaks with a peculiar dignity—his speech is exalted energy and endowed with all the charm of complete Retorick.' National Gallery of Canada, Ottawa, 5777. Purchased 1951.

THE LOYALISTS

The defeat of the British in Boston and the subsequent evacuation of the city by the British army under General Howe in early 1776 provided the northernmost colonies with their first wave of Loyalist refugees. Quebec received its first Loyalist exiles several years after Nova Scotia did; they were greater in number, and tended to be more militant, having experienced bitter fighting between Tories and Patriots. In Westchester County, New York, the Loyalist forces were known as 'cowboys' and 'cattle rustlers', while their patriot counterparts were called 'skinners' because of their tendency to skin victims of all possessions.[6] Some arrived in Quebec with Loyalist regiments, while others joined irregular military organizations (such as Butler's Rangers) after their arrival. Quebec served as a staging ground for frequent British guerrilla attacks on areas such as the Mohawk Valley of New York. In response to such raids, in 1779 the Americans mounted a major expedition into the land of the Six Nations Iroquois, led by General John Sullivan, who was ordered by George Washington to lay waste the countryside. The Iroquois, including Joseph Brant, were forced to retreat to Fort Niagara, where they appealed to the British for assistance.

Nova Scotia (including the future New Brunswick) and Quebec (including the Niagara district) received most of the Loyalists retreating during the war. As the fighting wound down and peace negotiations began in Paris, the British ruthlessly sacrificed their American allies and supporters. They gave in to demands from the United States delegates for the western lands claimed by the Native peoples. They agreed to allow the American government to shift responsibility for any Loyalist compensation to the states, which were not party to the treaty. Meanwhile, Loyalist refugees and soldiers were drawn to New York City—the last major centre of British power and authority in the new United States. There they waited anxiously for word about the peace negotiations, while agents fanned out across the remains of Britain's loyal American empire, from Nova Scotia to the Caribbean, in search of a refuge for them.[7]

By autumn of 1782 it was fairly clear that the losers in the peace settlement would be the Loyalists and the Native peoples. British commander-in-chief Sir Guy Carleton began to arrange for the movement of large numbers to Nova Scotia, and on 22 September 1783 he sketched out a policy for Loyalist relocation. He emphasized that land grants were to be 'considered as well founded Claims of Justice rather than of mere Favor', to be made without fees or further obligation.[8] He expected that families would receive from Nova Scotian authorities 600 acres (243 hectares) of land and single men 300 acres (120 hectares), as well as tools from New York stores.

These arrangements, it should be emphasized, were an improvised response to a rapidly emerging crisis: New York would soon be handed over to the Americans, and the thousands of Loyalists waiting there would have to be removed for their own protection. No provisions were made for those soldiers in the various provincial (or Loyalist) regiments recruited in America, but this oversight was corrected early in 1783, when the policy for civilians was extended to them. Regular British regiments disbanded in the colonies would receive similar land allotments. Neither Carleton nor the British made any attempt at a careful definition of Loyalism at this point. They assumed that all those who had congregated in New York qualified for assistance, as did many soldiers and sailors not in New York but about to be discharged in America. Subsequent policies adopted by the various colonies receiving Loyalists and other American settlers would further complicate the picture.

The question of qualification for compensation was far more difficult than that of immediate assistance.[9] Those whose property had been overrun by invading armies—whether in the loyal or the rebellious provinces—were not eligible for compensation. Almost by definition, the only people who could be compensated were those exiled Loyalists who had lost offices and property in the United States because of their publicly acknowledged political allegiance. The British never claimed that those compensated were the only true Loyalists. But such a conclusion was tempting.

American settlers continued to stream into the loyal provinces of British North America long after the initial transplantation of exiles in 1782–4. The distinction between Loyalists and post-Loyalists was no clearer than that between 'resident Loyalists' and 'refugee Loyalists' (only the latter were entitled to receive compensation). In Upper Canada, Americans (sometimes called 'late Loyalists') continued to pour into the province after 1790.[10] Some of the newcomers were pacifist Quakers and Mennonites attracted by promises of exemption from military service in Upper Canada. Others were fleeing the new American Constitution or Pennsylvania's repression of illegal whisky in the 1790s. Most, however, were probably apolitical settlers simply looking to take up land from public or private developers as part of the westward-moving frontier. Not until 1798 did the Upper Canadian government change its policy of permitting the American arrivals to take an oath of allegiance with few questions asked and adding them to the bounty rolls (lists of those eligible for government assistance) as 'United Empire Loyalists'.

DEMOGRAPHIC COMPOSITION OF THE LOYALIST REFUGEES

No complete demographic picture of the Loyalists of all the provinces that would become Canada—either refugee or resident—is currently available. A perfectly accurate one is probably impossible.

Tracing individual Loyalists back from Canadian settlement to their American and European origins is as difficult as keeping track of them after they first receive a grant of land.[11] Even the most detailed files—on refugees applying for compensation from the British government—are incomplete in important respects. Moreover, applicants to the Loyalist Claims Commission were hardly a representative cross-section of the newcomers.[12] Few of those granted land ever filed a claim, for example. The total numbers of those actually resettled by the British are uncertain. Nor do we know how many of those who received land grants actually took up their holdings.

What is clear is that not everyone who received land grants or other forms of local assistance was a civilian Loyalist refugee. Nearly half of those supported under the various Loyalist resettlement programs were disbanded soldiers. Most of these were American colonials who had formed the so-called 'Loyalist regiments'. But in both these units and regular army units, replacements had come from wherever they could be found. Historical investigation of the Loyalist regiments is still in its infancy.[13] As for the British regular army, it was an international mercenary force that included a number of units from George III's German territories (such as Hesse) and large contingents of Irish and Highland Scots who spoke little English. The civilian refugees often organized into private syndicates to acquire land (the Associated Loyalists, the Bay of Fundy Adventurers), while the disbanded soldiers tended to group together under their former officers.

Newfoundland officially received no Loyalist refugees, although a few may have ended up there. Cape Breton Island and the Island of Saint John took in about 1,000 each. The Loyalists arrived on the two islands some time after the initial period of transportation from New York to Nova Scotia in 1782 and 1783. Many had probably already received land (and been counted as Loyalists) in Nova Scotia, where about 35,000 Loyalists (including more than 3,000 loyal blacks) had arrived. More than 10,000 sought refuge in the colony of Quebec; most settled in what would become Upper Canada, around Kingston (Cataraqui) in the east and Fort Niagara in the west. Among these refugees were members of the Six Nations Iroquois who had been driven out of their homelands in New York State because of their refusal to abandon their traditional alliance with the British Crown. More than 2,000 exiles settled around Sorel near Montreal; until 1792 they were forbidden to settle in the Eastern Townships, ostensibly for military reasons.

An outside estimate of all the newcomers by 1800 (not all of whom would necessarily be defined as 'true Loyalists') would be 50,000—perhaps half of all the former American residents who chose to go into exile (the rest went to Britain, Florida—still British in the 1780s—and the Caribbean). Compared to the numbers of refugees from political turmoil in the modern Third World (two million or more in Rwanda alone), these numbers seem quite modest. In relation to the population of the United States at the time, however, they were substantial. The number of American residents who supported the British—perhaps 20 per cent of the total population of British origin—was considerably greater than the number that chose exile.

As many as half of Canadian Loyalists can be traced to New York. This was perhaps not surprising, given New York's proximity to Quebec and its role as a refuge for loyal Americans at the conclusion of the war. Not all Loyalists who were in New York in the early 1780s were necessarily long-term residents of the state. The proportion of New Yorkers was very high in some districts of resettlement. In eastern Ontario, for example, more than 80 per cent of the settlers came from New York and what would become Vermont.[14] Suggestive evidence indicates that many Loyalists from upstate New York had only recently immigrated to the American colonies as part of a massive wave of British immigration to America in the 1760s and 1770s, between the end of the Seven Years' War and the start of the

LOYALIST CLAIMS

In the years after the end of the American Revolution, commissioners travelled across the British North American colonies hearing claims for compensation from Loyalists. Following is the record of a claim heard in Saint John in 1787.

778. Case of ELIZTH. CAMPBELL, widow of Moses Campbell, now Elizabeth Finlayson, late of New York.

Claimt being sworn saith:

Her Husband was a native of Scotland. Had been a Seargent in war before last. Was settled on Lake Champlain when the Troubles broke out. On Major Allan Campbell's Lot between Crown Point & Ticonderoga. In the last Rebellion he joined Genl. Fraser immediately. Was afterwards employed in Indian Department. Continued to be employed till he died in 1781.

Produces Certificates from Genl. Fraser in strong Terms to entitle him to 8 Rations, with several Certificates to his Loyalty & activity & the service he rendered Genl. Fraser.

He has left a Widow, the Claimt. & 8 Children. Alexander, eldest son, now lives near Johnston—of age. Elizabeth Bland Allen. Nancy, now Mrs Sutherland. Catherine, Isabell, James & John. All of the Province.

4 Young Infants live with their Mother. Elizabeth Bland lives in this Town. Mr. Sutherland lives in Point Murellea Township. Allen in same Township, the other four live with their Mother.

He had 200 acres in Major Campbell's Lot, granted at the end of war before last. He had cleared about 20 acres, built an house, Barn & Outhouses. One of the Rebels now lives upon it. Does not know of any Confiscation or Sale. It was a good Tract but does not know how to value it, thinks £250.

Lost 2 horses, Wheat in the Barn, 100 Bushels, Carpenter's Tools, Household Furniture, farming utensils.

Most of these things taken by the Rebels when her Husband first joined Genl. Fraser.

Lost Hay, Boats, Buildings &c. Destroyed after General Burgoyne's Defeat. Does not know by whom they were destroyed.

Alexander Campbell appears, Eldest Son of James Campbell. Says he is 21 years of age. Entitled as he supposes to the Lands. Lives at Mr. Noel's, Shoemaker, in this Town.

CAPT FRASER, Witness: Says he knew the late Moses Campbell. Remembers he joined the Army in 1776 & Served the Campaign in 1777, he was a remarkably good man for his line of Life & active & Loyal.

Knew his Lot. It was about 5 miles above Crown Point. A tolerably good house, an appearance of Considerable Improvemts. He seemed in Circumstances to support his family tolerably well. Major Allen Campbell had a large Lot of Land there & Moses Campbell had been a Seargent in the same Regiment.

SOURCE: *Second Report of the Bureau of Archives for the Province of Ontario by Alexander Fraser, Provincial Archivist*, 1904, Part II (Toronto, 1905), 926–7.

American Revolution.[15] In eastern Ontario a full 17 per cent of the foreign-born Loyalists had arrived in North America within two years of the start of the war.[16] The same tendency towards recent arrival can be found among Loyalist claimants of compensation.[17]

Obviously, not all Loyalists were adult males. Ascertaining how many women and children accompanied the heads of households into Canadian exile (or, as in many cases, later joined them there) is extremely difficult. Available evidence suggests that most of the private soldiers granted land (including drummers and 'volunteers') were single men without families. Close to half of all officers, commissioned and non-commissioned, and more than half of civilian refugees resettled with their families.[18] We do know that 13 per cent of all Loyalist compensation claimants were women.[19] Since claimants were typically heads of households, it appears that as many as one in eight Loyalist households was headed by a female. Just over 30 per cent of eastern Ontario's adult Loyalists were women.[20]

Generalizing about the Loyalists is not easy. They had many reasons for loyalty, rooted in their particular circumstances. They were on one level a cross-section of American society, but on another level many were—for one reason or another—less thoroughly assimilated than the rebels into mainstream American culture and its values.[21] These less-assimilated Americans, often recent immigrants from Europe and perhaps suspicious of American pressures for conformity, may have felt that the British Crown offered a certain protection for their minority position. The American Revolution required a commitment to a complex ideological position based on the principles of the Declaration of Independence. Those who opposed it simply accepted the principle of loyalty to the Crown.

THE BLACK LOYALISTS

One long-neglected minority group among the exiles were the black Loyalists.[22] From the first days of the revolution, the British authorities had tried to recruit some of the colonies' half million slaves to fight against their masters, and in 1779—when the American South was becoming a theatre of war—the British commander-in-chief, Sir Henry Clinton, issued his famous Philipsburg Proclamation, promising to 'every NEGRO who shall desert the Rebel Standard, full security to follow within these Lines, any Occupation which he shall think proper'. Lured by the promise of freedom, thousands made their way to British lines. Of these, more than 3,000 had their names and personal details, including their stories of escape, recorded in a 'Book of Negroes' and were evacuated to Nova Scotia in 1783. Those who did not manage to escape, however, were not so fortunate: many slaves who were seized from their 'owners' and confiscated as property were simply resold by the British (when 43 were taken to Montreal in 1783, they were sold for an average price of £33.15).

Once the black Loyalists arrived in Nova Scotia, they desperately needed land, but they were relegated to the bottom of every list of those eligible for grants. At Port Roseway (later Shelburne), where land grants were delayed for several years, they had been given their own community of Birchtown to the northwest of the main settlement. Fully two-thirds of Birchtown's residents never received any land at all, and the few grants that were made were much smaller than Carleton had promised. This pattern persisted across the colony. Of the more than 3,000 black Loyalists transported to Nova Scotia—most of them males—only 1,155 received any land; the average size of these grants was less than 11 acres. Among the other disadvantages that the black Loyalists suffered, those in Nova Scotia were denied the right to trial by jury, and those in New Brunswick were not permitted to vote. In 1792 nearly half of the black Loyalists in Nova Scotia accepted with enthusiasm the chance to immigrate to the African colony of Sierra Leone.

■ 'A Black Woodcutter at Shelburne, Nova Scotia', by William Booth; watercolour, 1788. LAC, C-40162.

Not all the black newcomers were free. Some arrived as slaves brought to the loyal colonies of British North America by Loyalist masters. Usually listed in the muster rolls under the euphemistic term 'servants', most probably were household rather than field slaves. There were 90 such 'servants' counted in eastern Ontario in October of 1784, and 26 in the first muster of Loyalists on the Island of Saint John in June of that year.[23] According to one estimate, 1,232 slaves were taken to Nova Scotia with white Loyalist refugees.[24]

A number of black people, free and enslaved, appear in court records of this period. In 1786, for example, three indictments were found (for burglary and assault) by a grand jury on the Island of Saint John against Jupiter Wise, a household servant of Captain Burns.[25] The chief prosecution witness was James Stevens, a free black man who had met Wise in the course of organizing the escape of a number of slaves. Over the following decades, as the institution of slavery became a hotly contested issue in all the colonies of British North America, the courts consistently ruled against slave owners. The institution would gradually wither away, but without much evidence of enthusiastic abolitionism.

WOMEN LOYALISTS

Recovering the stories of Loyalist women has not been easy. Most of the surviving official records ignored them almost by definition. One place where women's stories could be found in some detail, however, was in the case files of the Loyalist claimants to the British government for compensation.[26] Of the 3,225 people in all the British American colonies who applied, 468 were women. In most files these women narrated their own stories of suffering during the American war. Their evidence suggests much about the lives that women lived in a highly structured patriarchal society, one in which married women enjoyed few rights. Although women claimants had considerable knowledge about property, particularly in the context of the home, most were not able to provide detailed information about their family's financial losses. Women usually

■ A view of Shelburne in 1789, showing houses used as barracks. Drawing by William Booth. LAC, C-10548.

were not kept informed financially by their husbands. The challenges they faced when suddenly they had to take over supervision of the family property or business were not made any easier by the ignorance in which most had been kept.

Women left behind, without male protection, when their men went off to fight—or to escape a tar-and-feathering—often faced threats and even abuse from 'patriots'. But exile brought troubles of a different kind; many claimants said that when they left their homes, their 'severest trials were just begun'. The loss of their homes and cherished possessions was probably more traumatic for Loyalist women than were the property losses suffered by the men—especially in the early period, when often there were no homes available for the newcomers. When Deborah Smith arrived at Shelburne, late in 1783, 'The snow was about two feet deep. . . . There were a number of houses abuilding, but none finished. . . . It looked dismal enough.'[27] Recreating a stable existence would also be more difficult for women. Loyalist men usually settled among friends and colleagues with whom they

already had personal relationships cemented by military service, but women were often without such support systems. Men also had many more opportunities than women to make new acquaintances outside the home.

While male Loyalists seeking compensation described themselves as 'distressed' or 'unhappy', women most commonly called themselves 'helpless'. The difference in terminology was significant. Men in exile did not perceive themselves as being alone, or in a situation beyond their power to control. But women did, casting themselves in what one scholar has recently called 'the language of enfeeblement'.[28] Men may have sacrificed for a principle, but the decision had been theirs to make. Women who had not been consulted about the political activities of their male relative, or involved in the decisions leading to exile and resettlement, had every right to be bitter. In most cases, their reasons for becoming 'Loyalists' had more to do with family and community ties than with abstract political principles.

Perhaps most unfortunate of all for female Loyalists, exile in the loyal provinces meant isola-

BARBARA RUCKLE HECK
(1734–1804)

Barbara Ruckle Heck was an anomaly in the early history of British North America: a legend in her own time. Given the difficulties of communication in the eighteenth century, the achievement of such a status was no mean accomplishment. She was born in Ireland, although her background was German. She belonged to a group of Palatine refugees who had been resettled by the British government in Ireland in 1709, as the 'Foreign Protestants' would be resettled in Nova Scotia in the early 1750s. Ruckle's particular group of Palatines was converted to Methodism by John Wesley in 1748, and it was as German-Irish Methodists that she and her husband Paul Heck immigrated to New York City in 1760. According to the story, around 1766 she turned angrily against friends who were playing cards in her kitchen. She threw the cards in the fire and set out to find a preacher who could save her from the fires of hell. The result was the foundation of the Wesley Chapel in New York, the first Methodist church in the city, which was opened in 1768. A few years later, the Hecks withdrew from New York City, which was apparently too worldly, and moved to the countryside at Camden Township, near Bennington, Vermont. When the American Revolution came, Paul Heck joined a Loyalist regiment, his farm was confiscated, and with other Palatine families the Hecks in 1785 sought refuge in Quebec in Township No.7 (Augusta). Their settlement served as the beginning of the Canada Conference of the Methodist Episcopal Church, and Barbara Heck's piety became well-known in Methodist circles of the time. It was said that she died on her knees, praying. Barbara would later become celebrated as the founder of Methodism in Canada. Interestingly enough, in many ways her life tells us more about Loyalism than about Methodism. The Hecks were typical of one stream of Loyalists: recent immigrants from Europe, of non-British background, and members of a religious minority likely to face persecution from patriotic Americans.

tion from all the anti-patriarchal republican ideas and language associated with the Revolution. Loyalist women not only lost their homes and families but were forced into an inflexible patriarchal straitjacket, and got lost to history.

ETHNIC LOYALISTS

As we have seen, not all the Loyalists had been born in British North America. The Anglican clergyman Jacob Bailey characterized his new neighbours in the Annapolis Valley as 'a collection of all nations, kindreds, complexions and tongues assembled from every quarter of the globe'.[29] One study has found that of the 1,422 compensation claimants living in North America, only 721—just over half—were native-born Americans.[30] A study of eastern Ontario produced similar findings, with American-born and foreign-born Loyalists virtually equal in numbers.[31] If one disregards the American–European distinction of birthplace and looks instead at ethno-national origin, nearly 30 per cent of eastern Ontario Loyalists were of German back-

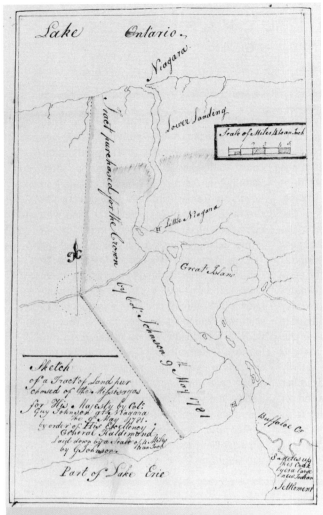

■ 'Sketch of a Tract of Land purchased of the Missisagas for His Majesty by Col. Guy Johnson at Niagara the 9th of May 1781'. In exchange for 300 suits of clothing, the British acquired 3 million acres of land for Loyalist settlers. Archives of Ontario RG 1-A1-1, vol. 1, 67.

Loyalists who moved north in the 1780s came from a wide range of backgrounds, and in many cases had little in common besides their experience of revolution and their allegiance to the Crown. The high percentages of Loyalists born outside North America and, in particular, recently arrived on the continent suggest that we should not overemphasize the cultural 'American-ness' of the Loyalists.

NATIVE LOYALISTS

In its own way the experience of the Native Loyalists paralleled that of the blacks. In Canada the best-known Native Loyalists were those from the Iroquois or Six Nations Confederacy, who ultimately settled in what would become southern Ontario.[33] Although some individual Mohawks supported the British—especially members of the Brant family, who had close connections with the Johnsons of upstate New York, long dominant in British superintendancy of the Iroquois people—most of the Six Nations had tried to remain neutral. The British put far greater pressure on the Iroquois to break their neutrality than did the Americans, arguing that the two peoples had long been united by covenant chain in perpetual alliance. Not all the Iroquois were persuaded. Their families were often as divided as European ones.

Like the Loyalists themselves, who got nothing more out of the peace negotiations than a vague promise that their claims would be taken to the several states for consideration, the First Nations were virtually abandoned by Britain in its haste to put an end to an expensive and unpopular war. When the British transferred to

ground. Another quarter were of Scottish stock. Substantial proportions of New Yorkers settling in western Quebec/eastern Ontario were Highland Scots and Germans.[32] In short, the

the Americans sovereignty over land south of the Great Lakes and as far west as the Mississippi River, they totally ignored First Nations' claims to most of this land. The First Nations could reasonably argue that they had never surrendered it in the first place. Even Britain's loyal friend Joseph Brant was bitter, declaring the British had 'sold the Indians to Congress'. Part of the problem was the gap between Aboriginal and European interpretations of landownership and sovereignty.

The general British attitude was well demonstrated by the efforts of colonial officials to accommodate Native refugees in what would become Upper Canada. To secure grants for them, Quebec Governor Frederick Haldimand hastily concluded a series of treaties purchasing several parcels of land from the Mississauga. But the land granted to the exiles did not necessarily match the land purchased.[34] Along the Grand River, for example, where 1,843 Native exiles were in residence by 1785, the government granted much more land than it had actually bought from the Mississsauga, thus adding insult to injury in a series of transactions that would never stand much close scrutiny. Moreover, the government of Upper Canada insisted that the Grand River land was earmarked solely for Aboriginal settlers, and could not be sold to Europeans. Joseph Brant maintained that if his people were truly equal to Europeans, they could do what they liked with the land. From the Native standpoint, this issue was never satisfactorily resolved.

LOYALIST ELITES AND COMPENSATION CLAIMANTS

If blacks and First Nations existed at the margins of the Loyalist fold, there was also a considerable Loyalist elite. Part of the story of that elite may be found in the records of the Loyalist Claims Commission. Receiving compensation did not necessarily make a Loyalist a member of the elite, but receiving a British pension certainly did, for pensions were paid in 'real money': pounds sterling. The largest group receiving pensions consisted of the officers of American regiments disbanded in 1783—a total of approximately 1,000, of whom perhaps 600 resided in British North America. These men collected their half-pay pensions regularly as long as they lived, and their widows received the same payments thereafter.

Some claims for compensation were filed in the colonies, others in London.[35] More than half of the colonial claims came from Quebec, mainly from ex-New Yorkers living in the future Upper Canada, even though only about 20 per cent of the Loyalists had settled there;[36] this bias has never been satisfactorily explained, although it may be that there were more claims agents active in that region. There was also a substantial difference in the size of claims filed on each side of the Atlantic. More than half of those resident in British North America submitted claims for less than £500 (854 of 1,426, or 66 per cent). Among former New Yorkers filing in America, more than 70 per cent claimed less than £500; among those filing in London, only 13.8 per cent (193 of 1,400) claimed for less than £500. American-based Loyalists were clearly less well-to-do than those settling in Britain.

A handful of older Loyalist leaders were appointed by the British as major officials in the loyal provinces: Edmond Fanning became lieutenant-governor of the Island of Saint John, John Wentworth became governor of Nova Scotia, William Smith was made chief justice of Quebec, and Charles Inglis became bishop of Nova Scotia. In addition, the administration of the new province of New Brunswick (created out of the upper part of Nova Scotia in 1784) was filled exclusively with Loyalists who had lost offices in the 13 colonies,[37] and a few Loyalist military officers were appointed to civil posts by colonial governors such as Fanning. But in most cases Loyalists did not automatically become the dominant political leaders in their new homes. This was particularly important in Upper Canada. Although Lieutenant-Governor John Graves Simcoe has often been called a 'Loyalist' governor, he was a British army officer whose patronage appointments went chiefly to fellow officers, only a few of whom were themselves Loyalists. In every province there was considerable factional infighting for political dominance. Members of the Loyalist elite fought among themselves, were challenged by the Loyalist rank and file, and in most provinces had to face an entrenched political group of non-Loyalists.

SETTLEMENT AND POLITICS

The three largest groups of Loyalist exiles from New York settled in three 'instant towns' in Nova Scotia and Quebec: Shelburne (formerly Port Roseway) on the southwest coast of the Nova Scotia peninsula; Saint John at the mouth of the Saint John; and Cataraqui (renamed Kingston in 1784) on the eastern shores of Lake Ontario.[38] The two Nova Scotia communities quickly (if temporarily) replicated the urbanity of New York itself. Initially, all these new centres experienced booms based on the availability of British money, but their long-range success would depend on their becoming the centres of some kind of economic activity in their regions.

Located on some of the poorest agricultural land in Nova Scotia and lacking any exploitable resource except fish, Shelburne quickly declined, its collapse assisted by problems with land grants in the area, including long delays in surveying. Saint John would find some economic sustenance in the rich agricultural hinterland of the Saint John River Valley and the new province's seemingly inexhaustible timber resources. Kingston would struggle on as an administrative centre, but with little vitality until well into the nineteenth century. Kingston even served briefly (1841–3) as the provincial capital, but the other two Loyalist towns were isolated from political power in their respective provinces. Loyalist newcomers also swelled the population of Charlottetown on the Island of Saint John, and founded Sydney on Cape Breton Island.[39]

The difficulty of obtaining good land helps to account for one of the most characteristic patterns in Loyalist settlement: few of the newcomers stayed where they were initially settled. The exceptions were the Loyalist military units (the King's Royal Rangers of New York, Jessup's Rangers, Roger's Rangers) that settled in eastern Ontario. In general, Loyalist military groups led by their own officers and united by similar backgrounds provided an element of coherence otherwise absent in many Loyalist settlements. Mobility in quest of better land was encouraged by administrators' failure to provide proper land grants and titles. Loyalists who had only recently arrived in America settled more readily in their new homes, perhaps because they had some experience with starting afresh. The American-born tended to become more quickly dissatisfied with their situation. The most stable newcomers were members of the office-holding elite, who tended to cluster in the provincial capitals.

If the Loyalists were geographically restless, they were also easily discontented and highly vocal in political affairs. Although only a fraction of the new arrivals would be formally compensated for the property they had lost in the United States—and those compensated seldom felt satisfied—all Loyalists felt that they had suffered for their allegiance to the Crown, and they insisted that they deserved both land and government assistance. Moreover, since most of the Loyalists had been accustomed to American-style democracy, they expected to be able to participate in the political process. Most ordinary North American colonists had supported colonial criticisms of British policy right up to the point of the open break with the mother country. Loyalists did not like arbitrary or oligarchic government, and they detested any landholding arrangement—such as leasehold, the seigneurial system, or the payment of quitrents—that was not freehold tenure.

Loyalist political activity thus took place at several levels simultaneously. At one level there were demands to be allowed to share in government. Quebec Loyalists complained bitterly about the absence of a representative assembly in

■ 'Encampment of the Loyalists at Johnston, a New Settlement on the banks of the St Lawrence River in Canada', watercolour by James Peachey, 6 June 1784. An officer in the 60th Regiment, Peachey was deputy surveyor-general at the time, surveying lots for disbanded troops and Loyalist refugees. 'Johnston' was the future Cornwall, Ontario. LAC, C-2001.

the province, and Nova Scotia Loyalists about the domination of the government by pre-revolution inhabitants. On another level, Loyalists were often divided among themselves politically. The chief internal divisions were two. One was between the old colonial office-holding American elite (most of whose members had gone into exile in England or Nova Scotia during the war) and a new one that had emerged in the course of the fighting, consisting mainly of officers of Loyalist regiments, many of whom had not been leaders before the war. This split overlapped with another split between the elite and the more articulate members of the rank and file, who sought a more democratic and open future.

THE LOYALIST IMPACT

The Loyalists' influence on the constitutions, politics, economy, and institutions of British North America was obvious and is easy to document. Their influence on the values and culture of British North America is more complex and problematic, although of great importance.

A combination of Loyalist resettlement and imperial restructuring following the loss of the American colonies completely remade British North America between 1784 and 1791. The Loyalist migration provided the experienced anglophone settlers that Britain had sought after 1763 to people the northern colonies and serve as counterweights to the francophones in Quebec. A first round of imperial reorganization took place in 1784. Cape Breton was recognized as a separate colony and, with the Island of Saint John, was placed under the authority of the governor of Nova Scotia. Disputes between newcomers in the north and the government of Nova Scotia resulted in the creation of New Brunswick as a separate colony in 1784, one that Loyalists could dominate—in the process showing what loyal men and women of ability could accomplish. Most Loyalists were either religious dissenters or totally unchurched. However, enough Loyalist leaders were Anglicans for the Church of England to become the established church of British North America and—with the help of the British government—to remain so for years to

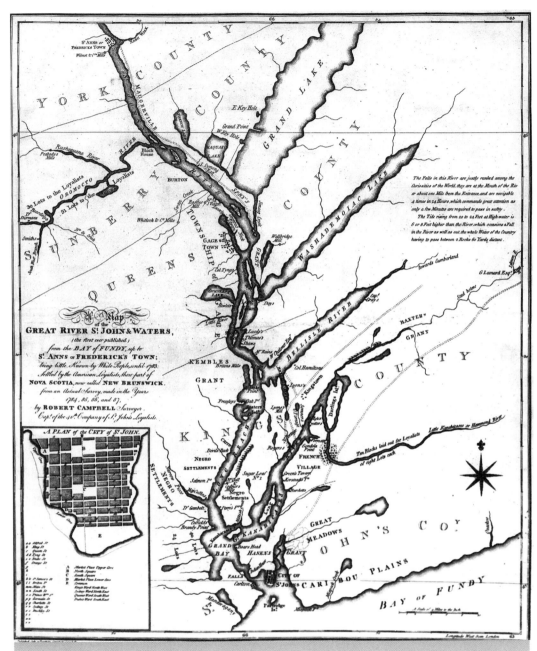

'A Map of the Great River St John & Waters', by Robert Campbell, published in London in 1788. The caption notes that the region was 'little known By White People until 1783 [and] Settled by The American Loyalists'. LAC, NMC-254.

come. Imperial reorganization was completed in 1791, when Upper Canada was separated from Lower Canada and both provinces were given representative government under the Constitutional Act. Intended to guarantee all the King's subjects in British America the same rights, and to provide new revenue for the Crown, the Constitutional Act was important for its acceptance of the 'French fact', but also for its recognition of the separate existence of an anglophone community to the west, which could now attract settlers who would not have considered moving to a predominantly French-speaking province.

The presence of the Loyalists remade the politics of British North America as well as its governments. The newcomers brought with them not only colonial political experience but the rhetoric associated with it. They were firmly committed to representative government and 'the rights of Englishmen' as found in what the Loyalist James Moody called 'that glorious Constitution to which he owed his security'. They also feared rebellion, which for Moody was 'the foulest of all crimes'.[40] They believed in order, hierarchy, and authority, including the right of the state to exercise its power without much restraint. Unlike the Americans, whose fear of unrestrained power led first to rebellion and then to the complex political arrangements worked out in the American Constitution (including the Bill of Rights), the Canadian Loyalists wanted government to play an active role in society and expected to benefit from it. At the same time, we must be careful to appreciate that the Loyalists were, in the language of the eighteenth century, 'True Whigs'. They could be fiercely critical when those governing them did not show 'due Regard to the British Constitution' or sought to invade 'our Liberties striking directly at the Vitals of our most excellent Constitution'. Like other Americans, most Loyalists were firmly opposed to tenancy. Many had been tenants on large estates in New York and were not anxious to repeat the experience.[41] Although landlords would continue trying to construct European-style estates in

British North America until well into the nineteenth century, Loyalist attitudes and demands for freehold land—to which the authorities acceded—set a pattern that became the norm.

We must also be careful about labelling the Loyalists as 'anti-American'. Many despised republicanism and hated the United States. But such hostility could hardly be extended to everyone born or brought up in what became the United States, or who shared American cultural characteristics, such as opposition to tenancy. After all, to object to Americans really meant to object to themselves.

In economic terms, the Loyalists' great gift to British North America was cash money in the form of British settlement assistance, compensation, and pensions.[42] It is impossible to calculate the total cost to Britain of resettling the Loyalists, but the bill was in the millions of pounds—and it came only a few years after an earlier British administration had recoiled from a far smaller bill for settling Nova Scotia. Close to half a million pounds' worth of compensation (in the form of drafts on the British Treasury) was paid to Loyalists resident in British North America between 1783 and 1793. These funds represented a substantial injection of capital into a frontier society.

Institutionally, the Loyalists not only made possible the establishment of the Church of England in British North America, but also pressed for places of higher learning in the colonies. William Smith of Quebec advocated a secular university for his province, and Benedict Arnold (who lived in Saint John as an unpopular Loyalist refugee from 1786 to 1791) spearheaded a premature—and unsuccessful—campaign for a university in New Brunswick. Charles Inglis, however, actually did found King's College in Windsor, Nova Scotia, transferring north the classical ideal of the elitist liberal arts college that the Americans had copied from Oxford and Cambridge.

When we look beyond institutions, the cultural contribution of the Loyalists to British North

BENEDICT ARNOLD

(1741–1801)

■ Benedict Arnold. Everett Collection/
The Canadian Press.

Born to an old Connecticut family fallen on hard times, Benedict Arnold ran away from home at an early age to join the army in New York. With peace, he ran an apothecary shop and a trading business out of New Haven, but he leapt to the defence of American liberties in 1775. He convinced Massachusetts to commission him as a colonel to lead an expedition against Fort Ticonderoga in New York, but circumstances forced him to share the command of the enterprise with Ethan Allen. The fortress surrendered without a shot. Arnold subsequently resigned rather than serve under another officer, but was soon leading another expedition across northern Maine in late autumn to capture Quebec. He ended up commanding the unsuccessful American

army at Quebec, being seriously wounded in the process.

During the first few months of the war against Britain, Arnold had established that he was a charismatic leader of men, recklessly courageous under fire, a superb field commander, but quick to take slights and very disputatious. These traits would follow him throughout the war. His superiors understandably saw him as impetuous and headstrong, the proverbial loose cannon. In the Burgoyne invasion of 1777, Arnold again personally led his troops into battle. But the American Congress was slow to reward Arnold with promotion, and questioned his accounts, leading to a court martial and reprimand. Arnold served as commander at Philadelphia beginning in 1778. This led him into Loyalist society in the city, which he found very congenial—he would marry a beautiful young Tory lady named Margaret Shippee—and to a flirtation with the British that ultimately culminated in October 1780 in his attempt to surrender his command at West Point, which he had personally requested from George Washington, to Sir Henry Clinton in return for £20,000. The plot was revealed when Major John Andre was captured with incriminating documents. The defector escaped by sloop down the Hudson River only minutes ahead of arrest. In a pamphlet published at the time, Arnold claimed that he had never supported independence, and that, moreover, he could not support a country aligned with Catholic France.

Several prominent Americans changed sides during the war, but Arnold was not only late, but had been unusually active on the rebel side, and had, moreover, sold out for cold cash. He moved with his family to England, but returned to New Brunswick in 1785 to rebuild his fortune. The Loyalists hated him, regarding him as untrustworthy. When his store burned to the ground in 1788, he sued his partner for slander for alleging that Arnold had deliberately set the fire himself. The court found the defendant guilty but awarded Arnold only token damages. Arnold soon returned to England. At one point he wrote the British government, 'there is no other Man in England, who has so great Sacrifices as I have done of Property, Rank, Prospects &c in support of Government, and no Man who has received less in Return.'[43] In 1797 he managed to acquire a large land grant of 13,400 acres in Upper Canada, but he always felt relatively unrewarded for his actions. Arnold's 'treason', of course, was felt much more seriously because of the nationalistic nature of the conflict in which it occurred; he was not simply changing sides, but 'betraying his country'.

America is more difficult to assess. On the whole, the Loyalists appear to have strengthened American cultural tendencies already existing in the Maritime region, while providing an alternative to the French culture in Quebec, particularly in the western region that was to become Upper Canada. We have already seen the Loyalist influence at work in landholding patterns and religion. Two other areas where it is still discernible are language and architecture. It would be challenged, of course, first by an anti-American backlash during the War of 1812, especially in Upper Canada, and then by massive immigration from the British Isles beginning after 1815. (We tend to forget that although the Loyalists were immediately followed by another wave of Americans, immigration to British North America in the nineteenth century was largely British.) But in the long run the Loyalists' American cultural patterns prevailed.

In language, the Loyalists helped to establish a North American variant of English in British North America that a subsequent half-century of British immigration could not erase.[44] Travellers in the years before the War of 1812 frequently commented on the Americanized pronunciation, vocabulary, and cadence so commonly found across British North America from Halifax to the Grand River. Canadians would always sound more like their neighbours to the south than their cousins across the water.

In architecture, the Loyalists contributed to the Canadian landscape the colonial-style wooden

Loyalist architecture: the Jonathan Odell house, Fredericton, c. 1785–95. Public Archives of New Brunswick P5/288.

farmhouse and the occasional early Georgian mansion.[45] Perhaps more important, they helped to introduce and popularize American house-building techniques, employing wood-frame and especially balloon-frame construction, unusual in timber-starved Europe and not found in French Canada.[46] According to one later European traveller on Prince Edward Island, all houses were built of wood, most with 'the wood set perpendicularly, and fixed to beams above and below, previously framed together'. In a 'frame-house' like this, he reported, the walls were covered with 'dressed boards nailed on horizontally, overlapping one another to keep out the wind and rain.'[47] The Loyalists also made the wooden fence, especially the pole fence, standard in British North America.

Finally, it has become part of the lore of Canadian political journalism that the Loyalists were responsible for the 'radical Toryism' that has often been seen as peculiarly Canadian.[48] According to this theory, the political culture of the Loyalists was American liberalism tempered by the conservative values of respect for author-ity, community, and strong government, and it was this Tory culture that enabled Canada to adopt radical-liberal policies—including medi-care and state-owned broadcasting—that are anathema in the United States. Unfortunately, this question has not yet been examined with the care it deserves.

CONCLUSION

Despite their obvious importance, the Loyalists have never been unequivocally accepted as one of Canada's founding groups. Much of the resistance has reflected either a Canadian reluctance to make heroes of Americans or a reaction against older, overstated elitist interpretations of Loyalism. Nevertheless, the Loyalists provided a substantial influx of new settlers between 1775 and 1791 (and beyond), which transformed the complexion of British North America. A complex multicultural group of conservative-liberal refugees, partly but not entirely American in origin, perhaps they deserve more recognition.

SHORT BIBLIOGRAPHY

Allen, Robert, ed. *The Loyal Americans: The Military Role of the Loyalist Provincial Corps and their Settlement in British North America, 1775–1791*. Ottawa, 1983. An excellent study of the military contribution of the Loyalists in relation to their resettlement in Canada.

Bell, David G. *Early Loyalist Saint John: The Origin of New Brunswick Politics 1783–1786*. Fredericton, NB, 1983. Focuses on the conflict between Loyalist elite and rank and file.

Brown, Wallace, and Hereward Senior. *Victorious in Defeat: The Loyalists in Canada*. Toronto, 1984. The best general synthesis available on the Loyalists in Canada.

Johnstone, C.M., ed. *The Valley of the Six Nations*. Toronto, 1963. A collection of documents about the resettlement of the Six Nations in Ontario.

Kimber, Stephen. *Loyalists and Layabouts: The Rapid Rise and Faster Fall of Shelburne, Nova Scotia, 1783–1792*. Toronto, 2008. A detailed account of one of the Loyalist boom towns, particularly good on the black Loyalists.

Knowles, Norman. *Inventing the Loyalists: The Ontario Loyalist Tradition and the Creation of Usable Pasts*. Toronto, 1997. A study that emphasizes the importance to Canada of Loyalist mythology.

MacKinnon, Neil. *This Unfriendly Soil: The Loyalist Experience in Nova Scotia, 1783–1791*. Montreal and Kingston, 1986. A detailed account of the Nova Scotia experience.

Moore, Christopher. *The Loyalists: Revolution, Exile, Settlement*. Toronto, 1984. Another useful overview of the Loyalists.

Potter-MacKinnon, Janice. *While the Women Only Wept: Loyalist Refugee Women*. Montreal and Kingston, 1993. The best study of Loyalist women in Canada.

Shenstone, Susan B. *So Obstinately Loyal: James Moody 1744–1809*. Montreal and London, 2000. A recent biography of an important Loyalist, a member of neither the elite nor the rank and file.

Walker, James St G. *The Black Loyalists: The Search for a Promised Land in Nova Scotia and Sierra Leone, 1778–1870*. Halifax, 1976. The most thorough account of the history of the black Loyalists.

STUDY QUESTIONS

1. Why was the evacuation of the black Loyalists so difficult?
2. What choices were available to the residents of the northernmost colonies of British North America in the face of the approaching civil war? What would you have done?
3. Should loyal residents of the northernmost colonies be regarded as Loyalists? If so, how would loyalty be defined?
4. Discuss the ethnic composition of the Loyalist migration.
5. What special problems did Loyalist women face?
6. How was Loyalist resettlement important to British North America?
7. Were the Loyalists the 'founders' of English-speaking Canada?
8. Defend Benedict Arnold's defection to the British in 1780.

CHAPTER TWELVE

Colonial Politics, War, and Rebellion, 1791–1840

British North America at the end of the eighteenth century was a loose collection of provinces, some of them only recently established and with little political experience or constitutional heritage either individually or collectively. Some (Newfoundland, Cape Breton Island) did not have the full apparatus of political institutions. Only Nova Scotia had a Legislative Assembly more than a generation old. While the Loyalists were familiar with assemblies and the politics associated with them, the French-speaking majority of the population in Lower Canada had no experience at all with representative government. By 1840, however, all the provinces of British North America had developed a sophisticated understanding of British political traditions. As the rebellions of 1837 and 1838 demonstrated, some of the population were unhappy with Britain's continuing failure to allow the colonists the autonomy to run their own affairs.

Colonial efforts towards liberation from imperial political tutelage came in several stages. Initially, the British authorities had the ultimate power. As a result of its experience with the United States, the mother country desired most earnestly to maintain stability and due subordination in its remaining North American colonies. The imperial system was still evolving; Britain

introduced the Colonial Office to serve as a link between colonies and Parliament only at the beginning of the nineteenth century. Colonial governments were at first dominated by an appointed elite. The elected assemblies gradually began to seize more power, but before 1820 organized leadership in the assemblies was sporadic, and only a few gadflies tried to challenge the rule of governors and councils as self-perpetuating oligarchies. After 1820, the assemblies became increasingly conscious of their potential power. In every province, the institutional apparatus of the assemblies grew, and an elite leadership developed that frequently shared a ruling-class ideology crossing colonial boundaries not only intellectually but practically as well. At the same time, the mix of the specific issues underlying popular political discontent could vary between colonies. Different configurations of conflict between agrarian and mercantile interests, various ethnic and confessional groups, and contending social classes produced quite different results from one colony to the next. One issue that was not contentious, however, was that women were required to remain politically in subordinate positions.

By the mid-1830s, 'reform' factions were contending for power with the oligarchies in every colonial legislature. These factions wanted to control the power of the purse (and hence

TIMELINE

1791
Constitutional Act of 1791 divides Quebec into Upper and Lower Canada, provides for separate legislatures.

1797
Riots in Lower Canada.

1806
William Cottnam Tonge expelled from Nova Scotia assembly.

1807
Robert Thorpe elected to assembly on slogan 'The King, the People, the Law, Thorpe, and the Constitution'.

1811
Loyal Electors suppressed in PEI.

1812
American invasion of Canada; death of Brock.

1814
Upper Canada legislature passes Alien Act. Treaty of Ghent.

1817
Rush-Bagot Agreement.

1818
Convention of 1818 fixes boundary between British North America and United States.

1819
Gourlay leaves Upper Canada.

1827
Upper Canadian legislature passes Naturalization Bill.

1831
Election riot in PEI.

1832
William Lyon Mackenzie presents grievances to Lord Goderich.

1834
Passage of 92 Resolutions in Lower Canada.

1837
British pass Ten Resolutions. Rebellions in Upper and Lower Canada. Lord Durham appointed governor general.

1838
William Cooper goes to London to gain escheat. Second rebellion in Lower Canada.

1839
Durham submits his report.

colonial administration), but they also wanted to revise their respective colonial constitutions in a variety of other ways. When the British authorities did not respond favourably to their demands, rebellions broke out in both Upper and Lower Canada in 1837. Although they shared certain elements of political ideology and constitutional discontent, these rebellions were essentially localized and easily suppressed. Nevertheless, they did persuade the imperial authorities that some constitutional adjustments would be required. Recommendations for change would eventually be made by Lord Durham (see Chapter 17).

THE SHAPE OF EARLY POLITICS

In pre-modern societies, government represented the highest expression of the culture of the classes capable of participating in politics on something resembling a full-time basis. Such was certainly the case for the elite groups actively involved in politics between the arrival of the Loyalists and the collapse of the oligarchies that had dominated the governments of the early period. A full-time political appointment—with salary, pension, and the chance to pass one's position on to a son or other kin—was the ultimate ambition of most men engaged in politics in these years. Gaining access to such a position was no easy matter, and given the ways in which the colonial political system conspired against either reform or change, it was not surprising that some critics ended up trying to bring the system down through open rebellion. The principal political institutions in the colonies were the governor, his council(s), and the assembly, with the Colonial Office the important element in the mother country.

One of the obvious characteristics of colonial government was that ultimate authority rested in Britain, which in this period was controlled by the landed aristocracy, with a bias towards order, tranquility, and the preservation of private property. The British government held an ultimate veto on every piece of colonial legislation (the 'royal disallowance'); made most major political appointments in the colonies (including governors and councillors) and paid for them through the civil list; and influenced colonial affairs in a variety of formal and informal ways, including the parliamentary legislation that made colonial preference possible. When the British organized a Colonial Office in the first decades of the nineteenth century, a colonial secretary sat in most (but not all) British cabinets, and supervised a small bureaucracy of civil servants who faithfully maintained the files of empire.[1] What the British government desired above all from its colonies was that they operate without causing crises great or small—certainly without introducing issues from afar that would influence the British political situation. Armed rebellions were taken seriously enough, although what British politicians wanted when they responded to such emergencies was resolution as quickly and expeditiously as possible. At one time, the Colonial Office was seen in Canada mainly as an obstructionist agency, but in recent years it has been rehabilitated, as historians have gained a clearer understanding of the many pressures working upon it.[2]

Most appointees to colonial governorships in British North America had some sort of administrative experience. All, however, found their situation impossible. A colonial governor was expected simultaneously to be the local representative of the British Crown (and hence ceremonial head of state) and the local head of government, the equivalent of a first minister heading the executive. Inevitably the governor would find himself torn between British orders and local demands. Whatever side he chose, there would be conflict, and since the prevention of conflict was one of his principal duties, its emergence would eventually lead to his recall. Governors had a chance of success in this system only by dominating both houses of the legislature, but they seldom had sufficient control of patronage to achieve this degree of control.

Governors worked closely with the network of colonial officials and merchants who made up their councils. Some colonies, such as Upper and Lower Canada, maintained a distinction between executive and legislative functions by having two councils, but in most provinces one council served both purposes. The councils, centres of the elite political establishments of the colonies, were more or less self-perpetuating oligarchies and were described in derisive terms by their critics: the 'Family Compact' in Upper Canada, the 'Château Clique' in Lower Canada, the 'System' in Nova Scotia and New Brunswick, and the 'Cabal' in Prince Edward Island. These groups were never as closely or tightly connected as their opponents professed to think, but in collaboration with the governor each did administer its colony and also served as the upper house of the legislature, with a veto over all legislation. In the first third of the nineteenth century the councils increasingly opposed any attempts by the popularly elected assemblies to wrest control of provincial affairs from their hands—sometimes by co-opting assembly leaders into their ranks. The various oligarchies tended to be composed of men of Tory stripe, who often referred to the levelling 'republicanism' of the American or French revolutionaries with a combination of disdain and fear. Only in Lower Canada and Newfoundland was the oligarchy composed of a different ethnic group than its critics. In Lower Canada the critics were chiefly French-Canadian, in Newfoundland frequently Irish.

The British had extended to their colonies the conventional constitutional theory of mixed or balanced government, in which—in a single bicameral legislature—the governor represented the monarchical element, the council(s) the aristocratic, and the elected assemblies the democratic. All three branches were to act in concert in their legislative endeavours, thus preventing one from becoming dominant. In practice the veto given to each element quickly frustrated the assemblies, which sought unsuccessfully to obtain the right to initiate taxation and to supervise financial expenditures. Lord Durham was quite accurate when he observed in 1839 that collision between the executive and representative branches of government was natural.[3]

In most colonies of British North America, the chief obstacle to the cosy working of elite politics was the popularly elected assembly. (Newfoundland was not granted an assembly until 1832, although once it obtained representative government it quickly joined the other colonies in the pattern.) But we must not confuse popular election or representative government with democracy in the modern sense of the term.

While the political franchise was relatively broad in most colonies, extending to most adult male property owners (perhaps 80 to 90 per cent of all adult males), only members of the local elites normally ran for election to the assembly, since only they could afford the time and money necessary to serve constituents in the often distant political capital. Assemblymen were not paid, and in most colonies they were not even reimbursed for their travel and living expenses. Most voters were prepared to accept this arrangement, and in most places a politics of deference was tacitly established, according to which only those near the top of the social pyramid were suited for political service.

Standard electoral practices in the early period included the blatant purchase of votes. Despite the theoretically broad franchise, only a relative handful of men ever voted in any assembly election—partly because polling was centralized at the chief market towns, balloting was not secret but open to public scrutiny, and the process was frequently manipulated by election officials (usually sheriffs) in favour of one candidate or another. Voters were bought with liquor and stayed bought, since they voted in public. Protests about electoral abuses were common, both in Lower Canada and elsewhere. As one Canadien candidate complained, following the Quebec City elections of June 1792 (which he lost by 26 votes): '62 Voters more on the spot presented themselves in my favor and formally protested even in the building where the election was held, from which they were chased by some gentlemen who demolished it by force.'[4]

Although women in the colonies, as in Europe, were denied the vote, they did become involved in political affairs. We do not know whether the Lower Canadian 'patriotes' who in 1837 tried to enlist women in a boycott of British imports succeeded, but at least two women took action on behalf of the establishment. Hortense Globensky of Ste-Scholastique brandished firearms to disperse the 'mob', and Rosalie Cherrier of St-Denis ripped down signs at a public

ELECTION MANIFESTOS, 1820

In the open system of polling, candidates usually stood before the electors and spoke to their candidacy before the polling officer called the voters forward one at a time to declare their preference. The following describes such an election in Montreal in 1820. George Garden was a Montreal businessman born in Scotland.

Wednesday last being the day fixed for the Election of the Members of the West Ward of the City, George Garden and L.J. Papineau, Esquires, were unanimously chosen as Members. The Returning Officer having read the writ and explained to the Electors the duty for which they were assembled, Mr. Papineau came forward and offered himself in a neat and appropriate speech from the Hustings. He commenced by stating that the reason they were called upon to discharge the duty of Electing Members of Parliament was the much lamented death of our late revered Sovereign [George III]. He next took a view of the great and progressive blessings the Canadas had enjoyed under his long and glorious reign, enumerating the inestimable privileges they now possessed, and their great capabilities for improvements which were daily progressing since they became part of the British Empire. To place this in its most vivid colours he contrasted it with the wretched state of Canada, while it was a Province of France, detailing how it was at that time kept as a military garrison for the purpose of making excursions on the neighbouring nations, and that all the advantages of soil, climate, and industry were totally neglected under the sway of the old French despots. He proceeded by a natural transition to mention the important duty of guarding those great privileges and blessings for the benefit of our children; and that there was no more effectual means of doing this than by fixing on judicious and proper representatives. This led him to touch upon the duties of representatives and to a description of a rigid adherence to the law which ought to be their continual rule of action. In conclusion, he said, having had the honour of representing them in their Parliaments, and feeling that [this was] a very distinguished and flattering career as they were the Electors of the most populous, most enterprising, most rich as well as the most intelligent part of Lower Canada, he again solicited their suffrages. Adding that it should be his study to attend to their interests, to the best of his abilities, if he again became the object of their choice.

He was followed by Mr. Garden, who excused himself from addressing the Electors at great length, from the circumstance of his being unaccustomed to speak in public. He modestly declined having any intimate knowledge of legislating, but hoped that from his long residence, and intimate discourse with many parts of the services, he would not be found unrepresentative of those things most conducive to their interests. He declared that if they elected him, he would be a rigid attendant to their wishes and endeavour to merit the confidence they would place in him.

SOURCE: *The Montreal Herald*, 1 July 1820.

demonstration and harangued the mob.[5] Women also played an active role in resistance against landlords in Prince Edward Island in the 1830s, although most of the known incidents involved efforts to protect their homes and property against seizure by legal officers.[6]

POLITICAL CONFLICT: EARLY OPPOSITION

Serious political conflict between the assemblies and the governing oligarchies was almost inevitable, given the constitutional arrangements. But it was much slower to develop in British North America than it had been in the thirteen American colonies half a century earlier. No tradition of constitutional political opposition had yet developed in British North America, and Britain itself offered very few precedents in this regard. In all the colonies, the oligarchies associated the aspirations of the assemblies with the levelling republicanism that had led to revolutions in both the United States and France. Criticism of government was immediately rejected, and critics were silenced by whatever means necessary, including violence—though in most cases the loss of office appears to have been sufficient.

Before 1815, criticism of the various colonial governments was only sporadic, and for the most part was expressed from within the ranks of the elite according to fairly clearly defined rules. It was acceptable to criticize one's opponents within the confines of the House of Assembly; not so acceptable to publish such criticisms in a newspaper; and totally unacceptable to organize any sort of campaign against the people in power. Only occasionally did an opposition turn to the general electorate for support, and never with a concerted effort over an extended period of time. The absence of persistence can be explained in part by the swiftness with which critics who became too vociferous were suppressed or co-opted by the government in power, partly by the difficulty of holding together loose coalitions of legislative opponents without any unifying, consistent political goal apart from replacing the ruling oligarchy from which most of them were excluded. Most of the early efforts at opposing the colonial governments were led by outspoken political gadflies who received precious little support from their colleagues: James Glenie in New Brunswick, William Cottnam Tonge in Nova Scotia, Robert Thorpe in Upper Canada, and William Carson in Newfoundland. The last three were all dismissed from public office for their political agitation. That all held major offices—and thought they could use them as platforms for criticizing those in power—says much about the absence of clear lines of authority in the political culture of the day.

The political experience of James Glenie (1750–1817) was symptomatic of the period before 1815.[7] New Brunswick had a built-in conflict between Saint John and Fredericton: the former the home of vociferous democratic loyalists and the latter—established in large part to insulate the government from radical elements—gaining support from the proto-aristocrats who resided in and around the capital. Glenie was a Scots-born former military officer (in the engineers) who had run into trouble with the concept of blind obedience on several occasions before settling in Sunbury County in 1788. Glenie wanted to pursue an aggressive trade in ships' masts, but soon ran afoul of Lieutenant-Governor Thomas Carleton (the brother of Guy Carleton) and the Loyalist elite of Fredericton. Deciding to fight the government from within the assembly—of which he was a member between 1789 and 1803—he proposed the appointment of new councillors who would be 'European Gentlemen very well qualified who will not be Tools like those recommended'. By 1795 he had begun a public campaign to make the public aware of the differences between the assembly's program and the administration's behaviour, carrying the news 'into every County and to every Man's door as much as possible'. The political issues at stake—hard to identify in retrospect—were chiefly connected with objections to the oligarchical way the government operated.

Among the abuses that Glenie decried were constant vetoes of assembly legislation by the Legislative Council, and wasteful spending by an internal clique. He agreed that 'our Legislature consists of three distinct Branches, like that of Great Britain', but insisted that the model did not apply in British North America, 'where two Branches of the Legislature are in a great measure thrown into one scale.' After some years of leading the assembly into deadlock with the government, Glenie was unable to sustain the opposition and in 1802 he was nearly defeated (winning with 101 votes against 87 for his opponent). The next year he disappeared from politics, and in 1805 he went to England. The opposition that Glenie had cobbled together was basically a loose collection of all those opposed to Thomas Carleton's Loyalist New Brunswick. He therefore counted among his supporters—briefly—religious dissenters, merchants, pre-Loyalists, residents of Saint John and the coastal area, and Loyalists out of power. But rhetoric alone could not hold such a coalition together in the absence of major issues.

NASCENT POLITICAL PARTIES

Only in Prince Edward Island (renamed in 1798) and Lower Canada did anything approximating a political party form before the War of 1812. From the very founding of the small island colony there had been political infighting, and the 1780s saw a brief attempt at an assembly-centred opposition to the corrupt government of Walter Patterson. The issue that struck the most responsive chord with the public was escheat, a legal process by which the Crown could recover lands previously granted to 'proprietors'. But other issues provoked the formation of a political organization called the Loyal Electors, which established itself in 1809 within a colony of 7,000 inhabitants, fewer than 300 eligible voters, and perhaps 50 members of the elite—officeholders, professional men, merchants, and large landholders—in residence. When the Loyal Electors proposed to consider 'proper legislative measures, to bring about the introduction of upright, independent men and persons of unimpeachable character in the House of Assembly'—the similarity to James Glenie's earlier call in New Brunswick is striking—the reformers quickly came into conflict

with the island's officials.[8] The octogenarian lieutenant-governor, J.F.W. DesBarres, appears to have supported the Electors.

On 18 October 1811 the province's attorney general sent DesBarres a legal opinion on the constitutionality of the society of Loyal Electors, which he described as a 'self created permanent political Body organized after the manner of Corporations and associated for the purpose of controlling the Representatives of the People in the House of Assembly, as well as the appointment of Public Officers'. Claiming that the society's purpose was to 'obtain possession of the whole power of Government', the attorney general declared that its views and principles were not 'consistent with the Genius and Spirit of our Constitution'.[9] As a result, the British government was easily persuaded that the Loyal Electors were a 'Confederacy of a very dangerous description'. The society itself was quickly suppressed, and Governor DesBarres and his advisers were dismissed—which was doubtless the object of the exercise. That any organization should be officially crushed for attempting to behave like a political party tells us much about the state of political theory in British North America in 1811.

Lower Canada was a particularly likely place for distinct political organizations to form, because religious and linguistic differences created both sharp divisions and informal political bonds quite different from the usual links based on conflict between 'ins' and 'outs' or political 'hinterland' and 'centre'. Political divisions developed when the English-speaking merchants who had dominated the first assembly elected after the Constitutional Act of 1791 found themselves outnumbered by an active group of French-Canadian political leaders, mainly from the ranks of the liberal professions. After 1800 the increasingly vocal Canadiens formed their own party in opposition to the alliance of officials and merchants that came to be known as the Château Clique. Each group had its own newspaper, and soon the Quebec *Mercury* and *Le Canadien* were thundering at one another across a growing gulf.

In 1805 a new land tax imposed to build a prison served as a focus for criticism of government, and Governor Sir James Craig attempted to suppress *Le Canadien*, which was feeling its way towards an ideology of opposition. However, the newspaper's editorial position in these early years, mainly articulated by its fiery editor, the lawyer and assembly member Pierre-Stanislas Bédard, supported British concepts of liberty and British institutional traditions, including the balance of powers.

For Bédard, writing in 1809, the British constitution represented:

> perhaps the only one under which the interests and rights of the various classes composing society are so carefully arranged, so wisely set off against one another and linked to one another as a whole, that they illuminate and sustain one another through the very conflict which results from the simultaneous exercise of the powers that are entrusted to [these classes].[10]

He argued, however, that the way in which power was administered in his province was wrong, for it did not reflect the balance of interests. He also recognized that such maladministration jeopardized the position of the governor in the balanced constitution, for 'it lays the king's representative open to the danger of losing the people's confidence through his ministers' errors'. At the same time—unlike his counterparts in colonies lacking the fundamental division between French and English that Lower Canada faced—Bédard also recognized that 'a governor cannot have the English party, the party of the government, on his side without adopting all its ideas, prejudices, and plans against the Canadians.' To Bédard's regret, his successor as leader of the Canadien party, Louis-Joseph Papineau, built more on this latter analysis than on the constitutional theory. When Bédard retired in 1819, he said that 'Mr. Papineau and Mr. Viger [another spokesman for the Parti Canadien] are no real friends of mine.'

THE WAR OF 1812

To nobody's real surprise, the United States declared war on Great Britain on 18 June 1812. American hostility to the British had been building for years over two sets of grievances. One set related to maritime matters. From 1806 the British navy had blockaded European seaports under the control of the French, thus preventing Americans from trading with Europe. Moreover, the British violated what the United States regarded as its rights as a neutral on the high seas, both by stopping American ships and by removing British subjects sailing them.

The second area of Anglo–American tension was the vast territory south of the Great Lakes that the British had transferred to the United States by the Treaty of Paris in 1783. Having surrendered it to the Americans, the British began to have sober second thoughts, chiefly because of their long-standing commitments to the First Nations of the region. As American settlers moved into the 'Middle Ground', the British were still dragging their heels on evacuating their forts and posts. Even after the posts were officially abandoned in 1796, following considerable diplomatic negotiations, the British continued to favour a Native military resistance to the Americans. Replacement forts were built on British North American soil, and the British were prepared not only to receive more Aboriginal refugees from their traditional hunting grounds but to back the creation of a confederate state proposed after 1805 by the Shawnee leaders Tenskwatawa ('The Prophet') and Tecumseh.[11] The chronological coincidence of British maritime harassment and British support of the western First Nations was naturally viewed by the American government as a co-ordinated policy. Meanwhile, a group of expansionist congressional leaders from the border states and territories called the 'War Hawks' were pressing for an invasion of Canada—territory they had long coveted.

In 1812 and 1813 a series of American armies invaded British North American territory,

■ Tecumseh, by 'S.W.', from J. Richardson, *War of 1812* (Toronto, 1902). Tecumseh's image has haunted the Canadian imagination, as this fanciful example suggests. LAC, C-3809.

American settlement.[12] By and large, the Canadian authorities did a reasonably good job of avoiding unnecessary witch-hunts during the emergency.[13] American armies were thrust back through the major entry points: the Detroit–Windsor corridor, the Niagara Peninsula, and Lake Champlain. British regulars, well led by several commanders, notably General Isaac Brock, and assisted by militiamen from both Upper and Lower Canada and Aboriginal allies, proved equal to much larger forces of American volunteers. The Upper Canadians came out of the war convinced that their militia had won the war virtually single-handed, and the British in Lower Canada discovered that the French Canadians provided more support for the British cause, including soldiers, than they had anticipated. The war was also fought on the Great Lakes, where both sides built navies from scratch, and in the fur-trading territory of the west, where Canadien voyageurs captured and held Fort Michilimackinac (on western Lake Huron). In the course of the hostilities, York (Toronto) was sacked, and Washington was burnt in retaliation. The British were unable to win control of the lakes, however, and both sides agreed to a peace acknowledging stalemate at Ghent (following which Andrew Jackson captured New Orleans with a ragtag army of buccaneers and adventurers).

The status quo ante bellum was quickly restored. Nevertheless, the War of 1812 had considerable impact upon British North America in several areas. One was in the domestic politics of Upper Canada. To the notions of loyalty to the British Crown dating from the period of the American Revolution was added a new ideological stream born of the War of 1812. The Tory elite of Upper Canada became convinced that the province had been in great danger, as much from the internal menace of American residents as from the external one of American troops. They carried over into the post-war period their belief in the necessity of the simultaneous suppression of political opposition and maintenance of social

mainly in the Canadas (the Atlantic region remained largely uninvolved). The Yankees expected the former Americans living north of the border to support them, and just enough did so to vindicate the British and Canadian authorities who had warned against permitting

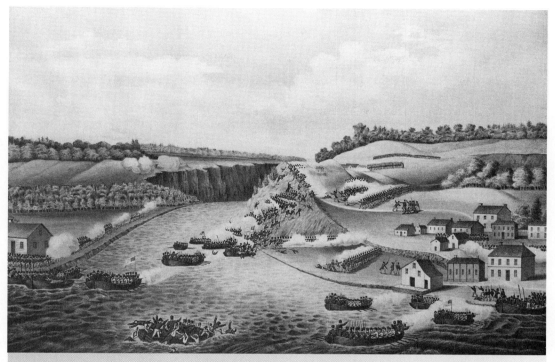

■ 'The Battle of Queenston. October 18th, 1813 [*sic*]', by Major James B. Dennis, coloured lithograph, c. 1866, after the original print published by J.W. Laird & Co., in London. The battle of
Queenston Heights actually took place on 13 October 1812. LAC, C-276.

harmony, by force if necessary. This belief would
serve as the basis for Upper Canadian Toryism
for several generations.[14]

The War of 1812 also had implications for
the First Nations people, many of whom had
supported the British. It was never quite clear
how a British victory would contribute to the
cause of Aboriginal unity or the dream of an
Aboriginal state, but it was certainly plain that
from the Aboriginal perspective, maintenance of
the status quo was a victory for the American
expansionists. The United States had used the
war to solidify its control of the 'Middle Ground'
and to push the First Nations further to the margins. One of the articles in the Treaty of Ghent
stipulated that both the United States and Great
Britain would endeavour not only to end hostili-

ties with the Native peoples but 'forthwith to
restore to such tribes or nations respectively all
possessions, right and privileges which they may
have enjoyed or been entitled to in one thousand
eight hundred and eleven, previous to such hostilities.'[15] This clause remained a dead letter. As it
became clear that the Britain was seeking détente
with the United States, many of the First Nations
living near the border reluctantly came to terms
with the Americans, while others retreated farther west to continue a resistance that they knew
full well was doomed.

Finally, in the aftermath of the War of 1812
(though not in the peace treaty itself) Britain and
the United States tidied up a number of contentious items, some of them left over from the
eighteenth century. In the Rush-Bagot Agreement

■ 'Surviving warriors of the Six Nations Indians', Brantford, July 1882. Jacob Warner, 92, John Turtle, 91, and John Smoke Johnson, 93, were veterans of the War of 1812. Seven decades later, the First Nations community still commemorated their participation in the war. LAC, C-85127.

of 1817—really an exchange of notes between Charles Bagot (British minister in Washington) and Richard Rush (acting American Secretary of State)—the two nations agreed to limit the number and size of naval armaments on the Great Lakes. And in 1818 the two governments negotiated an understanding about the western boundary—previously undefined—running clear across the continent from the Lake of the Woods to the crest of the Rocky Mountains along the 49th parallel (although the line would not be surveyed until the 1870s). The two governments also agreed to leave the disputed Oregon Territory on the Pacific slope open to a 10-year joint occupation. The same agreement confirmed American fishing rights in Newfoundland and Labrador.

POLITICAL CONFLICT AFTER 1815

UPPER CANADA

Not long after the end of the war of 1812, government leaders in Upper Canada felt the sting of another gadfly. Robert Gourlay was a self-declared agrarian radical. He had studied agriculture after receiving his MA in Scotland, and wrote an official report on the conditions of farm labourers in two English shires. By the time he arrived in Upper Canada (where his wife had inherited land), in 1817, land issues were causing much discontent. Crown reserves made huge areas useless; immigration from the United States had slowed down because of a decision to deny land grants to Americans; and militia veterans from the War of 1812–14, who had been promised land, had not received it.[16] Deciding to become a land agent, Gourlay applied for a land grant himself. He also prepared a list of 31 questions for resident landowners (drawn from Sir John Sinclair's *Statistical Account of Scotland*), which he was allowed to publish in the official *Upper Canada Gazette*, appended to an address in which he contrasted the possibilities of Upper Canada with its actual state. In a second address, in February 1818, he was more strident, encouraging American immigration—in defiance of government policy—and accusing the colonial government of 'paltry patronage and ruinous favouritism'. When he was refused a land grant (because he did not intend to settle in Upper Canada), his rage knew no bounds. His writings in the *Niagara Spectator*—against the 'vile, loathsome and lazy vermin of Little York', with special words of invective for Archdeacon John Strachan—reached a provocative climax in April 1818: 'It is not the men, it is the system which blasts every hope of good and till the system is overturned, it is vain to expect anything of value from change of representatives or governors.'[17]

To a considerable extent, the Gourlay business was a private quarrel among Scots. Gourlay was encouraged rather more than supported by a handful of Scottish merchants in the colony who generally kept a low profile. Lord Selkirk, who was engaged in his own struggle with the Canadian establishment over the fur trade, was also a supporter without a popular base.[18] Not surprisingly, Gourlay was hounded out of the colony by its political leaders, but he left it a twofold legacy: the rich fund of information gathered by his questionnaire and published in his *Statistical Account of Upper Canada . . .* (2 vols, London, 1822), which drew attention particularly to the large areas of unused land in the province; and his image as a political martyr to a ruthless oligarchy, which would help to inspire future efforts at reform.

Gourlay's opposition to the Family Compact looked backward to the era of individual opposition and ethnic quarrelling rather than forward to the age of organized reform. In the transitional period, Upper Canadian politics became extremely complex and confused. As a result of the election of 1824, the assembly of Upper Canada had a majority of members critical of the executive—for the first time in its history. The occasion for this result was at least partly the bitter cultural division between the oligarchy (which was resolutely British rather than English[19]) and the majority of the population (who were still probably American in origin and citizenship). This division was also to some extent sectional, for the eastern part of the province had been settled chiefly by Loyalists and Scots Highland immigrants, who backed the establishment, while the western part was mainly composed of Americans and Lowland Scots, who leaned towards reform. The critics in the assembly included Peter Perry, a public-spirited landowner of Loyalist background; Dr John Rolph, an English-born lawyer and doctor; and Marshall Spring Bidwell, an American-born lawyer. Bidwell's father, Barnabas Bidwell, had sat briefly in the assembly in 1821 but was expelled in 1822 after a bitter debate in which he was accused of being a fugitive from American justice; he insisted he was being persecuted because of his American origins.

In 1827 the Upper Canadian legislature, encouraged by the provincial government, had passed the Naturalization (or Alien) Bill, which refused British citizenship and its privileges to Americans who had not lived in the province for seven years, had declared allegiance to the king, and had renounced allegiance to the United States.[20] American-born residents found the last of these conditions particularly obnoxious. Many long-established Upper Canadians—the Bidwells, for example—could be considered aliens even though some of them sat in the assembly. Moreover, the legislation threatened the property titles of many people. In the election of 1828 the critics of the administration, now known as reformers, increased their numbers with the addi-

■ William Lyon Mackenzie, 1834, lithograph
published in *Canadian Military Events*, III,
337. LAC, C-24937.

tion of (among others) the American-born businessman Jesse Ketchum and the Irish-born Dr William Warren Baldwin—who was very much a member of the elite in the sense of being wealthy, educated, and a considerable landowner, but who was also a dedicated reformer, critical of the 'arbitrary, oppressive, and high-handed conduct of the Colonial Executive'.[21] These men were moderate reformers, most of them professionals who could debate with the Tories more or less as equals and mix with them socially.

Gentility was not a characteristic of another new member of the assembly in 1828, however. The self-styled independent William Lyon Mackenzie (1795–1861) was a Scots-born newspaper editor whose radical voice had been heard in his newspaper, the *Colonial Advocate*, since 1824. In many ways Mackenzie was the heir of Robert Gourlay. He had campaigned for this elec-

tion by distributing a pamphlet entitled 'The Legislative Black List of Upper Canada: or Official Corruption and Hypocrisy Unmasked', in which he rated members of the assembly according to the way they had voted in past sessions. When the new assembly convened, Barnabas Bidwell was chosen speaker of the house, but Mackenzie increasingly set the agenda, energetically exposing abuses and corruption on several fronts. Over the next nine years Mackenzie was to become increasingly disruptive for the other reformers, most of whom would gradually distance themselves from him, but he remained influential throughout the 1830s.

He had fertile ground on which to operate. Although Upper Canada had increased in population since the end of the War of 1812, and had created new townships, built new roads, schools, mills, and canals, and established a provincial bank, more and more people had political grievances. Many complaints were connected with the high-handed activities of that arch-Tory high Anglican, John Strachan, who maintained that the Church of England was the province's only safeguard against the rampant republicanism of the Americans. Even less popular than this anti-American stance was Strachan's insistence on the exclusive claims of the Church of England to the province's clergy reserves. According to the Constitutional Act of 1791, the clergy reserves—one-seventh of the public lands of Upper Canada—were to be set aside 'for the Support and Maintenance of Protestant Clergy'. The idea was that the reserved land would be rented out and the proceeds directed to the clergy—but renters were hard to find, since land was so easily purchased; thus large expanses of land sat unused, separating settlers from one another, creating drainage problems, and making it difficult to build and maintain roads. (The clergy reserves would finally be secularized in 1854; see Chapter 17.) Other complaints had to do with the executive's control of most of the revenues in the province. Of all the grievances, however, perhaps the most important was the fact that the governing elite, the Family Compact—with its fear of the 'unbridled democratic will' of the assembly and its rejection of anyone who criticized the government in any way—had a stranglehold on the province's politics.[22]

In the election of 1830 the reformers were greatly reduced in number, but their morale was sustained by Britain's election of a Whig government in 1831, and by the passage of the Reform Bill in 1832, the year Mackenzie visited London to meet the leading radicals and present his grievances to Lord Goderich, the colonial secretary. Mackenzie's spirits, and his hatred of the government, had risen to new heights when he published in the *Colonial Advocate* (1 Dec. 1831) a statement that was considered libellous: 'Our representative body has degenerated into a sycophantic office for registering the decrees of as mean and mercenary an executive as was ever given as a punishment for the sins of any part of North America in the nineteenth century.'[23] Mackenzie was expelled from the assembly, only to be triumphantly re-elected a few weeks later by the York County farmers and tradesmen who were his most loyal followers, and who presented him with a medal 'as a token of their approbation of his political career'. He was almost immediately expelled again, and re-elected—a pattern that was repeated several times over. Of those expulsions, Peter Perry was reported to have stated publicly that 'No two persons disapproved more at times of Mr. Mackenzie's occasional violence than Mr. Bidwell and himself, but they both supported him on principle, seeing that the people had been insulted in his person.'[24]

In March 1834 Mackenzie was elected the first mayor of Toronto, and in October he was returned to the assembly, which once again had a majority of reformers, now seen to be made up of both moderates and radicals. The two groups united in passing various reformist bills, but these came to nothing once they reached the Tory Legislative Council, Mackenzie then began to think about pressuring the government from outside the assembly. In the meantime, he per-

suaded that body to set up a Committee of Grievances, with himself as chairman, which allowed him to summon a parade of government officials and other citizens (from February to April 1835) to answer his pointed questions. The 500-page result, *Seventh Report from the Select Committee of the House of Assembly of Upper Canada on Grievances*, was jumbled, often inaccurate, and filled with impractical schemes, but nonetheless offered a highly detailed and revealing account of the condition of Upper Canada. Two thousand copies were printed, and it found its way to the new colonial secretary, Lord Glenelg. Receiving it as the voice of the assembly—Glenelg did not know that it had been only reluctantly endorsed, or that some moderate reformers, including Peter Perry, voted against it because of its inaccuracies and virulent exaggerations—he recalled Sir John Colborne, the lieutenant-governor.

THE RADICAL REFORMERS

The new generation of political critics that emerged in British North America between 1820 and 1840 were both more stubborn than their predecessors and more willing to invoke popular opinion in support of their attacks on the ruling oligarchies. Besides Mackenzie, three reformers stand out in this period: Louis-Joseph Papineau of Lower Canada, Joseph Howe of Nova Scotia, and William Cooper of Prince Edward Island. Of the four, only Howe would survive the turmoil he created with his political career intact. Mackenzie and Papineau would spend years in exile after frustration at their inability to change the constitutional system led them to sponsor abortive rebellions. Cooper would eventually drift off to California, his political movement having fizzled out with little to show for it. None of these men actually overturned the political system of the elites, but they made some inroads against it—anticipating in a variety of ways the gradual democratization of politics in British North America.

■ Louis-Joseph Papineau, lithograph by Antoine Maurin (1793–1860). LAC, C-5435.

All four reformers were radical-sounding in their rhetoric. Papineau—seigneur of Montebello on the Ottawa River, a lawyer, and member of the assembly since 1809 and three times its speaker—was the most socially conservative and Cooper the most profoundly democratic, but all four shared Cooper's ideal of the 'independent cultivator of the soil', condemning the commercial and merchant classes and expensive economic development by the public sector. All believed in equality of conditions—what has come to be called 'the level playing field'. In the 1830s, unable either to persuade the British government of the inadequacy of existing constitutional arrangements, or to alter the system by political agitation, both Papineau and Mackenzie turned to the ideology of Jacksonian democracy: the natural wisdom of the people, the natural aristocracy among men, and therefore the desir-

ability of rotation in office, to allow everyone a chance to govern. As Papineau explained, the aristocratic nature of the existing political constitution was inconsistent with the democratic nature of the social constitution in the Canadas, 'where every one is born, lives and dies a democrat; because every one is an owner; because every one has a small piece of property. . . .'[25]

What these reformers all shared was a desire to overturn the 'corrupt' ruling oligarchies and replace them with administrations that would be 'responsible to the province'[26] as represented in the House of Assembly. They also shared the agrarian assumption that public 'improvements' paid for out of the public purse or sponsored by the government, such as canals or banks, were imposed on taxpayers by the oligarchies and represented unnecessary financial burdens—in effect, that such measures amounted to 'class legislation'. For Mackenzie, the 'true source of a country's wealth' was 'labour usefully and prudently applied'; institutions such as banks might 'issu[e] promises to pay gold and silver on demand in almost unlimited quantity', but they did nothing 'to produce . . . wealth and prosperity'.[27] For Papineau in Lower Canada, it was bad enough that an active economic state was dominated by a mercantile class which promoted capitalism in all ways: that the merchants were British was even worse.

The struggle between commercial capitalism and agrarianism was a fundamental element in the politics of the time. These reformers were not precursors of socialism, for they had no conception that economic development could be directed by government on behalf of the people; nor did they have any overall conception of a positive role for the state in ensuring the well-being of its citizenry. Rather, they were nineteenth-century liberals who sought to reduce both the influence of government on the lives of the people and the temptation to insist on special privileges. As Mackenzie wrote in a broadside entitled *Independence* in late November 1837: 'We contend, that in all laws made, or to be made, every person shall be bound alike—neither shall any tenure, estate, character, degree, birth or place, confer any exemption from the ordinary course of legal proceedings and responsibilities whereunto others are subjected.'[28]

POPULAR POLITICS, POLITICAL VIOLENCE, AND REBELLION

POPULAR POLITICS

While the basic political confrontation may have been between the various elites contending for control of electoral politics, the common people—especially but not only enfranchised males—had their own agenda and played their own parts in the political process. In the 1790s the French Revolution had considerable impact in Lower Canada, especially among the habitants, who continued to feel a much closer connection to France than to Britain.[29] Popular resistance and rioting occurred on several occasions. In 1794, opposition to raising a militia (possibly to fight the Americans over the western posts) drew large armed mobs into the streets of Quebec City and Montreal. In Quebec's Charlesbourg district, those who did not favour the mobs were threatened with barn-burning and disembowelling. Another series of riots broke out in 1796–7, mainly over local issues such as the enforcement of corvées for road construction during the harvest season. Regular troops were summoned to disperse the crowds, which the authorities were convinced had been stirred up by French agitators. One of these agitators was David McLane, an American from Rhode Island who had been recruited by French agents in America; McLane was arrested, found guilty of treason, and summarily hanged and disembowelled.[30] Following this episode, Attorney General Jonathan Sewell observed that the habitants were now 'more observant of the laws than can be expected of the best subjects . . . and the roads are universally good in consequence.' Another consequence of the agitation was a growing conviction among the English authorities that the French-Canadian party in Quebec was encouraging revolution.

In general, the authorities feared any expression of popular sentiment through public gatherings—what the British called politics 'out of doors' of the legislature. When the electorate had to be persuaded to vote for one or the other of the elite factions, candidates usually relied on personal campaigning and use of the newspapers. Not often did popular sentiment lead to the formation of a political party devoted to the interests of ordinary people who made up the vast bulk of the voters. This had happened in Prince Edward Island, however, where the Escheat Party led by William Cooper emerged in the 1830s to call for land redistribution by which tenant farmers (a large proportion of the population of the island) would be able to own, rather than rent, the land they worked. In Upper Canada, petitioning became a favourite form of extra-parliamentary politics. When Robert Gourlay organized petitions in Upper Canada in the years following the War of 1812, the government responded with repressive measures, but such efforts became more acceptable after 1830. As Carol Wilton has emphasized, petitioning in Upper Canada was aimed more at influencing the policy of the British government than at producing a direct effect on the local legislature.[31] Such petitioning was well-organized and carried out through the form of well-advertised public meetings, and was usually tolerated. During the rebellions, of course, such meetings were again repressed.

The failure of the Escheat Party in PEI to achieve its goals despite its control of the local legislature forced it into orchestrating popular petitions to Britain. When petitioning failed to move the British authorities, the Escheat Party had no place to go, and Cooper gave up his agitation. In all provinces, the popular goals were usually expressed in moderate language—except during the periods of the French Revolution in Lower Canada and the rebellions in Upper and Lower Canada—but the resiliency of popular movements 'out of doors' did eventually help to restrict the worst excesses of the legislative politicians, particularly their use of libel laws and the power to expel troublesome assembly members as means of suppressing dissent. By 1840 it was possible for newspapers to report on parliamentary debates, for example, without drawing down the wrath of either the government or the legislature. Soldiers could still be called out to disperse crowds for very little reason, however.

THE PEOPLE AND JOSEPH HOWE

How popular support could work on behalf of the reformers is demonstrated by the 1835 libel case of Joseph Howe (1804–73). The son of a Halifax Loyalist printer, he was educated largely by his father. Through his own efforts, he entered the family firm in 1818, and in 1828, at the age of 24, he became a newspaper publisher. Like most early newspapers in British North America,

■ Joseph Howe in 1871. LAC, C-22002.

the *Novascotian* was from its inception well integrated into the culture of the day. The paper carried some international news, mainly gathered from newspapers brought to Halifax by merchant shippers, and reported on local politics in an official tone. It also pressed for local economic development and carried much mercantile advertising. Occasionally its publisher allowed himself to offer a bit of poetry or a literary essay, often his own. Gradually Howe became more daring in his remarks on local and provincial politics, always maintaining that reform was needed to bring the institutions of government up to British standards.

On 1 January 1835 the *Novascotian* printed a letter signed 'The People', in which it was charged that the magistrates of Halifax had 'by one strategem or other, taken from the pockets of the people, in over exactions, fines, etc., etc., a sum that would exceed in the gross amount of 30,000 pounds'. The targets of this allegation demanded that the governor prosecute whoever was responsible for it, and when Howe refused to name the author of the letter, he himself was charged with criminal libel. He consulted several lawyers, who told him 'there was no doubt that the letter was a libel [and that he] must make . . . peace, or submit to fine and imprisonment.'[32] At that time, any criticism that belittled public officials or disturbed public order was criminally libellous, and neither truth nor fair comment was a defence.[33] Nevertheless, after spending a week reading in the law, Howe believed that he did have a defence after all. Whether he acquainted himself with earlier British and American cases of liberty of the press is not known. In any event, he wrote to his wife that, if he 'had the nerve and power to put the whole case before a Jury, as it rested in [his] own mind, and they were fair and rational men, they must acquit.'[34]

When the court met, Howe quickly admitted all the facts of publication and went straight to the jury, without calling any witnesses. As a prominent layman, he had to be given a certain leeway by the court, and he made the most of it to argue his case. For over six hours he spoke (people had longer attention spans in those days), at several points reducing jurors to tears. As a legal defence the case he presented was irrelevant, for as the attorney general remarked when the court reconvened the following morning, Howe had 'stated a great variety of things which could not be evidence, which are mere hearsay, and which the court would not have permitted counsel to use.' The verdict would hinge on the charge to the jury delivered by the chief justice, who was among those that Howe had accused in his speech. But the chief justice refused to exercise his power. He merely told the jury:

> In my opinion, the paper charged is a libel, and your duty is, to state by your verdict that it is libellous. You are not bound by my opinion. . . . If you think that this is not a libel, as a consequence, you must think that it bears no reflections injurious to the complaining parties. If this is your opinion say so; I leave the case in your hands.[35]

Within ten minutes the jury had acquitted Howe. All Halifax celebrated, as if freedom of the press had been established in Nova Scotia and everywhere else. It had not. Only in 1843 did the British Parliament pass legislation permitting truth of the libel as a defence, and even after that date newspaper editors in British North America were constrained in what they could say about public officials and public life. The case of the *Novascotian* reminds us about the limits of action within the pre-modern political culture of British North America in the first third of the nineteenth century.[36]

POLITICAL VIOLENCE

Political violence was common throughout the first decades of the nineteenth century. Though sometimes spontaneous, often it was carefully calculated for partisan purposes. The age itself was violent, and elites often harnessed tensions—easily exacerbated by liquor, as well as ethnic and religious divisions carried over from the Old Country—for their own purposes. At one 1832 poll on Prince Edward Island, voters began to be noisy in mid-afternoon and threatened to pull down the hustings. They were quieted by threats, 'except when the Returning Officer was administering the Oath, which generally excited a noise'. Finally, at about 7 p.m., 'while the Returning Officer was speaking to an Elector as to his qualification, the Hustings were pulled down—the Deputy Sheriff and the Candidates thrown to the ground—and the Boards of which the Hustings were made, and the barrels which supported them, were thrown into the air—a barrel in falling struck the Returning Officer on the shoulder.'[37] A year later in Farmersville, Upper Canada, a political meeting was interrupted by a gang of Orangemen wielding a 'number of Shillalahs', in the course of which 'a number of persons received contusions and the Chairman was severely cut on the head.'[38] Occasionally members of the elite themselves engaged in mob activity, almost always in disguise: in 1826 a 'mob' of 15 young Tories, dressed as 'Indians', smashed William Lyon Mackenzie's printing press, partly in retaliation for his scurrilous attacks on leading members of the Family Compact.

Most large-scale violence erupted in conjunction with nominating meetings and electoral polling. It was most common in districts where ethnic or denominational conflict already existed, and was particularly intense where ethnic and denominational lines overlapped, producing what contemporaries usually referred to as 'sectarian' controversy. Before 1840, sectarian conflict was kept to a minimum in most regions by the tendency for cohesive ethnic and confessional groups to settle together in nodes of population separated from their neighbours by large expanses of 'waste' (wilderness) land. This settlement pattern meant that the conflicting groups hardly ever came together except on election day. In places like Newfoundland—where Protestant and Catholic, English and Irish, boat-owner and worker, tory and liberal, all contended together —violence, electoral and otherwise, was part of everyday life.[39]

THE REBELLIONS OF 1837

Before the 1830s, ordinary people were rarely at the centre of political events. Nevertheless, the dominant cultural expression in the British colonies between 1790 and 1840 was in politics, and in the late 1830s the elite culture suffered a crisis that—without transforming it—loosened it up and liberalized it a bit. This change was brought about in Upper and Lower Canada by rebellions against the elite leadership by various

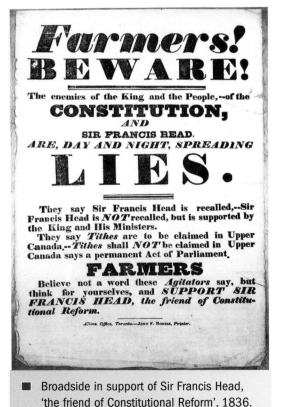

■ Broadside in support of Sir Francis Head, 'the friend of Constitutional Reform', 1836. Metropolitan Toronto Reference Library.

non-elite opponents. These uprisings can be viewed in a variety of ways: as political events, as cultural manifestations, as eruptions of subterranean pressures resulting from agrarian discontent both long- and short-term, or—in Lower Canada—as expressions of French–English animosity. To some degree they were all these things. Had the rebellions not been so quickly and brutally suppressed by the authorities, similar uprisings might well have broken out in the eastern provinces, particularly in Prince Edward Island, where agrarian and political discontents were also strong.

The rebellions of 1837 challenged the stable political culture of the elites in the Canadas. If home rule was one ambition of the reformers, the accommodation of partisan rivalries that extended beyond the ranks and ken of the governing elite was another. In Upper Canada, the assembly was infuriated by the discovery that Lieutenant-Governor Colborne, before he was recalled, had established 44 rectories for Anglican clergymen, encompassing some 21,000 acres. A select committee, headed by Peter Perry, was set up to investigate grievances. It criticized Colborne harshly, calling him a liar and a tyrant who had conducted 'our affairs' according to his own 'arbitrary and vindictive' will. The assembly voted to stop the supply of money for the everyday expenses of government. The new lieutenant-governor, Sir Francis Bond Head, responded angrily, reviewing and justifying his own policies, and calling the decision to stop supply a direct attack on the monarchy. A month later he dissolved the assembly, and in the bitterly fought election that followed, he actually campaigned against the reformers, most of whom—including Mackenzie, Perry, and the speaker of the assembly, Marshall Spring Bidwell—were swept out of office. Having won chiefly by convincing the electorate that to vote against him was tantamount to disloyalty, Head celebrated his victory. But in fact the result was a disaster, for without the moderates, who had now been effectively removed from politics, there was no one to curb the hotheads who were utterly frustrated by the system.

The political gridlock was even more serious in Lower Canada, where—unlike the reformers in Upper Canada—the Parti Canadien and its successor, the Parti Patriote, had fairly consistently dominated the lower house, and the party conflict had long since taken on ethnic overtones. The Parti Canadien was dominated by members of the regional elites, chiefly French-Canadian professionals with neither the hope nor the ambition to be co-opted into the ranks of the Château Clique—men such as Denis-Benjamin Viger, a Montreal lawyer and member of the assembly who financed *La Minerve*, a newspaper that published nothing to discourage the acceleration of rebellious activities in the province. Like the reformers in Upper Canada, the French Canadians spoke of autonomy for their province and the right to rule themselves, but they meant something different by those terms. What was needed, argued Papineau in December 1834, was a 'local, responsible, and national government for each part of the Empire, as regards settlement of its local interests, with supervisory authority held by the imperial government, to decide on peace and war and commercial relations with foreign countries; that is what Ireland and British America ask for.'[40] The reference to Ireland, rather than Upper Canada, was crucial. In February 1834, a list of 92 resolutions, prepared by Papineau and three others, was adopted by the assembly of Lower Canada and submitted to London. It catalogued grievances and requests, among them control of revenue by the legislature, responsibility of the executive to the electorate, and the election (rather than appointment) of legislative councillors. In 1836 in Upper Canada—when a letter from Papineau, attacking British governing authority, was read to the assembly—Mackenzie agreed with his fellow radicals in Lower Canada that action must be taken against the British. But in March 1837 the British Parliament replied to the 92 Resolutions with 10 resolutions of its own, in effect rejecting the assembly's demands: among other things, it allowed the governor to take funds from the provincial treasury without the assembly's approval.

Beyond their obvious political and constitutional significance, the rebellions were also manifestations of popular discontent. The role of agrarian issues in this discontent is uncertain. The traditional historical interpretation has focused on the mid-1830s collapse of the international wheat market, which put pressures on Upper Canadian farmers and even more pressures on Lower Canadian farmers, whose wheat economy was already in crisis. Rural districts had been restive for several years in both provinces, and in early 1837 protest meetings were held at which some farmers turned up bearing arms. However, not all historians agree on the extent to which agrarian distress fuelled the rebellion. Colin Read, for example, maintains that the farmers of western Upper Canada were relatively prosperous and that their discontent was more political than economic.[41] Allan Greer argues that it was the seigneurial system rather than the wheat market that motivated French-Canadian farmers to protest.[42]

In any event, to forestall unrest, in early November the colonial authorities in Lower Canada attempted to arrest Patriote leaders, who escaped into the country. Although the government forces lost the first armed confrontation, at St-Denis on 23 November, by mid-December they had established control. Meanwhile in Upper Canada, an attempted rural uprising near Brantford dispersed on 13 December when its leader, Dr Charles Duncombe, heard of the defeat of Mackenzie's motley group of protestors on 8 December at Montgomery's Tavern north of Toronto.[43] There is some suggestion that the authorities acted severely against the Brantford group at least partly because many of them were American-born.[44] Certainly the centres of the Duncombe uprising were in townships inhabited chiefly by people of American background.[45] Both Mackenzie and Papineau persistently

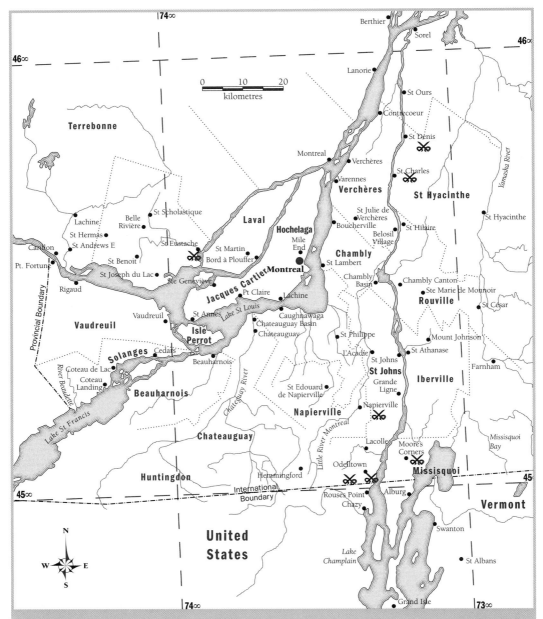

Southwestern Lower Canada in 1837, showing the region of Lower Canada in which the major fighting of the 1837 rebellion occurred. The battles, mainly the result of local rural uprisings, are marked with crossed swords. Based on a map from A.D. Decelles, *The Patriotes of '37: A Chronicle of the Lower Canadian Rebellion* (1916).

SAMUEL LOUNT
(1791–1838)

Born in Catawissa, Pennsylvania, Samuel Lount emigrated to Upper Canada with his family in 1811, but he spent the period of the War of 1812–14 in the United States. When he returned to Upper Canada he became a blacksmith, but also worked as a tavern-keeper and surveyor. A typical resident of the moving frontier, he was a jack-of-all-trades, moving in and out of farming and various artisan occupations, especially blacksmithing, and commercial ventures, including storekeeping and tavern-keeping. Well respected in his neighbourhood, he was reluctant to enter politics, but was elected MLA for Simcoe County in 1834, inevitably joining the reformers in the assembly.

Two years later he was defeated for the assembly by what he always regarded as corrupt practices, and his cynicism about Upper Canadian politics led him to respond favourably to an invitation from William Lyon Mackenzie to join him in producing a government more attuned to the people. Lount led a group of supporters to Toronto in late 1837, where he became Mackenzie's lieutenant, increasingly attempting to restrain his leader and minimize violence. When the 'rebellion' was put down, he attempted to flee in a boat across Lake Erie to the United States, but was blown back into Upper Canada and arrested.

Lount was tried for treason, and was caught by the special pardoning legislation (the Pardoning Act) passed by the government in early 1838. This Act allowed indicted prisoners from the 'late insurrection' to plead guilty and petition for clemency before they were

■ Execution of Lount and Matthews [date and artist unknown]. LAC, C-001242.

arraigned, thus enticing prisoners to confess their guilt in the hopes of escaping execution. This policy of legal entrapment was more than slightly unsavoury, to say the least. The government, arguing the need to make them examples, rejected out of hand Lount's appeal and that of another rebel, Peter Matthews, despite the fact that both men had large families. The government continued to refuse leniency to Lount and Matthews despite petitions for clemency signed by thousands of Upper Canadians, and they were hanged publicly in the courtyard of Toronto jail on 12 April 1838 before a large crowd. Their property was then confiscated.

denied that they had orchestrated the insurrections, although they wished to take credit for providing the initiative as leaders. Many of the rebels felt they had been goaded into action. Dr Wolfred Nelson, a supporter of Papineau, commented: 'You have to fight liars, whether with their own weapons or with trickery. Frankness is a fine thing among honest men and in private life; in public, it leaves us too exposed. I am annoyed by Mr Papineau's and Mackenzie's admission that we had decided to rebel. That is to justify our opponents and to deprive of any right to complain that we were attacked.'[46] Certainly the rural districts in Lower Canada had their own reasons for rising in arms against the government.[47] What appears clear is that when both Mackenzie and Papineau escalated legal agitation in 1837, most of the political reformers cautiously supported them. But when agitation turned to insurrection, many moderate members of the elite fell away, to be replaced by armed farmers with their own grievances.

Unfortunately for the rebels in both Upper and Lower Canada, their self-declared leaders had fairly narrow agendas for political change. Without plans for wide-ranging social and economic reconstruction, they sought little more than to replace the existing elites with themselves. Neither Papineau nor Mackenzie had any practical notion of how to turn a spontaneous uprising into an organized rebellion. Nor did either grasp the nature of the rural discontent. In Lower Canada the Patriote leaders considered their cause to be in the best interests of the French-Canadian 'nation'; but they were not truly committed revolutionaries, prepared to suffer and die for their beliefs. They were simply liberals.

In both the Canadas, the would-be rebel leaders became caught up in their own hysteria, panicked, and fled, leaving others to face the music. When Papineau heard that warrants had been issued for the arrest of the Patriote leaders, he dashed across the border dressed as a woman. His counterparts in Upper Canada were not much braver. Mackenzie fled at the first sign of trouble, clad in his greatcoat—his critics said—to ward off the bullets, while Charles Duncombe told his followers that only leaders would be prosecuted and forthwith made his way to Michigan, also dressed as a woman.

But the leaders were incorrect in thinking that only they were in danger. Indeed, just the reverse was the case. Although there were few real 'battles' in either province in 1837 or 1838, many rebels died in the course of the skirmishes. Moreover, the authorities were much harder on the rank-and-file rebels, many of whom were imprisoned, exiled, or executed, than on the leaders: eventually both Mackenzie and Papineau would be 'rehabilitated' and allowed to resume public life. Samuel Lount and Peter Matthews were entrapped by the Pardoning Act, when their confessions did not lead to leniency, but other Upper Canadian rebels were freed under its provisions; the British government had insisted that the Canadian authorities be as lenient as possible and provide a form of summary justice that avoided expensive and time-consuming public trials.

THE LOWER CANADIAN REBELLION OF 1838

To sort matters out, in December 1837 Britain appointed Lord Durham governor-in-chief of British North America. Durham arrived in Canada in late May 1838. In addition, fearing an invasion by Americans in league with exiled rebel leaders, the British increased the number of regular soldiers stationed in British North America. But the reinforcements did not arrive in time to prevent a second uprising in Lower Canada in November 1838, led by Wolfred Nelson, who returned from the United States with a few supporters and joined up with several thousand badly armed Patriotes at Napierville. The rebels were quickly routed by a much larger army under Sir John Colborne, who was now commander of the British forces in the Canadas. The government army did a good deal of burn-

DENIS-BENJAMIN VIGER
(1774–1861)

Denis-Benjamin Viger came from an upwardly mobile French-Canadian business family and was educated to the law, which he practised without much success. Eventually he would inherit a fortune in land, but while waiting he served as a militia officer in the War of 1812, wrote for newspapers, and became one of first full-time politicians in the legislative assembly of Lower Canada, which he entered in 1813. Viger soon joined the Parti Canadien, and became its active spokesman in the newspapers. He helped organize the *Canadian Spectator* in 1822, wrote a number of pamphlets, and in 1828 was part of a delegation to London that testified before a House of Commons committee on French-Canadian problems. Upon his return to Canada he was appointed to the Legislative Council, but soon after became the assembly's agent in England, with F.-X. Garneau (see p. 481 as his secretary. When the 92 Resolutions failed to convince the British government of the need for further reform, Viger returned to Canada where he was active in Patriote circles, but always behind the scenes. With L.-J. Papineau, he hoped that the British would come to terms without a need for bloodshed.

Viger's actual role in the rebellion of 1837 is largely a matter of conjecture, but he remained publicly visible and was not particularly persecuted despite his close ties with all the rebel leaders. His newspaper, *La Minerve*, was openly supportive of the rebellion. Viger replied to the Bishop of Montreal's pastoral letter of condemnation of the Patriotes in *La Minerve* in August 1837, pointing out the close connections between the Church and the British authorities. He counselled caution after the open riots of November 1837, but after the closure of *La Minerve*, in November 1837, he apparently bankrolled two newspapers that advocated resistance to the British. When the second uprising began in late 1838, the government quickly put him in prison, where he remained until 16 May 1840 without being officially charged with any crime. His health was severely damaged by the long confinement.

In 1841 he was elected to the assembly in the new province of Canada, and in 1843 he attempted to form a ministry with William Henry Draper under the supervision of Governor Metcalfe. He spent many months seeking to stabilize his government, but was defeated in the elections of 1844. He nevertheless continued as co-premier until June 1846. He was reappointed to the Legislative Council for a second time in early 1848, but never attended meetings. At best a shadowy figure in the rebellion, Viger was obviously not prepared to declare himself an all-out revolutionary. Rather, he was one of those Patriotes who hoped that the people would provide the raw material for a revolution that men such as himself could then shape and lead.

ing (for which Colborne was awarded the nickname 'Old Firebrand'), particularly in the county of Laprairie; describing 'the frightful spectacle of a vast expanse of livid flames', the Montreal *Herald* reported that it had been told 'not a single rebel house [was] left standing.'

■ 'St. Eustache—after we had burnt it . . . 1838', watercolour by Philip J. Bainbrigge (1817–81). LAC, C-11880.

Once again the government allowed the rebel leaders to escape and instead went after the rank and file.[48] This strategy probably reflected the governing elite's sense that there had been a conjunction of popular discontent along with the constitutional wrangling. This time 753 men were captured and 108 brought quickly to trial, resulting in 99 death sentences. In the end, 12 were executed and 58 were banished to Australia. This government response (although relatively mild for its time) was typical of both British North America and its successor, the Dominion of Canada: for many decades governments typically reacted to violent expressions of popular discontent with disproportionate brutality.

Meanwhile, in October 1838—barely six months after his arrival—Lord Durham had announced his resignation. He would submit his report on Canada in 1839 (see Chapter 17).

CONCLUSION

The politics of the period between 1790 and 1840 were dominated by several complex themes. The most obvious was the elite-level struggle for control of the political process. Yet at other levels of society, different dynamics were in play, most of which suggested a more profound popular discontent than traditional interpretations of the legislative conflict would allow. In Upper Canada, British and American residents (and their respective cultures) waged a sometimes desperate struggle for domination of the province—a struggle exacerbated by the War of 1812 and finally settled by the rebellions of

1837, in which the supporters of the British triumphed. To the west, the First Nations people had fought their own wars for their own agendas. In Lower Canada, the conflict was between a different set of cultures, French and English. At the same time, Prince Edward Island and Lower Canada experienced constant battles between landlords and tenants. Especially in the latter, the suppression of the rebellions of 1837 and 1838 marked the temporary triumph of the landlords.

SHORT BIBLIOGRAPHY

Buckner, Phillip A. *The Transition to Responsible Government: British Policy in British North America, 1815–1850*. Westport, Conn., 1985. The most authoritative study of the problem.

Calloway, Colin G. *Crown and Calumet: British–American Relations, 1783–1815*. Norman, Okla., 1987. Despite its subtitle, this study is mainly about Aboriginal peoples and policy.

Greenwood, F. Murray. *Legacies of Fear: Law and Politics in the Era of the French Revolution*. Toronto, 1993. A useful study of early Quebec politics with a legal emphasis.

———— and Barry Wright, eds. *Canadian State Trials, Volume II: Rebellion and Invasion in the Canadas, 1837–1839*. Toronto, 2002. Establishes the historical importance of the legal side of the rebellions.

Greer, Allan. *The Patriots and the People: The Rebellion of 1837 in Rural Lower Canada*. Toronto, 1994. Focuses on the popular dimension.

Manning, Helen Taft. *British Colonial Government after the American Revolution, 1782–1820*. New Haven, 1933. The classic study of its subject, never really superseded.

Read, Colin. *The Rising in Western Upper Canada, 1837–8: The Duncombe Revolt and After*. Toronto, 1983. Emphasizes the importance of other Upper Canadian uprisings besides that led by William Lyon Mackenzie.

Senior, Eleanor Kite. *The Rebellions in Lower Canada, 1837–8*. Stittsville, Ont., 1985. An important study of the military history of the Lower Canadian uprisings.

Sheppard, George. *Plunder, Profit and Paroles: A Social History of the War of 1812 in Upper Canada*. Montreal and Kingston, 1994. A revisionist analysis of the War of 1812 in the colony at its Canadian centre.

Stewart, Gordon T. *The Origins of Canadian Politics: A Comparative Approach*. Vancouver, 1986. A look at the question of Canada's political beginnings, based on modern research and thinking in American and British history.

Ward, John Manning. *Colonial Self-Government: The British Experience, 1759–1856*. London, 1976. An important general account, putting Canada into the imperial context.

Wilton, Carol. *Popular Politics and Political Culture in Upper Canada, 1800–1850*. Montreal and Kingston, 2000. A work that attempts to get away from the traditional story.

STUDY QUESTIONS

1. Why was Joseph Howe's defence in his 1835 libel trial such a tricky business?
2. What sort of colony would the British have viewed as ideal?
3. How did open polling affect early elections?
4. What were the key differences between the reformers before 1815 and after 1820?
5. Why was the War of 1812 important to Canadian development?

6. What did the 1814 Alien Bill make possible?
7. What were the chief issues in popular politics?
8. Why did political gridlock develop in the early 1830s?
9. Were the rebellions of 1837 totally unsuccessful?

CHAPTER THIRTEEN

The New Immigrants and Settlements: Peopling British North America, 1791–1860

■ Between 1790 and the early 1860s, the population of the British colonies in North America increased from 250,000 to more than 3,500,000. This tremendous growth played a part in both the beginning of serious discussions over the unification of British North America and a new push for westward expansion. While much of the population growth was the result of natural increase, especially in French Canada, a good deal of it was the product of immigration, mainly from Europe and particularly from the British Isles. The newcomers helped to transform British North America from a collection of colonies in which more than half the population of European origin spoke French to one in which by 1850 English predominated. Although francophones were still the majority in the St Lawrence region, once Lower and Upper Canada were joined, in 1840, English-speakers became the majority in the new united Province of Canada. In several areas—notably Cape Breton (which was a separate colony until it merged with Nova Scotia in 1820) and Prince Edward Island—more people spoke Gaelic than French.

Post-Loyalist immigrants to British North America were mainly Americans (in Upper Canada) and Scots Highlanders (in nearly all the provinces). Neither group was much wanted by the authorities, who feared the American influence in Upper Canada and thought that Highlanders who emigrated against the wishes of their landlords would not make good citizens. After the end of the Napoleonic Wars, however, both the government and the ruling/landlord classes in Britain once again began to think that the British Isles were becoming overpopulated. Increasingly they came to see emigration as both an alternative to public assistance for the poor and underemployed, and an outlet for superfluous farmers in an era of agricultural transformation. 'Shovelling out paupers' became standard practice for municipal authorities with large numbers on the poor rates. Nearly two million residents of the British Isles sailed to British North America between 1815 and the 1860s as part of a larger exodus to the United States and other British settlement colonies (in South Africa, Australia, and New Zealand). After 1849, some even travelled as far as the Pacific coast. Not all of the two million settled permanently in British North America—perhaps as many as half moved on to the United States, and some unknown number returned to Britain. But some of those who went first to the United States later made their way north to British North America. In 1853, for example, Canada West was the seventh most popular destination of immigrants arriving

TIMELINE

1791
Beginning of Napoleonic Wars closes Atlantic to immigration.

1801
Treaty of Amiens brings temporary peace to Europe. Immigration, especially from Highland Scotland, resumes.

1803
Parliament passes legislation regulating transatlantic passage. War with France resumes.

1811
Lord Selkirk begins recruiting settlers for his Red River colony.

1814
Black refugees arrive in Nova Scotia.

1815
Napoleonic Wars end. Various schemes of assisted emigration for soldiers and sailors organized.

1816
Settlement of Lanark County, Upper Canada, begins.

1819
Albion emigrants arrive in New Brunswick.

1823
Beginning of assisted Irish settlement in Upper Canada. More British regulation of the transatlantic passage.

1824
Canada Company organized.

1825
Robert Wilmot-Horton becomes dominant figure in British emigration policy debate.

1826
Hearings of Parliamentary Emigration Committee.

1828
Development begins on Huron Tract in Upper Canada.

1829
Edward Gibbon Wakefield advocates self-financing emigration.

1831
New Brunswick Land Co. founded.

1832
John Lewellin publishes pamphlet on emigration to Prince Edward Island. Petworth Emigration Committee established.

1833
Cholera epidemic in Lower Canada.

1834
New Poor Law bill introduced in England. British American Land Co. chartered.

1837
Petworth scheme ends.

at New York. In any event, a good many immigrants did put down roots in British North America in this period.

Folk memories of this great migration include many tales of suffering. Poor people told of being driven from their homes and taken

ADVICE FOR IMMIGRANTS

Numerous books and pamphlets were published between 1800 and 1860 devoted exclusively to advice for new immigrants. Most of the advice was useful. Few authors said anything about the passage itself or the difficulties of the transition process.

[Liverpool] is undoubtedly the best port to embark from, as vessels may there be met with at any time during the spring and summer months; and the expense of travelling to that town, even from places at a considerable distance, is not great . . . . In the winter and very early in the spring, there are also vessels constantly going to New York, from whence there are steam-boats to Albany, and a stage to Montreal, or to Sackett's harbour opposite Kingston, by Utica. This would be the best route for persons without families, or who had but little baggage, and who were desirous of leaving England in February or March. A considerable duty or per centage (as much, I believe, as thirty per cent) on the value of their baggage, is paid at New York by persons not intending to settle in the United States, but who were only passing through them in order to proceed to the British colonies. Persons with families, and a considerable quantity of baggage, had therefore better embark for Quebec; and the commencement of April would be soon enough to leave Liverpool, as vessels cannot proceed up the river St. Lawrence to Quebec before the middle of May, on account of the ice. . . .

Coarse warm clothing with flannel shirts, thick worsted or yarn stockings, and strong shoes or half-boots nailed, are most suitable for the climate of Canada in winter; and duck slops, duck trowsers, and calico or homespun linen shirts, for summer wear. Fur caps may also be brought out, as they are expensive here. Any old clothes will serve during the voyage out, and in travelling through the country. Beds may be taken out (without bedsteads). Curtains and curtain-rings, cords, blankets, sheets, warm rugs or coverlets, and several spare bed-ticks. All these latter articles are extremely dear in Canada. Scarcely any thing else need be provided, as all articles of hardware, axes suitable for the country, plough-irons, harrow-teeth, Dutch and tin ovens, tea-kettles, kettles for cooking meat in, &c., &c., &c. may be purchased at Montreal at nearly the same prices as in England.

Every thing should be well packed in strong boxes, cases, or trunks, the more portable they are the better, each not exceeding three feet in length, eighteen inches in breadth, and one foot in depth, made water-tight if possible, or in barrels about the size of flour barrels, also water-tight; and all to be well lashed up or corded. Beds, bedding, curtains, &c. &c., may be sewed up in a wool-sack or very coarse harden, with a strong cord round them; this is the most convenient and best method of taking out beds. China or other earthenware may be packed in tow or the refuse of flax. . . .

All spare money must be brought out in guineas or Spanish dollars, which may be purchased for good bills at any bullion office in Liverpool. Dollars are bought for about 4s. 4d. or 4s. 6d. each.

SOURCE: English farmer settled in Upper Canada, *A few plain directions for persons intending to proceed as settlers to His Majesty's province of Upper Canada, in North America* (London, 1820), as found in Harold Innis and A.R.M. Lower, eds, *Select Documents in Canadian Economic History 1783–1885* (Toronto: University of Toronto Press, 1933), 96–8.

■ 'A First Settlement', by W.H. Bartlett, engraved by J.C. Bentley, from N.P. Willis, *Canadian Scenery* (London, 1842), vol. II. LAC, C-2401.

advantage of by unscrupulous ship captains, before landing destitute in howling wildernesses. Even the better-off immigrants, with some money and education, often described the experience as an ordeal. No doubt part of the reason—particularly among the wealthier newcomers—was that most prospective immigrants had a highly idealized picture of the New World. Although the attractions of British North America may sometimes have been exaggerated, literally hundreds of pamphlets and manuals (as well as letters home from earlier immigrants) were available describing the harshness of the climate, the expense and labour required to clear a farm from the wilderness, and the

scarcity of amenities in most parts of the colonies. Apparently the immigrants simply refused to believe that such realities would apply to them.

Everything that happened in British North America in these years—the rebellions of 1837–8, the union of the Canadas in 1841, the gold rush on the Pacific slope in the late 1850s and early 1860s—took place against the backdrop of this massive movement of migration and resettlement. The vast majority of the leaders of British North America in the second third of the nineteenth century—Lower Canada excepted—were born in Britain or the United States.

TABLE 13.1

POPULATION OF BRITISH NORTH AMERICA, c. 1791–1860

	c. 1791	c. 1845	c. 1860
Newfoundland	15,000	96,000 (1845)	122, 638 (1857)
New Brunswick	20,000	155,000 (1840)	252,047 (1861)
Nova Scotia	40,000	202,000 (1838)	330,857 (1861)
Cape Breton	2,000	n.a.	n.a.
PEI	6,000	47,000 (1841)	80,857 (1861)
Quebec/Province of Canada	171,000	697,000 (LC, 1844) 432,000 (UC, 1840)	1,111,566 (CE, 1861) 1,396,091 (CW, 1861)
The West	n.a.	10,000 (1840 est.)	20,000 (est.)
Total	254,000	1,639,000	3,337,058

SOURCE: *Census of Canada, 1870–71* (Ottawa, 1876), IV, passim.

POPULATION AND IMMIGRATION NUMBERS

Early statistical data for British North America are notoriously unreliable—when figures are available at all. Censuses were taken at different times in different colonies; they were never complete; and the kinds of information they collected were limited. Furthermore, in many cases comparable data are not available. Nevertheless, the gross data that we have indicate that the population of European origin grew from over 250,000 in 1791 to over 1,600,000 in 1845, and to 3,337,000 in 1860 (see Table 13.1).

Data on the First Nations are far more limited: perhaps 50,000 Aboriginal people inhabited the settled parts of British North America in 1790, and in 1845 approximately 150,000 were living in the outlying territory administered by the Hudson's Bay Company. Of the population of European origin in 1791, 140,000 were of French origin and the remaining 110,000 of British ori-

gin. By 1845, the French population was around 600,000, and the British close to one million. By 1860, the francophone population was well over a million. In 1790, as many as half the people of British origin had arrived by way of the thirteen American colonies, but by 1845 those of American origin made up less than 10 per cent of the 'British' total, with extensive concentrations only in Upper Canada—where 32,000 in the 1842 census were listed as having been born in the United States—and Nova Scotia. For the francophone populations (Canadiens, Acadians, and Métis), the growth between 1790 and 1860 was the result almost exclusively of natural increase, but for anglophones natural increase was less important than massive immigration from the British Isles, particularly after 1815.

Immigration figures are even less reliable than population data. Records were not systematically kept for what is now Canada until well after Confederation, although after 1815 the British began keeping approximate track of their

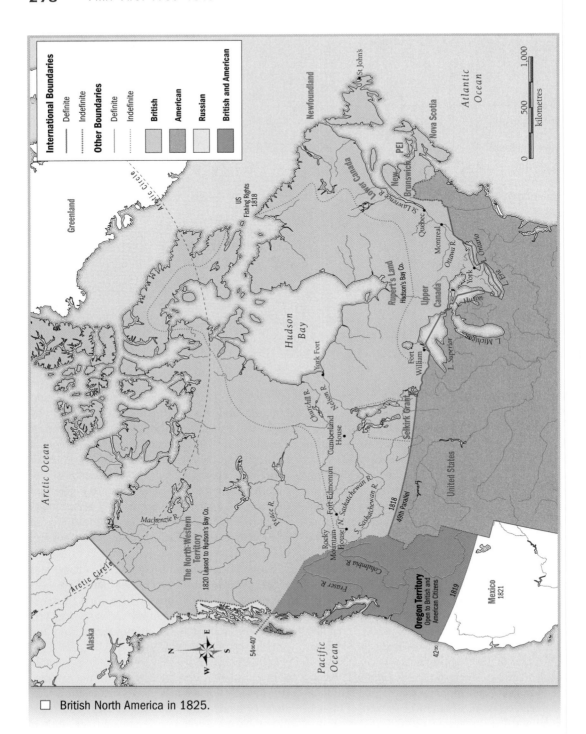

□ British North America in 1825.

emigrants. Nobody monitored the border between the United States and British North America. Since many emigrants from the British Isles sailed initially to British North America but had the United States as their ultimate destination, the British figures are singularly unreliable as indicators of the numbers that stayed in British America. Nevertheless, it is likely that more than 750,000 Britons settled in Britain's American colonies between 1791 and 1845, close to half of them from Ireland. Of the rest, English and Welsh together outnumbered Scots, but—given the relatively small population of Scotland—the Scots represented the British population that was statistically most likely to emigrate in this period. The fact that the newcomers came overwhelmingly from the British Isles did not mean that they were in any way a homogeneous group. Britain was really a collection of quite distinctive countries, most of which were connected for administrative and political purposes only. The bulk of the new arrivals came from the least-integrated parts of the British nation, particularly in a cultural sense. Some spoke languages other than English (Welsh, Gaelic, Erse, Cornish), and even those who spoke English usually did so with distinctive accents and vocabularies. Most belonged not to the Church of England or the Church of Scotland but either to dissenting Protestant denominations or to the Roman Catholic Church. Once in British North America, the Scots and Irish especially retained distinctive identities, which they have never entirely lost.

The immigration of 1791–1860 falls naturally into two periods. Between 1791 and 1815, the newcomers were about equally divided between Americans (the so-called 'late Loyalists' who settled mainly in Upper Canada) and British (with Highland Scots extremely prominent). These immigrants were relatively few in numbers, perhaps 20,000 in all. Most were small property-holders with enough capital to pay their own passage to the New World. The first wave of massive immigration began after 1815, when the

Napoleonic Wars ended, and was almost entirely British in origin. As the British attitude towards colonial emigration shifted from hostility to enthusiastic support, the numbers increased ever more rapidly, especially after 1830. According to British sources, 70,000 left Britain for British America between 1815 and 1820, 139,000 between 1821 and 1830, and 522,000 between 1831 and 1845. After 1840, the Irish and Highland Scottish famines fuelled an even greater influx of immigrants to British North America, which continued until 1855.[1] After 1815 the numbers of immigrants without capital would grow steadily as the cost of the passage declined and various British subsidization schemes came into effect. Earlier immigrants could expect to become farmers and landowners, partly because they had some money and partly because they could take full advantage of generous land grants offered by the various colonial governments. Later immigrants, however, often had to begin their new lives as labourers, whether in resource industries or on public works projects, which became increasingly common in the 1830s. In neither period was much attention paid to the prior claims to land of the First Nations, who were generally regarded as nomads with no entitlement to the territory they occupied.

THE EARLY PERIOD: 1791–1815

'LATE LOYALISTS'

Although the end of the 1780s is usually regarded as marking the conclusion of Loyalist resettlement in British North America, the movement of American settlers into the remaining British colonies continued well after that date. Some unknown number of the new migrants went to Lower Canada (Quebec), where the English-speaking population tripled from 10,000 to 30,000 between 1791 and 1812, without a commensurate anglophone immigration intake from Europe. Many Americans settled in Upper Canada, however. Some of the newcomers, often called 'Late Loyalists', were Quakers and Mennonites who had been attracted to Canada by the prospect of exemption from military service, but they were soon joined by a large influx of American pioneers drawn by the ready availability of land, whether from the government or from private entrepreneurs. Until 1798 the Upper Canadian government regarded these new arrivals as part of the 'United Empire Loyalist' contingent and allowed them to take an oath of allegiance with few questions asked. But as friction between Britain and the United States heated up in the later years of the Napoleonic Wars, Upper Canada became concerned about the 'American menace'.

By the time of the War of 1812, Americans composed as much as 80 per cent of an Upper Canadian population estimated by one contemporary at 136,000 in 1813.[2] Americans also accounted for 10 per cent of the population of Lower Canada, or about 30,000 people. Although, during the war, residents of American origin were certainly regarded by the authorities as potential collaborators with the enemy, the most important implications of the preponderance of Americans, especially in Upper Canada, were cultural. In any struggle for cultural dominance in Upper Canada, the Americans would obviously choose the culture with which they were most familiar. The result could well be a province culturally indistinguishable from the American states on the other side of the border—a situation that those of British background might well find unacceptable.

BRITISH EMIGRATION

Before 1815, immigrants from the British Isles came mostly from the Scottish Highlands and Ulster. But the British authorities were not pleased to see these people leave, and did not encourage their counterparts in the colonies to welcome them. One reason was that for most of the period Britain was at war with France, and those regions were major recruiting grounds for the army. Another reason was that, according to the mercantilist view that still prevailed in most British governing circles, population was needed at home and should not to be encouraged to leave. In 1803 a groundswell of concern over the loss of tenants from the landlords of the Scottish Western Highlands and Islands led to the passage of the first British legislation regulating the transport of emigrants across the Atlantic. Officially intended to improve conditions on the vessels carrying emigrants, in fact the law was cynically designed to raise the price of passage beyond the reach of most ordinary people.[3]

Reluctant to see emigrants leave in the first place, the British authorities did not press the various colonial administrations to welcome the new arrivals by offering them land or assistance. As a result of this policy—or, more frequently, the absence of positive policy—and the almost continual warfare of this period, immigration from the British Isles before 1815 was spotty, occurring only during the brief periods of peace, particularly between 1801 and 1803. Thus, American immigrants made up a particularly large proportion of the new arrivals in the early period. Meanwhile, on the east coast Acadians were able to re-establish themselves in large portions of New Brunswick, as well as in Nova Scotia and Prince Edward Island. By 1803 a religious census showed nearly 4,000 Acadians in Nova Scotia, nearly 700 in Prince Edward Island, and nearly 4,000 in New Brunswick.[4] Left virtually to fend for themselves, the Acadians had developed their culture and institutions before the authorities were fully aware of what was happening.[5]

Most of the Scots who immigrated before 1815 were drawn to the Maritime provinces, where beachheads of settlement had already been established, but some joined Scottish communities in eastern Upper Canada, especially in the Glengarry district. Many were Roman Catholics. In this early period, as later, previous settlement and kinship ties were important factors in the decision to emigrate and the choice of destination. The Scots arrived in large family

LORD SELKIRK ON HIGHLAND EMIGRATION

In every civilized country where landed estates are on a large scale we find no more people upon a farm than are reckoned necessary for carrying on the work that must be done upon it. This is the natural result of the operation of private interest. The proprietor lets his land to the tenant who will give him the highest rent for it; and the tenant manages it in the manner that he expected will produce him the most profit. For this purpose, he must raise as much produce, but with as little expense, as possible; to avoid expense, he must employ no unnecessary hands; must feed no superfluous mouths. The less of the produce is consumed upon the farm, the more he can carry to market.

. . . Where farms are very small, the proprietors will, in every situation, find it for their interest to throw several into the hands of one man. . . . One man constantly employed might accomplish all the work of cultivating several of these small possessions. When they are thrown together, the farmer is enabled, merely by diminishing the number of superfluous mouths, to send a part of the produce to market; and from the same land, without any addition to its fertility, to afford a better rent to the landlord.

The further enlargement of farms throws them into the hands of men of education and efficient capital, who, by following improved modes of cultivation, increase the productiveness of the soil: thus, according to the observation of Dr. Adam Smith, 'the diminution of cottagers, and other small occupiers of land, has in every part of Europe been the immediate forerunner of improvement and better cultivation.'

Such a revolution in the system of landed property must be accompanied by an entire change in the distribution of the inhabitants. The population must be cast into a new form. The class of small tenants will gradually disappear. . . . A few shepherds, with their dogs, will be sufficient for all the work of many. . . . The produce will no longer be consumed wholly upon the spot, in affording a scanty subsistence to an indolent contented tribe; but will supply, at a distance, the wasteful luxury of industrial crowds.

During the operation of this change, and the temporary derangement it occasions, much individual distress will unavoidably be suffered. A great part of the inhabitants must, in one way or another, seek for means of livelihood totally different from those on which they have hitherto depended. But the country affords no means of living, without a possession of land: they must look for resources, therefore, where there is a prospect of employment, and must bring their mind to the resolution of removing at least from their native spot. Two prospects present themselves. In the Low Country of Scotland, the wages of manufacturing labour; in America, the easy acquisition of land in absolute property. Of these alternatives, it is easy to perceive which will best suit the inclination and habits of Highlanders. . . . To those who can . . . afford the expenses of the passage and first settlement, the low price of land in America presents the prospect of speedily attaining situations and mode of life similar to that in which all their habits [are based]. Accustomed to possess land, to derive from it all the comforts they enjoy, to transmit their possessions from father to son, and to cherish all the prejudices of hereditary transmission, they must naturally consider themselves as born to a landed rank, and can form no idea of happiness separate from such a possession.

SOURCE: Untitled pamphlet, reprinted in J.M. Bumsted, ed., *The Collected Writings of Lord Selkirk 1810–1820* (Winnipeg: Manitoba Historical Society, 1987), 252–4.

groups, and successful settlement attracted more immigrants from the same districts. After 1806, when the closure of the Baltic timber region to Britain encouraged the development of the timber industry in British North America, the numbers of ships sailing westward across the Atlantic to pick up timber suddenly increased, and since most ship-owners found passengers preferable to ballast, the cost of the passage was reduced. (It would not increase until the 1840s, when a shift in British trade policy put an end to the favouritism shown North American timber in the British market.) Few immigrants were attracted to Lower Canada, however, in part because of the dominance of French culture, and in part because the seigneurial system made it difficult for newcomers to purchase freehold property except in the isolated Eastern Townships.

BLACK REFUGEES

In 1814, towards the end of the War of 1812–14, the commander of the British fleet on the Atlantic coast issued a proclamation offering shelter to all American residents who came to British ships or posts as refugees. Although he did not mention slaves, it was well understood that they were the targets of the proclamation. Indeed, by an international decision the United States was compensated for 3,601 slaves taken away from the southern states (mainly Maryland and Virginia). Most of these people were transported to Nova Scotia, where they joined some 1,500–3,000 other blacks who had made their way to Halifax during the war. As more refugees continued to arrive, the British authorities found themselves responsible for a wave of immigrants that the Nova Scotia assembly labelled as 'a separate and marked class of people, unfitted to this Climate, or to an association with the rest of His Majesty's Colonists'.[6]

Initially treated as new settlers, the refugees were gradually dispersed into the countryside and supplied with agricultural implements along with two years' worth of provisions. Beginning in 1815, however, they were treated under the Act

for the Abolition of the Slave Trade of 1808, which required only that the chief customs officer provide them with the same rations earlier given American prisoners of war in Halifax. Like the black Loyalists before them, the refugees were given 'tickets of occupation' for 10-acre lots. But most were not experienced farmers—as field hands, they were familiar only with plantation agriculture—and in any case the allotments of land were too small to support a family. Governor Dalhousie told the Colonial Office that the refugees were 'Slaves by habit & education, no longer working under the dread of the lash, their idea of freedom is Idleness and they are altogether incapable of Industry',[7] and the government began looking for somewhere else to send them. Some went to Trinidad in 1820, but many remained in Nova Scotia, where they had to depend on the public purse and private charity until well into the nineteenth century. In 1834, in the wake of emancipation in the West Indies, Nova Scotia tried to avoid similar problems by preventing the clandestine landing of liberated slaves in the province, but in 1836 the British government disallowed the legislation on the grounds that it was discriminatory.

Black refugees fared little better in New Brunswick, where an initial group of nearly 400 were sent in 1815. Some found employment, and when they requested land allotments, in 1816, they were given tickets of occupation to lots of 50 acres, not far from Saint John.[8] But the land was poor and stony (in the twentieth century the soil was found to be totally unsuited to agriculture), and had to be surveyed at their own expense. Moreover, they were forbidden from selling it. Not surprisingly, the 'Black Settlement' —or 'Willow Grove', as it came to be called—did not prosper.

Two points regarding the black refugees should be highlighted. First, they were consistently discriminated against. Given inadequate quantities of land that was unsuitable for farming in any case, they were denied title and therefore unable to sell it for other purposes. Second,

■ 'The Emigrant's Welcome to Canada', c. 1820. W.H. Coverdale Collection of Canadiana, LAC, C-41067.

many of the poor Irish, Welsh, and Scots Highlanders who immigrated via assisted settlement schemes between 1815 and 1830 were no more successful than the black refugees, even though they had access to considerably more public and private assistance. The truth was that settlers without capital and independent agricultural experience were unlikely to succeed in British North America, whether they were white, black, red, or green.

THE POST-WAR PERIOD, 1815–1860

The War of 1812–14 interrupted the flow of immigration, chiefly because the threat of privateering on the high seas reduced ocean traffic. After 1815, circumstances combined to reverse the resistance to emigration on the part of both the British government and the British landholding classes (the common people of Britain had always been enthusiastic about starting afresh in the New World, given half a chance). Immediately after the Napoleonic Wars, the cooling of the overheated wartime economy led to substantial unemployment; and even after the post-war depression had ended, a new round of industrialization and agricultural rationalization left many without work in their traditional occupations and places of residence. The growth of the factory system threw many traditional artisans out of work, and the new industrialists did not employ workers when they did not have orders to fill. For many villagers and small farmers, migration was inevitable—either within the British Isles to other forms of employment or to

North America, where there was at least a chance of continuing to work on the land.

As pressures on Britain's long-standing arrangements for poor relief increased, the search for solutions became urgent. In 1826 the influential *Edinburgh Review* argued that 'What is wanted is, the adoption of a system that will effectually relieve the immediate pressure of pauperism, without throwing it upon Great Britain and which will, at the same time, enable such further measures to be adopted as will ensure the future and lasting prosperity of the country.' More and more, emigration was seen as the answer. But whether this relocation project should be officially sponsored and funded by the British government was another matter. The boom in the North American timber trade provided the shipping capacity for the transatlantic movement of immigrants at a relatively low cost, and private entrepreneurs were brought into the picture in various capacities.

In British America the relationship between immigration and land policy—particularly the ways in which 'waste' or wilderness land was transferred from the Crown to individuals—was always close. The traditional British pattern was to devolve the cost of immigration onto the private sector. Before 1775 the government had reserved large grants of land for prospective sponsors of immigration, but after 1783 land was typically made available to anyone who applied for it, at the cost of the legal expenses. Occasionally, as in Nova Scotia and with the Loyalists, the British government sponsored settlement schemes. Advocates of 'assisted' emigration argued that such schemes should cover actual settlement on the land as well as the initial relocation. Underlying this argument were three assumptions: that the people so aided would need external support until their land was improved; that they would ultimately farm their own land; and that they should be required to pay back the investments made in them. There seemed to be no middle ground. Either the state paid for everything, including tools and provi-

sions, until the farmer became truly self-sufficient—which would take several years and could be done for only relatively small numbers—or it paid virtually nothing. Relatively few emigrants benefited from assisted emigration, either public or private, and most of the costs of transplantation—in terms of both money and suffering—had to be borne by the settlers themselves.

Although people immigrated for various complicated reasons, no doubt the principal one was to gain access to land, which was becoming increasingly difficult to obtain in the British Isles. Land meant different things to different people. For some it meant independence. As one former Glasgow weaver put it in 1821, in Scotland:

> I had to labour sixteen or eighteen hours-a-day, and could earn about six or seven shillings-a-week—here, I can, by labouring about half that time, earn more than I need: there, I was confined to a damp shop,—but here, I enjoy fresh air: there, after I had toiled until I could toil no more, I would have the mortification of being a burden,—but here, two or three years' labour will give me more than will keep me in sickness, as well as in health: there, it is all dependence,—here, it is a fair prospect of independence.[9]

Not all new arrivals hoped to become full-time farmers. Many sought to return to a half-remembered past when artisans had enough land to supplement their earnings with subsistence agriculture. Combining farming with some other occupation became quite common in British North America.

Politically and culturally, the increase in immigration from the British Isles after 1815 was momentous. Despite the War of 1812, the roots of the population of British North America in 1815 were as much American as British. While most residents of American background had not openly supported the United States during the war, the long-term implications for a politically autonomous British America were clear if the American influence continued to predominate.

So too were the cultural implications. The massive immigration between 1815 and 1845 confirmed both that British North America would continue to belong to the British Empire, and that British culture would be at least as influential as American culture in the various provinces.

PATTERNS OF POST-1815 IMMIGRATION

Five basic patterns of immigration and settlement can be identified in British North America after 1815. But they were not mutually exclusive: for example, a given family could receive assistance with the costs of transportation or settlement or both. Chronologically, the trend moved from public assistance in the 1820s to almost complete self-reliance in the 1840s, with several intermediate or transitional stages along the way.

Government-assisted immigration. As early as 1813 the British government began making plans for settling demobilized soldiers on waste land in its American colonies. The first formal scheme was launched in 1815 when the government advertised in Scotland, offering passage to Upper Canada, land grants of 100 acres for each head of family, agricultural implements at cost, and a publicly supported minister and schoolteacher for each community. The scheme was obviously not designed for the very poor: prospective emigrants had to put down a substantial deposit refundable in Canada two years after actual settlement. In the same year more than 700 passengers on four government vessels were sent to Quebec and housed over the winter in Cornwall at the government's expense; eventually they made their way to lands recently purchased from the Aboriginal people in Lanark County. By then, however, the newcomers had lost a year's planting time. To prevent them from leaving for the United States, the government had to continue providing assistance, and this proved so expensive that the ministry abandoned the scheme, awaiting 'a Season of less financial

Difficulty'. Subsequent ventures, including one involving unemployed weavers in 1819–20, required the co-operation of government and private emigration societies. In the case of the weavers, who also settled in Lanark County, the government advanced over £22,000 to them, and in 1836 was forced to cancel the debts.

Despite the British authorities' reluctance to invest large sums in settlement schemes, the problems of Ireland and its dispossessed tenant farmers were too pressing to ignore—at least in the mid-1820s. In 1823 the ministry of Lord Liverpool proposed public sponsorship of Irish emigration to Canada, offering to 500 acceptable applicants from the rebellious south of Ireland free passage, free land, and free conveyance to it. Irish landlords initially opposed the scheme, arguing that it would attract 'the most industrious and best disposed' of their tenants and recommending instead that only people 'connected with the disturbances' or from districts prone to violence be selected for emigration. This was an ongoing problem: the British ruling classes wanted overseas emigration to serve as a safety valve relieving the country of paupers and troublemakers, not as a siphon removing peaceable and industrious citizens. On the other hand, paupers and troublemakers did not usually make the most successful immigrants. In the case of the Irish plan, Peter Robinson—a prominent resident of York and brother of the attorney general of Upper Canada—was placed in charge of recruitment. He focused on County Cork, where the Insurrection Act was in force.[10]

In Ireland Robinson met some initial resistance, but he soon found 'a perfect mania for going to Canada'. A party of 568 left in July 1823, but did not arrive on their lands at Shipman's Mills (Almonte), in the Bathurst district, until October—too late to plant and nearly too late to build shelters for the winter. Local residents had to be employed to help the newcomers. Within two years, a third of the 182 families had departed. The average expense of settling one person had been more than £26. Two years later, in 1825, another 2,024 people were removed from 'the most disturbed part' of Ireland and transported to the future Peterborough, Ontario. In this case, a third of the adult emigrants died within three years, and there was much local violence between the Roman Catholic newcomers and the Protestant Irish already living in the district. Costs again were high, publicity about the venture negative, and the governor of Lower Canada spoke for many when he described the enterprise as having 'no other end than relieving the South of Ireland of a burden [and throwing it] upon the industrious classes of this young country.'[11]

The various government experiments with assisted emigration in the 1820s all demonstrated that the cost of establishing British settlers in British North America was high: even those who thought that the costs could be reduced estimated £60 for a family of five. But some members of the British government—particularly the parliamentary undersecretary at the Colonial Office, Robert Wilmot-Horton—insisted that such government sponsorship was essential, to rid the country of unwanted paupers. Wilmot-Horton's own emigration scheme, presented to several parliamentary committees and in 1828 to Parliament itself, called for the expenses of transatlantic resettlement to be paid by local authorities encumbered by poverty, via an annuity debited to the ratepayers. Three factors worked against Wilmot-Horton's scheme: local taxpayers were not enthusiastic about footing the bill; many people feared that populating British North America would only accelerate the colonies' union with the United States; and, finally, an attractive alternative plan emerged in the late 1820s. Its chief advocate was Edward Gibbon Wakefield, who focused less on emigration itself than on the disposal of colonial land. Unlike Wilmot-Horton's plan, which was attacked as nothing more than the 'shovelling out of paupers', Wakefield's scheme concentrated on land policy, abandoning the idea of giving land away in favour of charging a 'sufficient price' that

would not only ensure a revenue for colonial improvements but guarantee that those acquiring land would have some capital.[12]

Private assistance. After 1830 the British government backed away from publicly assisted emigration, chiefly because it was not willing to assume the cost. Serious consideration was given to legislation for parish-aided emigration in 1831 and again in 1834, largely to prevent rural unrest. But few English parishes were willing to take up the burden, and when such unrest did not materialize to the extent feared, the steam went out of the plan. Nevertheless, some parishes continued to support the concept of transporting and resettling prospective charges on the poor rates, and in some regions the rural crisis did turn nasty. In Sussex, for example, the protest activities of the legendary 'Captain Swing' led the Earl of Egremont, one of the region's largest landholders, to assist the parishes in transporting some 1,800 men, women, and children (mainly from the Petworth district of West Sussex) to Upper Canada in the years 1832–7. In Canada, the Petworth Emigration Committee received further help from the province, and the emigrants, mainly redundant agricultural labourers, settled chiefly in what is now southwestern Ontario, especially around London and Woodstock.[13]

We know a good deal about the Petworth scheme because the records of it are unusually complete and because a collection of the emigrants' letters home was edited for publication by the Reverend Thomas Sockett, the manager of the project.[14] Since the letters were clearly intended to justify the Petworth scheme and attract further immigrants to Upper Canada, it is impossible to know how accurately they reflect the settlers' true feelings. Nevertheless, the letters suggest that most were well pleased. The majority succeeded in obtaining work or a farm. On 30 July 1833, for example, Caroline Dearling wrote her parents: 'We have got 50 acres of land, at 3 dollars per acre: we have nothing to pay for 3 years. Our house will be done before long, then

PETER ROBINSON
(1785–1838)

Peter Robinson was born in New Brunswick to a prominent family among the newly arrived Loyalists from New England. In 1798 he moved with his family to Upper Canada. Robinson was active in the fur trade, and in 1812 personally raised a rifle company that fought with Brock and in the west during the War of 1812. With the help of his stepfather he became a businessman and land speculator in the years after 1812. Robinson's early career was not hurt by the fact that his brother, John Beverley Robinson, was attorney general of Upper Canada.

Elected to the House of Assembly in 1816, in 1822 Peter Robinson went to England and met with Robert John Wilmot-Horton, the colonial undersecretary who was seeking to send landless Irish tenant farmers to settle in Upper Canada. Robinson agreed to supervise the scheme, and thereafter visited Ireland regularly. He personally selected most of the immigrants and in 1823 accompanied them to their new homes in Upper Canada. However, he left them on their own almost at once, and was severely criticized when many of them abandoned the settlement in search of better opportunities. As a result, when in 1825 he travelled to the Newcastle area with another 2,024 immigrants, he tried to take a more hands-on approach. Getting the newcomers settled on their land proved to be complex and

difficult. Yet the Newcastle settlements appeared to be going well when Robinson testified before the 1826 and 1827 select committees on emigration orchestrated by Wilmot-Horton. At the hearings, Robinson testified to the high cost of assisted emigration, given the need to support the emigrants for several years in order to prevent them from leaving. In the end, he and others suggested that the expense was beyond the capacity of the government, and the program was discontinued. Before Wilmot-Horton left office in 1828, he ensured Robinson's appointment as commissioner of Crown lands and surveyor general of woods in Upper Canada, and a third appointment, as commissioner of clergy reserves, soon followed.

Because of the close relationship between land and immigration, Robinson became the major figure in Canadian immigration policy. Although the British government had withdrawn from large-scale assisted immigration, the land policy that Robinson administered was generous, and included employment for immigrants on Crown lands, especially during the bad years of 1832–3. Unfortunately, his open-handed policy and accountancy shortcomings left larger and larger bills behind, and in 1833 colonial officials stopped his salary briefly until he repaid some of the advances.

we are going to it. John can get work, he is a harvesting.'[15] Not all immigrants to British North America were so successful. Of course, the Petworth group had the advantage of considerable assistance. Furthermore, as hard-working,

experienced farmers, they were ideally suited for pioneering in Upper Canada.

The Petworth scheme was closed down when the Earl of Egremont died in 1837, but other landlord-sponsored emigration projects continued into the 1840s, especially from the Hebrides islands off the northwest coast of Scotland. Many of these islands had managed to support substantial populations in the earlier years of the nineteenth century, partly through the remittances sent home by soldiers in Highland regiments and partly through employment (collecting kelp, which was used in glass- and soap-making), supplemented by small-scale agriculture on tiny plots of land. After the Napoleonic Wars ended, however, both the remittances and the kelping business fell off, and the landlords tried to shift into other economic activities, mainly sheep-farming. A few landlords who felt some responsibility for the inhabitants of their lands paid for them to emigrate, mainly

■ Thomas Douglas, Earl of Selkirk. This portrait is said to be based on one by the Scottish artist Henry Raeburn, but the location of the original is unknown. LAC, C-1346.

to British North America. Although there were constant complaints from the colonies, which felt they were being used as dumping grounds for an indigent population, the Highlanders were resourceful and accustomed to making do within extended kinship communities. Most eventually found places in the Maritime provinces, though on land considerably less attractive than that in Upper Canada.

PRIVATE LANDHOLDERS AND LAND COMPANIES

Wakefield's ideas regarding land distribution were never fully implemented in British North America, although they underpinned the remarks on land policy in Lord Durham's famous *Report* of 1839; indeed, those remarks were drafted by Wakefield, who served as one of Durham's aides. But the notion of selling Crown lands to provide colonial revenue was always attractive, and it gained more support after Wilmot-Horton's emigration proposals were rejected.

Before the 1820s, most land was distributed through free grants to proprietors, who would develop the land and sponsor immigrants to settle on it. Over the years, this process underlay many of the large land grants made to proprietors in several colonies, including Prince Edward Island. But the costs of developing a wilderness were high, and individual private landlords such as Lord Selkirk or Thomas Talbot (in southwestern Upper Canada) were limited in what they could do. By the 1820s, privately funded land companies—which could raise larger amounts of capital than a single proprietor—partially replaced the earlier individual entrepreneur. Of the three largest companies—the Canada Company, the British American Land Company, and the New Brunswick and Nova Scotia Land Company—the earliest and most energetic was the Canada Company, in which the Scottish novelist John Galt played a leading role.[16] In 1826 this company purchased most of the Crown reserves and half of the clergy reserves in Upper Canada, and it later bought a large block of unsurveyed land on the shore of Lake Huron (the Huron Tract). Its payments for these lands—spread over 16 years—provided Upper Canada with a regular income. Although the Canada Company nearly went bankrupt on several occasions, and despite constant complaints that the payments and concessions were not commensurate, it did succeed in settling large numbers of people on its lands. One of its most important agents was William ('Tiger') Dunlop, who in 1832 published a popular guide entitled *Statistical Sketches of Upper Canada, for the use of Emigrants: by a Backwoodsman*.[17] The towns of Guelph, Galt, and Goderich were all founded on Canada Company land, and by 1840 boasted nearly 6,000 settlers, 23,000 acres under cultivation, and large numbers of gristmills, sawmills, tanneries, and distilleries.

The British American Land Company was incorporated in 1834 to develop and settle nearly 600,000 acres of Crown land in the Eastern Townships of Lower Canada. John Galt and Edward Ellice were its principal promoters. In 1837 Colonel Duncan McDougall advocated the establishment of 5,000 Highland Scots families on 150,000 acres of company land, at a cost to the British taxpayer of £227,500, on the grounds that the removal of protective duties on alkali had destroyed the kelp industry, much as the abolition of slavery had destroyed the sugar planters. The scheme did not win public favour, but the company did begin co-operating with Scottish landlords in making land available for emigrants whose former lairds agreed to pay for their passage. The company's success was limited by the availability of competing government lands, and gradually it moved into more diversified investments.

THE CANADA COMPANY,

Have nearly One Million Acres of Land,

OF THE FINEST DESCRIPTION,

For Sale, in the Huron Tract,

And persons desirous of purchasing can obtain all the necessary information, as to prices, situation of vacant Lots, and mode of application, from the *Land Agents*, appointed for that purpose, at the Company's Offices in,

Goderich, Stratford, & Hay.

The object which the Canada Company have principally in view in appointing those Agents, is that they may afford this information, for they have not been empowered to receive Money; persons, therefore, having to make payments, either on account of credit Instalments falling due, or first Instalments on new purchases, may lodge the money with the Bank of Upper Canada Agency in the *Town of London*, on account of the Canada Company, who will give them a Receipt for the same, which may be remitted to the Commissioners in Toronto as Cash, and by return of Post its receipt will be acknowledged; or should there be no Bank Agency in the neighbourhood, they may retain the money till the arrival of one of the Commissioners, who will attend at each Agency every second month, for the purpose of receiving money and issuing Location Tickets to purchasers; or they may forward the amount, at their own risk, by the Post from *Stratford* or *Goderich*, and which leaves the latter place each week for Toronto.

No person will be allowed to take up Land who is not prepared to *pay the first Instalment in Cash*, either by remittance in the manner here pointed out, or to the Commissioner on his periodical visits, and should this regulation not be complied with, the Lands will be immediately held as open for re-sale; nor will any person be allowed to hold Land who has not made a regular application for it through the Land Agent, and received his written permission to take possession of it on the terms here stated.

Canada Company's Office,
Toronto, 1st May, 1836.

Printed at the U. C. Gazette Office.

☐ An advertisement for Canada Company lands. Metropolitan Toronto Reference Library.

Finally, the New Brunswick and Nova Scotia Land Company was formed in 1831 to settle several large tracts in New Brunswick. Of the three major land companies, it was the only one that actually advanced money to emigrants (mainly Scots from the Isle of Skye). In its financial affairs, however, the New Brunswick Company —like its sister land companies—appears to have combined chicanery with bad management. None of these ventures was ever able to determine whether it had made a profit from land improvement and settlement. Nor is a modern assessment of their economic viability and financial operations possible.

THE TRANSATLANTIC TRANSPORTATION CONTRACTORS

From the beginning of the nineteenth century, many of the transatlantic immigrants travelled to North America on sailing vessels built for freight (especially timber) that were temporarily converted to accommodate passengers. Sometimes the owners of such vessels chartered them to contractors who then found the prospective passengers, and sometimes they advertised for emigrants themselves. In distressed areas the contractors often canvassed door-to-door.

The brig *Albion* was built for a Welsh merchant family named Davies, residing in Cardigan and trading out of Liverpool. Registered in March 1815, just at the end of the Napoleonic Wars, the *Albion* was a relatively small vessel—72 feet long by just 22 feet wide—with a maximum height of about 13.5 feet, one deck, two masts, and a burden reckoned officially at 166 tuns. Launching the *Albion* at the start of a lengthy economic crisis, the Davies family had to look far afield for cargoes. British North America offered plenty of timber, but it was hard to find an outgoing cargo, since timber was much bulkier than the finished goods exported to North America. Thomas Davies turned to the distressed farmers of Cardiganshire, whose land had been overused during the war and was now suffering from soil exhaustion. After the war, the bottom dropped out of the grain market, and not even the introduction of the Corn Laws (which protected the market but raised the cost of grain for consumers) offered much relief. In Cardiganshire the poor were reduced to 'swallowing barley-meal and water—boiling nettles, etc.'. Meanwhile, the landed proprietors sent 'their Bailliffs with Distress warrants to Distrain upon their poor tenants', secure in the knowledge that, with a rapidly increasing population, there would be no shortage of new tenants prepared to pay more

than their predecessors for the privilege of working the land.[18]

After a long period of rural unrest, the surplus population of Wales would eventually be put to work in the coal mines and factories of the Industrial Revolution, but in 1819 the prospect of starting again in America was attractive. However poor they might be, some displaced farmers still possessed farm equipment and livestock that they could sell for passage money. Thomas Davies distributed broadsides printed in English and Welsh, and found 180 passengers for the *Albion* to carry to New Brunswick. The voyages to America of the *Albion* were different from countless others of the period only in the fact that the participants wrote and published works about them. Someone, for example, wrote—in Welsh—a lengthy narrative about an 1818 passage to New Jersey, and among the passengers on the 1819 voyage was one who wrote a poem, 'Cân Sef Hanes y Brig Albion' ('Poem about the history of the Brig Albion'):

> I can tell you about New Brunswick,
> Which is so full of trees, right across it;
> I don't think there is anywhere in the whole world
> A better place to be found . . . .
> There are no rents or taxes here,
> Everyone owns his own property.
> O that the poor people of Wales
> Could be here, all of them.[19]

The reality that the passengers encountered on arrival was not so positive. Disembarking in Saint John, where they were unceremoniously dumped by the ship's captain, the newcomers had little money and no means of obtaining land. Most headed up the Saint John River to Fredericton, where they successfully petitioned the government for land and eventually received assistance from a local society that raised funds 'for the purpose of assisting the Welch families' through subscriptions and donations.

Others who were dumped by their ships were not so fortunate, especially after a series of cholera epidemics in the 1830s aroused widespread public hostility towards them. Nevertheless, many newcomers did arrive with considerable capital—or at least access to it—and the money they injected into the colonial economies became as important as any other single economic factor in the period.

UNASSISTED IMMIGRANTS

In addition to settlement assistance, the *Albion* passengers had the advantage of being a homogeneous group; having each other's company and support was probably a critical factor, especially since their cultural background set them apart from both the English- and the French-speaking communities of New Brunswick. Most new arrivals in British North America travelled alone, or at best in nuclear families, and for them the process of adjustment was often extremely difficult. Most immigrants to North America in the 1815–40 period probably paid their own way, out of modest savings. Virtually all the emigration manuals emphasized the relationship between capital and success in British North America. After 1845, however, increasing numbers of immigrants had been forced out of their homes by famine, poverty, and unemployment. For those people emigration was not a choice but an imperative.

In 1876 a tiny volume was published in Toronto, entitled *Life and Adventures of Wilson Benson. Written by Himself.* Born in Belfast in 1821, Benson arrived in Quebec with his young wife, Jemima, in 1841. They made their way to Brockville by barge and settled there with two sovereigns of ready money and a chest from which most of their personal possessions had been stolen on the last leg of the trip. According to Benson:

> My wife hired out to do general house work. However times were so bad I could not find a stroke of work to do, neither in the town nor in the country round about. My money was exhausted, and the

first night in Brockville I took lodging in a tolerably respectable looking tavern; but after getting to bed, the fleas and bed-bugs appeared to be at war which of them should take possession of me. This was my first experience of bedbugs.[20]

As his account suggests, the Bensons were forced to separate in order to find employment. Benson quickly moved through a variety of jobs, none of which lasted long. He tried storekeeping in Kingston and worked as a porter on a river steamer before opening a small store in Toronto and beginning a trade in fruit and vegetables with Kingston while still working on inland vessels. Not until 1851 were the Bensons able to settle on some waste land—and it was probably the death of his father in Ulster that provided the money to do so. By 1876 Wilson Benson was well satisfied: 'it is a source of extreme gratification to me, as it no doubt will be to all the pioneers of my early days, that their sacrifice of worldly comforts and exposure to toil and suffering have so largely contributed to the development of our country and the welfare of succeeding generations.' Others who were less successful in the quest to make a new life would no doubt express less satisfaction; but we hear mainly from those who did achieve their ambitions, not those who failed on the way.

Nor do we often hear about female immigrants. Although most new arrivals were male, females, too, came to British North America, and not only as wives or in family parties. In the nineteenth century, a single, unattached woman arriving in British North America could either look for a husband—in an environment famously short of females—or find employment as a servant.

The difficulty of the transatlantic passage remained unchanged from 1790 to 1860.[21] Even the lucky few who could afford cabin accommodation faced voyages of six to ten weeks, cooped up in small quarters and living on bad rations, at least towards the end. For the poor majority in steerage, the discomfort and health risks were

■ 'Wharf at Quebec', by James Pattison Cockburn, c. 1830. An officer in the British military, Cockburn arrived in Quebec around 1826 and travelled widely through British North America before publishing his book *Quebec and Its Environs* in 1831. LAC, W-571.

greatly increased. As conditions worsened in Britain, and especially Ireland, many emigrants were already malnourished when they sailed, and therefore particularly susceptible to contagious disease on overcrowded vessels. Increasingly, the bulk of the immigrant traffic passed through the port of Liverpool, where thieves and con artists preyed on those waiting to set sail. After 1825 the British government abandoned any serious effort to regulate the passage. Given that most new arrivals heading inland in British North America landed at Quebec, it should have been no surprise when the city experienced a series of epidemics in the 1830s, or that some residents

became convinced that the British government was deliberately dumping its unwanted poor on their doorstep. Conspiracy or not, mortality and suffering ran fairly high among the immigrants.

BLACK IMMIGRANTS

After 1815, most black immigrants to British North America headed for Upper Canada in search of refuge from slavery or extreme racial discrimination. As one contemporary popular song put it:

I'm on my way to Canada
That cold and distant land

The dire effects of slavery
I can no longer stand—
Farewell, old master,
Don't come after me,
I'm on my way to Canada
Where coloured men are free.[22]

Another song was supposedly sung by fugitives crossing into Canada at Niagara Falls:

Oh, I heard Queen Victoria say,
That if we would forsake,
Our native land of slavery,
And come across de lake,
Dat she was standing on de shore,
Wid arms extended wide,
To give us all a peaceful home,
Beyond de rolling tide.[23]

Not all the new arrivals were fugitives; indeed, most probably were not. Many from the northern cities were relatively prosperous freedmen hoping to escape racial discrimination. British America did provide a refuge from slavery, but it was by no means free of racism.

We can delineate three distinct periods of black immigration into the Canadas. In the first, before 1830, a mere trickle of individuals crossed the international border at either Windsor or Niagara Falls, usually without any organized assistance. In the second period, between 1830 and 1850, the exodus was increasingly well organized, involving white abolitionists as well as black activists committed to freeing their fellows from oppression. One key feature of this period was the development of the 'Underground Railroad': a complex network of organizations, individual men and women—black and white— and safe houses through which fugitives were smuggled northward and eventually across the border. Although its reputation for secrecy was well deserved, its operations were actually quite ad hoc, and its members seldom directly encouraged slaves to escape.[24] Another key development after 1830 was the active involvement of the white abolitionists who, for example, financed group settlements on the Upper Canadian side of the border. The final period began in 1850 with the American passage of the Fugitive Slave Law, aimed at facilitating the recapture of escaped slaves even on Canadian soil, and continued until the start of the American Civil War. Abolitionist activities intensified, as did clandestine immigration and passionate feelings on all sides. Even on the Pacific coast, spillover from eastern hostilities drove hundreds of black people from California to Victoria and the Gulf Islands, where they generally met with a favourable reception.

CONCLUSION

In the absence of any formal public policy, the settlement of British North America was largely completed through the successes and failures of individual immigrants from the British Isles between 1815 and 1860. Most were not destitute, but many arrived without enough money to take up land, at least immediately. By and large, the earlier arrivals probably succeeded more readily, partly because they brought more money with them, partly because there was more fertile and well-located land available to them than to those who followed. Together, these immigrants—part of one of the largest mass movements of human history—transformed the British North American colonies in the first half of the nineteenth century. They also injected a tremendous amount of money into the various colonial economies. Even if the average immigrant brought only £10, the total between 1815 and 1860 would amount to nearly £20 million. Filling the needs of new settlers developed into one of the most vibrant sectors of the colonial economy.

SHORT BIBLIOGRAPHY

Benson, Wilson. *Life and Adventures of Wilson Benson. Written by Himself.* Toronto, 1876. One of the few surviving autobiographies by an ordinary immigrant.

Bumsted, J.M. *The People's Clearance: Highland Emigration to British North America, 1770–1815.* Edinburgh and Winnipeg, 1982. Argues that early Scottish emigration was not necessarily forced by clearances, but was largely voluntary.

———. *Lord Selkirk: A Life.* Winnipeg, 2008. Attempts a balanced account of the pioneer in assisted emigration.

Cameron, Wendy, and Mary McDougall Maude. *Assisting Emigration to Upper Canada: The Petworth Project 1832–1837.* Montreal and Kingston, 2000. A recent study of English assisted emigration in the 1830s.

Cowan, Helen I. *British Emigration to British North America: The First Hundred Years,* rev. edn. Toronto, 1961. Still the standard overview.

Greenhill, Basil. *The Great Migration: Crossing the Atlantic Under Sail.* London, 1968. A judicious survey of a passage much more complex than it first appears.

Houston, Cecil J., and William J. Smyth. *Irish Emigration and Canadian Settlement: Patterns, Links, and Letters.* Toronto, 1990. A good account of Irish settlement, distinguishing carefully among several Irelands.

Johnston, Hugh. *British Emigration Policy, 1815–1830: 'Shovelling Out Paupers'.* Oxford, 1972. The best survey of British policy after the Napoleonic Wars.

Macdonald, Norman. *Canada, 1763–1841 Immigration and Settlement: The Administration of the Imperial Land Regulations.* London, 1939. Still the best work on the relationship of land and immigration.

Preston, Richard Arthur, ed. *For Friends at Home: A Scottish Emigrant's Letters from Canada, California and the Cariboo 1844–1864.* Montreal and London, 1974. An edition of letters that demonstrates the mobility of many emigrants.

Thomas, Peter. *Strangers from a Secret Land: The Voyages of the Brig 'Albion' and the Founding of the First Welsh Settlements in Canada.* Toronto, 1986. A work much richer than its title suggests.

STUDY QUESTIONS

1. What are the problems with early immigration statistics?
2. Who were the 'Late Loyalists'?
3. What effect did war have on immigration?
4. Is Lord Selkirk's explanation for Highland emigration satisfactory?
5. Why was the relationship between land policy and immigration so critical?
6. Did the British attitude towards emigration change in the first half of the nineteenth century? Why?
7. If you were contemplating immigration to British North America in the first half of the nineteenth century, what sorts of information would you want to have?

CHAPTER FOURTEEN

The Colonial Economy, 1791–1840

British North America came out of the American revolutionary period with an extremely limited economy in considerable disrepair. By the 1840s it could boast a very active, even vibrant, commercial economy based on rich natural resources and a growing transatlantic carrying trade. Without substantial economic growth, Britain's American provinces could not have attracted—and retained—the many new immigrants flooding into its seaports and filtering out to settle its 'waste' lands. Immigration and growth, of course, were mutually reinforcing. Economic development was always complex, and in most regions of European settlement it depended from the outset on natural resources.

Although the typical settler was a farmer, he seldom existed solely by growing and preparing his own crops for his own consumption. Fish, furs, timber, and grain were particularly critical as additional sources of income. Taken together with their ancillary reprocessing industries, these represented well over 90 per cent of all economic activity in British North America in this period. Such commodities, of course, required markets, and before the 1840s Britain's colonies found theirs chiefly in the United Kingdom and within the Empire, where trade policies tended to remain mercantilistic and favourable to colonial raw materials. In the 1840s, when Britain shifted to a policy of international free trade, British North America would have to make significant adjustments to its economic and commercial patterns. But for infant colonies rapidly expanding with new settlers, Britain's preferential treatment for raw materials constituted a major boost, and was at least as important as immigration in their economic growth.

The mother country also provided much of the capital with which British North Americans developed their resource base. Reliance on British investment may have led the colonies to concentrate on too small a range of activities, ultimately limiting their economic development. But for people desperately short of capital, investment in any form was a boon—and in any case there was little alternative. The United States' economy was not yet sufficiently mature to provide venture capital for foreign investment. The Americans were using what capital they generated chiefly to develop their own internal market, and subsequent patterns of American investment in British North America/Canada suggest that if the Americans had shown an earlier interest in their northern neighbours, their focus would have been on extending their own economy rather than gaining returns on investment, which was the immediate goal of at least some British investors.

TIMELINE

1791
New British Corn Laws.

1801
Aqueducts for Montreal opened.

1806
Napoleonic Wars close the Baltic to trade, leading to new timber laws in Britain.

1811
Fur-trade war begins in the West.

1812
Fort Astoria on Columbia River sold to the North West Company. Cunard and Son founded.

1815
Newfoundland fishery begins to stagnate. Sealing increases in importance. New Corn Law of 1815 protects colonial production.

1817
Bank of Montreal founded.

1818
Night watchmen introduced in Montreal.

1821
Merger of HBC and NWC. Bank of Upper Canada chartered. Lachine Canal begun.

1822
Americans have moved into Gulf of St Lawrence fishery.

1824
Fort Vancouver established.

1826
Rideau Canal begun.

1827
Fort Langley established.

1828
Corn Act of 1828 allows colonial advantage outside Europe.

1829
Welland Canal, linking Lakes Erie and Ontario, opened.

1832
York police force founded.

1833
Chambly Canal begun. Canadian ship *Royal William* becomes the first to cross Atlantic under mainly steam power.

1836
First steam vessel on Pacific coast.

1839
Cunard Line established.

FISH

Fish were the oldest and most consistently rewarding of British North America's resource commodities, having been successfully exploited since the early years of the sixteenth century.

Traditionally associated with Newfoundland, the fishery continued to dominate that colony's economic picture throughout the nineteenth century; but in the period 1790–1840 fishing also became important for Nova Scotia and the Gulf of St Lawrence, especially the Gaspé region of

Lower Canada. While Newfoundland continued to send most of its cod to Southern Europe, Nova Scotia exported much of its catch to the West Indies, where Britain was largely able to exclude the Americans and give her northern colonies some competitive advantage. Britain had also assisted the colonial fisheries to a limited extent in the peace negotiations that followed the American Revolution, when—although it allowed the Yankees to fish on the Grand Banks and in the Gulf of St Lawrence—it restricted their right to dry fish on unsettled British shoreline except in Newfoundland. Later, after the War of 1812, Britain would argue that the war had negated the rights given the Americans in 1783, further increasing Newfoundland production. The fishery was to remain a bone of Anglo–American contention for many years.

The exclusion of the Americans was not the only change that affected the Newfoundland fishery in these years. By 1815, ongoing warfare had killed the migratory fishery operating out of England's West Country, leaving control of fish production almost totally in the hands of Newfoundland residents, whose numbers grew rapidly as a result. West Country merchants moved into St John's, which became the commercial entrepôt for both the fishery and the island as a whole, gradually eliminating both English and Channel Islands interests.

Nevertheless, after 1815 the Newfoundland fishery entered a long period of stagnation, which forced Newfoundlanders to diversify. Moving into Labrador, they began combining fishing with sealing. Before 1815 sealing had never represented more than 10 per cent of the value of the cod fishery, but now it increased rapidly in importance. In 1818, 165,622 seals were taken; in 1831, the total was over 601,000, and dried cod and seal-oil exports were worth £360,000 and £197,000, respectively. Sealing employed 290 ships and 5,418 men in 1827. The markets for Newfoundland fish changed as well, with those in Southern Europe declining in volume after 1815, those in the British West

Indies holding steady, and those in British America and Brazil increasing substantially. Newfoundland faced increased competition, particularly from countries like Spain and Portugal, which had been major customers before 1815.[1]

While Nova Scotia did not directly compete with Newfoundland for world fish markets, its rise did prevent Newfoundland from gaining ground in the British West Indies trade. Nova Scotia merchants had access to more diversified cargoes, and even exported shiploads of ice to the Caribbean. Nova Scotia had gained its West Indian advantage during the breakdown of Anglo–American relations that culminated in the War of 1812, and after the war had persuaded Britain to restrict American trade with the Caribbean islands. In an attempt to expand the market for its fisheries, Nova Scotia experimented with bounties and worked hard at building up a carrying trade to the West Indies in goods from both the United States and British America. A fishery that in 1790 had been mainly for local consumption employed 10,000 men by 1830, and was in volume about one-fifth of the Newfoundland totals.

The Gaspé fishery suffered from several disadvantages in this period. As Americans were not prohibited from dry-fishing on unsettled coastlines, such as those of the Magdalen Islands, they were attracted to the Gulf of St Lawrence. Moreover, attempts to support and protect the fishery ran up against opposition from the Canadien agricultural interests that dominated the assembly of Lower Canada. According to Louis-Joseph Papineau, support for the Gaspé fishery 'encourag[ed] a species of industry the least proper for this country; for every fisherman they created they withdrew a cultivator from the soil, a pursuit that is infinitely more fit for Canada than any fishery.'[2] Clearly, the advocates of agriculture failed to appreciate the symbiotic relationship between farming and the resource economy in many regions. Nevertheless, several large merchant firms flourished in the Gaspé fishery; the biggest, Charles Robin and Co. at

Paspébiac, employed over 350 men between May and August and supported more than 800 families in the district.[3]

The fisheries of British North America grew substantially in the early years of the nineteenth century, when American competition was virtually eliminated. Although no appreciable expansion took place after 1815, the industry continued to employ a considerable workforce. It produced a significant export trade, which of course required many sailing vessels, large and small, and thus contributed both to the shipbuilding industry and to the carrying-trade capacity of British North America. Many colonial sailors learned their skills as young men working on small fishing boats.

FUR

That other traditional Canadian resource industry, the fur trade, was a very minor one in financial terms after 1790; its exports amounted to only a small fraction of the value of the Newfoundland fishery. Nevertheless, in a non-economic sense the fur trade was extremely important to British North America, since it anchored Great Britain's claim to sovereignty over much of the northern part of the continent, especially in the vast territory extending west of the Great Lakes across the prairies and the northern tundra to the Pacific slope. It was also important to some industries in England, particularly the hatting industry located around Stockport and Manchester, and to office operations, since the Bay supplied most of the goose quills with which English Bob Cratchits kept their accounts. In the years between 1790 and 1840 the fur trade extended its geographical reach both northward and westward, in the process gaining information about virtually the entire continent.[4] Meanwhile, by 1820 a bitter rivalry between the Montreal-based North West Company and the English-based Hudson's Bay Company came to a head. The battlefields were Lord Selkirk's colony at Red River and the rich fur-trading territory of

the Athabasca River system in what is now northern Alberta. Out of this commercial war came a new fur-trading company that, although it took the name of the Hudson's Bay Company, was actually a coalition of the two earlier rivals. This new company was allowed by the British government to administer most of British North America outside the settled areas.

THE NORTH WEST COMPANY

The Montreal-based fur trade—managed from the 1790s to 1821 chiefly by the North West Company—had always been inherently expansionistic, using its employees' canoeing and portaging skills to continue pressing into new territories offering higher-quality furs. After the American Revolution, the direction of the Montreal trade was largely in the hands of Highland Scots, but the labour force consisted almost exclusively of Canadien voyageurs and Aboriginal trappers. The Montrealers constructed an elaborate but flexible corporate organization to run the trade. They separated the marketing and trading functions, allowing successful traders who operated in the interior to rise rapidly to profit-sharing partnerships in the company. Unlike other resource industries in British North America, the fur trade always tended towards monopoly, to avoid competition in the actual process of trading with the Aboriginal suppliers. The North West Company itself represented the end product of several decades of amalgamation of smaller trading concerns, when cut-throat competition and violence were used to intimidate those unwilling to co-operate. The company always encouraged individual enterprise, particularly beyond the bounds of its normal trade. Among the feats of overland exploration accomplished under its auspices were the 1793 journey of Alexander Mackenzie to the Pacific and the 1808 descent to tidewater by Simon Fraser of the river that bears his name. By 1812 the company had successfully expanded to the Pacific coast in the wake of

■ The forts of the recently merged Hudson's Bay and North West companies at Pembina on the Red River, 1822. The NWC post, Fort Gibraltar, is on the left, the HBC post, Fort Douglas, on the right. Watercolour by Peter Rindisbacher. LAC, C-001934.

David Thompson's journey down the Columbia in 1811. Having taken over a trading post at Astoria, at the mouth of the Columbia, founded by an American fur company, after 1814 the Nor'Westers largely controlled the Pacific fur trade, which until then had been conducted chiefly by American traders arriving by ship.

Yet despite its rapid geographical expansion, the North West Company had serious problems in the early years of the nineteenth century. These included a substantial increase in transportation costs across a river network of more than 5,000 kilometres, as well as increasingly lengthy gaps between the time traders headed west with goods to trade for furs and the time the furs were taken to market in Europe. The company had no control over the depression in fur prices that resulted from Napoleon's closure of

the Baltic in 1807; nor was it able to eliminate all competition from the Hudson's Bay Company by reaching some agreement on the sharing of territory. Publicly the Nor'Westers insisted that the chartered monopoly of the HBC was irrelevant; but privately they knew they were interlopers— and that if the English company ever gained the full backing of the British government in asserting its charter rights, their Montreal-based trade would be in trouble.

THE HUDSON'S BAY COMPANY

For nearly 150 years the Hudson's Bay Company had paid very good dividends to its stockholders. Run from London by a board of directors who had never seen its fur-trading territories, the HBC was conservatively managed. Montreal-based competition from the Nor'Westers had forced the company to move inland from its posts on the Bay, but it had not yet expanded into the rich territory of the Athabasca, and its total share of the fur trade was relatively small. In 1809, however, Lord Selkirk and his family became important stockholders in the HBC, and they were determined to reinvigorate the company and diversify its trading activities. In 1811 Selkirk received a large grant (roughly 300,000 square kilometres) of western territory from the HBC and began to organize a settlement at Red River—in the very district where the canoe crews of their rivals stopped for provisions on the transcontinental journey between the St Lawrence and the western fur-trading areas. The Nor'Westers regarded the establishment of the colony as an open declaration of war, and by 1815 they, Selkirk, and the HBC were engaged in a desperate struggle for control of the West that continued for five years.[5] The British government refused to intervene officially in the dispute. By 1820 all three parties— the Nor'Westers, the HBC, and Selkirk—were physically and financially exhausted, and in 1821 the Nor'Westers joined their rivals, with the blessing of the British Colonial Office.

The new HBC enjoyed the benefits of the original company's charter, access to capital, and corporate management, with most of its expanded personnel in the field coming from the more energetic Nor'Westers. From 1821 to 1840, the Hudson's Bay Company attempted to maintain a monopoly position, not only in the territory of its historic charter but as far east as Labrador, as far southwest as the Willamette Valley (in the future state of Oregon), and as far north as Alaska and the Arctic. It was not successful on all fronts, but it did manage to control—economically and otherwise—most of the territory that would become western and northern Canada. At the same time the restructured HBC was increasingly used by the British government as an informal instrument of imperial policy. Unfortunately, the company's settlement efforts, particularly west of the Rockies, were not as successful as its fur-trading activities.

After 1821 the traditional product of the fur trade shifted from 'Made Beaver' (beaver pelts that Aboriginals wore next to their skins as clothing) to 'Parchment Beaver' (sun-dried out of doors). The former, with guard hairs naturally removed, were far more valuable. Why this shift occurred is not entirely clear, but it is probably connected with the economic pressures on the Natives and their increasing dependence on HBC trade goods, which meant they no longer wore skins. By 1850 'Made Beaver' was no longer listed on the shipping lists of the HBC.

One consequence of the disappearance of the North West Company was that Lower Canada (especially the ports of Montreal and Quebec) was forced to shift out of an industry that it had previously dominated; timber and wheat would become the wave of the future in eastern Canada and goods from the Bay were shipped via York Factory. Although the fur trade continued to be profitable for several generations, the main beneficiaries were British investors, and by 1840 the company stopped hiring Lower Canadians. Personnel for the trade now came either from Britain or from the settlement at Red River. Over-extended transportation routes continued to be a problem, but little of the traffic came through the east. HBC traders deliberately over-trapped the Columbia River basin to create a buffer zone between themselves and the Americans.[6] After 1821 the Pacific slope became increasingly important to the company, which established Fort Vancouver, on the Columbia River, as a major depot in 1824 and Fort Langley, on the lower Fraser, as a northern entrepôt in 1827. In 1836 the first steam vessel arrived at Fort Vancouver. The company pressed hard to reach self-sufficiency in foodstuffs at all its locations, and by the 1830s the Pacific posts had replaced Red River as the principal source of food. By 1832 Fort Vancouver had over 400 cattle and was producing 3,500 bushels of wheat, 3,000 of barley, 3,000 of pease, 15,000 of potatoes, and 2,000 of oats. New lines of trade, such as salmon-packing, were developed, and new

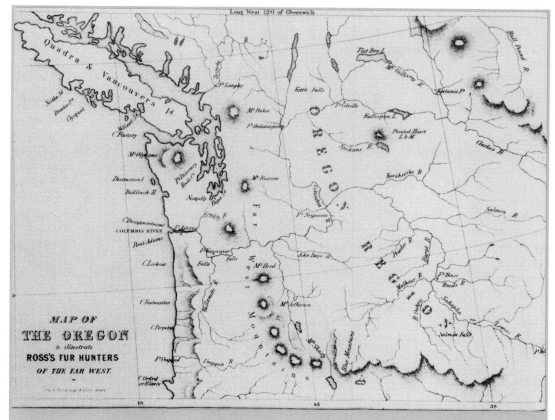

MAP OF
THE OREGON
to illustrate
ROSS'S FUR HUNTERS
OF THE FAR WEST

☐ One of the best accounts of the Oregon Territory was written by the fur-trader Alexander Ross after he retired to Red River with his Okanagan wife and their children (see Chapter 20). *Fur-Hunters of the Far West* was first published in 1853. This map is from the 1855 edition. Metropolitan Toronto Reference Library.

markets opened. In the late 1830s the HBC moved into California and the Sandwich Islands (Hawaii), and in 1839 it signed a deal with the Russians to supply their fur-trading company, the Russian American Company, with foodstuffs for 10 years.

The obvious agricultural potential of the Far West, especially the Willamette Valley, attracted the first American settlers in the late 1820s, and soon pioneers were trekking overland from mid-continent in covered wagons along the fabled Oregon Trail. The Hudson's Bay Company was able to freeze out American fur-trade competitors, but could not hold back the constant stream of American settlers. Residents of the Willamette Valley soon began organizing to demand territorial status and annexation to the United States.

Although the value of fur production was relatively low, and went into an absolute decline after 1840, the fur trade was crucial to the West, chiefly because furs were almost the only commodity that could be exported profitably in the early years. Politically and economically, the entire western and northern region was organized around the fur trade, as was much of Labrador. In the organized and settled provinces of British North America, however, the fur trade had little importance after 1821.

TIMBER

After 1790, fish and furs—the old staples of the northern colonial system—were rapidly joined and even exceeded in economic importance by timber and grain. Particularly in the early years of production, both commodities benefited from imperial policies that gave preferential treatment to goods from the colonies, especially in the large and lucrative British market. The first such policy was the British Corn Law of 1791. The colonial competitive advantage continued to grow even after the famous Corn Law of 1815, which partially cushioned British North America from the general prohibition on imports of wheat and wheat flour into Britain imposed in order to drive grain prices up. In a Corn Act of 1828, the mother country continued concessions to colonial wheat and flour made in 1825 and 1827.[7] By the 1840s, however, the British government began talking about reducing the differential duty scales on wheat, and in 1846 it effectively put an end to colonial preference in grain.[8] The pattern was similar in the timber trade, where differential duties were the 'sleeping partners of the Corn Laws'. The practice of giving duty advantage to colonial timber began in earnest with Napoleon's closure of the Baltic in 1807, and reached its maximum effect in the period 1813–19. Extremely high duties on non-colonial timber were reduced in the early 1820s, but British North America retained its distinct advantage until 1842, when the Peel ministry began to move towards free trade. A massive reduction in colonial preferences was introduced into Parliament in 1846, and thereafter the colonies' timber, like their grain, was forced to compete without much advantage in the British market. For most of the first half of the nineteenth century, however, the industry was shaped by the advantages first given to colonial timber as an indirect result of French actions.

Merchants in British North America constantly lobbied to secure continued or even enhanced imperial preference for their major resource exports in Britain. (Colonials may have been chained economically to the mother country, but they revelled in the chains.) Any hint of a change in imperial regulations sparked fears of economic disaster in the colonial mercantile community. But British policy was never intended to suit the colonies. Having provided these industries with advantages in the start-up phase, the mother country began moving towards free trade at a stage when the duties had served—or at least ought to have served—their economic purpose.

Every province of British North America, except Newfoundland, became actively involved in the timber trade, cutting down primary-growth forests as quickly as possible with no thought for conservation or reforestation. It was in New Brunswick, however, that the timber business was most pervasive, dominating every aspect of life. Starting at an extremely low level of production, the colony's exports of squared timber increased forty-fold within two decades, to 400,000 tonnes by 1821, and its dependence on timber became almost total. In 1827, for example, wood products accounted for over two-thirds of the value of all exports from Saint John. Expansion of settlement was closely connected to the opening of new timber territory, and jobs in the forests were available to recent immigrants who had no qualifications other than their willingness to work.

For a time, almost anyone could become a timberer. The industry soon came to be dominated by those local merchant entrepreneurs with access both to markets and to the expensive licences needed to cut on Crown land. Obtaining a licence required not only capital but political connections at Fredericton; and, not surprisingly, New Brunswick's timber princes became its leading politicians. By 1836–7, 12 men held nearly

■ These two photos from the New Brunswick lumber camps obviously post-date 1840, but there is no reason to think that conditions in the timber trade changed much in the course of the nineteenth century. From Adam Shortt and A.G. Doughty, eds, *Canada and Its Provinces* (Edinburgh, 1914), vol. 14. Metropolitan Toronto Reference Library.

half the province's licences. At a level below the large merchants, who were based in the port cities, a variety of local entrepreneurs—storekeepers, brokers, sawmill operators—organized the hundreds of small parties that spent the winter in the woods, cutting trees, and then in spring transported them by river to the ports. In some ways it was in the interests of the industry to do as much processing as possible on the spot, but the production of sawn planks (or 'deals') in place of squared timber developed only slowly. The British preferred squared timber; little capital was required to cut it, and it was easier than deals to handle and float downriver. Nevertheless, the shift to fully processed lumber was inexorable, and only strengthened the position of the people with capital at the apex of the timbering pyramid. By 1837 the sawmills of Samuel Cunard, in the Miramichi River Valley, were capable of cutting 42,471 feet (13,000 metres) of boards per day, 'the produce of 320 logs and 50 workmen'.[9] In New Brunswick, as in other prime timber country such as the Ottawa River Valley, the production of timber had become very much an industry.

GRAIN

All North American farmers needed at least one marketable crop, but—given the primitive state of transportation and the limited availability of markets—finding a profitable one was not easy. Hence the attempts by early colonial promoters to encourage specialty crops, such as flax or hemp. The growing overseas demand for wheat seemed to offer an ideal solution to the farmers' needs, and in the extensive agricultural lands of the St Lawrence Valley and Upper Canada wheat quickly became the dominant crop. Many Canadian farmers of the first half of the nineteenth century were at least as specialized in wheat production as their later prairie counterparts, exporting a substantial part of their production to international markets. Marketing wheat was much like marketing fish or timber. The producers had little connection with the

ultimate sale and distribution of the commodity and were almost totally dependent on the commercial acumen of the merchant exporters. In this period wheat had strong internal and external markets, and it was virtually the only crop that could be transported for long distances and exported successfully. In 1840—admittedly a very good year—the St Lawrence mercantile system exported, mainly to the United Kingdom, over 1,700,000 bushels of wheat and flour. Even so, Upper and Lower Canada had quite different experiences with wheat in terms of economic growth.

The soil in much of Upper Canada was relatively well suited to wheat, although the cash potential of the crop did tempt some farmers to try growing it in places where conditions were less favourable. Wheat prices depended on international and imperial variables. When prices were high, farming strategies were adapted accordingly, and since virgin land produced the best yields, farmers practised an exploitative form of agriculture that was not very different from the way timberers attacked the forests: instead of rotating crops, they exhausted the soil and moved on, eventually as far as the prairies. By 1840, with the output of Upper Canadian farmers reaching new heights, the handwriting was already on the wall for the colony's wheat economy. Within 10 years the best soil everywhere in the bread-basket regions would be exhausted, and average wheat yields had already fallen from 40–50 bushels per acre to under 20. Nevertheless, while the wheat boom lasted it contributed to both commercial development and capital accumulation in the colony. In the more prosperous districts west of Belleville, most of the major towns, such as Brantford and London, served as export ports or terminals while supplying the surrounding wheat-growing region. Since much of the western crop was shipped to overseas markets through Montreal via the St Lawrence, Upper Canadian wheat enabled Montreal to remain a major entrepôt, despite the uneven record of its Lower Canadian hinterland.

PHILEMON WRIGHT
(1760–1839)

■ Philemon Wright, c. 1800–10, by an unknown artist. LAC C-011056.

Philemon Wright was born in Woburn, Massachusetts. He fought with the Americans at the Battle of Bunker Hill in 1775, and subsequently moved to the Vermont frontier. In 1796 Wright bought land in Lower Canada. A year later he applied to the government in Quebec for a land grant on behalf of himself and a number of associates (fellow citizens of Woburn) and in March 1800 he led a party of 63 settlers to the township of Hull. Initially he had planned to establish himself as a squire in a new agricultural society, and he did pursue agriculture seriously: by 1820 he was one of British North America's first 'Wheat Kings', harvesting nearly 36,000 bushels of wheat on his farms—a count that doubled within a few years—and he also raised large numbers of cattle.

At the same time, however, he pursued a number of other interests: in innkeeping, milling, retailing, and, above all, lumbering. At first, much of the wood came from the land that the settlers were clearing for their crops, but gradually Wright acquired more land specifically for timber. Whether lumbering was simply an offshoot of his agricultural activities or the fulcrum of the entire enterprise is not entirely clear, but by 1806 he was floating rafts of squared timber down the Ottawa River to Quebec. Wright's operations were a classic example of economic integration, both horizontal and vertical. Not only did he have a piece of virtually every economic enterprise remotely related to Hull Township, but he controlled the production of timber from the woodlot to the point of sale on the St Lawrence.

Before 1830 Wright showed little interest in politics, although as an important member of the regional elite he had a good deal of local power. He was a militia officer, a justice of the peace, and after 1817 commissioner for the summary trial of small causes. It was Philemon Wright who asked the Royal Institution for Advancement of Learning to establish a school at Hull, and although he began life as a Congregationalist he gradually moved towards the Church of England. Wright was master of the first Masonic lodge established in Hull in 1813. He was elected to the assembly in 1830, sat for four years, and went home without having become a member of either the Legislative Council or the Château Clique. A perfect example of a 'Late Loyalist', Wright demonstrated how Yankee ambition and ingenuity could work in British North America.

Indeed, while Upper Canadian farmers flourished, their Lower Canadian counterparts passed through a series of crises in the first half of the nineteenth century. Through the end of the eighteenth century, Canadien agriculture had been fairly small-scale and diversified, producing for a limited local market with wheat as the major crop. When a substantial overseas market for Canadian wheat opened, early in the nineteenth century—before Upper Canada was capable of exploiting it—Lower Canada tried to meet the demand even though neither its soil nor climate was well suited to wheat. Land that in many cases had been farmed for generations, using bad agricultural techniques, quickly became exhausted when required to produce grain intensively, and the new lands were not very promising. By the 1830s (if not before) the rapidly increasing population was consuming more wheat than Lower Canada could grow. The result was a permanent wheat shortage. In the long run Canadien farmers would move out of wheat altogether, but in the short run its failure as a staple crop deprived Lower Canada of the cash income that might have served as the basis for urban and economic development, as it did in Upper Canada.[10]

Despite the obvious importance of wheat to many farmers, their dependence on it should not be exaggerated. Farmers everywhere in British North America also produced a variety of foods for their own consumption; livestock (cows, chickens, and pigs) and kitchen gardens were often tended by the women and children of the household. The vagaries of the international market could present serious problems for farmers who over-specialized or fell deep in debt. In such cases a prolonged decline in the price of wheat, such as occurred in the mid-1830s, caused considerable distress. Almost from the beginning, some well-located farmers were able to supply meat and produce to adjacent urban markets, or to send crops like potatoes to places such as Newfoundland that were chronic importers of food. In the Atlantic colonies particularly, where farms had been established before

the wheat boom and where neither land nor climate was well suited to that crop, mixed farming was fairly common. Nevertheless, Maritime farmers still devoted far more land to wheat and grain than was advisable.

WOMEN AND THE PIONEER ECONOMY

For many women in British America, the struggle to carve a farm out of the wilderness was the principal reality of life. For the minority who lived in the cities, the struggle took a somewhat different form. But for all women in the days before modern labour-saving devices, most work associated with the home meant long hours of heavy physical drudgery.

Perhaps the most obvious aspect of women's responsibilities was food preparation, starting with the yeast (or 'barm') for the bread that in the early days, before the construction of outdoor ovens, had to be baked in a fireplace kettle. In addition, however, women were responsible for much food production and preservation. Many fruits could be dried. (Samuel Strickland described one method: 'Plums, raspberries and strawberries are boiled with a small quantity of sugar, and spread about half an inch thick on sheets of paper to dry in the sun. This will be accomplished in a few days; after which the papers are rolled up, tied, and hung up in a dry place for use. When wanted for tarts these dried fruits are taken from the paper and boiled with a bit more sugar, which restores the fruit to its former size and shape.'[11]) Some vegetables were dried, others pickled; meat was usually dried, smoked, pickled, or salted. During the long winter months the staple diet consisted of salt pork, flour, potatoes, and corn, often dried. Women made soap and candles, they washed clothes, they tended the fires under the maple syrup. As life improved, there would be cows and fresh milk, chickens and fresh eggs. Both milk cows and chickens were usually tended by the women and children. Although conditions became less primitive over time—and the focus of production shifted from subsistence to the market—there was never any appreciable reduction in the work required of women to keep their families going.

In every household there was a rough division of labour by gender, which only became more categorical as the nineteenth century wore on. The woman's job was to produce food, clothing, and household necessities, and to perform a wide variety of services for other members of the family. At the same time, of course, she was also responsible for bearing and raising children. In a society in which infant mortality was high and farm labour from outside the family hard to come by, the pressure to produce large families was considerable. As John MacGregor put it in *British America* (1833): 'He who has the most numerous offspring, is considered to have the best opportunity of prospering, in a country where land is abundant, and in which the price of labour is high.'[12] Society recognized the advantages that marriage brought to the pioneer. John Howison noted in 1821 that 'Married persons are always more comfortable, and succeed sooner, in Canada, than single men; for a wife and family, so far from being a burden there, always prove sources of wealth. The wife of a new settler has many domestic duties to perform; and children, if at all grown up, are useful in various ways.'[13] Women were also expected to contribute in the male sphere when required (men did not normally reciprocate), and in many families such assistance was called for on a regular basis. At a time when British North America was still largely a resource society, men often left home for long periods to work in timbering, fishing, or fur-trading; from time to time they might also be called away on military service or political business. In their absence, women had to run households and farms, manage businesses, and generally keep the family going.

Some women might earn small amounts of cash by selling extra produce, such as eggs or butter, but otherwise their work was not remunerated. Moreover, women's contributions to the family's economic well-being were rarely taken into account in inheritance strategies. Typically, the family patriarch would leave his property to the eldest son, along with the responsibility for the maintenance of the widowed mother. Daughters usually counted for very little, and the position of widows was often quite precarious, although they did have control over any property that they had brought to the marriage.

THE MERCANTILE SYSTEM

MERCHANTS

Producing resource commodities anywhere in British North America would have been a futile exercise without the capacity to sell them on the international market. Here the merchant capitalist was critical, for it was through him that the production of the colonies flowed out and finished products flowed in. The merchant had to manage the movement of goods in both directions, either employing others to transport them or organizing his own shipping system. He needed reliable agents abroad. He also had to deal with the vagaries of an unsophisticated international credit system that essentially depended on his own ability to turn goods around in an environment where it often took years to realize any return on earlier investment. Merchants operated at various levels of volume and capital investment. The small merchant continued to find a place throughout the period, but as the resource trade grew, larger entrepreneurs were required—men like Samuel Cunard in Halifax. Large or small, mercantile entrepreneurship was both rewarding and financially dangerous. The risks were many, ranging from disasters at sea to miscalculations of the market, to creditors who would not pay their bills. The larger entrepreneurs were at greater risk than the smaller ones, and few merchant princes managed to leave their fortunes to their heirs. Because of the difficulty of finding trustworthy partners and agents, the extended family network continued to be the international basis of much mercantile activity.

One of the few great merchants who managed to leave a fortune to his heirs was Samuel Cunard (1787–1865), whose estate at his death was valued at somewhere between £350,000 and £600,000—in any case, a vast sum for the age. Cunard got his start in A. Cunard and Son, the Halifax firm of his father, founded in 1812, which was active in the timber and West Indian trades. The younger man engaged in a variety of enterprises in British North America, diversifying and protecting himself relatively well. But even he experienced a financial crisis when the steamship company he had created in 1839 with several Glasgow partners (the forerunner of the Cunard Line) failed to make the anticipated profits because of a British recession. Cunard found himself overextended, and in 1841 began mortgaging his property to raise cash; a year later he furtively slipped out of Halifax aboard one of his own steamships to avoid a writ of attachment for £2,000. The Cunard family scrambled to find the £4,000 it took to keep Samuel from being pushed into involuntary bankruptcy by one creditor. For many years thereafter, Cunard's creditors hampered his movements and prevented him from controlling his own enterprises; he liberated himself from them only in the 1850s.[14]

Atlantic merchants joined Cunard in emphasizing the carrying trade, though seldom in steamships. James Peake of Charlottetown emigrated from Plymouth to Prince Edward Island in 1823 and quickly became a major ship-owner and -broker, selling Island-built vessels in the British market. Peake concentrated on smaller vessels, mainly schooners, for resale, keeping the larger brigantines for his own use, chiefly in two trades: the timber trade between PEI/New Brunswick and England, and a general coastal trade, often between Nova Scotia and Newfoundland. He took advantage of 'fleeting opportunities' whenever possible—as in 1845, when he bought potatoes from PEI for a New England market where crops had failed. But the basis of his success was diversification: into stores that sold goods he imported, into marine insurance, into ship chandlery and outfitting (which grew out of both his retailing and ship brokerage operations), and into land speculation. Peake himself regarded it as his task 'to set an example and to encourage others to plan and build for the future in this place'. He added, 'Tho' others will no doubt have more capacity, still I feel it is my place, if I may say it, to be an engine, yet moderate.'[15]

COLONIAL MANUFACTURING

Merchants like James Peake were fully aware of their importance in the economic life of their regions. In the period 1790–1840, commercial activity was the 'engine' of British North America's economic system, filling the Atlantic Ocean with vessels that sailed east with resource commodities and west with manufactured goods and new immigrants. Nevertheless, two kinds of manufacturing activity did take place within the British colonies. One was the production for local markets of specialized goods that either could not be imported profitably or could not be imported at all. Every town had its saddler, every village its blacksmith; wheelwright Benjamin Chappell produced more than 700 spinning wheels by hand for the Prince Edward Island market in the early years of the nineteenth century. The second type of manufacturing involved the processing of resource commodities. Grain was distilled into whisky, brewed into beer, and milled into flour; wood cleared by farmers was burnt into potash, and timber was cut at sawmills into deals. Most of these specialized manufacturing enterprises were relatively small. The largest by far were the shipyards that transformed timber into sailing vessels.

Shipyards could be found anywhere in British North America at the junction of forests and open water; the commerce of the Great Lakes and the transatlantic traffic both required a good many sailing vessels. But no place depended more

■ Shipbuilding at Dorchester, New Brunswick, 1875. The technology of shipbuilding remained fairly constant throughout the nineteenth century. Over the years, Dorchester's river silted up, and the community is now landlocked. LAC, C-10103.

on shipbuilding than Saint John, New Brunswick. 'Whatever Saint John is,' commented one of its newspapers in 1848, 'it must be admitted that shipbuilding and the timber trade have made it.'[16] The shipbuilding industry there—as everywhere in British North America—was controlled by the craftsmen who built the vessels, not the merchants who ordered them. Sometimes a merchant like James Peake of Prince Edward Island would supply material and capital advances. But the shipyards themselves were owned and operated by master shipbuilders of limited resources. Before 1830, vessels built in British North America had a somewhat unsavoury reputation for bad workmanship and green wood, but as their quality improved, the demand for them grew both in the colonies and abroad. The marine craftsmen became extremely skilful, and entered

the elite among the artisans in Saint John and other places. Saint John was distinguished in the Maritime region for the large size of the vessels it produced. By 1840 its merchant fleet was the largest of any port in British North America, and most of it had been produced at home. Since shipbuilding was done outdoors, it was as seasonal as the resource economy itself.[17]

Shipbuilding was in many respects an ideal processing industry. It relied primarily on the rich timber resources that British North America had in abundance. It did not require excessive capital outlay for physical plant or materials, and its products could be sold inside or outside the colonies. The carrying trade was a major contributor to any mercantile economy and a major employer. But even during its heyday, the wooden-ship construction industry did not have

■ 'Brewer's Lower Mill; view down the Cataraqui Creek & Clearing made for the Canal. Sketch taken in 1829. Excavation for the Lock just commenced'; sketch by Thomas Burrowes. In 1827 the estimated cost of building the canal was £169,000; the final cost was £822,804. Archives of Ontario, CI-0-0-0-67.

a bright future; nor did it prove capable of generating industrial spin-offs. As early as 1840, when the industry was about to enter its golden age, technological developments in steam and iron were already foreshadowing the decline of wood. Moreover, most shipbuilders were content to import the finished goods employed in ship construction, such as iron fittings and sailcloth; hence, spin-offs into secondary manufacturing were rare. Through the 1840s the industry was simply a monument to the mercantile resource economy that had so dominated British North America from 1790 to 1840.

'INTERNAL IMPROVEMENTS'

Trade and commerce required infrastructure— what the Americans in this period called 'internal improvements'—of all kinds. Banks were necessary to provide a common medium of exchange, but several attempts to establish them in British North America before 1817 ran into political opposition from those who remembered earlier problems with French and Yankee paper money. Finally, the Bank of Montreal was founded in 1817, and was followed by the Bank of Upper Canada (chartered in April 1821, opened in July 1822) in York. Soon there were banks scattered across British North America, each operating independently. Banks issued their own paper money, which—unlike American currency—was usually fully backed with precious metal. The currency was usually denominated in dollars, although most businesses kept their books in pounds, shillings, and pence. Local currency had no monopoly, however. In most places, dollars and cents (American), 'dimes and yorkers' (British North American), pounds sterling (British), and pounds Halifax currency (British North American) circulated interchangeably at different rates of exchange. Residents of the colonies had to be numerate in order to make the necessary calculations.

Early commerce in British North America depended on access to the ocean, or at least to navigable waterways with ocean outlets. It was important to live near a dock or wharf. An expanding internal economy required roads, bridges, and canals to connect the bulk of the population with their markets and sources of supply. Most British North Americans wanted such facilities, but they did not necessarily want to pay for them out of taxes. Canals became the great craze after the American success with the Erie Canal, connecting the Hudson River with Lake Erie, opened in stages between 1820 and 1825. The Lachine Canal, begun in 1821 and finished in 1825, partially bypassed the rapids of the St Lawrence above Montreal. The Welland Canal, connecting Lakes Erie and Ontario, was opened in 1829.

The Chambly Canal, begun in 1833, bypassed rapids on the Richelieu River. And the Rideau Canal, linking Lake Ontario and the Ottawa River, was a military boondoggle: intended to facilitate the movement of troops between Kingston and Ottawa, it was paid for by the British government and built with little regard to expense between 1826 and 1832. By improving the St Lawrence River system and, in particular, access to Lake Ontario, the early canals helped the economy to shift from a transatlantic focus to an internal one—a process that would really take hold with the introduction of the railroad in the 1850s.

EARLY CITIES AND TOWNS

Trade and commerce, both international and internal, were the bases of urban growth in British North America in these years. Even in a

city such as Saint John, with its strong industrial component, the industry was founded on trade. For the most part, the major cities were the centres of both commerce and political activity, although it was easier for a city to flourish without a seat of government (e.g., Montreal or Hamilton) than without trade (e.g., Fredericton, the political but not the commercial capital of New Brunswick). Despite its picturesque location and its important role in local politics, Charlottetown in 1801 contained only about 45 families, including those of the officers of government and the garrison. No city dominated more than its own immediate region, and none was very large; Montreal, with a population of 40,000 in 1840, was at the top of the urban list. Nevertheless, from the 1790s to the 1840s most urban centres in British America grew rapidly. York, for example, contained 12 cottages in 1795—two years after its founding. Immigration halted during the War of 1812–14 and the population remained fairly static at 600–700 people. Although the town was occupied twice by the Americans in 1813, it enjoyed an economic boom and some merchants got rich. By the time York was incorporated and renamed Toronto in 1834, it had 100 shops, over 1,000 houses, and a population of 9,252.

All British North American towns and cities were still quite small in area as well as in population; many consisted of just a few tightly packed buildings huddled around port facilities. In 1834 Toronto was a rectangle bounded by Parliament Street on the east, Bathurst on the west, and the lakefront on the south, extending only about 100 metres north of Queen Street. In 1837 Anna Jameson described it as 'most strangely mean and melancholy. A little ill-built town [with] some government offices, built of staring red brick, in the most tasteless, vulgar style imaginable; three feet of snow all around; and the gray, sullen, wintry lake, and the dark gloom of the pine forest bounding the prospect.'[18] Montreal was little better. As one visitor described it in 1820, 'The whole city appears one vast prison'; in 1833

THE WELLAND CANAL

■ Welland Canal, Port Colborne, Ontario, 1885.
LAC C-00757.

As is well known, Canada is plentifully supplied with navigable waterways, some stretching for hundreds of miles. Unfortunately, there were many breaks in the waterway chain that made long-distance navigation somewhat problematic. An obvious early solution to connecting up the waterways was the canal, an improvement going back hundreds of years in Europe and elsewhere in the world. A few early canals were proposed and even constructed in the eighteenth century, notably at the Sault to aid the fur traders, but the great period of canal creation did not begin until the end of the second decade of the nineteenth century, when demand, capital, and sufficient labour availability combined to make construction possible. The first great canal—the Erie Canal—was proposed in the United States in 1817, nearly 400 miles long across New York State between Albany and Buffalo. It was supported strongly by government and would prove to be an almost instant success when completed in the 1820s.

Soon after the Erie Canal was proposed, the Canadian merchant W H. Merritt proposed a much less grandiose ditch between Lakes Ontario and Erie across the Niagara Peninsula, which became known as the Welland Canal. The Canadian government was interested, but not enough to invest money in the enterprise. Consequently, Merritt raised the funds by private subscription, more than half of it from the United States. At the end of construction the Canadian and British governments added token amounts towards the funding of the project. A differential of almost 300 feet between the lakes was solved with 40 locks, hastily and cheaply built. The whole process constituted a major

engineering feat, however. The canal was completed in 1833, but it experienced substantial difficulties. The chief one was that the Welland
Canal, like most Canadian engineering projects,
was constructed in advance of traffic demands.
It did not immediately make money. Because of
the haste and cheapness of construction, it
required constant repair and maintenance. The
money wasted on the Welland Canal was a constant theme of the reformers of the 1830s. W.L.
Mackenzie described the canal as a great hoax
perpetrated on the public. The development of
transportation in Canada is one of the neglected
fields of Canadian history.

another commented that 'the houses are all made
of grey stone so that the long narrow streets look
very dark.'[19] Americans were more impressed by
Montreal than Europeans were, perhaps because
its stone construction was rare in North America,
but even as travelled a European as Lord Selkirk
found the place attractive and substantial on his
1804 visit.

Urban conditions everywhere were still
fairly primitive in the 1830s, but they were

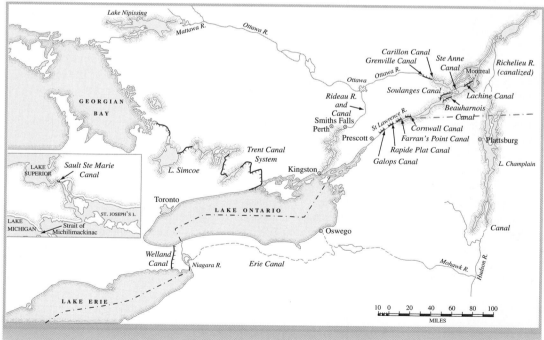

☐ Canadian canals. Adapted from G.P. de T. Glazebrook, *A History of Transportation in Canada*, vol. I, 77. (Toronto: McClelland & Stewart, 1966 [1938])

improving. Saint John, for example, began constructing a wooden sewer system, although before 1840 few householders hooked up to it, partly because of the entry fee. In the same decade the city acquired a piped water supply, which in turn improved its firefighting capacity. Toronto was fairly typical for 1830 in lacking sidewalks, drains, sewers, water supply, and street lighting—all improvements of the late 1830s and the 1840s. In Montreal, drinking

THE LOWER CANADA DEBATE OVER BANKING, 1831

In 1831 the Assembly of Lower Canada considered a banking bill. The debate was reported in the *Montreal Gazette*.

Mr Bourdages expected that the Hon Members who supported these bank Bills would content themselves, as they did last year, to tell us that we did not understand the matter, and that they alone understood it; but it was plain to every man of common sense and reflection that the Banks had done more harm than good. On the specie question, everybody must be convinced that they were the cause of its disappearance, as well as of what was called deteriorated coin being first introduced in large quantities and then banished. They first speculated upon sending for large amounts of it, and circulated them here and there, when it was *reformé* they got hold of it again and sent it back to be passed again at a profit, speculating thus both ways, pocketing the profits and leaving the mass of the people to bear the loss. . . .

Mr Bedard said that this was the very reason he was against Banks, because he and many more had no confidence in them. He believed the Banks had done great harm. Their only real use to the public was an Office of Discount, but they were of no use in that respect, for the Directors and stockholders absorbed all the money for discounts, and there was none left for others. If he was not mistaken, Directors and stockholders were not, in other countries, allowed to participate in the discounts. Before the Bank, young beginners got credit to go into business, and if they could not realise in time, their credit was bad; but now notes were taken, with which the merchant ran directly to the Bank to get discount. . . .

Mr De Montenach spoke from the experience of twenty years that he had lived in this country. We have seen quantities of gold and silver of the best assay in circulation, and in large quantities up to the very times the Banks were established; now we have comparatively no specie in circulation, and when we go to the Banks to get cash, we are paid in the worst kind of specie; that was perhaps the reason why the country people who formerly would take nothing but good silver, now even preferred notes. The practice of Directors discounting for each other had already been noticed; but it produced also the consequence that when a man of landed property, a man whose real wealth far surpassed the fictitious paper riches of these Directors, wanted to discount a miserable Bill of £100, he could not get it, whilst thousands were profusely given to people who perhaps were worth nothing. The country had not gained by the Banks, but lost. He did not, however, say it would be right, under existing circumstances, to put them down altogether; but their Charters ought to be revised with all circumspection. . . .

SOURCE: *Montreal Gazette*, 19 March 1831.

water was supplied through wooden aqueducts first introduced in 1801 and converted to cast iron in 1819; and rue Saint-Paul was lit with oil lamps from 1815 and with gas light after 1830.[20] Policing before 1840 was minimal, consisting of a few ward constables and a night watch. But Montreal got its first 24 'night watchmen' in 1818, and the Toronto police force was established in 1832—a few years ahead of Boston's. For most urban centres, the break between the eighteenth-century town and the nineteenth-century city occurred somewhere around 1840.

CONCLUSION

British America's extractive colonial economy, dependent as it was on international mercantilism, was an essential stage of development. But it was only temporary. By 1840 it was coming to an end, as British policy moved towards free trade. By then the provinces of British North America had to be prepared to move in different directions, and for the most part they did so. The social structure based on the resource-extraction economy, of course, would survive much longer.

SHORT BIBLIOGRAPHY

Acheson, T.W. *Saint John: The Making of a Colonial Urban Community*. Toronto, 1985. The best study of the development of an early city in British North America, one based on the timber trade and shipbuilding.

Bumsted, J.M. *The Fur Trade Wars: The Founding of Western Canada*. Winnipeg, 1999. An account of the struggle for control of the fur trade between the Hudson's Bay Company and the North West Company.

Cohen, Marjorie Griffin. *Women's Work, Markets, and Economic Development in Nineteenth-Century Ontario*. Toronto, 1988. A revisionist study of the economic activities of women in the nineteenth century.

Creighton, Donald. *The Empire of the St. Lawrence*. Toronto, 1956. The classic account of the commercial system of early Canada, unsympathetic to the aspirations of French Canada.

Innis, Harold A. *The Cod Fisheries: The History of an International Economy*. Toronto, 1954. The classic study, still not superseded.

Lower, A.R.M. *Great Britain's Woodyard: British America and the Timber Trade, 1763–1867*. Montreal, 1973. The standard overview.

McCallum, John. *Unequal Beginnings: Agriculture and Economic Development in Quebec and Ontario until 1870*. Toronto, 1970. An interesting comparative study that focuses on the relationship between agriculture and capital formation.

Ouellet, Fernand. *Economic and Social History of Quebec, 1760–1850: Structures and Conjectures*. Toronto, 1980. Quebec history influenced by the French schools of historians.

Ryan, Shannon. *Fish Out of Water: The Newfoundland Saltfish Trade 1814–1914*. St John's, 1985. A study based on extensive research.

Sager, Eric, and L.R. Fischer. *Shipping and Shipbuilding in Atlantic Canada, 1820–1914*. Ottawa, 1986. One of several studies resulting from a massively funded project in maritime history.

Samson, Roch. *Fishermen and Merchants in Nineteenth-century Gaspé*. Ottawa, 1984. The best account of the French fishery.

Wynn, Graeme. *Timber Colony: A Historical Geography of Early Nineteenth Century New Brunswick*. Toronto, 1981. A historical geographer's view of the timber trade in one colony.

STUDY QUESTIONS

1. What changes took place in the fisheries between 1790 and 1820?
2. What were the strengths of the North West Company?
3. Why did the British government support the Hudson's Bay Company after 1821?
4. How did the mercantile system work before 1840?
5. What were the characteristics of the shipbuilding industry?

CHAPTER FIFTEEN

Colonial Society, 1791–1840

Ultimately, a colonial economy based on natural resources depended on transatlantic and even international (as opposed to strictly British) trade. But a resource-based economy also had substantial implications for the society and its structure. The extraction and production of the raw materials of trade were a pre-industrial business, with seasonal rhythms determined by the nature of the commodity. Fish and grain required summer activity, while timber was cut in the winter and transported by river in the spring; the fur trade had its own yearly cycle. Initial production was usually in the hands of small-scale commodity producers (such as farmers and boat-owners) who exploited casual labourers and were in turn exploited by the merchants who took the commodities to market. Most primary-resource producers had little connection with their international markets and no control over the prices they received for their products, and as a result they usually tried to maximize production regardless of economic or environmental conditions.

As a small capitalist, the typical primary producer—whether boat-owner, farmer, or lumberman—identified himself with the commercial system rather than with his workforce, and this impeded the development of any working-class consciousness or the formation of any articulated class structure. Merchants had to be successfully entrepreneurial to survive, but they tended to find it difficult to move beyond their immediate commercial horizons into wider industrial activity. Recognizing the value of processing raw materials, merchants were prepared to invest in such processing within their own sphere of activity, but not outside it. The limited availability of capital further restricted their entrepreneurial range.

The resource society of the early nineteenth century was dominated by two elites, one centred on government (including military officers) and the other on commerce. It is not difficult to distinguish them, or to understand the sources of their power, even if they did have more in common than some of their rhetoric suggested. By far the majority of the population belonged to the non-elite: small shopkeepers, artisans, minor civil servants; proprietors of small industries such as gristmills, tanneries, soap factories, and breweries; and resource workers and farmers. In Great Britain a fundamental distinction existed between those who owned land and those who did not, but in British North America few 'landholders' possessed anything but farms in the process of becoming, and many were forced to hold other jobs, often working side by side with people who did not own any land at all.

Colonial society also contained large numbers of people who for one reason or another

TIMELINE

1792
Black Loyalists leave Nova Scotia for Sierra Leone.

1817
Maria Louisa Beleau dies in a Quebec hovel.

1818
'The Palace' is built for John Strachan.

1829
Black settlement formed at Wilberforce, Upper Canada. Death of Shawnadithit, the last Beothuk.

1833
English law limits the dower rights of women.

1835
Prince Edward Island establishes a divorce court.

1836
British Parliament holds inquiry on Aboriginal peoples in the Empire. Lieutenant-Governor Francis Bond Head of Upper Canada decides to remove Ojibwa to Manitoulin Island.

1837
Upper Canada passes Seduction Act.

1838
Jesse Happy case defines extradition principles in Canada.

1839
British Parliament passes Crown Lands Protection Act. Prostitution specifically mentioned in Lower Canadian statute.

either occupied an inferior position in the social structure and legal system or existed altogether outside them. Women were in the first category and First Nations in the second. Black people stood somewhere in between.

THE SOCIAL HIERARCHY

THE GOVERNING ELITE

At the top of the elite ranks of British North American society were the appointed officials of the colonial government, military officers, and the major merchants, who usually lived in the capital cities close to government. Foremost among the officials was the governor or lieu-tenant-governor—by virtue of his position, the size of his salary, and his station in Britain. The

first lieutenant-governor of Upper Canada was John Graves Simcoe, who founded York in 1793 and hoped to establish an aristocratic society there. Although Simcoe himself left Canada only three years later, his assistant, Peter Russell— who arrived as receiver-general of Upper Canada in 1793, was appointed to both the Executive and the Legislative Councils, and from 1796 to 1799 was administrator of the province—per-haps unintentionally helped to achieve that goal, creating an elite based at first on connections, but in time mainly on ability. Russell himself laid out the plans for York. In the process he acquired a large property stretching north from Queen and Peter Streets to Eglinton Avenue (including the present-day Russell Hill Road). To farm part of it, he brought over from England John Denison, who founded a leading Toronto family.

■ 'Part of York the Capital of Upper Canada on the Bay of Toronto in Lake Ontario', 1804, by Elizabeth F. Hale. Looking east along Palace (now Front) Street, this view shows Cooper's Tavern (at left, facing what is now Jarvis Street) and the houses of Duncan Cameron (a merchant), William Warren Baldwin, and William Allan. In the distance are the government buildings and blockhouse (with flag). LAC, C-34334.

Russell also brought his cousin John Wilcocks, the mayor of Cork, to York. Wilcocks, who became prominent as a merchant and the first postmaster, persuaded another Irish family to emigrate in 1798: Robert Baldwin Senior and his son, William Warren Baldwin, a doctor, lawyer, and architect who married Phoebe Wilcocks (the inheritor of the Russell property) and became very influential in Upper Canadian politics (as would his own son Robert). Other members of the elite, however, were native-born. John Beverley Robinson, the brilliant son of a Virginia loyalist whose father died when he was seven, was educated first in Kingston in a school run by John Strachan, an ambitious Scot who later became an Anglican priest and a powerful figure

in his own right. Robinson became solicitor general in 1815, attorney general in 1818, and chief justice in 1829, an office he held until 1862.

Anglophiles to a man, colonial officials, at least outside Lower Canada, modelled themselves on the British gentry. (The locally born Nova Scotia Supreme Court Justice, Thomas Chandler Haliburton, actually managed to retire to the mother country, although he had to write a number of best-selling books to do so.) Their houses—typically designed in late Georgian symmetry, with a columned front portico and extensive grounds—reflected their aspirations. Peter Russell's frame house on Front Street West, built for him in 1797 by William Berczy, was imposing enough to be given the name 'Russell

■ The Campbell House, Toronto, 1822.
Photograph by William Toye, 1993.

Abbey'. John Strachan's magnificent house, also on Front Street, was popularly known as 'The Palace' even before Strachan became archbishop of Toronto in 1839. Twenty years earlier, the year after it was built, his brother visiting from Scotland reportedly commented, 'I hope it's a' come by honestly, John.'[1] Those two dwellings disappeared long ago, but the degree of architectural distinction attained in the 'gentlemen's houses' of other members of York's colonial elite can still be seen in 'The Grange' (1817–18), home of D'Arcy Boulton, the son of a judge, and 'Campbell House' (1822), home of Judge William Campbell.

Not surprisingly, colonial officials also embraced British values. They believed in the balance of economic interests, and above all in order. As John Beverley Robinson argued in 1830, order 'lies at the foundation of good government in the social state. . . . by all who are concerned in making or administering the laws for this rapidly expanding country, it should be felt that we, in this generation, are laying the foundations of a social system which is to extend its advantages or entail the consequences of its imperfections upon millions who will soon succeed.'[2] Such men were well educated and usually

extremely able. But they governed British North America according to an extremely narrow and limited vision, and they were willing to do almost anything—short of soiling themselves in open graft and corruption—to prevent the growth of opposition to their views.

The most successful merchants—at York, men such as William Allan and Joseph Cawthra—shared the lifestyle of the major colonial officeholders, but not their status. One reason was that British ambivalence about 'trade' carried over to British North America. What really limited the social reach of the merchants, however, was the instability of their incomes, which could be greatly affected by conditions in the market. The British associated status with land because an income from landed estates was rightly regarded as far more permanent (and inheritable) than income from commerce or industry. British North America was never able to replicate the British landed aristocracy, since even the colonial official's income was limited to his lifetime. Offices were occasionally passed on from father to son, but only by dint of special pleading—not through inheritance. In theory, the seigneurs of Lower Canada ought to have been regarded as landed aristocrats, but the typical seigneur was a good deal like the typical Scottish country laird described by Sir Walter Scott in his novels: too poor to cut an impressive figure in the town, reduced to a slightly seedy rural gentility—especially after the Lower Canadian agrarian crisis of the 1830s.

Another difference between Canada and the mother country was the sheer availability of land: a backcountry farm in Upper Canada often had a larger acreage than the typical English estate. Although most landholders were more interested in speculation than status, the tendency to emulate British values meant that land never lost its symbolic importance. Dr William Warren Baldwin in 1815 built a house on an estate three miles west of York that extended north from present-day Queen Street as far as Eglinton Avenue. He described it a year later as follows:

■ 'The Falls of Montmorency (Quebec in the distance)', engraved by C. Hunt 'from a drawing by Lieut. Col. [J.P.] Cockburn' and published in 1833. LAC, C-095617.

I have a very commodious house in the Country —I have called the place Spadina, the Indian word for Hill—or Mont—the house consists of two large Parlours Hall & stair case on the first floor—four bed rooms and a small library on the 2d. floor—and three Excellent bed rooms in attick storey or garrett—with several closets on every storey—a Kitchen, dairy, root-cellar, wine cellar & man's bed room under ground—I have cut an avenue through the woods all the way so that we can see the vessels passing up and down the bay—the house is completely finished with stable &c and a tolerable good garden.[3]

The satisfaction in such a description is palpable.

Lacking a permanent upper class based on possession of land, British North America instead began developing a social structure based on wealth and conspicuous consumption, which might be temporary but was certainly visible. Not all social standing was based on money, of course. British North Americans had more regard for education, professional training, and the life of the mind than did many Britons, and the professional men—doctors, lawyers, clergymen, architects, surveyors, educators—who were concentrated in the largest towns and cities were admitted to the ranks of elite society, although usually in secondary positions.

THE REGIONAL ELITES

While colonial officials and the majority of merchants lived in the political capitals that doubled as the great commercial centres of British North America—York, Montreal, Halifax, St John's—a sprinkling of others assumed the functions of leadership in the hinterlands. Every province had its retired half-pay officers attempting to carve landed estates out of the wilderness, and Lower Canada had its seigneurs. Every British North American colony also had its local merchants and professional men, as well as a few prominent farmers with particular acumen or abilities, often exercised in the context of a church organization. Thus Elihu Woodsworth, a farmer and cordwainer (shoemaker) who was deacon of the Grand Pré Presbyterian Church in Wolfville, Nova Scotia, had a strong sense of his own worth, which was apparently shared by his fellows. Early in 1835, for example, he entered in his diary:

> Attended the Temperance Society in the evening. Was warmly solicited to join the Society—but I observed to them that the general disposition of mankind was to ascend in office rather than descend and as I had been President of a Temperance Society upwards of 20 years it would be rather degrading to become a private in my old age. . . . Mr. A. DeWolf said if I would allow my name to be put on the temperance records I then would be appointed President.[4]

Pecking orders in small villages were often different from the social hierarchies in the political capitals, however.

From the regional elites men were elected to the various houses of assembly, where they would represent the countryside and often contend with the governing elites for political control of the colony. The same class provided the men who served as local justices of the peace (or magistrates), and as militia officers as well. Sometimes such honours came as a consequence of local success, but in most instances appointments as magistrates or militia officers, made in the political capitals by members of the governing elite on principles never entirely clear, preceded other accomplishments. In most provinces these were alternative routes to regional prominence, which was recognized by election to the assembly and by appointment to permanent

local civil office. Before 1840, most members of the regional elites would have described themselves as farmers; however, 'farming' was a capacious category, and farmers often engaged in a variety of occupations, using diversification as a survival strategy.[5] Indeed, perhaps the most striking feature of most British North Americans was their lack of occupational specialization: over the course of a lifetime, most colonials would hold many different jobs, both in succession and simultaneously.

THE NON-ELITE

Identifying the elite is considerably less complicated than sorting out the remainder of British North American society. Theoretically, in a frontier society with so much 'waste' land available at relatively low cost, the bulk of the population ought to have been yeoman farmers, or at least on their way to that level. But such was not the case. One reason was that in many places—including Newfoundland, Prince Edward Island, and large parts of Lower Canada—freehold land was simply not available to be developed. A second reason was that unimproved freehold land, though often cheap enough to buy, cost a great deal—in labour and in cash—to develop. The less cash one had, the longer the process took. Without capital, a farmer could carve out of primary-growth forest only a few acres a year, at best, and in the 1830s the typical British North American farmer was probably still struggling to clear enough additional land to grow a marketable surplus. Employment in resource industries such as fishing and timbering offered an alternative to farming. But such employment was often exploitative, and might never pay enough to allow a worker to buy his own land. Even if it did provide a small landholder with the cash income he had not yet obtained from his farm, it would also slow down the process of clearing the land he needed to become a market farmer himself. And although the farmer with large marketable surpluses might be the envy of his peers,

■ 'Canada, Settler's house in the forest, on the Thames, nr London CW, April 1842', watercolour by Henry Francis Ainslie. Few farmers were able to clear more than 1.5 acres a year, and stumps were often left in the ground to rot, with crops growing up around them. LAC, C-000544.

market farming brought its own problems, connected with external prices and demand.

THE TRUCK SYSTEM

Further complicating the picture of the social hierarchy in British North America was the 'truck system' commonly employed almost everywhere in the resource industries. 'Truck' was an arrangement between a resource merchant and a supposedly independent resource harvester by which the merchant advanced capital (usually in the form of supplies) to the harvester in return for the fruits of the harvester's labour. In most resource industries, this system tended to be exploitative, since what the harvester was able to

provide to the merchant (fish, timber, buffalo robes) was seldom enough to pay for the advances received; therefore the harvester would fall deeper and deeper in debt to the merchant. The truck system was most common in the fishery, particularly in Newfoundland, where it led boat-owners into 'slavish servitude'. But it was common in the timber districts and the fur trade as well.

Although the producer or harvester remained theoretically independent, in truth his labour and his production were contracted for years in advance. Many producers never got out of debt and, therefore, were never able to market their resource harvest openly or receive the best price for it. Moreover, the system encouraged the producer to employ his entire family in hopes of increasing production enough to get out of debt. While some merchants may have deliberately manipulated the prices of goods—selling supplies high and buying harvests low—it would probably be a mistake to see the truck system as a deliberate conspiracy of merchants against producers. Truck did not so much create a pre-industrial producer culture as provide the only workable arrangement within one.[6] Those caught up in the truck system might be best described as 'quasi-dependent'; a good many such people existed in the resource economy.[7]

THE POOR

At the bottom of colonial society were the poor, who because they lacked capital were part of a dependent class, clearly recognized by their contemporaries as socially inferior. The poor fell into three categories—permanent, immigrant, and casual—and two major groupings: those who had relations or friends to look after them in their distress, and those who did not and therefore had to rely on public sympathy. While British North America was in some senses a 'land of opportunity' and a good country for the poor man, it was pitiless for those too young, too old, or too infirm to support themselves. In the winter of 1816–17 a child named Maria Louisa Beleau died in Quebec in a hovel described as 'NOT FIT FOR A STABLE. It is open in many parts of the roof, and on all sides. There is no other floor than the bare earth. It is a mere wooden shell; it has no window, nor any chimney. In the middle is a shallow hole made in the earth, in which there are marks of a fire having been made; and the smoke escaped through the open parts of the roof and sides.'[8]

A second category among the poor included recent immigrants who arrived without capital resources. Unable to find enough money to move on from the ports they arrived in, these newcomers (often Irish, and therefore less likely than English, Welsh, or Scots to meet sympathetic

locals) merged into the third category: the casually employed. Because of the seasonal nature of most work in Canada, the numbers of the unemployed were always highest in winter. Snow, ice, and cold weather slowed down most economic activity except in the timber industry, and even skilled artisans might be temporarily out of work in winter. In some places resident fishermen would be unable to work for seven months of the year. And in the West, Aboriginal people who came to be called 'homeguards' camped outside fur-trading posts in the coldest months in hopes of receiving assistance from the traders inside.

Winter was always the worst time to be poor. Food costs increased, and wood—no longer easily obtainable close to settled areas—became the largest single expense of the urban poor. Rural farmers could at least keep warm, even if they had no more money than the urban poor. Together, cold, malnutrition, and crowded housing were a ready-made recipe for the spread of illness in the winter. 'Relief' was provided for the poor partly out of charitable instincts, but largely to prevent their being driven 'by despair to commit depredations', or infecting the entire community with contagious disease.[9] The preferred form of relief was some sort of make-work employment, combined with charitable dispensations. Most charities sought to make relief so unpleasant that only the truly desperate would take it.

In the nineteenth century, British North American society tended to identify poverty as an urban problem, not only because it was more visible in towns but because rural poverty seemed difficult to understand. How could a family that was able to grow its own food and cut its own wood possibly be poor? In Lower Canada, however, the soil on many seigneuries had been abused for decades, and crop failures, low prices, overpopulation, and the unremitting exaction of seigneurial rents had rendered many habitant families more or less permanently impoverished by the 1830s. The principal causes of poverty in this period—unemployment, environmental conditions, and, in the case of Aboriginal people particularly, discrimination—remained untouched by a society that saw poverty as a moral rather than an economic issue.

OCCUPATIONAL PLURALITIES

Between the poor and the 'respectable' existed numerous occupational and social groups that defy ordering by any scheme except the most rigid and unrevealing of Marxist categories. British Americans could become caught in the truck system, or they could be exploited by unscrupulous landlords. Even if a worker was paid decent wages for part of the year, home was frequently a semi-developed farm on marginal land, or an improved farm of insufficient acreage to support a large or extended family. In most of New Brunswick, much of Prince Edward Island, and the Ottawa Valley, huge portions of territory were dominated by neither agriculture nor timbering, but a combination of the two. In these agro-forestry districts, timber-workers were not forced to join the urban unemployed in the summer off-season; instead, they worked their subsistence farms, trying to grow enough food to support their families. Nor did such farmers have to deal with the market, since their cash income came from outside employment. In some places, however, farmers who worked in the woods could be caught up in both tenancy and the truck system.

Conditions were similar in the French-Canadian parishes that before 1830 supplied large numbers of voyageurs for the fur trade. In 1814 a British traveller wrote of the parish of Sorel in the Lower Richelieu Valley:

> The country people in the vicinity are mostly employed as voyageurs in the North-west fur trade, and the cultivation of their farms is left to their wives and children. When they return home, they seldom bring more than enough to support them during the winter. The soil is thus neglected, and the town is badly supplied with provisions.[10]

The same description could have been applied to large parts of the resource economy. But, in fact, Sorel's problem had less to do with neglect than with the subdivision of extensive landholdings in response to rapid population growth after 1790. Neighbouring parishes producing for the market exported their surplus population, but Sorel's fur-trade income permitted its inhabitants to survive on holdings that were not large enough to be viable farms. Large areas of Nova Scotia, New Brunswick, Lower and Upper Canada (especially east of Kingston), and Prince Edward Island consisted of uneconomic farms that were kept operating on a subsistence level by women and children—whose labour went unpaid and unrewarded except when children beginning their own adult lives were given some part of the family property.

Even in districts with both exceptional soil fertility and access to markets, newly established farms rarely produced surpluses or prosperous farmers. As Catharine Parr Traill wrote of Upper Canada in 1838: 'Even a labouring man, though he have land of his own, is often, I may say generally, obliged to hire out to work for the first year or two, to earn sufficient for the maintenance of his family; and even so many of them suffer much privation before they reap their reward.'[11] Traill discovered from her own experience that few farms in the making were capable of feeding a family, let alone earning any return. She was advised to be patient and cheerful in the meantime.

Nevertheless, some advances towards prosperity were achieved in the rural areas. As with the elites, housing was a vivid indicator of such progress. Settlers generally moved from log shanties to log houses to permanent dwellings (often stone or brick). Many settlers reached the third stage around the end of the period of the resource economy. In 1831, Upper Canada had 36,000 dwellings, of which 75 per cent (27,000) were made of logs and fewer than 1,000 of brick and stone. Most houses were small, with total floor space varying from 300 to 600 square feet.

Size was a function of cost. When Lord Selkirk, at the beginning of the nineteenth century, solicited carpenters' estimates for building a house—'30 by 40—2 Stories (20 Feet sidewall) cellar and garret'—the quotations he received ranged from £925 to £1065. Typically, a substantial 'dwelling house' might measure 6 by 9 metres, with a kitchen added on at the back. Length of settlement—hence degree of prosperity—was the principal factor in the choice of construction techniques, although few British Americans lived for long in hewn-log houses (they preferred frame and board), and English newcomers were on the whole able to afford better houses than their Scottish and Irish counterparts, largely because they arrived with more money. In 1841 most Irish lived in shanties, reflecting both their poverty and the recentness of their arrival as immigrants.[12]

THE LAW

Understanding nineteenth-century law in British North America is not easy, for there were several legal systems in operation. The most obvious distinction concerned civil (as opposed to criminal) law: while the English-speaking colonies followed the English common law (based on custom and precedent), Quebec had been permitted to preserve the French civil code (based on Roman law, codified in statutes). In addition, however, First Nations societies had their own laws, by which their members were governed except when they were brought under the purview of one of the European systems. Furthermore, in the pre-Confederation period the only political authority in much of western and northern Canada was the Hudson's Bay Company. Questions of jurisdiction and the applicability of English law in the West were difficult to decide.

Jurisdictional differences affected the administration of the law as well. In the 'common-law' colonies, English statutes and precedents were applied except when overridden by local legisla-tion. In the course of the nineteenth century, Canadian legislatures modified increasing numbers of earlier laws, producing ongoing battles between the courts and the legislatures over who controlled the law. At the same time, the application of any law was subject to interpretation by judges and juries.

Canadian judges tended to be extremely conservative, attached to the common law and hostile to legislative change, which they often deemed to be motivated more by ephemeral public opinion than by immutable values. On the other hand, in some situations juries controlled the interpretation of both the law itself and the facts of the case. And because each colony controlled its own legislation for the administration of justice, there were some variations. In all the colonies, including Quebec, criminal law followed the English model.

DISADVANTAGED GROUPS

WOMEN

Between 1791 and the 1840s, as society in British North America became more settled and stable, the conditions of life for women changed as well—not always for the better. Materially, life for many women became somewhat easier as the rough conditions of pioneer and immigrant life gradually improved. At the same time, however, women lost much of the autonomy that they had exercised in earlier times. The culprits were essentially two loosely related developments. First, the expansion of courts and the increasingly regular use of the English common law added formal weight to patriarchal assumptions that put women, especially married women, in a legal position of inferiority to men; in French Canada, the civil law was based on similar patriarchal assumptions. Second, there was a simultaneous elevation of women to a 'pedestal' and an increasing tendency to sentimentalize their supposed virtue and innocence. Women found themselves treated as frail creatures in need of protection, both physical and moral.

The law in British North America in the first half of the nineteenth century reflected the society both in theory and in practice. It was quite different for men than for women. Women were citizens only in that they were inhabitants of British North America. Their civil rights had yet to be defined. Not merely discriminated against or ignored, most women were legal non-entities. Widows and adult spinsters were legally autonomous (the law called them *femme sole*), but underage or married women were without legal standing: their status was subsumed under that of their fathers or husbands. In keeping with the patriarchal principles of the English common law and the French Coutume de Paris, only males had full membership in the judicial and political community. Women were denied the vote—and therefore the right to participate in either the creation or the administration of the law. They could not be lawyers, judges, or magistrates, or even serve on the juries that decided other women's fates.[13]

Marriage—the norm for women in the nineteenth century—resulted in enormous disabilities. Because much of the law, whether English or French, had been developed to deal with property passing through the male line, it is hardly surprising that married women were not regarded as autonomous. Under the medieval common-law doctrine of 'coverture', a married woman in most instances had no right to a matrimonial home held in her husband's name or to property and income acquired in joint labour with her husband. Women did retain ownership of any real estate they brought into the marriage, but in most cases they were not allowed to manage it or receive any rent or profit from it. A married woman lost the right to all personal property except what was called 'paraphernalia' (clothing and personal ornaments). A married woman could not act as her own agent at law; she could not sue (or be sued), and was not permitted to conduct business apart from her husband except

with his consent. As Sir William Blackstone put it, 'In law husband and wife are one person, and the husband is that person.'

Most of British North America entered the nineteenth century with the patriarchal concept of marriage, entrenched in English common law, virtually unchallenged. Quebec had slightly different premises, but the effect was the same. Most Canadians regarded marriage as sacrosanct, and there was little public pressure to make its legal dissolution easy. Both Nova Scotia and New Brunswick did have courts of divorce, created in 1758 and 1784 respectively, and Prince Edward Island joined them in 1835. But Upper Canada had no divorce court, even though it granted several ad hoc petitions for divorce and debated the issue on several occasions. The civil code of Lower Canada was categorical: 'Marriage can only be dissolved by the natural death of one of the parties.' Grounds for divorce were confined to adultery except in Nova Scotia, which also recognized cruelty. Before 1840, fewer than 50 divorces had been granted across British North America. Informal separation was much more common, of course, and many a colonial left his family by the simple act of moving to the frontier.

Male and female adulterers were treated quite differently: in a man adultery was an understandable failing; in a woman it was a fall from virtue. A husband in effect possessed his wife's sexuality for life, and neither violence nor abandonment on his part could justify her in taking up with another man. The husband of a woman who had committed adultery had no natural duty to provide support and maintenance. In all the colonies, attempts to obtain judicial separations (and financial support in the form of alimony) often failed, even when abusive behaviour was involved. The courts consistently refused to act decisively in cases of abuse.

One aspect of Canadian civil law and practice with special relevance for women was the law governing the relationship between master and servant. This law did not apply within families, since the family was regarded as an eco-

■ 'A French Canadian Lady in her Winter dress and a Roman Catholic Priest', from John Lambert, *Travels Through Lower Canada and the United States of America in the Years 1806, 1807, 1808* (London, 1810). LAC, C-113742.

ous feature of the master–servant law was the tort for seduction, a popular legal action in nineteenth-century Canada. This tort had its origins in the common-law concern for the loss of services experienced by a master whose servant was (for example) beaten or enticed away. But by the nineteenth century the seduction law was most frequently applied in cases concerning daughters rather than servants. The ostensible legal ground for such action was that the seducer had deprived the master/father of the servant/daughter's services. Gradually, however, damages for parental dishonour took precedence. At the beginning of the century, it had to be proven that the defendant 'debauched and carnally knew' the plaintiff's servant or daughter, made her pregnant, and thus deprived him of services while imposing on him the costs of caring for her. The Upper Canada Seduction Act of 1837 spoke of seduced daughters, no longer required proof of service, and recognized that the real injury was the wound to the patriarchal parent's feelings.

nomic unit. (Even a daughter who had lived for years with her father and cared for him in the expectation of an inheritance had no legal claim to compensation. According to the judge in one such case in Upper Canada: 'this young woman could not be living any where else more properly than with her aged and infirm parent; and if she did acts of service, instead of living idly, it is no more than she ought to have done in return for her clothes and board, to say nothing of the claims of natural affection which usually lead children to render such service.') One curi-

The treatment of women under the criminal law paralleled that under the civil law. In cases where women were the offenders rather than the victims, the law had to face the disparity between the social ideals of feminine virtue and the reality represented by the offence—usually prostitution. On the other hand, first offenders usually received lenient sentences, perhaps in part because there were no prisons capable of incarcerating women separately from men. In one case, the judge explained that the jail was 'filled with women of the most abandoned and loathsome character, and I felt great reluctance at the idea of exposing this young girl to the contamination of such society which would probably prevent her from getting a respectable situation afterwards, and might ruin her future prospects in life.' Whether as offenders or as victims, non-virtuous women tended to get particularly short shrift from the courts either as offenders or victims, but the male dominance of the legal system worked against women under nearly all legal circumstances.

Prostitution was an enterprise rife with discrimination on the basis not just of gender but of class, race, and ethnic origin. The ultimate discrimination, of course, was that the law concentrated on the women, while male procurers, pimps, bawdy-house operators, and customers went virtually untouched. Following the English common law, British North America treated the keeping of a bawdy house as a nuisance. In the early period, the colonial legislation on prostitution dealt mainly with bawdy houses. Not until 1839 was prostitution mentioned specifically in a statute (in Lower Canada). The enforcement of prostitution laws was sporadic and capricious. Except in the larger cities there probably were not many prostitutes; at least, few were ever prosecuted.

By and large, women charged with criminal offences came from the lower orders of colonial society. Women appearing in the courts as victims represented only a slightly broader spectrum of the social fabric, probably because 'respectable' women risked sullying their reputations if they did so, however gravely they might have been wronged. Two distinctly different sorts of violent crimes against women can be identified: violence from the community and violence within marriage. In the latter case, as we have seen, rape could not be at issue because the courts were agreed that a husband could not rape his wife.

Rape and its variants—attempted rape, indecent assault, carnal knowledge, perhaps abduction—were not the only violent crimes committed against women within the community, but they were the most common. Whether or not a man was prosecuted in such cases, however, depended on circumstances and the attitudes of the court. Rape in British North America was governed chiefly by English law, which made it a criminal act punishable by death to 'ravish', 'rape', or 'unlawfully and carnally know'. Lawyers always regarded rape cases as difficult, since the accusation was easy to make and difficult to disprove. As a result, the courts tended to want evidence beyond the testimony of the victim and often reduced 'rape' to lesser charges.

The fundamental problem of women and the law—the gender inequality inherent in English common law—was never really addressed in British North America. Nor was the law's structural discrimination altered.

BLACKS

By the 1820s, slavery had been judicially abolished in British North America and the British government was consciously adhering to the judicial maxim that 'every man is free who reaches British soil.' Most of the black refugees went to Upper Canada, and Canadian courts held firm when slaveholders tried to use them to extradite refugees facing charges for crimes committed in the course of their escapes. In 1838 a case was heard in Upper Canada involving a Kentucky fugitive named Jesse Happy who had stolen a horse in the course of his escape, but left it on the American side of the border and then wrote to the owner telling him where to find it. In response to this case the British formalized the rule that former slaves could be extradited only if there was evidence of a criminal act that 'would warrant the apprehension of the accused Party, if the alleged offense had been committed in Canada'. Since there was no slavery in British North America after the 1820s, the refugee's supposed 'theft' of himself was no crime. In addition to legal security from extradition, the colonies provided black refugees, or those who were male property-holders, with full rights as citizens who could vote, serve on juries, and run for political office. In some cases and in some places, blacks had to fight to maintain these rights, but they usually emerged triumphant. There was much informal racism in the society, however; one black refugee once claimed that 'Canadian Negro Hate is incomparably MEANER than the Yankee article.'[14] More than 40 black communities were established in Upper Canada between 1825 and 1850, most of them by white philanthropists and church groups.

THE WILBERFORCE SETTLEMENT

The Wilberforce Settlement, named after the British abolitionist William Wilberforce, was founded in Lucan, Upper Canada, by New York Quakers in 1829, as a home for freed blacks. The following letter appeared in the New York-based abolitionist monthly paper, *The Liberator*.

Wilberforce Settlement,
U[pper] C[anada]

[17 September 1831]

Mr. Editor:

It will no doubt be gratifying to our friends who in different parts of the state of New York and elsewhere, have taken an interest in our welfare, and have aided us in effecting this infant settlement, to hear from us, to know how we are getting along; we therefore beg the favor of communicating to them, through the medium of your very useful paper, a short account of our affairs: Through the blessing of God, we have all enjoyed our usual degree of health. We have erected for our accommodations comfortable log buildings, and have a portion of our land in a state of cultivation; our crops at present continue to smile upon the labor of our hands; we shall raise the present year nearly enough to supply the present number of settlers. The people are industrious, and well pleased with their present location; and it is believed that none of them could be hired to go back to the states. Two religious societies have been organized, one of the Baptist, under the pastoral care of Elder Nathaniel Paul, and the other of the Methodist, under the care of Elder Enos Adams; and we are happy to add, that the utmost degree of harmony exists between the two churches. A sabbath school, under the superintendence of Mr. Austin Steward, late of Rochester, is in successful operation; and a day school for the instruction of the children, is taught by a daughter of Elder Benjamin Paul, late of the city of New York; and in addition to which, a temperance society has been formed, consisting of about thirty in number; and the voice of

the people is decidedly against ardent spirits ever being introduced as an article of merchandise among us. There are, however, a number of families who have emigrated from the states, whose pecuniary circumstances will not admit of their coming at present to join us, but are compelled to take lands in the neighboring settlements upon shares, and hundreds more in the states are longing to join us, but on account of their limited means are not able to carry their designs into effect. We feel grateful for past favors, but will not the eye of the Philanthropist be turned toward their condition, and his hand opened to supply their wants, that they may thereby be enabled to join their brethren, to help forward one of the most noble enterprises that ever was started, to elevate the too long degraded African, this side the Atlantic?

The annual election of the Board of Managers, whose duty it is to appoint agents, and to take the oversight of the general concerns of the settlement, took place July 11th, when the following persons were duly elected: Austin Steward, Benjamin Paul, Enos Adams, William Bell, Philip Harris, Abraham Dangerfield, Simon Wyatt. The newly elected board, considering the limited means of the colored people generally, and the absolute necessity of pecuniary aid, and in order to carry so desirable an object into effect, and to secure its permanent character, have reappointed Mr. Israel Lewis their agent to obtain collections in the states, and the

Rev. Nathaniel Paul, late of Albany, whose standing as a minister of the gospel, and whose devotedness to the cause of his colored brethren, are too well known to need any recommendation from us, to embark for England, for the same purpose. He will probably sail as soon as the necessary means shall be obtained to defray the expense of his voyage— and should a kind Providence smile upon the exertions of our agents, we have no doubt but in the course of a few years, that this settlement will present to the public such a state of things as will cheer the heart of every well wisher of the African race and put to silence the clamor of their violent enemies. By order and in behalf of the Board,

AUSTIN STEWARD, *Chairman*
Benjamin Paul, *Secretary*

SOURCE: From *The Liberator*, 17 September 1831. Reprinted in C. Peter Ripley et al., eds, *The Black Abolitionist Papers, Volume 2: Canada, 1830–1865* (Chapel Hill: University of North Carolina Press, 1986), 47–56.

Abolitionist sentiment increased everywhere after 1830, aided in large measure by the elimination of slavery within the British Empire in 1833. Canadian white abolitionists, most of whom were middle-class people belonging to evangelical Protestant denominations, were often assisted by their British counterparts.[15] Contemporaries downplayed the abolitionist work done by freed blacks themselves, particularly in Canada. Black communities in Amherstburg, Windsor, and Chatham were active in providing help for refugees. Blacks dominated many chapters of the Anti-Slavery Society of Canada, and many black lecturers toured the colonies denouncing slavery and raising money for abolitionist causes. What blacks wanted most in British North America was to be treated with dignity and equity, allowed quietly to assimilate into society.

One of the most important institutions that blacks brought with them to British North America was their religion. Slavery had worked against the formation of many family and community ties, but the slave owners were not able to prevent the establishment of Protestant churches. The relationship of Christianity and slavery was ambiguous from the beginning. Many masters opposed missionary activity among their slaves, fearing that conversion to Christianity might give the blacks dangerous ideas. But some evangelical ministers in the South, particularly after the 'Great Awakening' of the mid-1700s, insisted on extending religion to the black community. Throughout the colonial period, especially in the American South, most blacks worshipped with Europeans, but there were also many slave congregations that met in secret, free of the white ministers who sought to impose their values on the worship. Separate black churches developed distinctive forms of worship and music, reflecting the people's African roots through complex rhythms, emotional interventions, and call-and-response singing. The local black minister was usually an important community leader, and revered by his congregation.

FIRST NATIONS

Unlike black immigrants, the First Nations had no desire to assimilate into British North American society. They wanted to remain apart and continue to practise their traditional way of life, insofar as that traditional, pre-contact life remained possible.

The period between 1791 and 1840 saw a marked deterioration in living conditions for the Aboriginal peoples of eastern British North

'THE COLOURED PEOPLE OF HAMILTON' TO GOVERNOR CHARLES T. METCALFE

Hamilton, [Canada West]
October 15, 1843

Dear Sir[:]

We the people of colour in the Town of Hamilton have a right to inform your Excellency of the treatment that we have to undergo. We have paid the taxes and we are denied of the public schools, and we have applied to the Board of the Police and there is no steps taken to change this manner of treatment, and this kind of treatment is not in the United States, for the children of colour go to the Public Schools together with the white children, more especially in Philadelphia, and I thought that there was not a man to be known by his colour under the British flag, and we left the United States because we were in hopes that prejudice was not in this land, and I came to live under your Government if my God would be my helper and to be true to the Government. I am sorry to annoy you by allowing this thing, but we are grieved much, we are imposed upon much, and if it please your Excellency to attend to this grievance, if you please Sir. I have left property in the United States and I have bought property in Canada, and all I want is Justice and I will be satisfied. We are called nigger when we go out in the street, and sometimes brick bats is sent after us as we pass in the street. We are not all absconders[.] Now we brought money into this Province and we hope never to leave it, for we hope to enjoy our rights in this Province, and may my God smile upon your public life and guide you into all truth, which is my prayer and God bless the Queen and Royal Family.

The Coloured People of Hamilton

SOURCE: C. Peter Ripley et al., eds, *The Black Abolitionist Papers, Volume 2: Canada, 1830–1865* (Chapel Hill: University of North Carolina Press, 1986), 97–8.

America. Indeed, across the northern half of the continent, the conditions faced by indigenous people were directly related to the initial date of contact: the longer the Europeans had been present in a region (and the more settled it was), the more depleted and marginalized the Aboriginal population was. The British government after 1791 operated on the assumption that Aboriginal numbers in eastern North America were declining precipitously, in some areas to the point of extinction. Whether population decline facilitated dispossession and marginalization or vice versa has never been clear, but the two processes probably reinforced one another—and in any case, the result was the same. (This pattern was hardly confined to British North America. With reference to the Aboriginal people of Australia, Sir James Stephen, the legal adviser at the Colonial Office from 1813 to 1846, commented that 'we take possession of their Country, introduce amongst them the most profligate habits and the severest Law of Europe—and having tainted them with our vices and oppressed them with our injustice, we execute against them all the severity

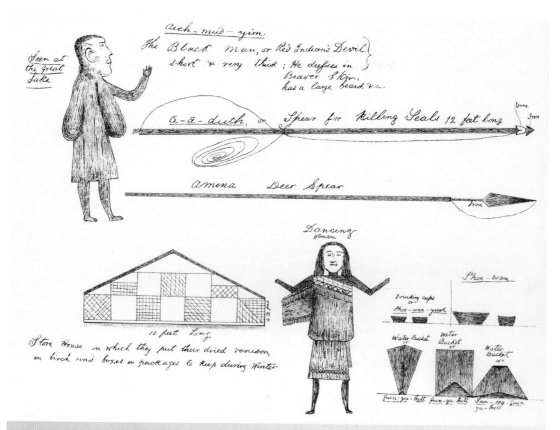

aich—mud—yim.

The Black man, or Red Indian's Devil
short & very thick; He dresses in
Beaver Skin,
has a large beard &c.

Seen at the Great Lake

ō-ā-duth, or Spear for killing Seals 12 feet long

amina   Deer Spear

Dancing Woman

Shoe-wan

Store House in which they put their dried venison,
in birch rind boxes or packages to keep during Winter

10 feet Long

■ Shanawdithit, born c. 1801, was the last known Beothuk. She died of tuberculosis in St John's in 1829. Before her death she made a number of drawings showing aspects of her people's culture. LAC, C-28544.

of our own Law merely for having too well learnt the lessons we have taught them.'[16])

Believing that the First Nations were in the process of disappearing, the British also believed that those individuals who remained needed to be integrated into European society as quickly as possible: first educated and 'civilized' by missionaries, then turned into farmers. At the same time, the British began to assume that Aboriginal people would not truly become part of the fabric of British America until they were fully integrated. Thus, they might be entitled to follow their own law, but as long as they did, they could

not be full citizens with voting rights. When the British Parliament passed the Crown Lands Protection Act in 1839, declaring First Nations lands to belong to the Crown, the result was to ensure that most Aboriginal people—who did not typically own land as individuals—were disqualified from voting under the property-based franchises in effect in most provinces, even if they had not been previously disenfranchised.

'Indian policy' was directed from the Colonial Office in London, largely because the British—suspecting that local settlers would not deal fairly with Native people—were reluctant to give colonial administrations a free hand.[17] But policy was rarely co-ordinated, and there was little overall imperial supervision. The first serious attempt at co-ordinating policy came as a result of a parliamentary inquiry in 1836 that examined the treatment of Aboriginal peoples throughout the Empire. British North America featured prominently in the 1,000-page report, which outlined a litany of abuses from every colony except Nova Scotia, where the government refused to provide information. Understandably, the committee concluded that Indian policy should remain under British control. It also recommended against making treaties with local bands, because the treaty process was so heavily weighted in favour of the government that it could not produce a satisfactory result. This recommendation was not implemented, however, and full treaty-making power was officially transferred to colonial governments in the ensuing years. Basically, each colony or province had its own Indian policy and administrative structure for implementing it. In some ways this local control may have been a good thing, since circumstances differed from one jurisdiction to the next, and almost any overall policy would have required exceptions. Together, however, an unjust treaty process and a tendency towards corrupt administration would leave First Nations people increasingly impoverished and restless.

The Atlantic Region. In general, Native populations in the Atlantic region had very few recognized land rights and thus very little protection from encroaching settlement. The hunting and fishing areas most prized by the Aboriginal people, chiefly coastline and river frontage, were also the areas preferred by the incoming settlers, who forced Native people out of their traditional food-gathering areas and rightly assumed that no government would try to stop them. As one group of settlers told the Nova Scotia government when they were warned off a Mi'kmaq reserve, they could 'hardly be supposed capable of accurately considering that the good faith of

the government towards the Indians renders it impossible to extend the same kindness and tenderness to them as it might were the trespasses committed upon unreserved Crown land'; in short, the squatters assumed that they could settle at will on unreserved Crown land.[18] Aboriginal populations, squeezed out of their hunting areas, their numbers already decimated by disease, were reduced in most places to a few hundred people at best, subsisting in dire poverty. When any land was set aside for them, it was almost invariably marginal, not suitable for cultivation—the sort of land otherwise considered suitable only for distribution to blacks.

Only a few Beothuk were still alive in Newfoundland in 1791, and with the death of Shawnadithit (c. 1801–29), the last Beothuk, the island's Aboriginal population was officially extinct. When Shawnadithit died, in St John's, not all her remains were interred: local surgeon William Carson presented her skull and scalp to the Royal College of Physicians and Surgeons in London, presumably for research purposes. For the British, the extinction of the Beothuk demonstrated that settlers could not be trusted, and that Aboriginal peoples needed paternalistic protection.

In contrast to Newfoundland, the adjacent Labrador coast had few European settlements, and the Native people were able to maintain much of their traditional way of life until well into the twentieth century. The European presence consisted almost entirely of fur-trading posts (often administered by the Hudson's Bay Company) and Moravian missions. Despite its geographic location, Labrador had more in common with the frontier West than the settled East.

The process by which Aboriginal populations were marginalized was well explained in 1794, by Nova Scotia's superintendent of Indian Affairs, George Monk, when he petitioned the colonial government on behalf of the Mi'kmaq. In earlier days there had been room for all, wrote Monk, and the Mi'kmaq had merely to learn to live in peace with the whites. By the century's end, however, settlement had eliminated their hunting grounds and there was no place left for them to go. Now the Mi'kmaq would have to be treated as objects of 'general relief'—at least until the authorities could 'rehabilitate the rising Generation to labour in some of the various works of farming till they know how to earn a livelihood for themselves.'[19] No wide-ranging land-cession treaty—with its reciprocal granting of reserve land—had ever been made with the Mi'kmaq, who by the nineteenth century began to press government for land. In 1820 some reserves were set aside by the council in each county, but they could not be settled until they had been surveyed. Some Nova Scotians advocated a policy of survey and agricultural assistance for the Indians. As one wrote to the *Novascotian*, in a letter signed 'Micmac': 'let not the lip be contemptuously curled at the idea that an Indian may become an industrious farmer.'[20] After 1827 the assembly annually voted small amounts for 'Indian relief', but all the Mi'kmaq received were handouts of provisions and land in the form of unsurveyed local reserves. Then in 1841 an aged chief named Peminuit Paul (1755–1843) wrote directly to the young Queen Victoria for assistance:

> I cannot cross the great Lake to talk to you for my Canoe is too small, and I am old and weak. I cannot look upon you for my eyes do not see so far. You cannot hear my voice across the Great Waters. I therefore send this Wampum and Paper talk to tell the Queen I am in trouble. My people are in trouble . . . . No Hunting Grounds—no Beaver—no Otter . . . poor for ever . . . . All these woods once ours. Our Fathers possessed them all. . . . White Man has taken all that was ours. . . . Let us not perish.[21]

Within five days of the receipt of this letter at the Colonial Office, a dispatch requesting more information was on its way to the lieutenant-governor of Nova Scotia. But further information took time to collect, and by the time it was available British ardour had cooled. This was typical

■ Demasduit was captured in 1819 by the English, who called her 'Mary March'. This watercolour, painted in the same year by Lady Henrietta Hamilton, the wife of Newfoundland's governor, is the only known portrait of a Beothuk. LAC, C-87698.

of the Empire, especially where indigenous peoples were concerned. Nevertheless, Nova Scotia in 1842 passed legislation for 'the Instruction and Permanent Settlement of the Indians' and created the post of Indian Commissioner (first held briefly by Joseph Howe). Some individual Mi'kmaq did receive specific parcels of land, but many objected to individual ownership. As one Crown lands commissioner wrote, they preferred 'to have everything in common, even their wigwams—they wish to be as children of the same family'. Few of them became farmers.[22]

New Brunswick did not have a separate office to deal with its Aboriginal population, which numbered about 1,000. A few reserves had been created following the establishment of the new colony in 1784; by 1838 there were 15 reserves totalling 61,293 acres, mostly on land unsuitable for farming, but there was still no reserve policy. As in Nova Scotia, squatters had simply moved onto any arable First Nations lands, and the Aboriginal people themselves resolutely refused to try farming on poor land.

The Canadas. Unlike the Atlantic region, the Canadas had substantial numbers of Aboriginal people, and they laid claim to substantial areas of land. Since 1763, the core of 'Indian policy' in the Canadas had been the notion of an orderly frontier.[23] In theory this policy involved a legal procedure for the orderly purchase of lands from the First Nations, the reservation for them of sufficient land on which to make a living, and the full application of legal rights under the law. This approach was adopted in part to symbolize the difference between Canada and the United States. It involved the application of the common law to everybody, including the Aboriginal people, because the common law was a bulwark of Tory ideology and because it provided a framework for good government. This law-centred approach was meant to avoid unnecessary violence and to promote acceptance of the new order. It worked better in theory than in practice.

The treatment of the Mississauga, whose hunting lands were in southern Ontario west of Lake Ontario, is one example of the problems that arose. In the 1780s the Mississauga agreed to surrender some of those lands to the Loyalists arriving from the United States. They did so not only because they expected that, in return, the British would provide an endless flow of 'presents', but also because they did not understand 'property' in the way that the British did; in other words, they did not realize that they were giving the British a good deal more than just the temporary use of their land. The agreements did not explicitly state that the Mississauga were giving up their rights to the territory's rivers, lakes, and minerals, and the

British negotiators assured them that they could still use the lands. The Mississauga believed they had temporarily 'rented out' the land, while the British believed their Aboriginal title had been extinguished. Not surprisingly, the Mississauga came to resent the transaction. As one told the mixed-blood missionary Peter Jones (Kahkewaquonaby) in the 1820s:

> Our fathers held out to them the hand of friendship. The strangers then asked for a small piece of land on which they might pitch their tents; the request was cheerfully granted. By and by they begged for more, and more was given them. In this way they have continued to ask, or have obtained by force or fraud, the fairest portions of our territory.[24]

As this complaint suggests, by the time the Mississauga had become aware of how the British understood the treaties, they were too weak to fight back. In 1805 they sold most of their remaining land, although this time they kept reserves on the rivers of the surrendered territory.

The Mississauga, with the assistance of Peter Jones, eventually created a successful agricultural settlement on the Credit River and resisted Canadian efforts to remove them to Manitoulin Island. Other missionaries and the Department of Indian Affairs in Upper Canada established more agricultural villages, usually complete with church buildings and schools. But most were ultimately regarded by the British as unsuccessful, particularly after 1830, when the policy emphasis shifted from assimilation to government paternalism and protection. The big change came in 1836, when Lieutenant-Governor Sir Francis Bond Head decided that attempts at assimilation were misguided; instead, he argued, 'the greatest kindness we can perform towards these Intelligent, simple-minded people is to remove and fortify them as much as possible from all Communication with the Whites.'[25] Head engineered the cession of several million acres of Ojibwa land in return for a promise that Manitoulin Island and its adjacent

PETER JONES
(1802–56)

■ Peter Jones (Kahkewaquonaby).
Peter Jones Collection, Victoria
University Library (Toronto).

Peter Jones ('Kahkewaquonaby' or 'Sacred Feathers' in Ojibwa, 'Desagondensta' or 'He stands people on their feet' in Mohawk) was born near Burlington, Upper Canada. His mother was the daughter of a Mississauga chief, his father a retired English surveyor. Brought up among the Mississauga until the age of 14, he was sent to school by his father, where he learned English and became known as Peter Jones. He was converted to the Methodist Episcopal Church at a camp meeting in Ancaster in 1823, became a trial preacher in 1827, and was ordained in 1833. (When invited by Archdeacon John Strachan to join the Anglicans, he refused.) Meanwhile, in 1826 he led a group of Mississauga—including many of his own family—to a mission village on the Credit River, where they cleared the land and successfully began farming; in 1829 he was elected a chief of the band. To raise money for mission activities (much of it for his own people), he toured extensively on the lecture circuit, usually dressed in 'Indian' garb. He travelled to the United States in 1829 and made several trips to Britain, where in 1831 he had an audience with the King and met his future wife, Eliza Field, who came to Canada and assisted her husband in his missionary work. In the late 1830s Jones and his people successfully resisted government pressure to move to Manitoulin Island. Nevertheless, some of the Credit band objected to the complete loss of Native identity that Jones preached.

In the 1840s Jones's health began to fail, and on his third British missionary tour, in 1845, he confessed to his wife that he was 'getting heartily tired of begging'. He also objected to posing as an 'Indian' when at heart he felt himself to be totally Europeanized. In 1847 he was able to lead 200 of his people to new land on the Grand River at New Credit, but his health continued to deteriorate. He spent his last years in a handsome brick villa constructed for him not far from Brantford. Jones published many sermons and speeches during his lifetime, and after his death Eliza Jones edited his diaries and papers for publication. Much of his most important work, however, was done in translating scripture and hymns into Ojibwa. Jones helped his people to survive by adapting to European ways; but he appears to have paid a heavy psychological price for his own efforts to function within both the Aboriginal and European worlds.

islands would be protected as 'Indian territory'. The Ojibwa knew full well that the deal was a bad one, but feared that if they did not agree they might lose everything. Many religious denominations in both Britain and British North America protested Head's reserve policy.

CONCLUSION

British North America between 1790 and 1840 had an economy based almost exclusively on a handful of staple resources and a social structure sharply divided between the elite and the non-elite. But clear social distinctions did not mean that the social categories were simple. The truck system, tenancy, and occupational pluralities complicated the picture, as did the legally inferior status of most women and the widespread prejudice against the black and Aboriginal peoples. Nor did the fact that British North America was a 'good poor man's country' mean that there was no poverty. Although, on the whole, social and economic conditions did improve for immigrants in the second generation, for first-generation immigrants without substantial capital, life could still be difficult.

SHORT BIBLIOGRAPHY

Backhouse, Constance. *Petticoats and Prejudice: Women and Law in Nineteenth-Century Canada.* Toronto, 1991. A valuable study of the legal status of women in the nineteenth century.

Brown, Jennifer. *Strangers in Blood: Fur Trade Company Families in Indian Country.* Vancouver, 1980. An important overview of the society of the fur trade.

Cadigan, Sean T. *Hope and Deception in Conception Bay: Merchant–Settler Relations in Newfoundland, 1785–1855.* Toronto, 1995. An analysis of the fishing society of Newfoundland.

Graham, Elizabeth. *Medicine-Man to Missionary: Missionaries of Change among the Indians of Southern Ontario, 1784–1867.* Toronto, 1984. An important revisionist work on the missionary impulse among Aboriginal peoples in Ontario.

Greer, Allan. *Peasant, Lord and Merchant: Rural Society in Three Quebec Parishes 1740–1840.* Toronto, 1985. A revisionist study of rural society in Quebec.

Haring, Sidney L. *White Man's Law: Native People in Nineteenth-Century Canadian Jurisprudence.* Toronto, 1998. Arguably the most important work on the First Nations that has appeared in recent years.

Hepburn, Sharon A. and Roger. *Crossing the Border: A Free Black Community in Canada.* Urbana and Chicago, 2007. A detailed study of one of the most successful black communities in Canada West.

Johnson, J.K. *Becoming Prominent: Regional Leadership in Upper Canada, 1791–1841.* Montreal and Kingston, 1989. The best study of the phenomenon of the regional elite.

Light, Beth, and Alison Prentice, eds. *Pioneer and Gentlewomen of British North America 1713–1867.* Toronto, 1980. A rich collection of documents on women in colonial Canada.

Pentland, H. Clare. *Labour and Capital in Canada: 1650–1860.* Toronto, 1981. A Marxist reading of colonial society in British North America.

Prentice, Alison, et al. *Canadian Women: A History*, 2nd edn. Toronto, 1996. The best overview of the history of women in Canada.

Silverman, Jason. *Unwelcome Guests: Canada West's Response to American Fugitive Slaves, 1800–1865.* Millwood, NY, 1985. An important general survey of the fugitive slave movement to Upper Canada.

Upton, L.F.S. *Micmacs and Colonists: Indian–White Relations in the Maritimes, 1713–1867.* Vancouver, 1979. A well-researched study along traditional lines.

Ward, W. Peter. *Courtship, Love and Marriage in Nineteenth-Century English Canada.* Montreal, 1990. An interesting and useful survey of courtship and marriage patterns among the elite.

Winks, Robin. *The Blacks in Canada: A History*, 2nd edn. Montreal, 1997. The essential work in black history, now a generation old, but recently revised.

Study Questions

1. What were the relationships between the economy and society in colonial Canada?
2. What distinguished the two elites of British North America?
3. What effect did the 'truck system' have on colonial society?
4. Why did conditions for women in British North America worsen as society became more stable?
5. How would you describe the legal position of women in British North America in the colonial period?
6. Why did the position of the First Nations deteriorate in the first part of the nineteenth century?
7. How could British North America be both a 'good poor man's country' and the home of so much poverty and social injustice?

CHAPTER SIXTEEN

Colonial Culture, 1791–1840

■ British North America was part of the British Empire, and the destination of millions of emigrants from the British Isles. Not surprisingly, British culture transplanted into North American pioneering conditions predominated in the period before 1840, although specifically American influences introduced by the Loyalists continued to make their presence felt.

The word 'culture' can mean many things. Used in the anthropological sense, it refers to the way people or peoples live and behave in their everyday lives. For example, the emerging concept of domesticity had a significant impact on British North American society in the pioneer period. But 'culture' can also refer to various forms of intellectual, aesthetic, and spiritual activity. Two institutions central to the expression and transmission of culture in this sense—the church and the school—were established in many regions before 1840. Typically, cultural production in early British North America was non-professional. Aspirations to 'high culture'— work of permanent value—had their centre in Nova Scotia, where they were exemplified in the literary activities of T.C. Haliburton and Thomas McCulloch. Some of the most robust writing in the pioneer period, however, was produced by fur traders and explorers. Vernacular or popular culture, produced for ordinary consumption or amusement without any particular eye to intellectual or aesthetic effect, flourished as well. In this chapter we will examine two areas of popular culture: musical activity and sports. The latter, especially, was more complex than simple colonial transplantation. It involved the importation of many sports from Europe, especially the British Isles; the subsequent remaking of them to suit a new environment; and often the exportation of the new product to the United States.

ANTHROPOLOGICAL CULTURE: THE RISE OF DOMESTICITY

As British North American society became more settled, and somewhat more urbanized, a trend emerged within the ranks of the middle and upper classes towards a clear separation of work and home life. Women withdrew into the privacy of the home, and the family became the central social unit for the transmission of culture, the maintenance of social stability, and the pursuit of happiness. This trend towards domesticity had begun among the elite, but gradually made its way into the middle class as the century went on. Increasing prosperity allowed more people to build bigger houses, within which could develop new notions of social space. Once it became possible to reserve specific rooms for specific func-

TIMELINE

1789
King's College founded at Windsor, Nova Scotia.

1801
Alexander Mackenzie's *Voyages from Montreal* published.

1807
First curling club organized in Montreal.

1809
William Berczy paints the Woolsey family.

1818
Founding of Dalhousie College in Halifax. First Bank of Montreal building erected.

1819
Bishop Plessis elevated to archbishopric. New Catholic dioceses created in Upper Canada and PEI.

1820
Daniel Harmon publishes his fur-trade journal in Massachusetts.

1821
First letter by Mephiboseth Stepsure appears in *Acadian Recorder*.

1824
First novel by a native-born Canadian published: *St Ursula's Convent*, by Julia Hart.

1827
King's College (Upper Canada) chartered.

1829
McGill College opens. Joseph Lancaster comes to Canada.

1830
William Lyon Mackenzie's *Catechism of Education* published.

1831
Osgoode Hall erected in Toronto.

1832
John Richardson's *Wacousta* published.

1833
Montreal Gazette reports on Mohawk–Iroquois lacrosse game.

1836
Haliburton's *The Clockmaker* published.

1837
Public ice hockey ('ice-hurtling') played in Montreal.

1838
First recognizable baseball game in British America played in Beachville, Upper Canada. Anna Jameson's *Winter Tales and Summer Rambles* published.

1840
First indoor curling facilities constructed in Montreal.

tions (and specific people), it also became possible to distinguish between 'public' and 'private' space. Instead of spending his life almost entirely in the public sphere, the husband and father now came 'home' from work to renew himself. With this new definition of the home as a masculine refuge came a new 'cult of true womanhood', emphasizing the woman's role as wife, mother, household manager, and fulcrum of the family. Increasingly, women were expected to confine their activities to the private sphere. As motherhood and housewifery were elevated to sacred female duties, it became one of the woman's chief functions to providing a moral sanctuary from the outside world. To some extent this function merged into male patriarchy's notion of women as frail and weak. As the Kingston *Gazette* put it as early as 1810:

> Women, it has been observed, are not naturally formed for great care themselves, but to soften ours. Their tenderness is a proper reward for dangers we undergo for their preservation; and the ease and cheerfulness of their conversation, our desirable retreat from the fatigues of intense application. They are confined within the narrow limits of domestic assiduity; and when they stray beyond the sphere, are consequently without grace.[1]

The idealization of home and family was accompanied by a new attitude towards human emotion, usually labelled 'sentimentalization'. Gone was the stoic silence with which earlier generations had faced the vagaries of family relationships. Now sentiment was openly avowed—at least with respect to approved topics and within widely accepted bounds of respectability. One of the most common occasions for the expression of sentiment was the death of a child. As one Victorian mother wrote, 'I never knew till I had a dear child how agonizing the parting with it would be, and when I saw its sweet face looking so calm and composed, I could scarcely realize the sad truth, that it was lost to me forever in this world.'[2] It was now possible in mourning to admit personal feelings. In 1841, soon after the death of his wife, Chief Justice Edward Jarvis of the Prince Edward Island Supreme Court wrote to her sister:

> My own feelings have now become so nervous & sensitive that I seem to participate as much in any anxieties of my friends as if it were my own case. I cannot shake off the dreadful weight & oppression which hangs increasingly upon my spirits & the slightest exciting cause wholly overpowers me. . . . The utmost indifference to every passing event & occupation possesses me & I cannot overcome it.[3]

Such an open expression of depression was a relatively new phenomenon, at least in middle-class society.

With the new freedom to express personal feelings of grief came a corresponding increase in expressions of affection and love. In the past, marriage had been seen mainly in terms of practical matters such as dowries, or family alliances, or labour in the fields. Now, however, the British (and British North American) middle classes talked openly about companionable marriage. Henry and Sarah Crease, on the eve of migration from Britain to Victoria in 1858, wrote to one another as 'My sweet wifey' and 'my own darling hubby'.[4] But of course tender phrases did not necessarily imply a relationship between equals. Men still thought that submissiveness and obedience were important qualities in a bride. One prospective groom in 1829 wrote to his mother telling her that his new wife would not only 'unite affection & prudence in her conduct as respects myself', but 'be an excellent & dutiful daughter-in-law'. Another man, contemplating marriage in 1832, hoped to find in his wife 'a true friend, a rational companion, and a useful assistant'.[5] James Robb, who had emigrated from Scotland to teach at the university in Fredericton, wrote his mother in 1840:

> Ellen and I are one. I have gained the best and sweetest of all wives, friends and companions. She is beautiful, she is good, she is fond and affectionate. She is, in short, the very person whom you yourself, my own dear Mother, would have selected as the fittest for your James. If I am ever to be happy, it will be with Ellen; and since the beginning of our union, my life has been one of

calm tranquillity and delight. I now have an object to live for, and one also worthy of all and more than all I can ever do for her. She is peaceful and gentle and more affectionate than a dove, in short, my Ellen is everything I could wish.[6]

For the most part women appear to have accepted the constraints that came with marriage—if not always easily. Marriage, wrote one prospective bride to her sister in 1830, 'costs me something even in prospect to give up my independence, my power of motion, my hermitage, my philosophizing life, my general utility & alas some of my more particular associations.' But, she continued, 'I am more and more contented to make these sacrifices. . . . it is perhaps the work assigned me by providence to promote his more important interests whilst I am at the same time convinced that I should in return incur no hindrance but receive assistance & encouragement

on my own onward progress towards the great goal.'[7] The effort at rationalization in these words is certainly apparent.

One of the most important consequences of the rise of domesticity, of course, was a narrowing of the approved life courses for middle-class women. The possibilities of a public career had never been very broad, but now virtually the only socially acceptable career for a woman of 'standing' was marriage—an institution that put her legally under the complete control of her husband. By the 1850s the ideal of the 'true woman' would have migrated as far west as the isolated Red River settlement. In a letter to his brother, William Ross described his notion of 'perfectly accomplished ladies': 'They can play elegantly on the Harp, guitar, piano, they sing melodiously and methodically. They can dance and waltz like true English dames, and I guess they can play the coquette too if that be any part of Ornamental

DANIEL HARMON'S FUR TRADE JOURNAL

Monday October 10, 1808 DUNVEGAN [ATHABASCA], which is a well-built Fort and stands in a pleasant situation, with Plains on either side of the River. Here is where my friend A.N. McLeod used to Winter, while in Athabasca and here I find my former companion & friend Mr. Frederick Goedike &c who past last Summer here—and about the fort are encamped a number of Iroquois-Hunters and Beaver Indians, who have been waiting our arrival. And at long last I have reached the place where I shall pass, God willing, the ensuing Winter, also Messrs. Donald McTavish, J.B. McTavish & Joseph McGillivray and thirty-two labouring Men, nine Women & several Children, which makes it differ much from the solitary place where I was last Winter. Here our princi-

pal food will be the Flesh of Buffaloe, Moose, Red Deer & Bears. We also have a tolerable Kitchen Garden, therefore we have what would make the most of People contented—that is those who only think of filling their greedy Bellies. As I have mentioned what we have to nourish our *bodies*, I must also add that we have a very good collection of Books to satisfy our *minds*, and if we are so disposed will make us grow wiser & consequently better. And to complete the whole the above mentioned Gentlemen are sociable & agreeable Companions—and now if I do not pass a pleasant & profitable winter it must be my fault. This evening I have past in agreeable chat with my friend Goedike of our transactions together in the Red River &c., &c.

SOURCE: Daniel Williams Harmon, *Harmon's Journal 1800–1819* (Victoria: TouchWood Editions, 2006), 103.

Education.'[8] Not all women, of course, wanted to be ornaments or decorations. Even in communities containing few women, however, the ideal of a domestic sociability was very strong.

CULTURAL INSTITUTIONS: RELIGION

Next to politics, religion was the most common form of cultural expression in the colonies of British North America. In the early nineteenth century, the human need for explanatory constructs capable of giving order and meaning to life was filled chiefly by various Christian churches. The francophone population was almost exclusively Catholic, while the English-speakers were both Protestant and Catholic. But other differences were perhaps equally important. One such division was between those denominations that supported the principle of establishment and those that did not. Another had to do with national origins: most of the francophone Catholics were Canadian-born, although an influential minority were refugees from the French Revolution; the anglophone Catholics came from the British Isles; and the Protestants came from both Britain and the United States.

THE ESTABLISHED CHURCHES

The elite culture of privilege was supported not only by the constitutional arrangements of the provinces of British North America, but also by the clergy of the established churches. Such support was one of the reasons the British government felt so strongly about the need for establishment in the American colonies. Indeed, an established churchman was almost by definition a supporter of the status quo. In Lower Canada, the quasi-establishment of the Roman Catholic Church put it squarely among the defenders of order and privilege. For many years it was tacitly agreed by government that the established church in Upper Canada—the one entitled to receive the financial support of the state—was

the Church of England. This understanding was of course devoutly upheld by Archdeacon John Strachan of York, who in 1824 expressed to Sir Peregrine Maitland, the lieutenant-governor, his belief that the form of worship and the doctrine of his church 'was the most pure form of Christianity existing in the world, certainly the most compatible with our form of government'.[9] Significantly, not only Anglicans but Presbyterians and Roman Catholics too were inherently conservative in their views. Like Strachan, Bishop Alexander Macdonell—his Roman Catholic colleague on the Legislative Council for many years—also believed in a social hierarchy.

For conservatives such as these:

> To meditate the establishment of equality . . . , that splendid delusion of the present age, the vision of the weak, and the pretext of the wicked, is in fact to meditate war against God, and the primary laws of creation. . . . In society inequality is just as natural as in the forest, but productive of much more salutary effects. Without inequality what would become of the necessary distinctions of parent and child, master and scholar, the employer and the employed?[10]

While Strachan and Macdonell would certainly have agreed with those sentiments, they were actually expressed in Halifax by a Presbyterian clergyman, Andrew Brown, in 1794. Strachan's account of social order differed only slightly from Brown's:

> Subordination in the Moral World is manifest and this appearance of nature indicates the intention of its Author. The beauty and advantages of this arrangement are obvious and universally acknowledged. . . . The various relations of individuals and Societies require a mutual exchange of good offices. . . . Hence it would appear that they who labour in the inferior departments of life are not on that account the slaves of their superiors. The Magistrate requires the aid of his people—the Master of his Servant. They are all

JOHN STRACHAN

(1778–1867)

■ Bishop John Strachan, 1847.
Toronto Public Library (TPL),
JRR T15000.

John Strachan evoked strong feelings among his contemporaries. For more than half a century he was simultaneously one of the most respected men in Upper Canada and one of the most detested. Strachan was born in Aberdeen, Scotland, and graduated from the University of Aberdeen. Shortly after his arrival in Canada in 1799, he took orders in the Church of England and began teaching at Cornwall. (The question of whether he had left the Presbyterian Church for the Anglican would later become a public issue; he claimed he had always been an Anglican.) Strachan used his school, which was attended by many sons of provincial officials, to begin to establish his position in Canadian society. In 1811 he accepted the offer of General Isaac Brock to become rector of York, with a salary plus other public emoluments. In late 1812 he formed the Loyal and Patriotic Society of Upper Canada, which raised funds to relieve disabled militiamen and their families. He negotiated with the Americans on two occasions when they invaded York in 1813. After the war, in 1816, he became a member of the province's Executive Council and used the post to dominate in the fields of education and religion for many years. He joined the Legislative Council in 1820.

Strachan wrote and published extensively on affairs of the day, including a vicious attack on the Earl of Selkirk and an immigrant's guide (released in 1820 under his brother's name). More important, he pressed for educational reform, including the establishment of common schools and a college in the province. Unfortunately, he was unable to divorce his educational campaign from his commitment to the established status of the Church of England. When, in 1825, he became associated with an effort to sell the clergy reserves, which would benefit only the Church of England, he wrote a letter falsely disparaging the work of every other denomination in the province. This letter would haunt him for years. In the spring of 1827 he returned from England with a charter for a new university, which was to be all too thoroughly controlled by the Church of England. According to a pamphlet written by Strachan, its main purpose was to educate clergymen for Anglican missionary activity.

By the later 1820s, Strachan had come to be seen as the evil genius behind the so-called Family Compact, although his political activities were actually becoming less important. When his membership on the two councils became a grievance for the reformers, he readily resigned from the Executive Council, but insisted on remaining on the other one. Despite his increased role in church affairs in the province, he could not gain the appointment as bishop until 1839, when he was given the post without stipend. Finally, in 1843, King's College opened with Strachan as president. But he was still attempting to monopolize the revenue from the clergy reserves, and he found his presidency of the college under constant attack. In 1849 he opposed the legislation secularizing the college and in 1850 he left for England to lobby for the charter for the University of Trinity College, opened early in 1852. He was eventually relieved of many of his duties as bishop by the election of a coadjutor in 1866.

Throughout his career in Upper Canada, Strachan had articulated the traditional Tory position: a belief in hierarchy, order, and the establishment of the Church of England. This position became increasingly untenable, but he revelled in controversy and managed to stave off the inevitable longer than anyone would have believed possible. Strachan seldom published anything that was not polemical, but his was a central voice in the ecclesiastical and educational affairs of his time.

dependent upon one another, as they subsist by an exchange of good offices. . . . The lowest order enjoys its peculiar comforts and privileges, and contributes equally with the highest to the support and dignity of Society.[11]

Established church leaders like Strachan, Jacob Mountain of Lower Canada, and Charles and John Inglis of Nova Scotia all understood that they needed to develop their churches at the local level in order to justify the public favour they received from the political elite of which they were part. All succeeded to a considerable extent, although a vigorous local presence did not necessarily translate into popular acceptance for the Church of England.

For those not associated with established churches—the majority in most provinces, although in Lower Canada Catholics were obviously overwhelmingly dominant—the pretensions of the ecclesiastical establishment, particularly in maintaining their traditional monopoly on marriage rites and education, were constant irritants that were frequently blamed on the oligarchic constitutional system, as were the clergy reserves in provinces that had them. Not all non-supported denominations opposed establishment; the main grievance of the Presbyterian Church—which was, after all, the established church in Scotland—was that the Church of England refused to share its public support. Dissenters chafed under arrangements that granted all Christians 'liberty of conscience' but denied their clergymen full powers to act in such matters as the solemnization of marriage. The Anglicans fought an unsuccessful rearguard action—by the 1830s it had lost any pretense to monopoly—but in the process it demonstrated its privileged position. The complaints of the Presbyterians were particularly telling.

Within the Catholic Church the years before 1840 saw a number of developments. In Lower Canada it further solidified its position as a privileged, quasi-established institution, especially under Joseph-Octave Plessis (bishop and archbishop, 1806–25), who was appointed to the province's Legislative Council in 1817.[12] Plessis continued to have trouble with shortages of priests despite the arrival of a number of French clerics exiled by the French Revolution. The exiles turned the church in an even more conservative direction in terms of attitudes towards law and authority. Plessis had to deal as well with lay opposition in parish administration, especially outside his own province, in the Maritime region. He also presided over the devolution of the church in British North America, as Rome in 1819 divided the diocese of Quebec to create new dioceses in Upper Canada and in Prince Edward Island, both headed by Highland Scots, and elevated him to an archbishopric. Plessis himself did not adhere to the ultramontane view that the church, as the guardian of moral law, must be heeded in all matters related to politics. But he did attempt, with some success, to strengthen the structure of his church by educating more clergy, obtaining government recognition of its legal position (not just in Lower Canada), and reforming its far-flung governance by creating more administrative units.

THE DISSENTERS

In every colony there were dissenters who objected not only to the conservative social vision of the established churches and their support of hierarchy and privilege, but also to the very formal view of God they promulgated. The most numerous dissenters were Methodists, whose itinerant ministers were constantly on the move, covering as large a circuit as possible; other dissenters included Baptists, some schismatic Presbyterians, and a handful of other groups, such as the Society of Friends (Quakers) and the Mennonites (who kept to themselves and did not enter any debates, political or religious).

In the opinion of John Strachan, the Methodists preached 'the Gospel from idleness or a zeal without knowledge. They are induced without any preparation to teach what they do not know, and which, from their pride, they disdain to learn.'[13] Strachan was scornful of the fact that there were no educational requirements for entering the Methodist ministry (a candidate had only to satisfy a Conference committee that he was familiar with a set list of books). Another important objection to Methodists, from the viewpoint of Strachan and other British conservatives, was that many of them were Americans and possibly republicans. Indeed, much of the cultural struggle between the British and the Americans in these years was played out in religious terms: both the Methodists and the Baptists in British North America were internally divided into British and American wings, and many of the other dissenting denominations experienced conflict among the different immigrant groups that made up their membership, as they sought some sort of acceptable British–American synthesis.

For most of the dissenting Protestants, the fundamental disagreements (both with the established churches and with one another) were epistemological, centring on how one came to know God. Many of the dissenters were evangelicals who believed that God had to be experienced emotionally rather than comprehended rationally. Spiritual feelings were 'awakened' at revivals (in the Maritime provinces) and 'camp meetings' (in Upper Canada). Such events were characterized by mass participation in a highly charged emotional atmosphere. Striving to inspire a crisis experience leading to conversion, the preachers emphasized 'Christ crucified' and often preached (as one witness put it) as if battling a swarm of bees. Naturally, those who preferred their religion rational, orderly, and sedate were appalled. Not only were the evangelicals irrational and passionate, but they were inherently populist in their attitudes. For many in the establishment, violent passion and populism went hand in hand with revolution.

CULTURAL INSTITUTIONS: EDUCATION

Another area of conflict between the privileges of the establishment and the needs of an expanding

■ Methodist camp meeting, Grimsby, Upper Canada, 25 August 1859. Archives of the United Church of Canada/Victoria University Archives, Toronto, 90.162P/2019 N.

population was education. In every colony, including Lower Canada, Crown lands had been set aside for the support of 'a Protestant clergy' and education, and both the disposition of these lands and the use of the resultant revenue became bones of political contention. In Upper Canada, John Strachan fought on behalf of the Church of England's exclusive use of the revenue from the clergy reserves, both against the pretensions of other (more or less) 'established' churches, such as the Church of Scotland and the Roman Catholic Church, and against efforts to use the funds for secular purposes.

Educational institutions were divided between the private universities, colleges, and academies designed to educate the few and the public schools intended to deal with the many. Over the former the established churches generally maintained close control, on the grounds that higher education involved far more than

mere technical knowledge. The exception was Dalhousie College in Halifax, founded by Nova Scotia's governor, Lord Dalhousie, in 1818 as a non-denominational alternative to the University of King's College at Windsor, founded by the Church of England in 1789. In the case of common and elementary schools, relations with the established churches, particularly the Church of England, were rather more complex and tenuous.

At the start of this period, the Church of England saw elementary schooling as the responsibility of a state church. Thus the views of Bishop Jacob Mountain in Lower Canada were reflected in the foundation in 1801 of the Royal Institution for the Advancement of Learning, intended to supervise schools within the province operating under Anglican auspices. Catholics, for their part, established private schools and supported a considerable array of institutions staffed by clerics and nuns. A bequest of land and £10,000 provided by the Montreal merchant James McGill[14] to establish a university led the Royal Institution in 1821 to grant a charter to McGill College, which opened in 1829. Meanwhile, Strachan had his own ambitions for a university in Upper Canada, intended mainly as a 'Missionary College' for the training of clergymen. In 1826, authorized by the provincial government, he went to England to obtain a university charter, and the next year a royal charter was announced for the University of King's College, which was to be firmly under the control of the Church of England, with the lieutenant-governor as chancellor and the archdeacon of York as president. (William Lyon Mackenzie's angry response to this announcement appeared in the *Colonial Advocate* on 11 October 1827.[15]) But Sir John Colborne, who arrived as lieutenant-governor in 1828, thought a university was premature, and opted instead for a preparatory grammar school; the result was Upper Canada College, founded in 1829. The plan for King's College lay dormant until after the 1837 rebellion. Strachan had earlier taken the lead in encouraging the legislature to appropriate money for the support of common schools, and he was president of the General Board of Education established in the colony in 1823 to supervise public education.

Despite the political manoeuvrings, several institutions of higher learning were established in British North America before 1840.[16] Most of them had religious origins and were fundamentally intended to train a learned clergy. The typical colonial institution of higher learning was a small college, with an enrolment of fewer than 100 male students. The level of education on offer was closer to that of a modern secondary school than a university (either contemporary or modern), although many modern Canadian universities trace their origins to this colonial period. The curriculum was basically classical, with emphasis on mathematics and ancient Latin and Greek. In French Canada the 'collèges classiques', carried over from the French regime, trained young men for the priesthood and the professions, especially the law. The author Philippe-Joseph Aubert de Gaspé wrote with considerable affection and respect about the Séminaire de Québec, where he had been educated at the end of the eighteenth century.[17] Both anglophone and francophone schools were chronically short of textbooks. Much reliance was placed on rote memorization. Few of the teachers had any scholarly pretensions beyond the classroom, and 'research' was virtually unknown.

Both the elite and ordinary folk could agree on the desirability of education, although for somewhat different reasons. As one Quebec citizens' petition of 1787 complained, government after the Conquest had not emphasized 'the education of youth, from whom heretofore civil officers, good militia officers, commercial persons, navigators, and intelligent tradesmen were formed. All, for want of a public education, remained in ignorance of the laws divine and human, of reading, writing, and even of the English language.'[18] Many farmers may have seen little advantage in sending their children to school, but others recognized that education was inseparable from upward mobility, a point that the Scots in particular had long understood. As William Lyon Mackenzie put it in his *Catechism of Education*, published in 1830, 'Intelligence is power', and the aim of education was to produce happiness. On the subject of free schools, Mackenzie argued:

> The beneficial effects attending such a system are incalculable. Additional stability would be given to free institutions, the sum of public and private happiness would be greatly increased; the power of the people extended; crime diminished; an inviolable respect for the laws maintained; and a constitutional vigilance more increasingly exercised, against all encroachments upon national or individual rights.[19]

Mackenzie also maintained that entrusting schooling to the government meant that young people were 'trained generally to habits of servility and toleration of arbitrary power, in so far as precept and example can influence their minds.' Fortunately, they also obtained 'those keys of useful knowledge, the faculties of reading and writing, by means of which, "the liberty of the press", and the intelligence of the age, they are prevented from becoming instruments of evil.'[20]

If for the common folk and their liberal-minded spokesmen education was the means of mobility and liberation, for the conservative authorities education was essential to inculcate social order. Indeed, Mackenzie himself valued the 'additional stability'—specifically, the reduction in crime and increase in respect for the law—that he saw as products of education. For those members of the elite concerned about order, such stability was even more urgently needed, although expense was also a concern. Two systems of education were thus brought to the colonies from Britain after 1815, both of which promised to teach large numbers of students at relatively low cost by relying on older children to pass on the lessons they learned by rote to their younger counterparts.

One scheme, the Bell system of National Schools (also called the 'Madras' system, since it was first employed in India), was fostered in Britain by the National Society for Promoting the Education of the Poor in the Principles of the Established Church, and promulgated in British North America by the Anglican Society for Promoting Christian Knowledge (SPCK); it carried the baggage of its sponsorship with it. The other scheme was the 'Monitorial' system promoted by Joseph Lancaster, a London educator who went to Lower Canada in 1829 and whose educational experiments in that province were supported by men as diverse as Papineau, Mackenzie, and Lord Aylmer (governor of Lower Canada, 1831–5). Unlike the Bell scheme, the Lancaster system had the merit of not being associated with any denomination. Neither system ever won sufficient favour to have a direct influence on the structure of education, although parts of both were eventually incorporated into the arrangements for common schools. Only in the 1830s did demands for broadly based public education—such as those led by the Methodist minister and educational administrator Egerton Ryerson in Upper Canada—become prominent anywhere in British North America, and the landmark School Acts belong to the post-1840 period.[21] (They will be considered in the next chapter.)

Before 1840 school curricula in British North America were extremely eclectic, reflecting the cultural diversity of the colonies and the absence of central direction. Immigrants from different backgrounds, whether in England, Ireland, Scotland, or the United States, brought with them different educational experiences, which were usually coloured by substantial biases of class, ethnicity, and denomination. Textbooks imported from Britain, the United States, and (in Lower Canada) France shared many common moral assumptions, but differed on such basic issues as spelling and the currencies used in arithmetic problems. Moreover, as those books increasingly reflected conscious efforts to promote nationalism and patriotism in their respective countries of origin, they became even less appropriate for use in British North America. Yet, before 1840 it was hard to conceive of a British American culture, much less a British American 'nation'.

CULTURAL PRODUCTION

Politics and religion aside, the cultural activities of the British North American colonies were as diverse and eclectic as the origins of their populations would suggest. A common stereotype identifies the period 1790–1840 as one of extremely limited and primitive cultural and artistic production, in no way to be compared with the flowering of literature, art, and music in Europe and the British Isles, or even the United States. But that stereotype reflects a particular set of assumptions about culture. In the area of high culture, indigenous work was understandably rare; foreign models were usually dominant. There was, however, a substantial folk culture, which included a well-established oral tradition of tales and songs handed down from generation to generation and from group to group. There was also a strong tradition of material culture. The uncluttered, functional lines of the simple pine furniture produced by anonymous craftsmen during the colonial period were disdained by later generations that preferred heavy ornamentation and highly polished wood veneers. Today, however, we recognize that the aesthetic values of those anonymous furniture-makers were on a level with their fine craftsmanship.

ELITE CULTURE

Today, much of the elite culture of British North America seems lacking in both originality and dynamism. Nor could it be otherwise. European models were imitated because high art and literature were European almost by definition. Indeed, most of the producers of elite culture were trained and educated abroad, as were most of the social elite of this period. Of the 538 people given entries in Volume VII of the *Dictionary of Canadian Biography*, covering those who died between 1835 and 1850—and including the leaders of British North America in the second quarter of the nineteenth century—fewer than 200 were born in the colonies, and most of those were born in Lower Canada. The remainder came chiefly from the British Isles and the United States (although some had been born to British parents living as far afield as India and Senegal). Even those young people who did grow up in British North America were taught by seniors who had been educated abroad, usually with an emphasis on slavish replication of acknowledged masters in both form and content. Outside the elite circles in the larger cities, there was little appreciation of artistic, literary, theatrical, or intellectual work for its own sake: what the public wanted was whatever contemporary European taste dictated. A few people in the larger cities made a decent living catering to the gentry and the leading merchants. But there was no substantial market for works of art or refinement.

Most high culture was produced by people who made their living in some other way, and in many cases they regarded their artistic activity more as a diversion or a by-product than as serious professional work. The scarcity of institutions of higher learning—and the limited aspirations of those that did exist—meant that they could not provide employment for many artists and intellectuals. In 1787, for example, David Owen, senior wrangler at Cambridge University and tutor to William Pitt the Younger, was attracted to New Brunswick by the prospect of a university appointment. When the university failed to materialize, he retreated to family property on Campobello Island, where he spent the remaining 43 years of his life as an eccentric hermit and semi-feudal landlord who occasionally

published in the newspapers of Saint John. We will focus here on literature as the exemplar of high culture in this early period.

The real intellectual and literary centre of British North America in this early period was Nova Scotia, the home of Joseph Howe, Thomas Chandler Haliburton, and Thomas McCulloch. By the 1830s the province was also home to three colleges and several important academies. It contained a number of subscription libraries founded in the 1820s, and literary and scientific societies organized in the 1830s. It supported numerous newspapers and, between 1826 and 1833, two literary magazines, the *Acadian* and the *Halifax Monthly*. The cement that held much of the literary community together was Joseph Howe, himself a poet and essayist as well as a newspaper publisher and printer. In 1829 Howe published *An Historical and Statistical Account of Nova Scotia* by his friend Haliburton, whose 'Sam Slick' sketches usually appeared in instalments in Howe's weekly *Novascotian* before they were published—also by Howe—in book form. Howe was a leading member of 'The Club', a group of writers in Halifax who often contributed to his newspaper. The common topic for Nova Scotia's best writing was the development of the province itself, and the usual approach was to make fun of Nova Scotians for their follies and foibles—gently in Howe's 'Rambles', which ran serially in his newspaper between 1828 and 1831, but satirically in the writings of Thomas Chandler Haliburton.[22]

Born in Windsor, Nova Scotia, Haliburton was a Tory in the eighteenth-century tradition of the squirearchy. After an early career as a lawyer and politician, he succeeded his father as a judge in the Inferior Court of Common Pleas in 1829, and in 1841 was appointed to the Supreme Court of Nova Scotia, where he served until his retirement to England in 1856. Haliburton nevertheless made time for writing, and his output was prodigious, beginning with *A General Description of Nova Scotia* (1823), which was enlarged into *An Historical and Statistical Account of Nova Scotia*. Haliburton's romantic account of

■ 'The Woolsey Family', William Berczy, 1809, oil on canvas. If the sitters in this portrait look oddly detached from one another, the reason is that the artist drew each one separately. Once all the figures had been transferred to the canvas, he painted in the background around them. National Gallery of Canada, Ottawa. 5875. Gift of Major Edgar C. Woolsey, Ottawa, 1952.

the expulsion of the Acadians inspired Long-fellow's *Evangeline* of 1847. In 1835–6, Haliburton wrote 21 sketches about Sam Slick—a literary character to rival those of Dickens. When the sketches first appeared in Joseph Howe's *Novascotian*, they became so popular that Haliburton enlarged them into *The Clockmaker; or The Sayings and Doings of Samuel Slick, of Slickville* (1836). Slick is a wise-cracking Yankee clockmaker from Connecticut who tours Nova Scotia gulling the gullible and commenting on Nova Scotia society, employing 'soft-sawder' and an understanding of 'human natur' in his dual role as con-man/commentator. He achieved international popularity when *The Clockmaker* was published by Joseph Bentley in London.

Possessed of a ribald and anecdotal sense of humour—the reader can sense that many of these sketches had their origin in the tavern—Haliburton can still be read with enjoyment today, particularly by those who know a little about the society he was satirizing. He created Sam Slick for a purpose, which was quite double-edged. Sam embodied the worst features of Americans (braggery and opportunism), but his criticisms of Nova Scotians grew out of his admiration of the best American traits (energy and entrepreneurial adaptability). Haliburton insisted that Nova Scotia was living beyond its means, exhausting itself in useless squabbling. Through Sam Slick he offered the Tory alternatives: collective adjustment to changing conditions and the development of existing resources. While he did not succeed in reforming his province, he created a memorable stage Yankee, with a colourful dialect and an unlimited fund of aphorisms and epigrams, who became one of the most popular comic literary characters of the nineteenth century.

After the first series of Sam Slick sketches, Haliburton extended his range and began using Slick to satirize the Americans and the British more than Nova Scotians themselves. The result was popular success but not much critical acclaim, at that time or since. A work without Slick, *The Letter-Bag of the Great Western; or, Life in a Steamer*, which appeared in 1840, was condemned for its descent into coarse popular humour, including uneducated dialect and frequent use of puns (although both had been features of the Slick books as well). The real problem was that, without Slick, Haliburton's reactionary Toryism was all too apparent. Haliburton would produce one more masterpiece, *The Old Judge; or, Life in a Colony* (1849), which the subtitle accurately describes. It is a nostalgic, rather romantic, but very vivid portrait of colonial society in the form of sketches and stories that reveal the narrative skills of their author at his best.

Some of the most robust writing in British North America came out of the fur trade.[23] Most of the leading traders were well-educated men who routinely kept journals of their activities, and many eventually published either the journals themselves or memoirs based on them. (Many such works would later be edited and published by various historical societies.) These works were extremely popular and influential. Alexander Mackenzie's book *Voyages from Montreal . . . to the Frozen and Pacific Oceans*—his journals of his inland voyages of exploration—was published in London in 1801. Subsequent editions appeared in New York and Philadelphia that same year, and the work was translated into French, German, and Russian. Another trader, the American Daniel Williams Harmon, produced (with considerable editorial assistance) A

■ Thomas Chandler Haliburton. LAC, C-6087.

Journal of Voyages and travels in the interior of North America . . . during a residence of nineteen years, in different parts of the country, published in Massachusetts in 1820. Harmon's account of fur-trade society and the moral dilemmas of the trader offered a fascinating glimpse into a world that would later be exploited fictionally by Robert Bannatyne and others. Not surprisingly, because of its total lack of literary and aesthetic pretensions, this fur-trade writing was hard-pressed to make its way into the canons of Canadian literature. The critical standards of later generations, as much as the limited imaginations of contemporary British Americans, cast early writing in an unfavourable light.

Several of the best-known writers of the colonial period were women from the gentry class who took up writing as one of the few socially acceptable outlets for females in colo-

■ Susanna Moodie. LAC, C-7043.

nial British North America. The first novel written in Canada was *The History of Emily Montague* (1769) by Frances Brooke, the daughter of an Anglican clergyman who arrived in Quebec in 1760 as chaplain to the British garrison there. The novel is made up of 228 letters, many of which describe aspects of Canada. Brooke also used the letters to advocate companionable marriage and education for women.[24] The first novel by a native-born British North American—*St Ursula's Convent; or, The Nun in Canada*, published in Kingston in 1824—was written by Julia Catherine Hart (née Beckwith) of Fredericton, New Brunswick. Nearly 150 subscribers paid 9s 4d for the two-volume work. Hart published several other novels, all of which were characterized by unrealistic, often fantastic, plots and settings. In *St Ursula's Convent* she tapped a rich vein of Protestant suspicions of what Catholics 'got up to' in con-

vents, although her tale contained more melodrama than immorality.

The works of the Strickland sisters were more polished. Both Catharine Parr Traill and Susanna Moodie wrote classic accounts of their experiences as immigrants in Canada.[25] Traill's *The Backwoods of Canada* (London, 1836) consists of 18 letters home to family and friends in Suffolk. It is a sensitive early account of the pioneer experience: never complaining, she leaves readers with the overall impression of a cheerful adaptation to the rigours of life in a previously unsettled area of Upper Canada, where she willingly made do with whatever was at hand. Upper Canada itself, however, is portrayed as a land 'with no historical associations, no legendary tales of those that came before', and the impenetrable forest all around her is 'desolate', 'interminable', 'a maze' that simultaneously isolates and liberates the author. Susanna Moodie's *Roughing It in the Bush: or, Forest Life in Canada* (1852) is the best known of a number of works in which Moodie offers trenchant (and often discouraging) descriptions of the pioneering experience. Moodie was particularly good at satirical descriptions of customs such as the work 'bee' and the 'charivari'.

Another successful writer was Anna Brownell Jameson. More willing to flout the gender rules of her society, Jameson was a well-published author in 1825 when she married the lawyer Robert Jameson. She did not accompany her husband when he received a judicial appointment to Dominica, and when she joined him in Upper Canada, in 1836, it was only a temporary arrangement while she attempted to negotiate a legal separation. While in Canada she travelled extensively, and the result of her journeys was the book *Winter Tales and Summer Rambles in Canada* (1838). Jameson deliberately set out to view her adventures with both a personal and a feminist eye. As she records under the date of 13 March 1837, 'In these days when society is becoming every day more artificial and complex, and marriage, as the gentlemen assure us, more and more extensive hazardous and inexpedient, women must find means to fill up the void of existence.'[26]

Most women from the elite classes did not attempt to publish their literary efforts; rather, they composed lengthy and fascinating letters to friends and family or kept diaries that remained among family papers and have only in recent years been published.[27] Similarly, a number of women drew and painted, but usually not for public consumption.

POPULAR CULTURE

The vernacular culture of the common people tended to be oral rather than written, dynamically traditional rather than mimetic, and craftsmanlike rather than artistic. Two further points need to be made about vernacular culture. First, much of it was transmitted or produced by people who had no particular sense that they were creating culture and no conscious awareness of aesthetic values. Second, the snobbishness associated with European-style high culture has until recently prevented us from appreciating the very real accomplishments of a cultural tradition that was far more relevant to British North Americans. A few brief examples must suffice.

For all the inhabitants of British North America, singing—whether religious hymns or secular songs—was an important part of daily life. Most of what was sung was inherited from Europe, both music and lyrics, although the latter were frequently altered over time to suit new circumstances. Aboriginal peoples had their own musical traditions, but these were not absorbed into the songs of the settlers. People sang as they worked in the fields, the voyageurs sang as they paddled their canoes, fishers sang as they cast their nets. From the time of Henry Alline onward, hymn singing was central to any revival meeting in British North America, and (at least in the period before 1840) hymn-singing was more a matter of remembering a familiar tune than of reading from a songbook or score. Whenever people got together around a fire or a stove in the

■ Catharine Parr Traill, August 1867. LAC, C-67346.

evening of a Canadian winter, songs were sung, poems were recited, and stories told. Many of the pioneers came from ethnic backgrounds in which the bard—usually a combination of poet and singer—represented an important folk memory.

One of the most tangible manifestations of vernacular culture was a rich heritage of craftsmanship in wood, a material that was readily available everywhere in British North America. We have only recently become more aware of this heritage, as examples of wooden sculptures—including the figureheads of the great sailing ships of the time, carved by anonymous craftsmen—have become available in many Canadian museums.[28]

■ 'Curling on the Lake near Halifax', colour lithograph by Henry Laurence Buckton, 1870. LAC, C-8774.

The ships themselves were monuments to the skills of carpenters and builders, and many regions produced their own versions of classic models. Schooners made on Tancook Island, off the coast of Nova Scotia, were famous on the eastern coast of North America, for example.

However imitative elite culture was in this period, popular culture continually suggested the rich possibilities for creative adaptation of the inherited past to the North American present. By 1840, for instance, Scottish settlers familiar with the sport of curling had imported the game into a climate ideally suited for it and had made great strides towards its popularization. The first organized curling club in British North America was founded in Montreal in 1807, and by 1840, when the first Canadian book on the subject—

James Bicket's *The Canadian Curler's Manual, or, an account of curling as practised in Canada*—was published (by the Toronto Curling Club), most urban centres had a club. Now structured by a clear set of rules, the game became so successful in British North America that sometime around 1840 the world's first indoor curling facilities were constructed in Montreal. As for ice hockey, one of its predecessors—'bandy', 'shinty', or 'hurley'—was known to have been played in Dartmouth, Nova Scotia, in the 1830s by members of the garrison. A public ice-hockey game ('the ice-hurtling game') was described in the *Montreal Gazette* in February 1837. Early accounts suggest that hockey could be played with dozens of individuals on either side, and rules were not very sophisticated. Not all the

A POEM BY JOSEPH HOWE

Shortly after the death of Joseph Howe, in 1873, Sydenham Howe—his ninth child and fourth son—assembled and supervised through the press a collection of his father's writings. On publication in 1874 it was entitled *Poems and Essays*, and offered a selection of Howe's serious and sentimental verse. The author's lighter verse, like the writings of T.C. Haliburton and Thomas McCulloch, often featured 'mild indelicacies' regarded as unsuitable for Victorian readers, and was probably more original than the material chosen for publication. Our selection is from the printed collection.

THE FLAG OF OLD ENGLAND
[A Centenary Song, written for the one hundredth anniversary of the landing of Lord Cornwallis at Halifax]

All hail to the day when the Britons came over,
And planted their standard, with sea-foam still wet,
Around and above us their spirits will hover,
Rejoicing to mark how we honor it yet.

Beneath it the emblems they cherished are waving,
The Rose of Old England the roadside perfumes;
The Shamrock and Thistle the north winds are
 braving,
Securely the Mayflower[30] blushes and blooms.

CHORUS:
Hail to the day when the Britons came over,
And planted their standard with sea-foam still wet,
Around and above us their spirits will hover,
Rejoicing to mark how we honor it yet.
We'll honor it yet, we'll honor it yet,
The flag of Old England! We'll honor it yet.

In the temples they founded, their faith is
 maintained,
Every foot of the soil they bequeathed is still ours,
The graves where they moulder, no foe has
 profaned,
But we wreathe them with verdure, and strew them
 with flowers!
The blood of no brother, in civil strife pour'd,
 In this hour of rejoicing, encumbers our souls!
The frontier's the field for the Patriot's sword,
And curs'd be the weapon that Faction controls!

Chorus—Hail to the day, &c.

Then hail to the day! 'tis with memories crowded,
Delightful to trace 'midst the mists of the past,
Like the features of Beauty, bewitchingly shrouded,
They shine through the shadows Time o'er them has
 cast.
As travellers track to its source in the mountains,
The stream, which far swelling, expands o'er the
 plains,
Our hearts, on this day, fondly turn to the
 fountains
Whence flow the warm currents that bound in our
 Veins.
 Chorus—Hail to the day, &c.

And proudly we trace them: No warrior flying
From city assaulted, and fanes overthrown,
With the last of his race on the battlements dying,
And weary with wandering founded our own.
From the Queen of the Islands, then famous in story,
A century since, our brave forefathers came,
And our kindred yet fill the wide world with her
 glory,
Enlarging her Empire, and spreading her name.
 Chorus—Hail to the day, &c.

Ev'ry flash of her genius our pathway enlightens—
Ev'ry field she explores we are beckoned to tread,
Each laurel she gathers, our future day brightens—

> We joy with her living, and mourn for her dead.
> Then hail to the day when the Britons came over,
> And planted their standard, with sea-foam still wet,
>
> Above and around us their spirits shall hover,
> Rejoicing to mark how we honor it yet.
> *Chorus*—Hail to the day, &c.
>
> SOURCE: *Poems and Essays Joseph Howe* (London, 1874), 56–8.

sports played were imports. The *Montreal Gazette* of 1 August 1833 reported on a lacrosse game between the Iroquois of Caughnawaga and the Mohawks of St Regis; the sport—originally called 'baggataway' or 'tewaarathon'—would soon be taken up by non-Aboriginal players. Baseball was first played in Canada in a recognizably modern form in Beachville, Upper Canada, on 4 June 1838 as part of a Militia Muster Day—a year before Abner Doubleday's famous game at Cooperstown, New York.[29]

CONCLUSION

Given the vastness of the country; its division into several colonies with populations of varying ethnic backgrounds; the presence of large numbers of recent immigrants in different stages of assimilation, as well as marginalized groups such as blacks and First Nations; and a very high residential and occupational turnover, it is hardly surprising that feelings of nationalism to rival those in the United States were slow to develop. For most British North Americans in 1840, the sense of place did not extend very far beyond their immediate surroundings. National identities were often traced back to Europe. Love for country was expressed in terms of love for one's province or colony, as reflected in the motto of Sir Walter Scott—'This is my own my native land'—which Thomas Haliburton attached to his history of Nova Scotia in 1829. No British American was more ardently patriotic than Haliburton's publisher, Joseph Howe. One of Howe's first editorials after he began publishing a newspaper in 1827 was entitled 'My Country', and in 1834 he lectured to an audience at the Halifax Mechanics' Institute on the subject 'Love of Country a Stimulus to Enterprise'. In this address Howe argued that it was an 'unerring law of nature' that the colonial-born would feel their strongest attachment and first allegiance to their native land. When Howe returned to Nova Scotia from a visit to England in 1838, he reminded his readers that however 'fascinated' he was 'by the splendours and novelties of an old nation', what he really loved was 'that small countrie that we wot of, far over the billow . . . that small spot of earth, between Cape Sable and Cape North'.[31] Similarly ardent expressions of patriotism could be found everywhere in British North America by 1840.

SHORT BIBLIOGRAPHY

Benson, Eugene, and William Toye. *The Oxford Companion to Canadian Literature in English*, rev. edn. Toronto, 1999. A recent reference work on the subject.

Fahey, Curtis. *In His Name: The Anglican Experience in Upper Canada, 1791–1854*. Ottawa, 1991. The best book on Anglicanism in the largest colony of British North America.

Gavreau, Michael. *The Evangelical Century: College and Creed in English Canada from the Great Revival to the Great Depression*. Montreal and Kingston, 1991. A revisionist study of the meaning of evangelicalism in education and society.

Klinck, Carl T., ed. *Literary History of Canada: Canadian Literature in English*, rev. edn. Toronto, 1976. The classic compendium of all aspects of Canadian literature from the beginning.

Lemieux, L. *L'Établissement de la première province ecclésiastique au Canada, 1783–1844*. Montreal, 1968. An important introduction to French-Canadian Catholic history.

Morrow, Don, et al., eds. *A Concise History of Sport in Canada*. Toronto, 1989. A useful collaborative introduction to the subject.

———— and Kevin B. Wamsley. *Sport in Canada: A History*. Toronto, 2004. A good introduction that relates the development of sport and games to the meeting of Native and settler societies and the activities necessary to settling and living on the land.

Sissons, C.B. *Church and State in Canadian Education: An Historical Study*. Toronto, 1959. An older classic, still useful for its subject.

Warkentin, Germaine, ed. *Canadian Exploration Literature: An Anthology*. Toronto, 1993. A useful anthology of a neglected topic.

Westfall, William. *Two Worlds: The Protestant Culture of Nineteenth-Century Ontario*. Montreal and Kingston, 1989. An excellent explanation of a complex subject.

Wilson, J. Donald. *Canadian Education: A History*. Toronto, 1970. Still the best survey of its topic.

STUDY QUESTIONS

1. What is meant by 'domesticity'?

2. What vision of society did the established churches hold?

3. Were the Presbyterians true dissenters?

4. What epistemological issues divided the Christian churches in nineteenth-century British North America?

5. How did education become a religious issue?

6. What, according to William Lyon Mackenzie, were the purposes of education?

7. Why was it so difficult for British North American artists to create original work?

8. Why might popular culture have been more vital and vibrant than high artistic culture in British North America?

9. What is the theme of Joseph Howe's poem 'The Flag of Old England'? Are the sentiments it expresses compatible with his love of Nova Scotia?

☐ Writing about Women's History

■ Today, anyone who examines a survey textbook in Canadian history published before the mid-1960s will be struck by its almost total neglect of women. Canadian history until that time was chiefly the history of men in suits and uniforms (with an occasional side glance at men in farmers' overalls or fisherman's boots). The big breakthrough in writing about the history of women in Canada came only in the 1970s and especially the 1980s, in the wake of the feminist movement that began in the later 1960s, when earlier feminists' demands for equal treatment for women in all spheres, including historical coverage, began to bear fruit.

But full equality was still a long way off, for even today women are still being slotted into an overall approach to Canadian history—the 'development of the nation' approach—that is fundamentally ill-suited to the full integration of women, especially in the period before the twentieth century. In general, the historiography of women has evolved in three stages, but there has been no neat, lockstep chronological pattern to this evolution. At each stage the theoretical underpinnings of the enterprise become more prominent. But some first-stage work is still being published alongside work from the third stage.

In first-stage studies, women are typically introduced into the story simply by including some references to them. This approach does not require any sophisticated feminist theory, and there is little evidence of theory in this literature. From the beginning it was clear that for the period before 1860, for example, researchers were unlikely to discover many previously neglected women in the public arena, although there were more female writers and artists than one might have imagined. In addition, women's work in several other occupations, notably as teachers, members of religious orders, and domestic servants, turned out to be a rewarding area of study. On teaching, see Alison Prentice, 'The Feminization of Teaching in British North American and Canada, 1845–75', in Susan Mann Trofimenkoff and Alison Prentice, eds, *The Neglected Majority: Essays in Canadian Women's History*, I (Toronto, 1977), 49–69; Janet Guildford, '"Separate Spheres": The Feminization of Public School Teaching in Nova Scotia, 1838–1880', in Janet Guildford and Suzanne Morton, eds, *Separate Spheres: Women's Worlds in the 19th-Century Maritimes* (Fredericton, 1994), 119–44. On an alternative route for women that also involved teaching, see Marta Danylewycz, *Taking the Veil: An Alternative to Marriage, Motherhood, and Spinsterhood in Quebec 1840–1920* (Toronto, 1987). On domestic service, see Marilyn Barber, *Immigrant Domestic Servants in Canada* (Ottawa, 1991), and Claudine Lacelle, *Urban Domestic Servants in 19th-Century Canada* (Ottawa,

1987). On the women writers, see, for example, Charlotte Gray, *Sisters in the Wilderness: The Lives of Susanna Moodie and Catharine Parr Traill* (Toronto, 1999).

In some cases, the apparent absence of women raised useful questions, such as the one that C. Lesley Biggs discusses in 'The Case of the Missing Midwives: A History of Midwifery in Ontario from 1795–1900', *Ontario History* 75 (1983): 21–35. In other areas, such as the western fur trade, historians have found that women played more important roles than they had been given credit for, as Sylvia Van Kirk demonstrated in her pioneering *Many Tender Ties: Women in Fur Trade Society 1670–1870* (Winnipeg, 1980). The concept of popular politics enabled scholars to find considerable evidence of political activity by women outside the electoral sphere, especially in the field of social reform (e.g., the temperance movement) or in politics 'out-of-doors'; see Gail C. Campbell, 'Disenfranchised But Not Quiescent: Women Petitioners in New Brunswick in the Mid-Nineteenth Century', in Guildford and Morton, eds, *Separate Spheres*, 119–44.

Second-stage research has concentrated on the position and treatment of women in their societies. It also began to consider factors such as race and class and how they modified the effects of gender. In the nineteenth century, for example, severe constraints were imposed on women not only by convention but by the law, as Constance Backhouse showed in her *Petticoats and Prejudice: Women and the Law in Nineteenth Century Canada* (Toronto, 1991). Although women's legal situation was reformed over the course of the century, the process of change was slow, and the legal disabilities that women faced had serious repercussions in every aspect of life.

Other areas of interest for second-stage historiography have been more conceptual in nature: for example, in the Victorian era, the cult of domesticity, the 'separate spheres' doctrine (according to which women's proper place was in the 'private sphere' of the home and public life was reserved for men only), or the tendency to put women on a pedestal that was hard to escape. The essays in Guildford and Morton, eds, *Separate Spheres*, are revealing on these points. On the economic implications of women's situation in the nineteenth century, particularly in the 'household economy' of the farm, see Marjorie Griffin Cohen, *Women's Work, Markets, and Economic Development in Nineteenth-Century Ontario* (Toronto, 1988).

Recovering the lives that women lived within that 'private sphere' became an important part of the major revisionist trend towards 'social history' in the post-1970 period. For source material, many historians looked to private diaries and correspondence, or memoirs and autobiographies of the time. Often, however, these researchers encountered the same problem that social historians everywhere have faced, for literate women of the elite classes (whose husbands were the men in suits and uniforms) were far more likely than ordinary women to leave written records of their lives. Several large bibliographic and archival projects did examine previously neglected court files, in which non-elite women figured more prominently; but court cases—almost by definition—reflected deviant or transgressive behaviour; for example, see Judith Fingard, *The Dark Side of Life in Victorian Halifax* (Halifax, 1989). In short, many of the lives available for study are atypical in one way or another. Pioneer farm women have been particularly hard to investigate. Women's history quickly came to focus on the separate cultures of women, emphasizing the small gains in autonomy that, cumulatively, began to make a difference.

In the third phase of writing about women's history, the difficulty of fitting women neatly into the conventional story can become an analytical tool in its own right. An excellent example is Adele Perry's *On the Edge of Empire: Gender, Race, and the Making of British Columbia, 1849–1871* (Toronto, 2001), a book that is firmly situated in contemporary theory. Focusing on British Columbia in the middle of the nineteenth century, Perry argues that the colony's 'gender and racial character challenged normative standards of nineteenth-century Anglo-American social life' (p. 3); that the scarcity of European women led to the development of 'male homosocial culture' on the one hand and 'mixed-race heterosexual relationships' on the other; that these characteristics created an extremely rough, violent society; and that it was in response to this roughness and violence that serious efforts were made to create an ordered and 'respectable' white colony. Perry acknowledges four different sorts of theoretical underpinnings to her analysis: gender theory; a Marxist materialism rooted in class relations; post-colonial insights into imperialism and race; and post-structuralist ideas about the 'historically constructed character of social relations'. For her, these four different bodies of theory all fit together. The British Columbia produced by her analysis also fits very well into current historiography of the British Empire in India, Africa, and the Antipodes, for the province's history reflects all the standard features of colonialism.

Another illustration of third-level analysis is provided by Cecilia Morgan in her *Public Men and Virtuous Women: The Gendered Languages of Religion and Politics in Upper Canada, 1791–1850* (1997). Morgan employs new theoretical constructions of gender and discourse (the language in which life was discussed and debated) to illuminate the relationships between men and women in colonial Upper Canada. Instead of two clearly separate spheres, public and private, she finds a substantial blurring around the edges where the spheres intersected, particularly in the areas of religion and associational life. She points out that gender analysis is not limited to the private sphere of women, but also can reveal how the masculine public sphere was constructed and maintained. For example, the language used for the 'masculine' business of politics was explicitly masculine in nature, whereas the language used in religious and social contexts was often more sympathetic to women. Similarly, the construction of 'social space' differed between the legislature and the temperance organization.

The three stages in the evolution of research into women's history have had an enormous impact on our understanding of Canada's development, particularly in the era before women became officially integrated into the public sphere.

The Charlottetown conference, 1864 (detail). Standing in front of the pillar on the left is Thomas D'Arcy McGee; in front of McGee to the left is George-Étienne Cartier; and seated on the step is John A. Macdonald. NAC, C-733.

PART THREE

■ 1840–1870

■ A new era began in 1839 with the publication of Lord Durham's *Report on the Affairs in British North America*, which recommended reforms including the union of Upper and Lower Canada and the introduction of some form of responsible government. The *Report*'s title represented one of the first semi-official usages of the term 'British North America'. Replacing expressions such as 'the British colonies of North America' or 'the Provinces of British America', the new term suggested that even though the parts were still autonomous, a larger abstract unity was beginning to form. We must be careful not to conceptualize everything that happened after 1839 as pointing towards Confederation. Nevertheless, developments in many spheres were beginning to intersect and form larger patterns.

Between 1840 and the early 1870s British North America was transformed from a collection of loosely connected colonies in the northeastern part of the continent, heavily dependent on the mother country both economically and politically, to a transcontinental nation with an internal economy that was rapidly diversifying and starting to industrialize. Spectacular technological advances such as the invention of the steam engine and the telegraph radically altered perceptions of distance. In 1866 an undersea cable first connected Newfoundland to Britain, and by 1870 the Montreal Telegraph Company had installed more than 30,000 kilometres of wire across eastern Canada. Although the West was still unconnected, it was now possible to communicate almost instantly across much of the continent and beyond. Perhaps the most important communications development of the early Victorian era was the public postal service—a reflection of advances not in technology but in state organization and administration.

The achievement of responsible government coincided with Britain's decision to abandon mercantilism in favour of free trade, and both suggested a loosening of imperial ties. In the Province of Canada particularly, Britain's disengagement sparked a desire for closer integration—economic if not political—with the United States, made possible in part by the achievement of diplomatic entente on several unrelated issues. After 1850, the trend towards continentalism encouraged the development of a new rail-based transportation network. In turn, railways helped to transform a commercial economy into an industrial one, and contributed to an increasing awareness of the West in the Province of Canada. Yet on the east coast the continuing success of the maritime industries, including shipbuilding and the carrying-trade, meant that the Atlantic colonies were still focusing more of their attention on Britain than on the North American continent.

By the 1860s, currents from several directions were encouraging some form of colonial union. The immediate impetus was a perceived political stalemate in the united Province of Canada. In addition, however, there was the American Civil War, which underlined the need for defence at a time when Britain was actively reducing its responsibilities in North America. And in the background were growing numbers of people with an interest in westward expansion. The result, of course, was the creation of the Dominion of Canada.

CHAPTER SEVENTEEN

Political and Administrative Reform, 1840–1860

The period from 1840 to the early 1860s was a crucial era in the constitutional and political development of British North America. The major recommendations of Lord Durham gradually came into effect. The Canadas were reunited as one province, with a single assembly supported by a complex departmental structure. The British government did not so much bring about responsible government as allow it to happen, but by the mid-1850s the assembly of virtually every province in British North America had achieved control over domestic government. In most provinces responsible government went hand-in-hand with a two-party system. But the situation was rather more complex in the united province, where two linguistic sections necessitated the creation of parallel political parties that were hard to keep synchronized, not only in practical terms but ideologically as well. The wild card was Canada West's new ultra-Protestant reform party, the Clear Grits, which would ultimately be led by George Brown. The arrival of the new party signalled the emergence of new confessional controversies in the 1850s.

The achievement of responsible government was at one time seen as the major constitutional development of this period, indeed of the entire pre-Confederation era. Recently, however, Canadian scholars have increasingly emphasized the importance of another development: the beginning of the administrative state. This process, involving the gradual growth of state responsibility in a variety of directions, was perhaps most marked in the Province of Canada. The administrative state was most often associated with various changes in public educational policy, but it also gained strength from efforts to centralize authority over government and to establish some control over information. The increase in statistical material generated by every province in British America was a tribute to the hold that the new notion of the state acquired over provincial bureaucracies.

REORIENTING POLITICS: THE ACHIEVEMENT OF RESPONSIBLE GOVERNMENT

According to the standard histories, the British government gradually resolved the constitutional problems of the 1830s in British North America over the following decades with the introduction of responsible government. For most of the second half of the nineteenth century and the first half of the twentieth, this constitutional development was seen as one of the most crucial aspects of Canadian history in this period—even the most crucial aspect—and as a process it literally

TIMELINE

1837
Invention of the postage stamp.

1839
Durham *Report* tabled in British Parliament.

1840
Upper and Lower Canada reunited, with a single legislature.

1842
Baldwin and La Fontaine appointed leaders of Canadian ministry. Newfoundland gets its own legislature (partly appointed, partly elected). British military presence in British North America reduced.

1843
First major Canadian School Act.

1844
Draper-Viger ministry is formed.

1846
Beginning of the 'asylum movement'.

1848
Reform administration in Nova Scotia achieves responsible government. Lord Elgin calls on Baldwin and La Fontaine again. Old constitution restored in Newfoundland.

1849
Elgin signs rebellion losses bill, accepting ceremonial status for governor. Rise of 'Clear Grits'. Legal reform in Canada West.

1851
PEI gets responsible government. Colonial governments take over post offices.

1853
PEI legislature passes Land Purchase Act.

1854
New Brunswick gets responsible government.

1855
Newfoundland gets responsible government. John Langton appointed chairman of Canadian Board of Audit.

1856
Vancouver Island gets assembly. 'Bible Question' on PEI. John A. Macdonald becomes Conservative leader in Canada.

1857
George Brown becomes Liberal leader in Canada West. Cartier gets bill through Canadian Parliament for a centralized uniform legal system.

1857
Joseph Cauchon reports on Crown lands.

1860
PEI Land Commission.

1861
John Jessop introduces Canadian-style education to British Columbia.

1871
British Columbia gets elected assembly and responsible government.

shaped many of the histories written during these years. Constitutional development in British North America, including the achievement of domestic autonomy in government and liberation from tight British imperial control, as well as the development of political parties and party government, led naturally to the unification of the nation in 1867, and that was how historians told the story.

Not all historians have agreed on the definition of responsible government. Earlier chroniclers assumed that it meant simply colonial autonomy, while later scholars insisted that it required imperial recognition of party government. Whatever the definition, responsible government is considered less crucial today than it was in the past, largely because more recent historiography has uncovered other important themes. We can now appreciate that the narrow focus on responsible government tended to downplay significant changes in the very nature of the state (which began to develop a highly bureaucratized administrative structure) and of the law (which was codified and regularized).

LORD DURHAM AND HIS REPORT

The British government's response to the insurrections of 1837 and 1838 was to dispatch a fact-finding commission, headed by Lord Durham, who was given extraordinary powers to settle the colonies down and bring about necessary reform. Though Durham did not remain in Canada long enough to effect much change, his famous *Report on the Affairs in British North America*, filed in January 1839, was a thorough and eloquent examination of the problems of the Canadas. The solution he advocated—on the advice of Robert and William Warren Baldwin—was responsible government. Otherwise, Durham did not propose any major alterations to the elite political culture in place everywhere in British North America, much less to most of the social and economic systems that lay behind it (the exception was land reform).[1] In addition, being more impressed by

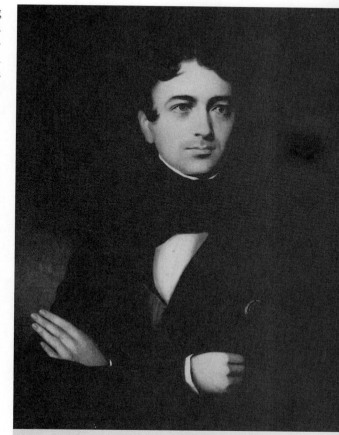

■ John George Lambton, Lord Durham, by Sir Thomas Lawrence. LAC, PA-2260.

the 'racial' conflict in North America than by other causes of discontent, Durham proposed the union of the two Canadas. As he wrote:

> I expected to find a contest between a government and a people. I found two nations warring in the bosom of a single state: I found a struggle, not of principles, but of races: and I perceived that it would be idle to attempt any amelioration of laws or institutions, until we could first succeed in terminating the deadly animosity that now separates the inhabitants of Lower Canada into the hostile divisions of French and English.[2]

either Upper or Lower Canada. Durham harboured the mistaken belief that the governors could maintain considerable power so long as they altered the makeup of their councils to reflect the shifting situation in the houses of assembly. He also mistakenly believed that French-Canadian culture was not strong enough to survive assimilationist pressures. Though for the most part he felt that the problems of the Canadas could be handled through constitutional reform, Durham did consider questions of land policy. He recommended an end to the landlords on Prince Edward Island, and strongly supported a general system of land reform based on the sale of Crown lands at a decent price.

THE CANADAS

For the Canadas, the process of constitutional reform began with the implementation of one of Lord Durham's main recommendations: the unification of Upper and Lower Canada into one legislature by Act of Parliament in July 1840, to take effect in 1841. Legislative union was not quite the same as a total merger; certain contentious aspects of administration, including the legal and educational systems, continued to operate separately. Nor did legislative union by itself satisfy Durham's other major recommendation: that the assembly have the right to decide on policy and its implementation through control of 'the persons by whom that policy was to be administered'. Neither Durham nor anyone else in British North America understood the importance of political parties in the politico-constitutional realm, or their crucial role in what came to be called 'responsible government'. This problem was compounded by Britain's desire to guarantee that local cabinet government would function with fairness and impartiality—two principles often ignored in partisan politics. The British were hesitant to release the various provincial governments entirely from their tutelage. The Colonial Office thus temporized by giving colonial governors more political freedom of

■ Robert Baldwin, portrait by Théophile Hamel. LAC, C-010671.

Once these two colonies were unified, the next step would be to assimilate the French Canadians into the English-Canadian culture.

In recommending that the internal government of the colonies be placed 'in the hands of the colonists themselves', Lord Durham dealt more with the relationship of colonies to the metropolis than with the details of local politics or constitutional arrangements. His assessment did not take into account the importance of political parties, or of political pluralism, in action than they had ever before enjoyed, actually encouraging them to serve as party brokers under the new arrangements. Governors of the Province of Canada were allowed to construct ministries, although local conditions forced them to accept in broad outline the personnel endorsed by the assembly.

In 1842 the new governor of Canada, Sir Charles Bagot, appointed two Reformers from Canada West and Canada East, Robert Baldwin and Louis-H. La Fontaine, both believers in responsible government, to form a ministry. He saw that the political alliance between these two Reform leaders made it necessary to admit French Canadians to the ministry. Although Bagot retained the right to select the chief minister(s), he stated that 'Whether the doctrine of responsible government is openly acknowledged or only tacitly acquiesced in, virtually it exists.' Bagot resigned in January 1843, however, owing to ill health, and died a few months later. His successor was instructed not to concede responsible government.

Sir Charles Metcalfe began his term as governor in a harmonious relationship with the Executive Council, supporting its decisions to make Montreal the capital of the Province of Canada and to grant a general amnesty for all offences except murder committed during the rebellion. But gradually a gulf formed between the governor and his ministers over a series of issues and mutual resentments. On 24 November 1843, after Metcalfe had made a Tory appointment, La Fontaine and Baldwin demanded that he not make another appointment without taking their advice—a principle that all the councillors considered essential to responsible government, and that Metcalfe saw as a surrender of the Crown's prerogative. Two days later all the councillors but one resigned. Metcalfe carried on alone until August 1844, when he formed a mainly conservative Executive Council, headed by William Henry Draper, the former attorney general for Canada West, and Denis-Benjamin Viger, the journalist-publisher

■ Louis-Hippolyte La Fontaine, lithograph by M. Desnoyers after a photograph. LAC C-036094.

from Canada East (see Chapter 12).[3] The governor then called a general election for November 1844, in which the ministry was sustained by a small majority; the government itself had now assumed the mantle of a party, formed around the remnants of the conservative anti-Reformers of the 1830s.

The next election was called in July 1847, and in January 1848 the Reformers won a sweeping majority: the Conservative ministry resigned. The new governor, Lord Elgin—who had arrived

12 months before with the instruction to concede responsible government—called upon La
Fontaine and Baldwin, as leaders of Reform parties in their respective constituencies, to form a
ministry, which was sworn in on 11 March 1848.
In placing himself, as a representative of the
Crown, above party politics and leaving government in the hands of leaders of an organized
party, Lord Elgin formally inaugurated responsible government in the Province of Canada. On
25 April 1849 he signed the Rebellion Losses
Act, the bill—passed in both houses of the legislature—indemnifying those in Canada East who
had suffered losses in the recent rebellions. The
immediate consequence of his so doing was that
Tory and Orange mobs hurled stones at him as
he departed, and that night the mobs burned the
Parliament buildings in Montreal. The capital
was thereupon moved to Toronto, which was to
alternate with Quebec City every four years.

Although the British authorities were prepared
to accept the dominance of the assemblies in other
colonies, they initially sought to prevent, then to
restrain, the development of a party system. But
despite London's best efforts, in the 1840s political
parties did coalesce, however loosely, around traditional local questions and local political dynamics.
Reformers found different issues to emphasize and
anti-Reformers responded in slightly different ways
from colony to colony, but the overall effect was the
emergence of two parties in each province differing
in their support of local reform. By and large the
anti-Reformers (the conservatives) found it more
difficult than others to acknowledge the need for
organization and party discipline, but they
achieved them.

THE MARITIMES

In 1847, the year Lord Elgin arrived in the
Province of Canada with a clear mandate to pre-
side at the inception of responsible government,
the governor of Nova Scotia, Sir John Harvey,
was steadfastly stonewalling any attempt to
reduce his political influence. A former governor

of Prince Edward Island (1836–7), Harvey maintained that the 'minor' colonies were:

> scarcely fitted for the strict application to them of
> a System of Government which not only contem-
> plates the materials for the machinery of two or
> more distinct administrations, but involves the still
> more startling proposition of the surrender of their
> offices by all the heads of the Civil Departments of
> the Government upon every Political change by
> which the possession of a Majority, however
> inconsiderable, in the representative Branch of the
> General Assembly is obtained by any party.[4]

Yet that surrender was exactly what he and other
governors were forced to accept. In fact, Nova
Scotia—where Joseph Howe had been agitating for
responsible government as a Reformer since
1836—finally achieved it after the election of 5
August 1847, which had been hard-fought on a
number of issues, including patronage and Crown
lands. The Reformers were victorious, and when a
Reform administration took office in late January
1848, the province became the first colony to
achieve responsible government. The Reformers/
Liberals not only insisted on control of the
Executive Council, but had a number of officeholders and magistrates dismissed—to be replaced
by government appointees—and took over management of Crown lands in return for a guaranteed
'civil list' of appointments to be paid for out of the
government budget. Self-government was granted
to the Province of Canada in March of that year, to
Prince Edward Island in 1851, and to New
Brunswick in 1854. Curiously enough, the
achievement of both representative and responsible government in the remainder of British North
America took much longer and involved complexities that until recently were not normally discussed in the standard constitutional histories.

NEWFOUNDLAND

The situation in Newfoundland was complicated
by a British attempt at alternative constitutional

arrangements in the 1840s. In 1842 that colony was given a legislature composed partly of elected and partly of appointed members, thus amalgamating the old Executive Council and assembly into one body. The experiment, however, was popular neither in Newfoundland nor in the British Parliament, and was never given a proper chance to work. In 1848 the old constitution was restored, and Newfoundlanders immediately began agitating for 'a form of Government based upon enlarged and fairly divided Representation—with a departmental Government and Executive Responsibility similar in character to that form lately yielded to . . . Nova Scotia'.[5] Although the British were reluctant to grant such a principle, Newfoundland eventually achieved its goal in 1855.

VANCOUVER ISLAND, BRITISH COLUMBIA, AND RED RIVER

Vancouver Island did not get an assembly until 1856, and that body did not begin serious conflict with its governor until after the retirement of James Douglas, its governor from 1857 to 1864. Between 1864 and 1866 the administration of his successor, Arthur Kennedy, saw the beginnings of the struggle over control of finances typical of developing colonies. But there was no constitutional resolution before Vancouver Island was joined with British Columbia (which had never enjoyed a legislative assembly) in 1866. The British authorities, who had imposed union on the two colonies, insisted that the new province of British Columbia—like Newfoundland earlier—was not ready for a fully elected representative government, much less a responsible one, and instituted an appointive Legislative Council instead. The old 'despotic' imperial notions obviously lingered on much longer than most Canadians would have liked to admit. An elected assembly (and responsible government) became one of the consequences of Confederation in British Columbia.

Red River never had an elected assembly, but it is worth noting that the establishment of such a body became one of the 'rights' demanded by the insurgents in 1869–70 from a Canadian government that had wanted to impose an appointed council in which it made most of the major appointments. Representative government would be written into the Manitoba Act (1870).

NEW POLITICAL AND CONSTITUTIONAL PROBLEMS

Although in the short run the constitutional adjustments of the 1840s seemed to work best in the Province of Canada—which, as the largest colony in British North America, was regarded as the bellwether—over the long haul the union of the Canadas and the achievement of responsible government brought some intractable new problems. The lower provinces, even Newfoundland, were sufficiently homogeneous to be able to live with a two-party system, particularly since the composition of the parties was fluid and constantly changing in response to events. But Canada was not so fortunate. The alliance in 1842 of Robert Baldwin and Louis-H. La Fontaine on a reform platform was in some respects illusory. It turned out that Canada East (the former Lower Canada) had slipped back into older voting patterns that were not very supportive of reform. The principle of governance by a coalition of parties from each of the two sections of the united province was inherently unstable. By the mid-1840s Canada East had become attached to the principle of the 'double majority', according to which the province had to be governed by an assembly majority in each of its two sections. Such an arrangement naturally appealed to Canada East's sense of nationality, but it also implied that political parties in the two sections would develop along parallel lines. So long as the principal issue remained the achievement of self-government, Reformers in the two sections could make common cause. But by 1850, when responsible government had become fully operational, new factors would emerge to complicate the Canadian political picture.

THE CLEAR GRITS

One complicating factor was the rise, at the end of the 1840s, of a new political movement in Canada West. It was a radical Reform group known as the 'Clear Grits', with whom the Grits (or moderate Reformers) eventually merged. The Clear Grits were purists, hence their name. As one of the group's founders, the Scottish-born David Christie, put it in 1849 to George Brown, publisher of the Toronto *Globe*, 'We want only men who are clear grit.'[6] Centred in the western districts dominated by Scots and Americans, the Clear Grits were thoroughgoing Reformers who embodied the traditional principles of Upper Canadian agrarianism. They were the heirs more of William Lyon Mackenzie[7] than of the moderate Robert Baldwin. They were democrats, populists, geographical expansionists, and opponents of close connections between church and state on Protestant rather than secularist principles. Furthermore—and ominously—they were hostile to French Canadians and did not hesitate to make their old-fashioned prejudices known. Colonial Secretary Lord Gray in early 1850 labelled them 'much the most dangerous party in Canada'.[8]

In 1840, when the population of Canada East was greater than that of Canada West, each section was given 40 seats, with the result that the anglophone element was over-represented. In 1849 the liberal Rouge party unsuccessfully demanded 'representation by population'. But when the census of 1851 showed that the population of the western section was greater, 'rep by pop' became a platform of George Brown, who stood as an independent Reformer in the general election in the autumn of that year—and was elected. The arrangement that had initially benefited Canada West quickly came to disadvantage it, producing a deadlock that would not be resolved until Confederation in 1867. The Grits perceived that French Canadians stood in the way of the successful adoption of their platform. As Lord Elgin, who was governor until 1854, quickly realized, 'If clear Gritism absorbs all the hues of Upper Canadian liberalism, the French, unless some interference from without checks the natural course of events, will fall off from them and form an alliance with the Upper Canadian Tories.'[9]

THE WITHDRAWAL OF FRANCOPHONE SUPPORT FOR REFORM

The growing pressures exerted by the Grits contributed to, but did not by themselves produce, another complicating development of the 1850s. This was Canada East's gradual withdrawal of support for the political principles of radical reform and the development of exactly the result Lord Elgin had feared: an alliance between the Canadian legislative majority and the Upper Canadian opponents of the Grits. By the 1850s Canada East had its own agenda, centred on the continued development of nationalist claims and the preservation of French-Canadian culture and society. By this time the leaders of the Catholic Church had come to recognize the importance of nationalism, and the necessity of separating it from its earlier reformist connections. In the process of separating nationalism and reform, the Grits—unwittingly—were extremely useful. The Grits' attacks on religious establishment were rooted in evangelical Protestant principles, and their great shibboleth was 'voluntarism': the idea that church and state should be separated, and that there should be no civil interference in ecclesiastical matters. In the Upper Canadian context, voluntarist arguments were directed against the efforts of the Anglican Church to control higher education and the clergy reserves. For example, in 1849 Robert Baldwin (a former student and parishioner of John Strachan) secularized the Anglican university that Strachan had founded: on 1 January 1850 King's College, Toronto, became the University of Toronto. The Roman Catholic hierarchy in Canada East did not want anything similar happening to their institutions.

CONFESSIONAL CONTROVERSIES OF THE 1850s

Ultra-Protestantism had many implications for the Catholic Church in Canada East. Supporters of voluntarism were not opposed to religion. Despite their rhetorical objections to church establishment, in practice they merely sought to replace one religious arrangement with a different one based on evangelical principles. But the Reformers were quite unable to appreciate the political import of that fact. Secularism, in their hands, was hardly neutral. At the same time that the voluntarists were seeking to free the state from 'religious' privilege, they were contemplating with equanimity the passage of legislation controlling the availability of alcoholic beverages and restricting work and other activities on the Sabbath. Such temperance and sabbatarian legislation was not approved by everyone, and certainly not by the traditional national churches. The voluntarist God might not be able to hold land or escape taxation, but He could be used to justify state intrusion in moral matters. Even secular schooling, by the 1850s, had acquired a religious dimension capable of dividing Protestants and Catholics, evangelicals and traditionalists.

The rise of denominational divisions as a factor in politics was not confined to the united province, although the sectional situation—with Roman Catholicism firmly entrenched in Canada East and evangelical Protestantism dominant in Canada West—gave such matters a special edge there. To a considerable extent denominational politics reflected the increasing democratization of the political process, for as the public began to play a greater role, politicians began emphasizing issues that would appeal to voters' cherished beliefs (or prejudices). The electorate was divided religiously in an era in which religious belief could not be treated as a matter of indifference, confined to church on Sunday morning or to observances within the sanctity of the home. In the legislatures, the context for the expression of such disagreement was usually public education.

Educational conflicts could take bizarre turns, as events in Prince Edward Island demonstrated, beginning in 1856. In that province the issue revolved around Bible reading in the schools, a practice that was demanded by the evangelical Protestants and opposed by the Roman Catholics, who did not have their own separate schools. Having integrated into the 'mixed schools' of the province, they actually favoured the continuation of 'godless', or non-sectarian, principles in them. The Bible question helped to realign Island politics, as Catholics and Protestant Liberals allied against evangelical Protestants, backed by the Tories. Many felt that the Tories, otherwise a declining force in politics, were pleased to fish in the troubled waters of confessionalism. In any event, the principal issue of the 1858 election was for many voters 'between Protestantism and Romanism', and a year later one prominent local newspaper commented that 'the two parties into which the people of this Island now are, and for some time to come will continue to be divided—[are] a Protestant and a Catholic party.'[10]

In Newfoundland as well, the contending parties wore denominational faces—the Liberals backed by the Roman Catholics and the Tories supported by the Protestants—although in that island province, as in the united Canada, religion and ethnicity were closely linked. In Newfoundland, Catholics were Irish and Protestants English in origin.

THE GROWING CANADIAN CRISIS

In Canada, La Fontaine and Baldwin retired from public life in 1851, and a new Reform government was confirmed in the general election of December 1851. George Brown was elected in the southwestern county of Kent and the ministry was now headed by Francis Hincks and Augustin-Norbert Morin. The Canada West Conservatives were led by Sir Allan MacNab, but the parliamentary leader and the brains of the party was John A. Macdonald, the Scots-born lawyer from Kingston who had been that city's member of Parliament since 1844. In June 1854, amid charges of corruption and extravagance, and procrastination over key issues, Parliament was dissolved. In the ensuing election Hincks and Morin, while winning the largest number of seats, did not win a clear majority; their minority government was soon defeated and they resigned. A coalition government was then formed, headed by MacNab and Morin; Macdonald (who did the real work of forming the new government) became attorney general for Canada West.[11] When unhappiness with his leadership forced MacNab to resign in 1856, Macdonald's leadership of the Conservatives was openly acknowledged.

On the Reform—now officially known as Liberal—side, George Brown took an increasingly prominent role. When, in May 1855, a new bill for separate schools in Canada West was passed at Quebec on the strength of the French-Canadian vote after many western members had left for home, the Grits were furious.[12] At this point Brown, arguing strenuously for representation by population, gained supporters from both the Grit and the Clear Grit factions, as well as from the more moderate Liberals. At a convention for unity in January 1857, Brown clearly emerged as the Liberal leader.

The double majority. Nothing unusual was suggested by the denominational, or even the 'racial' and sectional, nature of the divisions that existed in the Province of Canada. What was unusual was the ready acceptance of the principle of the double majority, which required that legislation affecting either Canada East or Canada West alone not be passed unless it received majority support from members having constituencies in the section in question—although it was unlikely that any ministry in either section could garner enough votes to make this work. Its acceptance was an open admission of the sectional—hence by definition incomplete—nature of the Canadian union. Sir Edmund Head, governor

from 1854 to 1863, quite properly regarded 'this quasi-federal question, which I am bound to treat as theoretically absurd', as an unnecessary complication—although he admitted that 'in practice it must be looked to'. Given the weakness of the Rouges in Canada East and the western strength of the Grits, as well as the difficulty of achieving co-operation between two disparate political groups already prejudiced against one another, the room for political manoeuvring, in the short run, was considerably reduced. The practice of Canadian politics had devolved into an exercise in ingenious compromising. In 1856 Macdonald, who had emerged as the supreme political operator, was able to forge a new coalition from among the moderate (some said pragmatic) Tories from Upper Canada, whom he led, and the Bleus of French Canada, led by George-Étienne Cartier. But the fact remained that Canada West was far more divided politically than Canada East.

Most Canadian political leaders could agree with Governor Head that the double majority was, as Macdonald put it in 1856, 'in the abstract indefensible'. It was also politically awkward if followed slavishly. For example, as a result of the December 1857 elections—when Macdonald scored a personal triumph in Kingston although the Brown Liberals, including Brown himself, won a clear victory, while in Lower Canada the Rouges were defeated by Cartier's Bleu Conservatives—the Macdonald-Cartier ministry continued in office. But the double majority would have required a coalition of Brown's Grits with Cartier's Bleus. It was not enough that sectional parties would have to govern in tandem; to make the system really work, the sectional parties with affinities for one another would have to be elected with majorities at the same time. Yet within the union the only alternative seemed to be 'rep by pop', which was hardly acceptable to the francophones of Canada East at a time when the population of Canada West was greater than their own and growing more rapidly.

John A. Macdonald would later describe the double majority with some affection, using another aspect of it to illustrate the working of a federal principle in Canada. Defending in 1865 the Seventy-two Resolutions that had been drafted at the Quebec Conference on confederation in October 1864 (the basis of the British North America Act), he argued:

> We, in Canada, already know something of the advantages and disadvantages of a Federal Union. Although we have nominally a Legislative Union in Canada—although we sit in one Parliament, supposed constitutionally to represent the people without regard to sections or localities, yet we know, as a matter of fact, that since the union in 1841, we have had a Federal Union; that in matters affecting Upper Canada solely, members from that section claimed and generally exercised the right of exclusive legislation, while members from Lower Canada legislated in matters affecting only their own section. We have had a Federal Union in fact, though a Legislative Union in name.[13]

As early as 1856 talk began to emerge of another alternative to the double majority: a proper federal union, perhaps even one that extended beyond the Canadas. In August 1856, Brown's *Globe* stated that 'If Upper and Lower Canada cannot be made to agree, a federal union of all the provinces will probably be the result.' By 1863 the political implausibility of the double majority had been accepted by most of the leading politicians of Canada. Some other version of union seemed the only solution.

THE RISE OF THE ADMINISTRATIVE STATE

One of the major developments of the middle years of the nineteenth century was the rise of a new kind of state, one that took on new responsibilities, created new sorts of administrative organizations, including a new professional bureaucracy, and acquired some new coercive capabilities. The emergence of this new activist, interventionist state was not confined to British America; it was much further advanced in Europe—especially in Britain, Germany, and Scandinavia—than anywhere in North America.[14] But the United States and British America shared in the climate of opinion that created the new state. That climate was partly humanitarian in impulse, as politicians sought to create new institutions to deal with some of the most obvious social effects of economic change, urbanization, and industrialization on the less fortunate members of society. But it also seems likely that the new middle class combined public-spirited concern with fear of the consequences, should the poor and unfortunate actually attempt to seize power or wealth or both. The excesses of the French Revolution likely remained alive in many minds throughout the nineteenth century, and certainly the rebellions of 1837–8 in the Canadas would have freshened the paranoia of the propertied classes in British North America. Despite the 'laissez-faire' rhetoric of the time, there can be little doubt that state activity did increase in many areas after 1840. But not all historians agree on the reasons for the phenomenon, and hence its meaning. Nor would all agree that the drive for the administrative state was deliberate and co-ordinated, or that its goal was 'social control'—coercive actions by dominant classes to maintain spheres of power.

Before 1867, the administrative state was most highly developed in the united Canada, and its rise is best documented for that province.

THE CROWN LANDS DEPARTMENT

In 1857 Joseph Cauchon, commissioner of Crown Lands, prepared an extensive report for the Legislative Assembly of Canada. Cauchon was an extremely hard-working and outspoken administrator, and his report indicated the complexities of the department under his supervision. There were mining claims on the northern shores of the Great Lakes, and the beginnings of land surveys in the Lake Superior area. The vast forests of the Huron–Ottawa Tract were now being exploited by timbermen under licence from the Crown Lands department. So-called 'colonization roads' were also being constructed in this tract in preparation for survey and settlement. In most of the older settlements of Upper Canada, land sales had fallen off, and Crown Lands' work now had more to do with contested claims over title. The Canadian Parliament had only that year given Cauchon's department responsibility for supervising the inland fisheries, and 30 'fisheries overseers' were at work policing the fishers. In Canada East, Crown Lands had responsibility for the administration of special tracts of land—the Jesuits' Estates, the Seigneury of Lauzon, the King's Domain. In addition, mining and timbering had to be regulated, along with an eastern fishery that involved not only lakes and rivers, but the Gulf of St Lawrence.

Such a vast domain required a large number of officials: surveyors, land agents, colonization road agents, timber agents and timber cullers, fisheries officials. The Crown Lands Department was a curious hybrid of the old disorganized colonial responsibilities of Upper and Lower Canada and the new regulatory concerns of the Province of Canada, governed under responsible government and eager to make every area of its activities pay its own way. Contradictory policies jostled everywhere. Should lands be sold to bring in revenue or to encourage settlement? Could natural resources be regulated without depriving the state of revenue or annoying the private entrepreneurs who dealt with the raw materials? Could sufficient revenue be preserved to support what the legislature expected to finance out of the resources at its disposal? Crown Lands was a department operating at the edge of the transition between the old Canada and the new. In this sense, it symbolized the political and administrative realities of the 1840–70 period.[15]

THE BLUE BOOKS

Beginning in 1822, governors in British North America were obliged to send to the Colonial Office annual summary reports on the colonies under their supervision. These reports, generally known as 'Blue Books', became increasingly detailed over time, and by the 1840s they included detailed censuses that in an earlier age might have been regarded as intrusive. By the early 1850s large quantities of statistical information were being collected and reported in all the British colonies in North America. Much of this material was not only forwarded to London but printed in the form of appendices to the various colonial legislature journals. This growth in official documentation reflected both the new needs of government and the increasing capacity of civil servants first to generate and then to manage the necessary records.[16] It helped to demarcate a new kind of state.

THE POST OFFICE

One of the most important developments of the early Victorian period in British North America was the creation of an inexpensive public postal service stretching from one end of the continent to the other. British North America had had a postal service since 1763, but it was both expensive and slow. Most people preferred to have their letters and packages delivered privately whenever possible, particularly since in the government-run post office system, the recipient (who often did not know a letter or parcel was coming) had to pay the postage. The big breakthrough had come in Britain between 1837 (when the postage stamp was invented) and 1840. The stamp made it possible to create uniform pre-paid postage-rate schedules based on weight, and by 1840 the British Post Office had been transformed into an increasingly popular and profitable operation based on the new transportation technology of railroad and steamship. In British North America, the British government transferred the postal system to colonial (i.e., provincial) control in 1851, leading to the introduction of those provincial postage stamps beloved of collectors. As in Britain, the colonial

TABLE 17.1

THE GROWTH OF THE BRITISH NORTH AMERICAN POSTAL SYSTEM, 1851–1871

Date	No. of post offices	Pieces of mail	Value of money orders	Savings value
1851	601	2.1 million	—	—
1861	1,775	9.4 million	$0.9 million	—
1871	3,943	53.7 million	$4.5 million	$2.5 million

SOURCE: Brian Osborne and Robert M. Pike, 'From "A Cornerstone of Canada's Social Structure" to "Financial Self-Sufficiency": The Transformation of the Canadian Postal Service, 1852-1987', *Canadian Journal of Communications* 13, 1 (1988): 3.

postal service grew rapidly in volume, profitability, and promptness of delivery after 1851. By 1857 it was possible to get a letter from Quebec City to Windsor in just over two days. The post office introduced new services. By 1861 it was possible to send money (in the form of money orders) through the mail, and by 1871 it was possible to save money at a postal savings bank. After Confederation the federal government would become responsible for postal service, and it had a system up and running by early 1868 (see Table 17.1).

The early post office was a highly profitable and much-appreciated operation. No province had any hesitancy about getting into the postal business or expanding its scope. The colonial post office was just one of many new services provided by provinces of British North America after 1840.[17]

ADMINISTRATIVE SERVICES IN THE UNITED PROVINCE

Lord Durham had echoed the views of many a colonial governor in his report's indictment of the inadequacy of the civil services of the Canadas, which were disorganized, unco-ordinated, and inefficient, as well as very much under the influence of political patronage. The lack of proper management from the top was one of the reasons that Durham had insisted on responsible government and its concomitant reform, the creation of a proper departmental system and chain of responsibility. His successor, Lord Sydenham, oversaw not only the union of the two Canadas but the reorganization of the administrative departments of government. Constitutionally, Sydenham and the Colonial Office wanted departmental heads to be responsible to the governor rather than the legislature, but in administrative terms he provided a new and more rational structure at the top, including the introduction of a Board of Works to oversee all public works in the province. The departmental framework he left behind in 1841 survived through virtually the whole Union period and on into the new national government. The dualism of the Union of 1841 was reflected administratively. Some departments were split in half at the top, but some, such as the Provincial Secretary's Department and the Education Office, had two completely distinct establishments, one for Canada East and one for Canada West. Francophones complained that a disproportionate number of the unassigned appointments went to anglophones—about two-thirds of the civil servants were English-speakers, not necessarily from Upper Canada—and there were con-

JOHN LANGTON
(1808–94)

John Langton was born in England. His father was a merchant who was able to take his family on a lengthy European tour before settling into effective bankruptcy in 1826, the year John entered Cambridge. After he graduated, an aunt subsidized his immigration to Upper Canada. He settled at Sturgeon Lake and spent some years in an unsuccessful business career, but eventually found keeping books for others a more congenial occupation. Elected to the provincial legislature as a Tory in 1851, he soon became a financial critic in the house.

In 1855, William Lyon Mackenzie returned from the wilderness to resume the critique of financial practices in the government that he had begun 20 years earlier. As chairman of the standing committee on public accounts, in 1855 Mackenzie issued a scathing report on government accounting. In response the government created a Board of Audit and John A. Macdonald appointed Langton, who surrendered his elected seat, to serve as its chairman. Thereafter, Langton spent many years attempting to assert legislative control over departmental spending and persuading a series of finance ministers, including A.T. Galt and William Cayley, to improve accounting practices. He was no political reformer; he simply worked to extend proper business practices to government finances, including double-entry bookkeeping and balance sheets, and to make these practices comprehensible to the legislators. Yet he also sought to be more than a bean-counter, and often strayed from the auditing of past expenditures into policy matters involving current and future spending. The

introduction of sound bookkeeping practices was a slow and tedious business, especially with the crucial Department of Public Works. Langton had to combine financial and political talent. In 1864 new legislation improved the position of the auditor by making him chairman of a seven-member board. Insofar as he made sense out of government accounting, Langton achieved a crucial political result, because proper accounts were essential if legislators were truly to control the purse strings of the government. Among his accomplishments was the introduction of statements of total income and expenditure, along with accounts of the government's cash position at the close of every financial year. He also struggled to differentiate between capital and income accounts. After 1864 Langton moved to introduce the concept of detailed estimates that bore some relationship to the final budget for each department. Among other things, this meant that departments would not be spending money that had not been authorized.

Gradually, Langton achieved a reputation as a competent and powerful civil servant, in many ways the most powerful civil servant in the Canadian government. It was Langton who originally organized the accounting system for the new Dominion and apportioned the debt between Ontario and Quebec. He became a member of the Civil Service Commission and secretary of the Treasury Board in 1868, and deputy minister of finance from 1870 to 1878. His departure from office was not free of criticism, for he had allowed Sir John A. Macdonald to manipulate the secret service funds. Despite this sorry conclusion, for most of his career Langton was the ultimate example of the new civil servant, devoted to establishing the order and fixed bureaucratic rules he regarded as necessary to prevent government from disintegrating into chaos.

stant frictions over language at the departmental level. A major development was the introduction of a Board of Audit in 1855, which gradually brought modern accounting practices to the administration of budgets. Arguably, it was only when a legislature could expect to see a direct relationship between its budgetary allotments and government spending that true responsible government had been achieved.

Not only were the departments rationalized, but over time they were greatly expanded. In 1842 there were 95 civil servants working in the central offices of the departments and 342 in the field. By 1852 those figures had grown to 176 in central administration and 704 in the field, and by 1867 to 354 in home offices and 2,306 in the field.[18] Although by modern standards these numbers are small, their growth reflected both increased population and increased duties and activities. One of the major assumptions of the period was that services had to be self-sustaining, recovering their own costs. Most of the civil servants remained political appointments, but after 1857 lip service was paid to competitive examinations and there was some insistence on appropriate skills. In Canada there were no major housecleanings when governments changed. After 1849, those in central administration simply had to move every four years as the seat of government shifted between Toronto and Quebec. All civil servants were supposed to work regular hours from 9:00 to 4:30, and salaries were more than competitive. Given the relative security of tenure in the colonial civil service, it was one of the most attractive places to work in the province. Its great drawbacks as a place of employment were a rigid seniority system and

the emergence of a bureaucracy based almost entirely on the generation of files of paper. Associated with the growth of the state bureaucracy was a greatly expanded state. A variety of state agencies set out to implement new policies and create new public institutions. Central departments often employed local government to help regulate and manage the new level of activity. Here only a few of the major developments can be examined.

REFORMS IN EDUCATION

Education was in a sense the flagship of the new state. There were several reasons for this. The importance of education and educational policy had long been a subject of debate in British North America. Many members of the elite came to agree on the value of an elementary general education as a means of assimilating immigrants (and Native people) and of preparing the population in general for a useful and productive life free of poverty, crime, and indolence. Most would have agreed with the educational reformer Egerton Ryerson, who in his 'Report on a System of Elementary Public Education for Upper Canada' (1847) asserted that 'A system of general education amongst the people is the most effectual preventative of pauperism, and its natural companions, misery and crime.'[19] From a somewhat different perspective, many citizens could agree that education would be of considerable benefit to them personally. Nevertheless, before the Union of the Canadas, state involvement in public education had been confined chiefly to the School Act of 1816, which enabled local districts to create schools and hire teachers who

JOHN JESSOP TO
EGERTON RYERSON, 1861

In 1859 John Jessop (1829-1901) travelled from Canada West to British Columbia, where he worked briefly in journalism and gold-mining before returning to teaching. In 1861 he wrote to Egerton Ryerson asking for advice about organizing a school in Victoria.

Victoria V.I.
August 16th 1861

Rev. E. Ryerson, D.D.
Chief Supt. of Schools &c &c

Rev. Sir

Having, at the solicitation of many of the citizens of Victoria, commenced a school and believing that a good opening presents itself for introducing the system of which you are the Honored Head, and under which I received my training during two sessions at the Provincial Normal School and more than five years as a common School teacher in different parts of Canada West, I am desirous of making it as efficient as possible and for that reason I have taken the opportunity of applying to you, through an old friend D. Ormiston B.A., for a supply of maps, charts, apparatus &c, &c, for the use of the school and for the benefit of the city of Victoria.

Our Common school here is very inefficient, while two others, one under the control of Bishop Hills of the Established Church, and another for Young Ladies in charge of the Sisters of Mercy have so much of the Sectarian element in their government as to make them distasteful to non-conformists of all denominations. A school, therefore, started and conducted exclusively on non-sectarian principles, as the one under my charge is and will be, and moreover carried on according to the admirable system of Canada West, cannot fail of soon becoming popular and flourishing. My object is to establish its reputation, and when the city is incorporated to fall in with the common school system that will then be adopted, and place myself at the head of the common schools of Victoria and Vancouver Island.

I believe I am the only person in the Island or in British Columbia that holds a first class Provincial certificate, or indeed one of any description from the Normal School. I have therefore a good opportunity in my present position to do a great deal toward placing the common school system here on a satisfactory basis.

I feel convinced you will, if possible, aid me in establishing an efficient school by sending from the Educational Department a good selection of Maps, charts, globes, phylosophical and chemical apparatus &c, &c, on the terms you supply them to schools under the control of your Department.

I have written Mr. D. Ormiston who with his estimable brother the Rev. Dr. Ormiston will I am sure interest themselves in anything pertaining to my success and advancement in life, on the subject and I have no doubt the requisite amount of funds for such a purpose will be advanced by either of those gentlemen.

I am desirous of obtaining this supply with as little delay as possible and for that reason would prefer having them shipped from New York per steamer for San Francisco as slow freight rather than sent round the Horn in a sailing vessel at a lower rate of freight, as the transit by way of the Isthmus would be at least three months quicker than the other mode of conveyance. . . .

I have the honor to be
Rev. Sir,
Your most obt. Servt,
John Jessop

SOURCE: *Canadian Historical Review* 29 (1948): 54-6.

could receive a provincial grant. An Education Commission in 1839 had reported on the sad state of education in the province. There were only 651 grant-aided schools and 14,776 pupils. In Lower Canada the state was even less involved in education, and many schools were sponsored by the churches. In 1838 a series of public letters by Jean-Baptiste Meilleur had outlined the parlous situation in Lower Canada. Across British North America, 'school promoters' like Meilleur, Egerton Ryerson in Upper Canada, John Jessop in British Columbia, and John Stark in Prince Edward Island agreed on the nature of the reform required—much of it based on foreign models— and corresponded regularly with one another.

In the 1840s education was transformed, particularly in what had been Upper Canada. The models were many, but clearly the Irish educational system was extremely important, with its system of public support and employment of school inspectors on a national level from 1831. The first major breakthrough in Canada was the School Act of 1843, which introduced a large-scale system of state grants monitored by local school inspectors who were responsible to a central education office. Three years later, a new School Act drafted by Egerton Ryerson created a central Board of Education with district superintendents to oversee local education under a chief superintendent. The central Board prescribed textbooks for use in the schools. The 1846 Act also provided for the establishment of a Normal

School to train teachers, which opened the following year in Toronto. Many revisions were subsequently made in the School Acts, but inspection was always included as the key to ensuring that standards were maintained. As Ryerson explained to an official from Indian Affairs in 1847, with reference to the organization of schools:

> The interference or control of the Government should be confined to that which the Government can do with most effect and the least trouble— namely, to the right of inspecting the Schools from time to time by an agent or agents of its own—to the right of having detailed reports of the School as often as it shall think proper to require them, at least once or twice a year; and the right of continuing or withholding the grant made in aid of these Schools. It is in this power over the grant, the exercise of which will be determined by the inspections made and the reports given, that the paramount authority of the Government in respect to these Schools will be secured.[20]

The principle of free public elementary education for all children, funded by a general assessment of property, with school inspections to ensure local compliance with central direction, was gradually extended across British North America, reaching the Maritimes provinces in the 1850s and British Columbia in the 1860s. Adoption of this system marked a major increase in state authority. Government-appointed

■ The Victorian era was fond of graphic illustrations of progress. Here four schoolhouses illustrate the improvements made from the early days of settlement to the 1860s: 1–2 'First Settlers' School-houses'; 3 'Country District School-house'; 4 'Village School-house'. From H.Y. Hind, *The Dominion of Canada: Containing a Historical Sketch of the Preliminaries and Organization of Confederation* (1869).

inspectors soon began to appear in other fields besides education, confirming the power of the state to control and standardize activities.

ASYLUMS

Another burst of state growth came with an increase in the public provisions made for orphans, the poor, and the mentally disturbed.[21]

For these less fortunate members of society, the state increasingly provided by establishing asylums—large public buildings to house (in effect to incarcerate) these people and insulate them from the outside world, partly for their sake but mostly for the sake of the world. The asylum gave the state total control of the inmate's environment, with a variable emphasis—depending on the reasons for institutionalization—on 'restraint' or 'res-

■ The Provincial Lunatic Asylum, Toronto, c. 1868. Metropolitan Toronto Library Board.

cue'. The idea of the orphan asylum was developed in the mid-nineteenth century. Although a Protestant Orphan Asylum was founded in Montreal in the 1820s, large-scale construction of orphan asylums did not begin until the 1840s, with Hamilton in 1846, Toronto in 1851, Saint John in 1857, Ottawa in 1864, and Brantford in 1869. The same period saw the construction of several 'lunatic' asylums. While Reformers talked about increased 'efficiency' and a new humanitarianism, the creation of the asylum (and the prison, which likewise developed in mid-century) also indicated an acceptance of public responsibility and an extension of new long-term coercive powers on the part of the state.

LEGAL REFORM

The emergence of the new state was accompanied by calls for a new legal culture appropriate to it. As the Quebec journal *Revue de législation et de jurisprudence* argued in 1846: 'The conquests which modern society has made in politics, science, the arts, agriculture, industry, and commerce necessitate the reform of the old codes which directed ancient societies. Everywhere, one feels the inadequacy of laws made for an order of ideas and things which no longer exists, and the need to remodel ancient systems and of promulgating new ones, in order to put ourselves at the level of society's progress.'[22] Canada East had already begun to revise its ancient institutions, introducing a land-registry system and redefining seigneurial tenure. Eventually George-Étienne Cartier shepherded a bill through Parliament in 1857 that called for the codification of the law and provided for the establishment of a uniform, centralized legal system throughout the province.[23] Legal reform came in Canada West in 1849 with the introduction into the Canadian House of Assembly of three major legal reform bills. One streamlined proceedings in the Court of Chancery, an equity court where decisions had for years been delayed by antiquated and cumbersome procedures. Another established a second Superior Court of Law to provide a more efficient appeal procedure. The third bill overhauled the law of evidence, chiefly to make more witnesses eligible to give testimony in both civil and criminal cases.[24] Inherent in legal reform and advanced legal thinking everywhere in British North America was a new awareness that the law was not simply a traditional set of principles discovered by judges, but an instrument for governing and regulating society in new ways. Instead of being eternal, law could be made, both by legislatures and by judges.

CONCLUSION

The political development of British North America between 1840 and the early 1860s was not limited to the introduction of responsible government. Political parties continued to evolve and new issues emerged, especially in the area of religion. It was true that the British hoped to reduce their colonial commitments (and their costs) in the wake of the establishment of internal self-government in the colonies, but the imperial authorities still had an extremely important role to play in the political system. Another parallel development to the establishment of responsible government saw the beginning, particularly in Canada, of the modern administrative state.

SHORT BIBLIOGRAPHY

Buckner, P.A. *The Transition to Responsible Government: British Policy in British North America 1815–59.* Westport, Conn., 1985. Now the standard study, detailed and elegantly argued.

Curtis, Bruce. *Building the Educational State: Canada West, 1836–1871.* Sussex and London, 1988. Argues the importance of educational policy for state formation in this period.

Dwivedi, O.P., ed. *The Administrative State in Canada.* Toronto, 1982. An early collection of essays dedicated to J.E. Hodgetts.

Greer, Allan, and Ian Radforth, eds. *Colonial Leviathan: State Formation in Mid-Nineteenth Century Canada.* Toronto, 1992. A collection of essays, informed by international thinking about the origins of the nineteenth-century state.

Gunn, Gertrude E. *The Political History of Newfoundland, 1832–1864.* Toronto, 1966. An older but reliable guide through the thickets of politics in Newfoundland in this period.

Hodgetts, J.E. *Pioneer Public Service: An Administrative History of the United Canadas, 1841–1867.* Toronto, 1955. A pioneering work, decades ahead of its time, on the administration of Canada.

Martin, Ged. *The Durham Report and British Policy: A Critical Essay.* Cambridge, 1972. An iconoclastic look at the Durham *Report*, arguing that it did not alter very much.

Monet, Jacques. *The Last Cannon Shot: A Study of French-Canadian Nationalism.* Toronto, 1969. The classic study of the emergence of nationalism in Lower Canada, under the watchful eye of the

Catholic Church.

Ormsby, W.G. *The Emergence of the Federal Concept in Canada, 1839–1845.* Toronto, 1969. Argues that federalism in Canada had its origins in the foundation of the Province of Canada.

Rooke, Patricia, and R.L. Schnell. *Discarding the Asylum: From Child Rescue to the Welfare State in English-Canada (1800–1950).* Lanham, Md, 1983. A good introduction to the changing views of social welfare and its role in Canada.

Stembridge, Stanley. *Parliament, the Press, and the Colonies, 1846–1882.* New York, 1982. The best book on British public opinion regarding the Empire in this period.

STUDY QUESTIONS

1. What was achieved with responsible government?

2. What were the issues at stake in the land question on Prince Edward Island?

3. What new political problems arose after the achievement of responsible government?

4. Why was the post office so important to colonial British North America?

5. What was the double majority?

6. Why did educational reform appear so crucial to Canada in the 1840s?

CHAPTER EIGHTEEN

Reorientation: British North America and the Empire after 1840

After 1840 the relationship between Great Britain and British North America was rapidly transformed. The change was initiated by the British government's decision to abandon mercantilist protectionism and embrace free trade. This alteration in global policy undoubtedly made it easier for the British to accept colonial responsible government, discussed in the previous chapter. It also forced the colonials to rethink their own commercial system. The Maritime colonies, enjoying the 'Golden Age of Sail', were satisfied with the status quo, but the Canadians quickly began to contemplate the United States as an alternative trading partner.

Although the imperial ties were loosened significantly between 1840 and the 1860s, it would be incorrect to assume that the British Empire was no longer important to British North America. The mother country still retained control over most of the northwestern section of the continent; it still appointed colonial governors; and it was still responsible for imperial defence. Despite their growing autonomy, the colonies probably never felt more attached to the Empire and the British monarchy than they did in 1860, when Queen Victoria's eldest son toured North America.

THE DEMISE OF MERCANTILISM

By 1840 the economy of British North America—based on the mercantilist principle of exploiting colonial raw resources for the international market, particularly in Britain—had reached its apex and was about to undergo considerable change. The most important factors in this change were clearly the British government's deliberate demolition of the imperial trading system that had prevailed since the seventeenth century; a shift into the burgeoning American market; and the rise of new technologies that began to resolve the transportation problems that had hindered internal development. Abandoning mercantilism, Britain moved to free trade and in the process wiped out the protectionist advantages she had previously extended to her colonies. As a result, the transatlantic trade based on the sailing ship, which had been the mainstay of all the colonial economies, became a regional matter. The Atlantic region continued to concentrate on the transatlantic economy within the British Empire, but the Canadians, thanks to the railway, began having visions of internal development and internal markets.

TIMELINE

1840

Political opinion in Britain begins to favour free trade.

1842

Colonial Office agrees to stay out of PEI land question in future. Strength of British army in British North America reduced.

1843

Fort Victoria founded. Corn Laws and Timber Laws repealed.

1848

Colonial Office responds unfavourably to Alexander Isbister's critique of the HBC.

1849

Vancouver Island created a colony. Colonial post office turned over to colonial governments.

1853

PEI passes Land Purchase Act.

1857

Parliamentary inquiry into renewal of HBC charter. Province of Canada begins recruiting immigrants in southern Germany.

1860

Prince of Wales tours British North America. PEI Land Commission appointed.

1861

Edward Watkin appointed president of Grand Trunk Railway.

1862

Hudson's Bay Company reorganized.

THE RISE OF FREE TRADE IN GREAT BRITAIN

The British mercantile system, which had essentially been in place since the first round of colonial expansion at the start of the seventeenth century, had been under attack since before the period of the American Revolution from a number of political and economic thinkers. The rebellion of the colonies merely substantiated the critics' basic argument. In 1776, for example, Josiah Tucker called mercantilism 'THE GREATEST INFATUATION' and pointed out, to those who bemoaned American separation, that England would be better off purchasing raw materials at the best possible prices than it had been when it paid bounties to encourage inferior colonial pro-

duction. 'When all Parties shall be left at full Liberty to do as they please,' Tucker wrote, 'our North-American Trade will rather be increased than diminished, because it is Freedom, and not Confinement, or Monopoly, which increases Trade.'[1] Adam Smith, in *The Wealth of Nations* (1776), presented a more thoroughly reasoned theoretical framework for free trade, along with a vision of international expansion based upon it. In the years following Smith, classical political economists in Britain—Malthus, Chambers, Ricardo, Mill—expanded on earlier critiques of mercantilism, always insisting that freedom worked best, even in the marketplace.

Despite the intellectual demotion of mercantilism in the first quarter of the nineteenth century, British governments found protectionism difficult to give up, since it artificially supported influential sectors of the economy, particularly the larger landholders. Eventually, however, the free-traders won, largely because of Britain's industrial successes after 1815. With the most dynamic industrial economy in the world by the 1840s, the British could no longer afford the luxury of protectionism, which limited their access to foreign raw materials; nor did they now need its converse, guaranteed colonial markets. By 1841 only 22 per cent of the British labour force was employed in agriculture, forestry, or fishing, as opposed to 35 per cent in 1801; and 40 per cent were employed in mining and manufacturing, up from 30 per cent in 1801. Cotton textiles accounted for about half of all British exports, and Britain had become the 'Workshop of the World'.

The overall strategy for the British economy had not changed since the seventeenth century. It still emphasized importing cheap raw materials and exporting finished goods to overseas markets, 'vast territories in North and South America, in the plains of Buenos Ayres, in the hills and dales of Australia and New Zealand'.[2] One of the leading free-traders, John MacGregor, originally from PEI, emphasized in his study *British America* (1832) that Britain's American colonies, especially the lands west of the Great Lakes, could support an enormous population and control 'the umpirage of the Western World'. What turned the British to free trade in the 1840s was the simple realization that it would work to their advantage. The ministry led by Robert Peel therefore gritted its teeth and systematically removed protection for grain (which the British called 'corn') and other raw materials (including timber), justifying the repeal of the Corn Laws by pointing to the famines of the 1840s and the resultant need for imported foodstuffs. 'I am fairly convinced', Peel wrote in 1846, 'that the permanent adjustment of the Corn Laws has rescued the country and the whole frame of society from the hazard of very serious convulsion.'[3] Ironically, British free-trade policies made possible a new wave of

British overseas expansion—this time economic rather than territorial. They also had a tremendous impact, perhaps more psychological than actual, on colonial merchants and their political allies, especially in the rich heartland of British North America. At the same time, Britain's industrial needs increased the need for international peace and bilateral understandings.

THE EARLY REACTION TO FREE TRADE IN BRITISH NORTH AMERICA

Most colonial merchants appreciated the nature of the revolution that had been underway in Britain for several years. In 1842 the Whig government in Britain proposed to modify the timber and sugar preferential duties, and in that year the *Quebec Gazette* summarized several generations of argument as follows: 'Our great ground of complaint is that British Acts of Parliament created the trade, caused capital to be invested in the trade, trusting to these acts, which by the uncertain character they now assume may ruin thousands. We never asked for protection; it was given on grounds of national policy.'[4] Those in Canada waited apprehensively for news about the future of the Corn Laws in 1846. The situation seemed particularly difficult because the Americans had been revising their own commercial legislation in 1845, remitting duties on goods imported into the United States from foreign countries and re-exported to Canada. As everyone rushed to export wheat and timber under the old system, the outcome was predictable: oversupply and the uncertainty resulting from the repeal of the Corn Laws and Timber Laws, both in 1846, led to a collapse of prices in 1847 that was to last for the rest of the decade. Wheat exports fell from 628,000 bushels in 1847 to 238,000 bushels by 1848, and flour exports dropped from 651,000 to 383,000 barrels. Further complicating matters for colonial governments was the arrival of thousands of impoverished Irish and Highland Scots immigrants, refugees from the Great Famine of the 1840s who brought sickness and expense to the colonies along with their anguish. The result of all these blows was a conviction that the old Empire had collapsed, indeed, had been subverted by the mother country. Canadians themselves helped to complete the demolition of the old mercantilism when they argued for the repeal of the British Navigation Acts, which regulated shipping, in favour of opening the St Lawrence to the Americans. Those shipping laws were abandoned by Britain in 1849.

Because the Province of Canada relied on wheat exports, the crisis seemed much more serious there than it did elsewhere in British North America, although all colonies turned instinctively from the mother country to that other obvious trading partner, the United States. Canadian policy in the 1840s, in the wake of British adoption of free trade, was to attempt to come to terms with the Americans. Indeed, in 1848 the Montreal Board of Trade insisted that Canadian–American interests 'under the changed policy of the Imperial Government are germane to each other, and under that system must sooner or later be politically interwoven.'[5] But the Atlantic Ocean and the Empire did not instantly go away.

THE GOLDEN AGE OF ATLANTIC SAIL

Despite the development of new transportation technologies, the wooden sailing vessel would remain the dominant means of shipping until later in the nineteenth century. Atlantic Canada enjoyed not only the raw materials but also the expertise in building and sailing such vessels that enabled it to benefit from both the local and the international need for a carrying trade.[6] The region's most important shipping advantage—its access to cheap vessels—was enhanced even in the early days of competition with iron steamers. In the 1860s, for example, a large new sailing ship could be purchased in Atlantic Canada for

one-quarter to one-half the price of an iron steamer built on the Clyde in Scotland. So long as the two remained relatively equal in speed and efficiency, sailing vessels remained profitable. For the Atlantic region, then, the key to expansion lay not in the traditional export of resources, but in the opportunity to carry goods produced anywhere in the world. Atlantic shipping flourished particularly during the early 1860s, when the United States was engaged in a bloody civil war and its merchant marine decreased substantially in size. One official in New Brunswick observed that 'the most advantageous branch of our trade in 1864 has probably been that of shipowning.'[7] Not only was Atlantic Canada's own merchant fleet substantial, but it supplied hundreds of vessels for British registry,[8] and the ships increased in size over the nineteenth century.

With hindsight it is possible to recognize the weaknesses inherent in the Atlantic carrying trade, even at the point of its greatest success and prosperity. The business was characterized by high risks and fairly rapid capital depreciation; the life expectancy of a wooden sailing vessel was no more than 15 years. Moreover, the trade was international, part of the transatlantic rather than the continental economy, and subject to international developments over which the Atlantic provinces had no control. The most important elements in the carrying trade, during its heyday, did not directly involve the economy of British North America at all; rather, it involved traffic with the United States and markets in Britain and Europe, transporting bulk commodities such as wheat, cotton, and petroleum. The Atlantic shipping industry was plugged into an international economy, and its success or failure was totally dependent on such factors as bulk freight rates and technological innovation by competitors. Nevertheless, the carrying trade was for some time a substantial and profitable economic enterprise, providing employment for thousands, both in the shipyards and on board the sailing vessels. It also produced an outward-looking international orientation, as opposed to the inter-

JAMES YEO
(1789–1868)

James Yeo was born in Cornwall, England. His father was a shoemaker, and James worked as a labourer before beginning a carting business around 1815. It failed, and upon remarriage after his first wife's death, James and his new wife immigrated to Prince Edward Island. There, Yeo worked for several West Country merchants, in particular Thomas Burnard Chanter. He established himself in Port Hill, Prince County, in the western part of the island, a district with some experience of ruthless and ambitious entrepreneurs. Yeo allegedly raised the capital to go into business for himself by collecting the bad debts of one of his employers and turning the money to his own purposes. He began with one merchant schooner and a small lumber business, and was soon shipbuilding; his first vessel, the *Marina*, was constructed in 1833. By 1840 he was ready to move into shipbuilding on a grand scale. Between 1833 and his death, Yeo's shipyards built over 150 ships, some of which were among the largest of their day, and his family was responsible for another 200. The Yeos contracted the building of their vessels to craftsmen at small shipyards all along the island's coast. Many of the ships were sailed to England in an unfinished state and completed at a family shipyard near Bideford. The Yeos thus took advantage of both Prince Edward Island's access to raw materials and England's access to the finishing hardware. Yeo cut timber everywhere on PEI, but especially in areas with absentee landlords who could not

protect their property. His wife managed a store at Port Hill, which engaged in the truck business and put many Islanders in the family's debt.

Gradually becoming a major landholder and proprietor, inevitably Yeo also became a major shipper of agricultural produce and timber from the island, acquiring large amounts of cash in the process. His trade with Britain seems not to have been much affected by the repeal of the Corn and Timber Laws. In a colony short of cash, Yeo's money turned him into a major local financier. Even the government borrowed from him, and by the 1850s one newspaper claimed that his wage bill was larger than the entire revenue of the government.

Yeo's success was based on a number of factors. He was extremely energetic and able, a man who could keep accounts in his head and make quick decisions. He was also ruthless in his exploitation of resources and people. Finally, he had an extremely loyal and hardworking family. Not only his wife but his sons and sons-in-law were all part of the family enterprise. One son ran the English shipyard that finished the ships, while other family members built and sailed ships. Although Yeo in later years was active in island politics, his involvement was a consequence of his business activities and not the cause of his success. He was always opposed to land reform for the island, and objected strenuously to responsible government.

nal, continental orientation of the Canadians; for Atlantic entrepreneurs, freight rates in Boston

were more important than territorial expansion into the western hinterland. While the Atlantic

■ Courtney Bay, New Brunswick, c. 1860. Many ships were built at this port near East Saint John. Provincial Archives of New Brunswick, P5-360.

provinces (not so much Newfoundland) were eager to expand transportation links with Canada, they were more interested in the implications for the carrying-trade between Europe and America than in the possibility of supplying an internal market with their own production.

BRITISH NORTH AMERICA IN THE NEW BRITISH EMPIRE

The imperial government conceded responsible government in British North America because it had little choice, given its unwillingness, in the era of free trade, to devote unnecessary amounts of money to colonial administration. There was a feeling in both the Colonial Office and Parliament that the separation of colonies, particu-

larly colonies populated with large numbers of British immigrants, was inevitable when those colonies had reached a point of sufficient 'maturity'. Equally strong was the feeling that the costs of imperial administration were an unnecessary drain on the public purse.

A student giving a cursory glance to the literature on the British Empire and British America between 1840 and the early 1860s could easily be forgiven for concluding that once responsible government had been conceded, nothing much happened on the imperial front until the British started thinking seriously about union (and autonomy) in the later 1850s. But that conclusion would not be entirely correct, for a number of reasons. In the first place, even if colonies like Canada were given internal self-government, the business of colonial administration would go on, albeit in a different context. The Colonial Office would continue collecting large annual volumes of papers dealing with individual colonies, and correspondence with Crown officials would still have to be maintained. Moreover, not quite all of British North America had yet acquired self-government; the Colonial Office still had responsibility for the West—British policy would create the colony of Vancouver Island in 1849, for example—and the ultimate authority concerning Aboriginal policy. As well, the British government still appointed colonial governors, and both it and they still had considerable moral authority in the colonies. In some cases the imperial government deliberately devolved its responsibilities as part of the reorientation process. Thus the British parliament passed enabling legislation for the hand-over of the colonial post office to local control in 1849, although the colonial governments did not take up their new post offices until 1851. Many of the problems created in earlier periods, such as the clergy reserves in Upper Canada, were thrashed out in the context of responsible government and were resolved by its achievement. Others, including the land question in Prince Edward Island, continued to fester, with Islanders convinced that the British government had created the problem in the first place and ought to settle it. And, finally, Britain was still in charge of the colonies' international affairs—including diplomatic relations with the United States, which encompassed such matters as the survey of the boundary line in 1857—and was responsible for both directing and financing the land and sea defence of British North America.

BRITAIN, THE HUDSON'S BAY COMPANY, AND THE WEST

The strength of the Hudson's Bay Company's position in the West lay in British policy concerning the Aboriginal peoples residing in the company's territories. As the parliamentary inquiry of 1836 into the state of Aboriginal peoples in the Empire had demonstrated (see Chapter 15), the emergence of competition in the fur trade had led to the use of liquor and other addictive substances as trade goods, and the arrival of European settlers inevitably resulted in dispossession of the First Nations. The inquiry's conclusions were instrumental in the decision of the British government in 1838 to renew the HBC's licence of exclusive trade for another 21 years. The Colonial Office hoped that in the long run the Native people would become farmers, but so long as they remained hunters and gatherers they needed to be protected from competition-related abuse and the encroachment of settlers. The Colonial Office thus rejected a 1847 'memorial' in which the mixed-blood Alexander Isbister complained about the 'harsh administration of the Hudson's Bay Company', claiming that his charges were much exaggerated.[9]

By the 1850s, however, the company's monopoly was under attack on a variety of fronts. British supporters of imperial expansion complained about its hidebound policies. Liberals who disliked monopolies on principle—among them William Gladstone—found much to criticize. As early as 1848, Gladstone had told Parliament, with respect to the HBC: 'There never was a case in which the evils of monopoly acquired a more rank development than in the instance of that Company. . . . the monopoly of land and trade was aggravated by absolutism in politics covered by the cloak of impenetrable secrecy.'[10] Perhaps most important, Canadian expansionists led by George Brown and Alexander Morris wanted the HBC replaced by some sovereign Canadian authority, so that its territory could be opened for settlement. Not surprisingly, with the company's trade monopoly up for renewal in 1858, a parliamentary inquiry was held in 1857, at which testimony was heard from all the interested parties, including a number of official representatives of the united province.

George Simpson and other HBC officials insisted that the territory in question was totally unsuitable for agriculture, chiefly because of the

REPORT FROM THE SELECT COMMITTEE ON THE HUDSON'S BAY COMPANY, 1857

1. The near approach of the period when the license of exclusive trade, granted in 1838 for 21 years, to the Hudson's Bay Company over that northwestern portion of British America which goes by the name of the Indian Territory, must expire, would alone make it necessary that the condition of the whole of its vast regions which are under the administration of the Company should be carefully considered; but there are other circumstances which, in the opinion of Your Committee, would have rendered such a course the duty of the Parliament and Government of this country.

2. Among these, Your Committee would specially enumerate,—the growing desire of our Canadian fellow-subjects that the means of extension and regular settlement should be afforded to them over a portion of this territory; the necessity of providing suitably for the administration of the affairs of Vancouver's Island, and the present condition of the settlement which has been formed on the Red River. . . .

7. Among the various objects of imperial policy which it is important to attain, Your Committee consider that it is essential to meet the just and reasonable wishes of Canada to be enabled to annex to her territory such portion of the land in her neighbourhood as may be available to her for the purposes of settlement, with which lands she is willing to open and maintain communications, and for which she will provide the means of local administration. . . .

11. As to those extensive regions, whether in Rupert's Land or in the Indian Territory, in which, for the present at least, there can be no prospect of permanent settlement, to any extent, by the European race for the purposes of colonisation, the opinion at which Your Committee have arrived is mainly founded on the following considerations: 1. The great importance to the more peopled portions of British North America that law and order should, as far as possible, be maintained in these territories; 2. The fatal effects which they believe would infallibly result to the Indian population from a system of open competition in the fur trade, and the consequent introduction of spirits in a far greater degree than is the case at present; and 3. The probability of the indiscriminate destruction of the more valuable fur-bearing animals in the course of a few years.

12. For these reasons Your Committee are of opinion that whatever may be the validity or otherwise of the rights claimed by the Hudson's Bay Company, under the Charter, it is desirable that they should continue to enjoy the privilege of exclusive trade, which they now possess, except so far as those privileges are limited by the foregoing recommendations.

SOURCE: *Report from the Select Committee on the Hudson's Bay Company* (London, 1857), iii–iv.

uncertainties of its northern climate. As Edward Ellice, for example, told the inquiry, 'I have no doubt that gentlemen who go out in the summer and look at the border of these rivers and see the fine pastures which they find for the buffalo, say, "These will make admirable farms," but they have not been there during the winter, and they have not considered the circumstances of the country with respect to fuel.'[11] Despite such testimony, the committee eventually concluded that the 'growing desire of our Canadian fellow-subjects that the means of extension and regular settlement should be afforded to them over a portion of this territory'—along with the pressures for change on the west coast and in Red River—meant that there should be a new regime. Canada should be allowed to annex such portions of the West as she could open and control, opined the committee. In the rest of the territory the HBC should continue its administration, in order to protect the 'Indian population from a system of open competition in the fur trade, and the consequent introduction of spirits in a far greater degree than is the case at present.'[12] The British committee also argued for continuation of the HBC's monopoly, in order to protect the 'more valuable fur-bearing animals'.

THE FOUNDING OF VANCOUVER ISLAND AND BRITISH COLUMBIA

One key development in the settlement of the West was the establishment of Vancouver Island as a British colony in 1849. Until then, Britain had been content to allow the HBC to act as the custodian of British interests and the Aboriginal population on the Pacific slope. But the company had come under attack, chiefly by James E. Fitzgerald, a clerk in the British Museum. Using knowledge acquired in the library's stacks to call attention to himself as a colonial expert, Fitzgerald published a scathing pamphlet in 1849, arguing that the country north of the 49th parallel, a 'frozen wilderness', had been exploited by the fur traders for their own purposes. He insisted that the prairie district—a 'broad belt stretching from Lake Superior, in a northwesterly direction to the Rocky Mountains'—was one region suitable for settlement, and that British Columbia and Vancouver Island were two others. Calling for an expedition to survey the West, both for settlement and for transportation links, he argued that 'Canada would become the line of transit for emigrants, for all the commerce which colonies in the interior would necessarily create,

instead of being, as she now is, planted against an impenetrable wall of desert, two thousand miles thick.'[13]

Fitzgerald was unsuccessful in his advocacy of a joint stock company to develop Vancouver Island, but his agitation did force the Colonial Office to permit the Hudson's Bay Company itself to organize a colony there. In January 1849 the island was leased to the HBC for an annual amount of seven shillings and the company was given five years to establish 'a settlement or settlements of resident [British] colonists' there.[14] In 1841, before the settlement of the western boundary, Governor George Simpson had sent James Douglas, who had been made chief factor the year before, from Fort Vancouver to establish a post on Vancouver Island as a fall-back position in case the Oregon Territory were lost. Douglas himself was of mixed blood, a 'Scotch West Indian' from the sugar islands, and his wife, Amelia Connolly, was the mixed-blood daughter of an HBC factor. He founded Fort Victoria in May 1843 as a fur-trading post, and returned to it in 1849 in his role as chief factor of the HBC, becoming governor in 1851 to succeed Richard Blanshard, who had discovered after his arrival, early in 1850, that Douglas held most of the real power.

The newcomers—mostly officers and clerks of the company and their families, joined by a handful of colonists—sought to reproduce the life of the British gentry on the Pacific slope. This was not easy. Getting to British Columbia by sea took many months, and the early colony was even more isolated than Red River in terms of access to trade and trade goods. The Colonial Office had encumbered Vancouver Island with the notions of Edward Gibbon Wakefield that land must be priced high (a pound an acre) and that settlement should be led by those who could afford to bring out labourers as settlers to work the lands. The trouble with such schemes was that the labourers were constantly abandoning their employers. Nevertheless, the 'Wakefield System' remained in place on the island until 1860, and over 17,000 acres (7,000 ha) of land

■ 'Vancouver Island, the Hudson Bay Co.'s Establishment, 1845', by P.M. O'Leary. LAC, C-4562.

were sold to 180 purchasers, most of whom had HBC connections. Many would retire with their mixed-blood families on Vancouver Island as an alternative to Red River. Much of the early agricultural work was done by the Puget's Sound Agricultural Company, which had been transferred from the Cowlitz Valley (in present-day Washington State) and had its own colonization program, involving four farms each managed by a 'gentleman bailiff' and worked by hired labour imported from Britain (mainly Scotland) for the purpose. A dour Scot, Kenneth McKenzie, was put in charge of farming operations, and he found himself constantly struggling with the pretensions of the bailiffs. 'Balls & parties every now & then for farmers in a new country will not do', he admonished one of his underlings, telling another: 'It is profits we want at as little outlay as possible.'[15] The company was astounded to discover that in 1853 one of its bailiffs spent eight times his annual salary on various expenses and purchases, including 1,606 pounds of sugar and 70 gallons of brandy, rum, whisky, and wine.

THE LAND QUESTION ON PRINCE EDWARD ISLAND

Another of those nasty hanging issues in which the imperial government was directly involved was the land question on Prince Edward Island. It had refused to allow the various escheat laws passed by the island's assembly to come into force, on the grounds that they infringed on the right of private property. Having disallowed the land legislation, the Colonial Office in 1842 stated that the imperial government would not interfere any further in the struggle between the landed proprietors and their tenants. Colonial Secretary Lord Stanley wrote to the island's lieutenant-governor on 14 July 1842, 'The duty of the

Government will be limited to enforcing a strict observance of the Law by the contending parties.'[16] The continuation of the land question in the form of an ongoing struggle between landlords and tenants was used as a reason for opposing the introduction of responsible government. The island was different from other provinces, argued its lieutenant-governor in 1848, because the land system meant that four-fifths of the population were ignorant tenants who were manipulated by designing politicians in their own interest. In a note written on this letter, a Colonial Office undersecretary observed that such arguments 'rather lead to the inference that the land question . . . should be settled as soon as possible, than that the island is otherwise unfit for responsible government.'[17] Responsible government was granted in 1851, but did not end the British government's involvement in the land question.

In 1853 the island's government passed a Land Purchase Act, under which the proprietors could sell their lands to the Crown. Many of the proprietors complained to the Colonial Office, insisting that the British government had to be the final court of appeal in 'extreme cases of injustice' where proprietorial lands were being undervalued for sale. Prime Minister Palmerston himself wrote to the Colonial Secretary on 19 December 1855 that 'The Owners have as good a right to their Property as you or I . . . have to our Estates, and it would be as unjust and of as bad an example to extinguish the Rights of these owners, as it would be to extinguish our Rights.'

In 1860 a Land Commission was appointed to investigate the question and to recommend a final solution. The commission, which included Joseph Howe, unanimously recommended that tenants, with a few exceptions, be allowed to purchase freehold land from their landlords, with arrears incurred before early 1858 forgiven.[18] The question of price was to be left in the first instance to negotiation between tenant and owner, and, if this proved unsatisfactory, to final arbitration. The proprietors argued against such a decision on the grounds that they had not agreed to allow third-party arbitration to set the prices for their lands. The British government agreed with the proprietors, and the Colonial Office initially refused royal assent to the Commission's recommendation until it had consulted with the Crown's law officers. Such consultation in 1863 merely confirmed the government's earlier decision.[19] Imperial authority had been employed to negate a colonial recommendation made by a commission formed with imperial approval. A different approach would have to be taken to resolve the question. Despite the acceptance of responsible government, there were obviously still some colonial situations in which the imperial government had considerable power.

DEFENDING BRITISH NORTH AMERICA

One of the major responsibilities—and major expenses—of the British Empire had long been to defend British America. In late 1840 this responsibility was the subject of a behind-the-scenes debate within the British military, which was particularly concerned about the ongoing costs. The Board of Ordnance in London protested the cost of maintaining 16 fortified posts in Canada alone. The commander of the army in North America insisted that Canada could not be protected without fortifications. Ordnance replied that successful defence depended more on the support of the people, concluding that 'if the inhabitants are not disposed to join us in endeavouring to repel an invading force, no extent of fortification would afford a certain security.'[20] The British government decided that it had an obligation to protect people who willingly remained with the Empire. Expensive fortifications continued to be built or extended—the Halifax Citadel, for example, begun in 1832, would not be completed until 1857, at a cost of more than £241,000[21]—but the pressure for economies continued as well; after all, the annual cost of a regular regiment of the line (with 953 officers and men) was

£46,000. In early 1842, the strength of the British regular army was reduced from a peak of 12,452 all ranks to 7,474 all ranks.

The diplomatic crisis between Britain and the United States over the Oregon Territory boosted the size of the establishment again, but the arrival of responsible government meant, as Lord Grey argued, that 'now the Canadians have self Govmt. so completely granted to them they ought to pay all its expenses including military protection.'[22] The government quickly backed down from such categorical statements, but Grey continued to press for a policy of 'cautiously proceeding to throw more of the Military expenditure upon the Colonies'.[23] Most of the cutbacks were made in Canada, which housed the bulk of the soldiers and was regarded as wealthy enough to protect itself. The other colonies were smaller and less capable of fending for themselves. The great naval base and garrison at Halifax were considered important for imperial rather than simply local reasons, and this would be equally true of the naval base at Victoria/Esquimalt, established in the 1860s.[24]

■ 'Fort Niagara from Fort Mississauga, Upper Canada', by Philip J. Bainbrigge. LAC, C-011899.

GARRISONS

Military garrisons—whether the large ones at Halifax, Quebec, and Kingston or the smaller ones in places like Montreal—were important parts of their local communities, for good and for ill. On the positive side was the money that a garrison injected into the local economy, in the form both of wages paid to the troops and of lucrative government contracts for construction, transport, and supplies. In the 1830s the Kingston garrison required 2,000 cords of firewood, 1,600 barrels of flour, 3,000 12-lb bundles of straw, and 4,500 pounds of beef tallow candles every year. Equally important was the contribution made by the soldiers—officers and enlisted men—to the cultural and social life of the community. Almost every garrison had a dramatic society, and major ones had military bands. The balls given by regiments were the high points of local social life, and invitations to the regimental mess were highly prized by townsmen. Soldiers were keen sportsmen, and garrisons helped to introduce and popularize British sports such as curling, cricket, fencing, and rowing, particularly after 1840, when the army adopted formal programs of physical training and sports. One officer argued that the 'best nurses of cricket in our colonies are the army and navy.'[25] The support given the local Anglican church by the garrison, especially the officer corps, was considerable. Finally, some of the soldiers discharged by garrisons—in Kingston, 1,258 soldiers between 1815 and 1865—would become residents of the community.

On the less desirable side, of course, were the establishments that emerged to provide soldiers with 'pleasure' in their off-duty hours. The Kingston council in 1841 complained to Lord

■ Regimental Dress, 93rd Regiment of Foot
Guards, 1838–48, by Frederick M. Milner
(1889–1939). LAC, C-5740.

Sydenham that in the town 'there was . . . a drinking shop for every 7th or 8th male adult, while the town was over-run with drunkards.'[26] A large garrison meant not only drinking establishments, but prostitutes as well. In 1851 the commander of the forces in Montreal wrote that the common soldier had 'no occasion to think for tomorrow . . . [and] no recreation but sensuality. His general haunts are the Grog Shop and Brothel.'[27]

DOWNSIZING

The size of the British military establishment in British North America was gradually reduced in the 1850s. Many of the smaller posts in Canada were abandoned, the naval presence on the Great Lakes was eliminated, and the dockyard at Kingston was closed, while the rank-and-file numbers in Canada were reduced to 4,732 and the size of the Nova Scotia command to 2,319. British expenditure on the army in British North America was briefly reduced from £464,056 in 1853–4 to £260,995 in 1854–5, and more

reductions accompanied the outbreak of war with Russia in 1854. The Reciprocity Treaty of that year suggested that there was no need to fear the Americans. By the end of 1855 there were only 1,887 imperial troops left in Canada, plus 1,086 in the Maritimes, and 311 in Newfoundland. The colonies grumbled, but did not move quickly to assume the costs or the responsibility for defence, although in 1855 the Legislative Assembly of Canada did pass a bill to establish a colonial militia, by a vote of 58 to 34. The British government continued to provide token numbers of troops in emergency situations in the later 1850s, and expenses again began climbing. Red River got a detachment of Royal Canadian Rifles in 1857 to defend the settlement against the Americans who had fortified the boundary at Pembina, and in 1858 Colonel R.C. Moody and a company of Royal Engineers (four officers and 150 other ranks) were sent to British Columbia. The Rifles proved useless and were withdrawn in 1861, but the 'Sappers' in British Columbia did yeoman service in various areas, including the construction of roads into the gold fields.

THE MILITIA

The establishment of volunteer militia forces in the several colonies brought mixed results. Not every colony was equally keen. In 1856 New Brunswick refused to re-embody its disbanded militia and argued that defence was an imperial responsibility.[28] In Canada the militias initially proved popular with the population, probably because the volunteers were paid five shillings a day for up to 10 days of annual drill, and drilling days were great social occasions. Volunteer companies were also popular in previously defence-less Prince Edward Island when they were created in 1859. Such units gave the public a chance to see colourful uniforms and parades, and gave officers a chance to use military titles before their names. But the provincial legislatures continued to drag their heels on defence appropriations. The opening of the American Civil War forced

TABLE 18.1

BRITISH MILITARY IN BRITISH NORTH AMERICA, 1861

	Officers	Other Ranks
Canada	611	12,341
NB	154	2,282
NS	147	2,738
Nfld	12	297

SOURCE: J.M. Hitsman, *Safeguarding Canada 1763–1871* (Toronto: University of Toronto Press, 1968), 172.

Britain to increase its garrison to 5,100 regular troops, and further increases were planned late in 1861 (see Table 18.1), following the diplomatic crisis known as the *Trent* affair, in which an American naval officer removed two Confederate diplomats from a neutral British merchant ship.

By 1861–2 army expenditures were £939,424 and a total of 12,949 troops were stationed in North America. Subsequent military developments will be discussed in Chapter 24.

BRITISH NORTH AMERICA AND THE BRITISH MONEY MARKET

Although Great Britain supplied substantial amounts of capital to British North America throughout the nineteenth century, it became a major secured lender only in the 1850s, with the financing of the Grand Trunk Railway.[29] British bankers had previously been reluctant to invest in either the British American colonies or their railways, but attitudes now changed. To some extent the shift was motivated by bad experiences with investment in the United States. The first colonial public utility company to be traded in London was a Jamaican railway in the 1840s, which was soon joined by the East Indian Railway and then by the Grand Trunk. The Grand Trunk—initially

intended to run between Montreal and Toronto—had first been projected in 1852 with great enthusiasm and hoopla. Ultimately, it was intended to connect by rail the eastern provinces of British North America with Canada, but the British government refused to guarantee loans, and the Canadian government, under Premier Francis Hincks, borrowed capital in British money markets against its own guarantees to develop a line from Montreal to the western end of Lake Ontario. Shareholders were promised a substantial annual dividend (11.5 per cent), and the initial offering was oversubscribed. But, like many such schemes, the Grand Trunk soon got out of hand, adding more track and borrowing more money. The contractors cut corners, and the traffic never measured up to the expectations (some called them claims) of the promoters. The Canadian government demanded and got its own gauge, to prevent its stock from running on American lines. However, it forgot the corollary: that American stock could not run on its track. By 1857 the government of Canada was in debt for the Grand Trunk to the tune of $25 million, and four years later the line's survival depended on public assistance, while the investors received no dividends.

The large banking firm of Barings and Glyns was the principal—indeed, virtually the only—conduit for moving British funds into Canada.[30] This firm consistently advanced money and charged Canada a lower rate of interest than it could have found on the open market. British investors preferred shares to bonds, and were always reluctant to invest in distant colonies, but they came to accept securities when they were secured by land grants and future earnings. The British financial system was greatly improved in the 1850s by the adoption of gold as the basis of the world monetary system. In any event, the major Canadian railroad—which required large amounts of capital and could make no profits until it was completed—could not have been built without substantial British investment. The funds simply were not available in either British North America or the United States. The British

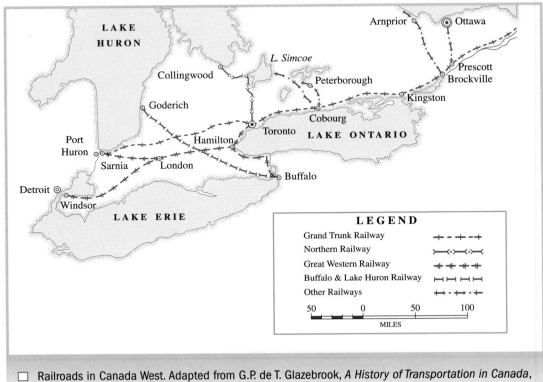

☐ Railroads in Canada West. Adapted from G.P. de T. Glazebrook, *A History of Transportation in Canada*, vol. I (Toronto: McClelland & Stewart, 1966 [1938])

bankers had nothing but trouble with the Grand Trunk, and eventually seized its property at the end of 1860, forcing the Canadian government to intervene by setting up a commission, which recommended setting aside revenue for creditors and economizing on operating expenses.[31]

BRITISH EMIGRATION

In one sense the transatlantic movement of people to British North America was a constant flow between the end of the Napoleonic Wars and Confederation, as we have seen. But beginning in the 1840s there were some new elements added to the mix. The annual totals of people leaving the British Isles increased substantially in the 1840s and 1850s, and the proportions heading initially to British North America decreased

equally sharply; most sailed for the United States (see Table 18.2). In 1857 the Province of Canada began actively recruiting immigrants in southern Germany, and substantial numbers of Western Europeans started coming to British North America in the later 1850s.

Meanwhile, the terrible famines of the 1840s pushed ever-increasing numbers of poor Scots and Irish people into overseas migration. Such emigrants usually had precious little money—so little that in the past they would have been unlikely to leave their homes. Now many were able to emigrate because their steerage passage was paid for by others—especially landlords and local authorities—and they would end up at the docks in North America virtual paupers. Even those who started out with some money often lost it in the process of emigration. The chief seaport for the transatlantic trade by the 1840s was Liverpool, which had rapidly became infamous as a centre of corruption devoted to separating emigrants from their money, however small the amount. Every person an emigrant came into contact with in Liverpool—from lodging-house keeper to passenger-ticket broker—expected a commission; in 1851, one former mayor of Liverpool charged that the emigrant was plundered at every stage and every step of the way from the moment he or she arrived in the port. According to the *Morning Chronicle* in 1850, even after the various sharks in Liverpool had drained the emigrant dry, 'they are loth to part with him entirely, and they write out, per next steamer, a full, true, and particular account of him—his parish, his relations, his priest, and his estimated stock of money' to a similar gang in America. The crowds at the docks at embarkation time were so intimidating and filled with pickpockets that many emigrants got on the wrong ship, or on the right one without their purses. Such was the obstacle course that emigrants faced before they even reached the open waters of the Atlantic, much less arrived on the North American side.[32]

TABLE 18.2

BRITISH IMMIGRANTS TO NORTH AMERICA, 1840–1865

Dates	To BNA	To US
1840-9	424,000	908,000
1850-9	252,000	1,626,000
1860-5	83,000	534,000

SOURCE: Helen I. Cowan, *British Emigration to British North America: The First Hundred Years* (Toronto: University of Toronto Press, 1961), 288.

Many emigrants could afford only the least expensive of steerage accommodation, aboard overcrowded third-rate ships carrying lifeboats crammed with cargo and baggage. One emigration manual of 1851 warned that the typical emigrant ship was worse than a slaver, which had a considerably greater interest in its cargo.[33] Unlike most American-built vessels heading for the States, many of those sailing to British America had not been built specifically for passengers,

■ 'Departure of the 'Nimrod' and 'Athlone' Steamers, with Emigrants on Board', *Illustrated London News*, 10 May 1851. Visual and Sound Archives Division, LAC, C-006556.

and were hauling people as ballast. Accommodations were makeshift at best. The passengers, who provided their own food and drink, were kept below deck, where they had to sleep, as one observer wrote, 'huddled together without light, without air, wallowing in filth and breathing a fetid atmosphere.'[34] Such conditions were ideal for incubating disease, and few vessels escaped contagion of one kind or another.[35]

REGULATION OF THE PASSAGE

Over the years, the British government had made sporadic efforts to legislate improvement in the conditions of the transatlantic passage. In so doing it had clearly established its responsibility for regulation. But the magnitude of the numbers forced abroad by the potato famine initially defeated all efforts at reform. The exodus was so great that after 1845 there were insufficient inspectors and emigration officers to deal with the increased traffic, and the government was reluctant to spend the money necessary to enforce the existing legislation. The British government was far too slow to respond to a crisis that had been predicted on all sides. By 1847, every passenger vessel arriving at Grosse Isle, the immigration station at Quebec, had lost some passengers to communicable disease, and thousands of immigrants were backed up on a small island, most sleeping on the open ground. It was later estimated that 70,000 Irish had left for Canada in 1847, of whom nearly one-third died and another third were still in Canadian hospitals at the end of the year.[36] There can be no question that the British authorities badly failed both their own people and their colonies in 1847.

■ In May 1851 the *Illustrated London News* published an article entitled 'The Depopulation of Ireland'. In this illustration, Irish emigrants about to leave their homes are shown receiving 'the priest's blessing'. LAC, C-3904.

The British government's immediate response to the crisis was to introduce new legislation and procedures that, on the whole, were less effective than those they replaced. On the other hand, the British North American provinces imposed draconian restrictions on immigration, and these were considerably more effective, reducing the flow of total immigration to the colonies from 109,000 in 1847 to 31,000 in 1848. The provinces doubled the immigrant tax; required substantial indemnifying bonds from the masters of ships carrying passengers deemed likely to become a public charge; and used the increased revenue to improve quarantine facilities. The British consolidated existing legislation regulating the passage in 1849, and continued to attempt (without much success) to improve conditions. A parliamentary commission reported in 1851 that existing legislation was not enforced, and was inadequate in any case. Its recommen-dation that larger vessels carry stewards to look after the welfare of the passengers was reflected in legislation the following year. Another parliamentary commission in 1854 discovered that although the government's efforts to regulate the passage had steadily increased, the loopholes that allowed abuse to continue had hardly been eliminated. Perhaps the greatest protection for the abusers was the common-law doctrine of the 'free contract'. Another major piece of passenger legislation—105 clauses, taking up nearly 30 pages in the book of statutes—was passed in 1855, and although it was not perfect, it did improve conditions on the passage, especially in tandem with other factors. One such factor was a reduced volume of passengers, which enabled the regulatory bureaucracy to function more successfully. Another was a gradual shift from sail to steam-driven vessels, even for steerage passengers, which shortened the voyage from weeks to

■ Irish emigrants awaiting departure on the quay at Cork, as depicted in the *Illustrated London News*, 10 May 1851. LAC, C-3904.

days, and was probably as important as regulation. The barn door was closed more than a bit tardily, however.

Interestingly, immigration after 1840 tended to mix together people from different places—first on board the vessels, then in the quarantine stations. No longer were whole communities or groups from one region of the British Isles arriving together. This new diversity would contribute to the development of a 'British' nationality in North America, as opposed to distinctive Scottish, Irish, Welsh, and English identities.

IMPERIAL SENTIMENT

At the same time that Great Britain was withdrawing from British North America, the anglophone population of the colonies was becoming more consciously and intensely imperialistic. A number of factors help to explain this paradox. Perhaps the most important was that—outside North America—the British Empire was reaching the height of its glory in the 1850s and 1860s.[37] During the 1850s Britain fought an imperial war with Russia in the Crimea and then crushed a widespread army insurrection (the Sepoy Mutiny) in India, which resulted in the elimination of the East India Company and the takeover of the administration of India by the Crown. Enthusiasm for the Empire was increased in Canada by the continuing arrival of immigrants from the British Isles, and in the Atlantic region by the success of transatlantic trade.

The Empire was also able to take advantage of the popularity of Queen Victoria and the royal family as symbols. The height of imperial enthusiasm in British America was probably reached during the 1860 tour of the Prince of Wales, the

■ Prince's Arches at CNE. City of Toronto Archives/TTC Fonds, Series 71, Item 5795 (Prince of Wales Gate, Exhibition (Executive Department) May 2, 1928.)

THE PRINCE OF WALES BEGINS HIS NORTH AMERICAN TOUR

The *Hero* and *Ariadne* [the Prince was aboard the latter] made it [into St. John's Harbour] about 4-30 on the evening of July 23, [1860] and anchored opposite the city at 7 P.M. They were received by a royal salute from the Citadel, by the ringing of bells, and by the lusty and loyal cheers of the populace of St. John's and the surrounding country, who crowded the wharves and every available spot where they could obtain a good view of the war-vessels. Flags were displayed in profusion, every house appeared decorated and illuminated, and the greatest enthusiasm prevailed among the whole of the inhabitants. In the evening an illumination took place, and which for magnificence was all that could be desired.

Tuesday morning (24th) was ushered in with naught but rain and dark foreboding clouds. By noon, however, everything had become bright and beautiful again, the sun appeared, and shone with increased lustre, adding to the scene of magnificence about to follow. Shortly after the Prince and suite, which was composed of His Grace the Duke of Newcastle, Secretary of State for the Colonies; Earl of St. Germains, Lord Chamberlain; Major General Hon. Robert Bruce, Governor to H.R.H.; Dr. Auckland, Physician to H.R.H.; G. Engleheart, Esq., Secretary to the Duke of Newcastle; Major Teesdale, and Capt. Grey, Equerries in Waiting, landed from the *Hero*. The booming of cannon from the citadel, the *Ariadne*, and the *Flying-Fish* and the cheers from the sailors and populace, proclaimed Albert Edward representative of our Queen. The yards of H.M. ships were manned, and the city and harbour presented a fine appearance, as every house and ship was decorated. Every body turned out in his best to do the Prince honour.

The landing took place on the Queen's Wharf, which was densely crowded with fashionably-dressed ladies, who hailed the Prince 'with their spotless handkerchiefs, and indulged in the warmest expressions of

joy and gladness.' The Prince and suite were received by the Governor, Sir Alexander Bannerman, who led them to carriages. The Masonic body, the St. George's, St. Andrew's, British Mechanics', Coopers', Temperance, Native, and Irish Societies, Phoenix Volunteer Fire Company, a Guard of Honour of the Royal Newfoundland Corps, and of the 1st, 2nd, and 3rd Volunteer Rifle Companies, composed the procession, which passed through many beautiful arches and gorgeous decorations, to the Government House, a fine substantial building.

At three o'clock His Royal Highness held a grand levee, when two hundred persons were presented; also many Addresses, but he replied to the whole, collectively, as follows:

I sincerely thank you for the Addresses presented to me, and for the hearty welcome received from you all on my landing on the shores of this the earliest colonial possession of the British Crown. I trust you will not think me regardless of your zealous loyalty if I acknowledge these Addresses collectively. It will afford me the greatest satisfaction to report to the Queen the devotion to her Crown and person unmistakeably evinced by the reception of her son, and so eloquently expressed in the Addresses from various bodies in this town and Harbor Grace. I am charged by the Queen to convey to you the assurance of the deep concern she has ever felt in this interesting portion of her dominions. I shall carry back a lively recollection of this day's proceedings and of your kindness to myself personally, but above all, of those hearty demonstrations of patriotism which prove your deep-rooted attachment to the great and free country of which we all glory to be called the sons.

He afterwards rode out to view the town, unattended.

A superb dinner and a grand ball were given in his honour during the evening. The ball was given at the Colonial House, which was beautifully decorated with flags, banners, and appropriate devices for the event. Thousands of persons attended, and the Prince danced until half-past one, opening the ball with Lady Brady, and dancing afterwards with Miss Grant, Mrs. Major Bailly, Hon. Miss. Kent, Miss E. Carter, Mrs. Ridley, Miss Mackarrol, Mrs. Young, Miss Robertson, Mrs. E.D. Shea, Miss C. Jarvis, and Miss. Tobin. The following is the list of dances:

1. Quadrille. 8. Lancers. 15. Varsovienne.
2. Quadrille. 9. Mazourka. 16. Schottische.
3. Waltz. 10. Waltz. 17. Quadrille.
4. Polka. 11. Quadrille. 18. Polka.
5. Quadrille. 12. Polka. 19. Galop.
6. Schottische. 13. Waltz and Galop. 20. Contra Dance.
7. Galop. 14. Lancers.

His Royal Highness remained in the room until three o'clock next morning. He seems to have pleased all parties (wherever he has visited), not only by his good looks, but by his affableness, unostentatious bearing, and good humour. The Duke of Newcastle and Earl of St. Germains, as on subsequent occasions, did not mingle in the festivities of the dance. They, as well as His Royal Highness, and the rest of the suite, were dressed in full uniform.

During the day, a magnificent Newfoundland dog was presented by the Newfoundlanders to His Royal Highness, together with a collar of massive silver, and a steel chain. The collar is beautifully wrought in silver, with the Prince's crest and motto, &c., and bears the following inscription:

'Presented to His Royal Highness, the Prince of Wales, from the inhabitants of Newfoundland.'

The name given the dog by the Prince is 'Cabot,' after the celebrated Sebastian Cabot, the discoverer of the Island, and, if tradition is to be credited, the continent of North America before Columbus had visited any part of the main land.

On Wednesday the 25th, the Royal party attended the Regatta, on the Lake Quidi Vidi near the city, and appeared to be well pleased with the entertainment.

At ten o'clock on the morning of the 26th, the Prince and suite took their departure from Newfoundland, riding on horseback to the wharf. The same procession escorted him away that welcomed him; but, on this occasion, they wore very different faces from those when he landed: then all was joy; now all was regret at losing him so soon. The streets were decorated as before, the bells rang forth a right merry peal, cannons roared, and the cheers of the multitude rang forth, far and near, as on his arrival. Every place was crowded; every one appeared in his best. The soldiers lined the wharf and streets, and the National Societies appeared in the procession in full regalia.

Every ship in harbour also did honour by displaying its bunting to the best advantage.

SOURCE: Henry J. Morgan, *The tour of H.R.H. the Prince of Wales through British America and the United States* (1860), 23-8.

18-year-old son of Queen Victoria, known affectionately as 'Bertie'. The royal tour—described as 'one grand state procession from Halifax to Hamilton'[38]—was the most important collective event in British North America before Confederation. Cheering crowds were to be found everywhere along the Prince's route, although in Canada West the tour organizers had trouble with the Orange Order, which tried to appropriate the Prince for its own sectarian purposes.

Even in French Canada, where the Catholic hierarchy expressed some complaints about the royal presence, a circular building was specially built, at considerable cost, for two great balls, one attended by 4,000 people and the other by 7,000. At every ball given in his honour, the future Edward VII danced the evening away. All observers were struck by the public's effusions of loyalty. One noted 'the extraordinary feeling of devotion and attachment to the Queen', and, according to an American reporter, the 'one sentiment distinguishing the people with respect to their royal visitor . . . was of admiration for the man, and loyalty to the throne'.[39] From this period date the etched and framed portraits of Queen Victoria that graced many houses in anglophone British North America.

CONCLUSION

British North America moved ambiguously away from its dependence on the British Empire after 1840. Some regions, such as the Maritime provinces, remained more consciously connected than others. Nevertheless, colonial developments in the West, the presence of British warships in the ports and British garrisons across the continent, the continuing influx of British immigrants, the royal tour of 1860—all served to remind residents of the colonies that the Empire remained an integral part of their lives, and that they were indeed British Americans.

SHORT BIBLIOGRAPHY

Cell, John W. *British Colonial Administration in the Mid-Nineteenth Century: The Policy-Making Process*. New Haven, 1970. Now the standard study.

Cowan, Helen I. *British Emigration to British North America: The First Hundred Years*, rev. edn Toronto, 1961. Old but still the best overview.

Edelstein, Michael. *Overseas Investment in the Age of High Imperialism: The United Kingdom, 1850–1914*. New York, 1982. A recent analysis.

Galbraith, John S. *The Hudson's Bay Company as an Imperial Factor*. Toronto, 1957. The classic statement of the imperial importance of the Hudson's Bay Company.

Knaplund, Paul, ed. *Letters from Lord Sydenham, Governor-General of Canada, 1839–1841, to Lord John Russell*. London, 1931. An interesting edition of correspondence.

Lucas, Sir Charles, ed. *Lord Durham's Report on the Affairs of British North America*, 3 vols. Oxford, 1912, repr. New York, 1970. The classic edition of the classic report.

MacDonagh, Oliver. *A Pattern of Government Growth 1800–1860: The Passenger Acts and Their Enforcement*. London, 1961. The most thorough study of the problem of regulating emigration.

Radforth, Ian Walter. *Royal Spectacle: The 1860 Visit of the Prince of Wales to Canada and the United States*. Toronto, 2004. A detailed investigation of the tour and its importance.

Semmel, Bernard. *The Rise of Free Trade Imperialism: Classical Political Economy, the Empire of Free Trade, and Imperialism, 1750–1850*. Cambridge, UK, 1970. A stimulating interpretation of the political economy of free trade.

Stacey, C.P. *Canada and the British Army 1846–1871*, rev. edn. Toronto, 1963. Still the standard account of its subject.

Stembridge, Stanley R. *Parliament, the Press, and the Colonies, 1846–1880*. New York, 1982. A useful analysis of British public opinion on colonial matters and the Empire.

STUDY QUESTIONS

1. What were the characteristics of the new economic order in British North America after 1840?

2. Why did the British turn to free trade?

3. How did Canadians react to the end of imperial protection?

4. What drove the economy of the Atlantic provinces in the years 1840–60?

5. In what ways did the British Empire remain involved in British North America after 1840?

6. What reason did the parliamentary committee of 1857 give for renewing the Hudson's Bay Company charter?

CHAPTER NINETEEN

Reorientation: British North America and the Continent after 1840

When the British had dismantled the mercantile system, their North American colonists naturally turned towards the United States, which at the time was more interested in settling its border with the British than in improving commerce. The resolution of the boundary issue was a major achievement of the early 1840s, and it would make possible closer relations between British North America and the United States in the years that followed. To everyone's surprise, however, neither the American government nor the American public responded very strongly to the outbursts of enthusiasm for annexation to the US coming from British North America in 1849 and 1850. In truth, the sectional divisions south of the border, which were again coming to the fore, made it difficult to attract support for the addition of new anti-slavery territory. Nonetheless, the 1840s had marked the beginning of a new set of relationships between British North America and the United States in one of the most important periods in Canadian–American relations.[1]

New attitudes took two forms in British North America in the 1850s, both directing the colonies' attention towards the continent and internal markets. One was an increasing interest in reciprocal trade with the US, which would lead to a Reciprocity Treaty in 1854. This treaty probably worked to the advantage of British

America, and was abrogated by the United States as soon as possible. The other was a westward thrust expressed not only in the construction of railways into the interior of the continent, but in a growing Canadian interest in the settlement potential of the vast prairie territory owned by the Hudson's Bay Company. The secession of the slave states in 1861 put annexation back on the American agenda, but in a new guise.

THE US BOUNDARY

In the nineteenth century, boundaries were among the most contentious issues between Great Britain and the United States. As the people whose territory was at stake, British North Americans were understandably concerned over the activities of Britain's diplomats, who seemed quite prepared to sacrifice colonial interests to a larger entente with the Americans. Nevertheless, the Anglo–American entente of the 1840s and 1850s settled the larger boundary questions, not necessarily in British America's favour.

THE WEBSTER–ASHBURTON TREATY

Although the Convention of 1818 had settled on the 49th parallel as the boundary in the region between Lake Superior and the Rocky Moun-

TIMELINE

1818
Convention of 1818 establishes boundary line to Rocky Mountains at 49th parallel.

1823
49th parallel surveyed at Pembina.

1830
Contentious boundary in New Brunswick/Lower Canada/Maine submitted to arbitration.

1838
Aroostook War on Maine-New Brunswick border.

1842
Webster-Ashburton Treaty resolves eastern boundary dispute.

1844
James K. Polk campaigns for US presidency with slogan '54-40 or Fight'.

1846
Oregon Boundary Treaty.

1849
Demands for annexation to US increase in Province of Canada.

1850
Fugitive Slave Law passed in US. Keefer's *The Philosophy of Railroads* published.

1851
Frederick Wilkins (Shadrach Minkins) escapes to Canada.

1852
Grand Trunk Railway incorporated.

1854
Great Western Railway opens. Reciprocity Treaty negotiated between Great Britain and US. Seigneurial system ended in Lower Canada.

1857
Survey of 49th parallel begins in Rocky Mountains.

1859
Americans occupy San Juan Island.

1860
Anderson extradition case heard in Canada.

1861
American Civil War begins.

---

tains, it left unresolved both the northeastern and far western borders.[2] Under the Treaty of Ghent (which ended the War of 1812) the New Brunswick–Lower Canada–Maine boundary was to be resolved through international arbitration. A large part of the problem was that the 1783 Treaty of Paris had drawn lines that did not match the geography of the region. Over time, the British became more assertive about their claims, and even expanded them. Neither side really felt comfortable with arbitration, however. The Americans' reluctance to submit to arbitration—which the British interpreted as a sign of the weakness of their position—was actually based on the conviction that no European party could understand the complexity of the issues. But the parties were no happier about the thought of trying to negotiate a compromise. In

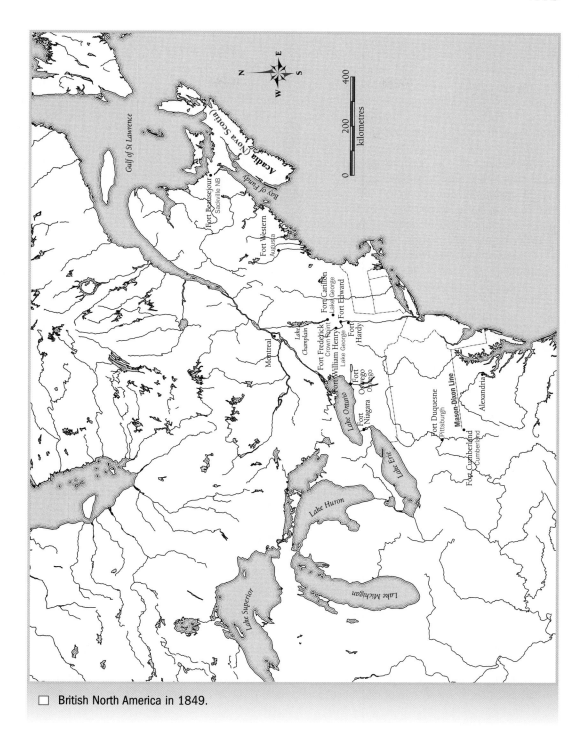

□ British North America in 1849.

early 1830 the boundary dispute was submitted to the King of the Netherlands, who decided that the protocols agreed to in advance by the disputants were 'inexplicable and impractical' and simply drew a line giving about two-thirds of the territory to the Americans. The American government did not accept this decision.

In the 1830s increasing friction developed in the Aroostook Valley over timbering rights; both sides rattled their sabres but they agreed to negotiate to avoid war. The desire of both parties to resolve matters was demonstrated by the fact that each side suppressed its official maps (which showed the area in question as belonging to the other party) in order to avoid public outcry over a compromise decision. The final arrangement, negotiated by Daniel Webster and Lord Ashburton in 1842, was—as Lord Ashburton wrote at the time—'a good and wise measure, and good and wise because it was fair'. Historians have generally

maintained that the most important aspect of the treaty was simply the fact that the two nations agreed to negotiate—and to compromise—despite the militancy of public opinion on both sides of the border. That compromise awarded a good deal of northern territory to the state of Maine, and would later force British American railway developers to build around American territory; the line would have been shorter had the land remained within New Brunswick.

THE OREGON BOUNDARY

The boundary problem was even more intense west of the Rocky Mountains, where the two nations had agreed in 1818 to share occupation until there was need for a formal decision. Many Americans had already settled in the Oregon Territory south of the Columbia River, and presidential candidate James K. Polk in 1844 had rat-

THE OREGON TREATY, 1846

Treaty With Great Britain In Regard To Limits Westward of the Rocky Mountains.

The United States of America and her Majesty the Queen of the United Kingdom of Great Britain and Ireland, deeming it to be desirable for the future welfare of both countries that the state of doubt and uncertainty which has hitherto prevailed respecting the sovereignty and government of the territory on the northwest coast of America, lying westward of the Rocky or Stony Mountains, should be finally terminated by an amicable compromise of the rights mutually asserted by the two parties over the said territory, have respectively named plenipotentiaries to treat and agree concerning the terms of such settlement—that is to say: the President of the United States of America has, on his part, furnished with full powers James Buchanan, Secretary of State of the United States,

and her Majesty the Queen of the United Kingdom of Great Britain and Ireland has, on her part, appointed the Right Honorable Richard Pakenham, a member of her Majesty's Most Honorable Privy Council, and her Majesty's Envoy Extraordinary and Minister Plenipotentiary to the United States; who, after having communicated to each other their respective full powers, found in good and due form, have agreed upon and concluded the following articles: —

Article I.

From the point on the forty-ninth parallel of north latitude, where the boundary laid down in existing treaties and conventions between the United States and Great Britain terminates, the line of boundary between the territories of the United States and those of her Britannic Majesty shall be continued westward along the said forty-ninth parallel of north latitude to the middle of the channel which separates the continent from Vancouver's Island, and thence southerly through the middle of the said channel, and of Fuca's Straits, to the Pacific Ocean: *Provided, however,* That the navigation of the whole of the said channel and straits, south of the forty-ninth parallel of north latitude, remain free and open to both parties.

Article II.

From the point at which the forty-ninth parallel of north latitude shall be found to intersect the great northern branch of the Columbia River, the navigation of the said branch shall be free and open to the Hudson's Bay Company, and to all British subjects trading with the same, to the point where the said branch meets the main stream of the Columbia, and thence down the said main stream to the ocean, with free access into and through the said river or rivers, it being understood that all the usual portages along the line thus described shall, in like manner, be free and open. In navigating the said river or rivers, British subjects, with their goods and produce, shall be treated on the same footing as citizens of the United States; it being, however, always understood that nothing in this article shall be construed as preventing, or intended to prevent, the government of the United States from making any regulations respecting the navigation of the said river or rivers not inconsistent with the present treaty.

Article III.

In the future appropriation of the territory south of the forty-ninth parallel of north latitude, as provided in the first article of this treaty, the possessory rights of the Hudson's Bay Company, and of all British subjects who may be already in the occupation of land or other property lawfully acquired within the said territory, shall be respected.

Article IV.

The farms, lands, and other property of every description, belonging to the Puget's Sound Agricultural Company, on the north side of the Columbia River, shall be confirmed to the said company. In case, however, the situation of those farms and lands should be considered by the United States to be of public and political importance, and the United States government should signify a desire to obtain possession of the whole, or of any part thereof, the property so required shall be transferred to the said government, at a proper valuation, to be agreed upon between the parties.

Article V.

The present treaty shall be ratified by the President of the United States, by and with the advice and consent of the Senate thereof, and by her Britannic Majesty; and the ratifications shall he exchanged at London, at the expiration of six months from the date hereof, or sooner, if possible.

In witness whereof, the respective Plenipotentiaries have signed the same, and have affixed thereto the seals of their arms.

Done at Washington, the fifteenth day of June, in the year of our Lord one thousand eight hundred and forty-six.

(signed by)

JAMES BUCHANAN

RICHARD PAKENHAM

tled American sabres with his campaign slogan of '54–40 or Fight', a reference to the latitude in degrees and minutes of the southernmost Russian boundary on the Pacific slope. American administrations of the 1840s were quite aggressive over continental expansion—the Polk government would go to war with Mexico in 1846 in the aftermath of the 1845 annexation of Texas—and the British were prepared to come to terms. Again a 'compromise' was reached, this one less even-handed than in the east.

Under the Oregon Boundary Treaty of 1846 the border across the Rockies to the Pacific was continued from the Great Lakes at the 49th parallel to the Pacific (exclusive of Vancouver Island). In return for conceding a dip in the boundary from the mainland to the southern tip of Vancouver Island, the Americans were given what was to become the State of Washington—a region previously occupied by the Hudson's Bay Company, in which there were virtually no American nationals. The forty-ninth parallel artificially bisected the Pacific slope, where mountain ranges and river valleys ran north and south rather than east and west. But apart from a few perfunctory protests from the HBC, British North Americans appear to have accepted this result without much outcry.

FUGITIVE SLAVES

Despite the diplomats' eagerness to avoid tensions, some frictions continued between the United States and British North America. Many were connected with the Underground Railroad that assisted fugitive slaves to escape to free American territory or to Canada, where courts normally held them to be emancipated.[3] The system was probably more significant for its symbolic value than for the actual number of slaves smuggled to freedom, but 'conductors' like Harriet Tubman became internationally famous and had substantial prices on their heads.

In 1850 the US Congress had passed the Fugitive Slave Law (see Chapter 15). In May of that year, a man named Frederick Wilkins escaped from his master in Norfolk, Virginia, and headed for Boston. The master learned of his former slave's whereabouts, and sent a 'slave catcher' to Boston to bring him home. The 'slave catcher' obtained a Boston warrant, had Wilkins arrested, and took him before a federal commissioner. A large group of blacks intervened, freeing him and removing him from the courtroom. Six days later, on 20 February 1851, Wilkins reached Montreal via the recently opened Vermont Central Railroad. He had crossed open ice twice, once for a distance of nine miles. In Montreal the former slave received a warm welcome from the community, renamed himself Shadrach Minkins, and was soon working as a barber. A later visitor reported that Minkins 'feels what he never felt previous to his residence in Canada, that he owns himself, and is perfectly safe from the impious clutch of the manhunter.'[4] In 1860 the extradition trial of another fugitive became the focus of international attention. In 1854 a slave called Jack Burrows had killed a man who tried to prevent his escape. He changed his name to John Anderson, but in 1860 he was arrested in Brantford, Canada West.[5] He was released on a technicality on the eve of the Civil War.

THE SAN JUAN ISLANDS

The United States and Britain had agreed in the Oregon Treaty of 1846 that, on the Pacific coast, the boundary would run through the 'channel which separates the continent from Vancouver's Island'. But disagreement emerged over the course of that channel. At stake was ownership of the various San Juan Islands (known in Canada as the Gulf Islands), and especially San Juan Island itself, which was militarily occupied by the United States in 1859 on the familiar grounds that American settlers needed protection. When the governor of British Columbia responded by dispatching a ship of war, the Americans would not allow the marines to land. The United States government was eager to avoid direct conflict,

HARRIET TUBMAN
(C. 1820–1913)

Harriet Tubman was born Araminta Ross, to slave parents on a Maryland plantation. As a child she worked in the fields and was subject to many abuses. On one occasion she was struck in the head by an object thrown by an overseer, and thereafter was subject to seizures. She took her mother's Christian name, Harriet, at an early age, and around 1844 married a freedman named John Tubman. In 1849 she escaped from the plantation and moved, without her husband, to Philadelphia, where she worked as a cook and began working with the Underground Railroad to liberate other slaves. She started with members of her own family. Although she was both illiterate and physically handicapped, Tubman never let these obstacles interfere with her activities. Indeed, they may well have provided cover for her many clandestine activities: who could be suspicious of such a person? In 1851, after the passage of the Fugitive Slave Act, Harriet moved to St Catharines, Canada West, but made a number of journeys back into the United States to lead fugitive slaves to freedom. In this period slaveholders were offering a reward of $40,000 for her capture, dead or alive.

In 1858 Tubman opened a boarding house in St Catharines, where the abolitionist zealot John Brown visited. In a letter to his wife, Brown described Tubman as 'the most of a man, naturally, that I ever met with'. Having rescued her own parents from Maryland, she settled them in a house at Auburn, New York, which she bought with the financial assistance of sympathizers, notably William Seward (later Lincoln's secretary of state). Although Tubman soon began using the Auburn house as a permanent residence, she

■ Harriet Tubman c. 1880. Library of Congress.

kept up her contacts in Canada and received financial assistance from there for many years. During the American Civil War she acted for the Union army in a number of capacities, including that of spy, but the American Congress refused to give her a pension. After the war she returned to Auburn, where she spent the rest of her long life. Tubman became a mythical figure in the black community from a relatively early period, especially after a biography was published in 1869; written by Sarah Elizabeth Hopkins Bradford, *Harriet Tubman: The Moses of Her People* describes her exploits in considerable detail, although they are essentially undocumentable.

■ Sappers of the Royal Engineers building a boundary mound, 1873. Glenbow Museum, NA-218-1.

but the acting secretary of war made clear that he would 'not suffer the national honor to be tarnished'. Although the two powers subsequently agreed to joint military occupation, the dispute was not finally settled until 1871.[6]

MAPPING THE BOUNDARY

Agreeing on a boundary line was not the same thing as physically establishing it.[7] On the prairies, for instance, an American surveying expedition in 1823 claimed to have determined by detailed astronomical observation the point on the Red River located at the 49th parallel. An oak post marked the spot, with 'G.B.' carved on the north side and 'U.S.' on the south. Even if it was accurate, however, one marker was hardly enough. Two years later, a surveyor acting under the Treaty of 1814 discovered that the 'most northwestern point of the Lake of the Woods',

which was supposed to mark the beginning of the boundary line, was under water and could not be precisely marked. Subsequent visits by both American and British surveyors to the Red River in the 1850s produced results differing by almost a mile. This was not much of a problem before Confederation, but it would become more serious later.

As for the west coast, the border line agreed to in the Oregon Treaty traversed some of the most difficult terrain in North America. The United States Topographical Engineers began its survey in 1857, and the Royal Artillery and Royal Engineers joined them a year later. The topography made it necessary to take occasional fixes at accessible points. Wide paths were hewed through the forests so that each point could be observed from the next. On one stretch between the Similkameen and Kettle rivers, there was so much local variation that it was agreed to adopt a mean parallel. The parties worked separately, and had great difficulty gaining access to much of the territory. Their relations with each other were cordial, but not particularly co-operative. There was some disagreement over the frequency of boundary markers, the Americans refusing to accept iron markers a mile apart because of the expense. The Americans would also refuse any deviation from the fixed parallel, thus isolating several bits of British territory accessible only through the United States. Correlating the findings of the two commissions would take until 1869, and the final survey of the boundary would not be completed until the 1870s.

THE ANNEXATION MOVEMENT

In 1849, in a fit of frustration, four of the leading English-language newspapers of Montreal, speaking for the mercantile community of Canada East, editorially supported annexation to the United States. The demand for annexation followed intense political debate over compensation for Lower Canadians who had lost property in 1837. The anglophone press viewed the Rebellion Losses Bill of 1849 with contempt, calling it 'the famous outrage, the damning insult to the loyal people of Canada, the Bill by which traitors, rebels, and murderers, are to be indemnified for supposed losses incurred by them in consequence of their crimes.'[8] Mass meetings in Montreal to protest the passage of the legislation led to a mob attack on the Parliament buildings, in the course of which they were set on fire and burned to the ground. Supporting annexation was another way of protesting against the current state of affairs, and while it may have seemed ironic that those who had so often proclaimed their loyalty to the Empire were now taking another tack, there was a certain logic to their argument.

As one annexationist manifesto explained:

The truth is, that between the abandonment by England of her former system of protection to Colonial produce, and the refusal of the United

The way Brother Jonathan will astonish the Natives.

ANNEXATION COMES IN BY THE RAIL, WHILE LIBERTY FLIES OFF IN THE SMOKE.

■ 'The Annexation Engine', from *Punch in Canada*, 1849. 'Brother Jonathan' was a term used by the British for the United States. This cartoon suggested that annexation would put an end to the privileges that French Canadians enjoyed under British rule. LAC, C-022325.

States to trade with us on a footing of reciprocity, Canada, to use the old proverb, is between the devil and the deep sea, and we must own—it may be perhaps from our terrible blindness—that we can see no way to get out of the scrape, but by going to prosperity, since prosperity will not come to us.[9]

The arguments will be familiar to most Canadians. 'What matter is it', asked one newspaper, 'whether you number yourself among the millions of Anglo-Saxons that obey our gentle Queen Victoria, or among those other millions who have delegated the supreme administration of their affairs for four years to plain old [US president] Zachary Taylor?'[10] The cause was occasionally taken up outside Montreal. The Toronto *Examiner*, for example, allowed that, 'However strongly many may cleave to British Connexion as a matter of choice, all agree that the great interests of the country must be sustained even at the sacrifice of such a connexion.'[11] The wide circulation of such views merely confirmed the opinion of those in Britain opposed to a political empire that ungrateful colonials would always leave the mother country at the first hint that their demands might be denied.

RECIPROCITY

Annexationism was far less widespread than the reciprocity movement, which flourished in the economic and commercial uncertainties of the late 1840s. Reciprocity became less popular as the depression that had accompanied the British shift towards free trade came to an end in 1851. Many British North Americans saw annexation less as a desirable end in itself than as the inevitable result of failure to achieve reciprocity. Canadians, especially those dependent on the wheat economy, viewed internal markets— among which they initially counted the United States—as the only alternative to the British markets that had been lost with the repeal of the Corn Laws. The leading Canadian spokesman for reciprocity, William Hamilton Merritt of St Catharines, argued the case in the Canadian parliament as early as 1846: 'Were our products admitted into their markets . . . the Canadian farmer would at all times be placed on an equal footing, in all respects with the western farmer . . . he would realize the advantages he possessed and resist any political change.'[12] In New Brunswick, where the timber industry was reeling from the ending of imperial preference in

1846, it was argued that reciprocity would allow colonial shipbuilders access to the American market and provide an outlet for the province's timber. Both Nova Scotia and Prince Edward Island were also enthusiastic, demanding that they be 'included in any measure of reciprocity that may be obtained for Canada.'[13] Only Newfoundland initially remained aloof, on the grounds that 'no advantage, to be derived from a reciprocal free trade with the United States of America, would compensate for the concession to the citizens of that Republic of a participation in the Fisheries of this Colony.'[14] But even Newfoundland would ultimately have its moments of enthusiasm.

In the United States, Israel D. Andrews published in 1851 the first of several reports favouring reciprocal free trade in natural products, stating that 'this measure recommends itself strongly to American interests and magnanimity.' Andrews saw the two countries as economically complementary, and maintained that a product controlled by an international market could not be protected by domestic duties. Thus Canadian wheat was no threat to American prices. Andrews was very bullish about the prospects of British North America as a market for American finished goods.[15]

When economic prosperity returned to British North America in the 1850s, reciprocity, like annexation, lost much of its support. But some kept the scheme alive, and the various colonial governments, especially the Province of Canada, began looking for ways of pressuring the Americans. In 1852 Newfoundland's assembly suddenly awoke to the possibility of being left out of a treaty. It insisted on inclusion at the same time that other provinces were having second thoughts, mainly over fishing concessions that the Americans considered an essential part of any trade negotiation. Although the British government generally supported reciprocal arrangements between British North America and the United States—partly on the grounds that any freeing of trade was a good thing, partly to encourage continuing Anglo–American entente, but mainly to please unruly colonials—the American government showed almost no interest in the matter until 1852, when the British government decided to toughen its fisheries policy. What little American political opinion existed concerning reciprocity was supportive, although for contradictory reasons. In the northern states reciprocity was seen as the first step towards the ultimate annexation of the British colonies. As an editorial in Horace Greeley's New York *Tribune* declared: 'Expansion in the direction of the north star—expansion for the purpose of union with more than two millions of liberty-loving slavery-hating people . . . is not a prospect to cry out against at the present moment.'[16] On the other hand, the southern states saw reciprocity as the only way to prevent annexation, which would seriously upset the delicate political balance between the states of the North and the South.

The Reciprocity Treaty as it was ultimately negotiated in 1854 by Lord Elgin, special envoy to the United States, was not a very broad-ranging free-trade agreement. It removed tariff and other barriers on a variety of enumerated goods, mainly raw materials common to both countries, such as grain, meat, flour, livestock, coal, fish, and fish oil. These had previously been the principal items both of export to the Americans and of import from them. The treaty did not remove barriers on finished goods ('dutiable items', as they were called), although the Americans hoped that the increased prosperity of British North America under the treaty would lead to greater imports. But the volume of trade in dutiable items did not increase, and several provinces (including Canada) increased duties, ostensibly for revenue purposes, during the life of the treaty. What the treaty did was open markets for raw materials in both directions, as well as make possible several re-export commodity trades abroad, such as the shipment of American wheat through Canadian ports. The result, of course, was much more beneficial to British North America than to the United States, which

explains why the Americans were so anxious to abrogate the treaty when its initial 10-year term expired. But it does not appear to have increased trade very much in either direction. British North America did not aggressively market its raw materials and agricultural produce in the United States, even during the Civil War years when prices and demand were high. In particular, the 'lower provinces' (the Atlantic provinces) failed to increase their exports to New England significantly. Nevertheless, impressive advantages did emerge in some aspects of trade for some regions and some commodities.

BRITISH NORTH AMERICA UNDER RECIPROCITY

Although the Reciprocity Treaty produced few important changes in the patterns of north–south trade, statistics are not the only way to measure impact. Psychologically, the arrangement was far more critical for British North America than for the United States. It encouraged merchants, entrepreneurs, and politicians—especially in the Province of Canada—to continue the process of rethinking their economic orientation: from an imperial context in which the British market was crucial to a continental context in which American and Canadian markets mattered most. Once turned from the traditional transatlantic economy to a continental one, Canada began to emphasize industrialization and the need to develop its own internal markets. Indeed, one of the principal reasons why American trade in dutiable items did not expand during the 10 years of the agreement was that the manufacturing capacity of British North America—again, particularly in the Province of Canada—grew substantially in this period. But the process of economic reorientation was not uniform across British North America. As we have seen, the period from 1840 to the early 1870s was the 'Golden Age of Sail', and the Atlantic provinces continued to prosper as part of the older transatlantic economy.

THE FISHERIES

From the American perspective, one of the key attractions of reciprocity was the chance to gain access to the inshore fishery of the Atlantic region. The British government had begun in the early 1850s to respond to complaints from the Maritime provinces about American competition in the fishery by enforcing a three-mile offshore limit against American fishermen.[17] The chief fish involved were not cod, but mackerel and herring. If nothing else, this offshore limit provided a quid pro quo for negotiation, although one that seemed to sacrifice the interests of the fishermen, especially the Nova Scotians. On the other hand, admitting the Americans was not an unqualified economic disaster. On Prince Edward Island, for example, the new regulations allowed the Americans to go ashore to dry their fish, giving the islanders an opportunity to make money supplying them with foodstuffs and other commodities. The American presence also provided capital for the growth of a native fishing industry. Both the numbers of islanders involved in the fishery and the value of their fish exports increased substantially after the Reciprocity Treaty.[18]

AGRICULTURE

While agriculture continued to fuel much of the economic vitality of British North America, particularly in central Canada, the period after 1850 saw several significant and related shifts in agricultural development. First, by 1850 Canada West had joined Canada East in reaching the limits of profitable wheat cultivation. Second, the commercial reorientation from international to internal markets, accompanied by great improvements in internal transportation through canals and railroads in the 1850s, permitted agriculture in Canada West to shift out of the grain monoculture and into mixed farming. The new produce from mixed farming, particularly in the dairy area (for example, butter and cheese), often found markets in Britain.

In 1854, the seigneurial system in the St Lawrence Valley was brought to an end by legislative fiat; traditional seigneurial obligations were replaced by a quitrent, and tenants were given the opportunity to purchase the lands they worked. As the old system was gradually eliminated, it became increasingly clear that agriculture would have to modernize if it was to meet the new market demands. As agriculture was transformed, the percentage of the total population of central Canada that depended on it decreased, from about 66 per cent in 1850 to less than 60 per cent by 1870.

The greatly expanding population of British North America throughout the mid-nineteenth century, combined with distinctly limited amounts of really productive agricultural land, meant that the opportunities for farm ownership quickly declined in most parts of the provinces. People in Canada became quite receptive to thoughts of westward expansion, particularly into the territory administered by the Hudson's Bay Company (see Chapter 20). Another result was a substantial out-migration to the United States (Chapter 22), beginning in Canada East in the 1840s and in the Atlantic region in the 1850s. This development would eventually put substantial pressure on the economies of the various provinces to find employment for intending migrants so that they could stay at home. By 1860, when the pressure was most keenly felt in Canada East, the problem had not yet hit the Atlantic region, which still thought of itself as dynamic and prosperous because of its international commercial success in shipbuilding.

CANADA AND THE RAILWAY MANIA OF THE 1850S

Unlike the Maritimes, the Province of Canada was becoming increasingly focused on the internal market, and improvements in overland transportation were essential to its development. Canals had proved inadequate to achieve the necessary integration, since they had to be tied to existing waterways. The new technology of the steam engine riding on rails, first developed in Britain in the 1820s and in the United States in the 1830s, was ideally suited to Canadian needs.[19]

Canadian railway expansion would not get underway in earnest until after 1850, by which time the old imperial system had already been demolished. The thrust for internal improvement was influenced by imperial reorientation; overseas linkages were not so important. British North Americans had recognized the potential advantages of railways since the 1820s, but had managed to construct only several short lines in the early years of the railway era. The Champlain and St Lawrence Railroad Company opened a line around the Richelieu Rapids in 1836, employing an imported steam engine and wooden rails. A railway around Niagara Falls was built in 1839, but with grades too steep for primitive locomotives. Several lines in Nova Scotia carried coal short distances. More ambitious projects were often discussed, one from Saint John to Quebec as early as 1827. The 1830s territorial disputes on the Maine–New Brunswick border prevented construction of a railroad from Saint Andrew's, New Brunswick, to Lower Canada, despite approval from the assemblies of both provinces and British financial support for a survey (the land surveyed went to Maine in 1842). A number of charters were granted in Upper Canada, but no construction was actually begun. By 1850, only 60 miles (100 km) of track were in operation in Canada. The obstacles were not technological, but financial and psychological. Railroads were expensive capital investments, few routes in British North America promised to be immediately profitable, and finding investors was no easy business—at least until the railway boom of the 1850s.

The most advanced thinking on railroads in Canada was expressed in a pamphlet by the civil engineer Thomas Coltrin Keefer, titled *The Philosophy of Railroads* (1850). Keefer was a St Catharines boy, educated at Upper Canada College in Toronto. He had apprenticed on the Erie Canal and worked on the Welland, but was basically unemployed in 1849 when he wrote a prize-winning paper that was published as *The Canals of Canada* (1850). This visionary pamphlet saw the St Lawrence waterway as the best outlet for the western interior, and proposed both free trade in agricultural products and a moderate tariff on manufactured goods to encourage industrialization. In *The Philosophy of Railroads*, written on behalf of the Montreal and Lachine Railroad, Keefer argued strenuously for the developmental advantages of rail. A born promoter, he described railroad stocks as ideal investments: 'if universal ruin be inevitable, they will be the last public works to succumb to the general prostration.'[20] He imagined railroads— those 'iron civilizers'—converting sleepy agricultural villages into manufacturing centres and bringing their inhabitants into the modern world. With reference to the St Lawrence and Atlantic Railway, he emphasized its importance to Montreal, 'inasmuch as it will pass for upwards of 100 miles through an agricultural country naturally depending upon Montreal for its supplies', and added: 'As an outlet . . . for the agricultural productions of the districts through which it passes, and as a means of supplying the city with firewood, vegetables, fruits and articles which without a Railway would not reach the market, (and as a means of promoting manufactures) it will be successful beyond a doubt.'[21] Although he put much of the emphasis on getting raw materials out of the interior, Keefer clearly recognized the railway's importance in supplying markets with manufactured goods.

In the 1850s a mania for internal development captured the imaginations of Canadian politicians and investors, who were encouraged by promises of the ultimate profits to be brought about by railroad construction. Keefer acknowledged that Canada was short on capital, but failed to add that railroads were extremely expensive to build, especially if the British practice of solid construction was followed (rather than the American one of building cheap and upgrading

THOMAS KEEFER
ON TECHNOLOGY

In 1854 the Canadian engineer Thomas Keefer lectured in Montreal on the future of the city. Here is the peroration to his address.

One great civilizing engine the Romans understood and employed—perfect roads. Constructed to convey the mail clad cohorts, the relentless Eagles, and the swift vengeance of the Roman Senate into revolting provinces, these noble roads were in the providence of God made the efficient and indeed the indispensable means of waging a spiritual warfare, and bore with jealous care the swift footed messenger of the Gospel of peace beyond the lofty Alps and the far distant Pyrenees. And may not we be entering upon those latter times, when many shall run to and fro and knowledge shall increase? And may not the vast, the almost incredible extension of the Railway system, the Electric Telegraph, and the Ocean Steamer over all the Christian Earth, be a forerunner—a necessary and an indispensable forerunner—to that second great moral revolution, the Millennium—'When the sword shall be beaten into a ploughshare and the spear into a pruning hood;—when nation shall not rise up against nation, neither shall there be war any more.' It may be a heresy—but is there not reason for a belief that the regeneration of the dark corners of the earth is to be accomplished, not through the pulpit alone, nor by sectarian schools—not yet the philosophy of cheap literature nor by miracles—but by a practical elevation of the people, to be brought about by a rapid development of Commerce and the Arts. Ignorance and prejudice will flee before advancing prosperity.

Wherever a railway breaks in upon the gloom of a depressed and secluded district, new life and vigour are infused into the native torpor—the long desired market is obtained—labour now reaps her own reward—the hitherto useless waterfall now turns the labouring wheel, now drives the merrier spindle, the cold and hungry are now clothed and nourished; and thus are made susceptible converts to a system the value of which they are not slow to appreciate. . . . Let then the bigot, the theorist, and the agitator ply their unprofitable trade—let them lay the flattering unction to their souls that they alone are engaged in the high and holy cause of moral elevation. Let them commiserate the apparently low aims, the ceaseless toil and drudgery of the practical mechanic;—but know for a certainty that bigotry and intolerance, agitation, and the highest order of speculative philosophy have existed in the midst of starving and uneducated masses;—that it is the Steamboat and the Railroad which has peopled the recent wilderness of the North West—and by granting facility of access and by securing a reward to labor, have diffused a degree of comfort and prosperity, unprecedented in history. Every new manufacture, every new machine, every mile of railway built is not only of more practical benefit, but is a more efficient civilizer, a more speedy and certain reformer, than years of declamation, agitation or moral legislation.

SOURCE: Thomas Coltrin Keefer, *'Montreal' and 'The Ottawa': Two lectures delivered before the Mechanics' Institute of Montreal, in January 1853 and 1854* (Montreal: J. Lovell, 1854), 30–1.

only as traffic permitted). The Canadian climate rendered the American practice highly dangerous, of course. British North America opted for

the British model, and the Great Western Railway, which opened in January 1854 between Niagara Falls–Hamilton–London–Windsor, cost $66,000 per mile; the Grand Trunk Railway, incorporated in 1852 to build a railway from Toronto to Montreal (later extended), cost $63,800 per mile. In the years 1852 to 1856, railway investment cost each person in Canada West $10 per year. By 1867 the total cost to Canada of 2,188.25 miles of track was $145,794,853, or roughly $66,000 per mile. From 1851 to 1860 three American states near Ontario—Ohio, Michigan, and Indiana—had built their lines for $35,000 per mile (about $4 per person per year).[22] In order to pay for construction, money had to be raised on the British exchanges, and governments had not only to guarantee the loans but eventually to contribute themselves. By 1860 the Canadian government alone had incurred a provincial debt on railway construction of over $20 million, not counting the costs borne by municipalities (see Tables 19.1 and 19.2).

Not only was construction expensive, but the sums of money involved in the manipulation of railway financing encouraged the worst in many businessmen and politicians (who were often the same people). This period has often been criticized for the lack of leadership—and the extent of venality—among its politicians. Allan MacNab, for example, who was seven times chairman of the Canadian assembly's railroad committee between 1848 and 1857 and served as the province's co-premier in 1854–6, was at various times president of three railway companies, chairman of another, and director of two more. It was MacNab who coined the immortal phrase, 'All my politics are railroads.' He profiteered in stock shares in his own companies, sold land to them at inflated prices, organized construction companies to build his roads, accepted 'retirement gifts' to leave boards of directors, and while co-premier took cash payments from railway companies. Although 'conflict of interest' was not yet a political concept, even his contemporaries regarded him as 'an excrescence which cannot be got rid of'.[23]

Interlocking directorates of politicians and businessmen, engaged in the various aspects of

■ Advertisement for the Grand Trunk Railway, c. 1864. LAC, 7569.

railroad construction, were common. So, too, were bribes to assembly members. Sir Edmund Hornby, who administered the Canadian business of the Grand Trunk, described the political manoeuvring over one unnamed railroad bill in his *Autobiography* (1928):

The Canadian Ministers were willing enough but weak—the majority a doubtful quantity, and although up to the last moment I felt there was a

TABLE 19.1

RAILWAYS OF CANADA

STATEMENT SHOWING THE COST, STOCK, BONDS, LOANS, FLOATING DEBT, AND DIVIDEND ACCOUNTS, OF CANADIAN RAILWAYS IN 1860
(COMPILED FROM THE REPORT OF THE INSPECTOR OF RAILWAYS)

Corporate name of railway	Cost of road and equipment	Capital stock paid in	Funded Debt			Government loan	Floating debt	Interest paid on debt in 1860	Dividends paid in 1880
			1st preference bonds	2d preference bonds	3d preference bonds				
Great Western and its branches	23,000,104.00	16,158,641.00	6,327,640.00	Included in 1st pref. Bds.		2,791,947.00*	–	528,254.00	3 per cent for six months
Grand Trunk and its branches	55,690,039.92	13,524,803.48	9,733,333.33	4,066,262.23	17,096,450.60	15,142,633.33	12,163,213.07	1,039,685.72	–
Northern (Toronto to L Huron)	3,890,778.68	823,818.50	491,046.67	1,092,566.68	287,481.35	2,311,666.67	–	55,545.21	–
Buffalo and Lake Huron	6,403,045.86	4,345,701.26	2,433,333.33	811,111.11	–	–	145,999.99	–	–
London and Port Stanley	1,017,220.00	935,542.00	399,400.00	120,000.00	–	–	77,770.00	–	–
Welland	1,309,209.92	710,299.60	486,666.67	243,333.33	–	–	211,851.93	–	–
Erie and Ontario	–	–	–	–	–	–	–	–	–
Port Hope, Lindsay and Beaverton, and branch	–	–	–	–	608,333.33	–	–	–	–
Cobourg and Peterborough	–	–	–	–	–	–	–	–	–
Brockville and Ottawa, and branch	1,901,000.00	207,000.00	–	648,000.00	–	–	–	280,000.00	4,968.00
Ottawa and Prescott	1,432,647.21	300,630.35	486,666.67	300,000.00	243,333.34	–	179,332.37	2,321.69	–
Montreal and Champlain, and branch	2,485,425.16	1,226,250.00	777,186.66	192,200.00	84,400.00	–	285,525.51	92,451.69	–
Carillon and Grenville	–	–	–	–	–	–	–	–	–
St Lawrence and Industry	50,171.00	42,300.00	–	–	–	–	909.00	48.00	2 per cent
Stanstead, Shefford, & Chambly	–	–	–	–	–	–	–	–	–
Peterborough & Chemung Lake	–	–	–	–	–	–	–	–	–
	97,179,641.75	**38,278,986.19**	**21,743,605.66**	**7,473,473.35**	**17,711,165.29**	**20,246,247.00**	**13,344,600.87**	**1,869,224.52**	

*The total amount borrowed from the Province by the Great Western Railway, on account of the Guarantee Law, was $3,755,555.18. In July 1858, this company repaid $957,114.45 of this amount.

Note: The length of roads for which there are no returns of cost in the above table is 172¾ miles, including eleven miles of Preston and Berlin, not running. The cost of these roads cannot be far from $5,000,000, and the total cost of Canadian Railways is over $100,000,000. The expenditure 'on capital account' is much greater than the 'cost of road and equipments'. In the case of the Grand Trunk Railway, the total expenditure is about $70,000,000—the difference representing interest and discount accounts, loss in working, etc. Of the Grand Trunk cost, $1,621,231.69 was on the Portland Division, and therefore not in Canada.

STATEMENT SHOWING THE EARNINGS, EXPENSES, INCOME, MILEAGE, NO. OF EMPLOYEES, AND NO. OF LOCOMOTIVES AND CARS ON CANADIAN RAILWAYS IN 1860
(COMPILED FROM THE REPORT OF THE INSPECTOR OF RAILWAYS)

Corporate name of railway	Total earnings in 1860	Total expenses in 1860	Net income for 1860	Earnings per mile per week	Expenses per mile per week	% of expenses to earn's	Total miles run exclusive of piloting, shunting & c.	Total persons employed on line	No. of locomotives	Passengers	Freight
				Deductions from returns						**No. of carriages**	
Great Western and its branches	2,197,943.34	1,993,806.00	204,043.00	122.51	111.13	91	1,261,604	2,049	89	127	1,269
Grand Trunk and its branches	3,349,658.18	2,806,583.17	533,075.01	58.72	49.20	84	8,195,064	3,118	217	135	2,538
Northern	332,967.01	260,466.56	72,500.45	67.40	52.72	78	280,035	370	17	20	801
Buffalo and Lake Huron	315,763.99	264,191.29	51,572.70	37.48	31.36	83	334,457	458	28	24	255
London and Port Stanley	29,385.57	23,256.02	6,129.75	23.55	18.62	78	41,300	38	2	2	50
Welland	64,554.40	51,274.35	13,280.06	49.64	39.44	79	47,810	104	4	4	87
Erie and Ontario	–	–	–	–	–	–	11,220	–	1	4	10
Port Hope, Lindsay and Beaverton, and branch	53,694.04	40,111.01	13,583.08	18.28	18.64	75	73,806	66	5	3	65
Cobourg and Peterborough	–	–	–	–	–	–	–	–	4	2	66
Brockville and Ottawa, and branch	53,801.10	34,427.25	19,373.85	16.30	10.42	64	53,715	74	3	8	79
Ottawa and Prescott	75,362.16	51,465.11	23,897.05	26.83	18.33	68	67,911	92	5	8	79
Montreal and Champlain	232,803.44	136,349.62	105,708.82	53.45	31.31	59	185,633	202	16	15	173
Carillon and Grenville	7,937.25	5,762.18	2,175.06	11.77	8.54	72	6,000	11	2	5	5
St Lawrence and Industry	8,796.00	7,819.00	978.00	14.08	12.50	88	12,440	24	2	5	5
Stanstead, Shefford, & Chambly	–	–	–	–	–	–	43,720	Leased by the Montreal & Champ.			
Peterborough & Chemung Lake	–	–	–					Worked by Cobourg & Peterborough			
	6,722,666.48	5,675,511.56	1,046,316.78	63.65	53.73	84	5,614,715	6,606	395	862	4,982

The improvement in the gross receipts of the first three roads since 1860, is as follows:

	1861		1862	
	Gross earnings	Earnings per mile	Gross earnings	Earnings per mile
Great Western	$2,266,864	$6,570	$2,686,060	$7,786
Grand Trunk	3,517,829	3,226	3,975,071	3,647
Northern	414,100	4,359	409,899	4,309

SOURCE: H.Y. Hind, *The Dominion of Canada* (Toronto: L. Stebbins, 1869).

TABLE 19.2
RAILWAY MILES OPENED IN
CANADA, 1850–1868

Year	Miles
1850	12
1851	63
1852	118
1853	444
1854	332
1855	335
1856	441
1857	103
1858	150
1859	520
1860	44
1861	9
1862	0
1863	0
1864	60
1865	0
1866	0
1867	35
1868	8

SOURCE: M.L. Bladen, 'Construction of Railways in Canada to 1895', *Contributions in Canadian Economics* 5 (1932): 43–60, as cited in L. Officer and L. Smith, 'Canadian-American Reciprocity Treaty', *Journal of Economic History* 28 (1968): 609.

money, and as I had no authority to bribe they simply abstained from voting and the Bill was thrown out. Twenty-five thousand pounds would have bought the lot, but I would rather somebody else had the job than myself. . . . Upon my word I do not think there was much to be said in favour of the Canadians over the Turks when contracts, places, free tickets on railways, or even cash was in question.[24]

In 1863, Thomas Keefer himself wrote of the boom period of railroad construction: 'No machinery could be better devised for launching a doubtful project . . . viewed as a commercial undertaking, than that possessed by the colossal railway contractors, the modern and unique results of the railway era.'[25] And, he added, 'During the Grand Trunk era of construction, from 1853 to 1859, the first Canadian age of iron, and of brass—the utmost activity was displayed in running into debt.'[26]

Construction over-runs were common and corruption was rampant. But, as Keefer emphasized, 'the great want of the Canadian railways [was] a paying traffic.' He was highly critical of expensive construction well in advance of settlement, resulting in what he called 'colonization roads'. By 1863, looking back on the proliferation of rail lines, Keefer would have preferred an alternative strategy of integrated 'national' railways, such as the Intercolonial, to link the lower provinces with central and western Canada. In his view, a national railroad would 'promote immigration, develop the resources, and provide for the defence of the country.' He recommended giving large endowments of land to companies willing to construct such roads, but admitted that without western immigrant traffic a Canadian road would have large numbers of cars travelling west as 'empties'—the landlocked equivalent of ships sailing in ballast.

All railway promoters insisted that their lines would promote manufacturing by reducing transportation costs to a minimum. As Keefer earlier had rhapsodized:

chance of getting the Bill through, I was always doubtful, since it was clear that some twenty-five members, contractors, etc., were simply waiting to be squared either by promise of contracts or

■ The Great Western Railway station, Hamilton, CW, c. 1850–60. LAC, C-019415.

A town has been built and peopled by the operatives—land rises rapidly in value—the neglected swamp is cleared and the timber is converted into sorts of wooden 'notions'—tons of vegetables, grains, or grasses, are grown where none grew before—the patient click of the loom, the rushing of the shuttle, the busy hum of the spindle, the thundering of the trip-hammer, and the roaring of steam, are mingled into one continuous sound of active industry.[27]

He might almost have been thinking of Collingwood (incorporated 1858), at the southern end of Georgian Bay, which was called by its early settlers the 'impenetrable swamp'. It was only a tiny village until 1855, when it became the northern terminus of the Ontario, Simcoe and Huron Railway. A similar success story awaited Ingersoll, 24 kilometres east of London, which prospered with cheese-making and agricultural-implement manufacturing after the arrival of the Great Western Railway in 1853.

Railroads certainly promoted travel into the heart of the continent. Despite many problems, by the early 1860s the Canadian rail lines were linked up to their American counterparts, and it was possible to travel from Quebec to Minnesota by rail.[28]

ATTITUDES TOWARDS THE UNITED STATES

Between 1840 and 1860, British North American attitudes towards the United States had softened considerably. British colonials still tended to be suspicious of the effects of too much democracy on the body politic, but they were now better informed of the workings of the American system and more willing to learn from the American example. The US Senate was the American institution most respected north of the border, chiefly because it was not directly elected, but was elected by the state legislatures. As the Toronto *Globe* observed in 1852, 'In the Senate of the United States is to be found its matured intellect and statesmanship; in its House of Representatives, its brawling demagogues and political intriguers.'[29] Whatever respect the American federal arrangements may earlier have enjoyed, the gradual degeneration towards civil war in the United States seemed to cast doubt on the wisdom of the American system, which came increasingly to be seen as giving too much power to the states and too little to the central government. Public opinion in British America was bewilderingly complex in its attitudes towards the two contending sections of the United States before 1860; however, most British Americans were clearly abolitionist in sympathy and thus favourably disposed to the North. On the other hand, prejudice against the loud and aggressive 'Yankee' (epitomized by Haliburton's Sam Slick) meant that the Southerners were often admired for their good manners, and their English and Scottish forebears, even by those who disapproved of slavery.

For both English and French Canadians, the Civil War plainly meant the failure of the American experiment in all its republican, democratic, and federal aspects. Initially sympathetic attitudes towards the government headed by Abraham Lincoln deteriorated as it became clear that the purpose of the war was to preserve the union, not to free the slaves. Moreover, many northern politicians and newspaper editors made it clear that any loss of southern territory could be easily compensated by territorial acquisitions north of the 49th parallel. Many newspapers in early 1861 actually advocated a union of the North with Canada as an alternative to war with the South, expecting such a result to be popular on both sides of the border. According to the New York *Herald* in February, 'The contracted views of the people of Lower Canada will be enlarged and expanded by an infusion of the Anglo-Saxon element and the energy of the people of the free States, who, being cut off from a Southern field of enterprise, must, by the law of their nature, expand northward and westward.'[30] The concept of 'compensation' had many supporters in the United States, but most British North Americans found it troubling, especially when they learned of the new Yankee words to 'Yankee Doodle': 'Secession first he would put down/Wholly and forever,/And afterwards from Britain's Crown/ He Canada would sever.'[31] By the end of 1861, many colonials simultaneously condemned the South for slavery and the North for not declaring it abolished. They applauded the arrival of British reinforcements to a garrison of only 4,300 regulars stationed in British North America, and, especially in Canada West, they advocated taking advantage of the North's problems in the West, where Confederate guerrillas were fighting.

CONCLUSION

By the early 1860s there were 11 independent railway companies in Canada West alone. Their construction had generated substantial amounts of economic spinoff, providing employment for many thousands of workers. Together with the Reciprocity Treaty, the railways contributed to a new economic orientation, at least in the Province of Canada, away from Europe and towards interior markets and sources for raw materials. Now increasing numbers of Canadians were turning their eyes to the West.

SHORT BIBLIOGRAPHY

Brown, S.F., and Robert Craig Brown. *Canada Views the United States: Nineteenth-Century Political Attitudes*. Seattle and London, 1967. A fascinating study of what Canadians thought about the United States in the nineteenth century.

Carroll, Francis M. *A Good and Wise Measure: The Search for the Canadian–American Boundary, 1783–1842*. Toronto, 2001. A recent, well-researched account of Anglo–American diplomacy and the various attempts to sort out the eastern boundary between Canada and the United States.

Collison, Gary. *Shadrach Minkins: From Fugitive Slave to Citizen*. Cambridge, Mass., 1997. A provocative biography of a fugitive slave and his subsequent life in Canada.

Creighton, Donald. *The Commercial Empire of the St. Lawrence, 1760–1850*. Toronto, 1937. Reprinted as *The Empire of the St. Lawrence*. Toronto, 1956. The classic study of the mercantile system developed in the Canadas and its disappearance in the face of free trade.

Keefer, T.C. *The Philosophy of Railroads*, ed. V.C. Nelles. Toronto, 1972. A wonderful piece of advocacy by one of the earliest Canadian boosters of the railroad.

Masters, D.C. *The Reciprocity Treaty of 1854*. Toronto, 1936. Reprinted Ottawa, 1963. Another classic study, never really replaced, of the economic agreement reached by Britain (on Canada's behalf) and the United States in 1854.

Shippee, L.B. *Canadian–American Relations 1849–1874*. New Haven, 1939. Despite its age, the best and most detailed overview of a complex period in Canadian–American relations.

Tucker, G.N. *The Canadian Commercial Revolution 1845–1851*. New Haven, 1936. Reprinted Ottawa, 1971. Another older work, still not superseded, which demonstrates how long it has been since a thorough evaluation of the economic history of this period was made.

Vinet, Mark. *Canada and the American Civil War: Prelude to War*. Vaudreuil-sur-le-Lac, Que., 2001. A recent study of the Canadian background to the American Civil War.

Winks, Robin. *Canada and the United States: The Civil War Years*. Montreal, 1971. The standard study of Canadian–American relations during the Civil War period, both well-researched and well-balanced.

STUDY QUESTIONS

1. Why were the North American boundary disputes relatively easy to resolve after 1840?
2. What part did fugitive slaves play in relations between British North America and the United States?
3. Why was the annexation movement of 1849 taken up more seriously in the United States than in Canada?
4. What exactly was 'reciprocity'? Why was it not more important to British North America?
5. What was Keefer's 'philosophy' regarding railroads?
6. Why were British Americans apprehensive about the prospect that the American South would secede?

CHAPTER TWENTY

The West and the North, 1821–1868

■ One of the best signs of the pace of British North America's development in the nineteenth century was the speed with which the region stretching from north of Georgian Bay to the Pacific slope ceased to be merely the 'back country' and became an object of great interest to politicians and governments. For much of the first half of the century, Rupert's Land was dominated by the fur trade, which was hardly a stable economic activity. A long-standing conflict between the North West Company and the Hudson's Bay Company—with Lord Selkirk's Red River settlement caught in the middle—was resolved in 1821 when the competitors merged to form a new Hudson's Bay Company. This new company held the vast plains for Britain over the middle years of the nineteenth century, while the First Nations were pushed further to the periphery and a mixed-blood society of great potential developed at the forks of the Red and Assiniboine rivers.

After mid-century, progress began to push on the prairie West from all directions. A single generation served to mark the time between unsettled and settled. When the British Parliament appointed a committee to investigate, it recommended that the region eventually be turned over to Canada. At the same time, scientists conducted studies in the West and agreed that much of the region was potentially useful for agricultural settlement. By 1859 the steamship, the newspaper, and the post office had all arrived at Red River virtually simultaneously.

In the late 1850s, the isolated colony of Vancouver Island, administered by the same Hudson's Bay Company that governed the West, was also struck by a sudden wave of settlers following a gold rush on the mainland. The results were a transformed Vancouver Island, a new Crown colony of British Columbia, and a new series of confrontations between the First Nations and European settlers.

THE LAND BETWEEN

Where did the West begin? This was no easy question to answer, because for the majority of people in eastern North America the West was more a construct of the imagination than a concrete geographical area. For most purposes, however, the West probably started somewhere around the Upper Great Lakes, certainly in the vast region above and beyond Lake Superior.[1] Until well into the nineteenth century, this territory was part of the western fur trade—and the rivalry between the North West and Hudson's Bay companies—not of British North America. The canoe-dominated supply lines from

TIMELINE

1820
Death of Lord Selkirk.

1821
Merger of Hudson's Bay Company and North West Company. George Simpson put in charge of North American operations.

1835
Council of Assiniboia established.

1836
Parliamentary inquiry into treatment of Aboriginal peoples in the British Empire.

1838
HBC's licence of exclusive trade renewed for 21 years. Major smallpox epidemic on prairies.

1840s
Métis join buffalo-robe trade.

1843
Fort Victoria founded.

1844
Franklin sets off on fatal Arctic expedition.

1848
Vancouver Island becomes a British colony.

1849
Vancouver Island leased to HBC. Sayer trial opens Red River to trade outside HBC.

1851
James Douglas becomes governor of Vancouver Island.

1857
Parliamentary inquiry investigates HBC monopoly in the West. Palliser and Hind expeditions arrive.

1858
Gold rush on Pacific slope. Colony of British Columbia established.

1859
Site chosen and cleared for New Westminster. First steamship, first newspaper, and first regular postal service arrive in Red River.

1861
Death of George Simpson.

1862
Gold strike on Williams Lake.

1864
Bute Inlet incident.

1868
Schultz jailbreak in Red River.

Montreal to the great fur-trade regions of the 'Petit Nord' on James Bay and the 'Grand Nord' in the Mackenzie and Athabasca areas had created the fur-trading community of Fort William on the western shore of Lake Superior; the administrative home of the North West Company, Fort William, before 1821, was probably the most populous permanent site in British North America west of Lake Erie. Its invasion and capture in 1816, by mercenaries led by Lord Selkirk, was the turning point in the commercial war between the two companies.

After the rivals' merger in 1821, both Fort William and the fur-trading region around Lake Superior gradually declined in importance. A commercial fishery was opened on Lake Superior in the 1830s, and mineral riches drew some attention in the 1840s, particularly when a rush to exploit copper deposits began in 1843. Canadian authorities found that they had absolutely no information on the region and no policy for dealing with frontier mining operations. By 1847 an investigation would disclose the chicanery involved in the staking out of mining claims. Aboriginal opposition to the miners helped in both bringing the region to the attention of the authorities and forcing Canada to take Crown title to it by negotiating a land treaty with the Ojibwa and Odawa inhabitants of the region, in which they transferred millions of acres to the Crown in return for promises of a reserve (consisting of Manitoulin Island and the many islands in Lake Huron). Nevertheless, as late as 1850 one observer described the Lake Superior region as 'notoriously barren and sterile', of no use except possibly for mining.[2] Even the forest cover was regarded as unimportant. The north was the home of the uncivilized fur traders, men without 'inspiration, natural wisdom, or moral health'.[3] Public interest preferred to concentrate on the lands north of Lake Huron, which surveyors reported held potential for agricultural settlement.

RED RIVER AND THE HBC TERRITORY

West of Fort William was another 650 kilometres of lakes and bogs, rock and trees, before the land flattened out into the vast prairies stretching to the Rocky Mountains. Much of this region—along with much of northern and western British North America—especially after 1821, was the bailiwick of the Hudson's Bay Company, which had been given its mandate to govern by the British Parliament. The human population between Lake Superior and the far side of the Rockies consisted of the tiny settlement at Red River, which after 1826 had become home to a number of prairie Métis; the Hudson's Bay Company, represented by a number of strategically located fur-trading posts; and the Aboriginal peoples who were still technically in control of the territory they inhabited.

RED RIVER

Even at the height of the fur-trade war, the major external threats to the Red River settlement had been environmental rather than human. Locusts (or grasshoppers) devastated the crops in 1818 and 1819, and in 1826 the greatest known flooding of the Red River virtually wiped out the settlement. The result of the flood was the departure of virtually the entire European population, which had included a party of Swiss who arrived in 1821 and the de Meuron mercenaries. Their place would be taken by current and former fur-trade employees, together with their mixed-blood families. After Selkirk's death in 1820 his executors administered the settlement until it was transferred to the HBC in 1835. Red River was governed by the Council of Assiniboia, made up of community members appointed by the HBC with some attention to representing the various interest groups. Although the settlers lacked representative government, they paid very little in taxes; import duties of 4 per cent and licence fees for sellers of alcoholic beverages provided the settlement's revenue. Justice was administered by the General Quarterly Court with a 12-man jury, normally consisting of six anglophones and six francophones.

The population grew slowly but steadily. It consisted largely of two groups: Métis (French-speaking Roman Catholics) and 'mixed-bloods' or 'country-born' (English-speaking Protestants, chiefly Anglicans), the former slightly more numerous than the latter. Despite continual conflicts over language, religion, and class, a promising multiracial society was developing on the

1, 2. A Swiss colonist with wife and children from the Canton of Berne. 3. A German colonist from the disbanded De Meuron Regt. 4. A Scottish Highland colonist.
5. An immigrant colonist from French Canada.

TYPES OF LORD SELKIRK'S SETTLERS IN 1822.

From a photo of black and white drawing of a Swiss Colonist, touched up by Mr. Lawson, artist of the *Manitoba Free Press.*

Courtesy of Dr. Doughty, Dominion Archivist.

■ 'Types of Lord Selkirk's Settlers in 1822': original drawing by Peter Rindisbacher, as 'touched up' and published in the *Manitoba Free Press* in the 1920s. Although the caption, added by the newspaper, identifies specific ethnic 'types', the models may actually have been family members and friends of the artist. Provincial Archives of Manitoba, N13832.

banks of the Red and Assiniboine rivers. There were not many racial problems, although some tension was created in the early 1830s by the arrival of the European wives of the leading HBC officers. As a result, the men usually had to 'turn off' the mixed-blood or Aboriginal women with whom they had had long relationships and many children, but without legal marriage. The discarded wives were understandably unhappy, and the newly arrived wives often looked down their noses at the mixed-bloods. Before 1860, however, Europeans were few in number and a distinct minority in the settlement.

The main problems were not originally linguistic, ethnic, or religious but economic, caused by the settlement's isolation. Red River was essentially an island, surrounded in all directions by unsettled prairie. The HBC was to some extent successful in its efforts to control commerce, and a regiment of British regulars was stationed in Red River in 1846 to protect the settlement from the Americans. But the HBC's limitations were made clear in 1849 by the failure of its prosecution of Pierre-Guillaume Sayer for illicit fur-trading; the outcome was, in effect, a victory for free trade for the Métis. Beginning in the mid-1840s, reformers within the settlement, mainly members of the Anglican clergy and their anglophone mixed-blood supporters, had begun to call for an end to HBC control; instead they demanded either Crown colony status for Red River or annexation to Canada. By the end of the 1850s, it was clear that Red River's isolation would not continue much longer. The first steamship docked at the settlement in 1859, having sailed up the Red River from Minnesota. The first newspaper in Red River, the *Nor'-Wester*, was begun that same year by two new arrivals from Canada, Robert Cunningham and William Coldwell. The railroad in the United States passed within 320 kilometres of the international boundary, and could be used by gold-seekers who travelled through Red River in 1862.

By the 1860s, ethnic tensions in the settlement were clearly on the increase. The arrival of more Canadians to join Messrs Cunningham and Coldwell increased the demand for annexation, and some of the newcomers were clearly hostile to Aboriginal and mixed-blood people. After the departure of the British regulars in 1861, the small local constabulary (consisting chiefly of a one-armed ex-army pensioner) was unable to keep the peace, and various prominent miscreants kept defying the court, either refusing to accept its decisions or allowing themselves to be broken out of the local jail by force. The Anglican clergyman G.O. Corbett was freed from incarceration by mobs on either side of his conviction for abortion in 1862. A series of incidents involved the leader of the pro-annexation 'Canadian Party' in Red River, John Christian Schultz. In 1868 the sheriff of Red River appeared at Schultz's store to collect pay-

ment of a debt. Following a struggle, Schultz was trussed up with rope from his own store. While Schultz was being carted off to jail, Constable James Mulligan attempted to maintain legal custody of the Schultz store. But Mrs Schultz asked him to leave, and when he refused, she ordered the shop nailed shut with nails and spikes, leaving the constable inside without food, drink, or heat. He was subsequently released, dehydrated but unharmed.

As her treatment of Constable Mulligan suggests, Agnes Campbell Farquaharson Schultz was a force to be reckoned with in her own right. She proved the point with her subsequent behaviour. At about one o'clock on the following Saturday morning, 18 January 1868, Agnes—who had been allowed to take food to her husband and remain with him—was joined by a party of about 15 men, who arrived with sleigh bells jingling at the doors of the jail at Lower Fort Garry. Later, her husband proudly told the following story himself, in a special edition of the *Nor'-Wester* (which by this time he owned):

> First, a party at the door to obtain peaceable entrance, then a request from the Doctor [Schultz] to let his wife out of the inner door of the prison, then a rush of the Doctor himself, who grappled with the constables who were barricading the door, then the upsetting of the jailer and the bolts drawn by the Doctor's wife, and then, as the expectant crowd saw the attack on the Doctor within, came the heavy thump of the oaken beam; soon the crashing of breaking timbers, and then the loud hurrah . . . and the escort of the Doctor to his home. It is well to know that no disreputable characters were among the party. When the constables, of which there are said to have been six, with eight 'specials', ceased to resist, the victors ceased their efforts, and no violence was used, but the breaking of the door, and the marks of a clenched fist on one of the special constable's face would not have been there had he not rudely assaulted Mrs Schultz in her endeavours to draw the bolts.[4]

ALEXANDER ROSS
(1783–1856)

Alexander Ross was born in Morayshire, Scotland. He came to Lower Canada in 1804 and worked as a schoolmaster there and in Glengarry. In 1810 he signed on as a clerk with the Pacific Fur Company, and sailed aboard the *Tonquin* for the Pacific Northwest, arriving in March 1811 to help establish Fort Astoria. He was subsequently put in charge of Fort Okanagan, at the juncture of the Columbia and Okanagan rivers, Here he met Sally, the Okanagan woman who would become his wife. Ross went to the North West Company when it took over the PFC in 1813, working mainly in the interior until his forced retirement to Red River in 1825. During the 1820s he had been expected to 'trap out' the Snake country—that is, to take out all the fur-bearing animals, to render the area unattractive to competing companies—but George Simpson did not believe that he was committed enough to the task. In the settlement he acquired a 100-acre grant near the Forks (in what is now called Point Douglas), where he farmed and traded, organizing York boats to Hudson Bay. Although George Simpson did not like him, he gradually acquired positions of responsibility. He became sheriff of Assiniboia in 1835 and a member of the Council of Assiniboia a year later. As sheriff and head of the Volunteer Corps of 60 men used as a police force in the 1840s, he refused to enforce the fur-trade monopoly of the HBC. He also served as governor of the jail and collector of customs. He and Adam Thom, the settlement's recorder or chief judge, fought for years over the question of the enforcement of the HBC monopoly. His demeanour was pedantic, and in

later years he was known in the settlement as 'the Professor'. In 1850 he was one of several judges who refused to continue their work as long as William Coldwell—whom they regarded as incompetent—remained in office. He fought for years to create a Presbyterian church in the settlement, finally succeeding in 1851, the year he retired from his major offices. Ross then had to fight to gain Presbyterian rights at the Anglican graveyard where the Scots had buried their dead for years.

In his later years Ross wrote three autobiographical books: *Adventures on the Columbia* (1849), on the founding of Astoria; *The Fur Hunters of the Far West* (1855), on his fur-trading activities in the interior of the Pacific slope; and *The Red River Settlement* (1856), still regarded by many as the best history of the Selkirk colony. Ross saw the settlement as an oasis of civilization in the midst of an alien and savage wilderness. These writings made him the pre-Confederation Northwest's most prolific resident author, and its finest as well. His prose style was straightforward and unembellished, but he had a good story and told it well. He may also have written the novel *Selma: A Tale of the Sixth Crusade* (1839). His career suggested the close relationship between the west coast and Red River in the first half of the nineteenth century, and his family was an excellent example of anglophone mixed-bloods in Red River entering into the world of Victorian respectability. Ross married Sally formally in 1828, and their children, particularly James, were all conscious of their Aboriginal heritage.

■ 'Half Breed Traders' c. 1872–4. Note the Red River cart at right. Provincial Archives of Manitoba, Boundary Commission collection, 164.

The fist had apparently belonged to Mrs Schultz, who was only one of several assertive women in Red River in the 1860s. About a year later Mrs Annie Bannatyne, a mixed-blood herself, publicly horsewhipped the Canadian poet Charles Mair over slurs Mair had published in eastern newspapers about mixed-blood women in Red River.

THE MÉTIS

Although the most concentrated population was probably to be found in Red River, people of mixed Aboriginal–European ancestry were present everywhere in North America, especially in places where the fur trade had been prevalent.

Originally the offspring of relationships between European traders and Aboriginal women, by the nineteenth century the Métis had gradually achieved a specific identity of their own, apart from the First Nations (a process that anthropologists call 'ethnogenesis'), particularly in regions like Red River and the American Midwest, where French traders had predominated. In British North America the situation was complicated by the presence of a second biracial population, descended from anglophone HBC traders and the women, mainly Cree, who congregated around the company's trading posts. Members of this group, who tended to be Protestants (usually Anglicans), were less likely to see themselves as a

HUNTING THE BUFFALO

THE SUMMER HUNT.

In another part of to-day's paper will be found a well-written article, the first of two communications to the columns of *The Nor'-Wester*, on the subject of the buffalo-hunt. The party to which our contributor was attached was what is known as the 'main-river band,' and was made up almost exclusively of hunters and their families residing on the Red River between Fort Garry and Pembina. Another expedition—the 'White Horse Plain Hunters'—taking its name from the district in which its ranks are for the most part filled, but including also many others living on the Assiniboine from its mouth to Portage la Prairie, its most remote settlement—went out about the same time; with what success we have not yet heard. It should be remarked that there are two seasons for hunting the buffalo—summer and autumn. Of the beef killed in the summer, a small quantity is dried in thin strips, and the remainder chopped up very small and made into pemmican—a highly concentrated and healthy food, much used by travellers and by the laboring part of the Red River population; whilst the cattle killed in the autumn are preserved fresh, by the action of frost, throughout the winter. Hence, the former is called the 'dried-meat hunt,' and the latter the 'green-meat hunt.' The flesh of the beast derived from the summer chase is turned to the most profitable account; on the other hand, the skin is more valuable in autumn, the animal at that time putting on his warm, thick coat to protect himself from the rigors of winter. The quantity of buffalo-meat annually slaughtered and cured throughout the country for pemican is something surprising. The Indians draw from the case their sole supplies. The Hudson's Bay Company's servants on the Saskatchewan have little else to depend upon, and when, as last year, this source fails them, are reduced to short-rations of horse-steaks and boiled dog. As we have already remarked, the strong, brawny arms and stout, muscular frames of our own people draw their chief support and nourishment from the same staff of life. To provide for all these demands requires great exertion; and thus it is that hundreds, we may safely say thousands in our midst make hunting the buffalo the great concern of their lives. The muster-roll of the main-river party alone swells to the dimensions of an army. Here it is—not simply derived from a mere approximation, but correctly ascertained by a close and careful count: 500 men, 600 women, 680 children; 730 horses, 300 oxen, and 950 carts. As may be supposed, such a formidable host, with appetites sharpened by the pure, invigorating breezes of the plains and the life-giving exercise of the chase, was capable of doing a vast amount of execution to the provisions; and one scarcely wonders on being told that two or three thousand fat carcases would barely serve them in food until they got home. The buffalo first appeared in sight in the neighbourhood of Bad Hill, about sixty miles from the boundary line, and in a run in which 220 hunters were engaged, 1300 buffalo were shot. The camp then moved southwards by the Sand Hills, until they came within five miles of the Little Souris River, and at this place they killed over 1,000. Here they stayed . . . the expedition moved back to Devil's Lake, where the more serious business of buffalo hunting was relieved by a bear, beaver, and deer hunt. This sport over—and good sport it was, several grizzly bears and a variety of lesser animals being made to bite the dust—a council was held and a resolution passed to go to the Couteau de la Prairie to hunt the buffalo which were still wanting to fill the carts. Mr. Chapin, a gentleman from Philadelphia, and Lieut. Whyte, R.C.R., accompanied the party, and, for young hunters, were unusually successful. Mr. Chapin killed ten buffalo, and Lieut. Whyte seven or eight.

SOURCE: *The Nor'-Wester,* 14 August 1860.

distinct people than were the French-speaking Catholic Métis. Many of the anglophone mixed-bloods identified more strongly with their European than their Aboriginal ancestors. As for the Métis, by the middle of the nineteenth century they were a third- and fourth-generation 'country-born' population and had little reason to identify themselves with the East or French Canada. For several generations the Métis had seen themselves as a 'nation', and a distinctive Métis flag had been raised over the region as early as 1815. By the mid-1800s it was clear to many Métis leaders that the old order would not last much longer. The buffalo were disappearing and settlement was advancing. The only real question remaining was whether the region would be integrated into the United States or British North America.

Whatever their origins, the 'halfbreeds'—as they were disparagingly called by many contemporaries—were by far the most numerous population in Red River; perhaps 55 per cent of the mixed-bloods were francophone Catholics, and 45 per cent anglophone Protestants. The relationship between the two linguistic groups has been much debated by historians. On the one hand, they worked together in the buffalo hunt, the principal Métis institution of the settlement. Twice each year, French- and English-speaking hunters joined to travel to the buffalo country in the northern United States, to shoot buffalo for food, pemmican, and hides. The two groups also intermarried and worked together in many business enterprises, including the considerable traffic in Red River that which grew up in the 1850s to connect the settlement with the United States. On the other hand, some of the Anglican clergy encouraged hostility between the Protestant mixed-bloods and the Catholic Métis. Contemporaries often assumed that the anglophones had settled down into European-style agriculture while the bison-hunting francophones remained closer to their Aboriginal heritage. But in truth there was little distinction between the two groups in terms of agricultural activity. If the francophones were

more active in the buffalo hunt, this tendency was less a reflection of their affinity with the Aboriginal way of life than of a rational decision that, in a place without a market for crops, hunting buffalo was more profitable than farming. Controversial at the time—and ever since—is the extent to which the Métis were entitled to share in the inheritance of their Aboriginal cousins.

THE HUDSON'S BAY COMPANY

Scattered throughout the fur-trading country were isolated trading posts, the only visible symbols of the Hudson's Bay Company's administration. During the period of fur-trade rivalry, the competitors usually matched one another, post-for-post, but under the governorship of George Simpson, who assumed effective North American control of the HBC in 1821 and held it until his death in 1860, the posts as well as the personnel were rationalized. Simpson was an energetic and peripatetic Scot, capable of travelling by canoe for weeks at a time, and he dominated his domain for nearly 40 years, although titular management of the HBC resided on Fenchurch Street in London, where the company had its home office and where its board of directors met every month. Simpson understood perfectly well that the company's special position in the West would not last forever, but he and the company managed to fight a relatively successful rearguard action against change and unnecessary encroachments that lasted until the sale of the company's territory to Canada in 1869. This defensive action took various forms. In regions subject to outside competition (usually American), the HBC generally tried to deplete populations of fur-bearing animals. In other areas, the company tried to conserve the resource by limiting trade. Perhaps most controversially, Simpson was always reluctant to support missionary activity among the First Nations, suspecting that missionaries would attempt to introduce 'civilization' and thus undermine the delicate environmental balance in the region.

ABORIGINAL PEOPLES IN HBC-ADMINISTERED TERRITORY

By the nineteenth century many Aboriginal people in the West had become highly dependent on the fur trade. Those who had escaped direct dependence—especially the parkland groups—had usually done so by concentrating on the bison hunt to supply provisions for the fur traders. The woodland peoples found it more difficult to reduce their reliance on many European articles. Nevertheless, everywhere in the West the Aboriginal people were able to manage and control the social change brought about by the fur trade. In British Columbia, the number and size of the potlatches increased, and new leaders arose who dealt with the traders. But the introduction of new wealth and new ideas was not necessarily disruptive. Other problems associated with the fur trade were more disturbing.

The animal populations of the HBC territory were steadily decreasing. Thus, opportunities for Aboriginal people in the fur trade also declined, despite efforts by the HBC to conserve resources in the woodland regions by, for example, limiting the use of steel traps. Beaver, moose, even the fish in the lakes and rivers began gradually to disappear, apparently because it did not take much to alter the environment.[5] The reasons for the decline of the buffalo population, well in advance of encroaching settlement, are not at all clearly understood. The HBC and other observers tended to blame overhunting of the bison for their skins. The 'buffalo robe' trade had been begun by American traders on the Missouri River early in the nineteenth century. Before 1830 as many as 200,000 skins were taken per year. The Métis hunt for meat had reduced the numbers of bison north of the 49th parallel long before 1820, and when Métis from British North America joined in the skin business after the 1840s, the pressure on the resource increased. On the other hand, it is also possible that the numbers of buffalo in those vast herds before the nineteenth century, which nobody was ever able

to count, were greatly exaggerated.[6] The latest historical study of the question suggests that many factors doomed the buffalo, but argues that the central cause was the creation by cultural and ecological interaction of new types of buffalo hunters, both Aboriginal and European.[7]

Although Aboriginal people in the West had been exposed to epidemic disease since first contact, the magnitude of the problem increased substantially in the nineteenth century. There had been a major smallpox outbreak in 1780–1 from the central prairies to the north-central woodlands, and the devastation it caused was exceeded when another outbreak occurred in 1838. This epidemic apparently spread from American trading posts on the Missouri River as Native people attempting to escape the disease instead carried it north. HBC traders in Saskatchewan worked desperately to inoculate the local population with cowpox vaccine, which had earlier been made available by the company. But the disease had a serious impact on the relative numerical strength of the various tribal groups: because the Cree had been largely spared in 1838, their population grew and expanded into many areas of the prairies abandoned by the Assiniboine. When another major smallpox epidemic occurred in the summer of 1869, less vaccine was available. There were also reports of the ravages of smallpox in British Columbia, although the numbers of those affected were much disputed by contemporary observers.[8] Smallpox epidemics were recorded in 1836, 1853, and 1862–3, and in 1847–8 a widespread epidemic of measles affected all of British Columbia.[9]

At the same time that the Aboriginal peoples of Hudson's Bay Company territory were facing these economic and demographic threats, it was the formal policy of both the British government and the company to leave them to their own devices.[10] The British had sovereignty over the West, but 'Indian' law and customs were regarded as part of the local law of the territory. No attempt was made to extend English law generally to the First Nations, and after the parliamentary report of 1837 on the treatment of Aboriginal peoples it became official British policy to regard the Queen's law and the Queen's peace as applying only to territory where British subjects actually lived, such as Red River. The HBC's own lawyers were not entirely convinced that the company had jurisdiction over the Aboriginal inhabitants. For their part, the First Nations insisted on maintaining their own law and their own jurisdiction, with considerable success. On the whole, they would be made subject to English criminal law only in cases involving Europeans or for offences committed on ground regarded as British. In such cases English justice could be quite harsh. Most of the people sentenced to death by British Columbia's 'hanging judge', Matthew Begbie, were Aboriginal, for example. Except in Red River, little if any Aboriginal land was sold to Europeans under the Hudson's Bay Company, and no treaties were made alienating Aboriginal land. The introduction of Canadian policy after 1870 would produce great changes.

SCIENCE ON THE PRAIRIES

While the British Parliament was considering the future of the West, two scientific expeditions—one British and one Canadian—set out to learn more about the region. The former was led by Captain John Palliser, an Irish landlord and adventurer who had spent a lifetime seeking excitement around the world. He had travelled in the American West in 1847 and 1848, bringing home a menagerie of wild animals, including three buffalo, an antelope, a bear, two Virginia deer, and a half-wolf 'Indian dog'.[11] Such a 'splendid chap', in the Victorian context, could hardly be denied when in 1856 he proposed to the Royal Geographical Society to survey a large portion of North America. The Society got the Colonial Office to contribute £5,000, to pay for two scientific assistants and two royal engineers. The British understandably wanted to know more about the western possessions that were

about to become the subject of a parliamentary inquiry. Lorin Blodgett, an American scientist, had published data in 1856 and 1857 suggesting that the prairies were hardly as barren as most people had imagined. Blodgett pointed out that what really mattered was not latitude but average temperature, and insisted that much of the region was 'perfectly adapted to the fullest occupation by cultivated nations'.[12] Eminent scientists were consulted, including Charles Darwin, and a team of experts was recruited for the expedition. The only amateur was Palliser, who formally received his commission during the parliamentary inquiry of 1857. The party left England on 16 May on the Royal Mail Steamer *Arabia*, docking in New York and then heading west via American railroad and steamer. At Sault Ste Marie they picked up two canoes with their voyageur crews, made their way by steamer across Lake Superior, and paddled to Lower Fort Garry on the Red River.

On 23 July of that same year the Canadian Exploring Expedition left Toronto for the West under the titular command of a retired chief trader of the HBC, George Gladman. Gladman was accompanied by Simon James Dawson, an engineer, and Henry Youle Hind, an English-born, Cambridge-educated professor of chemistry and geology at Trinity College, Toronto, who acted as geologist and naturalist. The sponsor was the Canadian government, eager to learn more about the northwest region that many were saying should be annexed to American territory.

The findings of these two expeditions served their purpose in expanding geographical knowledge and in helping to change the public perception of the West as unfit for human habitation. The final reports from Hind and Palliser, besides containing much scientific observation, acknowledged the great potential of the region. Indeed, an aura of 'impartial science' gave their findings great cachet in the eyes of enthusiasts for western expansion. Hind, in his *Reports of Progress; Together with a Preliminary and General Report on the Assiniboine and Saskatchewan*

Exploration Expedition (Toronto, 1859), waxed lyrical over the 'truly fertile valleys of the West', calculating that between Red River and the south branch of the Saskatchewan there were over 11 million acres of arable land. Palliser's *Papers Relative to the Exploration . . .* were also published in 1859, and after three more expeditions between 1858 and 1868, Her Majesty's Stationery Office published his *Journals, Detailed Reports, and Observations Relative to the Exploration* (1863) in an edition of fewer than 100 copies. Palliser made the same point as Hind, that millions of acres of the West were prime agricultural land, although he also identified what came to be known as 'Palliser's Triangle'—a drybelt area of the West that even today is the graveyard of farmers' hopes. Palliser also recognized how much easier it was to get into the British West via the United States, and he advocated building a 'railway on the British side of the line to the northward and westward, through the southern portion of "the fertile belt" to the Rocky Mountains as soon as the country showed signs of becoming sufficiently populated to warrant such an effort.'[13]

Both Palliser and Hind accepted long-standing assumptions that the northern prairie was an extension of the Great American Desert; but they insisted that parts of it were useful for settlement, and that a railroad was needed to open the region, particularly to connect Canada with the Pacific. Those in the Province of Canada who were interested in expansion found enough support in these studies to document their case. Science had now confirmed what continental expansionists had long known instinctively: not only was the Northwest suitable for settlement but, as the Canadian government insisted in 1864, it was 'capable of sustaining a vast population'.[14]

BRITISH COLUMBIA

While Victorian scientists made great claims for the potential of the prairie region, it was sheer serendipity that brought the Pacific slope to the attention of the world. One of Vancouver Island's chief problems as a colony was its isolation. A small European population was continually uneasy with the presence of the First Nations. As Adele Perry has recently pointed out, British Columbia may have been located 'on the edge of empire', but with its overwhelmingly male population and its disparaging attitude towards the local Aboriginal people, it was typical of Britain's imperial outposts in the Victorian era.[15] The colonists resented James Douglas, who as governor of the island (1851–63) made some effort to deal responsibly—if not exactly generously—with the Aboriginal people displaced by British newcomers. His predecessor, Governor Richard Blanshard, had distinguished himself by a heavy-handed action against a group of Newitty people accused of killing three sailors. Sending a message ahead of him that 'white man's blood never dries', he sailed north to their village and summarily destroyed it.[16] Intensely class-conscious and fearful, the early colonists shared Blanshard's belief that the Native people should be 'speedily coerced'. In a letter home in 1854, one settler cast doubt on Douglas's own ability to govern, given that he 'has spent all his life among the North American Indians and has got one of them for a wife'.[17] From the beginning, Douglas feared that the settlers' prejudiced attitudes would lead to trouble. He negotiated a series of treaties with the Aboriginal people around Victoria in order to protect the bulk of their land from European encroachment, but the colony seemed constantly in danger of going up in flames. Douglas's marriage to a woman of mixed Aboriginal–European ancestry was not an isolated case among Victoria's leading families. Many of the former fur traders who retired to Victoria with him had mixed-blood wives. They also had the money to buy into Victoria society, and expected their wives to join them in emulating the manners of English society.[18]

In 1857 gold was discovered on the mainland, along the Thompson and Fraser rivers. The California gold rush of 1848–9 was still

■ Lady Amelia (Connolly) Douglas and her husband, Sir James, both c. 1860. British Columbia Archives A-01234 and A-01227.

fresh in many people's minds, although when Governor Douglas exhibited a few grains of gold from the North Thompson at dinner in the HBC's mess hall, he seemed the only one to appreciate its importance as an instrument of 'great change and busy time'.[19] The amount of gold easily accessible was quite small by California standards, and the ensuing rush was a pale imitation of the American one. Nevertheless, hundreds of men, mainly from California, made their way to the interior of British Columbia in the spring of 1858—forever altering perceptions of the western colony as an isolated and useless appendage. Of the 450 men in the first rush inland, only 60 were British and fewer than a hundred were Americans (including 35 blacks); the rest were an international mix of professional gold-seekers.

The quiet and sleepy village of Victoria was transformed as more than 200 buildings were thrown up virtually overnight. Lieutenant Charles Wilson of the International Boundary Commission, who arrived in Victoria in July 1858, recorded in his diary:

> You are hardly safe without arms & even with them, when you have to walk along paths across which gentlemen with a brace of revolvers each are settling their differences; the whiz of revolver bullets round you goes on all day & if anyone gets shot of course it's his own fault; however I like the excitement very much & never felt better in my life. All the worst characters of the coast are crowding here in thousands, though only a month has elapsed since the discovery of gold, they have exported 8000 oz. from Victoria alone & reports from the mines of the mainland say they will far outrival the San Francisco ones.[20]

South of the 49th parallel, talk of American annexation spread rapidly. One popular American ditty was plain enough:

Soon our banner will be streaming,
Soon the eagle will be screaming,
And the lion—see it cowers,
Hurrah, boys, the river's ours.[21]

If the American threat had not existed, it would have had to be invented in order to justify Governor Douglas in his swift takeover of the mainland. In late 1857 he had declared that all gold mines in the interior were the property of the Crown and subject to licensing fees. Douglas had already taken the initiative to introduce British justice into a community of over 9,000 miners allegedly accustomed to American habits of vigilante law and the pursuit of sensual pleasures. According to Judge Matthew Begbie, even Englishmen resident in California had caught the American disease: 'There is usually to be remarked among such persons an alteration in voice, in tone and manner, and an accretion of prejudices, which, I think, render them less fit, and contrast unfavourably with the tone, manner and prejudices of Englishmen habitually resident in the United Kingdom.'[22]

The British government was forced to rush legislation through Parliament putting 'New Caledonia' (as the fur-trade district had been known) under the direct jurisdiction of the Crown, and the mainland colony of British Columbia was formally embodied with royal assent on 2 August 1858. James Douglas was appointed governor of the new colony, which was at first kept administratively separate from Vancouver Island. Douglas would subsequently write to Sir George Simpson with some satisfaction: 'Many changes have taken place in this Country since I had last [in 1841] the pleasure of travelling with you on the coast, and works of a perfectly stupendous character have been executed.'[23] Gold even produced the first books to be published on the west coast of British North America, Alfred Waddington's *The Fraser Mines Vindicated* and Kinahan Cornwallis's *The New Eldorado*. The latter included a useful map showing where gold was to be found. It proved surprisingly accurate.

The discovery of gold brought rapid, and unanticipated, changes to the Pacific coast. To the surprise of the local authorities, the miners, however rough in appearance, were not badly behaved. Judge Begbie, travelling in the interior to put the stamp of British justice on contentious cases, found them quite amenable. They were certainly a motley crew, described by one observer as 'Englishmen (staunch Royalists), Americans (Republicans), Frenchmen, very numerous, Germans in abundance, Italians, several Hungarians, Poles, Danes, Swedes, Spaniards, Mexicans, & Chinese.'[24] Another writer, slightly less ethnically precise, noted 'an indescribable array of Polish Jews, Italian fishermen, French cooks, jobbers, speculators of every kind, land agents, auctioneers, hangers on at auctions, bummers, bankrupts and brokers of every description.'[25] But every observer was impressed with the ethnic complexity. One German wrote of Fort Yale, 'It would have been difficult to find in one place a greater mixture of different nationalities', and added: 'The feminine population consisted of only six.'[26] The amount of gold obtainable on the Fraser with only a few hand tools and without capital investment was fairly small, and few prospectors became rich. One reported in the autumn of 1858 that although he was taking out $8 to $10 a day in gold, food was very expensive and he could not afford to send his family any money: 'I am too far in the mountains, it will cost more than $50.00 to send it and I would not be sure if you got it or not.'[27] Charles Major wrote to a friend in Sarnia, Canada West, in September 1858: '. . . if I, or any other, was to work as hard and live as meanly, I could make more money in Canada than I can here.'[28] Some settled down to work for mining companies with proper machinery, while others travelled across the new colony in search of fresh strikes. In any event, the need both to transport supplies into the interior and to take out the gold led to the rapid construction of wagon roads from the lower Fraser River, with the assistance of a contingent of Royal Engineers sent from Britain.

■ The Aurora gold mine, Williams Creek, BC, 15 August 1867, by Frederick Dally. Toronto Public Library (TPL), T14321.

In 1860 the gold rush extended northeastward into the foothills of the Cariboo Mountains, where a major strike was made at Keithley Creek. The next year Governor Douglas supervised plans for the construction of a long-distance road beginning at Fort Yale, passing through the Fraser Canyon to Lytton, and heading north from there. But when Billy Barker made a spectacular discovery, in August 1862, on Williams Creek—near where the town of Barkerville was later developed—the plans were extended to take the miners that far into the British Columbia interior.[29] Barker himself lived the high life and died in poverty. A few other early arrivals did well, one team of prospectors earning $10,000 apiece

for three months' labour. Most of the miners now arriving in British Columbia from abroad came up the coast by ship, often sailing around Cape Horn or crossing the isthmus of Panama. In 1862, however, a few parties travelled overland via Minnesota and Red River, crossing the prairies by Red River cart as well as horse and buggy. Some of those in the party led by Thomas McMicking completed the journey by rafting down the Fraser River. When McMicking drew up a statement of expenses at Quesnelle Mouth at the end of his journey, he commented, 'Our mining tools were the only articles . . . that we found to be unnecessary.'[30] Most of the gold required expensive equipment to extract, and

■ New Westminster, BC, 1863, photo by F. Claudet. British Columbia Archives, A-03330.

organized mining companies employing wage labour would take out far more gold than individual prospectors, who often had difficulty obtaining the simplest implements such as axes and shovels. Those who had been to the Cariboo complained that the journey to the diggings was hard, rough, and expensive. One correspondent to a Welsh newspaper in 1862 wrote: 'Let no-one think of coming here and taking a chance in the mines unless he has £100–£500 after reaching this place. Everything here for the maintenance of life is terribly expensive . . . . One meal of any kind costs 10s.'[31]

Many gold-seekers found employment and profits in other ways, because the economic spinoff from the rush was substantial for some time. James Thomson, a Scottish-born baker who had immigrated to Canada in 1844 and travelled widely in search of his fortune, headed for California in 1850. While he did not get rich, he made enough money from his efforts, mainly as a baker, to buy a farm in Edwardsburgh on the St Lawrence. He then made his way to the Cariboo in 1862. But he did not strike it rich in British Columbia either; as he reported to his wife, 'We can make about six dollars a day each, but our provisions cost us about two dollars per day each.'[32] Thomson spent most of his time sawing wood and cutting shingles before leaving British Columbia in late November. Arriving home before the end of the year, Thomson was lucky. Others complained of lack of employment. 'I had thought that if I did not succeed in getting gold that I should get work by the day fairly easily', wrote one Welshman to a newspaper at home, 'but quite the reverse, there is no work'; and the situation was no better in Victoria than in the gold fields, because 'so many have returned from the diggings.'[33] Evan Evans of Merthyr in Wales added, 'They return in their hundreds, some short of money, others without their health and strength and others because they have lost heart.'[34]

The rapid influx of people transformed Victoria and on the mainland led to the establishment of New Westminster, the capital of the new colony of British Columbia. Town lots in Victoria, after the inevitable real-estate boom, rose in value from $50 to $3,000. American firms, including Wells, Fargo and Co., quickly opened offices and stores, and a newspaper (the *Victoria Gazette*) was established. Tents gave way to ramshackle buildings constructed with lumber imported from Puget Sound. Mud was everywhere. Newly established churches openly competed for congregations. Despite the hurly-burly, the older English society in the town was able to maintain its pre-eminence. The site for New Westminster was chosen early in 1859 by Colonel Richard Moody, commander of the Royal Engineers. On a hillside, it had access to the Fraser River and was easily defended. Clearing the site for the new town, named by Queen Victoria herself, was not easy. The forest that covered the site was removed by Royal Marines in the spring of 1859. One new mid-summer arrival reported: 'Mighty trees were lying about in confusion, as though a giant with one sweep of his mighty arm had mown them down. Many of the trunks had been consumed by fire. Their charred remains were seen here and there. The huge stumps of the trees were still standing in most places . . . and between the prostrate trees and stumps there were a few huts, one small collection of wooden stores, some sheds and tents, giving a population of perhaps 150 people. This clearing continued up river to the extent of somewhat more than a quarter of a mile.'[35] The centre that developed was inhabited by a rough and ready collection of Canadians, British Americans, and Americans who had little in common except an inveterate dislike for the snooty ways of the English in Victoria. This hostility towards Victoria was part of the stock-in-trade of the local newspaper, the *British Columbian*.

A small group of black settlers had arrived on Vancouver Island in the 1850s, driven out of California by state efforts to legalize slavery. At first they were cordially received, and an immigrant society collected $2,500 to help them settle, mostly in Victoria and on Salt Spring Island. The black community in the colony was led in the 1860s by Mifflin Gibbs, who was a Victoria alderman and often acting mayor before his eventual return to the United States. In 1864 a corps of 'African Rifles'—founded in 1860 and consisting of three officers and 44 men, with blue uniforms and orange facings—was ordered disbanded by the government, apparently the victims of envy on the part of the white Vancouver Island Volunteer Rifles, founded in 1861. This began a campaign in Victoria of attempts to segregate the blacks, which led eventually to their dispersal, mainly back to the United States.[36]

Chinese immigrants began arriving in the colony from California in the late 1850s as a part of the gold rush. China had been opened to Europeans in the first half of the nineteenth century, and its enormous population encouraged the recruitment of contract labourers by visiting merchantmen. Some Chinese came voluntarily to British Columbia, while others were brought in to work in the mines and at other menial occupations. The new immigrants were overwhelmingly male, mainly from rural districts in southern China. They were largely unskilled and spoke little English. They came to North America as 'sojourners', temporary workers seeking to earn enough money to get back to their families. Cut off from the extended-family connections on which they had traditionally relied, the Chinese workers quickly developed voluntary organizations, often secret.[37] The white population regarded them as unassimilable, importers of every social vice imaginable, and unfair competition for employment. As early as 1860 the colonies of Vancouver Island and British

Columbia contained as many as 7,000 Chinese, although these numbers were not yet sufficient to make them targets for the intense racial hostilities they would later face.

HOPE, BRITISH COLUMBIA, IN 1860

In 1860 the 15-year-old Susan Louise Moir arrived with her family by steamer at Fort Hope. As Susan Allison, in later years she wrote a manuscript entitled 'Recollections of a Pioneer of the Sixties', which was subsequently edited and published by Margaret Ormsby.

Mrs. Landvoight told [me] that by the time she and her husband reached Hope two years before that their money was all spent and they had nothing left but a sack of flour, a can of jam, and a can of lard, and a small iron stove with a drum, a tent and some blankets. Otherwise, they were flat broke and amongst strangers, but she had an inspiration and put up the tent and stove and baked tarts and pies with the jam and sold [them] for twenty-five cents per slice. She made three dollars the first day—after that she could not make pies fast enough for her customers and soon added a cup of coffee—another twenty-five cents—and soon they were able to start a small store which now was a big one. She was a brave lady and did all she could to build the little town of Hope. . . .

The first house was occupied in Hope was a light timber frame with a lumber roof—lined and partitioned with cloth and paper. It was divided into two with this light partition and a blanket hung over a pole served for an inner door. Sheets served for window blinds. I can well remember how airy it was, the high Hope winds also raised the roof. Opposite was a stable with a fine horse that belonged to a man named Shannon. I believe he used part of it as a house. Next door was John Wirth's Hotel, and he was kind enough to allow us to use his well.

None of us knew how to wash clothes. We had a tin bath tub that we brought with us that we used for a wash tub and as we were ignorant as to the use of wash boards, we bent over the bath and rubbed with our hands till they bled and our backs felt broken. As we always wore white embroidered petticoats we had rather a bad time on washing day. Another difficulty was baking bread. At first Mrs. Charles was good enough to bake for us but we could not impose too long. We got a sack of flour and a can of 'Preston and Merril Yeast Powder' and when we went by directions managed to make fairly good bread, at least my mother did. We younger ones sometimes forgot to put in the baking powder and once in a hurry grabbed a can of sulphur by mistake and did not find out till the bread began to cook and we began to choke and splutter with the fumes. Then a man named Kilburn told us to use sourdough and bake in a skillet and when once we got on to that and did not let the bread stand too long we made a great success. . . .

With spring Hope woke up to life and activity. As head of navigation it really was an important place. Now we went to our new house. The things we had sent round the Horn arrived in due time. My sister's little piano, a plough, lamps, crockery and many other things, all useful and even ornamental for the house. Our beds were made of round poles and we used for blocks sawed off small logs, with a branch for a handle left on each for seats.

SOURCE: *A Pioneer Gentlewoman in British Columbia: The Recollections of Susan Allison*, ed. Margaret Ormsby (Vancouver: University of British Columbia Press, 1976), 8, 12.

The discovery of gold irreversibly altered life for the Native peoples of the Pacific slope, as serious mineral exploitation tended to do everywhere in British North America. Much of the remaining fur-trade territory—where the First Nations still followed their traditional ways of life, controlled their economic exchanges with Europeans, and, most important of all, retained control of their lands—was often not attractive for agricultural settlement. But remote and forbidding regions often contained great mineral wealth, and Aboriginal land claims and territorial rights were ignored in the rush to exploit the land itself. Unlike the earlier fur traders, the new arrivals, whether settlers or gold miners, tended to express intensely racist views concerning Aboriginal peoples. One British Columbia newspaper insisted that 'according to the strict rule of international law[,] territory occupied by a barbarous or wholly uncivilized people may be rightfully appropriated by a civilized or Christian nation.'[38] Few settlers would have disagreed with this proposition, or with the view that the 'indolent, contented, savage, must give place to the busteling [sic] sons of civilization & Toil.'[39]

One early symptom of the new situation was an incident that occurred at Bute Inlet in 1864, when a group of Chilcotin workers assisting a road construction crew killed (the contemporary newspapers preferred the word 'massacred') 13 white workers. The government moved quickly to dispense 'justice' to the culprits, who told one visiting clergyman that 'They meant war, not murder.'[40] In Victoria the murders were said to have been utterly without provocation. Governor Frederick Seymour himself wrote the Colonial Office to say that if the 'Indians' rose in war against the whites, 'I may find myself compelled to invite every white man to shoot every Indian he may meet. Such a proclamation would not be badly received here in the case of an emergency.'[41] In the interim, the British settled for summarily hanging eight Chilcotin accused of the crime. Only a few contemporaries fully recognized that the incident was part of the First Nations' response to their dis-

placement. Recovery from such a serious disruption would be extremely difficult.

Europeans by the late 1860s had begun penetrating parts of the interior of the province for settlement purposes. Both the Nicola and Okanagan valleys received pioneers, mainly from Britain. The Allison family moved to the Okanagan from Yale in 1866, and one young Irish immigrant wrote from Nicola Lake in 1868 that 'a young Englishman and I were the first two white men who came to this district', adding, 'when we came here our nearest neighbour was from 40 to 50 miles from us. Since then quite a number of settlers have located in the valley.'[42]

THE NORTH

Few British North Americans thought much about the vast Arctic region either as a potential source of raw materials or as part of a future nation. The Arctic was merely a footnote to the main development of British America. But during the nineteenth century a considerable amount of activity went on in the Far North, often at the instigation of the Royal Navy, which needed something for its officers to do after the end of the Napoleonic Wars in 1815. For most of the century, the goal was no longer commercial advantage but what the Admiralty described as altruistic scientific activity 'of the most liberal and disinterested' sort.[43] The first serious expedition was led by John Ross in 1818, and thereafter there was usually at least one Royal Navy vessel north of 60 at any point in the century. Because the Arctic was so difficult to access, most of these expeditions spent several winters in the ice. Loss of life could be heavy, and soon the greatest challenge for the captains was simply to return home with minimal casualties.

The most famous of those captains was undoubtedly John Franklin, who first commanded an expedition in 1819 that returned to England in the fall of 1822. Franklin and another Royal Navy sailor, Edward Parry, competed with one another for public glory until they teamed up in 1824 and actually produced some useful surveying work. There followed a series of dramatic incidents. In 1833 an English whaling vessel off Lancaster Sound (near Baffin Island) came upon three boats drifting in the sound. They contained a handful of emaciated men, the remnants of an expedition led by John Ross that had been given up for lost for several years. Ross himself was still alive. This party had survived for four years in the Arctic, thanks chiefly to the assistance of the Inuit. In 1844 Franklin returned to the region for a third time, carrying enough provisions for a three years' voyage through to the Pacific. The vessels of the Franklin expedition disappeared and no word was received from them. A relief party was not sent until 1848, by which time all the crew members were probably dead. Thereafter, a series of rescue missions were dispatched from Britain, each one grander and better prepared than the one before. Several experienced their own harrowing adventures.

Eventually, in 1853 some information about the fate of Franklin and his crew was serendipitously discovered by John Rae, a Scottish-born physician and explorer. Franklin's wife had encouraged several of the rescue attempts, and now raised by public subscription a fund to mount an expedition to bring home her husband's remains. This effort, led by Captain Leopold McClintock, sailed from England in 1857. McClintock managed to find a cairn with a note from the party in 1859, and subsequently came upon more traces of the ill-fated expedition, which he took home later the same year with news of their deaths. The 'fate of Franklin' had become a very popular topic in early Victorian Britain, and it has remained a favourite subject over the years, as various scholars and journalists have speculated on why such a well-prepared expedition proved such a disaster. One theory is that the men were victims of their extensive preparations, poisoned by the lead in the early tin cans used to preserve their food.[44]

■ Sir John Franklin, engraving c. 1845. LAC, C-1352.

CONCLUSION

The discovery of gold in British Columbia, the parliamentary inquiry of 1857 into the Hudson's Bay Company's charter, and the arrival on the prairies of two scientific expeditions might have seemed to have little in common except chronological proximity. What they signalled, however, was a recognition that the West was more than a vast desert of use only to the fur trade. Events moved extremely rapidly after the middle of the century, drawing the region to the attention of the land-hungry inhabitants of eastern British North America. Canada could think in terms of its own 'Manifest Destiny', its own transcontinental expansion. Settlement would, of course, mean even more profound changes for the Aboriginal population than the fur trade had brought.

SHORT BIBLIOGRAPHY

Fisher, Robin. *Contact and Conflict: Indian–European Relations in British Columbia, 1774–1860*. Vancouver, 1977. The standard work, older but reliable.

Isenberg, Andrew. *The Destruction of the Bison: An Environmental History*. Cambridge, 2000. A new study that comes to no definitive conclusions.

Karamanski, Theodore J. *Fur Trade and Exploration: Opening the Far Northwest 1821–51*. Vancouver, 1983. The best account of the northwestern fur trade.

Mackie, Richard S. 'The Colonization of Vancouver Island, 1849–1858', *BC Studies* 96 (Winter 1992–3): 3–40. The best modern study of the subject.

————. *Trading Beyond the Mountains: The British Fur Trade on the Pacific, 1793–1843*. Vancouver, 1997. An excellent synthesis of a complex period.

Marchildon, Gregory P., ed, *The Early Northwest* Regina, 2008. A useful collection of articles reprinted from *Prairie Forum*.

Morton, A.S. *History of the Canadian West to 1870–71*, 2nd edn. Toronto, 1973 (1939). Although old, this work is based on archival research and presents one of the few overviews of the early history of the entire West.

Pannekoek, Frits. *A Snug Little Flock: The Social Origins of the Riel Resistance*. Winnipeg, 1991. A controversial study of Red River society, arguing a sharp religious and ethnic division between Métis and mixed-bloods in Red River.

Ray, Arthur. *Indians in the Fur Trade*. Toronto, 1974. A pioneering study of the First Nations on the prairies.

Sterne, Netta. *Fraser Gold 1858! The Founding of British Columbia*. Pullman, Wash., 1998. A recent study of a relatively neglected event.

Wightman, W. Robert, and Nancy M. Wightman. *The Land Between: Northwestern Ontario Resource Development, 1800 to the 1900s*. Toronto, 1997. An important study of the region.

STUDY QUESTIONS

1. Was the area that is now northwestern Ontario a part of 'the West'?

2. What was distinctive about the Red River settlement?

3. Who were the 'Métis'?

4. Why did Britain allow the Hudson's Bay Company to continue its monopoly in the West?

5. Did the Aboriginal people flourish under HBC rule?

6. What was distinctive about settlement on Vancouver Island?

7. Why were the scientific expeditions to the prairies in the 1850s so important?

8. What was the significance of the gold rush for British Columbia?

9. How did Europe use the Arctic in this period?

CHAPTER TWENTY-ONE

Early Victorian Society, 1840–1870

In the middle decades of the nineteenth century British North American society was on the move. Not only were new immigrants constantly arriving, but settled populations were picking up and moving on, some to the United States, some to the new rural districts that were being created out of the wilderness, and many to the burgeoning Canadian cities. Meanwhile, the class structure of the society was beginning to take shape and even solidify, with the emergence of an urban working class and the rapid professionalization of certain skilled and educated segments of what was developing into a middle class. Ethnic–religious tensions increased substantially, sometimes erupting in open conflict. And as private organizations of all kinds—fraternal, humanitarian, religious, and even cultural—expanded, many people also began to organize groups for various purposes, from recreation to social reform.

MOBILITY

Probably the single most important social factor of the years 1840 to 1870 was the sheer extent of the movement of people responding to a variety of forces, both positive and negative. Movement into the prairie region would not begin in earnest until after 1870, but the population of Canada West had

been slowly creeping into the American Midwest since the early 1830s. We tend to associate geographical mobility with our own society, forgetting that the pattern of constant movement—of people constantly searching for a better life—existed in British America 150 years ago as well.

CANADA EAST/QUEBEC

The first sign of serious out-migration in Canada East came from seigneurial districts, the heartland of French-Canadian culture, language, and religion. There the agrarian crisis, combined with the failure and repression of the rebellions of 1837–8—which that crisis had helped to spark —drove many to leave their native province. Some of the migrants were political exiles, but most were young people, both male and female, impelled by the impossibility of finding affordable, productive land in the traditional seigneurial regions and pulled by the opening of textile mills in New England cities like Manchester, New Hampshire, Lowell, Massachusetts, and Woonsocket, Rhode Island. Almost any risk was preferable to the prospect of a lifetime on a farm of less than 100 acres—the future faced by the vast majority of inhabitants of the seigneuries. In the 1830s upwards of 40,000 left the province for the United States. That figure jumped to

TIMELINE

1838
British Americans celebrate Queen Victoria's coronation.

1840s
Sons of Temperance Lodges organized.

1845
Independent Order of Odd-Fellows brought to British North America.

1847
Riot in Woodstock, NB. Doctors in Canada West must be examined and certified.

1851
Wilson Benson settles in Grey County.

1852
John Snell has 100-acre farm in Peel County.

1857
St Patrick's Day parade in Toronto is secularized. Population of Montreal is 57,000.

1858
Irishman murdered in Toronto on St Patrick's Day.

1860
Prince of Wales tours British North America.

1866
Transatlantic cable laid.

1868
Regiment of Papal Zouaves raised in Quebec.

1869
Ontario establishes certifying College of Physicians and Surgeons.

90,000 for the 1840s and 190,000 for the 1850s. In the latter decade the legislative ending of the seigneurial system contributed to the population loss, which was understandably regarded as critical for Canada East; one cleric called it 'the cemetery of the race'. The people who left would respond rapidly to American assimilationist pressures, bringing an end to more than two centuries of ongoing expansion for the French-Canadian people. Today, visitors to those New England towns and cities can still see standing— usually empty and forlorn—the extensive brick buildings that once housed the nineteenth-century factories in which the French-Canadian migrants worked.

Not all those leaving the old seigneurial districts went to the United States. Thousands of other French Canadians moved into the Eastern Townships—originally intended as English-speaking enclaves within Canada East—while others continued to fill up unpopulated regions in the Laurentians and around Lac Saint-Jean. Colonization of these regions was promoted by both Church and state as an alternative to immigration to the United States. Antoine Gérin-Lajoie dramatized this movement in his novel *Jean Rivard*: the young protagonist decides against attempting to farm one of the small, over-worked properties in the seigneurial district and moves to the wilderness region of Canada East, where he pioneers a new and satisfying life close to the soil.

Because most of the land in the Townships was held by speculators, many of the first

French-Canadian settlers there started out as squatters. Once the region was opened by the railroads in the 1850s, sawmills and textile mills grew up rapidly along its rivers. In Sherbrooke the largest woollen factory in Canada—employing 500 workers—opened in 1866, giving French Canadians a chance to be exploited in their own province as well as south of the border. The arrival of larger numbers of French Canadians in the Townships helped drive many British settlers, often non-anglophone Gaelic-speakers from the Highlands of Scotland, farther west. As early as 1871 the former had come to outnumber the latter rather substantially. In the upper St Francis district of the Townships, for example, the French-speaking population grew from 9.7 per cent of the district in 1844 to 64.1 per cent by 1871.[1]

As well as moving out of the country or into regions like the Eastern Townships, thousands of people from Canada East, mainly francophones, moved into the expanding cities and towns of the province. Overall, the number of non-rural Québécois nearly doubled between 1851 and 1871, and the population of Montreal increased from 57,000 to 130,000. By 1871 Trois-Rivières had 124 manufacturing establishments employing just over 1,000 workers. The most significant change, of course, occurred in Montreal, where thousands of rural French Canadians, the majority of them female, moved in search of employment.

CANADA WEST/ONTARIO

Canada East was hardly alone in experiencing large movements of population, although the particulars varied from region to region. In the case of Canada West/Ontario, for example, most of those moving to the United States headed for the agricultural districts of the American Midwest, at least until the opening of Manitoba, in 1870, provided an alternative. A key factor behind the constant mobility was the inherent instability of that much vaunted institution the

family farm, which Canadians have always regarded as the keystone of rural society. The economic success of the family farm depended on the ability of family members to perform most, if not all, of the work. Large numbers of children were therefore desirable, and were by and large achieved. In Peel County, Ontario, between five and six children per family, of a total of eight or nine born, survived to maturity. A farm couple with five or six children had a chance of economic success. But they also faced increasing pressure both to expand their land-holdings and to reduce the number of prospective heirs. Young children represented a captive labour force, but as they grew up they would stay on the farm only on the understanding that they would eventually inherit enough land to become independent farmers themselves. In this male-oriented society, sons normally expected to inherit productive farmland, and their expectations could be deferred for only so long. Hence the tendency in all rural societies in British North America to send disproportionate numbers of female offspring (usually between the ages of 15 and 21) into the cities and non-agricultural work. If a family enjoyed the economic advantage of having several sons, it either had to provide sufficient landholdings for all of them or watch some of them leave to join their sisters in the cities.

In 1852, for example, farmer John Snell of Chinguacousy Township in Peel County was 41 years old, with eight children—four of them boys—under the age of 14. His farm of 100 acres (40 ha) had cost $1,300 to assemble, and he would add another 100 acres over the next few years. Although the farm was economically viable for a growing family, it was not large enough to provide for more than two sons, and at $60 per acre the cost of assembling more land for additional farms was prohibitive. Thus, while agricultural districts everywhere tended to produce large families, not all of the children could expect to be accommodated on the family farm, however prosperous. At the same time, the need

■ Settlers clearing land at New Denmark, New Brunswick, c. 1872. Provincial Archives of New Brunswick P5-167.

to provide for their children led farmers to increase their holdings whenever possible. Between 1851 and 1861 the average farm size in Peel County increased by 40 per cent, but the number of males aged 15 to 30 increased even more rapidly.[2]

Not every agricultural district, or every family within it, followed exactly the same pattern of development. Farms growing staple crops that required large acreages (such as grain) were less divisible than more complex mixed farms, although even the latter had a minimum size for viability. In time it became possible in Ontario, as it had always been in parts of French Canada and the Atlantic region, for families living on farms too small to be self-supporting to survive with the income provided by family members—often the family head and older children—employed off the farm. Yet for some members of the younger generation the pressure to depart was

always strong. On the other hand, farm families that did not enjoy a surplus of children put different pressures on the young, who could not leave because they were expected to take over the farm and help support their aging parents.

Under most circumstances women could not expect to inherit farms, even from deceased husbands; normally they could not even share in the proceeds of sale. The right of the male head of a household to own land, sell it, and control the inheritance of it was accepted in law and in practice everywhere in Canada, subject only to the right of the spouse to a share of the real estate during her lifetime. Few fathers chose to treat daughters equally with sons, however much they had contributed to the family's prosperity. Land went to the sons, and daughters could expect little more than a small cash bequest out of the liquid assets of the operation. Small wonder that young women were even more likely than their brothers to leave rural communities, although they did not usually travel so far. The accumulation and inheritance of land were key issues in rural society, and the economics of farming was an inherently destabilizing force in Canadian society for most of the population. Elder sons (and the women they married) could expect to become pillars of the community, local leaders in political, religious, and cultural terms, and perhaps even part of the rural elite in their community. But for most of the children of farmers, adulthood meant moving on, in search either of new land on which to begin the cycle again, or of non-agrarian opportunities.

Some new land within Canada West/Ontario was available to the north, and after mid-century settlers moved rapidly up to Georgian Bay, into the Muskoka country, and along the north shore of Lake Huron. Such settlers ignored the prominent outcroppings of the Canadian Shield and the shortness of the growing season. The father

of Stephen Leacock, for example, after unsuccessful attempts at farming in South Africa and Kansas, in 1876 settled his family near Orillia, in the Lake Simcoe region. Leacock's father soon abandoned his farm, leaving his wife and 11 children to survive mainly on family remittances from England.

Those who sought to grow grain, the staple crop of southwestern Canada West, usually moved west instead of north. At first they went to adjacent states of the American Midwest, such as Michigan and Illinois, where immigration from Upper Canada began in earnest in the 1830s. One community near London, originally settled by Welsh immigrants in the 1820s, was by the 1850s exporting most of its younger generation into the American grain belt. After the American Civil War a constant stream of Canadians made their way beyond the Midwest states onto the American prairies, contributing to the rapid settlement of states such as Nebraska and the Dakotas—though

JAMES THOMSON
(1823–95)

James Thomson led a nomadic existence and essayed a variety of occupations for many years in British North America. Born in Scotland, Thomson trained as a baker. He emigrated from Aberdeenshire to Montreal in 1841, and from there to Edwardsburgh, Canada West, still working as a baker. In 1849 he headed west to Chicago, where he clerked for a timber merchant, and a year later crossed the continent to California, where he tried gold mining but ended up baking again. Thomson returned to Edwardsburgh in the early 1850s, and at the age of 31 married, intending to settle down permanently as a

farmer. But by 1862 he was on the gold-dust trail again, working at a variety of occupations in the Cariboo until he returned virtually penniless in 1863. Thomson got a job as assistant bookkeeper in 1863 at the Edwardsburgh Starch Company. This time he stayed put, occasionally serving on the town council and ultimately, in 1881, becoming reeve of Edwardsburgh. His diaries and letters have been edited by Richard Preston as *For Friends at Home: A Scottish Emigrant's Letters from Canada, California and the Cariboo, 1844–1864* (Montreal and Kingston: McGill-Queen's University Press, 1974).

some of these families, or their children, would eventually cross the border again as the Canadian prairies were opened to settlement.

THE ATLANTIC REGION

The years before 1860 saw considerable internal expansion in the Atlantic region as some settlers moved into less desirable and more remote parts, while others moved into the major urban centres. Population growth rates overall continued extremely high, although in Nova Scotia—ominously—they began to decline as early as the 1850s. By the end of that decade very few of the older settled districts could support their natural increases in population, much less sustain incoming immigrants. In Newfoundland, for example, there was considerable movement out of the eastern districts into the largely unsettled western part of the island, and a vast increase in the seasonal migration into the Labrador fisheries; in some outports over two-thirds of the working males became seasonal workers in Labrador. Similar patterns existed in the Maritime provinces, as people in New Brunswick moved northward and in Prince Edward Island westward. But as the forests in these provinces became depleted, seasonal migration for timbering declined somewhat in intensity, and in the end, neither seasonal migration nor expansion onto new (and frequently marginal) land could ensure a livelihood for a growing population. As agriculture, fishing, and shipping began to reach the limits of their employment capacity, many young people migrated—either out of the region (usually to the United States), or to urban centres—in search of work.

There had always been some British North Americans who slipped across the border. But the 1860s saw the exodus from the Atlantic region, especially the three Maritime provinces, begin in earnest; probably only the uncertainties of the American Civil War prevented it from taking off before 1865. Whereas in the 1850s only a few districts were losing population, in the next decade over one-third of the counties in the Maritime

provinces experienced population losses. The correlation between rural counties (with economies largely dependent on farming and fishing) and depopulation was very high. The lost population moved in two stages: first from the countryside to the nearest town or city, and then out of the region entirely. While out-migration was a general phenomenon, Scots and Irish were over-represented in the exodus and Acadians under-represented. Most of those departing were young. One 1873 study of Nova Scotians going to the United States found that more than 20 per cent were under 15 years of age, and less than 15 per cent over 40. Significantly, considerably more than half (831 out of 1,524) were female, with the majority in the under-15 category. Most men leaving Nova Scotia were farmers and unskilled workers, although a minority came from artisanal trades declining in economic importance. By 1870 far more native Maritimers resided in the United States than in the other provinces of the new Dominion.

TRANSIENCY

The population on the move in the mid-nineteenth century did not consist only of a younger generation in search of agrarian opportunity. Another dimension was provided by a large group of transients, people who were constantly shifting from one frontier area to another, or from rural to urban and then back to rural. By and large, those who stayed in one place were reasonably successful. Those who kept moving tended to be failures, or at least people whose constant movement prevented them from becoming permanently established and hence successful. In Hamilton—an emerging city that has been as thoroughly studied for the mid-nineteenth century as any in North America—the correlation between transiency and poverty was remarkable. Similar findings over a similar period occur for Peel County, northwest of Toronto. In both rural Peel County and its market town, Brampton, persistence of residence was the most important factor in economic success measured by wealth. In Peel County, as in Hamilton at mid-century, residential persistence also meant that one was likely to have been involved with the community virtually since the beginning of its prosperity. Not all founders stayed, but those who did tended to prosper.

Transients have rarely been the subjects of biographical study. An exception is Wilson Benson (b. 1821), whose career was mentioned in Chapter 13. Beginning in Ireland at age 15, Benson changed his district of residence 11 times (six in Ireland and Scotland between 1836 and 1838 and five in Canada West between 1838 and 1851) before finally settling on a farm in Grey County in 1851 at age 30. He had changed occupations 29 times and apprenticed to at least six different trades in the 1830s and early 1840s, eventually moving back and forth between storekeeping and cooking seasonally on a lake vessel in the later 1840s. He was able to settle down only because of an inheritance.[3] In his later years, he also kept a store in his community.

A STRATIFYING SOCIAL STRUCTURE

By contributing to economic inequality in this period, transiency had some impact on social structure. But urbanization, industrialization, and immigration, combined with the exodus from the rural communities into the towns, created a working class. While the farming pioneers remained small-scale commodity producers indeterminately related to the solidifying class structure, the urbanized workforce swiftly turned into a landless proletariat. Over the middle decades of the nineteenth century, the older social structure of elites and non-elites became far more clearly stratified.

THE RISE OF THE RICH BUSINESSMAN

The potential for great gains in business has always meant the potential for great losses, and the mid-nineteenth century was no exception to the rule. Nevertheless, successful businessmen—including the ubiquitous bankers and the railway lawyers—were highly esteemed in this age of economic transformation, achieving high status partly by self-ascription and partly by their acknowledged economic and political power. That power was evident in all political arenas, but was uppermost at the municipal level, where businessmen formed a mutually supporting elite that took the lead in all aspects of the city's life, including its development and its land market. In this period, most business leaders were self-made men. This is not to say that they had risen from rags to riches, but they had achieved their positions in the community by their own efforts, without benefit of direct inheritance—though some merchant princes like Hugh Allan and the younger John Molson represented a second generation. Scots were over-represented in business ranks and Protestantism predominated. French Canadians and Irish Catholics were under-represented.

THE NEW PROLETARIAT

The rise of a working class will be discussed in detail in Chapter 23. Nevertheless, it is perhaps worth noting that similar inequalities of wealth existed in rural and urban areas alike. Fewer than two-thirds of farmers in 1871 Ontario owned land. Many of those without land were farmers' sons living at home, and the proportion of owners increased with age. Rural landlessness thus appears—at least in Ontario, and there are signs that the situation was similar elsewhere in British North America—to represent a process of land acquisition related more to the individual life cycle and the dynamic pattern of the family farm than to any sort of deep structural divide. The authors of the most recent and most detailed study of property in Ontario in the early Victorian period conclude that, relatively speaking, Ontario in 1871 was still a land of considerable opportunity—at least in terms of rural land acquisition.[4]

THE MIDDLE CLASSES AND THE RISE OF PROFESSIONALIZATION

It is an axiom of history that the middle classes are always rising. What historians must do is describe the unusual features of that rise in any particular period. The middle classes in early Victorian British North America included urban property-owners such as artisans and small merchants, substantial small-town merchants and small industrialists, and, in the rural areas, owners of large farms and boats. The relative dependability of income for professionals tended to set them apart from other members of the middle class. The beginning of professionalization is the particular development within the middle classes of the mid-Victorian period that we will highlight here.

As elsewhere in the educated occupations, the numbers of qualified practitioners were increased through formal education and at the same time stringent licensing requirements were imposed, often set by the profession itself. Nowhere was this process more advanced before 1870 than in the medical profession. Until the beginning of the nineteenth century, medicine was practised by many people besides those with suitable medical credentials; some simply declared themselves doctors, and others—such as midwives, who handled most births, and a variety of herbal healers—functioned in some sort of medical capacity. Canada had experienced a good deal of conflict over the licensing of doctors, partly because of differing educational systems in Canada East and Canada West, partly because of disagreements between doctors educated in Canada and those trained abroad.

The first medical school in Canada was opened in 1824 at the Montreal Medical Institution, which in 1829 became the faculty of medicine at McGill University. Medical schools and faculties were different from Colleges of Medicine, which were created to license doctors rather than to train them. Legislation requiring the examination and certification of potential practitioners passed the Canadian legislature in 1847. Ontario finally established a certifying College of Physicians and Surgeons in 1869, and was followed by other provinces in short order. One of the first acts of the Manitoba legislature, in 1871, was to create a Provincial Medical Health Board, which was responsible for setting examinations for licences to practise. The legislature initially grandfathered all those practising medicine in the new province into the Health Board without further scrutiny of credentials or capacities; this was typical of the way legislative licensing worked at first. Lawyers adopted a similar policy, and although the Law Society of Upper Canada (which came to regulate admission to the practice of law) was formed in 1797, most such provincial societies were created much later, between 1846 and 1877. Manitoba passed an 'Act to Regulate Admission to the Study and Practice of Law in Manitoba' in 1871. It permitted those who had been admitted to the profession elsewhere to practise in Manitoba as well, although many in the legislature objected to the automatic qualification of lawyers from other jurisdictions. When 10 barristers had been admitted to the practice, in December 1871, a Bar Society was formed to control future admissions.[5] Everywhere in British America, lawyers of the early Victorian period were usually trained as apprentices in working law offices; formal legal education in law schools did not become common until later in the century.

The rise of professionalism produced higher standards of practice—or at least guaranteed that practitioners had some appropriate training—but it also enabled the professions to control their numbers to some extent, and to create a public sense of professional status that justified relatively high incomes and raised esteem for their members. Clergymen and university professors, both of whom had lower incomes, joined doctors and lawyers as the leaders of the Canadian middle class. As we shall see later in this chapter, these professionals helped lead the new middle-class drive for respectability across British North America.

ETHNIC TENSIONS

From the arrival of the first Europeans in North America at the end of the fifteenth century, tensions had existed between peoples of different ethnic and cultural backgrounds—first between Aboriginal people and European newcomers, then between the colonials of the various European nations attempting to establish themselves. The conflict between the Catholic French Canadians and the Protestant population of New England was especially sharp, expressing itself both in war and in the taking of captives, but the conflict between the Acadians and the British was also severe. Ethnic tensions declined in much of British North America after 1763, although the populations of the settlements were no more homogeneous than they had been before. The main cause of this decline was residential segregation, often as a deliberate policy. Aboriginal people were separated from Europeans, while Europeans of different ethnic backgrounds were separated from one another in distinct settlement enclaves. The Germans in Nova Scotia had been moved to Lunenburg to segregate them from the remaining settlers in the province. The Acadians had escaped to the frontiers in the 1750s. And Quebec was divided in 1791 to allow anglophones and francophones to have their own distinct provinces in Upper and Lower Canada. At the beginning of the nineteenth century, British North America consisted of a series of isolated ethnic enclaves, often speaking distinct languages and consciously preserving a particular Old World heritage.[6]

During the first 40 years of the nineteenth century, the ethnic isolation of the peoples of British North America was steadily reduced, leading to increasing contact among potentially hostile peoples. The sheer increase in population made it difficult for enclaves to remain isolated, and the trend towards urbanization threw people of various ethnic origins together in one social and economic space. Meanwhile, a sharpening class awareness often expressed itself in ethnic terms, and increasing ethnic tensions in the Old World were imported to the New. One of the main arenas for ethnic hostility was Ireland, where Protestants and Catholics were becoming ever more aware of the antipathy between them. Irish problems in British America had been limited by the nature of the Irish immigration in the early years of the nineteenth century, when most of the new arrivals came from the mainly Protestant north of Ireland. But after the late 1830s and especially in the 1840s, when the potato famine drove hundreds of thousands of impoverished Catholic Irish across the Atlantic, the conflicting groups came into increasing contact with one another in many places in British North America. The larger port cities all received more than their fair share of the new Irish arrivals, but some sections of rural British America were equally affected, especially the Ottawa Valley and parts of the Atlantic provinces.

Probably the two areas most prone to ethnic unrest in the 1840s were the Ottawa Valley and large parts of New Brunswick. Both of these regions experienced substantial Irish Catholic immigration, but both were also affected by other ethnic or racial uneasiness as well. In New Brunswick a resurgent Acadian population was beginning to assert itself by 1840, and in the Ottawa Valley French and British Canadians were competing for land and power. During the 1840s, economic dislocation and uncertainty sparked increasing social violence.[7] For example, on 12 July 1847, some 300 members of the Orange Order in Woodstock, New Brunswick, assembled in front of their lodge hall and began a three-mile march to a Baptist church to hear a sermon. Many of the marchers were armed, since there had been tensions in the region for many months between Orangemen and Catholic Irishmen. While the Orangemen marched, Catholic Irishmen staged an armed counter-demonstration. A detachment of British troops arrived to keep the peace. The

Orangemen agreed that during their return procession they would leave their arms in a wagon following them, but otherwise defied the Riot Act. For their part, the Irish Catholics refused to disarm. When the two crowds met, a shot was fired and chaos ensued. The Irish Catholics suffered most of the casualties and probably all of the deaths, for which an exact number is not known. They also experienced most of the arrests and, ultimately, trials, which permitted the majority community to vent its hostility against them. The main result of the incident and its aftermath was a significant increase in the membership of the Orange Order in Carleton County, New Brunswick.[8] The Woodstock Riot was on the one hand an illustration of the sort of ethnic tensions possible in British North America at mid-century, and on the other hand an example of the sharpening tendency towards violence in colonial society. At the same time, it demonstrated some of the ways in which fraternal organizations had worked their way into the fabric of early Victorian British American society.

THE NEED TO BELONG

The early Victorian age in British North America was characterized by enormous expansion in the number of private associations devoted to non-occupational goals. Although the state, too, was growing, even in united Canada it did not weigh heavily on the lives of individuals in this period. Political allegiances were not as important to the average person as family, religion, and associational commitments. Churches continued to be most important. In Canada East/Quebec, the Catholic Church was overwhelmingly dominant. In the Atlantic region, Protestants and Catholics were more equally divided. Only in Canada West/Ontario were Protestants so clearly dominant in both numbers and power that the regional culture took on obvious Protestant dimensions; nevertheless, Ontario Culture was easily mistaken (especially by Ontarians) for Canadian Culture, particularly as it expanded westward onto the prairies.

By 1870 few British Americans, urban or rural, both male and female, could be found who did not belong to a good number of organizations in addition to their church. In an earlier period, before the 1830s, private fraternal societies had been organized, usually at the elite level, to provide or supplement municipal services such as water, light, firefighting, and library facilities. But by 1870 some organizations had virtually relinquished charitable and service activities in favour of providing entertainment and companionship for their members. The changing nature of fraternal societies was perhaps most marked in Ontario.

RELIGION

Catholicism. The early Victorian era was critical for Roman Catholicism in Canada.[9] Within French Canada the Church emerged as the leading voice of nationalist aspirations, and curés assumed positions of local leadership. English-speaking Catholics largely succeeded in separating themselves from their francophone colleagues within the administrative hierarchy. The early period of lay control—when, in the absence of local bishops and clergy, laymen enjoyed considerable autonomy—was over. The hierarchy had firmly re-established its control over the laity. Now the Church, particularly the francophone branch, was adopting the ultramontane stance—supporting absolute papal supremacy—that would characterize it for much of the next century. English-speaking bishops from the Maritime provinces were among those who tried to prevent the issue of papal infallibility from being decided at the Vatican Council of 1869–70. The divisions among the Canadian bishops at the Council were symptomatic of the divisions among Canadian Catholics. Although Protestants tended to view Catholicism as a monolith, Canadian Catholics were anything but homogeneous in their ethnic backgrounds, and were never able to speak with a single voice on any issue.[10] Even the French-speaking wing of the Church was not totally united, for Acadians and francophones in the West had quite different needs and institutions from Quebecers.

Despite the relatively accommodating attitude of the anglophone hierarchy within the Roman Catholic Church towards Protestants and their political dominance, hostility between Catholics and Protestants existed just beneath the surface in most provinces, and could erupt at almost any moment—as it did in the PEI 'Bible Question' of the 1850s (Chapter 17). Nevertheless, outside Quebec and perhaps Newfoundland, the Church tended to keep a relatively low profile and try to get along with other denominations.

In Quebec, one man symbolized the ultramontane Church of the early Victorian period. Bishop Ignace Bourget was consecrated coadjutor to the bishop of Montreal in early 1837, on the very eve of the rebellion, and succeeded to the see in 1840. He died in June 1885, at the end of the second Riel uprising, although he had retired a few years earlier. Bourget was always an active defender of both the papacy and the position of the Church in Canada.[11] He introduced the Roman liturgy with its effusive expressions of piety, fervently opposed the principles behind the European revolutions of 1848, and actively recruited priests, monks, and nuns both at home and abroad. Bourget expanded the ecclesiastical administration of his diocese, seeing that every parish had a resident priest and many a curate as well. As the numbers of secular clergy and lay religious increased, so did the numbers of children they taught. The clergy were now able to mobilize public opinion, as they did in 1868 when they helped to recruit 507 Zouaves in Quebec (and over $100,000 to support them) to serve in the papal army. The Church acquired a certain public flamboyance under Bourget, as evidenced by the new liturgical splendour, which was matched only by its orthodoxy and aversion to anything smacking of liberalism. He became the leading opponent of liberal thinking in the province, particularly as it was represented by the Institut Canadien, the Montreal centre for those intellectuals critical of

■ Bishop Ignace Bourget, c. 1871. LAC, C-49514.

the Church. Not surprisingly, Quebec bishops also strongly supported the doctrine of papal infallibility at the Vatican Council.

Outside Quebec and the francophone Church, a major development was the massive Irish Catholic immigration of the period after 1840, which helped remake the anglophone wing of the Church. No longer dominated solely by Scottish-born bishops, English-speaking Catholicism increasingly mirrored Irish piety and produced a new breed of authoritarian and authoritative clerical leadership that defended Catholicism within the larger society. Bishops like Michael Fleming in St John's and James Dunphy in Saint John reflected the new revival of Catholicism in British North America.

'THE BATTLE OF YORK POINT, 1849'

A major confrontation between Orangist and Irish mobs took place on 12 July 1849 in Saint John, New Brunswick. Nobody has ever known how many died in the fracas. Like many other such incidents, this one left behind it a song, which was later collected and published.

The Battle of York Point, 1849, St. John N.B. (by John Knox, eyewitness)

It was on the 12th of July, in the year of '49
Six hundred of us Orange boys together all did j'ine
To celebrate the Glorious Twelfth, in memory of
    our King
Who from popish chains and idol gods he did us all
    redeem.

(Chorus)
Then we will sing, our Orange boys, of courage bold
    and free,
Resolved to die before you fly from the popish enemy.

Then we marched down to Water Street, linked by
    heart and hand did go;
You would think it was a Paradise assembled
    here below;
Our freedom badge shone like the sun that lurks in
    the sky
And our music would delight you, whilst our Orange
    flags did fly. (Chorus)

Then we reached their green arch, the stones they flew
    like hail,
Our Orange balls caused some to fall, and some to
    turn their tail.
They ran like hunted horses, their hair stood up
    on end,
Whilst our Orange boys undaunted stood, their free-
    dom to defend. (Chorus)

Then we marched through the papist crowd, their
    stones we did defy,

For to meet our Orange Brethren on the Twelfth day
    of July,
And to let those popish rebels for them to think
    that we
Were some of the highest branches on King William's
    Orange tree. (Chorus)

Then we marched over to Indiantown, to meet our
    Brethren there,
The steamboat it saluted us with Orange voices
    so clear,
And everyone that passed us by would seem to make
    a pause,
But in their countenance you could read 'You're wel-
    come, Orange Boys.' (Chorus)

Now we all returned safe back again, our number
    to increase;
We thought to go through York Point, they would be
    all in peace;
But when we came to York Point the stones and bul-
    lets flew,
There were so many papists there as French at
    Waterloo. (Chorus)

Then we marched through York Point again, with
    guns and bullets all,
The papists, like pigeons off the housetops they did fall;
While they stopped at their stone heap, the brickbats
    for to throw,
Our Orange guns were levelled straight, and brought
    them all quite low. (Chorus)

Here is a health to our worshipful; all Protestants come join,
And celebrate the Glorious Twelfth, King William and the Boyne.

Come, join with us, all Protestants, these papists we defy,
And have your guns well primed, Orange boys, for the next 12th of July. (Chorus)

SOURCE: *The Sentinel Orange and Patriotic Song Book* (Toronto: Sentinel Publishing, 1935), 36, quoted in Scott See, *Riots in New Brunswick: Orange Nativism and Social Violence in the 1840s* (Toronto: University of Toronto Press, 1993), 211-12.

Protestantism. By 1840 Protestant denominations everywhere in British North America had largely cut themselves free from their roots in Britain or the United States. The major development of the early Victorian period, particularly in Ontario—where Protestantism emerged as a distinctive and all-embracing culture—was the construction of a broad alliance among the three major denominations: Anglicans, Presbyterians, and Methodists. This alliance was made possible

■ Orange Order parade along King Street, Toronto ca 1867. Toronto Public Library (TPL), T13222.

by the gradual elimination of the major points of public friction between the established churches and the dissenters, as the establishment ceased attempting to insist on exclusive state support and connection. Once the clergy reserves and the University of Toronto had been secularized, old hostilities melted away. Moreover, the Methodists became far more respectable and far less evangelical in their attitudes as the wilderness was settled. Camp meetings and itinerant preachers were replaced by church buildings and settled ministers in most denominations, and main-line Protestants discovered how much they shared.

The result was a Victorian Protestant value system that could be found everywhere in British North America, but was most pervasive in Canada West/Ontario. It emphasized the relationship between social stability and Protestant morality, which in turn was based on a firm belief in God and His millennium. It saw gradual social change as progressive, offering a way of understanding the changes facing the individual in the Victorian era. It recognized the need for a moral code based on the Ten Commandments, but one that was chiefly voluntary and personal. Protestant morality began with the individual Christian, but then was passed on to the community, which vigorously enforced its values.[12]

ORGANIZATIONAL LIFE

The Protestant churches were central to the development of a vast network of clubs, societies, and charities. By the mid-nineteenth century male governance in the churches was being implicitly challenged by the increasing proportions of women members. Evangelically oriented churches frequently employed their ladies' aid or women's auxiliary groups to sponsor missionary activity. Women usually supported such groups with their own money, kept separate from the larger funds of the church, and these missionary-aid societies offered many women their first opportunity at independent administration.

Beyond the churches, however, were many societies of less 'respectable' origin.

That most characteristic Canadian society, the Orange Order, could count the participants in its activities in the hundreds of thousands. It had been founded in Ulster in 1795 with the twin aims of defending Protestantism and maintaining loyalty to the British monarchy. Within a Protestant context the appeal was non-denominational, but religion was important, and the final requirement for membership in the early Orange Order was 'the strictest attention to a religious observance of the Sabbath, and also of temperance sobriety'.[13] In Canada the Order added to its politico-religious aims a strong fraternal aspect, providing rituals and social activities for its local members. By the early 1830s, the Orange Order had over 103 lodges, 91 of them in Upper Canada. Although Orangism came to British North America with the Irish, and served to some extent as an expression of Protestant Irish ethnicity, it became very popular with Scots in some provinces, and gradually took on a primarily WASPish air. At its height, the Orange Order probably never had more than 50,000 actual members, scattered across the continent and the social classes, but the membership numbers waxed and waned, and one estimate suggests that as many as one in three Protestant Canadians in the Victorian period had strong Orangist links. The Order had lodges everywhere, but was most important and influential in Canada West/Ontario.

Orangism has tended to be associated with public events—organizing parades on 12 July (the anniversary of William of Orange's victory over the Catholics in the 1690 Battle of the Boyne), opposing Roman Catholicism across a range of issues, demonstrating during the tour of the Prince of Wales in 1860, responding to the 1870 execution of Thomas Scott at Red River—and with the Irish. The Order's importance and influence rested, however, on the fact that it brought together Protestants of all origins and that at the local level it served as a focal point for social intercourse and conviviality. Lodges frequently held dinners to celebrate the 12th of July; in 1841, for example, the Woodstock, Canada West, lodge passed a resolution 'that a dinner be provided by Brother Love on Monday the Twelfth July, similar to that of last year, and that one shilling and three pence be taken from the funds of the lodge for each person present, to defray the expense of drinking standard toasts.'[14] As a 'secret' society it had elaborate initiation rites and a ritual, most of it borrowed from the Freemasons (who shared its anti-Catholic stance). The ritual appealed to men who spent most of their lives in mundane occupations and belonged to Protestant denominations that had very little ceremony in their church services. In the initiation ceremony for one of its graduated degrees:

> The door is . . . opened, and the Candidate (having the Bible in his hand) shall be introduced between his two Sponsors, each bearing an Orange Rod, decorated with Blue Ribbon, and one carrying, also, the Blue Book of the Lodge, with the Obligation thereon and open, and the other an Inkstand; he shall then be conducted to the side of the room, and then East, towards the Deputy-Master, before whom shall be burning one bright light; and before the Master there shall be placed eleven candles, in a semi-circle, and also one candle placed in the center of the circle. The eleven candles are not to be lighted until the Candidate has reached the Deputy-Master; the one in the center is not to be lighted.[15]

The Orange Order in its early days attracted a reputation for violence—especially in New Brunswick, where large numbers of Irish Catholics immigrated in the 1840s—and served as a lightning rod for various nativist hostilities.[16] By the late 1850s, however, the Canadian lodges were seeking to become more respectable, and were attempting to cut down on drinking and rowdyism. Now they put the emphasis on providing services for their members, including elaborate funerals. But if local fraternity was the key to Orangism's success, its public influence was enormous, particularly in Ontario.

The Orange Order was only the most prominent of the many fraternal organizations and voluntary societies that flourished in British North America. Most were semi-secret, with elaborate rituals based on Freemasonry. The Masons themselves expanded enormously in mid-century. As an example of the fancy regalia they displayed at funerals and public 'demonstrations', a member of a Lodge of Royal Arch Masons wore a scarlet robe trimmed with ermine, a white lambskin apron with a crimson and purple border, a crimson and purple sash, and various jewels of the order. Among the other organizations active in Canada were the Independent Order of Odd-Fellows (founded in England in 1813 and brought to British America in 1845) and the Order of the Knights of Pythias (founded in Washington, DC, in the early 1860s and brought to Canada in 1870). In the early Victorian period—roughly 1837 to 1870—there were no equivalent societies for Roman Catholics. Although most lodges had adjunct or parallel organizations for women, the most successful lodges were exclusively male and reaffirmed their members' masculinity as a part of the fraternal experience. By 1870 many Canadian men belonged to one or more of these organizations. The growth of fraternal benefit societies was a characteristic of an age of mobility. Membership offered social connections in a new community as well as status, entertainment, and, increasingly, assistance in time of economic or emotional need.

PUBLIC CELEBRATIONS AND SPECTACLES

Public feasting and celebrations were long-standing traditions in Western culture. By the early Victorian period such events had acquired more organization and regularity. In French Canada the feasts followed the Church calendar: the beginning of Lent was carnival time, and 24 June was St-Jean-Baptiste Day—the feast of the patron saint of French Canadians. In addition, both French- and English-speaking British North America celebrated various civic holidays, often specially proclaimed on an ad hoc basis. The coronation of Queen Victoria in 1838 was celebrated in Halifax with a massive parade, which included three regimental bands, a troupe of Highland pipes, and the Coloured Truckmen of Halifax, mounted.[17] The visit of the Prince of Wales to British America in 1860 was greeted with public celebration and spectacle in many places. Guy Fawkes Day on 5 November was associated with various public pranks, although its anti-Catholic origins limited its appeal and sometimes led to violence.[18] After 1867 the First of July (Dominion Day) became a public holiday. And the Queen's Birthday—24 May—was an extremely important civic occasion. In one town in Canada West, the day began with gun and cannon fire and continued with a procession featuring:

> . . . a motley crowd . . . mounted on horses of almost every conceivable color, size, age, and shape. One of them was mounted on a live unicorn, the horn apparently composed of a portion of a barber's pole. The appearance of this company was certainly most grotesque—some of the riders wearing hats something less than twelve feet in length, others wearing tin spurs of the greatest magnitude, and others again with coats of the most ludicrous cut and buttons of mammoth dimensions, and all wearing masks.[19]

A brass band led a noon-time parade to a site where team sports and athletic competitions were held, including a baseball game. Families picnicked at the park, and in the evening there was a banquet followed by theatrical events at the town hall. Late at night people massed in the streets for fireworks, followed by a torchlight procession.

As well as general public holidays there were various special days associated with ethnic groups: 12 July for the Orangemen and 17 March for the Catholic Irish, for example. Such occasions gave British North Americans an opportunity to enjoy marching bands and activities from mumming to street theatre. In Saint John two theatrical societies, the Calithumpians and Polymorphians, were created specifically for burlesque presentations at parades and processions.[20] Such societies also existed in other places. For many people these special days offered an excuse for the public consumption of alcoholic beverages, and particularly in the case of the Irish (both Protestant and Catholic) ethnic celebrations, an opportunity for a bit of rowdyism and violence as well. The St Patrick's Day parade in Toronto was a typical ethnic parade. It was organized by the Toronto St Patrick's Society, which had been founded in 1832. At its origin, the event had been primarily religious, with Irishmen parading to a mass at St Michael's

■ Daguerreotype of a group in costume for Saint-Jean-Baptiste day, Montreal, 1855. The four costumed boys represent (from left) the saint himself, 'an Indian Chief', Jacques Cartier, and 'a French-Canadian'. Photo by T.C. Doane. LAC, PA-139333.

■ 'A Fancy Ball at the Victoria Rink, Montreal', 1865-6, watercolour by Capt. F.G. Coleridge. LAC, C-102533.

Cathedral. In 1857, however, over 1,000 people had marched behind 400 members of the Young Men's St Patrick's Association. Instead of hymns, popular tunes were played, and secular symbols (shamrocks and harps) abounded. In 1858 an Irishman was murdered by Orangemen on St Patrick's Day. Thereafter, the newly organized Hibernian Benevolent Society orchestrated the parades, which displayed a new Irish militancy. In 1863 the Benevolent Society's band played a concert of Irish airs the night before the parade, and in the morning a crowd of several thousand marched from St Paul's Church on King Street to St Michael's Cathedral for mass. Bishop John Joseph Lynch delivered a sermon on the 'glorious saint' and the mission of the Irish diaspora, and then the crowd—larger now—marched back to St Paul's to hear speeches by prominent Catholic leaders, including Michael Murphy of the Hibernian Benevolent Society, who denounced the British and declared that 'three-fourths of the

Catholic Irish of this country would offer themselves as an offering on the altar of freedom.'[21] He concluded by declaring 'perfect satisfaction' with the laws of Canada, however. The crowd then broke into smaller groups and the parties continued well into the night.

Like many social activities in early Victorian British North America, the celebration of public events was chiefly a male business. Women may have worked behind the scenes sewing costumes and decorations, and women certainly thronged the streets for processions such as the one celebrating the visit of the Prince of Wales to Halifax in 1860. Occasionally, women even marched, especially in temperance parades. But the organization of these events was almost invariably in the hands of middle-aged middle-class men. Performance, at least before 1870, was also dominated by males, sometimes dressed up as females, and many burlesque routines explicitly mocked women.[22]

SOCIAL REFORM: TEMPERANCE

Heavy consumption of alcoholic beverages—beer, wine, and spirits—was a characteristic of early modern Europe and was brought to North America by the first settlers. Public drinking, at least for males, was a part of social conviviality, and in many towns and villages the alehouse (inn, tavern, saloon, pub) was probably the most important building. The public house served important social functions as the centre for the exchange of community information and as a male escape from the constricted quarters of the family, often providing amenities (heat, light, cooked food, conviviality) not available at home. Although women normally did not patronize public houses, in small places women (often widows) often owned and ran them. Soldiers and labourers in outdoor occupations such as lumbering were particularly frequent patrons. Almost any town had a large number of drinking estab-lishments, most of them small and nasty; Canada West in 1851 had 1,990 recorded taverns—one for every 478 people—and more unrecorded. Per capita consumption of whisky in Canada West in 1851 was three gallons per annum.[23]

Not surprisingly, many sought to reform drinking habits. At first much of the initiative for change came from the churches, especially in Britain and the United States, and reflected chiefly the interest of the middle classes who were increasingly embracing the notions of domesticity and respectability. The first temperance societies in British North America appeared in Nova Scotia in the 1820s.[24] In Upper Canada/Canada West, temperance took hold mainly in commercializing areas and was weakest in the agricultural regions, particularly among subsistence farmers. Temperance initially meant drinking in moderation, but soon came to mean abstinence (by the individual) and prohibition (by the state). By the 1840s the Sons of Temperance, which had originated in the

JAMES BROWN
TO HIS SON, 1858

My Dear James,

Although I have had very little communication with you for sometime past, on the disagreeable and heartrending subject of <u>intemperance</u>, I have never ceased to feel the greatest interest and anxiety with regard to you. Last night . . . I [was informed] that you were <u>wrong</u> again. . . . This struck me to the heart—drove all public matters out of my mind and made me not only sorry, but sick also! . . . And now, my dear James, what can I say to you that I have not said before? Or what can I do, in addition to what I have done already? . . . I begged of you many years ago, to join the Sons of Temperance, an association which although it cannot work miracles, has saved many. . . . It is a great advantage to the family that so many of them belong to the order, and an inexpressible <u>grief</u> to me, that you should be the exception. . . . Indeed, I know it is in <u>vain</u> to remonstrate with you now! If . . . the cases of violent death, and living misery which happen all around have no effect on you.

Yours in affliction, James Brown

SOURCE: Cheryl Lynn Krasnick, ed., *Drink in Canada: Historical Essays* (Montreal and Kingston: McGill-Queen's University Press, 1993), 21–2.

United States, was moving into British North America and organizing lodges that differed little from other fraternal organizations of the period—except that they served 'no liquor stronger than tea'. Samuel Leonard Tilley of New Brunswick and Charles Tupper of Nova Scotia were both important figures in temperance lodges, and temperance even played a role in the politics of the time.

In the beginning temperance was very much a Protestant movement, although in the late 1840s an anti-liquor movement led by the Catholic priest Charles Chiniquy was quite successful, especially among the more respectable members of Catholic communities in Canada East.[25] Temperance campaigns served a number of purposes in the early Victorian period. On one level they were part of a larger crusade against the vulgarity of earlier times. On another, especially in New Brunswick and Upper Canada, they represented a reaction against the arrival in those provinces after 1830 of large numbers of Irish immigrants. When Orange lodges sought to become respectable in the 1850s, one of their first campaigns was to eliminate liquor both from their own meetings and from public gatherings.[26]

CONCLUSION

British North American society and culture became more complex and multi-layered in the early Victorian period. Economic, political, and intellectual–aesthetic developments all had their impact on social structure, mobility, and both equality and opportunity. One key development was the growth of a middle class, which began to reorganize society to reflect its concerns, its ambitions, and its needs. In this process, institutions that offered a sense of belonging to the community were extended, and various reform movements (such as temperance) were introduced. The result was that British North America increasingly reflected the middle-class values that came to be associated with Queen Victoria.

SHORT BIBLIOGRAPHY

Breton, Raymond, and Pierre Savard, eds. *The Quebec and Acadian Diaspora in North America*. Toronto, 1982. An important collection of monographs on the dispersion of francophones in North America.

Courveille, Serge, and Normand Seguin. *Rural Life in Nineteenth-Century Quebec*. Ottawa, 1989. A useful synthesis of a substantial body of secondary material.

Darroch, Gordon, and Lee Soltown. *Property and Inequality in Victorian Ontario: Structural Patterns and Cultural Communities in the 1871 Census*. Toronto, 1994. A quantitative study of landholding based on nominal census returns.

Gagan, David. *Hopeful Travellers: Families, Land, and Social Change in Mid-Victorian Peel County, Canada West*. Toronto, 1981. The classic study of landholding in rural Canada West.

Guildford, Janet, and Suzanne Morton, eds. *Separate Spheres: Women's Worlds in the 19th-Century Maritimes*. Fredericton, 1994. A collection of articles on women in the nineteenth century.

Hansen, Marcus Lee. *The Mingling of the Canadian and American Peoples*. New Haven, 1940. The most detailed study of its subject, and still the best.

Hardy, René, and Normand Seguin. *Forêt et société en Mauricie: La Formation de la region de Trois Rivières, 1830–1930*. Montreal, 1984. A provocative regional microstudy of a lumber district in Quebec.

Little, J.I. *Nationalism, Capitalism and Colonization in Nineteenth-Century Quebec: The Upper St. Francis District*. Kingston, 1989. An important introduction to organized colonization in nineteenth-century Quebec.

Noel, Jan. *Canada Dry: Temperance Crusades before Confederation*. Toronto, 1995. A useful summary of temperance movements in early Canada.

See, Scott. *Riots in News Brunswick: Orange Nativism and Social Violence in the 1840s*. Toronto, 1995. The best microstudy of ethnic violence in nineteenth-century Canada.

STUDY QUESTIONS

1. What does the 1847 riot in Woodstock, NB, tell us about British North American society at the time?

2. Why were so many British North Americans on the move at mid-century?

3. Where were British North Americans moving to around 1860?

4. What is transiency (in the demographic sense) and why was it important?

5. Why was Irish immigration important to the Catholic Church?

6. What was the relationship between Protestantism and the voluntary society?

7. Why were public celebrations so common in early Victorian British America?

8. 'Temperance' was to some extent a code word for what tendencies in Victorian society?

CHAPTER TWENTY-TWO

Early Victorian Culture, 1840–1870

■ Virtually every diary or journal surviving from mid-nineteenth-century British North America records some sort of non-professional culture-making, whether at home or in the local community. A typical entry, from the diary that Charles Wilson kept in British Columbia in the 1850s, describes 'a very jolly day at New Westminster. . . . Seddall & Luard are first rate musicians & we had no end of waltzes, galops & songs to enliven us.'[1] In the days before entertainment came pre-packaged, almost every middle-class British North American (and a good many from other social ranks) knew how to make culture of some sort, whether playing a fiddle, painting a watercolour, writing a poem, or telling a story. The 'Canadian content' in such works, however, was often quite limited. This should not surprise us—after all, many people, at least in the English-speaking colonies, were recent immigrants whose very notions of culture had been formed in Europe.

CULTURAL INFRASTRUCTURE

The conscious cultivation of mind, creativity, and aesthetic tastes—which is what most people have in mind when they think of 'culture'—obviously does not come easily to a pioneer society living on the edge of a vast wilderness and spending most of its energy on survival. Such culture requires a complex infrastructure in order to flourish. Small parts of that infrastructure had been established almost from the beginning of settlement in North America, but full-fledged institutions supportive of culture developed only slowly, and the years between 1840 and 1870 were important ones in that process. Cities are crucial to the arts, for only they bring together sufficient numbers of people to provide an audience and sufficient wealth to make patronage possible. A number of other necessary cultural ingredients were either introduced or greatly extended in these years. At one time firm lines of demarcation would have been drawn between high culture and popular culture. But the current scholarly tendency is to blur the distinctions between the two, particularly at the margins.

BOOKS AND LIBRARIES

A colonial society was not normally a world of books. In earlier times, a handful of private individuals and institutions had accumulated relatively large collections, but it was not until the nineteenth century that the notion developed of a collection that might be collectively financed and made available to the public. Although the

TIMELINE

1818
Dalhousie University founded.

1824
Literary and Historical Society of Quebec founded.

1825
Theatre Royal opens in Montreal.

1830
First art exhibit in Halifax.

1834
First art exhibit in Toronto.

1838
Joseph Légaré's 'Galerie de Peinture' opens.

1839
Saint John *News* introduces a penny edition. 'Les Amateurs typographes' founded. First baseball game played in Upper Canada.

1841
Abraham Gesner opens museum in Fredericton.

1842
Dickens visits Montreal. Geological Survey of Canada established.

1843
Construction of St Patrick's Church begins in Montreal. Snowshoe club organized in Montreal.

1844
Institut Canadien founded in Montreal.

1845
First volume of Garneau's *Histoire du Canada* published.

1846
Halifax's Theatre Royal opens.

1847
Toronto Society of Arts founded. Longfellow's 'Evangeline' completed.

1848
Toronto's Royal Lyceum Theatre opens.

1850
University of Toronto secularized.

1852
P.T. Barnum's Menagerie and Museum appears in Guelph.

1853
'National' museum recommended for Province of Canada. George Brown publishes first daily newspaper in Toronto. Bellini's opera *Norma* presented in Toronto.

1859
Bishop Bourget issues pastoral letter against the theatre. Paul Kane's *Wanderings of an Artist* published.

1862
Literary journal *Le Foyer Canadien* founded; publishes *Jean Rivard* as a serial.

1864
Typographical Society of Quebec City opens reading room.

1869
First Ontario baseball tournament organized. George Beers publishes *Lacrosse, the National Game of Canada*.

modern public library was still several generations away, early versions of it emerged in a variety of places. (Curiously, there is no general history available of the development of libraries in Canada.) In many cities, subscription libraries were formed by subscribers who grouped together to buy books; the earliest of these had been established at the end of the eighteenth century. Such libraries were often associated with literary and historical societies (the prototype was the Literary and Historical Society of Quebec, founded in 1824). Mechanics' Institutes, which

originated in England in the 1820s, were brought to British North America later in the decade. Branches were opened in Montreal in 1828, York in 1830, and Halifax in 1831, and the network expanded significantly in the 1840s and 1850s; members of these institutions normally had access to both lending libraries and reading rooms. The Institut Canadien, founded in Montreal in 1844, created a library of major scientific, legal, and literary works as part of its effort to establish a formal French-Canadian culture. Symptomatic of the new trend was the cam-

■ The Mechanics' Institute, Toronto: the music hall as converted to a reading room, 1900. In the 1880s the Institute was taken over by the city and its library became the foundation of the Toronto Public Library system. Toronto Public Library (TPL), T12006.

■ The Fire Hall and Theatre Royal, Barkerville, BC, 1868–9. The theatre was on the second floor. Vancouver Public Library, Special Collections, photo no. 8636.

paign mounted by the British army after 1840 to equip every major garrison in British North America with a library. The united Canada established a provincial library in the 1840s, and libraries were founded as a matter of course by universities and colleges, which began to multiply after 1830. In 1863 the largest university library, at Laval, held 28,000 volumes, including 4,000 in medicine, 8,000 in science and literature, and 14,000 in theology.[2] In 1864 the Typographical Society of Quebec City opened a reading room with a collection of 1,000 books. A year later, New Westminster organized a public library, with books from the Royal Engineers' col-

lection forming the basis of the 'British Columbia Institute'. By the mid-1860s virtually every urban centre in British America could offer its citizens access to one or more large collections of books, as well as a reading room.

THEATRES AND PERFORMANCE HALLS

During the first half of the nineteenth century, most secular venues were makeshift structures, usually located in buildings designed for some other purpose and hastily converted to performance use. Before Confederation there were very few proper theatres, with stages and backstage accommodations. Naturally those that did exist were in the larger cities. Almost all were owned within the local community. Although the garrison at Halifax in 1789 constructed the New Grand Theatre, with boxes as well as open pits without seats in front of and behind the stage, the first building in British North America dedicated exclusively to theatrical performance was Montreal's Theatre Royal, which opened in 1825. Built by a syndicate headed by John Molson, the Theatre Royal seated 1,000, with two tiers of boxes, a pit, and a gallery, and included appropriate backstage facilities. The Royal Circus (renamed the Theatre Royal) opened in Quebec City the same year. Halifax's Theatre Royal, opened in 1846, could seat 160 patrons in its boxes. Toronto's first theatrical building was the Royal Lyceum, erected in 1848. The Royal Lyceum could accommodate an audience of more than 600, with pit seating, a balcony and gallery, and boxes on either side of the proscenium.[3] By 1850 there was a second-storey theatre in Hamilton, and in 1851 a private association began construction on the Music Hall in Quebec City, intended for concerts, plays, banquets, and public balls. Ottawa opened Her Majesty's Theatre in 1856. Victoria opened the Colonial Theatre in 1860. It seated 365 and 'was suitable for ladies; Indians and such ilk will have a corner to themselves.'[4] London acquired its Music Hall in 1866; located on the second floor of a large building, it had a flat floor and could seat nearly 600. But most urban centres settled for spaces in buildings not specifically dedicated to performance. As is often the case, we know most about Canada West. In smaller centres like Galt, Stratford, and Brockville, performance spaces were located in the local town halls, many of which were constructed in the 1850s. Peterborough opened Hill's Music Hall on the second floor of a market building in 1850. By 1870, however, most of the larger cities in Canada had acquired a proper theatrical venue.

MUSEUMS AND GALLERIES

Museums originated in the desire of acquisitive people, often with very eclectic tastes, to exhibit the 'curiosities' they had accumulated. The typical European museum was quite undiscriminating in what it put on display, and this characteristic was transferred to North America. In Philadelphia at the end of the eighteenth century, Charles Wilson Peale opened to the public a large collection of curiosities ranging from a mammoth's tooth to birds' nests used for soup. In 1810 John Scudder opened his American Museum in New York, and when Phineas T. Barnum took it over, in 1834, he used his showman's eye to develop the public's desire for the unusual. Barnum transformed the museum into a moneymaker, charging 10 cents for admission and exhibiting everything from great paintings to sideshow curiosities. Barnum also pioneered in using the museum as a venue for performances of everything from Shakespeare to minstrel shows. The earliest museums in British North America, often associated with the Mechanics' Institutes, were similarly eclectic in their offerings. In New Brunswick, for example, the geologist Abraham Gesner sought to open a provincial museum in 1841 to display his rock specimens, but when the government refused to finance it, Gesner found space in the Fredericton Mechanics' Institute; according to a catalogue of 1842, 'Gesner's Museum of Natural History' had a collection of 2,173 items. In Quebec, a collection created by the sculptor and gilder Pierre Casseur was purchased in 1836 by the government of Lower Canada and became the first public museum in Canada. Laval University opened an exhibit of its collections in geology and minerology in 1852. In York (Toronto), a 'Lyceum of Natural History and Fine Arts' was first proposed in the legislature of Upper Canada in 1833, but a provincial museum was not founded until 1853, with an eclectic collection of archaeological and fine arts specimens. That same year the geologist William Logan proposed to the Canadian Parliament the construction of 'an appropriate edifice especially planned as a National Museum', principally to house geological specimens.[5]

While many museums specialized in scientific exhibits, collections of fine art were also made available to the public, though not on a permanent basis. Halifax held its first art exhibition in 1830, when some 130 works borrowed from the community were displayed in two rooms and a corridor at Dalhousie College. 'Careful persons were employed to fetch and return the pictures without any expense to the owners; and no sticks, umbrellas or parasols were permitted to be taken into the rooms.'[6] This experiment was so successful that it was repeated in 1831, with works created mainly by members of the local art community.[7] The impetus for the Halifax exhibitions had come from a popular teacher of art in the city, William Harris Jones, who had arrived in Halifax from Britain in 1828. In 1832 the Quebec City painter Joseph Légaré opened his private collection of pictures and engravings, which filled his three-storey house, to the public. Six years later he opened the 'Galerie de Peinture de Québec' in the upper town; this 'temple of fine arts' not only exhibited works of art but provided a venue for musical performance and had a school of drawing and painting attached to it. Légaré and others were unsuccessful in establishing a national gallery in 1845, but in 1851 the artist again opened the top floor of his house to display his art collection, offering free admission to the public. Légaré's executors donated his collection of about 200 art works to Laval University in 1858. In the same period Montreal artists formed an organization in 1847, which in 1860 merged with the Art Association of Montreal. The new Art Association then launched a campaign for a permanent art gallery; that goal would not be realized until years later, but in the interim the group sponsored a series of temporary exhibitions.

In Toronto the Society of Artists and Amateurs held its first exhibition in the Assembly Chamber of the Parliament Buildings on Front Street in July 1834.[8] After a period of dormancy the society resurfaced in 1847 as the Toronto Society of Arts, founded 'for the promotion of the arts, and encouragement of native artists within the western portion of the province.'[9] The society cast its net wide, and sought to obtain 'from Europe a good collection of casts of the finest sculpture of antiquity, and specimens of classical compositions of foliage.'[10] The organizers understood the importance of patronage; among their patrons were the mayor and 'a long list of gentlemen' who 'consented to lend pictures from their galleries'. The four members of the management committee were all professional artists and architects, and the exhibition they mounted at the City Hall displayed 386 items exemplifying the applied as well as the fine arts, listed in a printed catalogue. It was a critical and popular success, although the Society was unable to follow it up.

NEWSPAPERS AND MAGAZINES

Newspapers and magazines were essential to the arts community in a variety of ways. Colonial newspapers provided space for budding writers and poets, occasionally printing or reprinting articles on the arts, as well as editorials calling for a greater cultural life as part of the process of building up the region. In 1829, for example, Joseph Howe's *Novascotian* printed an article by George Young entitled 'Freedom and the Fine Arts' and published a piece on Raphael's paintings in the Vatican. In addition, newspapers provided advance publicity for arts events and—most important, since artists cannot develop without some sort of feedback on their work—commented on them in critical reviews. By the time of the 1847 Toronto exhibition, citizens had access to 11 local newspapers, several of which actively covered the arts. Particularly important was the *British Colonist*, published by the Scottish-born Hugh Scobie. His rival newspaperman George Brown once described the *Colonist* as the 'literary common-sewer of Toronto', perhaps suggesting that Scobie was willing to entertain new ideas.[11] Like many another printer,

Scobie also set up as a 'Bookseller, and stationer, . . . bookbinder, lithographer, copperplate and woodengraver'. After 1843 he was able to produce lithographic prints and maps, and in the 1840s and 1850s he became an important publisher in Toronto, printing volumes of verse as well as a variety of almanacs and manuals.

Until the 1830s most newspapers had been published only once a week, but bi-weekly or tri-weekly editions became available in the larger cities beginning in the late 1830s. The Saint John *News* introduced a penny paper in 1839, and dailies started in the 1850s. Most early papers were four-page sheets and had relatively small circulations—usually not more than 1,000, although readership could be far greater. Susanna Moodie described the typical newspaper as 'a strange mélange of politics, religion, abuse, and general information. It contains, in a condensed form, all the news of the Old and the New World, and informs its readers of what is passing on the great globe, from the North Pole to the Gold Mines of Australia and California.'[12] One modern content analysis of four papers from 1849 corroborates this description. The Toronto *British Colonist* had an entertainment content of 3.2 per cent, considerably more than the Toronto *Globe* but not as much as Montreal's *La Minerve* at 4.6 per cent. George Brown published British North America's first daily in 1853, printing it on a steam-powered cylinder press, and by 1861 had reached the hitherto unheard-of circulation of 28,000. Brown also pioneered the regular serialization of popular fiction in British North America, including the works of Charles Dickens, and he aggressively pursued coverage of the arts, especially in the local community. All newspapers, especially the dailies, benefited from the introduction of telegraphy to British America in the late 1840s.

Most English-language newspapers did not routinely publish Canadian literature, especially fiction, preferring to concentrate on British and American work that could be copied from published editions. Few publishers were interested in Canadian authors, given the difficulties of defending their copyrights.[13] No shortage of literary magazines existed in British America after 1840. The problem was that few of them were able to survive for more than a few issues. Virtually the only successful literary magazine in English was *The Literary Garland*, published monthly in Montreal from 1838 to 1851 by John Lovell. Unlike many others, Lovell paid his contributors; Susanna Moodie 'actually shed tears of joy over the first twenty-dollar bill I received from Montreal.'[14] Publishing most of the leading authors resident in British America at the time, the *Garland* provided a forum of sorts for Canadian writing—although as Carl Klinck has pointed out, its focus was more 'Anglo-Bostonian . . . than Anglo-Canadian': in 1843, for example, its editor referred to local writing as the fruit of 'the seed of Old England and of New England . . . sown in Canada'.[15]

In Toronto, beginning in 1852, Henry Youle Hind edited *The Canadian Journal: A Repertory of Industry, Science and Art*, a magazine aimed at readers with a broader range of interests. In 1856 this magazine turned more academic, with Daniel Wilson of the University of Toronto as literary editor. In January 1858 Wilson published some Canadian work, including the poetry of Charles Sangster. Anglo-Canadian authors would probably have agreed with the Reverend E.H. Dewart in *Selections from Canadian Poets* (1864) that no country in the world paid so little attention to its own literature: 'Our mental wants [are] supplied by the brain of the Mother Country, under circumstances that utterly preclude competition.' Dewart added that 'Booksellers, too, because they make sure sales and large profits on British and American works, which have already obtained popularity, seldom take the trouble to judge of a Canadian book on its merits, or use their influence to promote its sale.'[16] Virtually the only way around this problem was to do as T.C. Haliburton did, finding publishers in Britain and the United States. But few writers were able to make that breakthrough.

The situation for native-born authors was somewhat better in French Canada, which had its language to insulate it from Britain and America and its culture to insulate it (to some extent) from France. Newspapers in French Canada were typically edited by journalists with broad literary pretensions, and were—despite their fierce political partisanship—perhaps more self-consciously literary and aesthetic than those in English Canada. After 1840, French-language papers routinely published indigenous writing, including full-blown plays intended as political satire rather than actual performance pieces. Most periodicals published in Canada East were blatantly nationalistic in intent. *Les Soirées Canadiennes* (1861–5) subtitled itself a 'compendium of national literature', and *Le Foyer Canadien* (1862–6) had as its objective to publish 'any Canadian work distinguished by originality in point of view, thought, or style'.[17]

In addition, a handful of scholarly and professional magazines were launched around the middle of the century, including *Canadian Agriculturalist* (1848), *Canadian Naturalist and Geologist* (1857), and the *Annals of the Botanical Society* (1860). Several medical journals were also begun, although most of them were short-lived.

LITERACY AND AUDIENCES

In history everything connects. Critical to the emergence of the daily newspaper and the development of a larger and more sophisticated arts community was the introduction of mass education in the 1840s, especially in anglophone British North America. As increasing numbers of people learned to read and write, the audience and market for the arts grew accordingly. Census data from 1861 suggest that more than 90 per cent of the people in Canada West knew how to read—a tribute to the early introduction of free schooling. Literacy rates were lower in Canada East, where over one-third of the population could not read, and in the Maritimes, where almost a quarter of the population could not read

and a third could not write. The 1871 census indicated that over 12 per cent of Ontarians could not write; the percentage for Quebec was almost 46 and for the Maritimes over 23. The figures indicate that French-Canadian culture remained much more oral than its English-Canadian counterpart. Naturally, the younger members of society were more literate than their elders, and in most places males were more literate than females. Raw literacy data do not, of course, tell us much about how individuals employed their skills.[18] Nevertheless, combined with the growth in libraries and the increasing availability of books and newspapers, the figures do suggest that British Americans were reading a good deal more by 1870 than they had been in 1840.

HIGHER EDUCATION

Higher education is important for culture because it stimulates interest in the life of the mind and in aesthetic matters. By 1867 there were 17 degree-granting institutions in the colonies, as well as a number of colleges that provided some higher education but did not actually give degrees. Every province (and even Red River) had at least a college or two, and several provinces (like Nova Scotia) had many. With a few exceptions, most of these institutions were small, with enrolments of under one hundred. With four exceptions—Dalhousie (1818), McGill (1821), New Brunswick (1828, secularized 1859), and the University of Toronto (founded 1827, secularized 1850)—institutions of higher learning were church-related and governed. One reason for the large number of small colleges and universities was that every major denomination insisted on having a place where its own students could be educated, mainly for the ministry, free from the doctrinal pollution of the competition.

Colonial institutions had their limitations. Many of the colleges were founded as 'academies', a category akin to modern high schools (some of which retain 'college' or 'collegiate' in their names today), perhaps offering a few of the

F.-X. GARNEAU
(1800–66)

❖

François-Xavier Garneau was born in Quebec City. His parents were poor and he was educated locally, spending several years at a Lancastrian school taught in a church basement. His parents could not afford to send him to the Séminaire de Québec, and he was unable to obtain a scholarship because he was never very sympathetic to the Church. Instead, he worked as a clerk at the Court of King's Bench until beginning to study as a notary at age 25. Over the years he informally acquired a considerable classical education, and began to write both poetry and fiction. In 1831 he visited London and Paris, then worked for over a year in London as secretary to Denis-Benjamin Viger. He began his first newspaper, *L'Abeille canadienne*, in late 1833, and when it failed two months later he went to work as a notary. For the next few years he moved from job to job, sometimes working as a notary, sometimes as a bank clerk, and after 1840 as a journalist and magazine editor. In 1842 he became French translator to the Canadian Legislative Assembly, a position that gave him free time for research and writing. From 1837 onward he was involved in nationalist politics.

In 1845 Garneau published the first volume of his great work, *Histoire du Canada depuis sa découverte jusqu'à nos jours* (3 vols, 1845–8), undertaken in response to the claim in Lord Durham's Report that French Canada was a place with no history and no culture. Drawing on archival research conducted in both Canada and the United States, he not only proved that Durham was wrong but provided French Canadians with a proud history and the foundations for a nationalism based on the theme of survival. At first many were offended by Garneau's

■ F.-X. Garneau. LAC, PA-74097

treatment of the Church, for his anti-clerical views and liberal support of freedom of thought and conscience led him to be highly critical of its role in New France—although he did appreciate its role as the guardian of French-Canadian nationality. Nevertheless, by 1855 his contemporaries had come to recognize his achievement and accept him as 'the national historian of Canada'.

Garneau also wrote large amounts of poetry, but little of it was collected during his lifetime, and therefore it was not properly appreciated. But he did publish various other writings over the years. Like many of the other leading intellectual voices of Canada in the middle years of the nineteenth century—both French and English—Garne au was largely self-educated and highly eclectic. Given the doctrinaire approach of institutional higher education at the time, this was probably a good thing.

most advanced students a year's worth of university-level curriculum. Only a few taught science seriously, partly because of the expense of proper laboratories, partly because higher learning had its roots in the traditional arts curriculum. Most of the colleges in this period would have continued to regard Latin and Greek as far more important than biology, and structured their curricula on a framework of theology and moral philosophy. Teachers or professors were often imported from Britain, and the various British traditions of higher education—not just of Oxford and Cambridge, but of Edinburgh, Glasgow, and Aberdeen in Scotland and Trinity College, Dublin—could be found in various places, depending on the origins of the founders. The Scottish tradition was particularly important, for it was broadly rather than narrowly humanistic, extending beyond classical languages and culture. Most teachers did not have higher degrees and had no interest in research or independent scholarship. They taught many hours a week, usually in lectures. Rote memorization remained the most important part of the instructional process. Virtually no graduate work was undertaken in the early Victorian college or university, even in a profession such as medicine.

LITERATURE

No doubt the most widely studied area of cultural activity is literature. This is unfortunate for the reputation of early Canadian culture in general, for virtually none of the fiction from the mid-nineteenth century is worth remembering, and the record is not much better in other literary genres. In Robertson Davies's satirical novel *Leaven of Malice* (1954), his hero, Solomon Bridgetower, is a young assistant professor who is preparing a critical edition of the works of Charles Heavysege (1816–76), 'Canada's earliest, and in the opinion of many, greatest dramatist'.[19] Davies probably chose Heavysege—who made his living as a carpenter—because the very name suggests a ponderous quality. In any case, poets

from that period are generally remembered only because they were literary pioneers, earnest toilers in the wilderness, or because they took an interest in the landscape of British North America and thus displayed a 'Canadian consciousness'. Most of the best writing in British North America in either language took the form of prose describing landscape, customs, and behaviour in the new land. While much of this literature, including the works of the sisters Susanna Moodie and Catharine Parr Traill, was published, a good deal of it—especially in English—remained in manuscript form. Many British immigrants, notably but not exclusively from the upper levels of society, regularly wrote long letters home describing their experiences in detail. Women were frequently the best correspondents.

Books and journals were easily available in cheap editions from Europe and the United States, and copyright law was not favourable to resident authors. Moreover, the linguistic divide reduced the already limited Canadian market even further. The same problems did not apply in the visual or performing arts.

THE PERFORMING ARTS

Canada has always provided more world-class performers than world-class creators—partly because performers are less likely than creators to be judged in terms of their 'Canadian content', and partly because performance has provided Canadians with opportunities to take part in world culture. The performing arts of theatre and music made great strides forward in the early Victorian period.

THEATRE IN ENGLISH CANADA

Theatre in English-speaking British North America always had to face a battle from the puritans who regarded the stage as the instrument of the devil, and performers—especially professional ones—as immoral if not criminal. Despite the disapproval, early Victorian audiences got to see an enormous variety of dramatic fare, performed by actors and actresses ranging from comedians to tragedians, some classically trained and others not.[20] Almost all of the plays were imported from Britain, Europe, or the United States. The works of Canadian playwrights like Heavysege or Charles Mair rarely made it to the stage; they were far too serious (Heavysege's *Saul* was never produced in his lifetime). The few local plays that were performed tended to be farces or satires written with particular audiences in mind. The principal early Victorian mode was melodramatic, with overblown gestures and expressions of emotion. Shakespeare was very popular, though invariably cut and trimmed to suit individual virtuoso actors. Apart from Shakespeare, drama fell into three categories: historical drama played in full costume; contemporary drama (which allowed 'contemporary' to stretch back into the late eighteenth century); and most popular of all, melodrama, combining suspense, adventure, and just deserts for the bad guys. After mid-century, plays based on novels such as *Uncle Tom's Cabin* (inevitably featuring Eliza and her baby leaping across the ice floes into Canada), *Lady Audley's Secret* (1863) and *East Lynne* (1865) were very popular, as was the temperance drama *Ten Nights in a Bar Room*. For comedy, the classics by Sheridan and Goldsmith were occasionally performed, but contemporary comedies—which came as close as they dared to involving sex— were more common, and knock-about farce was most popular of all. Theatrical audiences in British North America were apparently not usually as rowdy as those in Britain or the United States; however, there was always some audience participation—it was not until later in the century that theatres became as silent as churches until the end of an act. In 1862 a Montreal audience bombarded the actor Charles Fisher with apples, turnips, and eggs; later, outside the theatre, Fisher was attacked by a mob of nearly 500 people.

As well as the theatre proper, a variety of other theatrical entertainments also flourished in early Victorian British North America. A line between high culture and popular culture had not yet been clearly drawn, and thus much entertainment was included under the theatrical umbrella. Blackface minstrel shows were often performed after 1840, sometimes but not always by imported black companies. A handful of Toronto natives, headed by Colin 'Cool' Burgess, made reputations for themselves as blackface performers. The black community in Toronto in the early 1840s had attempted to discourage the introduction of 'certain acts, and songs, such as Jim Crow and what they call other Negro Characters', but without success.[21] In the 1850s a number of popular American minstrel shows toured Toronto, including Thomas D. Rice—the original 'Jim Crow'—who played a week at the Lyceum in 1853. In 1851 a minstrel troupe performed a benefit show for Shadrach Minkins (Chapter 19) in Montreal. In general, a minstrel show would include not only the well-known skits featuring the interlocutor and sidemen, but various dances, sing-alongs, and a variety 'olio'. One of the greatest circus performers—despite his Italianate name—was a Canadian.

Circuses were constantly touring Canada West in the summer. P.T. Barnum's Menagerie and Museum, featuring General Tom Thumb, appeared in Guelph in 1852. In 1864 a circus in Charlottetown distracted local attention from the delegations attending the conference at which the plan for Confederation was formed. And in 1867 G.F. Bailey announced in the Toronto *Globe* that his 'Metropolitan Quadruple Combination' would offer 'a Grand Morning Exhibition, On Wednesday, July 3, of all the attractions and specialities of the large and comprehensive Menagerie, including the comical Performing Elephants and the Lilliputian Baby Elephant from Africa. . . .'[22]

Most theatrical performances were produced by amateurs. Some of the best amateurs were associated with the major British garrisons at Toronto, Kingston, Montreal, and Halifax. In the earlier years of the century, soldiers often provided much of the available theatrical fare. Even

WILLIAM LEONARD HUNT, A.K.A. THE GREAT FARINI
(1836–1929)

William Hunt was born in New York in 1836, but grew up in Hope Township, Canada West. From an early age he was fascinated with the circus, and through his own efforts became a skilled funambulist (tight-rope or high-wire walker) and strong man. By the late 1850s Niagara Falls—already a major tourist attraction—had become a mecca for circus performers and carnival acts, and in 1859 Jean Francois Gravelet (the Great Blondin) achieved considerable fame by walking across the Falls from the American to the Canadian side on a three-inch rope. He subsequently performed other stunts on the rope, including pushing a wheelbarrow containing a small stove to the middle of the rope, where he proceeded to cook an omelette.

Hunt's first public feat came on 1 October 1859, when for $500, under the name Signor Guillermo Antonio Farini, he successfully walked the high wire across the Ganaraska River in Port Hope. Hunt did not use a balancing pole, walked blindfolded, and stood on his head in the course of his performance. Hunt subsequently issued a series of challenges to Blondin, but they went unanswered. Unfortunately, Blondin had accomplished most of his feats before Hunt began performing in public. One feat of Hunt that Blondin never equalled was lowering himself by rope from the tightrope across the Falls to the deck of the *Maid of the Mist* and then ascending back to the tightrope. This stunt took virtually superhuman strength and Hunt never repeated it. He performed twice each week at Niagara Falls in 1860, equalling or exceeding Blondin's stunts and collecting large sums of money in the process. Instead of cooking an omelette, for example, Hunt brought out a washtub, and washed handkerchiefs on the wire. But he never equalled the reputation of the Frenchman. Hunt subsequently added other daredevil stunts to his repertoire, including a failed attempt in 1864 to walk across the Falls just above the American side on a pair of customized stilts. He claimed that he served as a spy for the Confederate States during the American Civil War, and later insisted that in 1885 he had walked across the Kalahari Desert on foot. Circus historians take more seriously his claim to have invented the mechanism for the stunt called 'the human cannonball'.

smaller garrisons were typically active in theatricals. In 1868, Juliana Horatia Ewing, whose husband was an officer of the 22nd Regiment stationed in Fredericton, New Brunswick, wrote to her mother:

I have seen Bombastes for the 7th time. The 22nd have had some private theatricals—(last Friday) & very good fun they were. The man who acted Bombastes has such a prominent nose as [would be] a fortune to an actor, & he was capitally got up. Tell the boys He sang 'Kafoozlum' & I laughed as much as ever. There were several other comic songs in the regular style, but when they don't quite make you roar, they are dreary things. . . . Bombastes was very well done & I

Poster advertising Signor Farini as washerwoman. Buffalo and Erie County Historical Society.

Signor Farini crossing Niagara Falls on a tightrope, 1860. Niagara Falls Public Library, no. 10128.

laughed very much, though I don't care for burlesques: but their 'ladies' were made up splendidly. . . . The pretty one in the farce 'Done on both sides' was as pretty a girl as you could wish to see—but when she spoke in a deep bass voice, & with masculine abruptness it was awfully funny.[23]

Female impersonation was often a highlight of such entertainments, although many garrisons increasingly cast female civilians in female roles; in some cases garrison players sparked civilian companies into existence. British comedies and farces made up the typical garrison fare, but occasionally, heavier material, including Shakespeare, would be attempted.[24] Officers and men of

the British navy also were active performers, and the first European theatrical event ever staged in British Columbia took place aboard HMS *Trincomalee* in Esquimalt Harbour on 18 October 1853.[25] Contemporary reviews suggest that the quality of amateur performances varied, but in many instances performers may have fallen prey to that fine old Canadian tendency towards excessive expectation.

Troupes of touring professionals from Britain or the United States had begun to appear in British North America as early as the eighteenth century, and the construction of proper theatres encouraged a better quality of company to appear from abroad. Over the years, British North America hosted a veritable who's who of

■ 'The Lady of Lyons Burlesque', presented by the officers of the Halifax Garrison, 1872. Thomas Fisher Rare Book Library, University of Toronto.

theatrical talent from the English-speaking world, and a few giants like Sarah Bernhardt from outside it as well. Major performers appearing either alone or with their own touring companies began with the legendary Edmund Kean in 1826, and in the early Victorian period included Edwin Booth, Joseph Jefferson, Coquelin, and Helena Modjeska. Occasionally a native-born British American would win international acclaim. One performer from this period who made it big was Arthur McKee Rankin, who was born in Sandwich, Canada West, in 1841 and allegedly ran away from Upper Canada College to become an actor in 1861. By 1869 he was ready to tour with his own version of *Rip van Winkle*, in which he and his wife starred for many years on the road.

In many places court trials served as surrogate theatre.

THEATRE IN FRENCH CANADA

Not all puritans were English-speaking Protestants; the Roman Catholic Church also tended to disapprove of the theatre, at least in its commercial form, and as late as 1859 Montreal's Bishop Ignace Bourget issued a pastoral letter against it. Yet French-language theatre survived in Canada East, even if it did not always flourish.[26] During the 1830s three major theatrical figures had arrived in Canada from abroad. The first was Firmin Prud'homme, a Parisian who claimed considerable dramatic experience and worked with amateur companies on various plays, including his own *Napoleon on Saint Helena*. He even opened a school for acting, although his traditional style was compared unfavourably with that of British touring stars. The second was Hyacinthe-Poirier Leblanc de Marconnay, who arrived in 1834 and

A THEATRE REVIEW, 1862

In July 1862, the Garrison Amateurs of London, Canada West, presented three contemporary farces, two by J.M. Morton (*The Two Bonnycastles* and *Box and Cox*) and one by John Oxenford (*Only a Halfpenny*).

The Garrison Theatricals

Actors in Canada are scarce, but they would not have been scarce had they been much esteemed, and they would have been esteemed had they professed talents great enough to command esteem. We cannot say that the amateur performers we have lately seen in this city, have exhibited qualities sufficiently great to inspire the population with any deep love for theatrical performance. When we pay our money to see amateur performers, we buy the privilege of criticism, and if it pleases us to express our disapprobation of any particular actor, we have a perfect right, to do so in the ordinary manner, by means of the usual sibilations. If we did not exercise this privilege at the last performances of this Garrison, we abstained, from kind motives and not from a high estimate of the merits of the actors. We conceive that we have a right to expect that amateurs shall be somewhat perfect in their parts, and that the prompters shall not be heard throughout the house quite as frequently and very nearly as loud as the actor. Instead of sneaking towards the wings and leaning on the prompter for support, an actor should be 'Like strength, resounding on his own right arm.' He should have confidence in his memory and know the words of his part, or else he can never sustain the character. Our amateurs were sadly deficient— in this first of all necessaries and having to think too much about what sentences came next, they had no leisure to give to the grace and finesse of the actor. They were mere recitors [*sic*] with much assistance from the prompter, and not by any means, actors. We do not wish to particularise where all was bad, but the pre-eminence of badness ought certainly to be mentioned; and we can have no hesitation in assigning it to 'Box,' a more wooden Box than was never seen on any stage, not even an imitation of any previous Box. Without the vaguest apprehension of a point in the character— without life or energy, or bustle (if the sham women had possessed more of the latter it would have added to the effect of their make up)—a tamer representative of a part requiring great energy was never seen—it is quite inexcusable not to rehearse frequently before appearing in public. Frequent rehearsals would have disguised other inefficiencies, and would have made the best of the meagre talent the company possessed.

'This is no world in which to pity men,' but we did pity the men who must have felt their performance to be a sorry one, and we did also pity the audience who patiently bore as deep an infliction on their sense and temper. We hope the next amateurs who charge us for admission will think that they have a duty to perform to the paying public, and that they are, at the very least, bound to become as perfect as time and trouble can make them. With these remarks we close our friendly criticism.

SOURCE: *London Free Press*, 10 July 1862.

became active in anti-rebel journalism. He edited three different newspapers, but also wrote and presented plays at the Theatre Royal in Montreal, and in 1836 became president of the Amateur Canadian Dramatic Society. The third was Aimé-Nicolas Aubin (usually called 'Napoléon'), a Swiss who arrived in Canada in 1835 from the United States. Like Marconnay, Aubin was principally a journalist. He had been imprisoned for publishing a poem dedicated to the prisoners of 1837–8, and in 1839 he established a theatrical troupe called Les Amateurs typographes, which presented Voltaire's *Death of Julius Caesar* as well as his own plays in the face of much uneasiness among the authorities. In 1842 Aubin's group performed Pierre Petitclair's *La Donation*, the first play by a native-born French Canadian to be seen in Canada East. Thereafter, more indigenous work was probably performed in French Canada than in all the English-speaking colonies. Among the sources were the classical colleges, where amateur theatre began to take root in the late 1820s. By 1844 the Collège de Nicolet was able to produce Antoine Gérin-Lajoie's *Young Latour*—a dramatic retelling of the La Tour story (see Chapter 4)—with the author in the title role.

French Canada always had a predilection for the political, and newspapers of the post-rebellion period occasionally published political dialogues or little playlets. This trend reached its height in 1856, when *La Dégringolade* ('The Tumble' or 'The Fall' [of a ministry]), a play with 12 characters and 17,000 words, was serialized in four issues of the newspaper *L'Avenir*. In 1859 a French professional company arrived in Montreal offering a variety of contemporary plays, including vaudeville, melodrama, and comic opera. It was this commercial theatre that so angered Bishop Bourget, who requested that the clergy in his diocese 'please issue strict instructions, in your sermons, against attending Opera, the Theatre, the Circus, and other profane amusements which now constitute a real source of scandal for our towns and countryside.' There was little clerical opposition to indigenous theatre and amateur performance, however, and these continued to flourish in the province.

MUSIC

The occasional professional musician had managed to make a living in British North America before 1840, either as a member of a regimental band or as a combination of performer, teacher, and instrument-maker. There were some skilled amateurs and a few touring artists. But the early Victorian period saw the emergence of a much more widespread musical life.[27] Touring professionals now arrived in greater numbers. The English singer John Braham appeared in 1841, and by the 1850s the British colonies had heard the likes of Ole Bull (a violinist who appeared twice, in 1853 and 1857) and Jenny Lind (the 'Swedish Nightingale'). Brought to America by P.T. Barnum, Lind sang at Toronto's St Lawrence Hall on two evenings in October 1851, to audiences of a thousand people paying a minimum of $3.00 a seat. Her program included an aria from Bellini's *Beatrice di Tenda* and a cavatina from Meyerbeer's *Robert le diable*, and concluded with a Scottish ballad and a Norwegian folksong. Adelina Patti sang in British America in 1855 and 1860. A Berlin orchestra called the Germanians toured in 1850, giving nine concerts at Montreal's Theatre Royal during a two-week period; baskets were required to collect the bouquets at the end of each concert. Touring companies also performed Italian opera and light operettas. In 1853 the Artists' Association Italian Opera Company presented Bellini's *Norma* at Toronto's Royal Lyceum.

As the touring artists stimulated the public's appetite for music, concerts by local musicians became more frequent, usually featuring brief excerpts from a wide range of musical genres. Most of the skilled musicians were immigrants who had received their training abroad, and the most dedicated musicians often went abroad to make a decent living. Garrison bands continued to be important. In Montreal the band of the 23rd Regiment, considered one of the best in the country, was heard with enthusiasm by Charles Dickens in 1842. On the west coast, the band of the Royal Engineers brought new standards of musical performance when it arrived in the colony in 1859, and from that year until 1863, when it returned to Britain, it served New

Westminster in various guises: as a militia band, a fire-brigade band, a marching brass band, and even a dance band.[28] Brass bands were favourites everywhere in the colonies. The raising of the flag of the Métis provisional government in Winnipeg in 1869 was accompanied by a brass band from the local school in St Boniface. Brass bands were also routinely organized in Native communities and residential schools. Choral singing was also very popular, whether in church choirs or in choral societies. The Toronto Choral Society was founded in 1845.

Most of the compositions performed in the theatres and halls were imported, usually from Europe, as were many of the popular songs and dance tunes played—often on the fiddle—in the rural districts of both French- and English-speaking communities. When Johann Georg Kohl visited Canada in the 1850s hoping to collect traditional French-Canadian folksongs, he discovered that most of the material he gathered had been imported from France in recent times, though some had been written by members of the French-Canadian elite.[29] In 1853 James P. Clarke published a group of songs about the 'fair forest land' as a single extended composition entitled 'Lays of the Maple Leaf'. Clarke, who was born in Scotland and came to Canada in 1845, taught music at King's College and later the Toronto Normal School. Like most early musicians in British North America, he tried his hand at almost everything, from organ-mending to orchestral conducting. His compositions relied heavily on folksongs and melodies for their form and inspiration.[30] In French Canada, Ernest Gagnon collected the words and music of more than a hundred folksongs and between 1865 and 1867 published them as *Chansons populaires du Canada*. He also pioneered in attempting to use Aboriginal music in his compositions, particularly *Stadaconé, Danse sauvage pour piano*. Gagnon was another musical jack-of-all-trades who was, among other things, organist at the Quebec Basilica and teacher of music at Laval Normal School. Unlike Clarke, he was not strictly speaking a professional

for his entire career: in 1875 he became secretary to the Quebec Department of Agriculture and Public Works.[31]

DANCE

British Americans occasionally saw dancing on the stage in the form of pageantry set to music or divertissements within plays; they also saw the occasional touring professional dancer or troupe, such as the Petites Danseuses Viennoises, 48 dancing children who performed in Canada East in 1847. But most dance was a participatory activity rather than a spectacle. Social dancing was popular everywhere in the colonies, from the most remote outpost to the centres of government. In 1862 Viscount Milton and his party, touring west of Red River, stopped at a hamlet to attend a wedding. At one end of a small two-roomed house, he later wrote, were:

> two fiddlers, who worked in relays, the music being in most rapid time, and doubtless very fatiguing to the instrumentalists. The dance, in which about half-a-dozen couples were engaged when we entered, appeared to be a kind of cross between a Scotch reel and the 'Lancers', a number of lively steps, including a double-shuffle and stamp, being executed with great vigour. The dancing was dancing, and no mistake, and both the men and their fair partners were exceedingly hot and exhausted when the 'set' was finished.[32]

At the other extreme were the great balls given in the evenings during the Quebec Conference in 1864. Frances Monck, the wife of Governor General Monck's brother, reported on one such occasion: 'At French parties there are no fast dances, all quadrilles and lancers; it seems so odd. The R.C. Bishop won't allow "round dances". Six of the 25th [Regiment] string band played so well. So many old people I don't think I ever saw, and the older they were the more they danced.'[33]

ARCHITECTURE AND BUILDING

Architecture sits somewhat uneasily in the Pantheon of the Arts. While the design of buildings obviously has important aesthetic implications and impacts, a building also has to function in a practical sense, virtually independent of its visual appearance. Architects had a better chance of making a decent living than most other artists of the early Victorian period, especially when they took part in the construction as well as the design of a building. For that reason, architecture was a thriving enterprise in British North America. By 1840, architects in Britain's North American colonies had a number of styles from which to choose. The dominant Georgian style was now joined by several others: Classical, based on a revival of the forms of Greek antiquity; Gothic, based on a revival of the forms of medieval Europe; and Italian, based on a revival of the forms of baroque Europe. By and large, the Gothic and Baroque styles were more frequently seen in churches and colleges, and the Classical more often used in public buildings.[34]

Most of the great medieval models for the Gothic were cathedrals, so it is not surprising that ecclesiastics in British North America—especially Anglicans and Catholics—would turn to the style in the 1840s. An excellent example of early Gothic design is the Church of St Andrew's-on-the-Red (now in Lockport, Manitoba), which was designed and built by the stonemason Duncan McRae between 1845 and 1849. The first two buildings in the new full-blown Gothic style were St Anne's Chapel (1846–7) and Christ Church Cathedral (1845–53), both in Fredericton, NB. They were both designed by Frank Wills, a recent immigrant from Exeter who accompanied Bishop John Medley to New Brunswick in 1845; Wills later designed Montreal's Anglican Christ Church Cathedral (1857–60). The Cathedral of St John the Baptist (begun 1846) and St James Cathedral in Toronto—designed by Frederic W. Cumberland and begun in 1850—were both in Gothic style, as were a number of parish churches. St Patrick's Church in Montreal (1843–7), built to serve the city's Irish Catholic population, had a nave and side aisles, with a ribbed vault. While the Gothic style was occasionally used for Protestant churches in Canada East, French Canadians were not much attracted to it. Nevertheless, Victor Bourgeau's Église Saint-Pierre-Apôtre in Montreal (1851–3) was a very Gothic design, and Gothic elements found their way into the Catholic Cathedral of Saint Boniface at Red River, begun in 1839.

Born in 1809, Bourgeau was the son of a master wheelwright who somehow learned drafting skills, which enabled him to begin designing buildings in the 1840s. Although he began in the neo-Gothic tradition, he gradually shifted into

■ Christ Church Cathedral, Fredericton, in the 1860s. LAC, C-25544.

◼ Nineteenth-century row houses, rue Wolfe, Montreal. Photo by Jean-Claude Marsan.

the neo-baroque, partly under pressure from Bishop Bourget and the Jesuits to find a style different from that of the Anglicans. Bourgeau visited Rome in 1857 and briefly studied St Peter's Basilica. He did not think this design could be reproduced in small size, and advised Bourget against it. Although Bourgeau designed churches with baroque elements, the chief executor of the Bourget directive was probably John Ostell, who designed a number of edifices in baroque style, most notably Église Notre-Dame-de-Grâce in Montreal (1851–3). Bourgeau did assist Father Joseph Michaud in the design of the Cathedral Basilica of Saint-Jacques-le-Majeur in Montreal (begun 1870), which was a reduced version of St Peter's Basilica.

Self-consciously neo-classical elements were often added on to the older Georgian style that was still important for secular public buildings in British North America. The Charlotte County Courthouse (1839–40) in St Andrew's, New Brunswick, was typical, with a conspicuous classical portico providing a focus for its façade. The Kingston City Hall (1843–4) and the Bonsecours Market (1844–7) in Montreal were two other buildings with large neo-classical porticos. The Commercial Bank of the Midland District (1843–5) in Toronto and the Music Hall in Quebec City (1851–3) were more restrained in their adoption of classical elements, however, and over time restraint became far more a part of the mainstream of architecture for public buildings.

PRIVATE BUILDINGS

Housing in the early Victorian period became more elaborate for more of the population. Most houses in British North America were designed and built by craftsmen—carpenters and stonemasons—rather than architects. Some of these men may have had access to pattern books, but many probably relied on their memories to reproduce standard forms. The English row house became a common feature of cities in the English-speaking colonies after the 1850s; the duplex and triplex made their appearance in Montreal and other French-Canadian urban centres about the same time. In both cases the buildings tended to be tall and narrow, reflecting the cost of urban real estate and the consequent narrowness of lots. In all places, perhaps the most important development was the physical expression of the new ideal of domesticity, which gradually worked its way down the social scale.[35] As houses became larger, public spaces (for eating and talking) were increasingly separated from private ones (for dressing and sleeping), often by placing the public rooms on the ground floor and the bedrooms and private sitting rooms on the upper floors. By the 1840s outdoor privies were being replaced by indoor plumbing. Kitchens were transformed by the introduction of the cooking stove, which replaced the older fireplace. Although wood continued to be the most common building material, brick and stone were increasingly used in both urban and rural areas. British immigrants were consistently amazed at the use of balloon-frame construction techniques, which evolved in North America in the first half of the nineteenth century and were quite unknown in Europe. The balloon frame relied on the quantity of sawn lumber and nails used in construction for its strength, as opposed to the hewn timbers and mortise-and-tenon joining of timber-frame construction that required greater craft skills.

SCIENCE AND TECHNOLOGY

The early Victorian era marked the golden age of natural science in Great Britain—perhaps in the world—capped in the popular mind by Charles Darwin's *On the Origin of Species* (1859), which revolutionized people's thinking about the world in which they lived. In British North America there were few professional scientists and even

fewer of any international reputation. A handful of individuals taught aspects of science in the universities, a few were employed at the Geological Survey of Canada, and one or two were independent scholars. After the rebellions of 1837–8, there was a distinct decline in the pursuit of science by the bourgeoisie in Lower Canada, who may have put more of their energy into politics and the cultural struggle to prove Lord Durham wrong in his disparaging comments about French Canada. In 1876 Pierre Chauveau argued in his *Instruction publique au Canada* that while the anglophones had an affinity for mathematics and science, 'the French population looked to the moral and political sciences, to history, to literature, and to the fine arts.'[36] Chauveau's assessment of English Canadians may have been questionable, but his emphasis on the importance of the arts to French Canadians certainly was not.

Arguably the most original scientific thinker in British America in this period was George Paxton Young. One of the least well-known of the major figures, Young was born in 1818 and in early life published 10 mathematical papers, six in the *American Journal of Mathematics*, on the theory of quintic equations. This precociousness was typical of mathematicians, of course, although later in life Young did publish a paper entitled 'Boole's Mathematical Theory of the Laws of Thought' in the *Canadian Journal* in 1865. But mathematics was not a particularly fashionable branch of science in the nineteenth century. Young spent most of his working life as a minister, a professor at Knox College, a school inspector, and eventually a professor of metaphysics and ethics at University College Toronto from 1870 to his death, his mathematical contributions virtually forgotten.

Most of Young's scientific contemporaries were also employed full-time doing something else. There were many dabblers who were able to take advantage of the fact that the natural world of British America contained species and forms unknown in Europe or even the United States. Collecting unusual specimens for scientific institutions abroad became a pastime for many amateurs, and even some Hudson's Bay Company traders collected skins (mainly of birds distinct to the Arctic) for the Smithsonian Institution in Washington.[37] Charles Smallwood, a Montreal physician, was able to make a nice reputation reporting meteorological and astronomical phenomena from his home observatory, employing largely homemade instruments. The inventory aspect of science was what made most British American science possible.

The premier science of the early Victorian period was geology, and this was important to British America in many ways. It was geology that first raised questions about the biblical story of God and creation, questions that Darwin would pursue. Thus geological research provided the ideal scientific context for clergymen seeking to reconcile the new ideas with their faith. Because of the theoretical importance of relating the geological formations of North America to those of Europe—if the new theories were true, they should apply everywhere—geological research flourished between 1840 and 1870. Most of those British North Americans who made scientific reputations did so as geologists. Moreover, the practical utility of geology, particularly in the search for minerals to exploit, was obvious. Not surprisingly, the Canadian government spent most of its scientific budget on the Geological Survey of Canada, having been petitioned to do so by the Natural History Society of Montreal and the Literary and Historical Society of Quebec in 1841. The GSC was founded in 1842 to explore the province and uncover what was expected (quite rightly) to be great mineral wealth, particularly in the north. 'The object of the Survey is to ascertain the mineral resources of the country', bluntly stated William Edmund Logan, appointed in 1842 as the first geologist.[38] Logan managed to build a useful team of scientists, based originally in a Montreal warehouse, including a chemist (Thomas Sterry Hunt) and a paleontologist (Elkanah Billings). But the key to the success of the GSC was its field surveys, which produced accurate reports and maps basic to Canadian geology.

Perhaps the most important figure in technology was Abraham Gesner of New Brunswick. Born in 1797, Gesner conducted field surveys in the Maritime region, wrote, and lectured, while running a farm and practising medicine, before turning his attention to applied technology. Among his inventions were 'charcoal' briquettes made from compressed coal dust, a hydrocarbon fuel lamp, a process of asphalt paving, and 'coal oil' distilled from solid hyrocarbons. Like many other inventors north of the 49th parallel, Gesner had to move to the United States to find the capital to finance his discoveries. Thus his patents for kerosene were taken out in the United States and his book, *A Practical Treatise on Coal, Petroleum, and Other Distilled Oils* (1861), was published in New York.

In addition to its intellectual importance, science in early Victorian British America had a popular dimension as a public spectacle. Lectures featuring practical demonstrations of scientific principles were standard activities at any Mechanics' Institute. Beginning in 1841, James Paterson offered a series of lectures in Saint John on natural philosophy that included presentations on the pendulum, electricity, the steam engine, and pneumatics, illustrated with voltaic batteries and model steam engines.[39] In 1843 Abraham Gesner lectured in Saint John before an audience of 900 on 'Galvanism', demonstrating the principle with the help of a battery attached to an ox's head fresh from the abattoir. According to one observer, when electric current was applied, 'the head moved, the eyes winked, the jaws began to grind . . . as promised by the lecturer, and to the entire satisfaction of the audience.'[40] Gesner and Paterson openly competed for the public's attention; on one occasion the latter used electricity to set a miniature house on fire. Perhaps the most curious demonstration of the 'galvanic battery', however, came in 1869, at the conclusion of a meeting between residents of Red River and a band of visiting Sioux: the visitors were lined up and each was allowed to touch the ends of live wires

■ Caughnawaga (Kahnawake) Mohawks, lacrosse champions of Canada, 1869, James Inglis. LAC, C-001959.

for a dose of 'medicine'. One of the visitors fainted dead away, but most—we are told—seemed quite pleased, 'if highly astonished'.[41]

Science has always been regarded as a transnational endeavour and scientists as part of an international intellectual community. Curiously, however, one of its most significant effects in British North America was to reinforce the early Victorian trend towards national expansion and unification. As Suzanne Zeller has pointed out, geology in particular helped to identify the valuable mineral resources of the regions to the east and west of the province of Canada.[42] It was 'science' that, in the 1850s, convinced Canadians that the prairies were inhabitable. At the same time, science helped British Americans to think in terms of a larger continental whole, and science, notably natural history, provided a shared subject for people in all provinces.

POPULAR CULTURE

The term 'popular culture' does not refer only to the arts. It also has an anthropological sense, in which it is used to refer to the whole range of activities that engage ordinary people in their everyday lives. In recent years, Canadian historians have uncovered in the arena of popular culture an entire dimension of life that was previously ignored. Here we will examine just one of the many facets of life now being explored by historians for the period 1840–70: sports and games.

SPORTS AND GAMES

Sports and games served a number of purposes in early Victorian British North America/Canada. Organized sport was indisputably a male preserve in this period, one of the many (including the fraternal society) that emerged alongside the new concept of domesticity (Chapter 16). In addition to providing an opportunity for men to get together outside the home, participation in sports honoured the concept of 'manliness'. It also functioned as a kind of cement for community life, and as a focal point for the 'boosterism' so important to aspiring towns and villages. Much organized sport exemplified approved social values: fair competition in a wholesome atmosphere free of drinking and gambling. Finally, the sorts of sports in which individuals engaged helped to identify both their backgrounds (ethnic as well as socio-economic) and their aspirations. Fox-hunting (introduced by the British garrisons in the 1840s) was restricted to the elite, usually of British origin. Baseball was generally associated with the middle classes who sought to distance themselves and their communities from overt Britishness (although in 1870 the *Hamilton Spectator* described it as 'an imported game, . . . just a sandlot sport usually played by undesirables'[43]). Rowdier activities— boxing and cock-fighting, for example—were distinctly lower-class. And curling had a clear ethnic association with Scots.

A few sports had local origins. As we saw in Chapter 16, lacrosse began as an Aboriginal game. In 1856 the Montreal Lacrosse Club was organized, and by 1860 it had been joined by two others. The rules were codified in Montreal and promoted across the continent by a Montreal dentist named William George Beers, who by October 1867 had brought to life 80 lacrosse clubs with 2,000 members across the new Dominion. Two years later, the Mohawk team from Caughnawaga were the national champions. Beers sold lacrosse as a manly Canadian game, appropriate to the new country: 'there are none of the debasing accompaniments, the barroom associations of other games; there is no beastly snobbishness about it.'[44] Another obviously Canadian sport was snowshoeing, which became very popular in the 1860s, often among the summer lacrosse crowd. The Montreal Snow Shoe Club had been organized as early as 1843.

■ 'Two Women on Snowshoes', watercolour by Capt. Francis G. Coleridge, 1866. LAC, C-102427. Purchased with the assistance of a grant from the Minister of Communications under the Cultural Property Export and Import Act.

Even sports that had been brought from Europe by settlers and soldiers, such as curling, golf, and track and field, underwent substantial development and change in British North America. The rules for many popular sports and games were established between 1840 and 1870, although precise dates for particular sports are matters of contention. Efforts to codify games

■ A composite photograph of a baseball game in Tecumseh Park, London (Ont.), between the London Tecumsehs and the Syracuse Stars in 1871. The Middlesex County Courthouse can be seen in the distance. LAC, PA-031482.

reflected their increasing popularity—which in turn was caused not so much by the simple emergence of time for recreation as by the emergence of the concepts of leisure, play, and entertainment divorced from work. At the same time, the trend towards codification reflected not only the Victorian penchants for reform and organization, but the new ease of communication. Certainly by 1870 many sports and games familiar to us today had reached a stage of rule development that made them comprehensible to a modern Canadian. A fair number of regulations were designed to eliminate undesirable aspects of earlier sporting activity, such as drinking and rowdyism, gambling, and professionalism. What is really important, however, is the sheer quantity and exuberance of sporting activity on the part of both participants and spectators in the mid-1800s. The development of any of the major games followed roughly the same path.

Next to lacrosse, baseball was probably the closest thing to a 'national' game in Canada; it was much more popular than ice hockey, which required not only more equipment and more specialized skill (skating), but indoor facilities (arenas) in order to become a true spectator sport. (Plus, of course, ice hockey did not become a codified and organized sport until the 1870s.) Baseball was especially popular in Upper Canada. It competed with cricket as a ball game among children, and by the 1850s had begun to outpace cricket—now increasingly associated with the British-oriented gentry—in developing organized teams and attracting spectators. The baseball teams gradually came to use American rules, while cricket remained British in its structure. The ultimate key to its success, however, came in the 1860s with the establishment in communities across British North America of 'gentleman-amateur' ball clubs providing socially-oriented intra-club competition for young, Protestant, middle-class bachelors.[45] Soon the competition spread beyond communities. There was an unofficial Canadian championship by the early 1860s, and in the year of Confederation a team from Ingersoll, Ontario, won the junior championship at an American 'world' tournament. Woodstock hosted the first Ontario baseball tournament on Dominion Day in 1869.

By 1870 sport had evolved into a major component of public life in Canada. Several sports had codified their rules and developed increasingly complex organizations for competition. Facilities for spectators also were constructed, and large audiences could be assembled for major sporting competitions, which were still strictly amateur events.

CONCLUSION

The years 1840–70 saw two major developments in the cultural life of British North America. The first was the elaboration of an infrastructure that made it possible for cultural production to move beyond the immediate circle of the maker, into the world of consumerism and spectatorship. The second was the proliferation and increasing sophistication of all cultural forms; much of the work produced may not have been original, but the imitation of foreign models continued to improve. Some cultural production was indigenous and imaginative. Most aspects of culture had both a 'refined' and a popular dimension, the two not clearly separated, especially in the cities of the British colonies. At the same time, we should not forget that much cultural activity still went on at the individual and community levels, and was still participatory in nature. We should also remember that while particular cultural media were developing their own traditions, most conscious 'artists' and 'intellectuals' did not specialize, but worked across the media.

SHORT BIBLIOGRAPHY

Doucette, Leonard. *Theatre in French Canada: Laying the Foundations 1606–1867*. Toronto, 1984. The standard work in English for the early period.

Harper, J. Russell. *A People's Art: Primitive, Naive, Provincial and Folk Painting in Canada*. Toronto, 1974. A novel approach to art for the 1970s that emphasized non-traditional forms.

Harris, Robin. *History of Higher Education in Canada 1663–1960*. Toronto, 1976. Old but still the best overall account.

Kalman, Harold. *A History of Canadian Architecture*, 2 vols. Toronto, 1994. Comprehensive in its coverage.

Kallmann, Helmut. *A History of Music in Canada 1534–1914*, 2nd edn. Toronto, 1987. Offers a good deal of detail on the early period, although it lacks any overall thesis.

Key, Archie F. *Beyond Four Walls: The Origins and Development of Canadian Museums*. Toronto, 1973.

One of the few attempts to offer a synthesis of this field.

Klinck, Carl F., ed. *Literary History of Canada: Canadian Literature in English*, 2nd edn, vol. 1. Toronto, 1976. A co-operative compendium.

Metcalfe, Alan. *Canada Learns to Play: The Emergence of Organized Sport 1807–1911*. Toronto, 1987. A stimulating introduction to the development of sport in Canada.

Rutherford, Paul. *A Victorian Authority: The Daily Press in Late Nineteenth-Century Canada*. Toronto, 1982. Despite the subtitle, this volume includes much material on the earlier part of the century.

Saddlemyer, Ann, ed. *Early Stages: Theatre in Ontario 1800–1914*. Toronto, 1990. A collection of pioneering articles on the nineteenth-century stage in Ontario.

Vance, Jonathan, *A History of Canadian Culture*.

Toronto, 2009. The first full-length survey of Canadian culture, which Vance restricts almost exclusively to the arts.

Zeller, Suzanne. *Inventing Canada: Early Victorian Science and the Idea of a Transcontinental Nation*. Toronto, 1987. A work with a controversial argument—that science helped to unite British North America—and a good deal of material on colonial science.

STUDY QUESTIONS

1. What were the characteristics of cultural production in early Victorian British North America?

2. Why is cultural infrastructure so important to the development of a formal culture?

3. What was the role of the press in culture?

4. Would you have been a Canadian author in 1850?

5. Why were the performing arts arguably more advanced than other forms of artistic expression in British North America?

6. What contribution did military garrisons make to culture?

7. Is architecture one of the visual arts?

8. What were the characteristics of early Victorian science in British North America?

9. How did lacrosse develop as 'Canada's National Sport'?

CHAPTER TWENTY-THREE

Industrialization, 1850–1870

Industrialization began in British North America, notably the Province of Canada, in the 1850s. Not merely an increase in manufacturing, it marked a significant shift in the nature of such activity, involving new technology, new capital, and a new urbanizing workforce. Industrialization was an integral part of an economic transformation that inevitably pointed towards significant political changes. It also had many side effects. It spurred the quest for mineral wealth. It contributed to the rise of organized labour. It helped to increase economic inequalities and produce a new proletariat. Industrialization even led to changes in the legal profession.

THE RISE OF INDUSTRIALIZATION

The advent of industrialization in British North America coincided with the advent of railways. Railroads not only closed the distances between manufacturers and their markets, but were important markets for industrial goods themselves, as well as major industrial manufacturers in their own right. The Grand Trunk Railway, for example, began by building its own cars, and by 1857 decided to produce its own rails, constructing an iron foundry and rolling mill in Hamilton. By the late 1850s both the Grand Trunk and the Great Western were building their own locomotives in their own shops. In 1857 a journalist described the Great Western's car factory at Hamilton as 'the largest workshop of the kind, . . . perhaps, the most extensive manufacturing establishment of any description in Western Canada':

> The first room we entered seemed to be the general hospital, in which the sick giants were disposed in long rows and supported at a considerable height, with wooden blocks and beams. Passing in we came to two rows of ponderous machines. They were drilling machines, boring holes of various sizes through any thickness of metal. There were planing machines which dealt with iron and brass as if they were soft wood, and rapidly reduced the blocks of metal to the necessary form—machines which cut iron as if it were paper, and punched holes through quarter inch plates as easily as you would punch a gun-wad from a piece of paste-board.[1]

The Great Western's physical plant was huge: the carpentry shop was 50 metres by 25, and the body-building shop 90 metres by 15.

This kind of operation was a world away from the small-scale manufacturing businesses that British North America had known before the 1850s, most of which employed only a handful

TIMELINE

1854
Molson's Bank chartered. Montreal Steamship Co. incorporated.

1855
Great Western Railway appoints Aemilius Irving as its solicitor.

1856
H.A. Massey and Co. established.

1857
Grand Trunk Railway constructs iron foundry and rolling mill at Hamilton.

1858–9
Protectionist tariffs introduced in Canada.

1859
Fire destroys Halifax's downtown business district.

1861
Merchants' Bank of Canada chartered.

1862
First illustrated Massey catalogue.

1864
Merchants' Bank of Canada opens.

1865
Huge fire in Quebec City.

1870
Massey Manufacturing Co. incorporated.

1871
Canadian census lists 23,000 residents of Montreal and Hochelaga as 'industrial workers'.

---

of people producing for local markets. Even Prince Edward Island had its manufacturers, from individual craftsmen making spinning wheels to a brewery cum distillery. In the Province of Canada, manufacturing enterprises before 1850 had been small, scattered (nearly half of their workers lived outside the major towns), limited in variety (two-thirds of manufacturing workers in 1851 were involved in textiles, blacksmithing, and the resource trades), and generally undercapitalized. Like the manufacturers' markets, the sources of their raw materials were local: small foundries, for example, grew up near iron deposits. On the whole, in manufacturing establishments of this kind, owners and workers occupied the same physical space. Only shipbuilding was a large-scale industry before 1851, with seven shipyards in Quebec City alone (employing over 1,300 men) and several others in ports like Saint John. Small-scale manufacturing would continue to be the most important form of industrial organization in British North America throughout most of the nineteenth century.

The Province of Canada took the lead in industrialization in British North America, eventually becoming the metropolitan centre or 'heartland' controlling a vast resource 'hinterland'.[2] Among the advantages that Canada—especially Montreal and Canada West—enjoyed were ease of transportation through the Great Lakes–St Lawrence system; access to abundant raw materials not only in British North America but (under the Reciprocity Treaty of 1854) the United States; and a growing population, thanks to the opportunities for extensive agricultural settlement. Together, these factors provided the essential base for the infrastructure—canals,

SIR CASIMIR STANISLAUS GZOWSKI
(1813–98)

Casimir Stanislaus Gzowski was born in St Petersburg into a family of minor Polish nobility and followed the family profession of army officer in the Imperial Corps of Engineers. After becoming involved in a Polish rebellion in 1831, he fled to Austria and was imprisoned there. Two years later, the rebels were permitted to go into exile in the United States. There Gzowski learned English, apprenticed at law, and became an American citizen in 1837. In 1841 he surveyed the Welland Canal and proposed to William Hamilton Merritt a scheme for rebuilding the canal. Although he did not win the contract, he came to the attention of Governor Sir Charles Bagot, who had met Gzowski's father in Russia. Bagot offered him a job in London, Canada West, supervising roads and waterways. Gzowski worked on engineering projects of all sorts with the Canadian Board of Works. In 1846 he became a British citizen, and in 1849 he left the Board of Works to become a private engineer supervising railroad construction in a company run by Alexander Tilloch Galt, who later became a member of Gzowski's railway construction company. With Galt's political connections, Gzowski's firm was soon building railways

(including the Grand Trunk) and speculating in adjacent land as well. The partnership ended in 1857 because Galt and others feared fallout that might damage their political careers, but Gzowski carried on in the construction business and was soon diversifying into a rolling mill in Toronto and other ventures to supply material to the Grand Trunk. In 1855 he built an Italianate villa (with conservatories, greenhouse, and stables) on Bathurst Street in Toronto and began the process of self-transformation from a hard-driving entrepreneur to a respectable member of society. Gzowski had an increasing military interest. Although he managed to stay out of politics, he served as chairman of several government commissions and in the late 1860s helped in the founding of the Dominion Rifle Association. His last engineering success was a railway bridge across the Niagara River at Fort Erie, completed in 1873. In 1889 he became president of the Canadian Society of Civil Engineers. In later years, as honorary aide-de-camp to Queen Victoria, he got to wear a superb court uniform for his annual appearance at Windsor Castle. He became a KCMG (Knight Commander of St Michael's and St George's) in 1890.

railways, banks, communications systems—that would develop over time.[3] In addition, some contemporaries thought that the province benefited from protectionist policies such as the Cayley–Galt tariffs imposed in 1858–9, which raised the rates charged on many manufactured

goods normally imported from the US. Another theory, not often discussed by Canadian scholars, is that proximity to the American midwest—the first heavy-industry region in the US—gave Canada unusual opportunities for technological imitation.[4]

■ The Grand Trunk engine 'Trevithick' under construction at Point St-Charles, c. May 1859, by William Notman. LAC, PA-181101.

Two other keys to eventual industrial success lay in the proliferation of overlapping and interlocking business enterprises—often within a single extended family—and the accumulation of capital. The Molson family were characteristic entrepreneurs in the transitional period from commerce to manufacturing to industrialization,[5] with interests that extended far beyond the Montreal brewery that John Molson bought in 1786 (in fact, the brewery was never the largest in Montreal—though by 1863 the family's distillery was the largest in British North America). Going into the shipping business, in 1809 he launched the first steamship built in Lower Canada, the *Accommodation*, which was followed a few years later by the *Swiftsure* (1812) and the *Malsham* (1814). In 1822 the Molson family acquired majority control of the St Lawrence

Steamboat Co., which expanded to gain control of all shipping on the Ottawa River and the Rideau Canal. The Molsons were thus early pioneers in the steam revolution in Canada. In 1826 John Molson Jr was elected to the board of directors of the Bank of Montreal, and in 1836 he was appointed president of the Montreal Gas Light Co., which provided gas lamps for all the city's main streets. In the same year he co-founded the Champlain and St Lawrence Railroad, of which he was named president in 1836, the year the railroad was inaugurated. Molson's interest in iron technology also led him into iron-making, and in 1835 he began to manage the St Mary's Foundry, owned by his father, inheriting it when the father died the next year. (Though this foundry built heavy machinery, it had only seven employees.) In 1854 the Molsons, who had been

A QUEBEC BREWERY

In 1868, H. Beaumont Small produced a small book entitled *The Products and Manufactures of the New Dominion*. Here is a part of his section on breweries.

BREWERIES

Within the last ten or fifteen years, great improvement has manifested itself in the manufacture of malt liquor, and in the quality of the article produced. Formerly Kingston stood unrivalled in the production of a first class ale; but with a continually increasing English population in the west, the demand for a superior article became so great, that brewing has been largely entered into in all the cities of the Dominion; the places whose ales are most noted, being Kingston, Toronto, Montreal, Quebec, Hamilton, London and Prescott. The increased consumption consequently created a great demand for barley and hops; and the old pernicious system of mixing drugs to supply the deficiency of those staples, or for producing a body, has passed away. A pale malt from barley produces a beer equal to the finest Devonshire white ale, and hops both from England and of native growth, well picked and dried, give it that bitter taste which is so agreeable and so excellent to the health. . . . The following description of the brewery of J.K. Boswell, Esq., at Quebec, will give some idea of the manner in which a first class brewery is conducted. At this establishment 270,000 gallons are brewed in a year, of which large quantities are shipped to Newfoundland, the West Indies, and the neighbouring Eastern States. The buildings form three sides of a square. The first place that is seen entering from the office is the tun room, in which there is a large fermenting square vessel for porter, with two rows of cooling pipes all around, and a press vat for hops. In the fermenting room are four tuns of a large size. In the cooling room is a cooler having two horizontal fanners on the Edinburgh principle, propelled by the steam machinery of the establishment with twenty-eight windows or openings, steam cases on the roof, and a fire pipe to which is attached 220 feet of hose. In the Brewery room is a large mash tub with patent mash machinery, having four rows of steam pipes, and four arms to stir up and equalize the mass, a patent copper sparger having long arms perforated with holes to sprinkle on fresh liquor when needed. Off this room is a pair of malt rollers for crushing the dried malt, an elevator for carrying it to the hopper over head, a vertical engine of five horse power, and a large wort copper. Next comes the hop room, screen and elevators, dry room, kiln and two malt floors, each 91 feet long, having their floor of Roman cement made from the native rock. Below all are capacious fire proof vaults capable of holding 1200 hogsheads. Such is a cursory glance at one of the many large breweries of Quebec. . . .

SOURCE: H. Beaumont Small, *The Products and Manufactures of the New Dominion* (Ottawa, 1868), 137–8.

in the banking business for years, received a charter for the Molson's Bank, which would pay dividend rates of 8 per cent for most of the nineteenth century. They also owned a good deal of property in and around Montreal. Thus the Molson family embraced a great many of the activities that were bolstering the economy: brewing and distilling, steam navigation, iron-founding, railways, street-lighting, import–export, banking, and real estate.[6]

After 1850, as manufacturers developed larger plants, moved into markets outside their local areas, and began producing for export—an enterprise that required substantial capital investments—the changes in Canada were both rapid and profound. In the Montreal region, where industrialization was to advance most rapidly, most of the large firms with large capital investments were relatively recent creations, initially involved in clothing production (especially boots and shoes) and agricultural processing. By the later 1850s Montreal had moved aggressively into large-scale heavy-metal production and fabrication, building on the earlier foundries like St Mary's and importing iron ore and coal from the United States. By the mid-1860s the city had seven foundries and three rolling mills. Montreal industrialized rapidly for several reasons, but chiefly because of its labour supply and its access

to capital. One promotional pamphlet of 1856 made the city's case well. Among Montreal's advantages, according to the authors, were its commercial base and access to water-power. Another was:

> the density of the population of the surrounding districts. In many places the land has been subdivided until the holdings of each man are too small for profitable agriculture, and the people, deeply attached to the soil, are unwilling to leave the older settlements in the valleys of the St. Lawrence and Richelieu so long as they can obtain subsistence there. . . . No where are there found people better adapted for factory hands, more intelligent, docile, and giving less trouble to their employers, than in Lower Canada.[7]

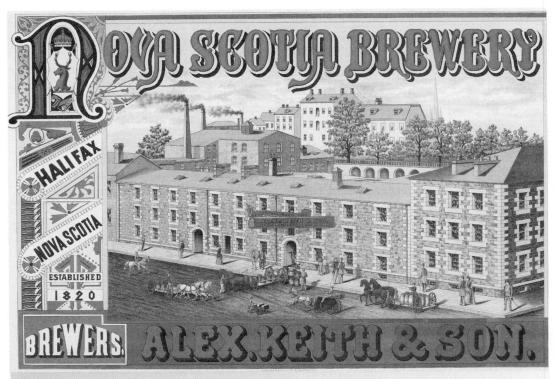

■ Nova Scotia Brewery, Halifax, established in 1820, lithograph c. 1890 by Maritime Steam Lith. Co. LAC, P11 (Peter Winkworth Collection of Canadiana).

The expansion of population and the subdivision of agricultural holdings—which had already begun in the 1830s and 1840s—drove some Lower Canadians into the factories of New England and others into the factories of Montreal. To take advantage of this new labour force, Montreal entrepreneurs needed capital, and they had little difficulty raising it in what was the largest money market in British North America.

Although the Molsons moved successfully into banking in the 1850s, the great Montreal financier and industrialist of the post-1850 period was Hugh Allan. Born in Scotland in 1810, into a family in the shipping trade between Glasgow and the St Lawrence,[8] he arrived in Montreal in 1826 and in 1831 joined an importing firm with shipping interests. Four years later he became a partner and, with his father's assistance, expanded the firm's shipping operations until it had the largest capacity of any Montreal-based firm, operating as part of the shipping interests of the Allan family. (In April 1863 it became H. and A. Allan—named for Hugh and his younger brother Andrew.) As president of the Montreal Board of Trade (1851–4), Hugh Allan pushed for a government-subsidized steamship line between Montreal and British ports that in addition to shipping imports and exports would provide mail service and transportation for immigrants. Raising capital from a syndicate, Allan formed the Montreal Ocean Steamship Co., incorporated in 1854, and two years later, with the help of Conservative politicians, secured the contract (and the £24,000 subsidy) to provide regular fortnightly service between Montreal and Liverpool in the middle of the year and from Portland, Maine, and Liverpool between November and May. By the 1870s the Montreal Ocean Steamship Company, now known as the Allan Line, held contracts to carry passengers into the interior, and Allan expanded into railway building.[9]

Meanwhile, in the 1850s and early 1860s Allan had also moved into financial institutions and manufacturing. He became particularly associated with the Bank of Montreal, serving on its board of directors from 1847 to 1857, and later established the Merchants' Bank of Canada (chartered 1861, opened 1864) as a family enterprise. (He ran the Merchants' Bank aggressively; it paid 10 per cent returns on capital stock—slightly better than the Molson Bank.) He was also active in a number of insurance companies, and had investments in many manufacturing concerns, including the Cornwall Woollen Manufacturing Co., the Montreal Rolling Mills, and the Canada Paper Co. The secrets of his success were twofold. First, he was increasingly able to employ his financial institutions to supply credit for his industrial enterprises. Second, he was perhaps the first Canadian entrepreneur to achieve both horizontal and vertical integration for his complex business empire. The Molsons had made tentative moves in this direction, but never appeared to understand completely what they had done. Allan was able both to diversify across enterprises and to control—to his profit—most of the steps in the final production within any operation. That he spoke French fluently and cultivated relationships with local French-Canadian elites was a distinct advantage.

In the 1850s and 1860s, Montreal's industrialization proceeded rapidly. The most important sectors were boot and shoe manufacturing, textile mills, tobacco factories, and the garment trade, for which much of the work was done in small establishments and private homes. The 1871 census classified 23,000 inhabitants in Montreal and the industrial suburb of Hochelaga as 'industrial workers', but—given the nature of the garment trade—the real total figure was probably a good deal higher. About one-third of the labour force was female, mostly working in tobacco and garments.

In Canada West, industrial development was more dispersed geographically and on a smaller scale than in greater Montreal.[10] No single entrepreneur was ever able to create quite so broad an empire as the Molson family or Hugh Allan. Typical was the Massey family. Born in 1798, Daniel Massey began in a small way to manufacture labour-saving farm implements and eventually steam engines and other machinery in Newcastle, under the name Daniel Massey and Co.[11] The business became H.A. Massey and Co. in 1856—the year Daniel died and his son Hart became sole proprietor—then the Newcastle Foundry and Machine Manufactory. It expanded and flourished under the direction of Hart Massey, who acquired production rights from the United States, between 1851 and 1861, for a mower, a reaper, a combined reaper and mower (a 'combine'), and a self-raking reaper.[12] (This was an early example of a Canadian enterprise importing American technology.) Hart succeeded in both manufacturing and marketing this equipment in British North America, using his early understanding of the need for effective advertising: the first illustrated Massey catalogue was issued in 1862. In 1870 the company was incorporated as the Massey Manufacturing Co., with Hart as president and his son Charles as vice-president and superintendent, and in 1879 the works moved to Toronto.[13]

The world economic depression that had contributed to the armed uprisings of 1837–8 lifted in 1841, and six years of prosperity and development followed for Canada West until another depression took hold in 1847 that lasted into the early 1850s. Prosperity was restored, particularly in Toronto, not only by the stabilization of the political situation, but also by the opening up of agriculture, timber, and trapping resources, and breweries and distilleries; by English investment, the development of banking and insurance systems, and immigration; and by gains in manufacturing. Some observers believed that one of the great advantages of manufacturing was its relative imperviousness to economic conditions. In 1865 the *Journal of the Board of Arts and Manufactures for Upper Canada* exulted that 'Whatever depressions or discouragements may hitherto have affected the material interests of Canada, nothing has thus far retarded the progress of manufactures. They, as a rule, have been continually advancing, as well in extent and

variety as in quality of articles produced.'[14] However, the increase in international traffic that had been expected to follow the Reciprocity Treaty proved illusory. Neither the opening of the St Lawrence to American trade nor the introduction of cross-lake shipping to New York by way of the Erie Canal and Hudson River gave much help to Canadian commerce.[15] The value of trade on the St Lawrence fell from $36 million per year in 1852–3 to $19 million in 1854, and averaged $24 million over the next six years. The tonnage of vessels using Canadian ports dropped precipitously, from 1,479,000 in 1854 to 870,000 in 1855. It was the railroad, railroad investment, and manufacturing—not reciprocity—that made Toronto the hub for the region. There were no large factories in Toronto in 1846. By 1871 large sectors of the economy had been industrialized. Workers had been concentrated in mechanized facilities employing a complex division of labour. The 1871 census showed 19 factories in Toronto employing more than 100 workers, and another 58 employing between 30 and 99 workers.[16] It was the largest single industrial producer among Ontario cities.

Even so, Toronto was never dominated by manufacturing the way Hamilton was. Having begun as a wholesale supplier for the agricultural hinterland to the west, Hamilton had become a railway centre in the 1850s, when Hamilton merchants bought into the Great Western and other lines, and by 1855 was specializing in metal fabrication—particularly, though not exclusively, connected with the railways. The presence of a pool of skilled labour helped to attract other enterprises, and the manufacture of heavy consumer items—including stoves and sewing machines—became the core of Hamilton's success. By 1864, 2,300 people were employed in 46 factories, almost half of which used steam-powered equipment. The fabrication of sewing machines was one of the wonders of the age. The *Hamilton Spectator* reported, 'The division of labour is here carried to the point of perfection; each particular part of the sewing machine is

D'ARCY MCGEE ON RECIPROCITY AND TARIFFS

In his newspaper *The New Era*, Thomas D'Arcy McGee, an Irish-Canadian journalist who only recently had settled in Canada from the United States, and who soon became an influential politician, a 'founding father', and the victim of Canada's first political assassination, wrote in 1858 of the need for balance in trade policy between open markets and tariff protection.

The word *protection*, used in relation to industry, has become odious in England. It was the selfish cry of a class already highly privileged—the landed aristocracy of England—and therefore it became hateful to the masses, who really wanted to be protected against the monopolists of the corn market. But protection is a good word, and expresses more than any other the true nature and end of a good government.

What we demand for native industry of Canada is not protection—at least no exploded English protection—but fair play. We demand that our workmen shall not be swamped, through the culpable remissness of our Legislature, in our own market. We demand that the reciprocity treaty shall establish a real reciprocity, and that if our markets continue to open to the mother country, our manufactures—be the same more or less—shall be as free to enter her ports. In short, we ask a Canadian tariff, in the interests of Canadian industry, and not of a few commissioned agents for foreign houses.

This is a question of employment and population, as well as of capital and currency. It is a question for farmers as for mechanics. The operation of such alterations to the tariff would be to encourage manufactures in Canada, and to sustain a large manufacturing population. That population is to be fed, and the money earned in the mill must find its way to the field. To create a domestic trade between the different classes of the same community, has been the first object of all national legislation. Diversity of pursuits and diffusion of wealth are the inevitable consequences of a well-balanced system, combining both artificial and agricultural employments. It is the immediate interest of the farmer on the Thames and Trent that the mill in his neighbourhood should be steadily at work; it directly affected him if it employs a hundred hands, fewer or more; —it therefore directly concerns him that the present tariff should not continue to allow into Canada the manufactures of other countries at from 5 to 15 per cent, while our manufactures in the United States and in England are mulcted at from 15 to 30 per cent.

The common fallacy is, that if you raise the duties on any given article, you make it dearer to the consumer. This would be the effect on articles which we could not, by any possibility, produce; for example, higher duties on teas and coffees would of course, enhance their price—the very thing we don't want to do. But to impose the same duties on certain descriptions of woolens, cottons, hardware, glass, furniture, leather, paper, books, &c, does not necessarily increase the price to the purchaser. The effect of a judicious system would be, *not to make them dear, but to make them here.*

SOURCE: T.D. McGee, *The New Era*, 1 April 1858.

handed over to a series of lathes, drills, punching machines, emory wheels, and no end of similar ingenious devices for lessening labour and giving accuracy to the work.'[17] A particular cutting machine ('a very complicated and beautiful piece of machinery') and a self-regulating planer were

■ Looking north from the corner of King and York streets, Toronto, 1858. City of Toronto Archives, SC-498-013.

the only ones of their kind in Canada, and had probably been imported from the United States. During the later 1860s the numbers of factory workers and steam-powered factories both increased substantially. In the 1871 census, Hamilton employed 4,456 'hands' in factories reflecting $1,541,264 in capital investment, paying wages of $1,329,712 and making products worth $5,471,494. More than 80 per cent of the firms involved employed more than 10 people.[18]

But Hamilton was exceptional in its industrial specialization. Elsewhere in Canada West, particularly outside the larger cities, much of the industrial growth was directly linked to the resource and agricultural sectors. In short, Canada West processed natural resources and served the needs of the rural community.[19] As one observer put it in the early 1870s:

Agriculture in its several branches has been, and is now, the foundation on which rests the entire industrial fabric of Ontario. On its prosperity all classes depend—and with a good crop or a bad one, business operations, the abundance of money, and the social comforts of our whole people rise and fall, as do the waters of the sea with the flow and ebb of the tide.[20]

Nevertheless, by the 1850s land shortages in Canada, combined with declining agricultural productivity, were leading on one hand to westward territorial expansion and on the other to industrial expansion based on the ready availability of cheap labour. Industrial expansion in turn produced pressures for larger markets. By the late 1850s many Canadian businessmen (and the politicians associated with them) saw the development of markets for industrial output as central to future policy. As the authors of *Montreal in 1856* argued, on behalf of the Montreal manufacturers, 'the sole difficulties with which they have to contend are a restricted market, and the competition of the larger, wealthier, and longer established factories in other countries.'[21] Thus, agricultural overpopulation created pressures for territorial expansion to provide new land for farmers, and at the same time gave rise to a class of urban workers who would form a new proletariat.

THE NEW RESOURCE INDUSTRIES

The gold rush that began in 1858 along the Fraser River presaged a new element in the resource economy of British North America: large-scale exploitation of the rich mineral wealth of the northern part of the continent, mainly geared to providing raw material and energy for the growing industries of British North America. Iron ore had been mined in small quantities since colonial times, and rich coal deposits in Cape Breton had been tapped since the 1820s. New technologies provided constantly expanding markets for British North America's mineral wealth, as well as new means of removing it from the ground. By the 1850s copper ore was being mined along Lake Superior. (The main problem hampering production—not resolved until later in the century—was the cost of transporting ore long distances for refining.) Petroleum was discovered in southwestern Ontario in 1857. There was an oil rush at Petrolia in 1862 after the discovery of a well that initially produced 3,000 barrels a day. By 1863 the production of crude oil in Canada ran to 100,000 barrels a year.

Small gold rushes also occurred in Nova Scotia in 1861 and in Canada East along the Chaudière River in 1863. Unlike timbering, which it gradually replaced as the principal economic activity and employer of labour in many isolated districts, mineral production tended to be extremely capital-intensive, requiring special-

GOLD REGIONS OF CANADA.

GOLD:
HOW AND WHERE TO FIND IT!

THE

EXPLORER'S GUIDE AND MANUAL OF PRACTICAL AND INSTRUCTIVE DIRECTIONS

FOR

EXPLORERS AND MINERS

IN THE

GOLD REGIONS OF CANADA,

WITH

LUCID INSTRUCTIONS AND EXPLANATIONS AS TO THE ROCKY STRATA, PECULIAR SHALE ROCKS, VEINSTONE, ETC, IN WHICH

GOLD, AND MANY OTHER VALUABLE MINERALS,

ARE TO BE FOUND IN THAT REGION;

WITH

EASY MODES OF DETERMINATION AND ANALYSIS,

ACCOMPANIED BY TWO

COLORED GEOLOGICAL MAPS.

BY HENRY WHITE, P.L.S.,
Author of the " Geology, Oil Fields, and Minerals of Canada West," etc., etc., etc.

TORONTO:
PUBLISHED BY MACLEAR & CO.,
17 KING STREET WEST.;
1867.

■ This 1867 guide, by Henry White, promised 'lucid instructions and explanations as to the rocky strata, peculiar shale rocks, veinstone, etc.', in which gold might be found. Metropolitan Toronto Library.

ized scientific knowledge, particularly of geological formations and refining techniques. Until the twentieth century, when international demand grew enough to justify the expense of local refining and long-distance transportation, production in Canada tended to be confined to a few minerals that were either valuable in relatively small amounts (like gold and silver) or particularly well located for outward transportation in bulk. Thus, by the 1850s Vancouver Island coal was shipped to California, and Nova Scotia coal to eastern American markets. But industrialization of the continent demanded large-scale mineral production, which in turn required transportation to and from the mines. Here, as in so many other areas, expansion of the railway system seemed critical.[22]

THE RISE OF ORGANIZED LABOUR

Industrialization inevitably made labour relations an important issue in British North America. The seasonal nature of work in the resource and construction industries had meant that the men they employed had little opportunity to organize themselves in order to address problems like bad working conditions or employer exploitation. Some workers just moved on, but others responded with general violence and rioting—often directed at targets other than the employer. Before 1850, more than 200 labour riots had taken place across the colonies, one-third of them involving men working in canal construction. In the same period only about 50 labour protests were sufficiently focused to be called strikes. Masons working on the Lachine Canal in 1823, for example, objected to working from 5 a.m. to 7 p.m. (They did not get the 12-hour day they sought, but their wages were raised.) Several times in 1844 workers on the Lachine Canal marched in a body to Montreal to vote. In October of that year 400 marchers clashed with cavalry and 27 men were arrested.[23]

Industrialization organized and steadied the labour market. Manufacturing tended to be more continuous than seasonal, and much of it was conducted indoors. Overhead costs encouraged employers to seek stabilization, and large labour pools developed. Industrial employers could afford higher annual wage bills than those in resource production, and in theory their overheads simultaneously provided workers with leverage and themselves with a drive to minimize labour costs. The rise of a capitalistic labour market settled the workers, but in reality did little for their bargaining position. Since those with some education and highly developed skills were in the strongest bargaining position, it is not surprising that labour organization first developed in British North America among people like printers. The York Typographical Society, for example, was founded in 1832. Although that good radical William Lyon Mackenzie initially supported it, by 1835 he had changed his tune: 'If all the journeymen were editors, and each had a press of his own, a more resolute, determined, . . . obstinate body would not be found on this continent.' His own workers had struck for higher wages, and Mackenzie railed against efforts 'to split up the community into so many selfish and mischievous monopolies.'[24]

Although trade unions emerged quite early in certain skilled industries—carpenters, for example, organized in Halifax in 1798, Hamilton in 1832, Montreal and Toronto in 1833, and Yarmouth in 1834—such unions almost never had any contact with one another, and could achieve only immediate and localized gains. Organization and communication were better in the Mechanics' Institutes, which had expanded greatly after 1840; but these were more like fraternal self-improvement societies, centred on their libraries, than militant unions. In Saint John, for example, the 'mechanics' (mostly waged artisans) had to fight for years to gain control of the Institute, which was able to mobilize tradesmen in non-union causes, such as campaigns for temperance or Sunday schools.

Throughout the 1840s and 1850s labour militancy, like the labour organization itself, was local, and extremely limited. Violence continued to occur among the unskilled navvies of the construction industry and the raftsmen of the timber industry, but it was seldom systematically organized. When labour showed signs of focusing its energies, the state quickly entered the picture. Despite business rhetoric about the free market in labour, few construction bosses objected to using informal spies to check on labour sentiment—or troops to enforce the peace. Navvies working on the canal projects of the 1840s were particularly restive, and a 'mounted police force' was created in 1845 to deal with labour violence on these quasi-public works projects. When the Great Western Railway began construction near Hamilton in 1851, the city raised a special police force to deal with labour troubles and built a large barracks to accommodate a contingent of mounted police. When a company was prepared to pay for a police force, it usually got one. Though the navvies were frequently able to win extremely short-term goals with their strikes and walkouts, they operated under distinct disadvantages when they attempted to behave in an organized fashion, not least because employers were willing to use the civil power to break strikes. By 1849 it was no longer necessary to demonstrate that there was a real and immediate crisis: an apprehended crisis would do. In that year the Montreal Mining Co. and the Quebec Mining Co., both active on Lake Huron, requested military assistance from the Canadian authorities to protect their operations from violence, and were almost immediately granted a contingent of troops.[25]

In the 1840s and 1850s, workers' trade or craft organizations tended to identify themselves solely with their individual trades, rather than with fellow workers in other trades in other places. But unity was regarded as central. As one manifesto of the Toronto Typographical Society (TTS) stated in 1847: 'We are knit together by ties that should be considered as indissoluble, being in the words of our motto, "United to Support"— not combined to Injure.'[26] The development of industrial activity, and the rise of factories employing mechanization in the 1850s and especially 1860s, brought significant changes to the still incipient labour movement. A handful of

international unions appeared that were occasionally British in origin (such as the Amalgamated Society of Engineers) though more frequently American (such as the International Molders Union). And unions with several local chapters—such as the Boot and Shoemakers Union and the Journeymen Cigarmakers Union—were organized. The TTS by 1865 was in contact with several British and American counterparts, and a year later it affiliated with the American National Typographical Union. The Knights of St Crispin (KOSC), the US-based union representing workers in the boot and shoe industry, organized nearly 30 chapters across British America from Saint John to Petrolia in the late 1860s. Craft unions led the way in strikes against employers. Mechanization was the most common grievance, but low wages and inflationary pressures were also factors. 'There can be no doubt that the dollar would go farther in a family twenty years ago than double that sum can be made to supply at the present day', grumbled one striking house carpenter in Halifax in 1864.[27]

Not all unions were devoted simply to industrial action; many were also fraternal bodies in the tradition of the crafts guilds. The rapid spread of the Knights of St Crispin in Canada underscores the workers' recognition of the problems introduced by mechanization and their desire to maintain older craft traditions. The KOSC organized social functions, provided a funeral benefit as well as funerals (with a special rite), and organized public processions and parades, in which its officers appeared dressed in special uniforms and carrying banners.[28] Public parades were frequently organized by worker organizations, giving those involved the opportunity to show off banners, uniforms, and emblems, as well as to demonstrate solidarity. One mass procession in Saint John in 1853 featured more than 5,000 marching workers, representing dozens of trades. A song written by a local printer was run off and distributed along the route of the march. Public demonstrations of this kind were characteristic of the era.

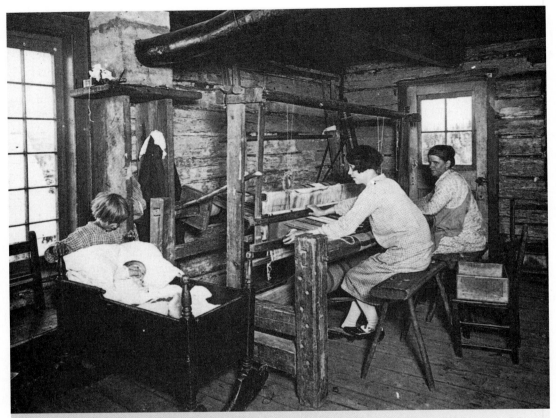

■ A mother weaving at home, with her children, Cap à l'Aigle, Quebec, c. 1910. Although this photograph comes from a later period, home-based piecework had long been a standard feature of the garment industry. LAC, PA-040744.

Mechanization was the principal issue behind labour organization, although the impersonality of the new factory system also created problems for labour, particularly as more and more juveniles and women were drawn into the labour market. In Montreal, for example, women and girls by 1871 constituted 34.5 per cent of the city's industrial workers; over 80 per cent of the workforce in the clothing industry; over 40 per cent in shoemaking; and over 60 per cent in tobacco processing. Young women were especially hard to organize because they typically worked only until they married, and many did piecework at home rather than at the factory.

THE CITIES AND URBANIZATION

Cities in the period 1840–70 continued to be dominated by commercial interests, but they were changing in a variety of ways. Connections between them improved as ever more sophisticated transportation networks of water and rail facilitated both regional and intra-regional commerce. Toronto, Montreal, and, in their own provinces, Halifax and Saint John became metropolitan centres, dominating their respective regions. The cities of British North America grew slowly but constantly in both population and expanse. Montreal, Toronto, and Hamilton in

THE HORSE IN INDUSTRIAL CANADA

❖

Although the nineteenth century was without doubt the age of steam, the railroad could not have done its work without the support of the horse. The two forms of motive power were not antithetical, but mutually supportive, at least in the days before the internal combustion engine (which, of course, was measured in terms of 'horsepower'). Industrial Canada's dependence on the railroad was, in turn, based upon its dependence on the horse, which was superior in carrying and pulling goods and people short distances where rail could not go. The number of horses employed in an area was in direct proportion to the number of railroad miles within it, and in agricultural regions the horse replaced oxen, not only pulling plows but also powering all sorts of farm machinery, such as reapers and harvesters. North America came to realize its reliance on the horse in 1872, when an equine influenza that began in Markham, Ontario, laid the horse population of

the entire continent low and brought business virtually to a halt. At this same time of major mutual dependence, the horse and the city were not entirely compatible. Long before the complaints of carbon-based fossil fuel pollution, urbanites hated the more tangible pollution of the horse, which left its mark on city streets, particularly unpaved ones, in the form of horse manure and urine. Adding to the deposits of horses used to draw freight were those of the horses who pulled the streetcars before their electrification. Farmers could use the manure to good purpose, while the city could only scoop it up and carry it away. Most urban dwellers greeted the introduction of 'horseless carriages' with much enthusiasm. The American Civil War was a war fought chiefly with horses, and there were far more horses and mules employed in World War I in Europe—over a million by the British and Commonwealth forces in 1918—than in 1861–5.

particular, which had been home to thousands of independent artisans, began to become major industrial centres. Most central cities still remained relatively small in area and in population, however; Toronto in 1860 was a built-up city of only about four square miles (100 ha) and a population of about 50,000, retaining its earlier mixture of commercial, residential, and industrial usages within the space of a few blocks.[29] The chief growth in population occurred in politically independent suburbs developed around the central city (see Table 23.1). The percentages of urban dwellers in most of the provinces of

British North America did increase during this period, although not as sharply as they would later in the century.

The middle decades of the century brought expansion in all sorts of municipal services, from water lines, sewers, and street railways to fire departments and police forces. Halifax constructed a pipeline from Long Lake to the centre of town in 1847. A street railway was first franchised in Toronto in 1861, with the first line on Yonge Street. Cities drew their populations both from the surrounding countryside and from immigration. In the mid-1840s, many of the

TABLE 23.1
POPULATION OF MAJOR CITIES OF BRITISH NORTH AMERICA, 1851 AND 1871

1851		1871	
Montreal	57,700	Greater Montreal	144,000
Quebec	42,100	Greater Toronto	115,000
Toronto	30,800	Quebec-Lévis	66,400
Saint John	22,700	Greater Saint John	41,300
Halifax	20,700	Greater Halifax	31,800
Hamilton	14,100	Ottawa–Hull	27,900
Kingston	11,700	Hamilton	26,900
Ottawa	7,700	London	18,000
London	7,000	Kingston	12,400

SOURCE: Paul Rutherford, *A Victorian Authority: The Daily Press in Late Nineteenth-Century Canada* (Toronto: University of Toronto Press, 1982), 11.

immigrants were poor Irish Catholics, who would provide much of the unskilled labour in most British North American cities.

One of the most important characteristics of those cities throughout their early history was their susceptibility to devastating fires (see Table 23.2). The main problems were the wood-frame construction of most of the buildings and a lack of the firefighting capacity required to contain fires and prevent them from spreading. Firefighting machinery was relatively primitive, and most fire departments were composed of volunteers. In the 1840–70 period virtually every large city had a fire that wiped out large portions of it. Saint John, New Brunswick, which had suffered from two major fires in 1837, one of which destroyed the business district, experienced two more in 1841, the first of which destroyed a shipyard along with 60 other buildings. Quebec City had a fire in May 1845 in which 1,050 buildings were destroyed and 20 lives lost, and a month later the St Jean parish of the city lost

1,200 houses and 40 lives. In June 1846 fire almost destroyed St John's, Newfoundland, leaving 12,000 people homeless and causing property damage into the millions. A fire in Montreal in July 1852 took 1,108 homes, caused millions of dollars in property damage, and left 15,000 people homeless. Quebec City was hit by fires again in the 1860s, with the largest in 1865 consuming 2,500 houses and 17 churches and convents; only four lives were lost, but 18,000 people were left homeless. After each of these disasters, citizens picked themselves up and rebuilt. Most of the new construction was still wood frame, but public buildings after 1840 were increasingly made of stone.

Although there was always a danger of fire in winter, because of the need for heat, Table 23.2 shows that the great fires all occurred in the warmer weather—often after periods of hot dry weather, when heat and evaporation turned wooden buildings into tinder. Together, improvements in construction materials and the

TABLE 23.2
MAJOR FIRES, 1840–1870

Location	Date	Buildings destroyed	Number left homeless
Saint John	1841	60 plus shipyard	
Boucherville	20 June 1843	140	100 families on relief
Quebec	28 May 1845	1,500–2,000	12,000
Quebec	28 June 1845	1,500	10,000
St John's	4 Oct. 1845	100	n.a.
St John's	9 June 1846	2,000	12,900
Toronto	7 Aug. 1849	n.a.	n.a.
Montreal	17 June 1850	190	n.a.
Fredericton	11 Nov. 1850	120	180 families
Montreal	8 July 1852	1,108	15,000
St John's	9 Sept. 1856	200	1,500
Halifax	9 Sept. 1859	business district	
Quebec	1865	2,500	18,000
Charlottetown	16 July 1866	100	30 families
Quebec	14 Oct. 1866	1,500	12,000–15,000

SOURCE: Adapted from John C. Weaver and Peter de Lottinville, 'The Conflagration and the City: Disaster and Progress in British North America during the Nineteenth Century', *Histoire Sociale/Social History* 13, 26 (November 1980): 418.

introduction of organized fire departments reduced the risk of fire after 1870.

THE NEW PROLETARIAT AND THE URBAN POOR

As Canadian cities began the transition from commercial entrepôts to industrial centres, they already contained significant inequalities of wealth and income. In Hamilton in the 1850s, for example, the most affluent 10 per cent of residents held 88 per cent of the propertied wealth within the city, received nearly 50 per cent of the income, and controlled about 60 per cent of the wealth. On the other hand, the poorest 40 per cent earned only 1 per cent of the income and controlled about 6 per cent of the wealth. Most of the poor in Hamilton were Irish and Catholic, doubtless recent arrivals to the province. Over half of the city's adult males did not own enough property to qualify for the vote, and few of the poor ever enjoyed any political office. Nevertheless, rich and poor in Hamilton still lived in close proximity to one another; the flight of the wealthy from the urban core had not yet begun.

■ 'After the Fire, Halifax', 1859, watercolour by Lefevre James Cranstone. LAC, C-036316.

In any Canadian city, before industrialization, considerable social and economic diversity could exist within a relatively small area. In Toronto in the 1840s, just one block away from a street sporting three gentlemen, three merchants, a professor, a broker, a registrar, a civil engineer, an auctioneer, and a widow was another street where there resided six labourers, two widows, a tailor, a shoemaker, a cooper, a moulder, an innkeeper, a clerk, and a carver.[30] Only with the emergence of a middle class sufficiently well-off to move out of the urban centre—and a working class sufficiently poor to cram into the buildings abandoned by the middle class—would the industrial city emerge, with its clear sectional divisions between rich and poor, and between one economic function and another. It was with industrialization that residential housing began to be differentiated on the basis of wealth. At the same time, economic functions began to be separated, with commerce remaining 'downtown' in the older urban core, and industry moving to the outskirts of the city as it then existed, where land costs were lower.

Rural migration to nearby cities and towns was substantial throughout British North America during this transitional period. Between 1850 and 1870 alone, the number of towns in Canada West with populations between 1,000 and 5,000 people more than doubled, from 33 to 69. Toronto, the largest city, grew commensurately, from around 30,000 in 1840 to 56,000 in 1870. Just over half of Toronto's residents were native-born Canadians, most of them drawn from the surrounding countryside. Toronto had a gender skew in favour of females, though not as substantial a one as Montreal, where women were drawn by domestic service and opportunities for employment in retail trade and manufacturing.

In the pre-industrial city the role of women and children within the labour force was fairly limited. In Hamilton in 1851, only 14 per cent of employed women were seamstresses and dressmakers; 72 per cent were domestic servants. And although adolescents entered the workforce at

TABLE 23.3

INDUSTRIES EMPLOYING FEMALES, ONTARIO, 1871

Industry	Females	Percentage of workforce
Tailors and clothiers	3,803	61
Dressmaking, millinery	2,023	95
Wool and cloth	1,535	42
Boots and shoes	704	11
Furriers and hatters	356	65
Cheese factories	332	37
Straw works	325	87
Cotton factories	303	61
Bookbinding	215	59
Tobacco working	176	25
Hosiery manufacture	174	71

SOURCE: Marjorie Griffin Cohen, *Women's Work, Markets and Economic Development in Nineteenth-Century Ontario* (Toronto: University of Toronto Press, 1988), 169.

the age of 14 or 15, young children were not particularly useful economically. The situation changed with industrialization. Machinery was used wherever possible. In the garment trade, which began the nineteenth century as a typical handicraft operation, the introduction of the sewing machine in the 1850s brought a revolution that made possible the employment of women (see Table 23.3). According to one estimate, a frock coat that took more than 16 hours to sew by hand could be machine-made in less than three hours.[31] Another aspect of industrialization—the division of labour into a series of simple, repetitive tasks—meant that children could now be employed for some kinds of work. In typecasting, for example, a machine produced the type at the rate of 200 characters per minute, but with small imperfections. Human labour could eliminate the imperfections. Young boys and girls could remove the small 'jet' left on each

type as its umbilical cord to the machine was severed, or rub the type on stone to smooth the surface. In Montreal, 25 per cent of boys between 11 and 15, and 10 per cent of girls of the same age, were part of the labour force in 1871.

From a factory owner's perspective, child labour meant big savings in wages. From the perspective of the child's family, in some cases it may have meant a chance to work together again the way farm families worked in the pre-industrial era. Many rural migrants seeking industrial work insisted that employers take on the entire family, particularly in the textile and garment trades. As one employer explained, 'a man will be working at the mill, and his daughter working there also, and he may have a small child, whom he desires to have there, for instance, in the spooling room. Often you don't want to take the child, but if you do not, he and his daughter will go out, and they will go to some mill where the whole three will be employed.'[32] While child labour may have served some social functions, however, its main purpose was to supplement meagre incomes. Many children were required to work, argued one charity worker, 'from the fact that their parents probably earn very little, not sufficient to keep a large family unless the little fellows are sent to work at tender years.'[33]

In the end, the most striking characteristics of families at the unskilled end of the industrial spectrum was their vulnerability to poverty.[34] Employers usually paid low wages, and felt little compunction about laying off workers—particularly in Montreal, where the port was closed to commerce every winter. Death or serious illness of the adult male wage earner was another calamity. The position of widows, particularly those without property, was very difficult.[35] Often the entire family had to work to make ends meet. To some extent the rural French-Canadian family was tailor-made for the industrial economy.[36] Not only were such families accustomed to working together, but they were used to sharing housing with kinfolk. As one Montreal observer put it, 'under the present state of things, overcrowding is inevitable, and only the cheapest and most inferior class of rookeries can be paid for out of the current rate of wages.'[37] Montreal had an especially high proportion of families who shared dwelling space with others; but such crowding was typical of the tenements of the labouring poor, with 'two to three families, or sometimes two families using one stove between them, and if there are several families, each family will have one room for a sleeping room, and use the kitchen for a dining room—the kitchen and stove in common with others.'[38] The family economy of rural Canada, especially rural French Canada, was thus carried over into the industrializing city. Within such families, of course, formal education was extremely limited; learning on the job was all that most children could expect. Opportunities for movement out of industrial poverty were also fairly limited, and had more to do with luck than with education.

ECONOMIC DEVELOPMENT AND THE LAW

As early as 1826, John Strachan observed that lawyers were 'emphatically our men of business'.[39] The truth of that observation became even more apparent as the nineteenth century wore on. Lawyers are recognized in Canadian history mainly for their role in politics, and the law has always been the most common occupation for legislators, before Confederation and after. Moreover, almost all lawyers of the nineteenth century combined their political careers with their legal ones, taking advantage of their political connections to assist their clients. But legal training and the practice of law were also extremely important to business and economic development in British North America in a variety of ways. Lawyers provided technical services necessary to business. They wrote the contracts essential to business activity and subsequently defended them in court. The vast majority of legal cases before most courts in British North America concerned matters of business, especially the honouring of contracts and the payment of debts. No businessman could operate without a good lawyer. By 1855, the Great Western Railway was paying Aemilius Irving an annual salary to serve as its solicitor. Some of his caseload had to do with competitors and suppliers, but much of it concerned questions of compensation: of those whose land had been affected by construction, or those injured or the families of those killed in accidents (frequent occurrences on early railways).[40]

Lawyers were also businessmen themselves, however, acting as entrepreneurs, developers, and principals in business organizations. John A. Macdonald was involved in a variety of business enterprises in the 1830s and 1840s, particularly in real-estate speculation. As business dealings became more complex in the canal and railway age, lawyers increasingly flourished as businessmen. Three of the original eight directors of the Welland Canal Co. had been lawyers. The great railroad manipulator Allan MacNab used both his law practice and his legal expertise to great advantage in his business dealings. Lawyers were—after merchants and businessmen—the most common members of boards of directors of the railways in Canada. Lawyers controlled railway management during the early years of railway expansion, both because their skills were needed to obtain charters in the first place and because their political clout was essential to keep them. Lawyers also lobbied inside and outside the corridors of power on behalf of their clients and their own economic interests. Perhaps even more important, lawyers helped to create the emerging administrative state in the Canadas.

The quintessential lawyer of the middle years of the nineteenth century was arguably George-Étienne Cartier.[41] Admitted to the bar in 1835 after articling for the Patriote lawyer Edouard-Étienne Rodier, Cartier practised in the bustling city of Montreal. Following the rebellion of 1837, in which he played some part, he fled to the United States for a year before returning to Montreal to a legal practice that increasingly included important corporate clients. Among those clients, by the early 1850s, was the Grand Trunk Railway Co., and it was Cartier who introduced into Parliament the bill that created it. He later insisted that he did not depend on the Grand Trunk for his livelihood, but as Canadian attorney general (1856–66) he consistently acted in its interests as well as those of another large client, the Seminary of Montreal, which was the city's most important pre-industrial corporation and a major landholder. In the same period he acted to reform the Civil Code and to rationalize the judicial process in Canada East through the Judicature Act of 1857. This last Act bureaucratized the courts in Canada East by establishing 19 judicial districts, each one with a jail and a courthouse. It was part of the process of creating Canada's new administrative state, but it also succeeded in creating new local employment for lawyers—as Cartier was well aware: 'Is the law which divides Lower Canada into several large

■ George-Étienne Cartier, photo by Notman & Son. William Notman (1826–91) immigrated to Canada in 1856 and set up a photographic studio in Montreal. He won many awards and left a collection of some 400,000 photographs, one of the greatest treasures of nineteenth-century Canadiana in existence. LAC, C-002162.

judicial districts disadvantageous for my compatriots? Doesn't this law permit a large number of young lawyers to distinguish themselves?'[42]

CONCLUSION

Exhaustion of eastern grain land, a shift from imperial to continental trade, the growth of industrialism, the expansion of railroad construction—all contributed, by the 1860s, to a new attitude on the part of many of the political and economic leaders of British North America. Some form of political unification seemed to be required that would make possible both westward expansion and eastern integration. The time was right for the creation of a national state out of the disparate colonies of British North America. Both external and internal pressures would help to complete the process.

SHORT BIBLIOGRAPHY

Bradbury, Bettina. *Working Families: Age, Gender, and Daily Survival in Industrializing Montreal.* Toronto, 1993. An exciting work on early industrialization in Montreal from the perspective of those employed by the factories.

Craven, Paul, and Tom Traves. 'Canadian Railways as Manufacturers, 1850–1880', *Canadian Historical Association History Papers* (1983): 254–81. A significant article on the importance of the railways to manufacturing.

Gilmour, J.M. *Spatial Evolution of Manufacturing: Southern Ontario, 1851–1891.* Toronto, 1972. A geographical study of manufacturing in southern Ontario, mostly concerned with later periods.

Goheen, Peter. *Victorian Toronto, 1850–1900: Patterns and Process of Growth.* Chicago, 1970. A geographer examines the ways in which Toronto expanded and grew in the second half of the nineteenth century.

Greene, Ann Norton. *Horses at Work: Harnessing Power in Industrial America.* Cambridge, Mass., 2008. An important revisionist study of the horse in the nineteenth century.

Katz, Michael. *The People of Hamilton, Canada West: Family and Class in a Mid-Nineteenth-Century City.* Cambridge, Mass., 1975. The first attempt to apply American quantitative methodology on a large scale to a Canadian subject (it is now unlikely to be replicated because of changes in funding practice).

——— et al. *The Social Organization of Early Industrial Capitalism.* Cambridge, Mass., 1982. A general theoretical examination of the social implications of early industrial capitalism, extending far beyond Canada.

Kealey, Gregory S. *Toronto Workers Respond to Industrial Capitalism, 1867–1892.* Toronto, 1980. A detailed examination of the Canadian experience in one city.

Pentland, H.C. *Labour and Capital in Canada 1650–1860.* Toronto, 1981. The classic introduction to early Canadian economic history from a Marxist perspective.

Taylor, Graham, and Peter Baskerville. *A Concise History of Business in Canada.* Toronto, 1994. A useful overview of Canadian business development.

Tulchinsky, Gerald. *The River Barons: Montreal Businessmen and the Growth of Industry and Transportation, 1837–53.* Montreal, 1977. An able analysis of the 'prequel' to industrialization in Montreal.

Wilton, Carol, ed. *Beyond the Law: Lawyers and Business in Canada, 1830 to 1930.* Toronto, 1990. A useful reminder that economic development requires infrastructure of various kinds, including the law.

STUDY QUESTIONS

1. What was the relationship between railways and industrialization?
2. Why did horses continue to be so valuable in the nineteenth century?
3. Why did the Province of Canada take the lead in industrialization in British North America?
4. Why was family enterprise still important in the 1860s?

5. Was labour organization necessarily inimical to industrial capitalism?
6. Why were nineteenth-century cities so susceptible to fire?
7. How did industrialization help to create a class of urban poor?
8. Why were lawyers so intimately involved with business enterprise?
9. What role did women play in the new industrial economy?

CHAPTER TWENTY-FOUR

Unification, 1862–1867

■ The political problems of the united Province of Canada in the early 1860s were the immediate stimulus for Canadian politicians to begin exploring the possibility of a larger union with the eastern ('lower') provinces at the famous Charlottetown Conference in September 1864. But Canadian politics was not the only reason for thinking about political unification, nor was the 'union' solution plucked from the sky. Ever since the Americans had separated from British North America in 1783, some people had advocated the creation of an integrated political unit on the British half of the continent.

Hopes for unification were encouraged by several developments in the years around 1860. The desire for western expansion and the development of a continental market played a part, but so did Britain's gradual withdrawal from the role of imperial protector. In the early 1860s, with the American Civil War underlining the need for military defence of British North America, British authorities began actively promoting the idea of unification as the solution to previous problems and the fulfillment of previous ambitions. Confederation was never inevitable; but neither was it an unanticipated result of a random combination of events.

THE IDEA OF UNION

EARLY SCHEMES

The political unification of the provinces of British North America—possibly under some sort of federal arrangement paralleling the American one—had been advocated ever since the days of the Loyalists. There was quite a lot of agreement on the form that such a union would take. Most of the early proposals were not very detailed, and thus could be supported in the abstract without a real commitment to a specific political philosophy. (Even the great anti-confederate Joseph Howe apparently supported the concept of unification in the 1850s. He was later roundly criticized for inconsistency, but this was of course unfair: support for a principle is quite different from support for a detailed proposal.) Occasionally, however, more specific proposals were put forward in response to specific political impasses. In 1821 and 1822, for example, when the mercantile leaders of Lower Canada pressed for political unification of the Canadas as a solution to the economic and constitutional problems resulting from the creation of the two Canadas in 1791, Upper Canadian Tories

TIMELINE

1821–2
Debate over unification of Upper and Lower Canada.

1823
J.B. Robinson submits plan for 'one grand confederacy' to Colonial Office.

1840
Act of Union for the Canadas, proclaimed the following year.

1849
Idea of a larger British North American union re-emerges.

1850
Henry Sherwood proposes 'A Federative Union of the British North American Colonies'.

1851
Sir Edmund Head proposes union scheme.

1857
D'Arcy McGee calls for a 'new Northern nationality'.

1858
J.C. Taché writes on union.

1861
American Civil War begins. *Trent* affair.

1864
Union gains clear victories over Confederacy in US Civil War. Ten-year period of Reciprocity Treaty ends. Brown, Macdonald, and Cartier form 'Grand Coalition' committed to union of British North America. Charlottetown Conference. Quebec Conference.

1865
Debates over union in Canada, Nova Scotia, New Brunswick, PEI.

1866
Rise of Fenian menace. New Brunswick and Nova Scotia legislatures approve union with 'better terms'. Delegates from Canada, New Brunswick, and Nova Scotia meet in London.

1867
British North America Act passed. Dominion of Canada proclaimed on 1 July.

responded with calls for a larger union. As John Strachan explained in 1824, in a parliament of all British North America, 'the French would be only a component part and would merge without any sacrifice of national vanity or pride &c.' For his part, Attorney General John Beverley Robinson had already submitted a plan for the unification of British North America into one 'grand confederacy' in 1823. 'It is believed that to unite the British North American Provinces by giving them a common legislature and erecting them into a Kingdom, would be gratifying all those colonies: that it would add to their security, confirm their attachment to the present government, and make wider the distinction between it and the republican institutions of their neighbours.'[1] Seeing unification as a stage in the colonies' progress towards full integration with the mother country, Robinson even resurrected an old Loyalist idea that British Americans should be represented in Westminster. Although the Colonial Office summarily rejected

Robinson's unification proposal as impractical—at the time, of course, Britain was still in its mercantilist phase, and a North American empire seemed worth maintaining—it is interesting to note that an internal commentator thought it contained 'within itself the germ of separation'.[2]

The idea of union resurfaced in 1849, when the British American League, a Loyalist organization opposed to increasing ties with the United States, advocated union with Britain as an alternative to annexation. By now circumstances had changed: the old colonial system had been dismantled. But Britain was not keen on allowing the colonies to be represented in Parliament. Even at this stage, very little thought was given to the possibility that union might lead to the creation of an independent and sovereign national state. The goal was simply colonial unification, not nation-building.

IN THE 1850S

By the 1850s the notion of the ultimate union of all the British North American provinces was part of the political culture of many (if not most) Canadians. The Tory politician Henry Sherwood published a series of letters in *The British Colonist* in 1850 proposing a 'Federative Union of the British North American Provinces',[3] and the subject was discussed regularly in the editorial pages of the Toronto *Daily Globe* as both natural and inevitable. The people of Canada and the Maritime provinces had much in common, as the paper noted in 1853:

> The question of their future destiny will begin to force itself on the mind of the people, as their numbers increase. Aspirations after a national name, a national position, a national literature will grow up in their bosoms, as soon as wealth and consequent independence reach every quarter of the country, through which they are now making giant strides. There will be a demand for the acquisition of new territory, a longing after a wider field, for the nation as it will then exist. The

natural outlet for this feeling will be in the union of the Provinces, and in the absorption of the territory which now rightfully belongs to them—we mean that of the Hudson's Bay Company. A magnificent state would grow from such a confederation under British protection, having all the life and activity of the American continent, yet retaining more of the virtues of the parent state than the neighbouring union, and avoiding many of the evils which afflict the Republic.[4]

By 1858 the vision had become sufficiently attractive that J.C. Taché, editor of the Bleu newspaper *Le Courrier du Canada*, in a book entitled *Des Provinces de l'Amérique du Nord et d'une union fédérale* accepted the inevitability of union, but insisted on the principle of confederation. The preservation of several separate but confederated governments was necessary, he argued, because of the diversity of the various Canadian provinces. Taché also discussed in detail the allocation of powers. The federal government would control all matters of material importance (money, post office, militia, for example), and the provinces would control all matters of moral importance (education, public charity, family life, agriculture, for example). This division reflected the thinking of Catholic Quebec, which obviously would have some effect on the final constitution.

Meanwhile, the imperial administrators at the Colonial Office and the governors of the various colonies were also finding the prospect of colonial unification and autonomy increasingly attractive, though for quite different reasons: not least were the efficiencies and economies that might result. From the British perspective, of course, the colonies had effectively been lost when they achieved responsible government. The remaining scraps of Empire were costly and exposed Britain to potential trouble. Sir Edmund Walker Head, lieutenant-governor of New Brunswick from 1848 to 1854 and governor-in-chief of Canada from 1854 to 1861, was a constant advocate of confederation, floating concrete proposals in 1851 and 1858. On 16 August

1858, Governor General Head announced that his government would open union discussions with the imperial and Maritime governments. But although the Cartier–Macdonald government of Canada was officially in favour of unification, its counterparts to the east were distinctly lukewarm, and Head was forced to drop the scheme. By the early 1860s, however, all the colonial governors had imperial defence as their most pressing priority, and all saw unification as a potential solution to their problems. In 1864 the lieutenant-governor of New Brunswick, Arthur Hamilton Gordon, pressed very hard for a colonial conference of New Brunswick, Nova Scotia, and Prince Edward Island to discuss Maritime union. Hoping that such a union might improve New Brunswick's insular political attitude and exposed military situation, he managed to generate enough enthusiasm that a conference was organized to meet in Charlottetown in September 1864.

As for the larger union, by 1860 there was considerable consensus, particularly in Canada, on the general blueprint. It would separate Canada East and Canada West, add the Maritime provinces (and perhaps Newfoundland), and expand into the West. The new federal government would have a bicameral legislature and provincial legislatures would remain. Federal powers would be general, provincial powers local. The union would remain a part of the Empire, as acknowledged through the appointment of a governor general representing the Crown. Responsible government would continue at both the federal and provincial levels. The details could be worked out when the time came. All that was needed was some spur to implement this consensus.

D'ARCY MCGEE AND A NEW CANADIAN NATIONALITY

By the 1850s the stirrings of what the Montreal *Pilot* called '*a true Canadian feeling*—a feeling of what might be termed *Canadian nationality*, in contradistinction to a feeling of mere colonial or annexation vassalage',[5] were evident. The extent to which this feeling reflected the growing strength of the Canadian state can never be known, but the sense of a new power emerging probably did lurk somewhere in the background. Even at this point the nature of the 'Canadian feeling' differed between Canada East and Canada West. The francophone press tended to define national sentiment narrowly, in terms of French Canada, whereas in Canada West the press had already begun extending the idea of nationality well beyond the borders of the province. Sometimes this idea was expressed in high-flown rhetoric, as in the Tory lawyer Alexander Morris's lecture *Nova Britannia* (1858), in which he called for a new national patriotism for British North America, 'this new Britannia, this rising power on the American Continent'. Often the idea was couched in terms of economic or cultural protectionism.

Thomas D'Arcy McGee, in his newspaper *New Era* (published in Montreal in 1857–8), called for revision of the 1854 Reciprocity Treaty on cultural grounds. In literature, according to McGee:

> The Americans have an advantage in this market. . . . The consequence is that Montreal and Toronto houses are mere agencies for New York publishers, having no literary wares to exchange with Harper, or Putnam, or the Sadliers, or Appleton. Economically, this is an evil; intellectually, it is treason to ourselves. If the design is to Massachusettsize the Canadian mind, this is the very way to effect that end; if, on the other hand, we desire to see a Canadian nationality freely developed, borrowing energy from the American, grace from the Frenchman, and power from the Briton, we cannot too soon begin to construct a Grand Trunk of thought, which will be as a backbone to the system we desire to inaugurate.[6]

McGee's *New Era*, though short-lived, was a major advocate of both British North American union—'The future political being of Canada is

■ Thomas D'Arcy McGee, 1868. LAC, PA-6109.

Montreal. Persuaded that the United States was bent on assimilating minorities such as the Irish Catholics, McGee believed that British North America should develop a different kind of political system. To a considerable extent he transferred his Irish nationalist ideas and reactions against his American experience to the Canadian scene. When he was elected to the Legislative Assembly of Canada in December 1857, representing the Irish and anglophone Catholic interests of Montreal, he issued his political manifesto:

> In entering into public life in this province, we do so with the strongest desire to preserve the individuality of the British North American colonies, until they ripen into a new Northern nationality. We shall judge of all proposed changes, not only by their own merits, but by their applicability to this end. Representation by population—the maintenance of the union of Upper and Lower Canada—a union under proper conditions with the Maritime Provinces and Bermuda—the annexation of Hudson Bay territory—the education, employment, and civil equality of all classes of people—in fact, every important topic that can arise ought to be viewed by the light, and decided by the requirements of Canadian Nationality.[7]

McGee's shopping list suggests the direction of thinking that was emerging in Canada by the end of the 1850s. Many of his principles were also accepted at the convention held by George Brown's Upper Canada Reformers in November 1859 at St Lawrence Hall in Toronto. Yet neither McGee nor Brown and his Reformers had necessarily committed themselves to such principles as a strong central government or legislative union. 'Under proper conditions' was a fairly vague phrase.

bound up most intimately with that of the maritime provinces', he wrote in 1857—and independence from the mother country. No doubt the idea of actual separation from Britain reflected McGee's Irish nationalism. At the same time he called for the 'speedy and secure establishment of the Canadian nationality'. Few British North Americans could be found in the 1850s proposing a more complete package of constitutional and intellectual change—union, independence, a new nationality—although the main components fitted together logically, almost inevitably.

Certainly no more ardent Canadian nationalist could be found than McGee, a Catholic Irishman who had come to North America in 1842 in the wave of Irish emigrants driven out of their homeland by famine (and what they regarded as British misrule). He worked in the United States as a journalist on Irish-American newspapers until 1857, when he moved to

THE ROAD TO CONFEDERATION

Feelings of ultimate inevitability do not necessarily lead to action. Once action has begun, however, they can help to move things along.

THE INTERNATIONAL SITUATION

The greatest spur towards national unification for British North America was the course of events in the United States, which rapidly altered both the continental and international balances of power. For years the Americans had been blundering towards the breakup of their federal union (another development that everyone seemed to feel was inevitable). That union fell apart with surprising suddenness in 1861, with the secession of the southern states into their own Confederacy and the beginning of the American Civil War. Even though most British North Americans found slavery abhorrent, a large segment of public opinion north of the border supported the Confederacy, for several reasons. French Canada could identify with the problems of a beleaguered minority, while English Canada had a long-standing hostility to American republican democracy as exemplified by the Union government of the northern states. Most Canadians could agree that it might be easier to live with a divided neighbour than a united one. As for the British, they found economic and political reasons for a neutral policy, which to the Americans seemed to favour the Confederacy—especially after the Americans seized Confederate diplomats off the British mail ship SS *Trent* late in 1861. Public opinion in the northern states, whipped up by American newspapers, was extremely hostile to both Britain and her colonies. Abraham Lincoln's government refused to back down and release the prisoners. The British hastily began to reinforce their garrisons in British North America. The stage was set for an Anglo–American war that could alter the history of the continent.

Despite clear provocation, the British government refused to take advantage of the *Trent* affair. Such forbearance demonstrated a genuine commitment to neutrality, but the military situation was such that Britain could not leave her North American colonies unprotected. Two scenarios seemed possible. In the first, the Confederacy would succeed in maintaining its independence, and the Union government would seek to replace the lost territory by turning its frustrated military machine northward to British North America. Alternatively, the Union government would defeat the secessionists, and then use its victorious army to annex British North America. The Americans could use as pretexts any number of incidents in which Britain and her colonies had 'supported' the Confederacy, including occasional raids on American territory by southerners based north of the border (the most notorious of these was made on St Alban's, Vermont, in 1864). From the British perspective, defending the colonies was expensive and dangerous, and although they sent troops there following the *Trent* affair, what they really wanted was for the colonials to organize their own defences and become sufficiently strong militarily to discourage the Americans from adventurism in the north.

In 1864 the military situation turned more dangerous for British North America as the Union forces gained clear victories over the Confederates. At the same time the decade-long reciprocity agreement was expiring, and motions were being made in the Congress to abrogate it. Although the Americans were hostile to British North America because of its perceived support of the Confederacy, the principal danger to reciprocity was a growing protectionism in the United States, combined with a conviction that the British colonies had benefited more from the treaty. In any event, the American Senate would vote for abrogation early in 1865.

THE CANADIAN COALITION OF 1864

The events of the American war influenced everybody's thinking. The difficulty experienced by the Canadian Parliament in organizing a military mobilization against the Americans (by building up the militia) was one of the factors that led George Brown to propose a political coalition with his long-time political enemies,

■ George Brown, 1880. Notman and Fraser/
LAC, PA-6165.

based on commitment to a British American federal union.[8] Brown, of course, needed no converting; unification had long been an explicit policy of his. Officially, at least, his enemies were equally committed to unification. The achievement of this 'Great Coalition'—combining the Conservatives under John A. Macdonald and the Bleus under George-Étienne Cartier with the Grits under Brown—broke the political deadlock. On 22 June 1864 Brown stood in the House of Commons for a major speech. He began, 'We have two races, two languages, two systems of religious belief, two sets of laws, two systems of everything', and concluded by proposing a coalition. His proposal was quickly accepted. The new government was able to move forward on a variety of fronts over the summer. The militia problem was resolved by providing funds and expanded units. More important, the outline of a new federal union was prepared, to

be presented to the conference of delegates from Nova Scotia, New Brunswick, and Prince Edward Island who were to meet at Charlottetown in September to discuss Maritime union. The *Trent* affair had stimulated interest in the completion of the Intercolonial Railway linking the Maritimes and Canada. But despite negotiations in 1862—involving Canada, Nova Scotia, and New Brunswick—that had agreed on a cost-sharing formula, the Canadians had continued to drag their feet on the project. A Maritime union that would enable the 'lower provinces' to negotiate on a stronger footing with the Canadians was debated in all three legislatures and occasionally discussed in the newspapers. Some voices called for a larger union. But Prince Edward Island made clear that its leaders could not be bothered to leave home to talk about union—hence the eventual choice of Charlottetown as the venue for discussions.[9]

THE VIEW FROM THE MARITIMES

It has never been clear where the Maritimes actually stood on the question of union—regional or national—at the time of the Charlottetown Conference in 1864. What we do know is that there was considerable support in the abstract for some sort of unification, tempered by two realities: a strong feeling that participation in a larger union must not work to the disadvantage of either the Maritime provinces or the region; and an equally strong, almost smug, feeling that the Maritimes were not doing so badly within the existing imperial system. The British may have been unhappy with the current operation of the Empire, but many people in the Maritimes found it quite acceptable. Most of the region's economic interests were transatlantic rather than transcontinental, and part of the problem of a British North American union was finding a way to provide the Maritimes with economic opportunities to replace those it enjoyed through its trade with the outside world under the umbrella of the British Empire. The Intercolonial Railway, of course, would make it possible to transport western products to the carrying trade of the Maritimes and at the same time offer the prospect of new markets for Maritime goods in the interior.

Historians sympathetic to central Canada have always tended to view the Maritime provinces as narrow-minded in their defence of entrenched local interests. This may have been partly the case, but such an interpretation really misses the point. The region was already a member of a larger political and economic system, known as the British Empire, which was a good deal more tangible in Halifax and Saint John than it was in Toronto or Montreal. The Maritimes had legitimate reasons for not wishing to surrender local autonomy to the powerful Canadians without receiving clear advantages in return. Ironically, many Maritimers feared a union that would merely cater to local interests. More than one newspaper joined the *Halifax Citizen* in expressing distrust of 'that combination of union and disunion—that expensive double machinery of government, that attempts to neutralize sectional feelings and interests through a general government while perpetuating those feelings by means of local legislatures.'[10]

Central Canadian historians have also refused to treat the opponents of union with much attention or respect. Before the advent of the *Dictionary of Canadian Biography*, precious few anti-confederationists made their way into standard Canadian reference works, and their opposition to confederation was ignored or downplayed. As is usually the case, the victors get to write the history. Though the anti-confederationist case may have been disproved by subsequent events—at least through 2010—at the time it was certainly not unreasonable to see the unification of British North America as an impractical visionary scheme, proposed by the Province of Canada to meet its needs but not really in the best interests of other, smaller colonies. Even a supporter of union could object to the specific terms worked out in 1864. As one New Brunswick legislator pointed out in the

debates over union in his province, 'This scheme had its origins in Canada; their necessities called for it, not ours.'[11] What analysis has been done of the backgrounds of those politicians and businessmen who opposed confederation indicates that the best predictor of attitudes towards the proposal fleshed out at Quebec was political allegiance. Anti-confederates in the provincial legislatures were far more likely to be Liberals than Conservatives, favouring grassroots democracy over economic development, and hostile to excessive centralism.[12] To some extent they reflected the suspicions of their constituents.

THE QUEBEC CONFERENCE

At Charlottetown the Canadians presented their scheme for a federal union to what seemed to be general approbation. But several problems were inherent in the proposals from the beginning. First, a central element in the Canadian initiative was the perceived need to circumvent the ethnic divisions of the united Canada, preferably by allowing the francophones their own province and then balancing that concession by adding more provinces to the union. It could be argued that the Canadian politicians of the early 1860s exaggerated the problems caused by the double majority rule. Were ministries in Canada really all that unstable? By comparison with Italian or Israeli ministries in the late twentieth and early twenty-first centuries, perhaps they were not. The Act of Union of 1840 gave the two ethnic groups a fair amount of autonomy, and if that structure had been allowed more time to evolve, ways around the perceived gridlock might have been found. On the other hand, were the problems with the constitutional structure of 1791 really caused by ethnic conflict or by other issues? In any event, John A. Macdonald and others found their ingenuity taxed to explain why this federal union would work when the American one had just failed, particularly since it was a given that, in any federal union operating on the basis of parliamentary responsible government and 'rep by pop', those provinces with smaller populations were likely to be overwhelmed.

The question of Senate representation proved critical, particularly at the second conference—which Newfoundland joined—held at Quebec in October 1864 to work out the details agreed to in principle at Charlottetown.[13] After Quebec, almost all the objections expressed in any part of British North America were not to the general principle of union, but to the specific terms worked out at that conference and the procedures used to implement them. Critics complained not about union itself, but about 'this union', which reflected the dominance of Canadian needs and Canadian thinking, and rode roughshod over the legitimate efforts of the smaller (Atlantic) provinces to protect themselves from the Canadian juggernaut. Critics also complained about the anti-democratic way in which ratification of the new arrangements was apparently to be orchestrated.

At the same time, many issues were never raised at Quebec, and many things were taken for granted that could later become grounds for objection. For example, when Macdonald moved at the conference that there be three sections to British North America—Canada West, Canada East, and the four Atlantic provinces, each section having 24 members in the Senate—the Atlantic delegates did not insist on equal representation for each province. In the discussions concerning the House of Commons, where representation was to depend on population, they had not balked at having only 46 seats (if Newfoundland were included) out of a total of 200. By comparison, the tripartite Senate division proposed at Charlottetown by the Canadians, which gave the Atlantic provinces collectively as much clout as one of the Canadian provinces, must have looked like a positive sharing of power. The immediate response from the East was a request to have the region's Senate representation raised to 32, partly because Newfoundland was now at the table. Eventually, the Quebec Conference returned to the Charlottetown arrangement—three sections of 24 members each—with another four seats allotted to Newfoundland. The Atlantic delegates did not try for equal Senate representation for each province because they understood that the Senate was not supposed to be an effective house of the legislature. Although responsible government was not discussed, it meant that legislative power had to reside in the House of Commons, whose majority would select the cabinet. Prince Edward Island made a big issue—without any success—over getting one more member of the Commons (six instead of five) than its population allowed.

A further debate came over the powers of the local legislatures. The majority case was stated by Charles Tupper of Nova Scotia: 'Powers—undefined—must rest somewhere. Those who were at Charlottetown will remember that it was fully specified there that all the powers not given to Local should be reserved to the Federal Government. . . . It was a fundamental principle laid down by Canada and the basis of our deliberations.'[14] But some delegates denied that the question had been settled at Charlottetown. Moreover, there was no necessary reason why the delegates at Quebec had to accept the principles laid down by Canada at Charlottetown, or why the federal government had to be given all the unspecified powers (an allocation that in theory made for a stronger rather than weaker central government). In fact, as Paul Romney has pointed out, both the federal and the local legislatures got specified powers and residual powers. The federal reserve read 'Generally respecting all matters of a general character, not especially and exclusively reserved for the Local Government and Legislatures', and that for the local governments was 'generally all matters of a private or local nature, not assigned to the General Parliament.'[15] Macdonald's explanation for the residual powers pointed to the failure of the American federal experiment, which had given the states the unspecified powers. But arguments based on the American example were always dangerous. Tupper was a good centralizing Tory, of course, and he was quite satisfied with a stronger federal government. But a number of Atlantic delegates objected to this arrangement. And those from Prince Edward Island became upset when a provision for money to buy out its landed proprietors (which apparently had been agreed to at Charlottetown along with the allocation of powers) was omitted from the final agreement for no very compelling reason.

However ungenerous the Quebec Conference was to Prince Edward Island, no one could accuse the Canadians of stinting on entertainment to woo the delegates. Both supporters and critics of Confederation could agree on the convivial atmosphere at Quebec, although they obviously took away different interpretations. 'Picture it ye enthusiasts!' wrote a Hamilton newspaper satirically. 'What a Canadian prospect and Arcadian delight. . . . a national Paradise. . . . Mr. Brown loving Mr. Galt, Mr. Galt loving Mr. Brown, and Mr. Macdonald loving everybody continually. What could be more lovely?'[16] According to *Barney Rooney's Letters*—a major anti-union publication from Nova Scotia, written in 'Irish' dialect—the conference came to life only after the delegates returned to the St Louis Hotel 'after a hard day's conspiracy', agreeing over the punch bowl that 'the well understood wishes iv [sic] the people are so notoriously in favour iv this scheme that it would be a reckless and infamous policy to put them to the trouble of expressing themselves.'[17]

As 'Barney Rooney' suggested, selling the Quebec scheme to the 'lower provinces' would not be easy, particularly since the supporters of Confederation were not willing to take the question to the public through an election or a plebiscite. The public debate was not very well informed, and the preliminaries to Canadian union produced no background documents in any way equivalent to the *Federalist Papers* (by James Madison, Alexander Hamilton, and company, 1787) that subsequent generations of

■ Charles Tupper. LAC, PA-6168.

■ John A. Macdonald, 1868. LAC, PA-6513.

Canadians could consult to understand what the country's founders intended. Some early debate did address the question of whether the proposed union was legislative, uniting all the assemblies under one, but most of the discussants had little real grasp of federalism in particular or political theory in general.

Historians have tended to downplay the debates that took place in both the newspapers and the legislative assemblies, emphasizing the larger forces at work instead of focusing on what are often seen as ill-informed commentaries and exchanges. Two points are worth making here. First, the debates do reveal quite plainly that no two com-

FRANÇOIS ÉVANTUREL
(1821–91)

François Évanturel was born at Quebec City, the son of a Frenchman who had fought for Napoleon before joining the British. Ordered to Quebec with the army, he was demobilized there in 1814. Young François studied at the Petit Séminaire de Québec, articled in a law office, and was called to the bar in 1845. He was active in the militia as well as the Societé Saint-Jean-Baptiste, and helped to found the Institut Canadien in 1848 before being elected to the Legislative Assembly in 1855 as a Liberal-Conservative, committed to the promotion of the North Shore Railway. Two years later he ran for the Assembly in one riding as an independent and in another as a Liberal, but lost in both. In 1861, however, he was elected again as a Liberal, and joined the John Sandfield Macdonald–Louis-Victor Sicotte cabinet. As minister of agriculture he attempted to reform his department and concentrated on colonization of unpopulated regions of the province.

In 1862 Évanturel was one of several Liberals who together purchased the newspaper *Le Canadien*, and five years later he became its editor and sole proprietor. The newspaper under Évanturel followed a line of unenthusiastic support for the government. In

the Assembly he participated in the Confederation debates as a moderate Liberal. Although he insisted that he was a friend of the Canadian administration and a supporter of the principle of confederation, he also warned that 'it may be so applied as to endanger and even destroy, or nearly so, the rights and privileges of a state which is a party to this Confederation. Everything . . . depends on the conditions of the contract.' Évanturel worried that a federation of the two Canadas alone, without the Maritime provinces, might not work well for French Canadians. His various speeches in the debates suggest that he was unable to decide whether union was really a good thing.

In 1867 Évanturel retired from politics to concentrate on his newspaper, but in 1871 he tried—unsuccessfully—to re-enter provincial politics as a critic of a government that he felt was too submissive to the federal administration. In 1872 he sold his newspaper to the Conservatives. Évanturel spent most of the remainder of his life in ill health, out of the spotlight, but in the mid-1860s he was a perfect example of a conflicted French-Canadian politician, one who suspected that the price paid for provincial autonomy might well have been too high.

JEAN-BAPTISTE-ERIC DORION
ON THE UNION

On 9 March 1865, Jean-Baptiste-Eric Dorion, brother of A.-A. Dorion and member for Drummond and Arthabaska, spoke in the debates over Confederation in the Canadian Parliament. Dorion was a Rouge, closely associated with the Institut Canadien.

. . . Why, Mr. Speaker, are we engaged this evening in discussing a Confederation of the Provinces of British North America? Because we had, last year, a Ministerial crisis, from which arose a proposal for the union of the two political parties who divided public opinion. The Macdonald–Taché Ministry, who represented the Conservative party in the country, had just been defeated in the Legislative Assembly; they were obliged to resign. It will be recollected that the Government were beaten on a question of maladministration of the public business. I allude to the advance of $100,000 made to the Grand Trunk Railway without authority of Parliament, for which act several members of the Cabinet were responsible. Could you inform me, Mr. Speaker, what has become of the $100,000 in question? Alas! It disappeared in the Ministerial crisis, and left us the extraordinary Coalition which now governs us, composed of men who for ten years treated each other as men devoid of political principle! . . .

They [the Maritimers] seem to be afraid of us, and notwithstanding the offers of money made to them, they will have nothing to do with a union. Our reputation for extravagance must be very bad to frighten them to that degree; and, no doubt, when they saw us spend in the course of a month or two, for receptions, in traveling and in feasting, sums equalling in amount the whole of revenue of Prince Edward Island, they must have gone back with a sorry idea of our way of managing public business. . . .

Now, let me justify my opposition to the projected change. I am opposed to the scheme of Confederation, because the first resolution is nonsense and repugnant to truth; it is not a Federal union which is offered to us, but a Legislative union in disguise. Federalism is completely eliminated from this scheme, which centres everything in the General Government. Federalism means the union of certain states, which retain their full sovereignty in everything that immediately concerns them, but submitting to the General Government questions of peace, of war, of foreign relations, foreign trade, customs and postal service. Is that what is proposed to us? Not at all. In the scheme we are now examining, all is strength and power, in the Federal Government; all is weakness, insignificance, annihilation in the Local Government! . . .

I am opposed to the scheme of Confederation, because by means of the right of veto vested in the Governor by the 51st resolution, local legislation will be nothing but a farce. They may try to make us believe that this power would be but rarely exercised, and that it differs in nowise from that exercised by the present Governor when he reserves bills for the Royal assent; but all the country knows that it would not be so. . . .

SOURCE: P.B. Waite, ed., *The Confederation Debates in the Province of Canada/1865* (Toronto: McClelland & Stewart, 1963), 147-9.

mentators had exactly the same understanding of the federal experiment that was being proposed or how it would work. This may have been partly a reflection of constitutional ignorance or lack of information, but it was also a product of the different sales campaigns that proponents of the scheme directed at different constituencies. Second, proponents themselves may have modified their conceptions of how it would work in the course of the debates. Such modification was perhaps most apparent with regard to the importance of the 'local' (the term was significant) legislatures. The original plan of the Canadians at Charlottetown had been to downplay the provincial bodies, but that soon became impossible. The result was a federal state quite different from the one most Canadian political leaders had anticipated.

People in Canada West and the Maritimes may have understood in a general way that the new union was to be centralist, but this was not the case in Canada East. While Macdonald and others were seeking to reduce the powers of the provincial legislatures to 'municipal' proportions, in French Canada a different apprehension was encouraged from the beginning. For example: 'The federal power will be sovereign, no doubt', wrote the *Courrier de St-Hyacinthe* in September 1864, 'but it will have power only over certain general questions clearly defined by the constitution. This is the only plan of confederation which Lower Canada can accept. . . . The two levels of government must both be sovereign, each within its jurisdiction as clearly defined by the constitution.'[18] The proponents of union in Canada East emphasized how Confederation would give French Canadians their own province. As George Cartier's *La Minerve* put it: 'as a distinct and separate nationality, we form a state within the state. We enjoy the full exercise of our rights and the formal recognition of our national independence.'[19] The general acceptance of this argument meant that little French-Canadian opposition was to be found when the union was debated in the Canadian legislature. The chief critic of the scheme in Canada East was Christopher Dunkin, an English-speaking Protestant MLA from the Eastern Townships.

THE DEBATES OVER UNION

Proponents of Confederation generally agreed that provincial acceptance of the new constitu-

tional arrangements could be achieved by legislative fiat, without recourse to 'the people'—a classic Tory position. Hence the main forums for discussion of the scheme were the debates within the provincial assemblies. What these demonstrated above all was the success of the union supporters in capturing most of the positive ground. Critics like Dunkin and A.-A. Dorion, leader of the Rouges and also an MLA, could dissect the Quebec proposals and reduce them to rubble—as Dunkin did in two four-hour speeches to the Canadian Parliament in 1865—but they had virtually no constructive replacements to offer. Dunkin argued that the scheme amounted to 'a disunion between Upper and Lower Canada', to which he objected strenuously.[20] He also attacked the proposal for a Legislative Council (or Senate) presented at Quebec as lacking any organizing principle beyond the desire to prevent its numbers from resting on population. Dunkin further insisted that 'the Federal system is simply inconsistent with the first principles that must prevail in a properly organized British responsible central government', but he did not describe those principles in detail.[21] Apart from suggesting that the 1841 union of the Canadas be preserved and somehow used as the basis for a larger confederation—a position that most of his colleagues had rejected—he had no real alternatives to suggest.

NEWFOUNDLAND

Newfoundland's bipartisan representatives returned from the Quebec Conference in favour of union, but two powerful groups in the province opposed it. The major merchants of Water Street feared the economic consequences of joining a unified British North America, and the Roman Catholic population, most of whom were of Irish background, feared that they would suffer as their ancestors had when Ireland was joined to Great Britain by the Act of Union in 1801. A vote was taken in the Assembly in early 1865 on a clause in the Throne Speech calling for 'a calm examination' of the union proposal. It disclosed that the legislators were about equally divided, and the government of Premier Hugh Hoyles decided to refer the question to the electorate. But union was not a priority issue in the 1865 election because nobody chose to press it. According to one observer, the feeling against Confederation was 'much more unanimous than in either New Brunswick, Nova Scotia, or Cape Breton'.[22] Much of the opposition was directed specifically at Orangist Canada West, although Newfoundland nationalism also played a part.

The St John's Chamber of Commerce in 1865 argued that the Confederation plan was designed to ease Canada's political difficulties, provide more resources for the defence of that province, and allow the Maritime colonies access to continental markets: 'it is difficult to see what interest this Colony can have in any one of these objects to justify the sacrifice of its independent legislative position and the assumption of a share of the enormous expenditure that must be incurred for the support of the General Government.'[23] Such expenditures would require higher tariffs, and would not provide any new markets for the Newfoundland fisheries. Newfoundlanders agreed that Great Britain would have to defend them, and, indeed, many suspected that a closer connection with Canada would attract more trouble than it would avoid. Pro-confederates had few specific counter-arguments to offer. They could point to the colony's economic difficulties and the impoverishment of its people, but they could not demonstrate how joining a new mainland confederation would help the island except through better communications and possible access to new capital. As a result, Newfoundland showed little interest in union in 1867. It would not see an election fought on confederation until 1869.

PRINCE EDWARD ISLAND

In Prince Edward Island the issue was simple. The population was small (although the popula-

tion density was the highest in British America), and likely to remain so. With the principle of representation by population built into the Quebec proposals, the island would have no clout in the federal legislature. Moreover, it appeared that the local legislature would be reduced to the equivalent of a town council, and the island would not be sufficiently compensated for 'the surrender of a separate Government, with the independent powers it now enjoys'. Prince Edward Island, like Newfoundland, recognized that Confederation favoured Canada's interests more than its own, and chose not to pursue union after the Quebec Conference.

NEW BRUNSWICK

The situation in New Brunswick and Nova Scotia was considerably more complex—and more volatile. Premier S.L. Tilley returned from the Quebec Conference to face such a storm of criticism that he refused to present resolutions supporting Confederation to the existing house. The Saint John *Telegraph* commented, 'If Confederation comes, it will be a six months' conception and a sickly child.' Tilley's arguments that the British government was behind the union and pushing hard only confused the province. In New Brunswick, as one Canadian reporter wrote in 1864, 'Party politics do not run high. There are no great questions dividing parties and the battles of Parliament are mainly of a personal nature, except where railway matters are introduced.'

Indeed, the Intercolonial Railway was a matter of high politics. Although it symbolized a continental commercial connection favoured by the manufacturers of Saint John, that connection was a mixed blessing. In the 1865 election called by Tilley to settle the issue, one poster put the question thus: 'Do you wish Canada Oats, Beef, Pork, Butter, etc. to come into this country at one half the price you are now receiving? Do you wish the whole Revenue of this country to be handed over to . . . the dishonest Statesmen of Canada?'[24] According to the Saint John *Freeman*, that revenue would be used to open the West.[25] At the same time, the selection of the route that the Intercolonial would take through New Brunswick was an important matter, for politicians recognized that those districts served by the railway were the most likely to prosper from it. The political leader of opposition to union, A.J. Smith of Dorchester, was critical of a scheme cooked up in the 'oily brains of Canadian politicians', and as an alternative proposed continuing reciprocity with the Americans—provided the Yankees would agree. He might have been better off with a program he could control, but in the election of 1865, Smith and his colleagues still blew the pro-Confederation government of Tilley away.

A non-partisan government—one newspaper described it as 'A queer mixture of Tories and Liberals'—whose only platform was opposition to union with Canada was not likely to do much or last long.[26] The Smith administration was back at the polls in April 1866. This time the campaign was conducted against the background of threatened invasions of British North America, particularly New Brunswick, by thousands of Irish nationalists calling themselves Fenians— many of them veterans of the American Union army who had kept their arms when disbanded. Most of their activities amounted to nothing more than a nuisance, aimed at destroying British American property in retaliation for British policy in Ireland, but some Fenian leaders wanted a full invasion that would hold territory to ransom for Irish independence.

If the Fenians had not existed, the pro-Confederation forces would have had to invent them. But there was just enough truth in the rumours circulating to fuel everyone's fears about American aggression and Irish volatility. Many in New Brunswick joined the Roman Catholic Bishop of Arichat (on Cape Breton), who wrote to Charles Tupper on 12 April 1866: 'Altho' no admirer of Confederation on the basis of the Quebec Scheme, yet owing to the present great emergency and the necessities of the times, the union of the Colonies, upon a new basis, we receive with pleasure.'[27] Smith had been to Washington, where he was unable to wring any politically usable concession from the Americans. The Smith government resigned in April 1866 after Lieutenant-Governor Gordon supported a resolution from the Executive Council in favour of Confederation. At the same time, there were reports of several thousand well-armed Fenians along the border from Machias to Calais in Maine. The lieutenant-governor dissolved the House on his own initiative.

Smith was repudiated by the New Brunswick electorate. He had no positive program to offer and was unable to make much out of the lieutenant-governor's collusion with the Executive Council and the pro-confederationists, even though the lieutenant-governor had exercised the arbitrary power of dissolution. The opposition was able to claim that Smith was disloyal to the Crown (which favoured union), and—more to the point—the Fenians lent weight to the confederationist claim that union was necessary to protect everything New Brunswick stood for. The Fenian leader in Maine, Bernard Killian, had certainly helped the confederationist cause by declaring that it was his purpose to obstruct unification of British North America. The new administration headed by Tilley introduced a motion favouring union, albeit not the union of the Quebec Resolutions: rather, union 'upon such terms as will secure the just rights and interests of New Brunswick, accompanied with provision for the immediate construction of the Intercolonial Railway.' From this point on, New Brunswick's opposition to union melted away. Given the province's location, it is not surprising that its people had always been ambivalent about Confederation and replacement of the traditional imperial vision with a continental one. The Fenian threat and British support for Confederation provided excuses for replacing the Smith government, which in office had exemplified no vision whatsoever.

NOVA SCOTIA

The situation was different in Nova Scotia, where the opposition to union was both more intense and longer lasting. The most populous and most prosperous of the Atlantic provinces, with a mixed economy spearheaded by a shipping industry that was still extraordinarily profitable and successful, by the mid-1860s Nova Scotia had a merchant marine of 350,000 tons—one ton of shipping for every one of its 350,000 inhabitants. With its ships able to sail anywhere in the world under the protection of the British Empire, Nova Scotia had little enthusiasm for continentalism. Surely, argued Joseph Howe, the leading spokesman for the anti-confederationists, there was no need to replace London as Nova Scotia's capital. 'We may not seek for another in the backwoods of Canada, and may be pardoned if we prefer London under the dominion of John Bull to Ottawa under the dominion of Jack Frost.' Howe's vision was simple—'You go down to the sea in ships and a flag of old renown floats above them, and the Consuls and Ministers of the Empire are prompt to protect your property and your sons in every part of the world'[28]—but unfortunately the Empire was no longer interested in the role of protector.

The province's lieutenant-governor in the years following the Quebec Resolutions, Sir Richard MacDonnell, wrote that the Great Coalition ministry in Canada 'seems not to have cared how Canadian—selfishly Canadian, they may have appeared to Bluenose who is very happy as he is.' The government headed by Charles Tupper in 1864 was unpopular, and embraced union as a policy that might keep it in office. But as the Halifax *Herald* put the matter after the Quebec Conference, 'We have the trade of the world now open to us on nearly equal terms, and why should we allow Canada to hamper us?'[29] In Nova Scotia that question was not an easy one to answer. Nova Scotians opposed to Confederation initially attacked on two fronts: first, any union was ridiculous, and second, this

union smacked too much of Canadian interests, giving Upper Canada rep by pop, Lower Canada provincial autonomy, and the Maritimes nothing but grief.

Before long the opposition had moved the discussion to economics and finance. As one Halifax newspaper soberly observed:

> The financial portion of the Confederation scheme is its important feature. Since no real Union is in contemplation, but rather a careful bargain between Canada and the Lower Provinces—free trade and an Intercolonial line offered by the former, and a Union which will loosen Canada's political deadlock by the latter—the fiscal portion of the agreement assumes a gigantic importance.[30]

Nova Scotians spent far more time on the details of the finances than on the principle of the bargain. Nevertheless, early in 1865—after Howe had raised his powerful voice in opposition and Tilley's pro-union government in New Brunswick had been defeated—the Tupper government backed off from introducing motions on confederation with Canada.

A variety of circumstances helped to put unification back into contention in Nova Scotia, but the main factors were the same ones as in New Brunswick: British pressure and the Fenian threats. Even the opposition gave in a little. The anti-confederationist William Annand, a friend of Howe, wrote to A.J. Smith in March 1866: 'Like yourself, I desire no political Union with Canada, because I feel that the Maritime Provinces, in any scheme that may be matured, must be seriously injured by a connexion with a colony which must necessarily exercise a preponderating influence over all the others.' In the event that circumstances forced union, he added, 'let it be one that has some more redeeming features than the Quebec Scheme.'[31] Tupper seized on the Fenian threat and waffling opposition to introduce a motion ignoring the Quebec Resolutions and calling for a 'scheme of union' in which 'the rights and interests of Nova Scotia' would be ensured. It passed 31–19 after a debate in which every member of the House put his views on the record. Unlike their counterparts in New Brunswick, the opponents of Confederation in Nova Scotia did not at this point disappear. They went on to complain about the Tupper government's failure to refer the matter to the voters, and in 1867 they would elect full slates of candidates, provincially and federally, committed to taking Nova Scotia out of the union of which she had become a part.

OPPOSITION TO THE QUEBEC RESOLUTIONS

Neither Nova Scotia nor New Brunswick liked the Quebec Resolutions, and the actions that their legislatures took in support of union quite pointedly avoided endorsing the resolutions themselves. The pro-confederationists in these provinces found it politically expedient to talk about renegotiating terms, but they allowed the Canadians to offer a slightly better financial deal without changing any of the features of the Quebec Resolutions that had been found wanting in so many quarters. In short, the legislatures in Nova Scotia and New Brunswick accepted the principle of union with Canada, but not the union worked out at Quebec—and yet what they got was the Quebec model with all its imperfections. All but the most ardent unionists in the Maritimes recognized that the Quebec proposals consigned their provinces to political impotence, and hardly anyone was surprised later, when the region's voices in Ottawa were ignored.

Given the strength and cogency of the opposition to Confederation in Nova Scotia and New Brunswick, how did these provinces end up as part of the union? The answer is—as Annand suggested to A.J. Smith in 1866—that circumstances forced them into it. Among those circumstances were British pressure and Fenian threats. More critical, however, was the failure or

inability of the anti-confederationists to offer any viable or appealing alternatives. Given Britain's attitude in the mid-1860s, the status quo was not really an option, and some kind of union was probably inevitable. The opposition's best bet would likely have been to propose serious changes to the Quebec Resolutions. But that would have required a concerted effort at political co-operation—something more than occasional carping in the newspapers and on the floors of the assemblies. In the end, only the Canadians were sufficiently well organized, and they got what they wanted.

CONFEDERATION BECOMES A REALITY

In November 1866, delegates from Canada, Nova Scotia, and New Brunswick—the three provinces committed to union—met in London to work out the final details: basically, the Quebec Resolutions, with more money (and an Intercolonial Railway) for the Maritimes. The possibility that Prince Edward Island, Newfoundland, the North West, and British Columbia might join later was written into the final draft of the Constitution (an earlier draft had specified only Prince Edward Island and Newfoundland). The delegates generally agreed that the new country should be called by the name of its largest component, thus openly declaring its importance in the union and creating confusion for students of Canadian history ever after. Under pressure from the Colonial Office, which in turn was under pressure from the Americans, they scrapped John A. Macdonald's preferred terminology, 'Kingdom of Canada', in favour of the less monarchical 'Dominion of Canada'. 'Dominion' was a somewhat vague word with connotations of power and sovereignty. In March 1867 the legislation they prepared—the British North America Act, the final drafting of which was done by legal experts of the British government—passed quickly through the British Parliament, the MPs

CONFEDERATION!

THE MUCH-FATHERED YOUNGSTER.

■ Cartoon by J.W. Bengough from his *Caricature History of Canadian Politics* (Toronto, 1886) I, 317.

■ The Parliament Buildings, Ottawa, 1866. LAC, PA-6998.

barely looking up from the order paper as they voted. Since many critics of union had complained that relying on the British Parliament to create the new country was a step backward from responsible government, the perfunctory nature of the action was probably just as well. The Queen signed the bill into law on 29 March 1867; the date of proclamation was to be 1 July. Joseph Howe, who had been in London lobbying against the legislation, returned to Nova Scotia and wrote:

> We must submit of course, because we cannot fight the British Government, but if the Queen's troops were to withdraw I would die upon the Frontier rather than to submit to such an outrage. . . . Our first duty will be to punish the rascals here who have betrayed and sold us. If they are convinced that the Canadians are disposed to act fairly, we may try the experiment.[32]

Howe thus admitted defeat from the outset.

CONCLUSION

To nobody's surprise, the Governor General, Lord Monck, called on John A. Macdonald, the politician everyone associated with the union, to be the first Prime Minister. On the morning of the first of July—a day of celebration and military parades in all the four provinces of Canada—the new country was proclaimed in the recently completed Parliament Buildings in Ottawa. Macdonald and other founders received knighthoods. Launching the new nation was not the same as ensuring its success, of course.

SHORT BIBLIOGRAPHY

Ajzenstat, Janet, et al., eds. *Canada's Founding Debates.* Toronto, 1999. The legislative debates in the Atlantic provinces have never been published. This work provides a selection of them, but unfortunately is organized by topic rather than by province, which minimizes the internal context.

Browne, G.P., ed. *Documents on the Confederation of British North America.* Toronto and Montreal, 1969. The best and most easily available collection of documents on Confederation.

Creighton, Donald B. *The Road to Confederation: The Emergence of Canada, 1863–1867.* Toronto, 1967. An account of Confederation by one of the leading historians of his generation. The author's impatience with any obstacles to Canada's achievement of its destiny is palpable.

Martin, Ged, ed. *The Causes of Canadian Confederation.* Fredericton, 1990. A collection of essays, including the best analysis of the anti-confederates presently available.

———. *Britain and the Origins of Canadian Confederation 1837–1867.* Vancouver, 1995. The best account of the British background of Confederation.

Moore, Christopher. *How the Fathers Made a Deal.* Toronto, 1997. A more skeptical modern account of Confederation, although still basically in the nation-building mould.

Morton, W.L. *The Critical Years: The Union of British North America, 1857–1873.* Toronto, 1964. A well-balanced account of the Confederation years, covering a longer period of time, before and after 1867, than Waite or Creighton.

Silver, Arthur I. *The French-Canadian Idea of Confederation, 1864–1900.* Toronto, 1982. An excellent analysis of the meaning of Confederation in French Canada, based on extensive newspaper research.

Waite, P.B. *The Life and Times of Confederation, 1864–1867: Politics, Newspapers, and the Union of British North America.* Toronto, 1962. A well-written account of the Confederation movement, based chiefly on the newspapers of the time.

———, ed. *The Confederation Debates in the Province of Canada 1865.* Toronto, 1965. A judicious abridgement of the huge volume of *Parliamentary Debates on the Subject of the Confederation of the British American Provinces* (Quebec, 1865; repr. 1951).

STUDY QUESTIONS

1. What sort of British North American union, if any, could have been predicted by 1860?
2. What did contemporaries see as the outstanding questions to be resolved in such a union?
3. What international factors in the 1860s increased the urgency of unification?
4. To what extent was Confederation a Canadian scheme?
5. What role did Fenianism play in Canadian unification?
6. Outline the opposition case against Confederation. What were its weaknesses?
7. What to your mind was the single most important factor bringing about Confederation?

☐ Writing about the History of Confederation

■ Why do students take courses in Canadian history and read textbooks like this one? The reasons vary, but most students will say that they think they should know something of their nation's history. Most citizens would agree. In fact, many Canadians believe that courses in Canadian history should be mandatory, and a good number would like to ensure that students are taught a version of the nation's history that they can be proud of. On the whole, however, Canadians are not as overtly patriotic as Americans, and most understand that not everything in our past has been positive. Yet even if some negative features can be tolerated, certain topics in Canada's history are by nature so sacrosanct that it is difficult to reappraise them honestly.

One of those sacrosanct topics is the making of the Canadian federation in the 1860s. For any country, the process of national unification is important, and in many cases it is mythologized, made larger than life. Canada has seen less overt myth-making than most nations. But this does not mean that the historical interpretation of the Confederation period has not been subtly affected by the desire to make the story a positive one. Any classroom discussion of the preconceptions that students bring to the subject of Confederation will show the extent to which mythology has crept into the picture. Not surprisingly, most students expect the Confederation story to be consistent with their notion of Canada as a great democracy. The 'founding fathers' ought to be men of foresight and vision, not manipulation and sordid backroom deals.

The historiography of Confederation has been dominated by three tendencies: a concentration on the progressive building of a nation, to the neglect of other problems raised by the subject; an insistence on interpreting that nation-building process in the most favourable light possible, regardless of evidence to the contrary; and, finally, a reluctance to take a fresh look at the Confederation story in the light of new concerns. One of the best strategies for arriving at a favourable interpretation has been to avoid any serious effort at explanation. Thus, Confederation has generally been seen as the product of specific political, economic, and military problems in the 1860s, to which national unification offered a solution. As a result, there has been considerably less skepticism in the historiography, both older and newer, of Confederation than one might ordinarily expect. Questions about this interpretation were virtually non-existent in the histories written in the 1960s, most of which were inspired by the approaching centennial celebrations of 1967, but it has always been rare. The tendency has been to isolate the Confederation period from what preceded and followed it.

By concentrating almost exclusively on the 1860s, historians have been able to treat national unification as a separate incident in Canadian history rather than as a seamless part of a larger picture that may be subject to reinterpretation.

As it is, our understanding of the 1860s is still essentially dominated by the analysis advanced at the time. The chief political problem, therefore, is seen as the instability of the parliamentary process in the Province of Canada. Whether the Canadian Parliament really was so unstable has not been carefully examined; nor has the possibility that the political grouping that promoted Confederation was not so important as has been assumed. Perhaps only Paul Romney, in his *Getting It Wrong: How Canadians Forgot Their Past and Imperilled Confederation* (Toronto, 1999), has seriously challenged the conventional wisdom on the reasons behind the drive for unification. In the economic realm, the need for a larger market has been emphasized, but the context in which the colonial economies were operating at the time of Confederation—the early stages of industrial capitalism—has not played much role in the discussion. As for military difficulties, the possibility that these were greatly exaggerated for political effect is seldom raised. The supposed Fenian threat, in particular, has been largely accepted at face value.

Among the casualties of the nation-building myth were, until very recently, the opponents of Confederation, who were charged with parochialism, negativism, cynicism, lack of vision, and ignorance of the theory behind federalism. Until the research was done for the *Dictionary of Canadian Biography*, we knew little about the careers of many individual anti-confederates, and virtually nothing about their specific objections. No one has discussed the subsequent fates of these men: did they fall into disrepute? did they continue in politics at the provincial level?

How these 'losers' were eliminated from the story is not at all clear; nor is it clear whether such 'losers' are worth examining in more detail, since their actions and ideas are not important. While Quebec historians have always been allowed to criticize Confederation from a separatist perspective, until recently the literature has not been so lenient towards critics from outside Quebec; there was a reluctance to allow the opposition any credibility, to admit that Quebec was given a different interpretation of the British North America Act than the other provinces were, or to acknowledge that some elements of Quebec society—notably the clergy—played an important role in persuading the province to accept union. Indeed, the opponents of union have usually been criticized for virtually every sin but political realism and common sense. In recent years, however, we have come to recognize that the opposition had a perfectly legitimate case. The union was imposed on the other provinces by the Province of Canada, and it was not necessarily a good deal for them. Curiously, even the constitutional debates of the 1970s and early 1980s did not provoke much revisionist thinking about the original British North America Act. In the context of the 1990s debate over federalism, however, the anticonfederate critique began to make a good deal more sense than it had in the past, and our view of the unification process became considerably less rosy.

Confederation was not the result of any popular mandate. One searches in vain for any concrete evidence of public support for nation-building in the 1860s. The National Library's website 'Confederation for Kids' admits that 'some groups of people were not given the chance to participate in the talks or to have their opinions heard'; but the 'groups' in question here are women and Natives people, and the suggestion is that other British North Americans did participate and were heard. Yet, in fact, the failure to consult the people was one of the chief criticisms of the Confederation movement. That failure has usually been explained by reference to the doctrine of parliamentary supremacy—but no scholar has really explored the anti-democratic implications of this doctrine. Moreover, in the new nation's first election the opposition in several provinces, especially Nova Scotia and New Brunswick, actually elected men committed to taking their constituencies out of the union. This opposition in the early federal Parliament is regarded as no more than a minor embarrassment for the ministry of Sir John A. Macdonald and has not been well studied.

One of the chief advantages to the narrow periodization of Confederation was that it allowed historians to avoid discussing western expansion (which was extremely racist and blatantly colonialist) as a central part of the story. The acquisition of the West could be seen as a consequence of Confederation rather than as part of the process; the treatment of the Métis in Red River could be omitted from the Confederation story; and the First Nations could be left out with a simple observation that they were not players.

Only in recent years have historians begun to look at national unification as a goal pursued by self-interested politicians who manipulated the political process to their own ends. There is still no real agreement on why union came about as it did, when it did, or, more particularly, on what led some politicians to fasten onto the idea and others to reject it. We do not understand clearly how the 'Fathers' started with one centralized conception of federalism and ended with another, more sympathetic to the provinces. No careful study has ever been made of the understanding of American federalism in British North America, particularly as reflected in the debates over Confederation in the various legislative assemblies. We do not even have a full text of those debates in all the provinces. No scholar has ever attempted to place Canadian Confederation in the context of national movements of unification in nineteenth-century Europe (especially in Germany and Italy). No one has tried to write a serious counterfactual analysis of Confederation—what would have happened to British North America without it? Most of the literature concentrates on regional divisions; otherwise, it assumes that all the players shared a common set of assumptions. Few attempts have been made to examine ideological (as opposed to geographical) divisions, or to investigate the role that other factors (generational or class differences, for example) might have played.

In short, Confederation historiography seems ready for a good shakeup. But we will probably not get one until another serious constitutional crisis raises new questions about the past for debate.

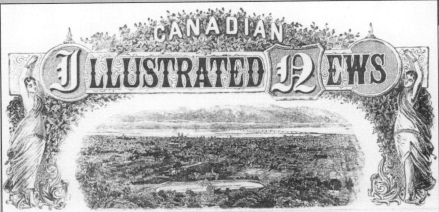

CANADIAN ILLUSTRATED NEWS

Vol. I.—No. 13.]   MONTREAL, SATURDAY, JANUARY 29, 1870.   [SINGLE COPIES, TEN CENTS. $1 PER YEAR IN ADVANCE.

"THE SITUATION"—See next page.

☐ 'The Situation', cover of the *Canadian Illustrated News*, 29 January 1870. Miss Red River must decide between the US Hotel, with its disreputable, apparently indifferent Uncle Sam, and the Hotel Canada, where a respectable lady offers a warm welcome. Library and Archives Canada (LAC), C-48653.

PART FOUR

■ 1867–1885

■ When the Dominion of Canada began its formal existence on 1 July 1867, one of the main purposes behind the act of confederation—to separate the old united Canada (East and West) into two provinces—was achieved. The new country had little idea of its future direction beyond a general sense of a 'manifest destiny' to expand and create a new political entity stretching from coast to coast. In 1867, however, it was not at all clear that such a project could actually be carried out. Within six years Canada would gain three new provinces and a vast western hinterland. But Canadians had very little experience at continental empire-building, and they made some serious blunders in their efforts to take over and administer the vast territories that they purchased from the Hudson's Bay Company in 1868. They also blundered in their first efforts to bring in Prince Edward Island, and only financial pressures led the tiny Island to join Confederation in 1873. (Newfoundland would remain unpersuaded until 1949.)

By 1873 Canada in theory stretched from Atlantic to Pacific, but a vast expanse of the West was virtually uninhabited and lacked any sort of communication links with the East. The West would have to be settled, and a railway constructed to connect the country. The challenges were not merely physical. New policies had to be developed to accommodate the new provinces, and a sense of national identity needed to be encouraged that would be capable of transcending strong provincial loyalties. Nor did everyone agree on what sort of a nation Canada should become: centralized or decentralized, part of the British Empire or autonomous.

In November 1885, two events took place—within a few days of one another—that were to become powerful symbols for the young country: the last spike of the transcontinental railway was driven at Craigellachie, BC, uniting east and west; and the Métis leader Louis Riel was executed for 'treason', dividing not only Aboriginal and white but also French- and English-speaking Canadians.

CHAPTER TWENTY-FIVE

The Completion of Confederation, 1867–1873

The first day of July 1867 certainly marked a beginning in the development of the Dominion of Canada. But in a larger sense it was only an interim point. The new union consisted of four provinces—carved from the three that had created it—and Sir John A. Macdonald's government was conscious that a lot of British territory on the continent had been excluded. The new government was also quite obviously the old Canadian coalition, with a few Maritime faces, organized into the old Canadian departments and using buildings erected in Ottawa for the old Union of the Canadas. Furthermore, several of the new government's first responsibilities involved 'old' rather than 'new' business. The malcontents from Nova Scotia would have to be pacified, the strays would have to be rounded up, and the promise of westward expansion would have to be fulfilled. Over the next half-dozen years three new provinces would be added, a fourth retained—and a fifth positively refused to join. Each situation was different, and few generalizations are possible. About the only thing the five provinces had in common was a singular lack of enthusiasm for the new union. By 1873 Canada would be a very different country, physically and demographically, than it had been in 1867. The possibilities for future development would be far more apparent.

THE ATLANTIC PROVINCES

NOVA SCOTIA AND NEW BRUNSWICK: PACIFYING THE ANTI-CONFEDERATES

When Joseph Howe returned from London in 1867, the anti-confederate movement in the Maritimes was stymied. A petition for reconsideration of Nova Scotia's membership in Confederation, although supported by John Bright (one of the leading Reformers in Westminster), was easily defeated in the British Parliament by a vote of 183 to 87. In September Nova Scotians elected pledged anti-confederates to all its seats, federal and provincial; but this was hardly a long-term solution. Like the provinces that had not joined, Nova Scotia (and New Brunswick) could only hope for 'better terms'. Howe led a repeal delegation to London in early 1868, but got no support from the British government and became disillusioned with British politics and politicians. Prime Minister Macdonald wrote Howe several times in the early autumn of 1868, emphasizing the government's dilemma: if he did not complete his cabinet and appoint officials, the government could not operate, and if he appointed unionists, he would be working against the public will.

TIMELINE

1865

Newfoundland assembly debates Confederation.

1866

British Columbia and Vancouver Island are united.

1867

The Dominion of Canada is proclaimed on 1 July. Parliament rejects petition for reconsideration of Nova Scotia's membership in Canada. William McDougall introduces resolutions for Canadian expansion.

1868

Joseph Howe leads repeal delegation from Nova Scotia to London.

1869

Howe reluctantly supports Confederation. Newfoundland debates prospective terms of union. This is the main campaign issue in 1869 election, which sees union candidates defeated. Howe joins Canadian cabinet. Governor Musgrave moves from Newfoundland to British Columbia. Métis led by Louis Riel organize resistance to Canadian takeover and set up provisional government.

1870

PEI rejects Canada's offer of 'better terms'. Execution of Thomas Scott. Debate over union in Legislative Council of British Columbia. Negotiations between BC and Canada over union. Red River admitted to Confederation as province of Manitoba. Wolseley expedition 'invades' Manitoba.

1871

British Columbia enters Confederation. PEI begins railroad construction.

1872

Responsible government comes to British Columbia. PEI opens union question.

1873

PEI delegation secretly negotiates terms with Canada. PEI joins Confederation.

Howe fully recognized the awkwardness of everyone's position. He was under pressure from some of the extremists to embrace independence or American annexation. In January 1869 Howe wrote Macdonald acknowledging his acceptance of the 'situation'. He then travelled to Ottawa (via Portland, Maine) to renegotiate Nova Scotia's debt and subsidies, thus providing 'better terms'. Howe's support for Confederation, however reluctant, was the key breakthrough in Nova Scotia. He could not prevent the formation of the Nova Scotia Repeal League and declarations (in the *Halifax Chronicle*) that 'We will not endure Union with Canada, we shall pay no taxes to the Dominion Government, except when we are forced to by the bayonets.'[1] But he could provide a conduit and a connection between the federal government and the province. Although he probably did not do his reputation much good—at the time or since then—by allying himself with Macdonald, his acceptance of the reality of the union and his refusal to engage in useless opposition were probably among his most important and statesmanlike acts.

In February 1869 Howe ran as a pro-confederate—in a hotly contested federal by-election—in Hants County. Despite a serious bout of bronchitis, which made campaigning difficult, he won with a comfortable majority and headed off to Ottawa. Within weeks he was sitting in the cabinet. In Ottawa, Howe's task was to attract the support of Nova Scotia MPs to the government, which he did gradually through local patronage. In 1871 he wrote a series of letters in support of confederation that were published in the course of the provincial elections, which substantially reduced the majority of the 'Nova Scotia Party' led by William Annand. In 1872 the Nova Scotia government started an active railroad building program, and after the Liberals under Alexander Mackenzie replaced the Tories in Ottawa in 1873, Nova Scotians increasingly spoke of a working alliance with the federal government. Gradually the Nova Scotia government abandoned its overt anti-confederate stance, and Nova Scotia MPs in Ottawa became allied with the two major federal parties, although residual resentment would surface from time to time over the years.[2]

PRINCE EDWARD ISLAND

THE LAND QUESTION

Most provinces had more than one reason for accepting Confederation. For Prince Edward Island an important motive was settlement of the long-standing land issue. As one Island newspaper put it, 'only let any government, legislative, federal, or mongrel, but offer 200,000 pounds sterling, to buy out the proprietors' claims, and give them [the people] free lands, and tell [them] their taxation will not be increased, and we believe the Islanders almost to a man would hold up both hands for the union.'[3] The Island's dele-

gates thought they had a commitment for that sum from the Canadians (chiefly George-Étienne Cartier). But when George Coles, the PEI delegate to the Quebec Conference, tried to write this condition into the Quebec Resolutions, his request was rejected; he then told the delegates 'they might as well strike Prince Edward Island out of the constitution altogether.'[4] Coles later declared himself against Confederation, and he was far from alone. In late 1864 the journalist Edward Whelen, one of union's main supporters, told A.T. Galt that the Island was totally against union; and the journalist Edward Reilly, denouncing the Quebec Resolutions as 'a scheme of spoliation for the Island', declared that resolution of the land issue was the *sine qua non* of the Island's entry into the union.[5]

Meanwhile, an organized movement of opposition to the proprietors called the Tenant League was becoming increasingly militant. In 1865 troops were required to quell sporadic outbreaks of disorder across the Island, and the British insisted the Island would have to pay for the troops itself. The Island government complained that the reason for the Tenant League's existence was the imperial government's failure to resolve the land question. When the House of Assembly and Legislative Council debated union again in May 1866, again most of the speakers opposed it. Among them was a farmer named Cornelius Howatt, who argued that Islanders 'would be such a small portion of the confederacy, our voice would not be heard in it. We would be the next thing to nothing. Are we then going to surrender our rights and liberties? It is just a question of "self or no self". Talk about a local Legislature. It would be a mere farce.'[6] In July the Island government bought the 212,885-acre (86,152-hectare) Cunard estate, initiating the policy of land purchase that would eventually prove to be the solution to the issue.

In London in August of 1866, at the imperial government meeting to finalize Confederation and prepare a final draft of the British North America Act, Premier J.C. Pope met privately with the Nova Scotia and New Brunswick delegates. Telling them that the Quebec terms were 'unjust, unfair and illiberal' to the Island, he added that, 'if they wished the people of Prince Edward Island to consider the matter at all, they must be prepared, in the first place, to enable us to extinguish Proprietary Rights, and to place us in as good a position as if our lands were crown lands.'[7] The delegates agreed unanimously that if the Island legislature would send delegates to arrange a plan that could be worked into the British North America Act, they would support the granting of whatever amount was necessary to purchase the proprietary rights, up to $800,000. The Canadian cabinet subsequently discussed this proposal and decided that the offer could be binding only if it were inserted in the BNA Act, which the cabinet had no power to do without legislative approval. If PEI joined, the land question could be discussed in a liberal spirit in London, and 'a strong representation to the first Government and Parliament of the United Provinces in favor of their granting compensation agreed upon by them'.[8] This response was seen by the Island government as unfavourable, and in October the *Islander* newspaper printed a letter from former Premier Robert Haythorne mocking 'the paltry bribe of £3 currency per head' and advising Islanders to reject the offer.[9] Lieutenant-governor George Dundas wrote to the Colonial Office that he thought a majority of the Island government would have accepted a proper offer. But that government was defeated in early 1867—partly because of the union question, partly because of its repression of the Tenant League—and the new government of George Coles voted to raise the cash required to buy out the proprietors on its own. In addition to this fundraising effort PEI proposed a reciprocity treaty with the Americans, who in August 1868 sent a committee to Charlottetown to discuss the idea. The talks went very well—and when the Colonial Office learned of them it panicked, partly because a separate agreement might endanger a larger Canadian initiative with the

United States on reciprocity, and partly because such a deal might enable PEI to remain independent. A disapproving dispatch was sent accusing the Island of exceeding its authority. Many PEI legislators resented that interference, which they took as evidence that the British wanted to force the Island into union with Canada.

NEGOTIATING 'BETTER TERMS'

In the end, the Americans did not pursue the treaty, but the prospect was enough to galvanize the Canadian House of Commons into considering the PEI issue. Action would probably have been taken had not Alexander Mackenzie, then a leading member of the opposition, been vehemently opposed. However, the Governor General of Canada and three Canadian cabinet ministers happened to visit the Island for a holiday in the summer of 1869, and they met with the provincial government. By now the Island had another premier, once again Robert Haythorne, who told them not only that 'the land question is the chief public question'[10] but that Canada would have to persuade Islanders that it did not intend to take more money from PEI than it spent there. As a result of those discussions, in December 1869 the Canadian government offered the Island generous terms, including a per capita debt allowance of $25; a special subsidy to cover local government; and an 'efficient Steam Service for the conveyance of Mails and Passengers' between the Island and the mainland, winter and summer, providing 'continuous communication'. It also promised that Canada would seek compensation from the imperial government for the Island's lack of Crown lands, and that if that request was refused, the Dominion itself would lend the Island $800,000 to help it deal with the land question.[11] Nevertheless, the Haythorne government summarily rejected the Canadian offer (always known as 'better terms') on the grounds that it did not resolve enough of the outstanding issues. Most observers agreed that union with Canada would require a full solution to the land question, not merely a loan to the Island government.

In 1871 the PEI legislature began on a course of active railway construction. The main objection to railway building was that it would lead to union with Canada. As one opposition legislator put it, 'the intention of the Government is to construct a railroad from one end of the Island to the other, saddle the Colony with a debt relatively heavier than that of the Dominion, then enter the Dominion and give up the Railroad.'[12] Between contracting overruns and the demands of every village for rail service, the province found that its debentures were unacceptable on the London market. Union with Canada was the only way to maintain the public credit, and the Dominion seized the opportunity when Premier Haythorne reopened the question of union late in 1872. In February 1873 a secret delegation headed by Haythorne stole off to Ottawa—in the night, by iceboat—and quickly agreed to a deal. The terms seemed generous on Canada's part. Not only did the Dominion assume the Island's debts and liabilities, but it agreed to pay a debt allowance, an annual grant, and a subsidy. Although all railroads under contract and construction became Dominion property, the Island would receive up to $800,000 in lieu of Crown lands to complete the purchase of proprietorial property, and continuous communication with the mainland was guaranteed. As Sir Leonard Tilley explained the Canadian offer in the House of Commons, 'the great local works there having been completed, there could never be any large local expenditure in the future, and it was in consideration of this fact that the Dominion Government had granted such liberal terms.'[13] All but one of the Island's legislators voted to accept the Canadian offer: the crusty old Cornelius Howatt refused to make the vote unanimous. (Over a century later, 'Cornelius Howatt, Superstar!' would become the symbol for an Island organization that questioned the positive rhetoric surrounding the centennial of PEI's entry into Confederation.)

On 1 July 1873, just before noon, the sheriff of Prince Edward Island, accompanied by some ladies and gentlemen, stepped forward on the balcony of the Colonial Building (where the Charlottetown Conference had been held nine years earlier) and read the proclamation of union. According to the *Patriot* newspaper, the audience below consisted of three people. After the reading, those on the balcony gave a cheer; the three persons below 'responded never a word'. Prince Edward Island settled down to become what it had known all along it would be: the smallest, least powerful, and poorest province within the Confederation.

NEWFOUNDLAND

In 1864 Newfoundland had in effect invited itself to the Quebec Conference, but the colony of 130,000 people scattered along the seacoast of a large island had found a decision on union too divisive to pursue. By the later 1860s, however, deteriorating economic conditions seemed to make the prospect of union more attractive. A series of bad years in the cod fishery,[14] mainly in the inshore areas, led the merchants to stop doing business on credit—'It is not our duty to maintain paupers', proclaimed one firm[15]—and the collapse of the truck system caused enormous suffering. Economic diversification was obviously essential, and those Canadian markets became increasingly inviting. Fearful of another Nova Scotia, Governor Anthony Musgrave and his Council agreed that it would be dangerous to pursue the project without 'a nominal reference to the body of the people'.[16] In 1869, therefore, the Assembly debated the proposed terms of union. None of the late applicants for entry would have any opportunity to alter the fundamental conditions of Confederation; all they could do was add 'terms'. Newfoundland's terms were fairly demanding (John A. Macdonald would later complain that they were far too great). In addition to the framework provided in the British North America Act, Newfoundland wanted the Dominion to pay the salaries of its leading officials; assume its public debt; provide subsidies for the support of local institutions; and pay $175,000 in return for the transfer of ungranted and unoccupied lands, mines, and minerals; as well as provide an exemption on export taxes, continuance of a garrison at St John's, special subsidies for the fishery, an annual subsidy to the government to replace lost income, and guaranteed steam communication with the mainland for both Newfoundland and Labrador. These terms were debated but then set aside pending 'an appeal . . . to the people at the next General Election'.[17]

An election is never ideal as a plebiscite, since other issues can intrude on the central question and influence the result. Other factors can also make a difference: for example, timing. Premier Frederick Carter delayed calling the election until after the spring fishery on the grounds that it would be unfair to hold an election when so many Newfoundlanders were away at sea; he wanted no charge of undue manipulation. Unfortunately, by the summer of 1869 the economy was looking up, and the opposition had had the benefit of five years (since 1864) to mobilize its forces. Turnout was unusually high—almost 10 per cent higher in most ridings than in the election of 1865. However, the Catholic vote was still firmly opposed to union— the confederate Ambrose Shea, running in a Catholic area, was greeted at Placentia by a priest and populace carrying pots of pitch and bags of feathers—and the Protestant vote split fairly evenly, as did the merchants'. In the end only nine confederates were elected, to 21 antis. Confederates blamed their defeat on the tactics of the opposition, which had predicted that the colony would surrender £618,000 to Canada in revenues in order to get £617,000 from Canada in subsidies and even spread rumours that Newfoundland children would be used as wadding for Canadian cannon. Perhaps the greatest argument against the scheme was fear of the unknown. Most contemporaries thought

intelligent people (read the elite) for the most part supported Confederation and the 'ignorant people' opposed it. Ultimately, however, it is impossible to tell whether the election reflected Newfoundlanders' true feelings about union. What is clear is that neither Canada nor the British government was sufficiently concerned about Newfoundland to seek to undo the conclusion reached in 1869; they were content to wait for Newfoundland to come around. The colony would from time to time show signs of a change of heart, but never quite managed one until 1949, and then under extraordinary circumstances.

THE CREATION OF MANITOBA AND THE NORTH-WEST TERRITORIES

CANADA MOVES TO EXPAND

On 4 December 1867, less than six months after the new Dominion of Canada had begun life as a nation, the MP from Lanark North (Ontario), William McDougall—one of the coalition Liberals who remained in the Confederation government—introduced seven resolutions into Parliament that were designed to set the stage for expanding the fledgling nation across to the prairies and out to the Pacific. The debate that followed was marked both by profound ignorance of the region and by extreme partisanship—and helps explain why the Canadian government would have so much trouble taking control of the West. Objections came from two separate quarters. One group, the opposition proper—the few remaining supporters of George Brown (who had failed to gain a seat in Parliament himself)—complained about the cost of expansion. The other, consisting of most of the Nova Scotia members and a number from New Brunswick, led by Joseph Howe, wanted relations between the Maritimes and the union government sorted out before embarking on a project of continental expansion that would make Maritime secession more difficult. Both groups agreed on the ultimate desirability of a continental nation. But not just yet.

The fact that a local population already existed in Red River was not completely ignored, either by McDougall in his resolutions or by the participants in the subsequent debate. But what was said about that population made it clear that Canada had no understanding of the local issues involved. Several supporters of the resolutions argued that the local people were entitled to liberation from the oppressive administration of the Hudson's Bay Company. Obviously they had read the *Nor'-Wester* newspaper's editorials, without realizing that these represented the opinions of only a small minority of Canadians resident in the settlement. Mr Chipman of New Brunswick used the occasion of the debate to remind the House of how the Maritimes had been dragooned into Confederation, posing a single rhetorical question—'were all the inhabitants of this territory willing to come into the Union, or were they to be dragged in against their will also?' and then sitting down. Dr Thomas Parker, a Tory representing Wellington Centre, Ontario, delivered a long, rambling speech in which he advocated taking possession of the territory on the sole principle of the 'right of a settler's spade' to cultivate the earth, arguing that the 'Indians' had been expelled from eastern Canada on that principle and that he saw no reason to treat the 'white savage'—apparently a reference to the mixed bloods—with any more consideration than the 'red' one. Parker had some qualms about purchasing the HBC charter, 'divorcing half a continent condemned . . . to sterility, unchristianity and barbarism', and many of his listeners agreed. On 11 December an opposition amendment was defeated by 104 to 41. The resolutions were then read and passed.[18] With expressions of ignorance and racism, the Canadian Parliament had endorsed westward expansion and the bringing of civilization to the Northwest.

In 1868 William McDougall accompanied Sir George-Étienne Cartier to London to negotiate the transfer of the region to Canada. The HBC bargained hard, but eventually agreed to sell the territory, including Red River, to Canada in return for £300,000 in cash, generous land grants—45,000 acres (18,210 hectares) around each trading post and what eventually amounted to 7,000,000 acres (2,832,800 hectares) scattered throughout the West—and the right of continued trade without hindrance. The negotiations were completed in March 1869, and the takeover was scheduled to take place on 1 December. Unfortunately, none of the parties involved—Canada, the British government, or the HBC—felt any need to consult formally or informally with either the Red River government (the Council of Assiniboia) or the residents of Red River at any point in this process. What the Canadians had in mind for the land acquired from the HBC (eventually divided into Manitoba and the North-West Territories) was a temporary colonial administration, to be run by a lieutenant-governor and an appointed council of seven to 15 members, with all previous functionaries and public officers continuing in their duties. The legislation prepared for the transfer was not very specific about details such as land policy. The Canadian government appointed McDougall the new territory's first lieutenant-governor and gave him a team of carpetbagging officials and councillors, none of whom had ever set foot in the West. The *Montreal Herald* described them as 'six Canadian adventurers . . . going there to try to make their fortunes in the scramble which is likely to take place for any good thing which might turn up, in the way of town lots, mines, or especially valuable agricultural territory'. Even the *Globe*, which had long supported western expansion, acknowledged that 'If William McDougall is sent to Fort Garry with a ready-made council composed of men utterly ignorant of the country and the people, the strongest feelings of discontent will be aroused.'[19] Naturally, the Canadian government did not bother to inform anyone in the West of the new arrangements.

The government proceeded to compound its

mistakes by dispatching in advance of the transfer a team of surveyors to prepare the way for an influx of settlement. Bishop A.-A. Taché of Red River, on his way to the Vatican Council in Rome, stopped in Ottawa to warn the Canadians of their errors. But Cartier brushed the warnings aside; as the Bishop later described their meeting, 'he [Cartier] knew it all a great deal better than I did, and did not want any information.' The survey team was officially welcomed by the local governor of the HBC in Red River, William Mactavish, who nonetheless warned that 'as soon as the survey commences the Halfbreeds and Indians will at once come forward and assert their rights to the land and probably stop the work.'[20] The leader of the team, John Stoughton Dennis, then made a difficult situation worse by attempting to survey occupied land in the settlement first. Nor was this the only provocation on the part of the Canadians: an earlier party, building a road from Lake of the Woods to the settlement, had been involved in a number of racial incidents, and some of the road crew were discovered trying to buy land from the Métis and Indians. By early September the American consul in Winnipeg was telling Washington that most of Red River was hostile to the plan for Canadian annexation. He thought an uprising unlikely, however, because the people had no political experience or talent for organization. At about the same time, McDougall ordered 100 Spencer carbines and 250 Peabody muskets to be sent to Fort Garry along with ammunition suitable for 'such Police and Volunteer Force as may be necessary'. Whether he had been warned by the leaders in Red River that trouble was brewing is not clear. By the early autumn of 1869, however, the Canadians were clearly perceived as a threat to the land, language, and religion of the local inhabitants, the Métis.

THE MÉTIS RESISTANCE

At this point Louis Riel emerged to lead the Métis. Born into a respected local family in 1844

and named after his father, who led a successful Métis protest against the HBC in 1849, the young Riel spoke out publicly against the surveys. Then in October 1869, while the surveyors were running their line south of Fort Garry through the land of André Nault, Riel led a party of neighbours to Nault's farm, where they stood on the surveyors' chain and told them to stop. This act was Riel's first resistance to Canada's acquisition of the HBC's territory. Soon after, Joseph Howe, the Canadian secretary of state for the provinces, arrived in Red River on an informal fact-finding expedition. Although Howe did not talk officially with any of the leading figures in the eventual uprising, he discovered that Red River already had a government (the Council of Assiniboia, created by the HBC in 1835) and a court system that had been functioning smoothly for years, and that many of the local people deeply resented Canada's interference.

In the meantime William McDougall was already on his way west to assume office. In late October, in the middle of a snowstorm, McDougall and Howe met as they were heading in opposite directions across the prairie, but Howe did not stop to brief the prospective lieutenant-governor. In Red River the newly formed National Committee of the Métis resolved that McDougall would not be allowed to enter the country, and sent him a message, which he received as he was approaching Pembina, on the American border: 'The National Committee of the Métis orders William McDougall not to enter the Territory of the North West without special permission of the above-mentioned committee.'[21] This warning—dated 21 October 1869 and signed 'Louis Riel, Secretary'—was Riel's second act of resistance to Canada. When the Council of Assiniboia summoned Riel to explain his actions, he replied that the Métis were 'perfectly satisfied with the present Government and wanted no other'; that they 'objected to any Government coming from Canada without their being consulted in the matter'; and that they 'would never admit any Governor no matter by whom he might be appointed, if not by the Hudson's Bay Company, unless Delegates were previously sent, with whom they might negotiate as to the terms and conditions under which they would acknowledge him'. Finally, Riel insisted that his compatriots were 'simply acting in defence of their own liberty', and 'did not anticipate any opposition from their English-speaking fellow countrymen, and only wished to join and aid in securing their common rights.'[22]

In early November Riel and a large party of his men walked into Upper Fort Garry, the Hudson's Bay Company fort, and took possession of it. The Métis then invited the anglophone mixed bloods to meet with them to 'consider the present political state of this Country and to adopt such measures as may be deemed best for the future welfare of the same.'[23] Delegates from the two groups would meet several times in November and debate subsequent actions. The English-speakers wanted to admit McDougall— who by now was marking time in a shabby residence at Pembina—and then negotiate with him, but Riel and his people insisted that negotiations must come first. On 27 November the Canadian government informed Britain that it would delay the transfer of the territory until the unrest died down. Prime Minister Macdonald understood perfectly well the consequences of any precipitate action, and on the same day wrote to McDougall warning him against any attempt to assume his position as lieutenant-governor, since that would automatically put an end to the authority of the Hudson's Bay Company:

> There would then be, if you were not admitted into the country, no legal government existing, and anarchy must follow. In such a case, no matter how the anarchy is produced, it is quite open by the law of nations for the inhabitants to form a government ex necessitate for the protection of life and property, and such a government has certain sovereign rights by the *ius gentium*, which might be very convenient for the United States, but exceedingly inconvenient to you.[24]

Unfortunately, communications with the Northwest still took a minimum of two weeks in winter, and this time lag would prove fatal.

Although he had been instructed to wait for an official warrant, on 1 December 1869 the impatient McDougall issued a proclamation extending the Queen's writ to Red River. When the Métis and mixed-blood delegates received this document, they decided to prepare a declaration of 'rights' as a preliminary to negotiations with Canada. The declaration was drafted by Riel, probably with the assistance of some Americans then in Winnipeg looking to encourage the Métis to negotiate with Washington. The list of rights began with the right of the people to elect their own legislature, with the power to pass all local laws, with a two-thirds majority overriding an executive veto. No act made by the Dominion Parliament would be binding on the territory without the consent of its legislature. All local officials were to be elected by the people. The document also called for a free homestead and pre-emption land law, providing cheap land for new settlers (a very American provision) and full bilingualism in both the legislatures and the courts, with 'all Public Documents and Acts of the Legislature' to be published in both French and English (very Canadian). Finally, the document demanded full and fair representation in the Canadian Parliament, and the continuation of 'all privileges, customs and usages existing at the time of the transfer'. The delegates of the two mixed-blood groups agreed that these were 'fair'. Where they disagreed was on the question of whether they could negotiate with Canada on the basis of this declaration. The anglophones were prepared to deal, but Riel and the Métis insisted that Canada had to come to the bargaining table with these rights embodied in an Act of Parliament as a preliminary to negotiation. When the mixed bloods refused to accept this position, Riel told them to 'Go, return peacefully to your farms. Rest in the arms of your wives. Give that example to your children. But watch us act. We are going to work and obtain the guarantee of our rights and of yours. You will come to share them in the end.'[25]

THE DECLARATION OF A PROVISIONAL GOVERNMENT

On 7 December Riel and his men surrounded the store owned by the leader of the 'Canadian party', Dr John Christian Schultz, where a number of Canadians had barricaded themselves. They took Schultz and 48 others to Fort Garry as prisoners, and the next day Riel issued a 'Declaration of the People', announcing the creation of a provisional government to replace the Council of Assiniboia. He, as president, offered to negotiate with Canada on the terms for Red River's entry into Confederation. A Métis flag—a fleur de lys and a shamrock on a white background—was raised over Upper Fort Garry on 10 December. Riel had done exactly as Macdonald had predicted. By now the Canadian press generally appreciated the extent of blundering involved, but the government could not bring itself to admit that it had been wrong in its approach to the transfer from beginning to end. Instead of sending emissaries fully empowered to negotiate with Riel, Canada sent a series of envoys with no authority to make any promises. On 27 December Donald A. Smith—the head of the Hudson's Bay Company in Canada, who had been appointed by Macdonald to explain to the people of Red River how Canada intended to govern the country and to report on the disturbances—arrived at the settlement and suggested a mass meeting of the inhabitants. Two such meetings were held, on 19 and 20 January 1870 —outdoors, in the bitter cold. Smith won over some of the crowd with his assurances that Canada would not interfere with the property, language, or religion of the people of Red River, but was forced by Riel to admit that he had no power to negotiate. Smith therefore agreed to take back to Canada a statement of what Red River regarded as essential to its acceptance of Canadian authority. Riel then proposed a convention of 40 representatives, equally divided

■ Louis Riel, a carte-de-visite studio portrait taken in Ottawa following his election as member of Parliament for Provencher, Manitoba, in 1873. LAC, 002048.

between the two language groups. At these meetings a new 'List of Rights' was debated, and Riel's provisional government was endorsed by the convention. In early February the remaining Canadian prisoners at Upper Fort Garry were released (some had already escaped), and three delegates were appointed to go to Ottawa to negotiate provincial status for Red River within Confederation.

Meanwhile, on 12 February 1870, a group of Canadian settlers, led by one of the surveyors, Major C.A. Boulton, and including several of the escaped prisoners, left Portage la Prairie to join a party led by Dr Schultz (another escapee) at Kildonan, a few kilometres from Fort Garry. The

■ Louis Riel at the centre of his provisional government, sometime in early 1870. Top row, left to right: Bonnet Tromage, Pierre de Lorme, Thomas Bunn, Xavier Page, Baptiste Beauchemin, Baptiste Tournond, and Thomas Spence. Middle: Pierre Poitras, John Bruce, Riel, John O'Donoghue, and François Dauphenais. Front: Robert O'Lone and Paul Proulx. LAC, PA-12854.

plan was to liberate the remaining prisoners, but Riel released them first, so the armed parties disbanded. However, on 17 February a small force of Riel's Métis arrested and imprisoned a number of the Canadians who were on their way back to Portage, including one named Thomas Scott.

Until now, Riel's strategy and tactics had been little short of brilliant. He had managed to keep the two mixed-blood groups, French- and English-speaking, together under the aegis of the provisional government, which was arguably necessary to maintain order in the settlement. Despite some talk about negotiating with the Americans—probably mainly for effect—Riel and his people clearly wanted Red River to be

admitted to Confederation, and had worked out their terms. In Ottawa, the Canadian cabinet agreed on 11 February to accept delegates from Red River and negotiate with them. But it was also agreed that if negotiations broke down, a military force would be necessary, and steps were taken with the British government to organize such a force, to consist of British regulars and Canadian volunteers.

THE EXECUTION OF THOMAS SCOTT

At this point Louis Riel made a mistake. When the prisoner named Thomas Scott became unruly, Riel allowed a Métis tribunal to conduct a

■ 'The Execution of Scott', 1870, from *Canadiana Military Events*, III, 429. This version of the event, in which Scott is casually dispatched with a pistol shot to the head, reinforces the Anglo-Canadian idea that his death was less a matter of formal execution than of cold-blooded murder. LAC, C-118610.

trial and sentence him to death.[26] Riel accepted the sentence, commenting that 'We must make Canada respect us.'

At the 1873 trial of Ambroise Lépine, who was charged with Thomas Scott's murder, Joseph Nolin under oath provided an account of Scott's trial on 3 March 1870. It is the only properly authenticated account in existence.

Scott was tried on the evening of the third of March; at the council that tried him Lépine presided; the other members of the council were Janvier Richot, André Nault, Elzéar Goulet, Elzéar Legemonière, Baptiste Lépine, and Joseph Delorme; I was secretary of the council; Scott was not present at the beginning; some witnesses were examined to state what evil Scott had done; these witnesses were Riel, Ed Turner, and Joseph Delorme; don't recollect any other witnesses; do not recollect nature of the evidence; Scott was accused of having rebelled against the Provisional Government and having struck the captain of the guard; Riel made a speech, I think against Scott; after the evidence had been heard Scott was brought before the council; Riel asked me to read to Scott what had passed before the council; did not, as I had written nothing; Riel then explained the evidence to Scott, and he was condemned to death while he was there Riel explained the sentence to Scott, and asked him if he had any defence to offer? Scott said something but I forget what; Riel did not ask Scott whether he had any witnesses; there was no written accusation against Scott; the work of the Council was done in about three hours; the Council sat about 7 o'clock; took some notes of the evidence; wrote them out regularly, and gave them to the Adjutant General; Richot moved and Nault seconded that Scott deserved death; Lépine said he would have to be put to death—the majority want his death and he shall be put to death; that closed the business of the council; Riel explained to Scott his sentence; and asked him if he had any request to make or wanted to see a minister? I do not remember what answer Scott made; Riel said if the minister was at the Stone Fort he would send for him; Riel said he would send Scott up to his room, that his shackles would be taken off, and that he would have pen, ink, and paper to write what he wished to; Riel told Scott that he would be shot next day at 10 o'clock; I do not know what Scott said; he was then taken to his room; when the vote was taken Baptiste Lépine objected to taking the life of Scott; he said they had succeeded so far without shedding blood and he thought it better not to do so now; Ed Turner took Scott to his room; saw Lépine next morning about 8 o'clock; Lépine told me to write a verbal report of the proceedings of the Council; Riel came to see the report and said it was not formal; Riel then dictated the report; it was made from notes of the evidence; don't remember what Riel changed; gave it to Lépine when written. . . .[27]

On 4 March 1870, Scott was taken outside the gates of Fort Garry. His eyes were bandaged and he was shot by a firing squad. Riel apparently did not think much about this event, although it was the first fatality that had occurred in the course of Red River's resistance. But the execution of Scott was to have enormous repercussions in Ontario, which had apparently been searching desperately for an excuse to condemn Red River. When word of Scott's death reached Ontario, a secret society named 'Canada First' undertook to orchestrate a public response. Inspired by the memory of D'Arcy McGee, who had been assassinated on the steps of the House of Commons on 7 April 1868, the members of Canada First believed in the need to inculcate a national spirit. They also believed in Canadian westward expansion and in the innate superiority of white Anglo-Saxon Protestants. Led by George Denison, the Canada Firsters—who included Charles Mair and John Schultz—organized their public campaign around the fact that Thomas Scott had been a member of the Orange Order. Soon all Ontario was up in arms about the murder of an innocent young Orangeman whose only offence was held to be his loyalty to Canada.

THE MANITOBA ACT AND THE WOLSELEY EXPEDITION

By the time the three-man delegation from Red River arrived in Ontario, the entire province was inflamed against Riel and the provisional government. Canada refused to meet officially with the delegates, led by Abbé Noel Ritchot, and negotiations were conducted in private. However, Ritchot was able to obtain the government's agreement to implement most of the 'List of Rights', and the Manitoba Act was quickly passed in May 1870—even if the Canadian government thought it had been forced to accede at the point of a gun. The Act granted provincial status to Manitoba (the name favoured by Riel), a province of only 1,000 square miles (2,590 square kilometres), with 1,400,000 acres (566,560 hectares) set aside for the Métis and bilingual services guaranteed. The Scott execution provided the Canadian government with an excuse to deny Riel and his lieutenants an official amnesty for all acts committed during the 'uprising'; although the Red River delegates who negotiated with Canada always insisted that such an amnesty had been promised as part of the unofficial settlement, there was nothing in writing. Instead of becoming premier of the province he had created, Louis Riel would go into long-term

AMBROISE LÉPINE
(1840–1923)

❖

Ambroise Lépine was born in St Boniface, the son of a well-to-do French-Canadian farmer and a Saskatchewan Métis woman. Educated at St Boniface College, he was hardly the illiterate 'savage' he was later made out to be by Canadians in Manitoba. In 1859 he married Cécile Marion, with whom he would have 14 children. The Lépines farmed a river lot (number 272) not far from the Riel family, but Ambroise also participated in the buffalo hunt. He was described as being 'of magnificent physique, standing fully six foot three and built of splendid proportion, straight as an arrow, with hair of raven blackness, large aquiline nose and eyes of piercing brilliance'.

In 1869 Lépine became an important figure in the uprising against the Canadian annexation of Red River, not surprising in view of his family position and hunting prowess, as well as his imposing size. He returned to the settlement around the end of October, just in time to be ordered to the border to make sure the Ottawa-appointed governor, William McDougall, did not cross it to assert Canadian control over the territory. Nobody knew who was in charge of this party, he later remembered, 'and I was made leader'. Lépine very nearly did not get his assignment right. He initially allowed McDougall to cross the border on 1 November, and then returned the next day to escort him back into the United States. Lépine continued to be associated with Louis Riel, and was the leader of the group who surrounded the Schultz house and store in early December. On 10 December he helped Riel and W.B. O'Donoghue raise the flag of the

■ Ambroise-Dydime Lépine, photographed in 1884. Glenbow Museum, NA-2631-3.

provisional government over Upper Fort Garry, and on 8 January he was named adjutant general of the provisional government, with the responsibility for the administration of justice—the equivalent of the chief of police in the settlement. He later represented St Boniface in the Convention of Forty, which met to formulate the demands to be made of the Canadian government, and chaired the Military Council of the convention.

It was Lépine who led the Métis forces out of Upper Fort Garry to confront the men from Portage la Prairie returning from a military gathering at Kildonan in February 1870. The Métis were on horseback and the Portage group on foot. The latter surrendered. Their captain, Charles Arkoll Boulton, was initially condemned to death by Riel, but was reprieved. Later, Lépine presided at the hearing that sentenced Thomas Scott to death, casting the deciding vote in favour of execution over the objections of his brother, Baptiste. The next day, he refused to listen to pleas for Scott's life and stood by stoically as the Canadian was shot by a firing squad.

When the Canadians took over Manitoba in late August of 1870, Lépine went on the run with Riel, whom he helped to raise a Métis militia force against a possible Fenian invasion in 1871. Later that year he was paid by the Canadian government to leave Manitoba with Riel, but he soon returned, and in 1873 he was arrested at his home for the death of Scott. His trial, which was really intended to test the government's case against Riel, ended in a conviction for murder by a mixed jury. Lépine did not testify at the trial, but issued a statement that denied the competence of the court to try him, insisting that his actions had been as a member of a de facto government; both assertions were dismissed by the court. He was sentenced to be hanged, but the Canadian Governor General commuted the sentence to two years in prison and permanent loss of civil rights. Lépine declined an amnesty conditional on leaving Manitoba for five years, and decided to serve his sentence. Released in 1876, he spent the rest of his long life in poverty and obscurity. He was conspicuous by his absence from the rebellion of 1885. In 1909 he helped A.-H. Trémaudan in the writing of a history of the Métis nation.

exile.[28] Whether Ottawa would uphold the land guarantees it made to the Métis remained to be seen, but the prospects were not good, for after passing the Manitoba Act it still dispatched a military expedition to Red River.

In August 1870 Riel was waiting at Fort Garry to hand over the government of the new province to Canada, but the leader of the expedition, Colonel Garnet Wolseley, insisted on entering the settlement as the commander of a conquering army. Realizing that they would be treated as rebels and murderers, Riel and several of his associates went into hiding. 'Personally,' Wolseley wrote, 'I was glad that Riel did not come out and surrender, . . . for I could not then have hanged him as I might have done had I taken him

prisoner when in arms against his sovereign.'[29] Troops dragged some guns from the fort and fired a royal salute of 21 guns as the Union Jack was run up the flagpole. A small group of half a dozen spectators gave three cheers for the Queen. What followed was anticlimactic. In the end, the main function of Wolseley's volunteer troops was to protect the rebels from vengeful Canadians (among them some of the troops themselves). One of the volunteers brought with him a warrant for the organization of a new Orange Lodge; organized in September 1870, by February 1871 it claimed a membership of 110 'good men and true' opposed to Catholic 'bigotry' in 'this priest-ridden country'.[30] Also in September 1870 Adams Archibald was formally installed as lieutenant-governor of Manitoba. Whether this new entity, still occupied by the Canadian military, was a fully autonomous province was an open question.

THE NORTH-WEST TERRITORIES

Manitoba aside, the rest of the territory transferred to Canada by the Hudson's Bay Company—the North-West Territories—was initially administered under the legislation passed by the Canadian Parliament in 1869, before the Red River resistance. The lieutenant-governor of Manitoba also served as the lieutenant-governor of the Territories. The temporary legislation of 1869 was renewed without change in 1871. Not until 1872 was a territorial council appointed. Of its 11 members, only two resided in the Territories; the other nine lived in or near Winnipeg, where the council's initial meetings were held. Only in 1905 would the region achieve provincial status as Saskatchewan and Alberta.

BRITISH COLUMBIA

UNION WITH VANCOUVER ISLAND

The process by which British Columbia entered Confederation lacked some of the drama of the events in Red River–Manitoba, but it had its own complexities. The two colonies of British Columbia and Vancouver Island had been joined by the British government in 1866 in the hope of resolving some difficult economic and political problems.[31] As Governor Frederick Seymour had reported to the Colonial Office in 1865, 'separated it seems difficult for one Colony to flourish without inflicting some injury on the other.'[32] By the mid-1860s the gold rush along the Fraser River was over and the influx of miners and their money had dried up. Indeed, the movement was now in the other direction, making it difficult both to collect taxes on the mainland and to raise capital in Victoria, the population of which fell from as many as 10,000 to 3,000 by the mid-

1860s. The legislative assembly of Vancouver Island had battled for some time to gain control over finances, but without much success. As the economic recession deepened, the Vancouver Island Assembly found the possibility of legislative union attractive. A leading member of the Assembly, a Nova Scotia-born journalist calling himself Amor De Cosmos (William Alexander Smith), introduced motions in January 1865 for the union of the two colonies. The idea of union was quickly accepted in Westminster, but the Colonial Office chose to incorporate Vancouver Island into British Columbia and give the new colony, under Governor Seymour, a Legislative Council with a mix of elected and appointed members rather than an elected assembly. The debts of the two colonies at union were quite unequal; British Columbia owed more than $1,000,000, Vancouver Island less than $300,000. Seymour was known as a profligate spender, and many in Victoria feared for the future. On the day the union was proclaimed, the former governor, Sir James Douglas, wrote in his daughter's diary: 'The Ships of war fired a salute on the occasion—A funeral procession, with minute guns would have been more appropriate to the sad melancholy event.'[33]

DEBATING CONFEDERATION

The first contentious topic for the new Legislative Council was the location of the new capital. When Dr John Helmcken, the former speaker of the Vancouver Island Assembly, managed to steer through a motion choosing Victoria, Governor Seymour lost his temper at the vote, dismissing several members and disparaging Victoria as the home of 'a half alien, restless population, ill at ease with itself'.[34] Also at this first sitting of the Council, Amor De Cosmos—who found the union no improvement—introduced a resolution calling for the eventual admission of British Columbia into the Canadian Confederation. A full debate of the issue followed. Although most of the councillors cautiously refused to take any

■ Victoria, looking east along Fort Street from Langley Street, c.1862. Royal BC Museum, BC Archives, A-02999.

action, the proposal received additional impetus when, on 29 March 1867—coincidentally, the same day the British North America Act was passed by the British Parliament—the American government arranged to purchase Alaska from the Russians, touching off howls in the American press for the annexation of British Columbia.

Officially the colony was notified in November 1867 that no action could be taken on union with Canada until the HBC territory had been incorporated into the Dominion, an event that would take longer than anticipated. Early the next year, a committee appointed at a public meeting in Victoria composed a memorial to the government of Canada pointing out that the colony had no mechanism for determining the wishes of the people through the legislature, and calling on Canada to take immediate steps itself to bring British Columbia into the union.[35] The Canadian government replied through S.L. Tilley, Minister of Customs, who on 25 March 1868 wrote that 'The Canadian Government desires union with British Columbia, and have opened

communications with the Imperial Government on the subject of the resolutions, and suggests immediate action by your Legislature and the passage of an address to her Majesty requesting union with Canada.'[36] Although the Victoria memorial claimed that the only opposition to union with Canada came from a handful of American annexationists, many of the colony's officials—who had only just moved to Victoria from New Westminster and feared losing their appointments—were also unhappy about the idea. 'I suppose there is little doubt we shall have Confederation sooner or later,' wrote one such official, 'but it appears to me that our only chance is to work together, & battle against it until a satisfactory provision is made for us.'[37] On Dominion Day 1868, a large open-air meeting at Barkerville called for 'some organized and systematic mode of obtaining immediate admission into the Dominion of Canada', as well as the elimination of 'the present irresponsible autocracy'.[38]

At the meeting in December 1868, Dr Helmcken made an effort to reform the Legisla-

■ 'The Hurdies, German Dancing Girls at Barkerville', 1865, photo by Charles Gentile. Brought to Canada by a contractor who then had to be paid back for their passage, these 'hurdy-gurdy girls' were not prostitutes, but were hired out to dance with lonely men and persuade them to buy drinks. Royal BC Museum, BC Archives G-00817.

tive Council by increasing its elective members and by regulating official salaries. The officials sitting on the Council resisted, and also supported a resolution postponing discussion of union with Canada. Back in Ottawa, Prime Minister Macdonald was annoyed by this obstructionism; suspecting a Yankee conspiracy, he talked of replacing Governor Seymour. Conveniently, however, Seymour died in June 1869. He was replaced by Anthony Musgrave, the former Governor of Newfoundland. For years Musgrave

had tried unsuccessfully to steer Newfoundland towards union with Canada, and he was discreetly ordered by the Colonial Office to bring his new colony into Confederation: in particular, Lord Granville told him to use 'no expressions which would indicate intention . . . to overrule the wishes of the community', but at the same time to recognize the importance attached 'to the early adhesion of British Columbia to the North American confederation' by the British government, which therefore 'would wish your language and polity to be such as are likely to conduce to that end'.[39] Musgrave arrived in British Columbia in August 1869, having travelled mainly by rail from Halifax to New York to San Francisco and then by steamer to Victoria. His journey was a suitable demonstration of the utility of a transcontinental railroad.

The colony that Musgrave was to govern consisted of some 10,500 settlers (6,000 white males, 2,600 white females, and 1,900 Chinese, mostly men) and roughly 50,000 Aboriginal people. Most of the European and Asian population clustered around Victoria, which was the only substantial town: New Westminster had fallen from over a thousand to only about 600 people after the government had moved to the island, and a thin line of settlement along the Fraser River up into the Cariboo was becoming thinner. The colony was expected to support itself without financial aid from Great Britain—it got only about £1,200 in naval charges and other funds from the British in 1868—and it had cut its budget substantially. Its economy was in transition: the official yield of gold was down from over $4 million in 1863 to $2.5 million in 1868, but the value of forest product exports rose from $3,416 in 1861 to $252,154 in 1869, and the value of coal exports went up to $119,820 in 1869.[40] Farming and fishing had also expanded. Still, the economy continued to depend heavily on the extraction of raw materials.

Musgrave's Legislative Council had 22 members, 13 chosen by the Governor (five government officials and eight magistrates) and nine elected by the inhabitants. Although this was hardly government by the people, a variety of approaches—petitions, public meetings, newspaper debates, and private lobbying—served to make public opinion known to the government. Musgrave thought this arrangement well suited to the colony, but the elected representatives wanted responsible government and favoured union with Canada in the hope that, in Musgrave's words, 'it may be possible to make fuller representative institutions . . . part of the new arrangements'.[41] A convention of 26 delegates meeting at Yale in September 1868 had urged immediate union with Canada and the establishment of representative and responsible government. In early 1870 the Legislative Council passed a motion calling for union with Canada, providing satisfactory financial terms could be arranged, and began another round of debates on the subject in March.

Like the debates held by other late entrants into Confederation, these were quite different from the ones that had preceded the drafting of the British North America Act. British Columbia could not hope to influence the shape of the union; all it could determine was the terms on which it would join. The debate was in some ways odd. The leading spokesman for union was the Attorney General, Henry Crease, who had earlier opposed it, while the opposition to the plan was led by former supporters. The reasons for this inversion were connected with internal politics. In fact, those who now argued against union did so because they wanted the questions of popular elections and responsible government settled beforehand, whereas those who now argued in favour of union were members of the government party who were satisfied with the local status quo. One speaker successfully moved for postponement, saying:

> We are told that we are not fit for Representative Institutions or Responsible Government. Then we shall go into the Dominion as a Crown Colony—bound hand and foot. The few Members that will represent us at Ottawa, will not have the power to do anything for us. I do not trust the Politicians of Ottawa. . . . I would rather remain as we are, with some Change and modification in our Government.[42]

A similar point was made by Dr Helmcken: 'We are a Colony of England; and I don't know that many people object to being a Colony of England; but I say that very many would object to becoming a Colony of Canada.'[43]

THE REMINISCENCES OF
DR JOHN SEBASTIAN HELMCKEN

In 1892 Dr John Sebastian Helmcken (1824–1920) of Victoria wrote a lengthy memoir of his experiences. The manuscript ended up in the Provincial Archives of British Columbia in Victoria, and was edited for publication by Dorothy Blakey Smith, appearing in print in 1975. Here Helmcken discusses the election of 1868, fought over the issue of Confederation.

. . . [A] general election was ordered; Confederation being the burning question, everyone rampant on one side or the other; of course the American element being against the Union. At this time no distinct terms had been proposed, but if I recollect rightly De Cosmos and the colored man Gibbs and [John Norris] had been to the 'Yale Convention'; a Convention for the purpose of an organization for Confederation purposes. The Convention was ridiculed and lambasted by opponents—the colored man [Gibbs] having a good share. By the bye I had been a means of getting the coloured man elected to the House of Assembly and really he was in some measure a superior man and very gentlemanly withal. I think he claimed being a West Indian.

I came out against Confederation distinctly, chiefly because I thought it premature—partly from prejudice—and because no suitable terms could be proposed. The tariff was a sticking point: although we had at this time a tariff but could change it to suit ourselves. Our income too would be diminished and there at this time appeared no means of replenishing it by the [British] North America Act. Our population was too small numerically. Moreover it would only be a confederacy on paper for no means of communication with the Eastern Provinces existed, without which no advantage could possibly ensue. Canada was looked down upon as a poor mean slow people, who had been very commonly designated North American chinamen. This character they had achieved from their necessarily thrifty condition for long years, and indeed they compared unfavourably with the

Americans and with our American element, for at this time and previously very many liberal-handed and better class of Americans resided here, many in business—some on account of the Civil War necessitating their remaining even after the frightful internecine killing had ceased. Our trade was either with the US or England—with Canada we had nothing to do. Of course my being an Anti-confederationist, led to my being dubbed an Annexationist, but really I had no idea of annexation, but merely wished the Colony to be let alone under HM Govt and to fight her way unhampered. I had nothing whatever to do with annexation petitions, and so not know who signed them—tho I have heard that some who now hold or have held official positions have done so. This petition doubtless went to the President of the US but no one has ever been able to see a copy of it since, altho it is said to exist in Victoria somewhere. There is no doubt the Americans had a contempt for Canada and this feeling extended to the colonists.

I suppose the election was one of the fiercest ever fought in Victoria, everyone seemed crazy, I among the number—these were the days of great excitements. I had the British and American elements and Jewish element on my side and after a time the election came on. Numberless ladies wore my colours, red, white and blue, in shape according to their taste, the men likewise. Ladies were at the windows waving their handkerchiefs, every hack in the place was frightfully busy. The polling went actively on, but there were no rows, or if there were, they were insignificant. Various committees had districts under control; they had to get the voters up and were responsible therefore. The cry went round that both sides had a number of voters locked up and were feeding them with whisky, to get them into proper trim; altho this accusation was not strictly true, still voters came to the polling place, where the Courts of Justice now stand, in files. Notwithstanding all this there were no rows outside the polling places, the matter was too serious for this. At length 4 o'clock struck—the polls closed; everyone tired—thirsty, hoarse and expectant. The Anti-confederates had won handsomely. . . .

SOURCE: Dorothy Blakey Smith, ed., *The Reminiscences of Doctor John Sebastian Helmcken* (Vancouver: University of British Columbia Press, 1975), 246-8.

■ Described by Dr Helmcken as 'a superior man and very gentlemanly withal', Mifflin Gibbs was born to free parents in Philadelphia in 1823 and arrived in Victoria from California in 1858. A successful businessman, by 1867 he was chairman of the finance committee of the Victoria City Council. Royal BC Museum, BC Archives B-01601.

On 14 March the debates turned to the admission terms proposed by Musgrave and the Executive Council. Everyone agreed that Canada should be liable for the debts of the colony and grant it a large subsidy. The first real question was over land communication with the East. While the government wanted a railway begun within three years of union, some members wanted a section between Yale and New Westminster to be constructed within three years, and an amendment to this effect was carried. Governor Musgrave subsequently reported to Britain that 'If a Railway could be promised, scarcely any other question would be allowed to be a difficulty',[44] but he may have overstated the case. In fact, the greatest debate concerned a seemingly innocuous Clause 15, according to which 'The Constitution of the Executive authority and of the Legislature of British Columbia shall, subject to "The British North America Act, 1867", continue as existing at the time of Union, until altered under the authority of the said Act.' A motion calling for the introduction of representative institutions and responsible government irrespective of Confederation failed, as did a proposed amendment calling for a constitution based on principles of responsible government to be introduced coincident with entry into Canada. Clause 15 was eventually passed as read. Interestingly, the question of administrative responsibility for the colony's Aboriginal population never arose in the debates.

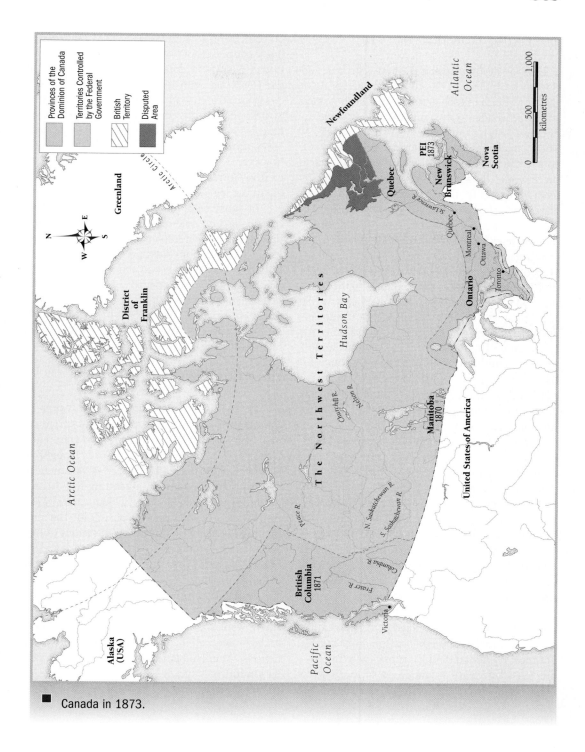

Legend:
- Provinces of the Dominion of Canada
- Territories Controlled by the Federal Government
- British Territory
- Disputed Area

Atlantic Ocean

Newfoundland

PEI 1873

Nova Scotia

New Brunswick

Quebec

St. Lawrence R.

Quebec

Montreal

Ottawa

Toronto

Ontario

Greenland

Arctic Circle

District of Franklin

Hudson Bay

The Northwest Territories

Churchill R.

Nelson R.

Manitoba 1870

United States of America

Arctic Ocean

Peace R.

N. Saskatchewan R.

S. Saskatchewan R.

Columbia R.

British Columbia 1871

Fraser R.

Victoria

Alaska (USA)

Pacific Ocean

1,000

500

kilometres

0

Canada in 1873.

ENTERING CONFEDERATION

The negotiations between British Columbia and Canada took place in Ottawa in the late spring of 1870.[45] The Manitoba Act had just been passed and the Canadian government's military expedition was setting out for the Red River territory. The Canadians were generous to a fault. Of course the debt could be wiped out. Of course there would be subsidies and grants, as well as federal support for the naval station at Esquimalt. Naturally British Columbia would get responsible government. Clause 15, as amended by the joint delegations, stipulated that although the existing constitution would continue until altered, it was understood 'that the Government of the Dominion will readily consent to the introduction of Responsible Government when desired by the inhabitants of British Columbia, and it being likewise understood that it is the intention of the Government of British Columbia under the authority of the Secretary of State for the Colonies, to amend the existing constitution of the Legislature by providing that a majority of its members should be elective.'[46] And of course the province would have a rail link with Canada—to be begun within two years and completed within 15. Governor Musgrave was astounded at the generosity of the terms. 'And then the Railway, Credat Judaeus! is guaranteed without a reservation! Sir George Cartier says they will do that, or "burst".'[47] The promise was certainly audacious (and in the end BC had to promise that it would not insist on the terms, especially regarding the railway, to the letter), but it was hardly surprising. For a variety of reasons, some political and some economic, Canada needed a transcontinental railroad to match the lines being rapidly constructed across the United States. As predicted, the railway guarantee wiped out most of the remaining opposition to union— but not all: 'We are a conquered country,' wrote

one official on 19 July 1871, '& the Canucks take possession tomorrow.'[48] The following day British Columbia entered Confederation as the sixth province with Joseph Trutch as lieutenant-governor. Trutch had opposed the introduction of responsible government and continued to drag his heels on constitutional change, actually appointing the first premier himself. Finally, however, on 23 December 1872 Amor de Cosmos formed the first ministry fully responsible to the legislature.[49]

In most respects the new province would remain largely isolated from Canada until after the railway was completed in 1885. Nevertheless, Confederation did have several effects for British Columbia. One was the development of a new land policy that opened the province up for massive pre-emption rights for those who had 'squatted' on land, as well as free land grants. Another was the transfer to the Dominion of responsibility for 'Indian policy'.

CONCLUSION

By 1873 Canada was—at least on paper—a transcontinental nation. A number of provinces had been added to the union, however reluctantly, and at least one had already sought to leave and been pacified. Had the government in Ottawa not succeeded in extending the original union of the Canadas, Nova Scotia, and New Brunswick as expeditiously as it did, the new nation's future might have been in serious doubt. Today most Canadians are happy to celebrate the events of 1867, but the next few years were equally important.

At the same time, the Canadian government had demonstrated a marked clumsiness in the way it went about its westward expansion and in its treatment of the inhabitants of the western regions. This clumsiness was to haunt the new nation for many years to come.

SHORT BIBLIOGRAPHY

Beck, J. Murray. *Joseph Howe*, vol. 2, *The Briton Becomes Canadian, 1848–1873*. Montreal and Kingston, 1983. The standard biography of Joseph Howe, judicious and well-balanced.

Bescoby, Isabel. 'A Colonial Administration: An Analysis of Administration in British Columbia, 1869–71', *Canadian Public Administration* 10 (1967): 49–104. The fullest and most detailed account available of the public history of British Columbia in the years 1869–71.

Bolger, Francis. *Prince Edward Island and Confederation, 1863–1873*. Charlottetown, 1964. The standard account of the Island and Canada.

Bumsted, J.M. *The Red River Rebellion*. Winnipeg, 1995. A study of the troubles in Red River that does not always put Louis Riel at centre stage.

Debates on the Subject of Confederation with Canada. Victoria, n.d. Transcripts of the BC legislative debates on union.

Hiller, James. 'Confederation Defeated: The Newfoundland Election of 1869', in James Hiller and Peter Neary, eds, *Newfoundland in the Nineteenth and Twentieth Centuries: Essays in Interpretation*. Toronto, 1980. The only detailed analysis of the 1869 Newfoundland election in which Confederation was defeated.

Morton, W.L., ed. *Alexander Begg's Red River Journal and Other Papers Relative to the Red River Resistance of 1869–70*. Toronto, 1956. A contemporary view of the Red River business.

———, ed. *Manitoba: The Birth of a Nation*. Winnipeg, 1965. A collection of contemporary documents, including Father Ritchot's journal of the actual negotiations with Canada.

Shelton, W. George, ed. *British Columbia and Confederation*. Victoria, 1967. A useful collection of essays on various topics connected with Confederation and the Pacific province.

Stanley, George F.G. *Louis Riel*. Toronto, 1963. The standard biography, well-researched and balanced in its interpretation.

STUDY QUESTIONS

1. In the end, did the antis in Nova Scotia have any choice but to accept Confederation?
2. Why did PEI change its mind about Confederation in 1873?
3. Why were Newfoundland merchants not enthusiastic about Confederation?
4. Why did the Newfoundland Irish oppose union?
5. What reasons lay behind the uprising in Red River in 1869?
6. What did Riel and the provisional government in Red River want from Canada?
7. What issues were involved in British Columbia's entry into Confederation?

CHAPTER TWENTY-SIX

■ Envisioning the New Nation, 1867–1885

■ In addition to completing the takeover of the northwestern part of the continent, the governments of Sir John A. Macdonald and Alexander Mackenzie gradually developed some national policies with which to govern the new Dominion. Before 1867, a good deal of energy had been devoted to arguments in favour of the union, but few attempts had been made to spell out the specifics of a vision for the new nation. Indeed, it turned out that there were several visions floating around, none of them acceptable to everyone. At the same time, most of the new nation's concrete policies were naturally carried over from the earlier Canadian system, with occasional adjustments to accommodate the other provinces. Among the most important developments were the emergence of a system of national political parties and the smooth transition, in 1873, from Macdonald's bipartisan coalition government to the Liberals under Mackenzie within the constitutional traditions of responsible government. Cultural developments in this period were significant as well.

THE QUEST FOR NATIONAL POLICIES

Sometimes, of course, the interests of the new nation's parts had to be sacrificed to larger concerns, one of which was Anglo-American entente. After the reciprocity agreement had been abrogated in 1866, both Nova Scotia and the new Canadian government after 1867 tried to keep American fishermen outside a three-mile offshore limit. However, since there were other tensions with the US, the imperial government was unhappy about this additional strain on relations with the US. One problem concerned a raiding vessel built by Britain for the southern states during the Civil War: in return for the losses the *Alabama* had inflicted on the North, the Americans were only half-facetiously demanding the cession of British American territory. Another concerned the Fenian raids launched from American soil into Canada in 1866 and 1870. Accordingly, in 1871 the British government made John A. Macdonald a member of an international joint commission set up in 1870 to deal with the fisheries question and advised the Canadians to give up their claim to a three-mile limit—though only 'in return for an adequate consideration'. Sir Charles Tupper, representing Nova Scotian interests, argued that fishing rights should not be sold only for a 'money consideration', but the British were eager to settle their differences with the Americans (or at least have them brought to international arbitration), and were quite willing to sacrifice Canadian (really

TIMELINE

1868
Canadian National Series of readers introduced into Ontario schools.

1870
Dominion Notes Act passed.

1871
Canada signs the Treaty of Washington. Bank Act passed.

1872
Ontario Society of Artists formed. Passage of Dominion Lands Act.

1873
Pacific Scandal. Macdonald government resigns. Alexander Mackenzie leads new Liberal government. North West Mounted Police established.

1875
Supreme Court of Canada established.

1876
Treaty Six signed at Fort Carlton. Indian Act of 1876 passed by Canadian Parliament.

1878
Macdonald's Conservatives returned to power.

1880
Royal Canadian Academy of Arts and National Gallery of Canada established.

1881
John Bourinot publishes *The Intellectual Development of the Canadian People*. First western real estate boom, in Winnipeg.

1882
Royal Society of Canada established. *Picturesque Canada* published.

1883
Qu'Appelle Settlers' Rights Association calls for reform.

1884
Mercier tables resolutions on federal encroachments on provincial power. First Nations hold Thirst Dance in Saskatchewan on Poundmaker's reserve. Louis Riel invited back to Canada. Riel sends long petition to Ottawa.

1885
Battle of Duck Lake (March). Battle of Batoche (May). Treason trial of Louis Riel (July). Eight Aboriginal warriors executed for their part in the uprising (November). Public gathering in Montreal protests Riel execution. Last spike in CPR line driven at Craigellachie, BC, on 7 November. Riel executed nine days later.

Maritime) interests to that end. The British view prevailed, and Macdonald signed the Treaty of Washington, seeing his signature as recognition of Canadian diplomatic autonomy and the treaty itself as marking the Americans' recognition of Canada as a separate entity.

On the domestic front, the new country's banking system grew rapidly after Confederation, from 123 chartered bank branches in 1868 to 279 in 1879 and 426 by 1890, representing some three dozen banks. The two most important pieces of banking legislation were the Dominion Notes Act of 1870 and the Bank Act of 1871. The former allowed the government to issue circulating notes of small denominations only partly backed by gold and silver, while the latter established central control over the banking system, specifying the capital requirements for banks, prohibiting new foreign-owned banks, and providing general regulations, including standards for the issuing of bank notes. High capital requirements together with federal policy restricted the number of bank charters granted and encouraged the acquisition of new branches rather than the creation of new banks. Canada was integrated into the international gold standard, but the government would share responsibility for the issuing of currency (and control of the creation of money) with the banks until well into the twentieth century. Canada did not create a central bank until 1934.

Confederation suggested an economic future that was generally encouraging to foreign investment. From its inception, Canada was able to import large amounts of capital to help create its economic infrastructure, including $166 million (7 per cent of the gross national product) in the years 1871–5.[1] Between 1865 and 1869, Canada raised $16.5 million in Great Britain, a figure that rose to $94.6 million in 1870–4, $74.7 million in 1875–9, and $69.8 million in 1880–4.[2]

One of the principal economic arguments for Confederation had been the opportunity for further railway expansion, and railroads were a prime target of foreign investors. Construction of the Intercolonial Railway through New Brunswick began in 1867, but the Macdonald government was slow to move on the greatest of all, the transcontinental line, mainly because of the enormous expense involved in building it so much in advance of population needs. The problem was that the railway was essential to improve communications with the West, and to some extent the railway promise made to British Columbia was intended to cast the die. Following the usual scuffling, Parliament awarded the charter in 1873 to Sir Hugh Allan's Canadian Pacific Railway Company. Then the Pacific Scandal broke. Allan had provided the government with money—more than $350,000—for its 1872 election campaign, and Macdonald was unable to avoid the charge of corruption.

In November 1873 his government resigned and was replaced by a Liberal government headed by another Scot, a former stonemason turned building contractor named Alexander Mackenzie. Canada's first government had been bipartisan, and the British North America Act had not formalized either responsible government or political parties within the Constitution. Earlier parties were provincial rather than national. In the early 1870s Mackenzie therefore had to construct a federal opposition party from the bottom up, gathering in those who dropped gradually away from the governing party of Sir John A. Macdonald. Once in office, Mackenzie took a more gradual approach to building the transcontinental line. In addition to using public funds, he was prepared to encourage private interests to hook up with American western lines, and trains began running from Minnesota to Winnipeg late in 1878. By that time Mackenzie's dour earnestness had worn thin with the voters, and the probity of his government was not enough to save it in the 1878 election. Nevertheless, he had made a genuine contribution to national politics by insisting that his Liberals were a national alternative to Macdonald's Conservatives, and proving it by governing for five years without having the country fall apart. Moreover, the Mackenzie administration had finished much of the agenda begun in 1867. Federal administration of justice was functioning. The Maritimes had become part of the nation. The Mounted Police were introducing Canadian sovereignty into the western interior. A Supreme

Court was in place, although perhaps not the Court envisioned by Sir John A. Macdonald.

ESTABLISHING A SUPREME COURT

The Macdonald government introduced a bill for a higher Dominion Court over the winter of 1868–9, apparently as a trial balloon. It was based on the American Supreme Court, provided for extensive original jurisdiction not involving appeals as well as a mechanism for appeal, and was intended as another centralizing institution for the new confederacy. However, as Oliver Mowat, the vice-chancellor of Ontario, pointed out to Macdonald later in 1868, 'You have the power of disallowing provincial statutes; you appoint the Provincial Governors, and you appoint also the Provincial Judges. The reasons therefore for which it was necessary in certain cases to have original jurisdiction to the Supreme Court in the United States are entirely inappropriate to our nation.'[3] Mowat doubted whether section 101 of the British North America Act authorized such a court, or whether it was appropriate that such a court could rule on provincial law 'which is not the *law of Canada*'. Other critics insisted that only provincial legislation could establish authority over the provinces. Even with a restricted jurisdiction, judges in the various provinces, especially Quebec, were dubious. Macdonald dropped his scheme, but it was picked up again by the Mackenzie government in 1875.

Instead of imposing a court on the nation, the Liberals sought to find a legitimate place for it within Canada's political institutions. They focused on the current need to appeal Canadian constitutional disputes to the Privy Council in England, which was not in keeping with a truly independent nation. A bill creating the Supreme Court carried in 1875 by a vote of 112 to 40 despite increasing hostility from the Colonial Office. Clause 47 ended appeals to the Privy Council based on statute, but not those based on the royal prerogative, and the latter were by

far the most common and contentious; Edward Blake, in England to plead the case for the Court, acknowledged that clause 47 was not important. The Liberals had trouble staffing the new Court, both because of partisanship among the judges and because of their known hostility to the institution of such a court. In the end, the Liberals had pressed for a new national identity but had accepted something considerably less. Sir John A. Macdonald allegedly quipped that he 'would rather be a dead premier than a live chief justice.'[4]

MACDONALD'S NATIONAL POLICY

On his return to power, Macdonald recognized the nationalist temper of the times and worked very hard to re-establish a direct connection in the public mind between his party and the process of nation-building. A certain decisiveness and flamboyance were all part of the Tory image. Even before the election, Macdonald had found his platform, introducing into the House of Commons a resolution 'That this House is of the opinion that the welfare of Canada requires the adoption of a National Policy, which, by a judicious readjustment of the Tariff, will benefit and foster the agricultural, the mining, the manufacturing and other interests of this Dominion.'[5] Macdonald invented neither the policy nor the term used to describe it. Both went back well into the traditional economic policy of the Province of Canada, which had begun using a tariff as an instrument of both protection and revenue in the late 1840s. Nor did Macdonald ever articulate the version of the National Policy later described by some economic historians and textbook writers. He certainly recognized connections between tariffs, manufacturing, employment, and 'national prosperity'. He also wanted a transcontinental railway and the western settlement necessary to make it a reality. But all these were traditional elements of Canadian economic expansionism.[6]

What Macdonald achieved was masterful,

nonetheless. He succeeded in persuading a large number of Canadians that policies strongly driven by the economic interests of some individuals were in the best interests of the nation as a whole, and he identified the party he led with the successful construction of that nation. The fact that many in the opposition party had quite a different vision of the meaning of Confederation, based on provincial rights, certainly helped in this identification.

PROVINCIAL RIGHTS

The development of nationhood in the years after 1867 did not mean that all Canadians shared the same vision of the new state.[7] To put it simply: was Canada an indissoluble new entity or was it the product of a compact among the provinces that they could modify or even withdraw from? Since the time of the debates over Confederation in the 1860s, many had disagreed over the nature of the union. While most Canadians in 1867 saw Confederation as creating a strong central government, the legislatures of the provinces had not been eliminated, and they would quickly reassert more than a mere 'local power'. As early as 1865 the arch-critic of Confederation, Christopher Dunkin, had prophesied that 'In the times to come, when men shall begin to feel strongly on those questions that appeal to national preferences, prejudices and passions, all talk of your new nationality will sound but strangely. Some older nationality will then be found to hold the first place in most people's hearts.'[8] Even John A. Macdonald had admitted in Parliament in 1868 that 'a conflict may, ere long, arise between the Dominion and the States Rights people.'[9]

The movement to support a 'provincial rights' interpretation of the new nation was spearheaded by Ontario, but it could have begun anywhere—including in Nova Scotia among those who wanted out of the Confederation deal. In any event, as early as 1869 Ontario became distressed at 'the assumption by the Parliament of Canada of the power to disturb the financial relations established by the British North America Act (1867), as between Canada and the several provinces'.[10] Not surprisingly, it was the old Reform party of Canada West, in the persons of George Brown, Edward Blake, and Oliver Mowat, that took the lead in demanding—as Blake put it in 1871—'that each government [dominion and provincial] should be absolutely independent of the other in its management of its own affairs'.[11] The Rouges of Quebec soon made similar demands, calling for recognition not only of Quebec's 'provincial' rights but of 'national' rights for French Canadians. Before long, Liberals in most provinces—many of whom had either opposed Confederation or been lukewarm about it—had embraced provincial rights as a way of expressing their discontent with the prevailing vision of the union.

The provincial rights movement often seemed interchangeable with Ottawa-bashing for local political advantage, motivated by nothing more than the desire to pressure the federal government into fiscal concessions. In time the movement would obviously come to be dominated by Quebec and issues of cultural nationalism. This was not the case in the beginning, however. In 1884, for example, the Honourable Honoré Mercier tabled resolutions in the Quebec legislature stating merely that 'the frequent encroachments of the Federal Parliament upon the prerogatives of the Provinces are a permanent menace to the latter.'[12] Expressions of cultural nationalism in the ensuing debate went no further than one backbencher's assertion that 'Le Québec n'est pas une province comme les autres.'[13] As we shall see, the Riel affair of 1885 would push Quebec towards arguments of cultural distinctiveness, and when Mercier—by this time Premier of Quebec—invited the provinces to the Interprovincial Conference in 1887 to re-examine the federal compact, the five provinces in attendance could reach broad agreement on demands for better terms and constitutional change.

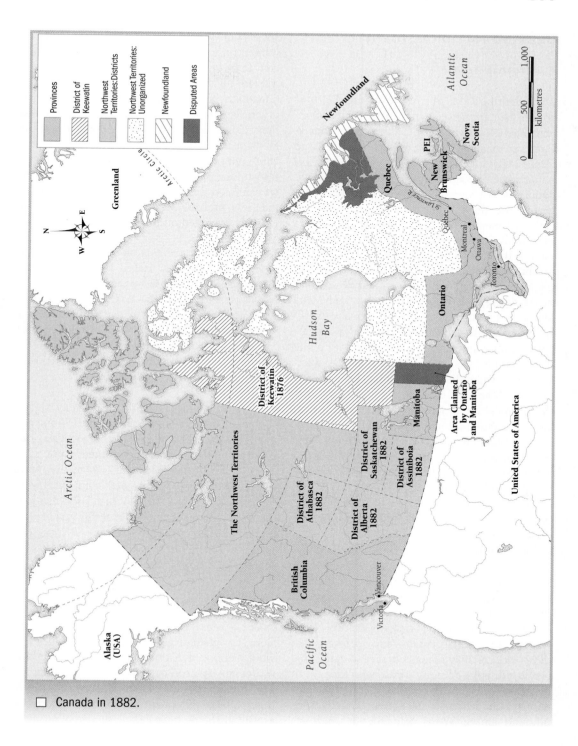

Canada in 1882.

SEEKING NATIONAL IDENTITY

CANADA FIRST

The identification of the emerging cultural nationalism, in the years immediately after 1867, with the movement that called itself 'Canada First' is in many ways unfortunate, for the Canada Firsters did not have a monopoly on national sentiment. Nor was their version of nationalism a very attractive one. One of the group's founders, Robert C. Haliburton, was an early exponent of the idea that Canadians were heirs to the glorious destiny of the 'Aryan' northmen of the Old World, and the Canada Firsters' position in the Red River controversy, for example, was plainly racist. They looked down their noses not only at Aboriginal people and Métis but at the French as well, seeing them as a 'bar to progress, and to the extention of a great Anglo-Saxon Dominion across the Continent'.[14] While these notions went together with Canadian westward expansion, they were fortunately not totally typical of the conscious development of Canadian nationalism. The French-Canadian poet Octave Crémazie, for example, lamented ironically that Canada's major literary languages were of European origin, arguing that 'if we spoke Huron or Iroquois, the work of our writers would attract the attention of the old world. . . . One would be overwhelmed by a novel or a poem translated from the Iroquois, while one does not take the trouble to read a book written in French by a native of Quebec or Montreal.'[15]

The major problem with most of the early expressions of a larger Canadian nationalism, even when they were not openly racist, was that they tended to visualize the new nation as seamlessly uniting the old colonies of British North America in a single entity—and to forget that those old colonies contained several quite disparate cultural traditions. Those who thought in pan-Canadian terms were almost entirely anglophone assimilationists. Manitoba's Chief Justice Edmund Burke Wood told the St Andrew's Society in Winnipeg in 1874 that 'Here we wanted no race, nationality, church, sect or religion to be dominant or in the ascendant; but we wanted all to be British subjects; all to be Canadians, all to be Manitobans, whatever his origin, language, race or pedigree.'[16] But Wood himself was not particularly sympathetic to the Métis or the Franco-Manitobans, and his underlying notion of Canadian identity was firmly British. The place of French Canada in the nation was an interesting question. In one draft letter to the press, probably written in 1870, Charles Mair virtually exploded on this subject:

> Ontario and the English-speaking people of Quebec have been milked long enough. . . . Thank God there is such a thing at last as a purely national feeling in Canada. There is a young and vigorous race coming to the front, entirely in earnest, and which is no longer English, Scotch or Irish, but thoroughly and distinctly Canadian. . . . It means strict justice to the French and nothing more—a fair field and no favour.[17]

The French language, claimed Mair, stood in the way of Canadians ever becoming a 'homogeneous people'. For these early nationalists, the condescending English represented more of a threat than did the Americans, whom they considered weak and 'effeminate' compared with their manly northern neighbours. They also saw the United States as the home of the 'grab' and a hotbed of political corruption.[18]

INTELLECTUAL DEVELOPMENT

JOHN BOURINOT

Politicians were not alone in endeavouring to create a sense of Canadian nationality. There were no guarantees that political unification would create a nation, particularly given the competing interpretations of the meaning of Confederation. Intellectuals and artists played their parts as well, providing rhetorical flourishes as well as the more mundane service of creating national institutions in which the arts could flourish. In 1881, for example, the chief clerk of the House of Commons, John Bourinot, published a book entitled *The Intellectual Development of the Canadian People: An Historical Review*, the first of his many works on history and Canadian government. Born in Sydney, Nova Scotia, in 1837, he was educated at the University of Toronto and then founded the *Halifax Herald* in 1860, becoming chief reporter of the Nova Scotia Assembly in 1861. In 1868 he moved to Ottawa to join the Hansard staff of the House of Commons, attracted—like many other intellectuals—by the economic opportunities and wider horizons that Canada seemed to offer after Confederation. In his book Bourinot sought to counter the tendency to deprecate the intellectual efforts of Canadians at home and abroad. Canada had moved 'beyond the state of mere colonial pupilage', he argued, implying that the cultural products of the new nation were just as worthy of respect as its political achievements.

Bourinot argued chiefly from advances in education and literacy. He began by writing in glowing terms of the free and accessible public education available in most provinces, and of the country's 21 colleges and universities. He pointed out that $64 million had been spent on public schools across the Dominion since 1867, adding that in 1839 about one in 13 young British North Americans had been attending school, while the proportion of young Canadians in school in 1881 was one in four. Newspapers were another sign of intellectual development, increasing from 65 in all British North America in 1840 to 465—56 of them dailies—in 1880. Fond of argument from sheer numbers, Bourinot wrote that in 1879, 4,085,454 pounds of newspapers at one cent per pound 'passed through the post offices of the Dominion', and over 30 million copies of newspapers were circulated annually in Canada through the mails.[19] He concluded with a chapter on literature, which catalogued a number of French-Canadian historians and poets—including Léon-Pamphile Lemay, Octave

Crémazie, Benjamin Sulte, and Louis-Honoré Fréchette, whose elegy 'Les Morts' he compared favourably to Victor Hugo's work—and offered a handful of English-Canadian writers, mainly from the Maritime region. The 'firm, broad basis of general education', Bourinot concluded, meant 'a future as full of promise for literature as for industry'.

Some of Bourinot's comments, especially about French Canada, sound extremely patronizing to the modern ear. He noted the 'greater impulsiveness and vivacity of the French Canadians' and was pleased to remind his readers that they were descendants of Normans and Bretons, 'people [who] have much that is akin with the people of the British Islands'. The idea of similarities between the French and the British was in the air in Bourinot's day, as Canadians attempted to define a new national identity after Confederation. At the same time he insisted on the existence of 'a national French Canadian sentiment, which has produced no mean intellectual feats'. On balance, 'in the essential elements of intellectual development, Canada is making not a rapid but certainly at least a steady and encouraging progress, which proves that her people have not lost, in consequence of the decided disadvantages of their colonial situation, any of the characteristics of the races to whom they owe their origin.'[20] In many ways Bourinot's book reflects the Victorian worship of Progress. Yet the very fact that in 1881 someone should have attempted to trace the intellectual development of the Canadian people indicates some of the distance covered in what the author himself saw as the movement from raw frontier colonies to civilized nation. That development, however, was hardly the simple progression that Bourinot sought to document.

EDUCATION

As Bourinot's comments suggest, if Canadians of his time had been asked to comment on their cultural accomplishments, they would surely have pointed with pride to their school systems—in particular, their accessibility and uni-

ISABELLA VALANCY CRAWFORD
(1850–1887)

❖

Isabella Valancy Crawford was born on 25 December 1850 in Dublin, Ireland. Her father, a surgeon who also studied the law, appears to have been a scapegrace member of a well-to-do family. Probably a heavy drinker, he migrated with his family to Wisconsin around 1854, and later moved first to Paisley and then to Lakefield, Canada West. In Lakefield young Isabella grew up as a companion to Catharine Parr Traill's daughter Katherine and was educated at home by her parents. Her father was convicted of the misappropriation of funds while serving as township treasurer in Paisley in the mid-1860s, and the ensuing stigma appears to have weighed heavily on his family, especially Isabella. In 1869 he set up a medical practice in Peterborough.

Local legend described his daughter as 'eccentric' before the death of her father in 1875. Like many another gentlewoman of the time, she managed to establish a modest career as a writer, mainly for Toronto newspapers, in order to support her mother and sister. Eventually the family moved to Toronto, where Isabella found more outlets for her writing, publishing prose and poetry in newspapers under a variety of pseudonyms and moving from one lodging house to another. Virtually all her life would be spent in genteel poverty. In 1884 she collected 43 of her poems in a volume entitled of *Old Spookses' Pass, Malcolm's Katie and Other Poems*, of which she published 1,000 copies at her own expense. Despite a number of positive reviews in British journals, only a handful of copies were ever sold. Nevertheless, she continued writing, mainly fiction of the women's romance variety for American popular magazines, and one of her novels was serialized in the *Evening Globe* in 1886.

Isabella Valancy Crawford died in 1887 after catching a bad cold. Not until well after her untimely death was she recognized as one of Canada's most important poets. Transferring the Tennysonian tradition of narrative poetry to pioneer Canada, she was extremely sensitive to Aboriginal legends, and had a highly developed sense of Canadian identity, which has led to her association with the 'Confederation Poets'. In a poem entitled 'The Camp of Souls', she wrote:

> White are the wigwams in that far camp,
>> And the star-eyed deer on the plains
>> are found;
> No bitter marshes or tangled swamp
>> In the Manitou's happy hunting-
>> ground!
> And the moon of summer forever rolls,
>> Above the red men in their "Camp of
>> Souls."

Much of her poetry was concerned with the role of suffering in life. A complete edition of her work is still not available. For a biography based on the limited material available, see Elizabeth McNeill Galvin, *Isabella Valancy Crawford: We Scarcely Knew Her* (Toronto, 1994).

CHARLES G.D. ROBERTS'S 'CANADA'

In 1886 Charles G.D. Roberts published a small volume of verses in Boston entitled *Divers Tones*. The following is one of the first poems in the book.

Canada

O Child of Nations, giant-limbed,
    Who stand'st among the nations now
Unheeded, unadorned, unhymned,
    With unanointed brow,—

How long the ignoble sloth, how long
    The trust in greatness not thine own?
Surely the lion's brood is strong
    To front the world alone!

How long the indolence, ere thou dare
    Achieve thy destiny, seize thy fame—
Ere our proud eyes behold thee bear
    A nation's franchise, nation's name?

The Saxon force, the Celtic fire,
    These are thy manhood's heritage!
Why rest with babes and slaves? Seek higher
    The place of race and age.

I see to every wind unfurled
    The flag that bears the Maple-Wreath;
Thy swift keels furrow round the world
    Its blood-red folds beneath;

Thy swift keels cleave the furthest seas;
    Thy white sails swell with alien gales;
To stream on each remotest breeze
    The black smoke of thy pipes exhales.

O Falterer, let thy past convince
    Thy future,—all the growth, the gain,
The fame since Cartier knew thee, since
    Thy shores beheld Champlain!

Montcalm and Wolfe! Wolfe and Montcalm!
    Quebec, thy storied citadel
Attest in burning song and psalm
    How here thy heroes fell!

O Thou that bor'st the battle's brunt
    At Queenston, and at Lundy's Lane,—
On whose scant ranks but iron front
    The battle broke in vain!—

Whose was the danger, whose the day,
    From whose triumphant throats the cheers,
At Chrysler's Farm, at Chateauguay,
    Storming like clarion-bursts our ears?

On soft Pacific slopes,—beside
    Strange floods that northward rave and fall,—
Where chafes Acadia's chainless tide—
    Thy sons await thy call.

They wait; but some in exile, some
    With strangers housed, in stranger lands;—
And some Canadian lips are dumb
    Beneath Egyptian sands.

O mystic Nile! Thy secret yields
    Before us; thy most ancient dreams
Are mixed with fresh Canadian fields
    And murmur of Canadian streams.

But thou, my Country, dream not thou!
    Wake, and behold how night is done,—
How on thy breast, and o'er thy brow,
    Bursts the rising sun!

SOURCE: Charles G.D. Roberts, *Divers Tones* (Boston: Lothrop, 1886), 2–5.

■ 'Lock no. 1, new Welland Canal', from *Picturesque Canada* (1882). LAC, C-083047.

versality. British North America's first Free Public Education Act, under which schools were fully financed by the state, was passed in Prince Edward Island in 1852, but in the post-Confederation period all the provinces moved to public funding and schooling became increasingly universal. Public financing allowed the colonial governments and their provincial successors to provide centralized control over education. These small bureaucracies were part of the administrative state that began to develop in the 1840s and continued growing through the Confederation period. Attempts by these centralized agencies to control denominational schools in the same way that they did public ones would lead to much controversy over the next years.

The greatest issue in education in the period immediately after Confederation arose in New Brunswick and involved not control over denominational schools but an effort by those schools themselves to gain some privileges. Section 93 of the BNA Act guaranteed educational rights to Ontario Catholics and Quebec Protestants, but in the Maritime provinces allowed only those privileges sanctioned by law before unification. In a famous court judgement in New Brunswick in 1873, Chief Justice Ritchie declared that the privileges of local Catholics before 1867 did not exist by law. The remedy, said Ritchie, was within the power of the legislature, not the courts. But the legislature was in the control of English-speaking Protestants. Following serious riots in the Acadian community of Caraquet in 1875, an attempt was made to find a remedy in the Canadian House of Commons. But to amend section 92 of the British North America Act, under which education was left to the provinces, would have set too dangerous a precedent. And there the matter stood.

Indeed, education was one of the most divisive issues in the new nation, and educational diversity was still the norm. Canada East had been somewhat slower than Canada West to move towards universality, and most of its schools continued to be dominated by both clerical teachers and clerical values, although Protestants were able to establish their own institutions in Quebec, particularly after education was reorganized in 1875. In Ontario a Canadian National Series of Readers was introduced as early as 1868, based on the Irish National Readers but 'greatly improved and Canadianized'.[21] Of course, using material published in Canada and adapted for Canadians was not the same as promulgating a strident or even standard Canadian nationalism in the schools. In the short run, English-Canadian educators tended to Canadianize by emphasizing 'the rich heritage of British history . . . reflected in our national escutcheon'.[22]

CULTURAL DEVELOPMENT

In various fields of the arts and letters, stirrings of cultural nationalism could be observed as Canadians attempted to break through the hard ground of the new nation's traditional colonial mentality, which tended to look to Great Britain and the United States for cultural models and directions.

THE CONFEDERATION POETS

The search for an essential 'Canadian-ness' went on in many corners of the new Dominion, but nowhere did it meet more success than in the somewhat remote New Brunswick town of Fredericton, home of the University of New Brunswick. There the rectory of St Anne's Parish (Anglican) produced Charles G.D. Roberts, while not far down the road lived his cousin Bliss Carman. Along with Ottawa's Archibald Lampman and Duncan Campbell Scott, William Wilfrid Campbell, and Isabella Valancy Crawford, these individuals made up the 'Confederation Poets', a designation invented by modern literary critics for the first 'school' of Canadian poets to wrestle with Canadian themes—notably the local or regional landscape and sometimes its deterioration—with some skill and sensitivity.[23] The Confederation poets were internationally known (in their day), familiar with American and European literary traditions, and not always much concerned with Canadian identity. Both Roberts and Carman eventually moved to the United States, and Roberts, in 'The Poet Is Bidden to Manhattan Island' (1886), explained why: 'Your poet's eyes must recognize / The side on which your bread is buttered!'[24]

THE ROYAL ACADEMY OF ARTS

Curiously enough, it was the painters rather than the writers who took the lead in organizing national groups to maintain professional standards and publicize Canadian art. The Ontario Society of Artists, formed in 1872 and incorporated in 1877, took the lead in this effort. It was instrumental in the formation of the Royal Canadian Academy of Arts in 1880—in collaboration with Governor General Lord Lorne—and in the establishment that same year of the National Gallery of Canada. The Academy not only held an inaugural exhibition in Ottawa, but planned others in

Toronto, Montreal, Halifax, and Saint John. As one of the founding academicians wrote, 'We are bound to try to civilize the Dominion a little.'[25] The year 1880 was doubly important in art circles, for in that year the Canadian Society of Graphic Art was also founded.

The first president of the Royal Canadian Academy, the painter Lucius O'Brien, was art director of an elaborate literary and artistic celebration of the young nation, *Picturesque Canada* (1882), which was based on the highly successful books *Picturesque America* and *Picturesque Europe*. It was the idea of two Americans, the Belden brothers, who had established themselves in Toronto. The editor of the project—George Monro Grant, the principal of Queen's University —stated in the Preface: 'I believed that a work that would represent its characteristic scenery and history and life of its people would not only make us better known to ourselves and to strangers, but would also stimulate national sentiment and contribute to the rightful development of the nation.' The two large volumes of *Picturesque Canada*— which can sometimes be found in second-hand bookshops—contained 540 illustrations. They included wood engravings based on paintings and, for the West, engravings of photographs of serene vistas, fulfilling the promise of the title. The descriptive texts by Grant, Charles G.D. Roberts, and others presented an idealized, complacent view of the cities, towns, and regions of Canada, praising the present and pointing to their glorious future. *Picturesque Canada* was a monument to the optimism of the time.[26]

THE ROYAL SOCIETY OF CANADA

The Royal Society of Canada was founded in 1882 to promote research and learning in the arts and sciences.[27] Again Lord Lorne provided much of the impetus, replicating a British institution to establish the importance of cultural accomplishments in creating a sense of national pride and self-confidence. He was the first of several governors general to make significant contributions to Canadian cultural nationalism; in

1936, for example, John Buchan (Lord Tweedsmuir) would help to introduce the Governor General's awards for literature. Lorne himself was an intellectual who painted and wrote poetry. The society was to be self-selective, with membership by invitation only, and bicultural, with a separate section for 'Littérature française, Histoire, Archéologie', although the scientific sections had 'no distinctions of race or language'. Its first president, J.W. Dawson, principal of McGill University, emphasized in his presidential address a sense of national purpose, especially 'the establishment of a bond of union between the scattered workers now widely separated in different parts of the Dominion'. At an early meeting Thomas Sterry Hunt, a charter member and later president, spoke of 'a new departure in the intellectual history of Canada' and added that 'the brightest glories and the most enduring honours of a country are those which come from its thinkers and its scholars.'[28] However romantic that statement may be, what is important is Hunt's emphasis on the country as a whole. Like the Royal Canadian Academy, the Royal Society had its headquarters in Ottawa.

THE NORTH-WEST TERRITORIES

Despite efforts to encourage a sense of nationhood that might transcend the barriers of cultural difference and geographical distance, the fact remains that the new Canadian nationality remained fragile, more than a little precious, and very racist. In addition, at least outside French Canada, it mainly expressed the prejudices and ideology of British Ontario. Many believed that the crucible for the new Canadian nationality, and the nation itself, was in the vast unsettled expanse of territory west of the Great Lakes that had been obtained from the Hudson's Bay Company. Here Canada had insisted from the beginning on controlling both the land and the natural resources, subject only to negotiations over the rights of the Aboriginal inhabitants. Here Canada would govern its own colony and make its own policy, free of the compromises required to bring older provinces into Confederation. And here its limitations would be most clearly evident.

The interests of the Canadian government in the Northwest, particularly under Sir John A. Macdonald, were focused on agricultural settlement, both as an outlet for excess eastern population and as a stimulus to the development of a truly transcontinental nation. Several problems faced the Dominion in the Northwest, however. In the first place, the government did not have the money to develop the territory as quickly as it, and the incoming settlers, would have preferred. The attempt to finance the building of a transcontinental railway had helped to push the Macdonald government out of office. Finding the large number of surveyors necessary to survey the land in advance of settlement, and the money to pay them, proved extremely difficult. Paying the compensation required to extinguish Aboriginal title to the land was almost impossible. In the second place, at the time of the transfer of the western territory to the Dominion in 1870, Quebec had assumed that western expansion was mainly Ontario's business. It was therefore surprised to discover that the West had a significant French-speaking Roman Catholic population: the Métis. As the government struggled with the Riel insurrection in Red River and then the new province of Manitoba, Quebecers became increasingly protective of the rights of French Canadians, including the Métis, in the region. The federal government's treatment of Riel became a major issue for Quebec, where it was widely believed that Riel was persecuted for being a French Canadian. The interpretation of Riel's career is still contentious today, and the arguments have not changed much since the nineteenth century.

WESTERN LAND AND SETTLEMENT POLICY

In 1872 the Canadian Parliament passed the Dominion Lands Act, based in large measure on the American Homestead Act. The insistence on a homestead act had been one of the 'rights' demanded by the people of Red River in 1869 and 1870. The legislation also regularized the Dominion Lands Survey, which had been in operation since 1869. The survey system continued the 640-acre square section that set the pattern for the landscape of the Prairie provinces. Under the Lands Act, any male farmer could obtain a quarter-section, 160 acres (65 hectares) of land, for $10 upon his agreement to cultivate 30 acres (10 hectares) and construct a permanent dwelling house within three years of registration. The law also allowed the farmer an additional quarter-section for an additional $10. This was designed to compensate the farmer for lack of rainfall and other drawbacks in much of the West. The homestead arrangement was not very important for settlement before 1890, because most of the best arable land on the prairies was initially held by the CPR, the HBC, and in reserve for the Métis.

In its eagerness to get the prairies populated, Canada also encouraged the settlement of various ethnic communities from Europe, usually through promises to immigrant leaders to provide blocks of land for self-contained ethnic settlement. The first successful negotiations along these lines were carried out with Russian Mennonites beginning in 1872 and 1873. These Mennonites, members of a Protestant pacifist sect founded in the sixteenth century, were from Prussia and Poland. They had left their homes because of military conscription in the eighteenth century. Catherine the Great of Russia offered them generous terms of resettlement, including land, freedom of religion, their own separate schools, and permanent exemption from military service. By the 1870s, however, Russian nationalism was threatening the Mennonite independence and communal lifestyle.

The Canadian government offered similar inducements to the earlier Russian ones: exemption from military service, religious liberty, control of education, free homesteads of 160 acres, and the right to purchase additional land at one dollar per acre. Canada set aside two blocks of townships for the Mennonites in southern Manitoba: one block of eight townships was on the east side of the Red River southeast of Winnipeg, and another block of 12 townships (the 'West Reserve') was along the international boundary west of the Red River. The blocks of reserves made plain to the Mennonites that they could live in their own village communities (and hold land in common) apart from their neighbours. About 8,000 Mennonites settled in 1874 in Manitoba.

The other ethnic group allowed by the Canadian government to establish itself as an autonomous community before 1885 was that of the Icelanders. People from Iceland had begun drifting to Canada in substantial numbers in the early 1870s, motivated both by volcanic eruptions and land shortages in their homeland. The first immigrants settled in Ontario and Quebec but were dissatisfied with their situation. In the spring of 1875 a party of Icelanders travelled west to find satisfactory land for a block settlement they had been promised by the Canadian government. The land they chose was on the west side of Lake Winnipeg, stretching from present-day Selkirk to Hecla Island and including the modern town of Gimli. This territory was north of the boundary of the province of Manitoba and was thus in the relatively ungoverned North-West Territories of Canada, where the newcomers were able to establish the Republic of New Iceland, an autonomous settlement with its own laws and judicial system. The Canadian government accepted a provisional council set up by the Icelanders and allowed them to produce a fully articulated system of self-government with four districts (*byggdir*), each governed by a council of five people headed by a reeve, culminating in a governing council (*Thing*). This republic became part of Manitoba when the boundaries of the province were expanded in 1881, but self-government remained in effect until 1887. Schools were established in New Iceland only months after arrival of the immigrants, with instruction being conducted in Icelandic.

Although the territory chosen for New Iceland was ideal for access to fishing on Lake Winnipeg, it was some of the poorest agricultural land in the region. Moreover, the Icelanders were struck with a devastating smallpox epidemic in 1876, transmitted by Aboriginal peoples to Icelanders who also lacked immunity to the disease. Spring flooding on Lake Winnipeg occurred between 1876 and 1880. When a major religious dispute among the settlers emerged in the late 1870s, outward migration began. Many Icelanders went either to North Dakota or to the burgeoning city of Winnipeg.

THE MOUNTIES

The North West Mounted Police, based on the Irish constabulary, were established in 1873 to act as a quasi-military agency of the Canadian government in the West. Its officers, drawn from the elites of eastern Canada, were committed to the notion of public stability that associated crime and violence with the 'lower orders' and Native people. Red coats were chosen for uniforms because the Native people still held a traditional respect for the British Army. The 'Mounties' moved into the West ahead of the settlers and have always symbolized a peaceful process of westward expansion, in contrast to the violence of the 'wild' American West. Certainly in Canada there was less individual violence, but peace was often imposed through state intervention and control.

THE ABORIGINAL PEOPLE

On the surface, Dominion policy concerning the Native inhabitants of the North-West Territories was simple and sensible. Canada acknowledged the Aboriginal rights to land of the 'Indians'—though not the Métis—and was prepared to negotiate treaties extinguishing those rights in

STEPHEN LEACOCK'S 'MY REMARKABLE UNCLE'

The first real estate boom in the new Canadian West began in Winnipeg in 1881. It was the harbinger of many similar phenomena in the ensuing years, and was treated later with affectionate humour by Stephen Leacock, who wrote of his uncle, a man who truly behaved much as his nephew described. E.P., as he was known, couldn't really be much exaggerated.

The most remarkable man I have ever known in my life was my uncle Edward Philip Leacock, known to every so many people in Winnipeg fifty or sixty years ago as E.P. His character was so exceptional that it needs nothing but plain narration. It was so exaggerated already that you couldn't exaggerate it. . . . all the talk was of Manitoba now opening up. Nothing would do E.P. but that he and my father must go west. . . . They hit Winnipeg just on the rise of the boom, and E.P. came at once into his own and rode on the crest of the wave. . . . In less than no time he was in everything and knew everybody, conferring titles and honours up and down Portage Avenue. In six months he had a great fortune, on paper; took a trip east and brought back a charming wife from Toronto; built a large house beside the river; filled it with pictures he said were his ancestors, and carried on in it roaring hospitality that never stopped.

His activities were wide. He was president of a bank (that never opened), head of a brewery (for brewing the Red River), and above all, secretary-treasurer of the Winnipeg and Hudson Bay and Arctic Railway that had a charter authorizing it to build a road to the Arctic Ocean, when it got ready. They had no track, but they printed stationery and passes, and in return E.P. received passes all over North America. . . .

Naturally E.P.'s politics remained conservative. But he pitched the note higher. Even the ances-

tors weren't good enough. He invented a Portuguese Dukedom (some one of our family once worked in Portugal)—and he conferred it, by some kind of reversion, on my elder brother Jim who had gone to Winnipeg to work in E.P.'s office. This enabled him to say to visitors in his big house, after looking at the ancestors—to say in a half-whisper behind his hand, 'Strange to think that two deaths would make that boy a Portuguese Duke.' But Jim never knew which two Portuguese to kill.

To aristocracy E.P. also added a touch of peculiar prestige by always being apparently just about to be called away—imperially. If some said, 'Will you be in Winnipeg all winter, Mr. Leacock?' he answered, 'It will depend a good deal on what happens in West Africa.' Just that; West Africa beat them.

Then came the crash of the Manitoba boom. Simple people, like my father, were wiped out in a day. Not so E.P. The crash just gave him a lift as the smash of a big wave lifts a strong swimmer. He just went right on. I believe that in reality he was left utterly bankrupt. But it made no difference. He used credit instead of cash. He still had his imaginary bank, and his railway to the Arctic Ocean. Hospitality still roared and the tradesmen still paid for it. Any one who called about a bill was told that E.P.'s movements were uncertain and would depend a good deal on what happened in Johannesburg. That held them another six months.

SOURCE: Stephen Leacock, *My Remarkable Uncle and Other Sketches* (Toronto: McClelland & Stewart, 1965 [1942]), 15–17.

■ Inspection of NWMP lancers at Fort Walsh, Cypress Hills, 1878. LAC, C-18046A.

exchange for reserves, often located on the most marginal and least fertile land. These treaties not only freed the more desirable land for settlement, but enabled the Canadian government to continue to pursue its pre-Confederation policy of settling First Nations people on the land as farmers in the hopes of eventually assimilating them into mainstream Canadian society. In 1876, for example, the Plains Cree of central Saskatchewan gathered at Fort Carlton to consider the terms of the government's Treaty Six. Their chief, Poundmaker (Pitikwahanapiwiyin), objected to the terms, arguing that the government should be prepared to do more than provide small plots of land, livestock (especially oxen), and farming implements. If Ottawa expected his people to become good farmers, it should also provide

training and other forms of assistance, particularly after the buffalo disappeared. Lieutenant-Governor Alexander Morris, who had presented the terms for the treaty, considered this suggestion as an example of pure greed, and it was pushed aside.[29] Nevertheless, Poundmaker signed the treaty, and three years later accepted a reserve on the Battle River. Another important Plains Cree leader, Big Bear (Mistahimaskwa), held out for six years. But by December 1882 his people were starving, and he agreed to sign.

After most of the Aboriginal bands on the prairies had signed the numbered treaties, the government consolidated the laws regarding Aboriginals into one omnibus piece of legislation, the Indian Act of 1876. This Act made Aboriginals wards of the state and regulated the sale of their land. The Aboriginal peoples of the West were caught in an inexorable process of change. The buffalo were rapidly disappearing, the victims of over-hunting, the arrival of settlement and new technology, and probably some sort of bovine disease epidemic. Whatever the reasons, most Aboriginal leaders knew that their traditional way of life was disappearing forever. But the Department of Indian Affairs expected them to become self-sufficient virtually overnight. It did not supply the reserves with enough food to prevent starvation and disease, and it complained when the desperate people slaughtered their livestock for something to eat. The reserve lands tended to be marginal, the assistance supplied was inadequate, and the attitude of many of the Indian agents (the government's representatives on the reserves) was basically unsympathetic. By the early 1880s, the West was a virtual powder keg of Aboriginal discontent. Cree leaders in what is now Alberta sent a letter to Sir John A. Macdonald (who was Minister of the Interior and head of Indian Affairs as well as Prime Minister) telling him they were destitute and that their motto was, 'If we must die by violence let us do it quickly.' The winter of 1883–4 was particularly severe, and many were starving. Some Indian agents wrote to Ottawa, but nothing was done. In June 1884 Big Bear and his followers, with many others, travelled to Poundmaker's reserve for discussions, after which some 2,000 people took part in the religious ritual known as the Thirst Dance.

THE MÉTIS

Like the First Nations, the Métis were systematically pushed to the margins. The Macdonald government had created Manitoba as a province only under duress, and the Prime Minister regarded the mixed-bloods as needing merely to be 'kept down by a strong hand until they are swamped by the influx of settlers'.[30] And swamped they were. As thousands of new settlers, mainly from Ontario, arrived in the

■ The Plains Cree leader Poundmaker (Pitikwahanapiwiyin; 1842–86) was named for his skill at constructing the pounds (pens) used to trap bison. LAC, C-001875.

province, the land rights that had been guaranteed to the Métis were gradually whittled down, and much of the land itself—about 2 million of the 2.5 million acres (809,370 out of 1,011,715 hectares) promised the Métis in 1870—ended up in the hands of speculators. By 1885 Ontario-born settlers outnumbered Métis five to one in Manitoba, and only 7 per cent of the province's population was of mixed-blood origin. The extent to which deliberate government policy was responsible for the plight of the Métis has been one of the most bitter historical controversies ever seen in Canadian historiography,

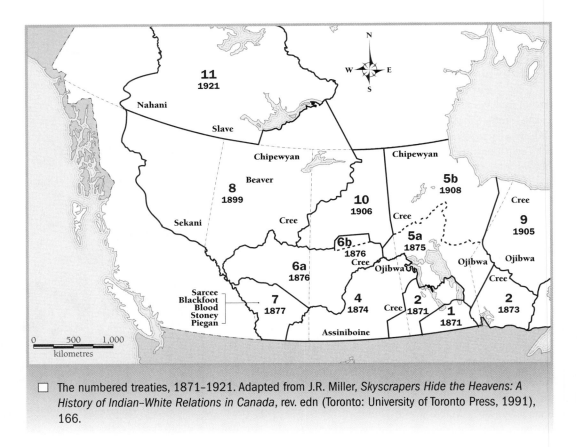

□   The numbered treaties, 1871–1921. Adapted from J.R. Miller, *Skyscrapers Hide the Heavens: A History of Indian–White Relations in Canada*, rev. edn (Toronto: University of Toronto Press, 1991), 166.

and the last word has not yet been written on the subject.

Many Métis headed farther west, often to the Saskatchewan Valley, where they formed several mission settlements, including Qu'Appelle, Batoche, and Duck Lake.[31] But the buffalo were becoming scarce. French, English, and Scottish mixed-bloods in the region demanded grants similar to those given to the mixed-bloods under the Manitoba Act. As in Red River a decade before, the arrival of government surveyors sparked fear and uncertainty as to whether the river lot holdings of the Métis would be allowed to survive in a square survey system. Part of the problem was that the surveying was not happening fast enough, not just for the Métis (who sought exemptions from it), but for the European

settlers as well. By the early 1880s, the Europeans in the region were becoming as restive as the First Nations and the Métis, although for different reasons. Their concerns were more political. In March 1883 the Qu'Appelle settlers' rights association passed resolutions calling for parliamentary representation, land law reform, proper legislation for settlers, and government assistance for immigrants. In December of that year a Manitoba and Northwest farmers' union was organized in Winnipeg. A motion for repeal of the BNA Act and the formation of a 'new confederacy of the North-West Provinces and British Columbia' was only barely defeated. A Bill of Rights was drawn up, which was summarily rejected in Ottawa.

In the late spring of 1884 the despairing

■ Big Bear trading at Fort Pitt, an HBC post on the North Saskatchewan River, 1884. In the same year the post was taken over by the North-West Mounted Police. In April 1885, in the course of the uprising, Big Bear's band attacked the fort, which they evacuated and then burned. LAC, PA-118768.

Métis turned to their old leader, Louis Riel. He had apparently put his life back together after several years of exile in the United States and institutionalization for mental disturbance in Quebec asylums between 1876 and 1878. Riel had become an American citizen and was teaching in St Peter's, Montana—where he had married and started a family—when a delegation from the Saskatchewan country visited him on 4 June. They told him of all the grievances that were burdening the peoples of the region, explained that agitation was developing against the Canadian government, and pleaded with him to return and lead them. Within a month, Riel and his family were in Batoche and he was initiating a peaceful movement of protest against Canadian policies.

By December 1884 Riel and W.H. Jackson (secretary of the North-West Settler's Union) had drafted a long petition, with 25 sections, which they sent to Ottawa. The document concluded by requesting that the petitioners 'be allowed as in [1870] to send Delegates to Ottawa with their Bill of rights; whereby an understanding may be arrived at as to their entry into confederation, with the constitution of a free province'.[32] Ottawa acknowledged receipt of the petition, but made no other response. Riel was mistaken in thinking the tactics that had worked—under special conditions—in 1869–70 could be repeated 15 years later. He was equally mistaken in believing that he had the support of all the people in the region. As soon as signs of armed confrontation appeared, the European settlers quickly dissociated themselves from Riel's movement, and the First Nations moved in their own direction, attacking European settlements in several places.

THE NORTH-WEST REBELLION

Events took a menacing turn on 18 March 1885, when Riel and some of his men strode into the Walters and Baker store in Batoche. Riel announced, 'Well, gentlemen, it has commenced.' 'What has commenced?' asked Walters. 'Oh, this movement for the rights of the country', was the reply.[33] The visitors then helped themselves to ammunition and provisions. On 21 March Riel sent a letter to Superintendent L.N.F. Crozier of the North West Mounted Police at Fort Carlton, which was manned by a force of Mounted Police and volunteers. The missive demanded that the fort surrender, on pain of attack by Riel and his men. Crozier refused. On 26 March, Gabriel Dumont, Riel's military 'general', intercepted a small detachment from Fort Carlton near Duck Lake. When Crozier heard of this action he left the fort with as many men as he could muster. This force met Riel and 300 Métis on horseback before it reached Duck Lake. Startled, Crozier gave an order to fire. Thirty minutes of gunfire exchanges followed, during which lives were lost on both sides.

The Métis, who outnumbered Crozier's men, forced them to retreat. Gabriel Dumont later recalled this confrontation in vivid detail:

> They had to go through a clearing so I lay in wait for them, saying to my men: 'Courage, I'm going to make the red coats jump in their carts with some rifle shots.' And then I laughed, not because I took any pleasure in killing but to give courage to my men.
>
> Since I was eager to knock off some of the red coats, I never thought to keep under cover and a shot came and gashed the top of my head, where a deep scar can still be seen. I fell down on the ground and my horse, which was also wounded, went right over me as it tried to get

away. . . . When Joseph Delorme saw me fall again, he cried out that I was killed. I said to him, 'Courage! As long as you haven't lost your head, you're not dead!' . . .

> While we were fighting, Riel was on horseback, exposed to the gunfire, and with no weapon but the crucifix which he held in his hand.[34]

Riel wrote a letter to Crozier blaming him for the battle. 'A calamity has fallen upon the country yesterday', he insisted. 'You are responsible for it before God and man.'[35] He then appealed to the Cree to assist him. He got more than he had anticipated. Poundmaker's men broke into buildings in Battleford, terrifying settlers, and the Cree warrior Wandering Spirit (Kapapamahchakwew) led a band that attacked Frog Lake, killing nine.

Prime Minister Macdonald was determined to crush this uprising quickly[36] and sent a military force under Major-General Frederick Middleton—by way of the new Canadian Pacific Railway—to put it down. Many of the troops came from Winnipeg militia units composed of ex-Ontarians.[37] Lieutenant-Colonel William Otter relieved Battleford, but was fired on by Aboriginal warriors at Cut Knife Hill and had to withdraw. A battle with the Métis at Fish Creek delayed the march on Batoche, where Middleton intended to confront Riel. But on 9 May the Canadian force of 800 men arrived at Batoche, where they quickly defeated Riel, Dumont, and about 200 armed Métis. The uprising was over by 12 May. Dumont fled to the United States and Riel was arrested.

THE AFTERMATH OF REBELLION

A formal charge of high treason, carrying the death penalty, was laid against Riel on 6 July. Even though Riel was now an American citizen, the Canadian government insisted that his activities had been treasonable and made the charge stick.[38] The trial began on 28 July at Regina.[39] Many Canadian historians have characterized it as a political trial, infamously coloured by the

■ Riel in the prisoner's box. He addressed the court twice during his trial, once after all the evidence had been presented (when he spoke for more than an hour) and once before sentence was pronounced. LAC, C-1879.

government's determination to see Riel found guilty and executed (on the other hand, Thomas Flanagan, in his book *Riel and the Rebellion: 1885 Reconsidered*, argues that the government behaved quite properly[40]). In any case, Riel passionately denied a plea of insanity proposed by his lawyers, who failed to present the defence argument that Riel himself insisted on: that the uprising was justified. The jury found him guilty, in effect rejecting the insanity plea, but recommended mercy. Ottawa dismissed two appeals, and Riel was hanged on 16 November 1885. A number of other leading rebels received lesser sentences.

If Riel was treated without sympathy by the Canadian government, the punishments meted out to the First Nations, who were regarded as having joined Riel's resistance rather than acting on their own initiative, were equally severe.[41] The Macdonald government used the rebellion and the violence committed by the leaders of the First Nations as pretexts to crush the protests against the failure to observe the negotiated treaties. Eight warriors were executed in late November 1885, and before the courts were finished, more than 50 others were sentenced to imprisonment. Among the leaders, Poundmaker stood trial for treason and was sentenced to three years in prison. Released after a year, he died four months later. Big Bear received a similar sentence, but was released after a year and a half. Wandering Spirit was hanged. The trials were conducted in a highly improper manner. Few of the accused were properly represented in court, and translation was inadequate for people who understood little English and less of Canadian law. Most First Nations leaders and people tried to remain clear of the Métis uprising, but this did not save them from a campaign of repression, in the late 1880s and after, mounted by Assistant Indian Commissioner Hayter Reed, who maintained that the rebellion had abrogated the treaties and proceeded to introduce a series of policies that made the First Nations totally dependent on the largesse of Canada.

At the time of his death Riel was already one of the most controversial figures in the nation's history. Contemporaries argued over whether he was a murderous traitor or a martyr, the saviour of his people. For French Canadians as well as Métis he symbolized resistance to Anglo-Saxon domination, and later generations would see him as symbolic of still other values, including a general resistance to the imperialism of central Canada. The execution of Riel had a lasting impact on Canada, particularly in Quebec, where it served to strengthen French-Canadian nationalism and turn voters away from the Conservative Party. On 22 November 1885, at a huge gathering in the public square in Montreal called the Champ de Mars, Honoré Mercier, the Liberal leader in Quebec, joined Wilfrid Laurier in denouncing the government action. 'In killing Riel,' Mercier said, 'Sir John has not only struck at the heart of our race but especially at the cause of justice and humanity which . . . demanded mercy for the prisoner of Regina, our poor friend of the North-West.'[42] Laurier added rhetorically, 'Had I been born on the banks of the Saskatchewan . . . I myself would have shouldered a musket to fight against the neglect of governments and the shameless greed of speculators.' But when Mercier proposed that French Canadians leave the two major parties and form one of their own, Laurier disagreed: 'We are a new nation,' he said, 'we are attempting to unite the different conflict elements which we have into a nation.

Shall we ever succeed if the bond of union is to be revenge?'[43] Laurier argued that Mercier's proposal would destroy Confederation.

THE COMPLETION OF THE CPR

The defeat of the Métis and the public execution of Louis Riel were only two of the reasons the year 1885 was so significant in the history of Canada, especially the West. On 7 November 1885, nine days before Riel's death, the last spike was driven at Craigellachie in eastern British Columbia, marking the completion of the Canadian Pacific Railway. The CPR had been resurrected in 1881 as a hybrid corporation controlled by private capitalists and financed chiefly by the state—which, along with public subsidies, gave it about 25 million acres (more than 100,000 square kilometres) of land along its right-of-way, as well as other concessions. The wisdom of rail construction in advance of settlement—building what T.C. Keefer had called 'colonization lines'—was actively debated at the time, particularly given the inducements needed to convince hard-headed businessmen to proceed, but the Macdonald government defended the railroad on the grounds of national interest. Since this concept is not measurable in quantitative terms, it is impossible to know whether the financial price was too high.

What we can say with certainty is that the construction of the CPR was a spectacular feat, attributable in part to the engineers in charge and in part to the managerial skills of William Van Horne. The actual construction, however, was carried out chiefly by the 6,500 Chinese labourers who were specially imported for the job. Many died, and those who survived were summarily discharged when the work was completed. Macdonald had defended Chinese immigration in 1883, arguing that it would 'be all very well to exclude Chinese labour, when we can replace it with white labour, but until that is done, it is better to have Chinese labour than no labour at all.'[44] With the completion of the CPR,

MEMORANDUM ON 'THE FUTURE MANAGEMENT OF INDIANS', JULY 1885

In 1885, a number of Indian bands in the North-West violently attacked post and forts at the same time as the Métis were engaged in battle with Canadian troops. The Canadian government responded to this violence in kind, both in terms of formal court action against the offenders, and in terms of a tougher policy. This memorandum was written by the Assistant Indian Commissioner, Hayter Reed, to his superior from Regina in July. It became the basis for the new policy.

Regina
July 20th/85

Memorandum for the Honourable the Indian Commission relative to the future management of Indians

1. All Indians who have not during the late troubles been disloyal or troublesome should be treated as heretofore; as they have not disturbed our treaty relations, and our treatment in the past has been productive of progress and good results.

2. As the rebellious Indians expected to have been treated with severity as soon as overpowered, a reaction of feeling must be guarded against. They were led to believe that they would be shot down, and harshly treated. Though humanity of course forbids this, unless severe examples are made of the more prominent participants in the rebellion much difficulty will be met with their future management, and future turbulence may be feared. It is therefore suggested that all leading Indian rebels whom it is found possible to convict of particular crimes, such as instigating and citing to treason, felony, arson, larceny, murder, etc., be dealt with in as severe a manner as the law will allow and that no offences of their most prominent men be overlooked.

3. That other offenders, both Halfbreed and Indian, who have been guilty of such serious offences as those above mentioned should be punished for their crimes in order to deter them from rebellious movements in future.

4. That the tribal system should be abolished in so far as is compatible with the treaty, e.g., in all cases in which the treaty has been broken by rebel tribes; by doing away with chiefs and councillors, depriving them of medals and other appurtenances of their offices. Our instructors and employees will not then be hampered by Indian consultations and interferences, but will administer direct orders and instructions to individuals; besides by this action and careful repression of those that become prominent amongst them by counselling, medicine dances, and so on, a further obstacle will be thrown in the way of future united rebellious movements.

5. No annuity money should be now paid any bands that rebelled, or any individuals that left well disposed bands and joined the insurgents. As the Treaty expressly stipulated for peace and good will, as well as an observance of law and order, it has been entirely abrogated by the rebellion. Besides this fact, such suggestion is made because in the past the annuity money which should have been expended wholly in necessaries has to a great extent been wasted upon articles more or less useless and in purchasing necessaries at exorbitant prices, entailing upon the Department a greater expenditure in providing articles of clothing, food

and implements, not called for by the terms of the Treaty, than need have been entailed if the whole of the annuity money had been well and economically applied to the purchase of such necessities. All future grants should be regarded as concessions of favour, not of right, and the rebel Indians be made to understand that they have forfeited every claim as 'matter of right'.

SOURCE: Blair Stonechild and Bill Waiser, *Loyal till Death: Indians and the North-West Rebellions* (Calgary, 1997), 250-3.

the Canadian government moved swiftly to limit Chinese immigration.

Despite the high costs, the positive aspects of the CPR far outweighed the negative for most Canadians at the time. On 4 July 1886 the first through passengers from Montreal arrived in Port Moody, British Columbia. A journey that only a few years before would have taken several months—sailing around the southern tip of South America or travelling overland by Red River cart—had taken just seven days. The railroad became the physical symbol of a transcontinental nation that now existed in fact as well as in the abstract.

■ The first transcontinental passenger train arrives at the foot of Howe Street in Vancouver, 23 May 1887. City of Vancouver Archives, CAN.P.78, N.52.

CONCLUSION

The West was to be an anglophone colony of Canada. Not only were First Nations, Métis, and Chinese cast aside as quickly as possible, but French Canadians were not supposed to move there in any substantial numbers. Most Quebecers in the years after Confederation considered the West important mainly in commercial terms, or as a better destination than the United States for Quebec migrants. As *L'Opinion Publique* (Montreal) stated in 1879: 'For five years English emigration has flooded Manitoba, and French emigration has been pretty well nil. . . . The North-West, founded and settled by the French, is destined, like the rest of North America, to be English.'[45] The francophone response to the execution of Louis Riel, however, was hardly so fatalistic. By 1885 Quebec public opinion was prepared to believe in theories of anti-French conspiracies.[46] National consolidation was arguably completed in 1885, but much Canadian 'nationalism' still bore the distinctive mark of the Ontario WASP. Two cultures, French and English, were being firmly set in opposition to each other. Trying to satisfy the country's two major components was the most challenging task facing the Canadian government.

SHORT BIBLIOGRAPHY

Beal, Bob, and Rod MacLeod. *Prairie Fire: The 1885 North-West Rebellion*, 2nd edn. Toronto, 1994. The best overview of the 1885 rebellion.

Berger, Carl. *The Sense of Power: Studies in the Ideas of Canadian Imperialism, 1867–1914*. Toronto, 1970. A pioneer work in Canadian intellectual history, still not superseded.

————. *Honour and the Search for Influence: A History of the Royal Society of Canada*. Toronto, 1996. A useful account of the development of a crucial national institution.

Bumsted, J.M. *Louis Riel v. Canada: The Making of a Rebel*. Winnipeg, 2002. A recent attempt at a balanced view of Riel.

Cook, Ramsay. *Provincial Autonomy, Minority Rights and the Compact Theory 1867–1921*. Ottawa, 1969. The standard study of the alternative vision of Confederation.

Lamb, W. Kaye. *History of the Canadian Pacific Railway*. New York, 1977. The best overview of the CPR currently available.

Neufeld, Edward P. *The Financial System of Canada, Its Growth and Development*. Toronto, 1972. The standard study of a complex subject.

Pór, Jonas. *Icelanders in North America: The First Settlers*. Winnipeg, 2002. An account of the early settlement of Icelanders in America.

Reid, Dennis. *Our Own Country Canada: Being an Account of the National Aspirations of the Principal Landscape Artists in Montreal and Toronto, 1869–1890*. Ottawa, 1979. An interesting piece of art history, relating the art to larger political and intellectual currents.

Sprague, D.N. *Canada and the Métis, 1869–1885*. Waterloo, Ont., 1988. A controversial account of the way in which Canada treated the Métis.

Stonechild, Blair, and Bill Waiser. *Loyal till Death: Indians and the North-West Rebellions*. Calgary, 1997. A superb analysis of the First Nations and the 1885 rebellions.

Swainger, Jonathan. *The Canadian Department of Justice and the Completion of Confederation*. Vancouver, 2000. A fine study of a much neglected topic.

Warkentin, John. 'The Mennonite Settlement of Southern Manitoba', Ph.D. thesis, University of Toronto, 1960. A thorough scholarly study of a complex question.

STUDY QUESTIONS

1. What was the National Policy?

2. What was the basic thrust of the provincial rights movement?

3. Comment on John Bourinot's arguments concerning 'the intellectual development of the Canadian people'. Do they really address the question?

4. Why was it difficult to develop a sense of Canadian nationalism?

5. Was the West treated fairly by the Canadian government after Confederation?

6. Is there a difference between being commissioned by the Canadian government to write a study of the military events of 1885 and being commissioned by the Canadian government to help prepare a brief in a court case regarding land claims?

7. What was the secret of E.P. Leacock's success?

INTRODUCTION

1. Arthur Marwick, *The Nature of History* (London and Basingstoke, 1970), 114.
2. E.H. Carr, *What Is History?* (Harmondsworth, 1964), 103–4.
3. D.A. McArthur, in *Ontario Historical Society Papers and Records* 21 (1924): 207.

1 THE PEOPLES OF EARLY NORTH AMERICA

1. This tale is adapted from the version in Deanna Christensen, *Ahtahkakoop: The Epic Account of a Plains Cree Head Chief, His People, and Their Struggle for Survival, 1816–1896* (Shell Lake, Sask., 2000), 3–14.
2. For the ice sheets, see R. Cole Harris, ed., *Historical Atlas of Canada: Volume I: From the Beginning to 1800* (Toronto, 1987), plate 1.
3. Liz Bryan, *The Buffalo People: Prehistoric Archaeology on the Canadian Plains* (Edmonton, 1991), 6–8.
4. T. Dillehay and M. Collins, 'Early Cultural Evidence from Monte Verde in Chile', *Nature* 332 (10 Mar. 1998).
5. Tom Dillehay, *Monte Verde: A Late Pleistocene Settlement in Chile*, 2 vols (Washington, 1997), II.
6. John Sorenson and Martin Raish, eds, *Pre-Columbian Contact with the Americas across the Oceans*, rev. edn (Provo, Utah, 1996); Barry Fell, *Bronze Age America* (Boston, 1982); Mark K.Stengel, 'The Diffusionists Have Landed', *Atlantic Monthly* (Jan. 2000), 35–48; Knud Fladmark, 'The Feasibility of the Northwest Coast as a Migration Route for Early Man', in A. Bryan, ed., *Early Man in America* (Edmonton, 1978). See also the bibliography to this chapter.
7. This paragraph and the one following are based chiefly on Reid A. Bryson and Wayne M. Wendland, 'Tentative Climatic Patterns for Some Late Glacial and Post-Glacial Episodes in Central North America', in William J. Mayer-Oakes, ed., *Life, Land and Water: Proceedings of the 1966 Conference on Environmental Studies of the Glacial Lake Agassiz Region* (Winnipeg, 1967), 271–98.
8. Ibid.; see also V.K. Prest, 'The Late Wisconsin Glacial Complex', in R.J. Fulton, ed., *A Canadian Contribution to IGCP Project 24*, Geological Survey of Canada, Paper 84–10 (1984), 21–36.
9. Olive Patricia Dickason, with David T. McNab, *Canada's First Nations: A History of Founding Peoples from Earliest Times*, 4th edn (Toronto, 2009), 51–2.
10. Ibid., xiv.
11. Margaret R. Conrad and James K. Hiller, *Atlantic Canada: A Region in the Making* (Toronto, 2001), 16.
12. Bruce Trigger, ed., *Handbook of North American Indians*, vol. 15, *Northeast* (Washington, 1978).
13. See Harris, ed., *Historical Atlas of Canada*, I, plates 2–8.
14. J.V. Wright, *The Ontario Iroquois Tradition* (Ottawa, 1966); Conrad Heidenreich, *Huronia: A History and Geography of the Huron Indians* (Toronto, 1971).
15. Bryan, *The Buffalo People*, 32–53, 81–4.
16. See Harris, ed., *Historical Atlas of Canada*, I, plates 2–8.
17. Dickason, with McNab, *Canada's First Nations*, 40.
18. Robert McGhee, *The People of the Arctic* (Vancouver, 1996).

2 CONTACTS AND ENCOUNTERS

1. Bruce Trigger, 'Early Native Responses to European Contact', *Journal of American History* 77, 4 (1991): 1195–1215.
2. Urs Bitterli, *Cultures in Conflict: Encounters between European and Non-European Cultures, 1492–1800*, trans. Richie Robertson (London, 1989).
3. The key work is Henry F. Dobyns, *Their Number Become Thinned: Native American Population Dynamics in Eastern*

North America (Knoxville, Tenn., 1983). But see also D. Ann Herring, 'Toward a Reconsideration of Disease and Contact in the Americas', *Prairie Forum* 17, 2 (1992): 153–66.

4. J.B. Waldram, D.A. Herring, and T.K. Young, 'Contact with Europeans and Infectious Diseases', in Waldram, Herring, and Young, *Aboriginal Health in Canada* (Toronto, 1995), 43–64.

5. Virginia P. Miller, 'Aboriginal Micmac Population: A Review of the Evidence', *Ethnohistory* 23, 2 (1976): 117–27.

6. V.P. Miller, 'The Decline of Nova Scotia Micmac Population', *Culture* 2, 3 (1982): 107–20.

7. I am indebted to James Axtell's 'Babel of Tongues: Communicating with the Indians', in his *Natives and Newcomers* (New York, 2000), 47–75, for the discussion that follows. But see also Stephen J. Greenblatt, *Marvellous Possessions: The Wonder of the New World* (Chicago, 1991), 86–118, and Robin Ridinton, 'Cultures in Conflict: The Problem of Discourse', in his *Little Bit Knowing Something* (Vancouver, 1991), 186–205.

8. June Helm, 'Matonabbee's Map', *Arctic Anthropology* 26, 3 (1989): 28–47.

9. *Dictionary of Canadian Biography* (*DCB*), IV, 523–4.

10. Richard Glover, ed., *A Journey from Prince of Wales's Fort in Hudson's Bay to the Northern Ocean 1769.1770.1771. 1772* (Toronto, 1958).

11. C.S. Mackinnon in *DCB*, IV, 339–42 at 340.

12. *DCB*, IV, 523.1.

13. Sylvia Van Kirk, *Many Tender Ties: Women in Fur-Trade Society, 1670–1870* (Winnipeg, 1980).

14. Emanuel J. Deschsel, '"Ha, Now Me Stomany That": A Summary of Pidgination and Creolization of North American Indian Languages', *International Journal of the Sociology of Language* 7 (1976): 63–81; Robert A. Hall, *Pidgin and Creole Languages* (Ithaca, NY, 1966).

15. Quoted in Peter Bakker, 'Two Basque Loanwords in Micmac', *International Journal of American Linguistics* 55 (1989): 259.

16. Marc Lescarbot, *The History of New France containing the voyages, discoveries, and settlements made by the French in the West Indies and New France . . . from one hundred years ago until now . . .* , trans. W.L. Grant, intro. H.P. Biggar, 3 vols (Toronto, 1907, 1911, 1914), II, 24.

17. John C. Crawford, 'What Is Michif? Language in the Métis Tradition', in Jacqueline Peterson and Jennifer S.H. Brown, eds, *The New Peoples: Being and Becoming Métis in North America* (Winnipeg, 1985).

18. Deanna Christensen, *Ahtahkakoop: The Epic Account of a Plains Cree Head Chief, His People, and Their Struggle for Survival 1816–1896* (Shell Lake, Sask., 2000), 230.

19. Patricia Seed, *Ceremonies of Possession in Europe's Conquest of the New World, 1492–1640* (Cambridge, 1995), 9, 31.

20. Ibid., 41–68.

21. Timothy Foote, 'Where Columbus Was Coming From', *Smithsonian Magazine* (Dec. 1991): 32.

22. Father Pierre Biard, in Reuben Gold Thwaites, ed., *The Jesuit Relations and Allied Documents: Travels and Explorations, 1610–1791*, 73 vols (Cleveland, 1896–1901), I, 173.

23. Peter Moogk, *La Nouvelle France: The Making of French Canada—A Cultural History* (East Lansing, Mich., 2000), 25–7.

24. Joyce Marshall, ed., *Word from New France: The Selected Letters of Marie de l'Incarnation* (Toronto, 1967), 341.

25. Chrestien Le Clercq, quoted by Cornelius Jaenen in 'The Indian Problem in Canadian History', in J.M. Bumsted, ed., *Documentary Problems in Canadian History*, 2 vols (Georgetown, Ont., 1969), I, 21.

26. Moogk, *La Nouvelle France*.

27. Brian J. Given, *A Most Pernicious Thing: Gun Trading and Native Warfare in the Early Contact Period* (Ottawa, 1994).

28. See Arthur Ray and Donald Freeman, *'Give Us Good Measure': An Economic Analysis of Relations between the Indians and the Hudson's Bay Company before 1763* (Toronto, 1978).

29. Patricia Seed, 'Taking Possession and Reading Texts: Establishing the Authority of Overseas Empires', *William and Mary Quarterly* 3rd ser., 49, 2 (1992): 183–209.

30. Francis Jennings, *Ambiguous Empire: The Covenant Chain Confederation of Iroquois and Allied Tribes with English Colonies from its Beginnings to the Lancaster Treaty of 1744* (New York, 1984).

31. In 1750 the British Parliament passed an Act for Regulating the Commencement of the Year, and for Correcting the Calendar Now in Use, which switched the system of days in Britain and its colonies from the Julian calendar to the Gregorian calendar on 1 January 1752. Before this time, the English system of days was unreformed, following the Julian calendar. The first day of the year was 25 March, and so February fell in 1703 by the Julian calendar and in 1704 by the reformed Gregorian one. Hence, dates here and throughout, shown as, e.g., 1703/4, indicate the Julian/Gregorian years for particular events that occurred in the 1 January–24 March period.

32. James Axtell, 'The Scholastic Philosophy of the Wilderness', *William and Mary Quarterly* (1973), and his *Natives and Newcomers: The Cultural Origins of North America* (New York, 2001), 189–213.

33. Quoted in Axtell, *Natives and Newcomers*, 213.

34. See the discussion of captivity in John Demos, *The Unredeemed Captive: A Family Story from Early America* (New York, 1995).

35. Calvin Martin, *Keepers of the Game: Indian–Animal Relationships and the Fur Trade* (Berkeley, 1978).

36. Anna Rooth, 'The Creation Myths of the North American Indians', *Anthropos* 52 (1957): 497–508.

37. Franz Boas, 'Mythology and Folk-Tales of the North American Indians', in his *Race, Language and Culture* (New York, 1940), 451–90; Alan Dundes, *The Morphology of North American Indian Folktales* (Helsinki, 1964).

38. Ella Elizabeth Clark, ed., *Indian Legends of Canada* (Toronto, 1950), 150–1.

3 EARLY EUROPEAN APPROACHES

1. See, for example, Farley Mowat, *Westviking* (Toronto, 1965).

2. Gwyn Jones, 'The First Europeans in America', in J.M. Bumsted, ed., *Interpreting Canada's Past*, 2 vols (Toronto, 1993), I, 2–19.

3. Gwyn Jones, *The Norse Atlantic Saga: Being the Norse Voyages of Discovery and Settlement to Iceland, Greenland, America* (London, 1964); Gwyn Jones, trans., *Eirik the Red, and other Icelandic Sagas* (Toronto, 1995); Kirsten A. Seaver, *The Frozen Echo: Greenland and the Exploration of North America, ca. A.D. 1000–1500* (Stanford, Calif., 1996); Jane Smiley, ed., *The Sagas of Icelanders* (New York, 2000).

4. William W. Fitzhugh and Elisabeth I. Ward, *Vikings: The North Atlantic Saga* (Washington and London, 2000).

5. T.J. Oleson, *Early Voyages and Northern Approaches 1000–1632* (Toronto, 1963).

6. Fitzhugh and Ward, *Vikings*, 266–8.

7. R.A. Skelton et al., *The Vinland Map and the Tartar Relation* (New Haven, 1965); Robert McGhee, 'The Vinland Map: Hoax or History?' *The Beaver* 67, 2 (Apr.–May 1987): 37–44, reprinted in Bumsted, ed., *Interpreting*, I, 20–30.

8. Peter Firstbrook, *The Voyage of the Matthew: John Cabot and the Discovery of North America* (Toronto, 1997), 44.

9. Evan Jones, 'Bristol and Newfoundland 1490–1570', in Iona Bulgin, ed., *Cabot and His World* (St John's, 1997), 72–81.

10. See plans in Firstbrook, *Voyage of the Matthew*, 66–7.

11. Bulgin, ed., *Cabot and His World*, 85–111; Peter E. Pope, *The Many Landfalls of John Cabot* (Toronto, 1997).

12. J.A. Williamson, ed., *The Cabot Voyages and Bristol Discovery Under Henry VII* (Cambridge, 1962), 128.

13. D.B. Quinn, ed., *New American World: A Documentary History of North America to 1612*, vol. 1 (New York, 1979), 180.

14. E.G.R. Taylor, 'Master Hore's Voyage of 1536', *Geographical Journal* 77 (1933): 469–70; *DCB*, I, 371–2.

15. Quoted in Lawrence Wroth, *The Voyages of Giovanni da Verrazzano 1524–1528* (New Haven, 1970), 142.

16. Quoted in *DCB*, I, 165.

17. H.P. Biggar, ed., *The Voyages of Jacques Cartier* (Ottawa, 1924), 65.

18. Ibid.,106–7.

19. Ibid., 169–71; James Pendergast and Bruce G. Trigger, *Cartier's Hochelaga and the Dawson Site* (Montreal and London, 1972).

20. J.E. King, 'The Glorious Kingdom of Saguenay', *Canadian Historical Review* 31 (1950): 390–400.

21. H.P. Biggar, ed., 'A Collection of Documents Relating to Jacques Cartier and the Sieur de Roberval', *Publications of the Public Archives of Canada* 14 (1930).

22. Biggar, *Voyages of Jacques Cartier*, 264–5.

23. André Thevet, *Cosmographie Universelle* (Paris, 1558), cited in *DCB*, I, 423.

24. D.B. Quinn, 'Columbus and the North: England, Iceland, and Ireland', *William and Mary Quarterly* 3rd ser., 44, 2 (1992): 278–97; Olaf Uwe Janzen, 'The European Presence in Newfoundland, 1500–1604', in Bulgin, ed., *Cabot and His World*, 129–38.

25. Robert McGhee, *The Arctic Voyages of Martin Frobisher: An Elizabethan Adventure* (Montreal and Kingston, 2001).

26. Ian Friel, 'Frobisher's Ships: The Ships of the North-Western Atlantic Voyages, 1576–1578', in T.H.B Symons, ed., *Meta Incognita—A Discourse of Discovery: Martin Frobisher's Arctic Expeditions, 1576–1578*, 2 vols (Hull, Que.: Canadian Museum of Civilization, 1999), 299–352.

27. Quoted in *DCB*, I, 317.

28. Vilhjalmur Stefansson, ed., *The Three Voyages of Martin Frobisher in Search of a Passage to Cathay and India . . .* (London, 1938), I, cvi.

29. Kirsten A. Seaver, 'How Strange Is a Stranger? A Survey of Opportunities for Inuit–European Contact in the Davis Strait before 1576', in Symons, ed., *Meta Incognita*, 523–52.

30. *DCB*, I, 317.

31. Ibid.

32. Robert Baldwin, 'Speculative Ambitions and the Reputations of Frobisher's Metallurgists', and Bernard Allaire, 'Methods of Assaying Ore and Their Application in the Frobisher Ventures', in Symons, ed., *Meta Incognita*, 401–504.

33. Daniel Francis, *Discovery of the North: The Exploration of Canada's Arctic* (Edmonton, 1986); L. Neatby, *In Quest of the Northwest Passage* (New York, 1958).

4 THE ATLANTIC REGION TO 1670

1. Calvert to Charles I, 19 Aug. 1629, reprinted in Gillian Cell, ed., *Newfoundland Discovered: English Attempts at Colonisation, 1610–1630* (London, 1982), 295–6.

2. James I of England was also James VI of Scotland.

3. Cell, *Newfoundland Discovered*, 96.

4. Quoted in D.B. Quinn, *England and the Discovery of*

America, 1481–1620 (New York, 1972), 347.

5. *DCB*, I, 390–2.

6. Luca Codignola, *The Coldest Harbour of the Land: Simon Stock and Lord Baltimore's Colony in Newfoundland, 1621–49* (Montreal and Kingston, 1988).

7. *DCB*, I, 421.

8. Quoted in Christopher Hibbert, *The English: A Social History 1066–1945* (London, 1987), 183–4.

9. William Vaughan, *The Golden Fleece* (London, 1626), the third part, 14, 9.

10. Gillian Cell, *English Enterprise in Newfoundland 1577–1660* (Toronto, 1969), 83–5.

11. G.P. Insh, *Scottish Colonial Schemes, 1620–1686* (Glasgow, 1922); John Reid, *Acadia, Maine, and New Scotland: Marginal Colonies in the Seventeenth Century* (Toronto, 1981), 21–40.

12. Quinn, *England and the Discovery of America*, 317.

13. G.C. Moore-Smith, 'Robert Hayman and the Plantation in Newfoundland', *English Historical Review* 33 (1918): 21–36.

14. Peter Edward Pope, 'The South Avalon Planters, 1630 to 1700: Residence, Labour, Demand and Exchange in Seventeenth-Century Newfoundland', Ph.D. dissertation, Memorial University of Newfoundland, 1992.

15. In general, see Reid, *Acadia, Maine, and New Scotland*.

16. *DCB*, I, 422.

17. Marcel Trudel, *The Beginnings of New France, 1524–1665* (Toronto, 1973), 68.

18. Marc Lescarbot, *Nova Francia: A Description of Acadia, 1606*, translated by P. Eronelle, 1609, with an introduction by H.P. Biggar (London, 1928), 90, 43. This is a contemporary translation of the Acadian part of Lescarbot's *Histoire de la Nouvelle France* (Paris, 1609).

19. See also Elizabeth Jones, *Gentlemen and Jesuits: Quests for Glory and Adventure in the Early Days of New France* (Toronto, 1986).

20. See M.A. MacDonald, *Fortune & La Tour: The Civil War in Acadia* (Toronto, 1983).

21. Naomi Griffiths and John Reid, eds, 'New Evidence on New Scotland', *William and Mary Quarterly* 3rd ser., 48 (1991): 502–7.

22. *DCB*, I, 597.

23. Nicholas Denys, *The Description and Natural History of the Coasts of North America* (Toronto, 1908), 136–7. (A translation of the second volume [*Histoire naturelle des peuples . . . de l'Amérique Septentrionale*] of his two-volume account of Acadia published in 1672.)

24. *DCB*, I, 383; see also MacDonald, *Fortune & La Tour*.

25. *DCB*, I, 514.

5 CANADA TO 1663

1. Quoted in W.I. Grant, ed., *Voyages of Samuel de Champlain: 1604–1618* (Toronto, 1907), 131.

2. The word 'Quebec' comes from the Algonquian word meaning 'where the river narrows', and first appeared on a French map in 1601.

3. Quoted in Grant, ed, *Voyages*, 136.

4. Quoted ibid., 165.

5. *DCB*, I, 367–8.

6. Marcel Trudel, *The Beginnings of New France, 1524–1663*, trans. Patricia Claxton (Toronto, 1973), 118–81.

7. Quoted in Edna Kenton, ed., *The Jesuit Relations and Allied Documents: Travels and Explorations of the Jesuit Missionaries in North America (1610–1791)* (New York, 1954), 23. A recent selection of the Jesuit letters is available in Allan Greer, ed., *The Jesuit Relations: Natives and Missionaries in Seventeenth-Century North America* (Boston and New York, 2000).

8. H.P. Biggar, ed., *The Works of Samuel de Champlain* (Toronto, 1922–3), vol. VI, Appendix VII, 378–9; translation.

9. Quoted in *DCB*, I, 330. A league was a variable measure, usually about 5 kilometres.

10. *DCB*, I, 517.

11. The name 'Canada' comes from the Iroquoian word 'kanata', meaning a village. It was used by Cartier's Native guides in 1535 to refer to Stadacona and gradually extended to refer to all of the country along the St Lawrence. But as many contemporaries emphasized, Canada was not synonymous with New France, which included all the French possessions in North America.

12. David Hackett Fischer, *Champlain's Dream* (New York, 2008).

13. Quoted in Karen Anderson, *'Chain Her by One Foot': The Subjugation of Women in Seventeenth-century New France* (London and New York, 1991).

14. Thwaites, ed., *Jesuit Relations*, XXII, 183–5.

15. Peter Goddard, 'The Devil in New France: Jesuit Demonology, 1611–1650', *Canadian Historical Review* 78 (1997): 40–62.

16. Mary Anne Foley, '*La vie voyagère* for Women: Moving beyond the Cloister in Seventeenth-Century New France', *CCHA Historical Studies* 63 (1997): 15–28.

17. François Dollier de Casson, *A History of Montreal, 1640–1672*, trans. and ed. Ralph Flenley (1928), 99.

18. Kenton, ed., *Jesuit Relations and Allied Documents*, 181.

19. Quoted in Carole Blackburn, *Harvest of Souls: The Jesuit Missions and Colonialism in North America, 1632–1650* (Montreal and Kingston, 2000), 118.

20. Dollier de Casson, *History of Montreal*, 155.

21. See Cornelius J. Jaenen, *Friend and Foe: Aspects of French–Amerindian Cultural Contact in the Sixteenth and Seventeenth Centuries* (Toronto, 1976); Bruce Trigger, *The Children of Aataentsic: A History of the Huron People to 1660*, 2 vols (Montreal, 1976); Denys Delâge, *Bitter Feast: Amerindians and Europeans in Northeastern North America, 1600–64*, trans. Jane Brierley (Vancouver, 1993).

22. Quoted in Anderson, *'Chain Her by One Foot'*, 124.

23. Reuben Gold Thwaites, ed., *The Jesuit Relations and Allied Documents* (Cleveland, 1896–1901), X (1636), 93–5.

24. *DCB*, I, 349.

25. *DCB*, I, 266–75.

26. Quoted in Leslie Choquette, 'Ces Amazones du Grand Dieu: Women and Mission in Seventeenth-Century Canada', *French Historical Studies* 17, 3 (1992): 627–55.

27. Nadia Fahmy-Eid, 'The Education of Girls by the Ursulines of Quebec during the French Regime', in Wendy Mitchinson et al., eds, *Canadian Women: A Reader* (Toronto, 1996), 38; see also p. 34 above. For an analysis of Marie that emphasizes her inability to escape her European background and assumptions, see Natalie Zemon Davis, *Women on the Margins: Three Seventeenth-Century Lives* (Cambridge and London, 1995), 63–139.

28. Quoted in *DCB*, I, 357.

29. Patricia Simpson, *Marguerite Bourgeoys and Montreal, 1640–1665* (Montreal and Kingston, 1997).

30. Elizabeth Rapley, *The Dévotes: Women and Church in Seventeenth-Century France* (Montreal and Kingston, 1990).

31. See 'Jansenism' and 'Jansenist Piety' in *New Catholic Encyclopedia* (New York, 1967), 7, 820–6.

32. Quoted in *DCB*, I, 131.

33. Arthur T. Adams, ed., *The Explorations of Pierre Esprit Radisson: From the Original Manuscript in the Bodleian Library and the British Museum* (Minneapolis, 1961).

34. Ibid., 39.

35. Ibid., 75.

36. Pierre Hurtubise, 'Jansenism, Gallicanism, Ultramontanism: The Case of François de Laval', in J.M. Bumsted, ed., *Canadian History before Confederation: Essays and Interpretations*, 2nd edn (Georgetown, Ont., 1979), 61–76.

37. *DCB*, I, 487.

38. Joyce Marshall, *Word from New France: The Selected Letters of Marie de l'Incarnation* (Toronto, 1967), 259.

39. Ibid., 265. For a further discussion of witchcraft and related matters in New France, see R.L. Séguin, *La Sorcellerie au Québec du XVIIe siècle* (Montreal, 1971). The French background is treated in Robin Briggs, *Communities of Belief: Cultural and Social Tension in Early Modern France* (Oxford, 1989).

40. Ibid., 288–9.

41. Yves Landry, *Orphelines en France pionnières au Canada: Les Filles du roi au XVIIe siècle* (Montreal, 1992).

42. Ibid., 214.

43. Quoted in W.J. Eccles, *Canada Under Louis XIV 1663–1701* (Toronto, 1964), 4.

6 CANADA 1663–1763: GOVERNMENT, MILITARY, ECONOMY

1. The English translation by J.R. Forster, *Travels into North America . . .* , 3 vols (Warrington, UK, and London, 1770–1), was republished with additional material as Adolph B. Benson, ed., *The America of 1750: Peter Kalm's Travels in North America*, 2 vols (New York, 1927), which was reprinted by Dover, 2 vols (New York, 1966).

2. François Furet, *Revolutionary France, 1770–1880*, trans. Antonia Nevill (Oxford, 1991), 3–14.

3. Yves Zolvanty, ed., *The Government of New France: Royal, Clerical, or Class Rule?* (Toronto, 1971); Terence Crowley, '"Thunder Gusts": Popular Disturbances in Early French Canada', *Canadian Historical Association Historical Papers* (1979): 11–31.

4. Order of the Bishop of Quebec, Ville Marie, 26 Apr. 1719, Library and Archives Canada (LAC), Robinson Collection, II, 34, translated and quoted by Cameron Nish and Pierre Harvey, eds, *The Social Structures of New France* (Toronto, 1968), 16.

5. Quote in Peter Moogk, *La Nouvelle France: The Making of French Canada* (East Lansing, Mich., 2000), 210.

6. Cornelius J. Jaenen, *The Role of the Church in New France* (Toronto, 1976); W.J. Eccles, 'The Role of the Church in New France', in Eccles, *Essays on New France* (Toronto, 1987), 26–37.

7. Jack Verney, *The Good Regiment: The Carignan-Salières Regiment in Canada, 1665–1668* (Montreal and Kingston, 1997).

8. Quoted in W.J. Eccles, 'The Social, Economic, and Political Significance of the Military Establishment in New France', in Eccles, *Essays on New France*, 111.

9. Baron de Lahontan, *Mémoires de l'Amérique septentrionale* (1703), quoted in J.M. Bumsted, ed., *Documentary Problems in Canadian History*, I (Georgetown, Ont., 1969), 45.

10. Ibid.

11. Ibid.

12. Quoted in Eccles, *Essays on New France*, 114.

13. Quoted in Bumsted, ed., *Documentary Problems*, I, 48.

14. Quoted in W.J. Eccles, *The Canadian Frontier 1534–1760*, rev. edn (Albuquerque, 1983), 104.

15. Ibid., 105.

16. Louise Dechêne, 'L'Évolution du régime seigneurial au Canada: le cas de Montréal aux XVIIe et XVIIIe siècles', *Recherches Sociographiques* 12, 2 (1971): 143–83. See also Sylvie Dépatie et al., *Contributions à l'étude du régime seigneurial canadien* (Ville La Salle, 1987).

17. Catherine Desbarats, 'Agriculture within the Seigneurial Régime of Eighteenth-Century Canada: Some Thoughts on the Recent Literature', *Canadian Historical Review* 73 (1992): 2–29.

18. R. Cole Harris, *The Seigneurial System in Early Canada: A Geographical Study* (Toronto, 1966); Marcel Trudel, *The Seigneurial Regime* (Ottawa, 1963); Morris Altman, 'Seigniorial Tenure in New France, 1688–1739: An Essay on Income Distribution and Retarded Economic

Development', *Historical Reflections* 10 (Fall 1983): 334–75.

19. Cameron Nish, *Les Bourgeois-gentilhommes de la Nouvelle-France, 1729–1748* (Montreal, 1968).

20. See the entries on Boucault and Charly Saint-Ange in *DCB*, III.

21. J.F. Bosher, *The Canada Merchants, 1713–1763* (Oxford, 1987); Kathryn Young, *Kin, Commerce, Continuity: Merchants in the Port of Quebec, 1717–1745* (New York, 1995); Dale Miquelon, *New France, 1701–1744: A Supplement to Europe* (Toronto, 1987).

22. Adam Shortt, *Canadian Currency and Exchange under French Rule* (Montreal, 1974).

23. Jacques Mathieu, *La Construction navale royale à Québec, 1739–1759* (Quebec, 1971); Albert Tessier, *Les Forges du Saint-Maurice, 1729–1883* (Trois Rivières, Que., 1952).

24. *DCB*, IV, 471–3.

25. Allan Greer, *Peasant, Lord, and Merchant: Rural Society in Three Quebec Parishes 1740–1840* (Toronto, 1985).

26. Hubert Charbonneau et al., 'Le Comportement démographique des voyageurs sous le régime français', *Histoire Sociale/Social History* 21 (1978): 120–33.

7   CANADA 1663–1763: POPULATION, SOCIETY, CULTURE

1. Quoted in H.A. Innis, *The Cod Fisheries: The History of an International Economy* (Toronto, 1940), 136–7.

2. R.C. Harris, 'The Extension of France into Rural Canada', in J.R. Gibson, ed., *European Settlement and Development in North America* (Toronto, 1978).

3. Leslie Choquette, *Frenchmen into Peasants: Modernity and Tradition in the Peopling of French Canada* (Cambridge, Mass. 1997), 21.

4. Peter Moogk, 'Reluctant Exiles: Emigrants from France in Canada before 1760', *William and Mary Quarterly* 3rd ser., 46, 3 (July 1989): 463–505.

5. Quoted in Allan Greer, *The People of New France* (Toronto, 1997), 13.

6. E.B. Greene, *American Population before the Federal Census of 1790* (New York, 1932).

7. Yves Landry, *Orphelines en France pionnières au Canada: Les Filles du roi au XVIIe siècle* (Montreal, 1992).

8. Quoted in Hubert Charbonneau et al., *The First French-Canadians: Pioneers in the St. Lawrence Valley* (Newark, Del., 1993), 24.

9. Greer, *People of New France*, 87–8.

10. Adolph B. Benson, ed., *The America of 1750: Peter Kalm's Travels in North America*, 2 vols (New York, 1927, 1966), II, 416–17.

11. Alison Prentice et al., *Canadian Women: A History* (Toronto, 1988), 41–64; Le Collectif Clio, *L'Histoire des femmes au Québec depuis quatre siècles* (Montreal, 1992), 19–145.

12. Jacques Henripin, *La Population canadienne au début de*

XVIIIe siècle (Paris, 1954).

13. Quoted in J.M. Bumsted, ed., *Documentary Problems in Canadian History*, I (Toronto, 1969), 23.

14. Jan Grabowski, 'French Criminal Justice and Indians in Montreal, 1670–1760', *Ethnohistory* 43, 3 (Summer 1996): 406–29.

15. Greer, *The People of New France*, 87–8.

16. 'Mémoire on the Present State of Canada Attributed to Bougainville, 1757', trans. Cameron Nish and Pierre Harvey in their *The Social Structures of New France* (Toronto, 1968), 76.

17. Quoted ibid., 75.

18. Benson, ed., *America of 1750*, II, 554.

19. R. Cole Harris, 'The French Background of Immigrants to Canada before 1700', in J.M. Bumsted, ed., *Interpreting Canada's Past*, vol. 1: *Pre-Confederation*, rev. edn (Toronto, 1993), 108–21.

20. Philippe Barbaud, 'Retour sur l'énigme de la francisation des premiers Canadiens: Le Choc des patois en Nouvelle-France', in *APART: Papers From the 1984 Ottawa Conference on Language, Culture and Literary Identity in Canada*, in *Canadian Literature* (suppl. 1) (May 1987): 51–7.

21. Luc Chartrand et al., *Histoire des sciences au Québec* (Montreal, 1978).

22. I.K. Steele, *The English Atlantic, Sixteen Seventy Five to Seventeen Forty: An Explanation of Connection and Community* (New York, 1986).

23. Quoted in Helmut Kallmann, *A History of Music in Canada 1534–1914* (Toronto, 1960; rep. 1987), 12.

24. Ibid., 84–5.

25. Dennis Reid, *A Concise History of Canadian Painting*, 2nd edn (Toronto, 1988), 11.

26. Benson, ed., *America of 1750*, II, 448.

27. Harold Kalman, *A History of Canadian Architecture*, 2 vols (Toronto, 1994), I, 63–4.

28. Ibid., 72.

29. Marius Barbeau, *Jongleur Songs of Old Quebec* (Toronto, 1962).

30. Loris Russell, *Everyday Life in Colonial Canada* (London, 1973), 126.

31. Diana de Marly, *Dress in North America*, vol. 1: *The 'New World', 1492–1800* (New York and London, 1990), 61–84.

32. Kalman, *History of Canadian Architecture*, 40.

33. Benson, ed., *America of 1750*, II, 460.

34. Jean Palardy, *The Early Furniture of French Canada* (Toronto, 1965).

35. Jay A. Anderson, 'The Early Development of French-Canadian Foodways', in Edith Fowke, ed., *Folklore of Canada* (Toronto, 1976), 91–9; Jean-François Blanchette, *The Role of Artifacts in the Study of Foodways in New France, 1720–60* (Ottawa, 1981).

36. Anderson, 'Early Development', 95.

37. Benson, ed., *America of 1750*, II, 511.

8   THE PERIPHERIES OF THE EMPIRES, 1670–1760

1. N. Dièreville, *Relations of the Voyage to Port Royal in Acadia or New France*, trans. Alice Webster, ed. with notes by J.C. Webster (Toronto, 1933), 95; A.H. Clark, *Acadia: The Geography of Early Nova Scotia* (Madison, 1968).

2. Dièreville, *Relations*, 66.

3. Ibid., 183–4.

4. See Naomi E.S. Griffiths, *The Contexts of Acadian History 1686–1784* (Montreal and Kingston, 1992); Jean Daigle, *Acadia of the Maritimes: Thematic Studies from the Beginning to the Present* (Moncton, NB, 1995).

5. Quoted in *DCB*, III, 566.

6. D.C. Harvey, *The French Regime in Prince Edward Island* (New Haven, 1926).

7. Earle Lockerby, 'Colonization of Île St-Jean: Charting Today's Evangeline Region', *The Island Magazine* 47 (Spring–Summer 2000): 20–30.

8. A.J.B. Johnston, *Control and Order in French Colonial Louisbourg, 1713–1758* (East Lansing, Mich., 2001); Eric Krause et al., *Aspects of Louisbourg: Essays in the History of an Eighteenth-Century French Community in North America* (Sydney, NS, 1995).

9. Quoted in J.B. Brebner, *New England's Outpost: Acadia before the Conquest of Canada* (New York, 1927), 86 ff. See also Griffiths, *Contexts of Acadian History*, 33–61.

10. 'Representation of the State of His Majesty's Province of Nova Scotia', 8 Nov. 1745, LAC, A27.

11. Quoted in Brebner, *New England's Outpost*, 187.

12. George T. Bates, 'The Great Exodus of 1749 or the Cornwallis Settlers Who Didn't', *Collections of the Nova Scotia Historical Society* 38 (1973), 27–62.

13. Quoted in W. Bell, *The 'Foreign Protestants' and the Settlement of Nova Scotia: The History of a Piece of Arrested British Colonial Policy in the Eighteenth Century* (Toronto, 1961), 344n.

14. Ibid., 109n.

15. Ibid., 436–7.

16. Ibid., 417–42, especially 435.

17. C. Grant Head, *Eighteenth-Century Newfoundland: A Geographer's Perspective* (Toronto, 1976), 73.

18. Ibid.

19. Ibid., 76–7.

20. Quoted in J.B. Brebner, *The Explorers of North America, 1492–1806* (London and New York, 1933), 200.

21. *DCB*, I, 394.

22. Pierre Margory, ed., *Découvertes et Etablissements des Français dans l'ouest et dans le Sud de L'Amérique Septentrionale* (Paris, 1879–88), II, 181–5.

23. Quoted from the historian Charlevoix in *DCB*, I, 183.

24. Francis Parkman, *La Salle and the Discovery of the Great West*, rev. edn (Boston, 1891).

25. Richard White, *The Middle Ground: Indians, Empires, and Republics in the Great Lakes Region, 1650–1815* (Cambridge, 1991).

26. Gilles Havard, *The Great Peace of Montreal of 1701: French–Native Diplomacy in the Seventeenth Century*, trans. Phyllis Aronoff and Howard Scott (Montreal and Kingston, 2001).

27. Catherine M. Desbarats, 'The Cost of Early Canada's Native Alliances: Reality and Scarcity's Rhetoric', *William and Mary Quarterly* 3rd ser., 52, 4 (Oct. 1995): 609–30.

28. Quoted in White, *The Middle Ground*, 176.

29. Natalie Maree Belting, *Kaskaskia under the French Regime* (Urbana, Ill., 1948), 39.

30. *DCB*, I, 80–4.

31. Quoted in Sylvia Van Kirk, *'Many Tender Ties': Women in Fur-Trade Society, 1670–1870* (Winnipeg, 1980), 70. See also *DCB*, II, 627–3.

32. Arthur J. Ray and Donald Freeman, *'Give Us Good Measure': An Economic Analysis of Relations between the Indians and the Hudson's Bay Company before 1763* (Toronto, 1978).

33. L.J. Burpee, ed., *Journals and Letters of Pierre Gaultier de Varennes de la Vérendrye* (Toronto, 1927), 54.

34. Ibid., 85.

35. Compare, for example, E.E. Rich, *The Fur Trade and the Northwest to 1857* (Toronto, 1967), 82–95, and Nellis M. Crouse, *La Verendrye: Fur Trader and Explorer* (Toronto, 1956).

9   A CENTURY OF CONFLICT, 1660–1760

1. By about 1720, the Five Nations had been joined by the Tuscaroras, who had fled north from the Carolinas to escape further conflict with the colonists there, and thereafter the Iroquois Confederacy became the League of Six Nations. See Olive Patricia Dickason, with David T. McNab, *Canada's First Nations: A History of Founding Peoples from Earliest Times*, 4th edn (Toronto, 2009), 129.

2. *DCB*, II, 400.

3. The best modern biographies are Nellis Crouse, *Le Moyne d'Iberville: Soldier of New France* (Ithaca, NY, 1954), and Guy Frégault, *Iberville le conquérant* (Montreal, 1944).

4. See, for example, Peter Edward Pope, 'The South Avalon Planters, 1630 to 1700: Residence, Labour, Demand and Exchange in Seventeenth-Century Newfoundland', Ph.D. dissertation (Memorial University of Newfoundland, 1992).

5. See John Demos, *The Unredeemed Captive: A Family Story from Early America* (New York, 1994).

6. Ibid.

7. John Winthrop to Fitz-John Winthrop, Boston, 1707,

Collections of the Massachusetts Historical Society 6th ser., 3 (1889): 387–8.

8. Gerald S. Graham, ed., *The Walker Expedition to Quebec, 1711* (London, 1953).

9. Quoted in Ian Steele, *Guerillas and Grenadiers: The Struggle for Canada, 1689–1760* (Toronto, 1969), 41.

10. G.M. Wrong, ed., *Louisbourg in 1745: The Anonymous Lettre d'un Habitant de Louisbourg* (New York, 1897), 15.

11. Quoted in John A. Schutz, *William Shirley* (Boston, 1961), 101.

12. Quoted in George Rawlyk, *Yankees at Louisbourg* (Orono, Maine, 1967), 154, 156.

13. James Pritchard, *Anatomy of a Naval Disaster: The 1746 French Naval Expedition to North America* (Montreal and Kingston, 1995).

14. The Duke of Bedford to Mr. Stone, 10 Nov. 1746, British Library Additional Manuscripts 32713, 426–7.

15. Pritchard, *Anatomy*, 225.

16. John Brenner, 'Canadian Policy towards the Acadians in 1751', *Canadian Historical Review* 12 (1931): 284–7.

17. Max Savelle, *The Origins of American Diplomacy: The International History of Anglo-America, 1492–1763* (New York, 1967), 373–86.

18. Most of the documents in the Acadian affair, including the minutes of this meeting, were published by Thomas B. Akins in *Selections from the Public Documents of the Province of Nova Scotia* (Halifax, 1869).

19. Quoted in J.B. Brebner, *New England's Outpost: Acadia before the Conquest of Canada* (New York, 1927), 220.

20. Ibid., 222.

21. 'Journals of Colonel John Winslow', *Collections of the Nova Scotia Historical Society* 4 (1883): 113–246.

22. The latest detailed survey of this war, clocking in at 861 pages and written from an American perspective, is Fred Anderson, *Crucible of War: The Seven Years' War and the Fate of Empire in British North America: 1754–1766* (New York, 2001). But see also Frank W. Brecher, *Losing a Continent: France's North American Policy, 1753–1763* (Westport, Conn., 1998); Francis Jennings, *Empire of Fortune: Crown, Colonies, and Tribes in the Seven Years War in America* (New York, 1988), which tells the story from the Aboriginal perspective; and Seymour I. Schwartz, *The French and Indian War 1754–1763: The Imperial Struggle for North America* (New York, 1994), which is copiously illustrated.

23. See, for example, Ian Steele, *Betrayals: Fort William Henry and the 'Massacre'* (Toronto, 1993).

24. Earl Lockerby, 'Deportation of the Acadians from Île-St-Jean, 1758', *The Island Magazine* 46 (Fall/Winter 1999): 17–25; Lockerby, 'The Deportation of the Acadians from Île St-Jean, 1758', *Acadiensis* 27, 2 (Spring 1998): 45–94.

25. Quoted in Brebner, *New England's Outpost*, 135.

26. Quoted ibid., 257.

27. Kimberly Maynard Smith, 'Divorce in Nova Scotia 1700–1890', in Jim Phillips and James Girard, eds, *Essays in the History of Canadian Law*, vol. 3: *Nova Scotia* (Toronto, 1990), 232–71.

28. Quoted in C.P. Stacey, *Quebec, 1759: The Siege and the Battle* (Toronto, 1959), 134.

29. Ibid., 144–5.

30. Quoted in Gordon Donaldson, *Battle for a Continent: Quebec 1759* (Toronto, 1973), 89.

31. Quoted in Stacey, *Quebec, 1759*, 118.

10 Expansion and Contraction, 1760–1782

1. Verner W. Crane, ed., 'Hints Relative to the Division and Government of the Conquered and Newly Acquired Countries in America', *Mississippi Valley Historical Review* 8 (1922): 371.

2. Quoted in R.A. Humphreys, 'Lord Shelburne and the Proclamation of 1763', *English Historical Review* 41 (1934): 258–64.

3. Deposition of Martha Walker, 24 Dec. 1764, PRO CO 42/4, ff. 216–17.

4. Quoted in Hilda Neatby, *The Quebec Act: Protest and Policy* (Toronto, 1972), 38–9.

5. Ibid., 40.

6. Thomas Gage Papers, 5 July 1772, William Clements Library, University of Michigan.

7. Quoted in Richard White, *The Middle Ground: Indians, Empires and Republics in the Great Lakes Region, 1650–1815* (New York and Cambridge, 1991), 258.

8. Ibid.

9. Gregory Evans Dowd, *A Spirited Resistance: The North American Indian Struggle for Unity, 1745–1815* (Baltimore and London, 1992), 33–7; William R. Nester, '*Haughty Conquerors*': *Amherst and the Great Indian Uprising of 1763* (Westport, Conn., 2000), 36–8.

10. White, *The Middle Ground*, 307.

11. Quoted in George Stanley, *Canada Invaded, 1775–1776* (Toronto, 1977), 27.

12. Ibid., 29.

13. Quoted in Robert Hatch, *Thrust for Canada* (New York, 1979), 84, 85.

14. Quoted in Stanley, *Canada Invaded*, 103.

15. Quoted in Gwynne Dyer and Tina Viljoen, *The Defence of Canada: In the Arms of the Empire 1760–1939* (Toronto, 1990), 49.

16. Ibid., 50.

17. Quoted in Ernest A. Clarke, 'Cumberland Planters and the Aftermath of the Attack on Fort Cumberland', in Margaret Conrad, ed., *They Planted Well: New England Planters in Maritime Canada* (Fredericton, 1988), 49.

18. Ernest A. Clarke and Jim Phillips, 'Rebellion and Repression in Nova Scotia in the Era of the American Revolution', in F.M. Greenwood and Barry Wright, eds,

Canadian State Trials: Law, Politics, and Security Measures, 1608–1837 (Toronto, 1996), 172–220.

19. Ernest Clarke, *The Siege of Fort Cumberland: An Episode in the American Revolution* (Montreal and Kingston, 1996).

20. C. Grant Head, *Eighteenth-Century Newfoundland: A Geographer's Perspective* (Toronto, 1976), 197.

21. Ibid., 180.

22. John D. Barnhart, ed., *Henry Hamilton and George Rogers Clark in the American Revolution* (Crawfordsville, Ind., 1951); White, *The Middle Ground*, 366–412.

23. John Dunmore, *French Explorers in the Pacific*, 2 vols (Oxford, 1965–9).

24. Robin Fisher and J.M. Bumsted, eds, *An Account of a Voyage to the North West Coast of America in 1785 & 1786* (Vancouver and Toronto, n.d.).

11 LOYALTIES AND LOYALISTS, 1775–1791

1. *DCB*, V, 513–14.

2. Allan S. Everest, *Moses Hazen and the Canadian Refugees in the American Revolution* (Syracuse, 1976).

3. Harold A. Innis, ed., *The Diary of Simeon Perkins 1766–1780* (Toronto, 1948), 134.

4. Ibid., 145.

5. J.M. Bumsted, *Henry Alline 1748–1784* (Toronto, 1970), 38.

6. John Shy, *A People Numerous and Armed: Reflections on the Military Struggle for Independence* (New York, 1976).

7. Esther Clark Wright, *The Loyalists of New Brunswick* (Fredericton, 1950), 18–67; Neil MacKinnon, *The Loyalist Experience in Nova Scotia 1783–1791* (Kingston and Montreal, 1986), 16–26.

8. Quoted in Wright, *The Loyalists of New Brunswick*.

9. J. Eardley-Wilmot, *Historical View of the Commission for Enquiring into the Losses . . . of the American Loyalists* (London, 1815); L.F.S. Upton, 'The Mission of John Anstey', in Esmond Wright, ed., *Red, White and True Blue: The Loyalists in the Revolution* (New York, 1976), 135–48; Hugh Edward Egerton, ed., *The Royal Commission on the Losses and Services of American Loyalists 1783 to 1785* (New York, 1969).

10. Fred Landon, *Western Ontario and the American Frontier* (Toronto, 1967).

11. Jo-Ann Fellows, 'The Possibilities for Quantitatively-Oriented Research on the Loyalists in Canada', in Wright, ed., *Red, White and True Blue*, 169–74

12. Eugene Fingerhut, 'Use and Abuse of the American Loyalists' Claims: A Critique of Quantitative Analysis', *William and Mary Quarterly* 3rd ser., 25 (1968): 245–68.

13. Robert Allen, ed., *The Loyal Americans: The Military Role of the Loyalist Provincial Corps and Their Settlement in British North America, 1775–1784* (Ottawa, 1983).

14. Maria Susan Waltman, 'From Soldier to Settler: Patterns

of Loyalist Settlement in "Upper Canada", 1783–1785', MA thesis (Queen's University, 1981).

15. Hazel C. Mathews, *The Mark of Honour* (Toronto, 1967); Elua L. Lapp, *To Their Heirs Forever* (Belleville, Ont., 1977).

16. Waltman, 'From Soldier to Settler', 62.

17. Wallace Brown, *The King's Friends: The Composition and Motives of the American Loyalist Claimants* (Providence, RI, 1965), 287–344.

18. J.M. Bumsted, *Land, Settlement and Politics on Eighteenth-Century Prince Edward Island* (Montreal and Kingston, 1987), 98–120; MacKinnon, *This Unfriendly Soil: The Loyalist Experience in Nova Scotia 1783–1791* (Kingston, Ont., 1986), 53–66.

19. Mary Beth Norton, 'Eighteenth-Century American Women in Peace and War: The Case of the Loyalists', *William and Mary Quarterly* 3rd ser., 33 (1976): 386–409.

20. Waltman, 'From Soldier to Settler', 32.

21. William Nelson, *The American Tory* (Toronto, 1961).

22. James St.G. Walker, *The Black Loyalists: The Search for a Promised Land in Nova Scotia and Sierra Leone, 1783–1870*, rev. edn (Toronto, 1992); Ellen Gibson Wilson, *The Loyal Blacks* (New York, 1976).

23. Waltman, 'From Soldier to Settler', 32; Jim Hornby, *Black Islanders* (Charlottetown, PEI, 1991), 2–3.

24. Phyllis Blakeley and John Grant, eds, *Eleven Exiles: Accounts of Loyalists of the American Revolution* (Toronto, 1982), 272.

25. Harry Holman, 'Slaves and Servants on Prince Edward Island: The Case of Jupiter Wise', *Acadiensis* 12 (Autumn 1982): 100–4.

26. Norton, 'Eighteenth-Century American Women'.

27. Quoted in Mathews, *The Mark of Honour*, 112.

28. Janice Potter-Mackinnon, *While the Women Only Wept: Loyalist Refugee Women* (Montreal and Kingston, 1993), 144.

29. Quoted in J.M. Bumsted, *Understanding the Loyalists* (Sackville, NB, 1986), 34.

30. Brown, *The King's Friends*, 287–344.

31. Waltman, 'From Soldier to Settler', 61.

32. Ibid., 55.

33. Barbara Graymont, *The Iroquois in the American Revolution* (Syracuse, NY, 1972).

34. C.M. Johnston, ed., *The Valley of the Six Nations* (Toronto, 1964).

35. Brown, *The King's Friends*, 287–344.

36. Howard Temperly, 'Frontierism, Capitalism, and the American Loyalists in Canada', *Journal of American Studies* 13 (1979): 16.

37. Ann Condon, *The Envy of the American States: The Loyalist Dream for New Brunswick* (Fredericton, 1984).

38. Marion Robertson, *King's Bounty: A History of Early Shelburne, Nova Scotia* (Halifax, 1983); David G. Bell,

Early Loyalist Saint John (Fredericton, 1983); Larry Turner, *Voyage of a Different Kind: The Associated Loyalists of Kingston and Adolphustown* (Belleville, Ont., 1984).

39. Robert J. Morgan, 'The Loyalists of Cape Breton', *Dalhousie Review* 55 (1975): 5–23.

40. Quoted in W.S. MacNutt, 'The Narrative of Lieutenant James Moody', *Acadiensis* 1, 2 (Spring 1972): 72–90.

41. Sun Bok Kim, *Landlord and Tenant in Colonial New York: Manorial Society, 1664–1775* (Williamsburg, Va., 1978).

42. Temperley, 'Frontierism'.

43. *DCB*, V, 35.

44. Morton W. Bloomfield, 'Canadian English and Its Relation to Eighteenth-Century American Speech', *Journal of English and German Philology* 47 (1948): 59–67.

45. Peter Ennals and Deryk Holdsworth, 'Vernacular Architecture and the Colonial Landscape of the Maritime Provinces—A Reconnaissance', *Acadiensis* 10 (1981): 86–106.

46. Brian Lee Coffey, 'The Pioneer House in Southern Ontario, Canada: Constructional Material Use and Resultant Forms to 1850', Ph.D. dissertation (University of Oregon, 1982).

47. D.C. Harvey, ed., *Journeys to the Island of St. John* (Toronto, 1955), 97.

48. Gad Horowitz, *Canadian Labour in Politics* (Toronto, 1968).

12 COLONIAL POLITICS, WAR, AND REBELLION, 1791–1840

1. The originals of those files, collected in large leather-bound ledger volumes, are still to be found in the Public Record Office in London, where they may be consulted by researchers.

2. 'The Colonial Office and British North America, 1801–50', *DCB*, VIII (Toronto, 1985), xxiii–xxxvii.

3. C.P. Lucas, ed., *Lord Durham's Report on the Affairs of British North America* (Oxford, 1913).

4. *Quebec Gazette*, 5 July 1792, quoted in Jacques Monet, ed., 'Electoral Battles in French Canada, 1792–1848', in J.M. Bumsted, ed., *Documentary Problems in Canadian History* (Georgetown, Ont., 1969), I, 175.

5. Allan Greer, *The Patriots and the People: The Rebellion of 1837 in Rural Lower Canada* (Toronto, 1993), 200–20.

6. Rusty Bitterman, 'Women and the Escheat Movement: The Politics of Everyday Life on Prince Edward Island', in Janet Guildford and Suzanne Morton, eds, *Separate Spheres: Women's World in the 19th-Century Maritimes* (Fredericton, 1994), 23–38.

7. *DCB*, V, 347–57. All Glenie quotations are from this article.

8. Quoted in J.M. Bumsted, 'The Loyal Electors', *The Island Magazine* 8 (1980): 12.

9. Ibid.

10. Quoted in *DCB*, VI, 41–9. All Bédard quotations are from this article.

11. Gregory Evans Dowd, *A Spirited Resistance: The North American Indian Struggle for Unity, 1745–1815* (Baltimore, 1992); Robert S. Allen, *His Majesty's Indian Allies: British Indian Policy in the Defence of Canada, 1774–1815* (Toronto, 1992).

12. George Sheppard, *Plunder, Profit, and Paroles: A Social History of the War of 1812 in Upper Canada* (Montreal and Kingston, 1994).

13. Paul Romney and Barry Wright, 'State Trials and Security Proceedings in Upper Canada during the War of 1812', in F.M. Greenwood and Wright, eds, *Canadian State Trials: Law, Politics, and Security Measures, 1608–1837* (Toronto, 1996), 379–405.

14. David Mills, *The Idea of Loyalty in Upper Canada 1784–1850* (Montreal and Kingston, 1988).

15. Quoted in Allen, *His Majesty's Indian Allies*, 169.

16. S.F. Wise, 'The Origins of Anti-Americanism in Canada', Fourth Seminar on Canadian–American Relations at Assumption University of Windsor, 1962.

17. Quoted in *DCB*, V, 347–57.

18. See J.M. Bumsted, *Lord Selkirk: A Life* (Winnipeg, 2008).

19. English culture was confined to England, while British culture encompassed all parts of the British Isles.

20. Paul Romney, 'Re-Inventing Upper Canada: American Immigrants, Upper Canadian History, English Law, and the Alien Question', in Roger Hall et al., eds, *Patterns of the Past: Interpreting Ontario's History* (Toronto, 1988).

21. Quoted in *DCB*, VII, 40.

22. Quoted in Gerald M. Craig, *Upper Canada: The Formative Years 1784–1841* (Toronto, 1963), 205.

23. Quoted in David Flint, *William Lyon Mackenzie: Rebel against Authority* (Toronto, 1971), 78.

24. Quoted in Craig, *Upper Canada*, 219.

25. Quoted in *DCB*, X, 573.

26. The phrase, from September 1830, is Mackenzie's. But the idea of responsible government was first articulated in 1828, in letters written to colonial authorities by William Warren Baldwin, influenced by his son Robert—under whose ministry in the Province of Canada (shared by Louis-H. La Fontaine) it came into effect in 1848.

27. Margaret Fairley, ed., *The Selected Writings of William Lyon Mackenzie* (Toronto, 1960), 217.

28. Ibid., 233.

29. F.M. Greenwood, *Legacies of Fear: Law and Politics in the Era of the French Revolution* (Toronto, 1993).

30. F.M. Greenwood, 'Judges and Treason Law in Lower Canada, England, and the United States during the French Revolution, 1794–1800', in Greenwood and Wright, eds, *Canadian State Trials*, 241–95.

31. Carol Wilton, *Popular Politics and Political Culture in Upper Canada, 1800–1850* (Montreal and Kingston,

2000).

32. Quoted in J. Murray Beck, *Joseph Howe* (Montreal and Kingston, 1982), I, 130.

33. F. Murray Greenwood and Barry Wright, 'Parliamentary Privilege and the Repression of Dissent in the Canadas', in Greenwood and Wright, eds, *Canadian State Trials*, 409–49.

34. Beck, *Joseph Howe*, 134.

35. Ibid., 140.

36. Barry Cahill, 'R. v. Howe (1835) for Seditious Libel: A Tale of Twelve Magistrates', in Greenwood and Wright, eds, *Canadian State Trials*, 547–76.

37. *P.E.I. Assembly Journals*, 1832, Appendix A.

38. *Brockville Recorder*, 14 Mar. 1833.

39. Linda Little, 'Collective Action in Outport Newfoundland: A Case Study from the 1830s', *Labour/Le Travail* 26 (Fall 1990): 7–35.

40. Quoted in *DCB*, X, 574.

41. Colin Read, *The Rising in Western Upper Canada: The Duncombe Revolt and After* (Toronto, 1982).

42. Greer, *The Patriots and the People*.

43. Ibid.

44. Fred Landon, *An Exile from Canada to Van Diemen's Land: Being the Story of Elijah Woodman Transported Overseas for Participation in the Upper Canada Troubles of 1837–38* (Toronto, 1960).

45. Read, *The Rising in Western Upper Canada*, 178–9.

46. Quoted in Fernand Ouellet, 'The 1837/38 Rebellions in Lower Canada as a Social Phenomenon', in J.M. Bumsted, ed., *Interpreting Canada's Past* (Toronto, 1986), I, 211.

47. Greer, *The Patriots and the People*.

48. Both Papineau and Mackenzie were eventually allowed to return to Canada, and they were elected to the Canadian legislature in 1848 and 1851, respectively. Nelson returned to the legislature in 1844. Duncombe ended up a state legislator in California.

13 PEOPLING BRITISH NORTH AMERICA, 1791–1860

1. Population data come from volume IV of the 1871 Canadian census; immigration data from the appendices in Helen I. Cowan, *British Emigration to British North America: The First Hundred Years* (Toronto, 1961).

2. Michael Smith, *A Geographical View of the Province of Upper Canada* (Hartford, Conn., 1813).

3. J.M. Bumsted, *The People's Clearance: Highland Emigration to British North America, 1770–1815* (Edinburgh and Winnipeg, 1982), 129–44.

4. Jean Daigle, ed., *The Acadians of the Maritimes* (Moncton, NB, 1982), 166.

5. Ibid., 50–9.

6. Quoted in Robin Winks, *The Blacks in Canada: A History*, 2nd edn (Montreal and Kingston, 1997), 116.

7. Ibid., 122.

8. William Spray, 'The Settlement of the Black Refugees in New Brunswick 1815–1836', in Phillip Buckner, ed., *The Acadiensis Reader* (Fredericton, 1985), I, 148–64.

9. Robert Lamond, *A Narrative of the Rise and Progress of Emigration from the Counties of Lanark and Renfrew to the New Settlements in Upper Canada* (Glasgow, 1821), 103–4.

10. Wendy Cameron, 'Selecting Peter Robinson's Irish Emigrants', *Histoire Sociale/Social History* 9, 17 (May 1976): 29–46.

11. Quoted in Helen I. Cowan, *British Immigration before Confederation* (Ottawa, 1968), 79.

12. Hugh Johnston, *British Emigration Policy, 1815–1830: 'Shovelling Out Paupers'* (Oxford, 1972).

13. Wendy Cameron and Mary McDougall Maude, *Assisting Emigration to Upper Canada: The Petworth Project 1832–1837* (Montreal and Kingston, 2000).

14. Wendy Cameron, Sheila Haines, and Mary McDougall Maude, eds, *English Immigrant Voices: Labourers' Letters from Upper Canada* (Montreal and Kingston, 2000).

15. Ibid., 145.

16. Thelma Coleman with James Anderson, *The Canada Company* (Stratford, Ont., 1978); H.B. Timothy, *The Galts: A Canadian Odyssey: John Galt, 1779–1839* (Toronto, 1977).

17. W.H. Graham, *The Tiger of Canada West* (Toronto and Vancouver, 1962).

18. Quoted in Peter Thomas, *Strangers from a Secret Land: The Voyages of the Brig 'Albion' and the Founding of the First Welsh Settlements in Canada* (Toronto, 1986), 75.

19. Ibid., 139.

20. Wilson Benson, *Life and Adventures of Wilson Benson. Written by Himself* (Toronto, 1876), 18.

21. Edwin C. Guillet, *The Great Migration: The Atlantic Crossing by Sailing-Ship 1770–1860* (Toronto, 1963).

22. Quoted in C. Peter Ripley, ed., *The Black Abolitionist Papers: Volume II: Canada, 1830–1865* (Chapel Hill and London, 1986), 3.

23. Quoted in Winks, *The Blacks in Canada*, 243.

24. Larry Gara, *The Liberty Line: The Legend of the Underground Railroad* (Lexington, Kentucky, 1967).

14 THE COLONIAL ECONOMY, 1791–1840

1. Shannon Ryan, *Fish Out of Water: The Newfoundland Saltfish Trade 1814–1914* (St John's, 1985).

2. Quoted in Harold Innis, *The Cod Fisheries: The History of an International Economy*, rev. edn (Toronto, 1954), 211.

3. David Lee, *The Robins in Gaspé, 1766–1825* (Markham, Ont., 1984).

4. See, for example, Theodore J. Karamanski, *Fur Trade and Exploration: Opening the Far Northwest 1821–1852* (Norman, Okla., 1983).

5. See J.M. Bumsted, *Fur Trade Wars: The Founding of Western Canada* (Winnipeg, 1999).

6. Richard Somerset Mackie, *Trading Beyond the Mountains: The British Fur Trade on the Pacific 1793–1843* (Vancouver, 1997).

7. Donald Creighton, *The Commercial Empire of the St. Lawrence* (Toronto, 1956), 243–4.

8. Susan Fairlee, 'British Statistics of Grain Imports from Canada and the U.S.A., 1791–1900', in David Alexander and Rosemary Ommer, eds, *Volumes Not Values: Canadian Sailing Ships and World Trades* (St John's, 1979), 187–8.

9. Graeme Wynn, *Timber Colony: A Historical Geography of Early 19th Century New Brunswick* (Toronto, 1980).

10. John McCallum, *Unequal Beginnings: Agriculture and Development in Quebec and Ontario until 1870* (Toronto, 1980).

11. Quoted in E.C. Guillet, *Early Life in Upper Canada* (Toronto, 1933), 196.

12. Quoted in Marjorie Griffin Cohen, *Women's Work, Markets, and Economic Development in Nineteenth-Century Ontario* (Toronto, 1988), 73.

13. Quoted in Innis, *The Cod Fisheries*, 71.

14. *DCB*, IX, 172–86.

15. Lewis Fischer, '"An Engine, Yet Moderate": James Peake, Entrepreneurial Behaviour and the Shipping Industry of Nineteenth Century Prince Edward Island', in Lewis R. Fischer and Eric Sager, eds, *The Enterprising Canadians: Entrepreneurs and Economic Development in Eastern Canada, 1820–1914* (St John's, 1979), 97–118.

16. Quoted in Wynn, *Timber Colony*, 153.

17. T.W. Acheson, *Saint John: The Making of a Colonial Urban Community* (Toronto, 1985).

18. Anna Jameson, *Winter Studies and Summer Rambles in Canada* (Toronto, 1966), lxxxii.

19. Edward Talbot, *Five Year's Residence in Canada* (London, 1824); quoted in Jean-Claude Marsan, *Montreal in Evolution: Historical Analysis of the Development of Montreal's Architecture and Urban Environment* (Montreal, 1981), 146.

20. Ibid., 145.

15 COLONIAL SOCIETY, 1791–1840

1. Quoted in Eric Arthur, *Toronto: No Mean City*, 3rd edn, revised by Stephen A. Otto (Toronto, 1986), 44.

2. Quoted in Patrick Brode, *Sir John Beverley Robinson* (Toronto, 1984), 175.

3. Quoted in Arthur, *Toronto*, 42–3.

4. Watson Kirkconnell, ed., *The Diary of Deacon Elihu Woodworth* (Wolfville, NS, 1972), 7.

5. On regional elites, see particularly J.K. Johnson, *Becoming Prominent: Regional Leadership in Upper Canada, 1791–1841* (Montreal and Kingston, 1989).

6. Sean T. Cadigan, *Hope and Deception in Conception Bay: Merchant–Settler Relations in Newfoundland, 1785–1855* (Toronto, 1995).

7. Peter Russell, *Attitudes to Social Structure and Mobility in Upper Canada, 1815–1840* (Lewiston/Queenston, Lampeter, 1990), 7–8.

8. Quoted in Judith Fingard, 'The Winter's Tale', in J.M. Bumsted, ed., *Interpreting Canada's Past* (Toronto, 1986), I, 255.

9. Quoted in Judith Fingard, 'The Relief of the Unemployed Poor in Saint John, Halifax, and St. John's, 1815–1860', in David A. Frank and Phillip Buckner, eds, *The Acadiensis Reader*, rev. edn (Fredericton, 1988), I, 197.

10. Quoted in Allan Greer, *Peasant, Lord, and Merchant: Rural Society in Three Quebec Parishes 1740–1840* (Toronto, 1985), 186.

11. Catharine Parr Traill, *The Backwoods of Canada* (London, 1836), 101.

12. Brian Lee Coffey, 'The Pioneer House in Southern Ontario, Canada: Constructional Material Use and Resultant Forms to 1850', Ph.D. dissertation (University of Oregon, 1982).

13. This section is based on Constance Backhouse, *Petticoats and Prejudice: Women and Law in Nineteenth-Century Canada* (Toronto, 1991).

14. Quoted in Gary Lee Collison, *Shadrach Minkins: From Fugitive Slave to Citizen* (Cambridge, Mass., 1997), 177. In general, see Jason H. Silverman, *Unwelcome Guests: Canada West's Response to American Fugitive Slaves, 1800–1865* (Millwood, NY, 1985).

15. Allen Stouffer, *The Light of Nature and the Law of God: Antislavery in Ontario 1833–1877* (Montreal and London, 1992).

16. Quoted in Sidney L. Harring, *White Man's Law: Native People in Nineteenth-Century Canadian Jurisprudence* (Toronto, 1998).

17. Ibid.

18. Ibid.

19. Quoted in L.F.S. Upton, *Micmacs and Colonists: Indian–White Relations in the Maritimes, 1713–1867* (Vancouver, 1979), 84.

20. Ibid., 87.

21. Ibid., 89.

22. Ibid., 96.

23. See Harring, *White Man's Law*.

24. Quoted in Donald B. Smith, 'The Dispossession of the Mississauga Indians: A Missing Chapter in the Early History of Upper Canada', reprinted in Bumsted, *Interpreting Canada's Past*, I, 299.

25. Quoted in Olive Patricia Dickason, with David T. McNab, *Canada's First Nations: A History of Founding Peoples from Earliest Times*, 4th edn (Toronto, 2009), 205.

16 COLONIAL CULTURE, 1791–1840

1. Quoted in Katherine M.J. McKenna, 'Options for Élite Women in Early Upper Canadian Society: The Case of the Powell Family', in J.K. Johnson and Bruce Wilson, eds, *Historical Essays on Upper Canada* (Ottawa, 1989), 403.
2. Quoted in J.M. Bumsted, 'The Household and Family of Edward Jarvis, 1828–1852', *The Island Magazine* 14 (Fall–Winter 1983): 24.
3. Ibid., 23.
4. Kathryn Bridge, *Henry & Self: The Private Life of Sarah Crease 1826–1922* (Victoria, 1996), 64, 68.
5. Quoted in Peter Ward, *Courtship, Love and Marriage in Nineteenth-Century English Canada* (Montreal and Kingston, 1990), 158.
6. Alfred G. Bailey, ed., *The Letters of James and Ellen Robb: Portrait of a Fredericton Family in Early Victorian Times* (Fredericton, 1983), 52–3.
7. Ibid.
8. Quoted in J.M. Bumsted and Wendy Owen, 'The Victorian Family in Colonial British North America', in Bumsted, ed., *Interpreting Canada's Past: Pre-Confederation*, vol. 1, 2nd edn (Toronto, 1993), 511.
9. Quoted in David Flint, *John Strachan: Pastor and Politician* (Toronto, 1971), 85.
10. Quoted in S.F. Wise, 'Sermon Literature and Canadian Intellectual History', in J.M. Bumsted, ed., *Canadian History before Confederation: Essays and Interpretations* (Georgetown, Ont., 1972), 257.
11. Ibid., 261.
12. *DCB*, VI, 586–99.
13. Quoted in Flint, *Strachan*, 89.
14. McGill was the brother-in-law of John Strachan's wife by her first marriage. Strachan had advised McGill to leave this bequest, was a trustee of his will, and was on the board of the planned university, of which he hoped to become principal.
15. Margaret Fairley, ed., *The Selected Writings of William Lyon Mackenzie* (Toronto, 1960), 93–4.
16. D.C. Maaters, *Protestant Church Colleges in Canada: A History* (Toronto, 1966).
17. *A Man of Sentiment: The Memoirs of Philippe-Joseph Aubert de Gaspé 1786–1871*, trans. Jane Brierley (Montreal, 1988).
18. Quoted in L.F.S. Upton, ed., 'The Quebec School Question, 1784–90', in J.M. Bumsted, ed., *Documentary Problems in Canadian History*, 2 vols (Georgetown, Ont., 1969), I, 104.
19. Quoted in Fairley, *Selected Writings of William Lyon Mackenzie*, 84.
20. Ibid.
21. J. Donald Wilson, 'The Ryerson Years in Canada West', in J. Donald Wilson et al., *Canadian Education: A History* (Toronto, 1970).
22. M.G. Parks, ed., *Joseph Howe's Western and Eastern Rambles: Travel Sketches of Nova Scotia* (Toronto, 1973).
23. Germaine Warkentin, 'Exploration Literature in English', in Eugene Benson and William Toye, eds, *The Oxford Companion to Canadian Literature*, 2nd edn (Toronto, 1999), 372–80; Germaine Warkentin, ed., *Canadian Exploration Literature: An Anthology* (Toronto, 1993).
24. Ann Edwards Boutelle, 'Frances Brooke's *Emily Montague* (1769): Canada and Woman's Rights', in Veronica Strong-Boag and Anita Clair Fellman, *Rethinking Canada: The Promise of Women's History*, 2nd edn (Toronto, 1991), 51–8.
25. Charlotte Gray, *Sisters in the Wilderness: The Lives of Susanna Moodie and Catharine Parr Traill* (Toronto, 1999).
26. Quoted in Thomas M.F. Gerry, '"I am Translated": Anna Jameson's Sketches and *Winter and Summer Rambles in Canada*', *Journal of Canadian Studies* 25, 4 (Winter 1990–1): 37.
27. See, for example, Margaret Conrad et al., eds, *No Place Like Home: Diaries and Letters of Nova Scotia Women 1771–1938* (Halifax, 1988).
28. J. Russell Harper, *People's Art: Naïve Art in Canada* (Ottawa, 1973).
29. Don Morrow et al., *A Concise History of Sport in Canada* (Toronto, 1989), 109 ff.
30. The mayflower is the emblem of the province of Nova Scotia.
31. D.C. Harvey, ed., *The Heart of Howe: Selections from the Letters and Speeches of Joseph Howe* (Toronto, 1939), 49–66.

17 POLITICAL AND ADMINISTRATIVE REFORM, 1840–1860

1. Janet Ajzenstat, *The Political Thought of Lord Durham* (Montreal and Kingston, 1988).
2. Gerald Craig, ed., *Lord Durham's Report* (Toronto, 1963), 22–3.
3. Viger had an ambiguous relationship with the revolutionary movement in Lower Canada and was imprisoned from 4 Nov. 1838, when Sir John Colborne proclaimed martial law, until 16 May 1840—although he was never charged.
4. Quoted in P.A. Buckner, *The Transition to Responsible Government: British Policy in British North America 1815–59* (Westport, Conn., 1985), 301.
5. Quoted in Gertrude E. Gunn, *The Political History of Newfoundland, 1832–1864* (Toronto, 1966), 113.
6. Quoted in *DCB*, XI, 169.
7. Mackenzie was pardoned in the general amnesty of February 1849. While his brief visit to Toronto in March, to test the waters, provoked some violence, he returned with his family in May 1850 to stay and

become rehabilitated as an ally of the Grit radicals. In the spring of 1851 he stood in a by-election to fill a vacant seat in Haldimand County, and won—over his opponent, George Brown.

8. Quoted in J.M.S. Careless, *The Union of the Canadas: The Growth of Canadian Institutions 1841–1857* (Toronto, 1967), 166.

9. Quoted ibid., 169.

10. Quoted in Ian Ross Robertson, 'The Bible Question in P.E.I.', in Philip A. Buckner and David A. Frank, eds, *Atlantic Canada before Confederation* (Fredericton, 1985), 282.

11. There were sectional attorneys general, of course, because there were two different systems of law and two different court systems in effect in the Province of Canada.

12. Education, like law, remained the responsibility of the sections in the Union.

13. Quoted in Careless, *The Union of the Canadas*, 202.

14. Oliver MacDonagh, 'The Nineteenth-Century Revolution in Government: A Reappraisal', *Historical Journal* 1 (1958): 52–67; Richard Corrigan and D. Sayer, *The Great Arch: English State Formation as Cultural Revolution* (Oxford, 1985).

15. J.E. Hodgetts, *Pioneer Public Service: An Administrative History of the United Canadas, 1841–1867* (Toronto, 1955), 118–27.

16. Bruce Curtis, 'The Canada "Blue Books" and the Administrative Capacity of the Canadian State, 1822–67', *Canadian Historical Review* 74, 4 (1993): 535–65.

17. Kenneth S. Mackenzie, 'Canadian Postal History Sources', *Archivaria* 9 (Winter 1979–80): 151–77.

18. Hodgetts, *Pioneer Public Service*, 36.

19. Quoted in Alison Prentice and Susan Houston, eds, *Family, School, and Society in Nineteenth-Century Canada* (Toronto, 1975), 69.

20. Quoted in Bruce Curtis, 'Class, Culture and Administration: Educational Inspection in Canada West', in Allan Greer and Ian Radforth, eds, *Colonial Leviathan: State Formation in Mid-Nineteenth-Century Canada* (Toronto, 1992), 103–33. See also Curtis, *Building the Educational State: Canada West, 1836–1871* (London, Ont., 1988), and Curtis, *True Government by Choice Men? Inspection, Education, and State Formation in Canada West* (Toronto, 1992).

21. Patricia T. Rooke and R.L. Schnell, *Discarding the Asylum: From Child Rescue to the Welfare State in English-Canada (1800–1950)* (Lanham, Md, 1983).

22. Quoted in John A. Dickinson and Brian Young, *A Short History of Quebec*, 2nd edn (Toronto, 1993).

23. Brian Young, 'Positive Law, Positive State: Class Realignment and the Transformation of Lower Canada, 1815–1866', in Greer and Radford, *Colonial Leviathan*, 50–63.

24. John D. Blackwell, 'William Hume Blake and the Judicature Acts of 1849: The Process of Legal Reform at Mid-Century in Upper Canada', in David Flaherty, ed., *Essays in the History of Canadian Law* (Toronto, 1981), I, 132–74.

18 BRITISH NORTH AMERICA AND THE EMPIRE AFTER 1840

1. Quoted in Bernard Semmel, *The Rise of Free Trade Imperialism* (Cambridge, 1970), 23–4.

2. Ibid., 132.

3. Ibid., 145.

4. *Quebec Gazette*, 22 Apr. 1842, quoted in A.R.M. Lower, *Great Britain's Woodyard* (Montreal, 1973), 88.

5. Quoted in Donald G. Creighton, *The Empire of the St. Lawrence* (Toronto, 1956), 369.

6. L.R. Fischer and Eric W. Sager, *Merchant Shipping and Economic Development in Atlantic Canada* (St John's, 1982).

7. Quoted in Eric W. Sager and L.R. Fischer, *Shipping and Shipbuilding in Atlantic Canada 1820–1914* (Ottawa, 1986), 8.

8. Eric Sager with Gerald Panting, *Maritime Capital: The Shipping Industry in Atlantic Canada, 1820–1914* (Montreal and Kingston, 1990).

9. J.M. Bumsted, 'The Colonial Office, Aboriginal Policy, and Red River, 1847–1849', in Bumsted, *Thomas Scott's Body and Other Essays on Early Manitoba History* (Winnipeg, 2000), 91–114.

10. *Parliamentary Debates*, 3rd ser., vol. CI, cols 270 and 272 (18 Aug. 1848).

11. *Report from the Select Committee on the Hudson's Bay Company* (London, 1857), 331–2.

12. Ibid., iii–iv.

13. James E. Fitzgerald, *An Examination of the Charter and Proceedings of the HBC* (London, 1849), passim.

14. Quoted in Richard Mackie, 'The Colonization of Vancouver Island, 1849–1858', *BC Studies* 96 (Winter 1992–3): 6.

15. Quoted in Margaret Ormsby, *British Columbia: A History* (Toronto, 1958), 102–3.

16. CO 226/63/201–2.

17. CO 226/73/373.

18. Ian Ross Robertson, ed., *The Prince Edward Island Land Commission of 1860* (Fredericton, 1988).

19. Ian Ross Robertson, *The Tenant League of Prince Edward Island 1863–1867* (Toronto, 1996).

20. Quoted in J.M. Hitsman, *Safeguarding Canada 1763–1871* (Toronto, 1968), 142.

21. John Joseph Greenough, *The Halifax Citadel, 1825–60: A Narrative and Structural History* (Ottawa, 1977), 116.

22. Quoted in Hitsman, *Safeguarding Canada*, 152.

23. Ibid, 153.

24. Barry Gough, *The Royal Navy and the Northwest Coast of North America 1810–1914* (Vancouver, 1971).

25. Quoted in Elinor Kyte Senior, *British Regulars in Montreal: An Imperial Garrison, 1832–1851* (Montreal, 1981), 177.

26. Quoted in John W. Spurr, 'Garrison and Community, 1815–1870', in G. Tulchinsky, ed., *To Preserve and Defend: Essays on Kingston in the Nineteenth Century* (Montreal and Kingston, 1976), 107.

27. Senior, *British Regulars*, 149.

28. David R. Facey-Crowther, 'Militiamen and Volunteers: The New Brunswick Militia 1787–1871', *Acadiensis* 20, 1 (Autumn 1990): 148–83.

29. L. Cottrell, *British Overseas Investment in the Nineteenth Century* (London, 1975).

30. Philip Ziegler, *The Sixth Great Power: A History of One of the Greatest of All Banking Families, the House of Barings, 1762–1929* (New York, 1988).

31. Ibid., 226.

32. Terry Coleman, *Passage to America: A History of Emigrants from Great Britain and Ireland to America in the Mid-Nineteenth Century* (London, 1972), 63–84; Edwin C. Guillet, *The Great Migration: The Atlantic Crossing by Sailing-Ship 1770–1860*, 2nd edn (Toronto, 1963), 43–65.

33. *The Emigrant's Manual* (Edinburgh, 1851).

34. Quoted in Coleman, *Passage to America*, 100.

35. For a full-length discussion of one communicable disease, see Geoffrey Bilson, *A Darkened House: Cholera in Nineteenth Century Canada* (Toronto, 1980).

36. Oliver Macdonagh, *A Pattern of Government Growth 1800–1860: The Passenger Acts and Their Enforcement* (London, 1961), 183.

37. A.W. Rasporich, 'Imperial Sentiment in the Province of Canada during the Crimean War 1854–1856', in W.L. Morton, ed., *The Shield of Achilles: Aspects of Canada in the Victorian Age* (Toronto, 1968), 139–68.

38. N.A. Woods, *The Prince of Wales in Canada and the United States* (London, 1861).

39. Gardner D. Engleheart, *Journal of the Progress of H.R.H. the Prince of Wales* (n.p., n.d.,), 69; Kinahan Cornwallis, *Royalty in the New World: or, the Prince of Wales in America* (London, 1860), 47–8.

19 BRITISH NORTH AMERICA AND THE CONTINENT AFTER 1840

1. L.B. Shippee, *Canadian–American Relations 1849–1874* (New Haven, 1939).

2. Francis M. Carroll, *A Good and Wise Measure: The Search for the Canadian–American Boundary, 1783–1842* (Toronto, 2001).

3. Mark Vinet, *Canada and the American Civil War: Prelude to War* (Vaudreuil-Sur-Le-Lac, Que., 2001).

4. Quoted in Gary Lee Collison, *Shadrach Minkins: From Fugitive Slave to Citizen* (Cambridge, Mass., 1997), 188.

5. Robert C. Reinders, 'The John Anderson Case, 1860–1:

A Study in Anglo–Canadian Imperial Relations', *Canadian Historical Review* 56, 4 (1975): 393–415.

6. James McCabe, *The San Juan Water Boundary Question* (Toronto, 1965); Hill Dawson, *The War That Was Never Fought* (Princeton, NJ, 1971).

7. In general, see the opening chapter to John E. Parsons, *West on the 49th Parallel: Red River to the Rockies 1872–1876* (New York, 1963), and George F.G. Stanley, ed., *Mapping the Frontier: Charles Wilson's Diary of the Survey of the 49th Parallel, 1858–1862, while Secretary of the British Boundary Commission* (Toronto, 1970).

8. Quoted in Gilbert Tucker, *The Canadian Commercial Revolution 1845–1851* (Ottawa, 1970), 131.

9. Ibid., 135.

10. Ibid., 136.

11. Ibid., 139.

12. Quoted in D.C. Masters, *The Reciprocity Treaty of 1854* (Ottawa, 1963), 5.

13. Ibid., 9.

14. Ibid., 10.

15. Tucker, *Canadian Commercial Revolution*, 110.

16. Quoted in Masters, *Reciprocity Treaty*, 42.

17. Harold A. Innis, *The Cod Fisheries: The History of an International Economy*, rev. edn (Toronto, 1965), 405–7.

18. Kennedy Wells, *The Fishery of Prince Edward Island* (Charlottetown, 1986), 121–30.

19. Douglas McCalla, 'Railways and the Development of Canada West, 1850–1870', in Allan Greer and Ian Radforth, eds, *Colonial Leviathan: State Formation in Mid-Nineteenth-Century Canada* (Toronto, 1992), 192–229.

20. Quoted in T.C. Keefer, *The Philosophy of Railroads*, ed. H.V. Nelles (Toronto, 1972), 6.

21. Ibid., 27.

22. Douglas McCalla, *Planting the Province: The Economic History of Upper Canada 1784–1870* (Toronto, 1993), 209–10.

23. Quoted in *DCB*, IX, 526.

24. Quoted in George de T. Glazebrook, *A History of Transportation in Canada*, 2 vols (Ottawa, 1964), I, 169.

25. Keefer, *Philosophy of Railroads*, 141.

26. Ibid., 158–9.

27. Ibid., 9.

28. J.J. Hargrave, *Red River* (Fort Garry, Man., 1871), 27–56, describes one such journey in 1862.

29. Quoted in S.F. Wise and Robert Craig Brown, *Canada Views the United States: Nineteenth-Century Political Attitudes* (Seattle and London, 1967), 79.

30. Quoted in Robin Winks, *Canada and the United States* (New Haven, 1960), 29.

31. Ibid., 50.

20 THE WEST AND THE NORTH, 1821–1868

1. W. Robert Wightman and Nancy M. Wightman, *The

Land Between: Northwestern Ontario Resource Development, 1800 to the 1900s (Toronto, 1997).

2. Quoted ibid., 33.

3. Quoted in Elizabeth Arthur, 'Beyond Superior: Ontario's New-found Land', in Roger Hall et al., eds, *Patterns of the Past: Interpreting Ontario's History* (Toronto, 1988), 134.

4. Quoted in J.M. Bumsted, *Thomas Scott's Body and Other Essays in Early Manitoba History* (Winnipeg, 2000).

5. Arthur Ray, *Indians in the Fur Trade* (Toronto, 1974), 216 ff.

6. Frank Roe, *The North American Buffalo* (Toronto, 1951).

7. Andrew C. Isenberg, *The Destruction of the Bison: An Environmental History, 1750–1920* (Cambridge, 2000).

8. Robin Fisher, *Contact and Conflict: Indian–European Relations in British Columbia, 1774–1860* (Vancouver, 1977), 44–5.

9. Robert T. Galois, 'Measles, 1847–1850: The First Modern Epidemic in British Columbia', *BC Studies* 109 (Spring 1996): 31–43.

10. David T. McNab, 'Herman Merivale and Colonial Office Indian Policy in the Mid-Nineteenth Century', in Ian A.L. Getty and Antoine S. Lussier, eds, *As Long As the Sun Shines and Water Flows* (Vancouver, 1983), 85–103.

11. While in New Orleans, when a professional musician had failed to appear, Palliser had sung both male parts in a charity performance of a Handel oratorio.

12. Lorin Blodget, *Climatology of the United States, and of the Temperate Latitudes of the North American Continent* (Philadelphia, 1857), 529.

13. John Palliser, *Journals, Detailed Reports, and Observations Relative to the Exploration, by Captain Palliser* (London, 1863), 18.

14. Quoted in Douglas Owram, *Promise of Eden: The Canadian Expansionist Movement and the Idea of the West 1800–1900* (Toronto, 1980), 69.

15. Adele Perry, *On the Edge of Empire: Gender, Race, and the Making of British Columbia, 1849–1871* (Toronto, 2001).

16. Fisher, *Contact and Conflict*, 52–4.

17. Quoted ibid., 59.

18. Sylvia Van Kirk, 'Tracing the Fortunes of Five Founding Families of Victoria', *BC Studies* 115/116 (Autumn–Winter 1997–8): 149–79.

19. Quoted in Margaret Ormsby, *British Columbia: A History* (Toronto, 1958), 142.

20. Quoted in Beth Hill, *Sappers: The Royal Engineers in British Columbia* (Ganges, BC, 1987), 6.

21. Ibid., 142.

22. Quoted in Tina Loo, 'The Road from Bute Inlet: Crime and Colonial Identity in British Columbia', in Jim Phillips et al., eds, *Crime and Criminal Justice: Essays in the History of American Law* (Toronto, 1994), V, 135 n.6.

23. Ibid., 163.

24. Ibid., 170.

25. Ibid., 141.

26. Dr Carl Friesach, *Ein Ausflug nach Britisch-Columbien im Jahre 1858*, translated and quoted by Robie L. Reid in 'Two Narratives of the Fraser River Gold-Rush', *British Columbia Historical Quarterly* 5 (1941): 227.

27. Quoted in Doug Fetherling, *The Gold Crusades: A Social History of Gold Rushes, 1849–1929* (Toronto, 1997), 81.

28. Quoted in Reid, 'Two Narratives', 230.

29. This was the famous Cariboo Road, between Yale and Barkerville. An impressive construction supported by pilings or crib-work, or cut through rock, it was completed in 1863.

30. Quoted in *DCB*, IX, 518. See also M.S. Wade, *The Overlanders of '62* (Victoria, 1931); Richard Thomas Wright, *Overlanders 1858 Gold* (Victoria, 1980).

31. Quoted in Alan Conway, 'Welsh Miners in British Columbia', *British Columbia Historical Quarterly* 20 (1957): 63.

32. Quoted in Richard Preston, ed., *For Friends at Home: A Scottish Emigrant's Letters from Canada, California, and the Cariboo, 1844–64* (Montreal, 1974), 305.

33. Quoted in Conway, 'Welsh Miners', 62.

34. Ibid., 63.

35. Quoted in Hill, *Sappers*, 45.

36. John Norris, *Strangers Entertained: A History of the Ethnic Groups of British Columbia* (Vancouver, 1971), 237–42.

37. Ibid. 209–12; Peter S. Li, *The Chinese in Canada* (Toronto, 1988).

38. Quoted in Fisher, *Contact and Conflict*, 104.

39. Ibid., 105.

40. Quoted in Judith Williams, *High Slack: Waddington's Gold Road and the Bute Inlet Massacre of 1864* (Vancouver, n.d.), 99.

41. Ibid.

42. Quoted in Cecil Houston and William Smyth, *Irish Emigration and Canadian Settlement* (Montreal and Kingston, 1990), 321.

43. Quoted in Daniel Francis, *Discovery of the North: The Exploration of Canada's Arctic* (Edmonton, 1986).

44. Owen Beattie and John Geiger, *Frozen in Time: Unlocking the Secrets of the Franklin Expedition* (Saskatoon, 1988).

21 EARLY VICTORIAN SOCIETY, 1840–1870

1. J.I. Little, *Nationalism, Capitalism, and Colonization in Nineteenth-Century Quebec* (Montreal and Kingston, 1989), 17.

2. Ibid., 44–5.

3. Wilson Benson, *Life and Adventures of Wilson Benson. Written by Himself* (Toronto, 1876).

4. Gordon Darroch and Lee Soltow, *Property and Inequality in Victorian Ontario: Structural Patterns and Cultural Communities in the 1871 Census* (Toronto, 1994).

5. Dale and Lee Gibson, *Substantial Justice: Law and*

Lawyers in Manitoba 1670–1970 (Winnipeg, 1972), 77–9.

6. See J.M. Bumsted, 'The Cultural Landscape of Early Canada', in Bernard Bailyn and Philip D. Morgan, eds, *Strangers within the Realm: Cultural Margins of the First British Empire* (Chapel Hill and London, 1991), 363–92.

7. Scott W. See, *Riots in New Brunswick: Orange Nativism and Social Violence in the 1840s* (Toronto, 1993); Michael S. Cross, 'The Shiners' War: Social Violence in the Ottawa Valley in the 1830s', *Canadian Historical Review* 54, 1 (1973): 1–26; Michael S. Cross, 'Stony Monday 1849: The Rebellion Losses Riots in Bytown', *Ontario History* 63, 3 (1971): 177–90.

8. Scott See, '"Mickeys and Demons" vs. "Bigots and Boobies": The Woodstock Riot of 1847', *Acadiensis* 21, 1 (1991): 110–31.

9. Jacques Monet, *The Last Cannon Shot: A Study of French-Canadian Nationalism, 1837–50* (Toronto, 1969); Terrence Murphy and Roberto Perin, *A Concise History of Christianity in Canada* (Toronto, 1996).

10. Terrence Murphy and Gerald Stortz, eds, *Creed and Culture: The Place of English-speaking Catholics in Canadian Society, 1750–1930* (Montreal, 1993).

11. *DCB*, XI, 94–105.

12. William Westfall, *Two Worlds: The Protestant Culture of Nineteenth Century Ontario* (Montreal and Kingston, 1989).

13. Cecil J. Houston and William J. Smyth, *Irish Immigration and Canadian Settlement: Patterns, Links, and Letters* (Toronto, 1980), 4.

14. Quoted in Christopher J. Anstead, 'Fraternalism in Victorian Ontario: Secret Societies and Cultural Hegemony', Ph.D. dissertation (University of Western Ontario, 1992), 111–12.

15. Quoted ibid., 122.

16. See, *Riots in New Brunswick*.

17. Bonnie Huskins, 'Public Celebrations in Victorian Saint John and Halifax', Ph.D. dissertation (Dalhousie University, 1991), 181.

18. Michael Cottrell, 'Green and Orange in Mid-Nineteenth-Century Toronto: The Guy Fawkes Day Episode of 1864', *Canadian Journal of Irish Studies* 19, 1 (1993): 12–21.

19. Quoted in Nancy Barbara Bouchier, '"For the Love of the Sport and the Honour of the Town": Organized Sport, Local Culture, and Middle Class Hegemony in Two Ontario Towns, 1838–1895', Ph.D. dissertation (University of Western Ontario, 1990), 119.

20. Huskins, 'Public Celebrations', 198

21. Quoted in Michael Cottrell, 'St Patrick's Day Parades in Nineteenth-Century Toronto: A Study of Immigrant Adjustment and Élite Control', *Histoire Sociale/Social History* 25, 49 (May 1992): 58.

22. Bonnie Huskins, 'The Ceremonial Space of Women: Public Processions in Victorian Saint John and Halifax', in Janet Guildford and Suzanne Morton, eds, *Separate Spheres: Women's World in the 19th-Century Maritimes* (Fredericton, 1994).

23. Cheryl Krasnick Warsh, '"John Barleycorn Must Die": An Introduction to the Social History of Alcohol', in Warsh, ed., *Drink in Canada: Historical Essays* (Toronto, 1993), 3–27.

24. Jan Noel, *Canada Dry: Temperance Crusades before Confederation* (Toronto, 1995).

25. Jan Noel, 'Dry Patriotism: The Chiniquy Crusade', in Warsh, ed., *Drink in Canada*, 27–42.

26. Glenn J. Lockwood, 'Temperance in Upper Canada as Ethnic Subterfuge', in Warsh, ed., *Drink in Canada*, 43–69.

22 EARLY VICTORIAN CULTURE, 1840–1870

1. Quoted in Beth Hill, *Sappers: The Royal Engineers in British Columbia* (Ganges, BC, 1987), 79.

2. Robin S. Harris, *A History of Higher Education in Canada 1663–1960* (Toronto, 1976), 80.

3. Robert Fairfield, 'Theatres and Performance Halls', in Ann Saddlemyer, ed., *Early Stages: Theatre in Ontario 1800–1914* (Toronto, 1990), 215–87.

4. Quoted in Stella Higgins, 'British Columbia and the Confederation Era', in W. George Shelton, ed., *British Columbia and Confederation* (Victoria, 1967), 25.

5. Quoted in Archie F. Key, *Beyond Four Walls: The Origins and Development of Canadian Museums* (Toronto, 1973), 124.

6. Quoted ibid., 130.

7. Jim Burant, 'Art in Halifax: Exhibitions and Criticism in 1830 and 1831', *RACAR: Revue d'art canadienne/Canadian Art Review* 8, 2 (1982): 119–27.

8. Carol Lowrey, 'The Society of Artists and Amateurs, 1834: Toronto's First Art Exhibition and Its Antecedents', *RACAR* 8, 2 (1982): 99–118.

9. Quoted in Carol Lowrey, 'The Toronto Society of Arts, 1847–48: Patriotism and the Pursuit of Culture in Canada West', *RACAR* 12, 1 (1986): 3.

10. Ibid., 4.

11. Quoted in *DCB*, VIII, 789.

12. Quoted in Paul Rutherford, *A Victorian Authority: The Daily Press in Late Nineteenth-Century Canada* (Toronto, 1982), 38.

13. The problem of copyright was one of the negative aspects of colonial literature. Copyright in British North America relied on the Imperial Copyright Act of 1842, amended in 1847. Foreign publishers could reprint any Canadian book without compensation, and American publishers reprinted British books in cheap editions for export to Canada on payment of a small duty. A Canadian author could lose his British copyright if the

physical quality of his Canadian publication was regarded as falling below British standards.

14. Quoted in Carl F. Klinck, ed., *Literary History of Canada: Canadian Literature in English*, 2nd edn (Toronto, 1976), I, 195.

15. Ibid., 160.

16. Quoted ibid., 197.

17. Quoted in William Toye, ed., *The Oxford Companion to Canadian Literature* (Toronto, 1983), 464.

18. Harvey J. Graff, *The Literacy Myth* (New York, 1979).

19. Robertson Davies, *Leaven of Malice* (Toronto, 1980), 163.

20. In general, see Robertson Davies, 'The Nineteenth-century Repertoire', in Saddlemyer, *Early Stages*, 90–122.

21. Quoted in Gerald Lenton-Young, 'Variety Theatre', in Saddlemyer, *Early Stages*, 176.

22. Quoted ibid., 174.

23. Margaret Howard Blom and Thomas Blom, eds, *Canada Home: Juliana Horatia Ewing's Fredericton Letters, 1867–1869* (Vancouver, 1983), 95–6.

24. Leslie O'Dell, 'Amateurs of the Regiment, 1815–1870', in Saddlemyer, *Early Stages*, 52–89.

25. James K. Nesbitt, ed., 'The Diary of Martha Cheney Ella, 1853–1856', *British Columbia Historical Quarterly* 13 (1949): 105.

26. In general, see Leonard E. Doucette, *Theatre in French Canada: Laying the Foundations 1606–1867* (Toronto, 1984).

27. Helmut Kallmann, *A History of Music in Canada 1534–1914*, 2nd edn (Toronto, 1987), 91–118.

28. Dale McIntosh, *History of Music in British Columbia, 1850–1950* (Victoria, 1989).

29. This is fairly typical of so-called folk material, much of which, when carefully examined, proves to be of quite recent origin.

30. *DCB*, X, 172–3.

31. *DCB*, XIV, 385–9.

32. Viscount Milton and W.B. Cheadle, *The Northwest Passage by Land, Being the Narrative of an Expedition from the Atlantic to the Pacific* (London, 1901), 162.

33. W.L. Morton, ed., *Monck Letters and Journals 1863–1868: Canada from Government House at Confederation* (Toronto, 1970), 157–8

34. Harold Kalman, *A History of Canadian Architecture*, 2 vols (Toronto, 1994), I, 257–318.

35. Peter Ward, *A History of Domestic Space: Privacy and the Canadian Home* (Vancouver, 1999), 24–41.

36. Quoted in R.A. Jarrell, 'The Rise and Decline of Science at Quebec, 1824–1844', *Histoire Sociale/Social History* 10 (1977): 90.

37. Debra Lindsay, ed., *The Modern Beginnings of Subarctic Ornithology: Northern Correspondence with the Smithsonian Institution, 1856–68* (Winnipeg, 1991).

38. Quoted in *DCB*, X, 448.

39. Martin Hewitt, 'Science as Spectacle: Popular Scientific Culture in Saint John, New Brunswick, 1830–1850', *Acadiensis* 18, 1 (Autumn 1988): 91–119.

40. Quoted ibid., 99.

41. J.M. Bumsted, *Red River Rebellion* (Winnipeg, 1996), 109–10.

42. Suzanne Zeller, *Inventing Canada: Early Victorian Science and the Idea of a Transcontinental Nation* (Toronto, 1987).

43. Quoted in Nancy Barbara Bouchier, '"For the Love of the Sport and the Honour of the Town": Organized Sport, Local Culture, and Middle Class Hegemony in Two Ontario Towns, 1838–1895', Ph.D. dissertation (University of Western Ontario, 1990), 35.

44. Ibid., 36.

45. Ibid., 260–6.

23 INDUSTRIALIZATION, 1850–1870

1. Quoted in Paul Craven and Tom Traves, 'Canadian Railways as Manufacturers, 1850–1880', *Canadian Historical Association Historical Papers* (1983): 254–81.

2. L.D. McCann and A. Gunn, eds, *Heartland and Hinterland: A Geography of Canada*, 3rd edn (Scarborough, Ont., 1998; first published, 1982).

3. Donald Kerr, 'The Emergence of the Industrial Heartland, c. 1760–1960', in McCann and Gunn, eds, *Heartland and Hinterland*.

4. A point suggested by Glen Williams, *Not for Export: The International Competitiveness of Canadian Manufacturing*, 3rd edn (Toronto, 1994).

5. B.K. Sandwell, *The Molson Family, etc.* (Montreal, 1933); Merrill Denison, *The Barley and the Stream: The Molson Story* (Toronto, 1955); S.E. Woods, *The Molson Saga* (New York, 1983).

6. Gerald Tulchinsky, *The River Barons: Montreal Businessmen and the Growth of Industry and Transportation, 1837–53* (Toronto, 1977).

7. Quoted in John McCallum, *Unequal Beginnings: Agriculture and Economic Development in Quebec and Ontario until 1870* (Toronto, 1980), 96–7.

8. *DCB*, XI, 5–15 (by Brian Young with Gerald J.J. Tulchinsky).

9. Allan's connection with the Canadian Pacific Railway, and his involvement in the notorious Pacific Scandal of 1873, are discussed in Chapter 26.

10. Douglas McCalla, *Planting the Province: The Economic History of Upper Canada, 1784–1870* (Toronto, 1993), 216–39.

11. *DCB*, VIII, 621–2 (by Michael Bliss).

12. *DCB*, XII, 700–9.

13. Peter Cook, *Massey at the Brink: The Story of Canada's Greatest Multinational, and Its Struggle to Survive* (Don Mills, Ont., 1981).

14. Quoted in Bryan Palmer, *A Culture in Conflict: Skilled Workers and Industrial Capitalism in Hamilton, Ontario,*

1860–1914 (Montreal and Kingston, 1979), 14–15.

15. L. Officer and L. Smith, 'Canadian-American Reciprocity Treaty', *Journal of Economic History* 28 (1968): 619–21.

16. Gregory S. Kealey, *Toronto Workers Respond to Industrial Capitalism, 1867–1892* (Toronto, 1980), 29, 25.

17. Quoted in Palmer, *A Culture in Conflict*, 16.

18. Ibid., 16–17.

19. Craig Heron, 'Factory Workers', in Paul Craven, ed., *Labouring Lives: Work and Workers in Nineteenth-Century Ontario* (Toronto, 1995), 499.

20. Quoted in R.L. Jones, *History of Agriculture in Ontario, 1613–1880* (Toronto, 1946), xi.

21. Quoted in McCallum, *Unequal Beginnings*, 97.

22. Jeremy Mouat, *Metal Mining in Canada, 1840–1950* (Ottawa, 2000), 7–28.

23. H.C. Pentland, *Labour and Capital in Canada 1650–1860* (Toronto, 1981), 192.

24. Quoted in Bryan D. Palmer, *Working-Class Experience: The Rise and Reconstitution of Canadian Labour 1800–1980* (Markham, Ont., 1983), 33–4.

25. Pentland, *Labour and Capital*, 193–4.

26. Quoted in Steven Langdon, 'The Emergence of the Canadian Working-Class Movement, 1845–1867', in J.M. Bumsted, ed., *Interpreting Canada's Past* (Toronto, 1986), I, 352.

27. Quoted in Palmer, *Working-Class Experience*, 81.

28. Kealey, *Toronto Workers*, 40–4.

29. Peter G. Goheen, 'Currents of Change in Toronto, 1850–1900', in Gilbert J. Stelter and Alan F.J. Artibise, *The Canadian City: Essays in Urban History* (Toronto, 1966), 82–3.

30. Ibid.

31. Robert McIntosh, 'Sweated Labour: Female Needleworkers in Industrializing Canada', in Wendy Mitchinson et al., eds, *Canadian Women: A Reader* (Toronto, 1996), 150.

32. Quoted in Bettina Bradbury, 'The Family Economy and Work in an Industrializing City: Montreal in the 1870s', in J.M. Bumsted, ed., *Interpreting Canada's Past*, 2nd edn (Toronto, 1993), 147.

33. Ibid., 96.

34. Bettina Bradbury, *Working Families: Age, Gender, and Daily Survival in Industrializing Montreal* (Toronto, 1993).

35. Bettina Bradbury, 'Surviving as a Widow in Nineteenth-Century Montreal', *Urban History Review* 17, 3 (1989): 148–60.

36. Bettina Bradbury, 'The Fragmented Family: Family Strategies in the Face of Death, Illness, and Poverty, Montreal, 1860–1885', in Joy Parr, ed., *Childhood and Family in Canadian History* (Toronto, 1982), 109–28.

37. Bradbury, 'The Family Economy', 157.

38. Ibid., 158–9.

39. Quoted in Carol Wilton, ed., *Essays in the History of Canadian Law: Beyond the Law: Lawyers and Business in Canada, 1830 to 1930* (Toronto, 1990), 3.

40. Jamie Benidickson, 'Aemilius Irving: Solicitor to the Great Western Railway, 1855–1872', in Carol Wilton, ed., *Inside the Law: Firms in Historical Perspective* (Toronto, 1996), 100–21.

41. Brian Young, 'Dimensions of a Law Practice: Brokerage and Ideology in the Career of George-Étienne Cartier', in Wilton, ed., *Essays*, 92–111.

42. Cartier, quoted ibid., 110.

24 UNIFICATION, 1862–1867

1. Quoted in Patrick Brode, *Sir John Beverley Robinson: Bone and Sinew of the Compact* (Toronto, 1984), 90–1.

2. Ibid., 91.

3. L.F.S. Upton, 'The Idea of Confederation: 1754–1858', in W.L. Morton, ed., *The Shield of Achilles: Aspects of Canada in the Victorian Age* (Toronto, 1968), 184–207.

4. *Daily Globe* (Toronto), 25 Oct. 1853.

5. *Pilot* (Montreal), 6 Apr. 1850.

6. Quoted in A.S. Rasporich, ed., 'National Awakening: Canada at Mid-Century', in J.M. Bumsted, ed., *Documentary Problems in Canadian History* (Georgetown, Ont., 1969), I, 240.

7. Quoted in Robin Burns, 'D'Arcy McGee: A Father of Confederation', ibid., 250.

8. For a succinct summary of the traditional view, see Paul G. Cornell, *The Great Coalition June 1864* (Ottawa, 1966).

9. For a succinct summary of the traditional view, see Peter B. Waite, *The Charlottetown Conference* (Ottawa, 1966).

10. Quoted in Peter B. Waite, *The Life and Times of Confederation, 1864–1867: Politics, Newspapers, and the Union of British North America* (Toronto, 1962), 80–1.

11. Quoted in Walter C. Soderlund et al., 'Attitudes towards Community Formation in British North America: The Atlantic Provinces and the Province of Canada Compared', *British Journal of Canadian Studies* 5, 1 (1990): 67.

12. Ibid., 57–76.

13. For the traditional view, see W.M. Whitelaw, *The Quebec Conference* (Ottawa, 1966).

14. Ibid., 95.

15. Quoted in Paul Romney, *Getting It Wrong: How Canadians Forgot Their Past and Imperilled Confederation* (Toronto, 1999), 99.

16. Ibid., 98.

17. William Garvie [editor of the *Halifax Citizen*], *Barney Rooney's Letters on Confederation, Botheration and Political Transmogrification* (Halifax, 1865).

18. Quoted in A.I. Silver, 'Confederation and Quebec', in J.M. Bumsted, ed., *Interpreting Canada's Past* (Toronto, 1986), I, 408.

19. Ibid., 412.
20. *Parliamentary Debates on the Subject of the Confederation of the British North American Provinces* (Quebec, 1865), 483.
21. Ibid., 503.
22. Quoted in James Hiller, 'Confederation Defeated: The Newfoundland Election of 1869', in Hiller and Peter Neary, eds, *Newfoundland in the Nineteenth and Twentieth Centuries* (Toronto, 1980), 70.
23. Ibid., 73–4.
24. Quotes from Waite, *Life and Times of Confederation*, 232–3, 240.
25. W.S. MacNutt, *New Brunswick: A History: 1784–1867* (Toronto, 1963), 424.
26. Quoted ibid., 431.
27. Quoted in Waite, *Life and Times of Confederation*, 268.
28. Quoted in J. Murray Beck, *Joseph Howe Anti-Confederationist* (Ottawa, 1965), 15.
29. Ibid., 194.
30. Ibid., 207.
31. Ibid., 226–7.
32. Ibid., 294.

25 THE COMPLETION OF CONFEDERATION, 1867-1873

1. Quoted in J.M. Beck, *Joseph Howe*, vol. 2, *The Briton Becomes Canadian, 1848–1873* (Kingston and Montreal, 1983), 250.
2. Kenneth G. Pryke, *Nova Scotia and Confederation, 1864–1873* (Toronto, 1979).
3. *The Protestant*, 1 Oct. 1864.
4. George Coles's letter in *The Examiner*, 3 Dec. 1864.
5. *The Examiner*, 9 Dec. 1864.
6. Quoted in Francis Bolger, *Prince Edward Island and Confederation, 1863–1873* (Charlottetown, 1964), 139.
7. Quoted ibid., 156.
8. Ibid., 158.
9. *Islander*, 26 Oct. 1866.
10. Quoted in Bolger, *Prince Edward Island*, 199.
11. Ibid., 200–1.
12. Ibid., 218.
13. Quoted in Frank P. MacKinnon, *The Government of Prince Edward Island* (Toronto, 1951), 136.
14. Nobody ever seemed to conclude from various shortages of cod in the nineteenth century that the fishery might be a non-renewable resource.
15. Quoted in James Hiller, 'Confederation Defeated: The Newfoundland Election of 1896', in James Hiller and Peter Neary, eds, *Newfoundland in the Nineteenth and Twentieth Centuries: Essays in Interpretation* (Toronto, 1980), 75.
16. Musgrave to Buckingham, 17 Feb. 1868, Public Record Office, London, CO 194/177, 24.
17. *Journals of the House of Assembly*, 1869, 33–6.

18. J.M. Bumsted, *The Red River Rebellion* (Winnipeg, 1996), 11–15.
19. Quoted ibid., 45.
20. Ibid., 49.
21. Quoted in George F.G. Stanley, *Louis Riel* (Toronto, 1963), 63.
22. Ibid.
23. Quoted in Bumsted, *Red River Rebellion*, 71.
24. Macdonald to McDougall, 27 Nov. 1869, Public Record Office, London, CO 42/678.
25. Quoted in Bumsted, *Red River Rebellion*, 94.
26. What Scott's offence was has never been clear. See my 'Thomas Scott and the Daughter of Time', *Prairie Forum* 23: 2 (Fall 1998): 145–70, and 'Why Shoot Thomas Scott? A Study in Historical Evidence', in *Thomas Scott's Body and Other Essays in Early Manitoba History* (Winnipeg, 2000), 197–210.
27. *Preliminary Investigation and Trial of Ambroise D. Lepine for the Murder of Thomas Scott: being a full report of the proceedings in this case before the Magistrate's Court and the several Courts of Queen's Bench in the province of Manitoba* (Montreal, 1874).
28. The Métis leaders, including Riel, were eventually granted amnesty in 1875. Riel's was conditional on his being banished from the country for five years.
29. Quoted in Bumsted, *Red River Rebellion*, 217.
30. Quoted in Cecil J. Houston and William J. Smyth, *The Sash Canada Wore: A Historical Geography of the Orange Order in Canada* (Toronto, 1980), 58.
31. Vancouver Island had incorporated the colony of Queen Charlotte Island in 1858, and British Columbia had annexed the colony of Stikine Territories in 1863.
32. Quoted in Margaret A. Ormsby, *British Columbia: A History* (Toronto, 1958), 217.
33. Quoted ibid., 219.
34. Ibid., 224.
35. Alexander Begg, *History of British Columbia from Its Earliest Discovery to the Present Time* (Toronto, 1894), 376.
36. Quoted ibid., 377.
37. Quoted in Ormsby, *British Columbia*, 228.
38. Quoted in Begg, *History of British Columbia*, 379.
39. Quoted in Isabel Bescoby, 'A Colonial Administration: An Analysis of Administration in British Columbia, 1869–71', *Canadian Public Administration* 10 (1967): 54.
40. Paul Phillips, 'Confederation and the Economy of British Columbia', in W. George Shelton, ed., *British Columbia and Confederation* (Victoria, 1967), 51–3.
41. Quoted in K.A. Waites, 'Responsible Government and Confederation', *British Columbia Historical Quarterly* (BCHQ) 6 (1942): 100.
42. Quoted ibid., 103.
43. Quoted in Derek Pethick, 'The Confederation Debate of 1870', in Shelton, *British Columbia*, 182.
44. Quoted in Ormsby, *British Columbia*, 245.

45. Willard E. Ireland, ed., 'Helmcken's Diary of the Confederation Negotiations, 1870', *BCHQ* 4 (1940): 111–28.

46. Quoted in Waites, 'Responsible Government', 118.

47. Ibid., 248.

48. Quoted in Ormsby, *British Columbia*, 250.

49. W.N. Sage, 'From Colony to Province: The Introduction of Responsible Government in British Columbia', *BCHQ* 3 (1939): 1–14.

26 ENVISIONING THE NEW NATION, 1867-1885

1. A.I. Bloomfield, *Patterns of Fluctuation in International Investment before 1914* (Princeton, NJ, 1968), 42–4.

2. M. Simon, 'New British Investments in Canada 1865–1914', *Canadian Journal of Economics* 3 (1970): 241.

3. Quoted in Jonathan Swainger, *The Canadian Department of Justice and the Completion of Confederation* (Vancouver, 2000), 112.

4. Ibid., 121.

5. Quoted in W.T. Easterbrook and M.H. Watkins, eds, *Approaches to Canadian Economic History* (Ottawa, 1962), 238.

6. R. Craig Brown, 'The Nationalism of the National Policy', in Peter Russell, ed., *Nationalism in Canada* (Toronto, 1966), 155–63; John H. Dales, *The Protective Tariff in Canada's Development* (Toronto, 1966).

7. J.R. Miller, 'Unity/Diversity: The Canadian Experience: From Confederation to the First World War', *Dalhousie Review* 55 (Spring 1975): 63–81.

8. *Parliamentary Debates on the subject of the Confederation of the British North American Provinces* (Ottawa, 1951), 511.

9. Quoted in Ramsay Cook, *Provincial Autonomy, Minority Rights and the Compact Theory 1867–1921* (Ottawa, 1969), 10.

10. Ibid., 11.

11. Ibid., 13. See also Donald Swainson, ed., *Oliver Mowat's Ontario* (Toronto, 1972).

12. Ibid., 31.

13. Ibid., 33.

14. *Toronto Globe*, 4 Aug. 1870.

15. Quoted in A.W. Rasporich, 'National Awakening: Canada at Mid-Century', in J.M. Bumsted, ed., *Documentary Problems in Canadian History*, vol. 1 (Georgetown, Ont., 1969), 225.

16. *Manitoba Free Press*, 7 May 1874.

17. Quoted in Carl Berger, *The Sense of Power: Studies in the Ideas of Canadian Imperialism, 1867–1914* (Toronto, 1970), 58–9.

18. Ibid.

19. The federal power that probably touched most Canadians immediately after union was control of the postal service. In 1867 the Dominion took over the operation of 3,477 post offices, which became 13,811 by the Great War in 1914. It almost immediately lowered rates from 5.5 cents to 3 cents per half-ounce on letters; by 1899 the rate was 2 cents per ounce. Post office patronage greased the wheels of party patronage, and Canadians saved their money in the postal savings banks. Throughout the first half-century of Confederation, the Canadian post office made money, while providing efficient public service to every inhabitant of the Dominion.

20. Bourinot, *The Intellectual Development of the Canadian People: An Historical Review* (Toronto, 1881).

21. Quoted in Neil McDonald, 'Canadianization and the Curriculum: Setting the Stage, 1867–1890', in E.B. Titley and Peter J. Miller, eds, *Education in Canada: An Interpretation* (Calgary, 1982), 97.

22. Ibid., 100.

23. An anthology of their work and critical comment upon it, edited by Tracy Ware, is in *A Northern Romanticism: Poets of the Confederation* (Ottawa, 2000). See also Malcolm Ross, ed., *Poets of the Confederation: Carman/Lampman/Roberts/Scott* (Toronto, 1960); George Woodcock, ed., *Colony and Confederation: Early Canadian Poets and Their Background* (Vancouver, 1974).

24. Ware, *Northern Romanticism*, 79.

25. Quoted in Moncrieff Williamson, *Robert Harris 1849–1919: An Unconventional Biography* (Toronto, 1970), 64.

26. For a further discussion of this theme, see Dennis Reid, *Our Own Country Canada: Being an Account of the National Aspirations of the Principal Landscape Artists in Montreal and Toronto, 1860–1890* (Ottawa, 1979), 298ff.

27. Carl Berger, *Honour and the Search for Influence: A History of the Royal Society of Canada* (Toronto, 1996).

28. Quoted in The Royal Society of Canada, *Fifty Years' Retrospect, 1882–1932* (Toronto, 1932), 91–2.

29. For a detailed account of the negotiation of Treaty No. 6, see Deanna Christensen, *Ahtahkakoop: The Epic Account of a Plains Cree Head Chief, His People, and Their Struggle for Survival, 1816–1896* (Shell Lake, Sask., 2000), esp. 217–312.

30. Quoted in D.N. Sprague, 'The Manitoba Land Question, 1870–1882', in J.M. Bumsted, ed., *Interpreting Canada's Past*, vol. 2 (Toronto, 1986), 4.

31. David Lee, 'The Métis: Militant Rebels of 1885', *Canadian Ethnic Studies* 21, 3 (1989): 1–19.

32. Quoted in *DCB*, XI, 746.

33. Quoted in Hartwell Bowsfield, *Louis Riel: The Rebel and the Hero* (Toronto, 1971), 116. Other studies of Riel—who has been the subject of more biographical attention than any other figure in Canadian history—include George Stanley, *Louis Riel* (Toronto, 1963); Thomas Flanagan, *Louis 'David' Riel: Prophet of the New Land* (rev. edn, Toronto, 1992); and my *Louis Riel v. Canada: The Making of a Rebel* (Winnipeg, 2001).

34. Bowsfield, *Louis Riel*, 121.

35. Ibid., 122.

36. The best survey of the rebellion is Bob Beal and Rod Macleod, *Prairie Fire: The 1885 North-West Rebellion*, 2nd edn (Toronto, 1994).

37. Bruce Tascona and Eric Wells, *Little Black Devils: A History of the Royal Winnipeg Rifles* (Winnipeg, 1983), 25–53.

38. See my 'Louis Riel and the United States', *American Review of Canadian Studies* 29, 1 (1999): 17–42.

39. A transcript of the trial is in Desmond Morton, ed., *The Queen v. Louis Riel* (Toronto, 1974).

40. Rev. edn (Toronto, 1998). For the other side, consult George R.D. Goulet, *The Trial of Louis Riel: Justice and Mercy Denied* (Calgary, 1999).

41. Blair Stonechild and Bill Waiser, *Loyal till Death: Indians and the North-West Rebellions* (Calgary, 1997).

42. Bowsfield, *Louis Riel*, 153.

43. Quoted in Barbara Robertson, *Wilfrid Laurier: The Great Conciliator* (Toronto, 1971), 50–1.

44. Quoted in Peter Li, *The Chinese in Canada* (Toronto, 1988), 29.

45. Quoted in A.I. Silver, *The French-Canadian Idea of Confederation, 1864–1900* (Toronto, 1982), 147.

46. In general, consult ibid.

Abenaki, 179

Aboriginal peoples, 3–20, 33, 35–7; alliance with French and, 159–61; in Atlantic region, 10–11, 334–5; in British Columbia, 16–18, 443, 450; British North American society and, 324, 331–8; British policy and, 202, 208–10, 215, 394; childrearing and, 35–6; concept of property and, 33, 35; creation myths of, 3–4; Dominion policy and, 586, 588–9, 595–6; early record of, 5–8; as explorers, 26–7, 195; European contacts and, 21–39; European disease and, 23; European explorers and, 43, 46, 48, 50–5, 56; fur trade and, 83, 89, 97, 217–18; Great Lakes region and, 12–13; guns and, 33; HBC and, 435, 441–2; imperial wars and, 170, 172, 179; knowledge of, 24; as Loyalists, 223, 228, 230, 236–7; missionaries and, 61, 84–5, 92–4, 98; myths of, 38; names of groups of, 8, 10; New France and, 79, 83, 84–5, 88–92, 130; North-West rebellion and, 592, 593–4; numbers of, 23, 193, 277, 332–3; Plains region and, 13–16; Pre-Cambrian Shield region and, 12; rights of, 193–4, 195, 333, 334; sexual mores of, 36–7; spirituality and, 37–8; sport and, 495; stereotypes and, 194; sub-arctic and arctic regions and, 18–19; views on Europeans and, 30–3; War of 1812 and, 253, 255; writing history of, xiv–xv, 192–5; see also specific groups

Acadia, 66–77, 141, 144–53; British and, 147–8, 153; expulsions from, 180–3, 184–5; government of, 14; oath and, 148, 181–3; war and, 177–80; see also Nova Scotia

Act for the Abolition of the Slave Trade, 282

adultery, 327

Agona, 50

agriculture, 295, 304–6, 322–3, 325; Aboriginal peoples and, 12–13, 588; in Acadia, 144–5; family farm and, 455–7; HBC and, 394–6; industrialization and, 508–9; in New France, 79, 83, 106, 113–16; in North-West Territories, 585; reciprocity and, 422; on Vancouver Island, 397

Alberta, 563

alcohol, 470–1

Alexander, Sir William, 63, 70, 71

Algonquian language group, 10, 16

Algonquin people, 83

Allan, Hugh, 459, 505, 574

Allan, John, 214

Allen, Ethan, 211, 242

Alline, Henry, 223, 226–7

American Revolution, 210–21, 223; Atlantic region and, 213–15; invasion of Canada and, 211–13; western region and, 215

Americas: European 'discovery' of, 44–56

Amherst, Jeffrey, 184, 190, 200–1, 208

Andrews, Israel D., 420

Anglicans: see Church of England

Annand, William, 537, 538, 550

annexation: US and, 411, 419–20, 444–5

anti-confederate movement, 548–50

Anti-Slavery Society of Canada, 331

Archaic culture, 8

Archibald, Adams, 562–3

architecture: early Victorian, 490–2; Loyalists and, 243–4; in New France, 134, 137–9

Arctic: expeditions to, 45, 55–6, 450–1

Argall, Samuel, 69–70

Arnold, Benedict, 211, 213, 224, 242–3

art(s), 583–4; galleries and, 478; in New France, 133–4; performing, 476–7, 482–9

Articles of Capitulation, 200–1

assemblies, colonial: see legislatures, colonial

Assiniboine people 16

asylums, 384–5

Athapaskan language group, 16, 18

Atlantic region, 144–58, 295–8; Aboriginal peoples and, 10–11, 334–5; American Revolution and, 213–15; anti-confederates in, 548–50; colonization of, 59–78; Confederation and, 525, 528–9, 534–8; after Confederation, 548–53; golden age of sail and, 391–3; immigration and, 280, 282; population mobility and, 458; responsible government in, 372–3; after Seven Years' War, 203–4; see also specific colonies, provinces

Attiwandaronk people, 12

Aubert de Gaspé, Philippe-Joseph, 349

Aubin, Aimé-Nicolas, 487–8

Axtell, James, 195

Baby, François, 209

Backhouse, Constance, 361

Baffin, William, 56

Bagot, Charles, 371

Bailey, Alfred, 194

Bailey, Jacob, 235

Baldwin, Robert, 319, 369, 370, 372, 375

Baldwin, William Warren, 258, 319, 320–1, 369

Baltimore, Lord, 59–61, 71, 73
Bank Act, 574
Bank of Montreal, 310, 505
banks, 310–11, 502, 505, 574
Bank of Upper Canada, 310
Bannatyne, Annie, 438
Bannatyne, Robert, 353
Baptists, 347
Barings and Glyns, 401
Barker, Billy, 446
Barney Rooney's Letters, 531
baseball, 358, 495, 496–7
Beauharnois de la Boische, Charles de, 161
beaver, 'Made/Parchment', 300
Bédard, Pierre-Stanislas, 253
Beers, William George, 495
Begbie, Matthew, 442, 445
Bell system, 350
Benson, Wilson, 291, 459
Beothuk people, 10, 334
Berczy, William, 228
Beringia, 5–7
Best, George, 56
Biard, Pierre, 69
Bicket, James, 356
Bidwell, Barnabas, 257, 258
Bidwell, Marshall Spring, 257, 264
Biencourt, Charles de, 67, 69, 70
Bienville, Jean-Baptiste le Moyne de, 159
Big Bear, 588, 593
Biggs, C. Lesley, 361
Bigot, François, 119, 201
Birchtown, NS, 232
Blackfoot people, 16
black people, 329–31, 332; immigration and, 282–3, 292–3; as Loyalists, 223, 232–4; as refugees, 282–3, 329; on Vancouver Island, 448
Blake, Edward, 576
Blanshard, Richard, 396, 443
Bleus, 376
Blodgett, Lorin, 442
'Blue Books', 378
Board of Audit, 380, 381
books, 473–6, 482; *see also* literature
Borah, W.W., and S.F. Cook, 193
border, US–Canada, 256, 411–19
Boucault, Nicolas-Gaspard, 115–16
Bougainville, Louis-Antoine, 110, 112–13
Boulton, C.A., 557, 562
Bourgeau, Victor, 490–1
Bourgeoys, Marguerite, 88, 95, 99
Bourget, Ignace, 463, 486, 488
Bourinot, John, 578–9
Braddock, Edward, 183
Bradford, Sarah Elizabeth Hopkins, 417
Brant, Joseph, 215, 228, 237
Brébeuf, Jean de, 87, 89, 133
breweries, 502, 503
Briand, Jean-Olivier, 205, 211
Britain: British North American policy and, 200–3; colonial economy and, 295; colonial government and, 246–8; Confederation and, 524–5; empire and, 141, 143; free trade in, 389–90; Hudson Bay and, 164–6; Newfoundland and, 156–7; relationship with Canada after 1840, 388–410; US relations and, 411; war with France and, 170–91; War of 1812 and, 253–6; *see also* England

British American Land Company, 288, 289
British American League, 524
British Columbia, 395–6, 443–50; Confederation and, 563–70; responsible government in, 373
British Isles: immigration from, 273–5, 279, 280–2, 283–92, 402–6
British North America: British empire and, 388–410; British money market and, 401–2; colonial period of, 197–359; constitutional problems in, 373–7; culture in, 340–59; economy of, 295–316; free trade in, 390–1; immigration and, 123–7, 273–94; imperial sentiment and, 406–9; military and, 398–401; political opposition in, 251–3, 256–71; political reform in, 367–77; politics in, 246–72; society in, 317–39, 453–72; as term, 365
British North America Act, 582–3
Brooke, Frances, 354
Brown, Andrew, 344, 346
Brown, George, 394, 478, 479, 576; Confederation and, 527–8; reform and, 374, 375–6
Brown, John, 417
Brûlé, Étienne, 96
buffalo, 14, 439, 440, 441
Buillion, Madame de, 88
Burke, Edmund, 206, 208
Burrows, Jack, 416
Bylot, Robert, 56

'Cabal', 248–9
Cabot, John, xi, 45–7
Cabot, Sebastian, 46
Calvert, George, *see* Baltimore, Lord
Campbell, Gail C., 361
Campbell, William Wilfrid, 583
Canada: *see* British North America; Canada East; Canada West; Dominion of Canada; Lower Canada; New France; Upper Canada
Canada Company, 288–9
Canada East, 370–2; civil service in, 379–81; double majority and, 373, 376–7; law reform in, 519; population mobility in, 453–5; reform and, 374; religion and, 375
'Canada First', 560, 578
Canada West, 370–2; civil service in, 379–81; double majority and, 376–7; population mobility in, 455–8; religion and, 375
Canadian Pacific Railway, 574, 594, 596
'Canadian Party', 436
canals, 311, 312–13, 501, 510
Cape Breton Island, 141, 142, 146, 202; Loyalists and, 230, 239
card money, 117–19
Carheil, Étienne de, 174
Carignan-Salières regiment, 110, 170
Carleton, Guy, 205–6, 207–8, 211, 213, 229
Carleton, Thomas, 251
carnival, 137
Carr, E.H., xiii
carrying trade, 307, 309–10, 391–3; *see also* shipping
Carson, William, 251
Carter, Frederick, 553
Cartier, George, 534
Cartier, George-Étienne, 376, 386, 519, 528, 554
Cartier, Jacques, 21, 47–55
Cataraqui (Kingston), ON, 238
Cayuga people, 83
census: in Acadia, 144–5; in British North America, 277; on Île Saint-Jean, 146; in Illinois, 162–3; in Nova Scotia, 203–4
Chambly Canal, 311
Champlain, Samuel de, 32, 66, 71, 96; Quebec and, 79–83, 85–6
Champlain and St Lawrence Railroad Company, 422, 502

Chandler-Haliburton, Thomas, 319
charivari, 137
Charlottetown, 311
Charlottetown Conference, 522, 528
Charly Saint-Ange, Louis, 116
Château Clique, 248–9, 252
Chauveau, Pierre, 492
Chauvigny, Marie-Madeleine de, 87
Chauvin de Tonnetuit, Pierre de, 61, 62, 66
Cherrier, Rosalie, 249–50
Chilcotin people, 18
children: Aboriginal, 35–6; family farm and, 455–6, 457; industrialization and, 512, 516–18; in New France, 129–30
China: immigration from, 448–9, 594, 596
Chiniquy, Charles, 471
Chipewyan people, 18
Christie, David, 374
Church of England, 239, 241, 344–7, 348
churches, 490–1; *see also* religion; specific sects
circuses, 483, 484
cities, 311–15, 512–15
civil service: Canada East and West and, 379–81
Clark, George Rogers, 215
Clarke, James P., 489
class: colonial, 321–3, 324–5; early Victorian society and, 459–61; middle, 460–1; sport and, 495; upper, 248–9, 251–3, 254–5, 264, 317, 318–21, 459; working, 459, 515–18
Clear Grits, 367, 374, 376
Clinton, Henry, 232
clothing: in New France, 137
coal, 509
Colbert, Jean-Baptiste, 105, 107, 108, 113, 125
Colborne, John, 264, 268–9, 348–9
Coldwell, William, 436, 437
Coles, George, 550–1
College of Physicians and Surgeons, 460
colleges, 480–2, 579
Colonial Office, 246, 248, 333–4; British North America and, 393–8; Confederation and, 524–5, 538; responsible government and, 370–1, 378, 379
colonization: absentee, 59–61; Atlantic region and, 59–78; charters and grants and, 61; early French, 52–4; motives for, 59–64; New France and, 79–103; unwanted populations and, 62–3
'colonization roads', 378
Communauté des Habitants, 89
Company of One Hundred Associates (Compagnie de la Nouvelle France), 73, 75, 76, 83–4, 85–6, 89, 99
Confederation: early ideas of, 522–4; historiography of, 542–4; international background to, 527; local legislatures and, 530–1
Confederation poets, 583
Conseil Souverain, 108
Conservatives, 375–6
Constitutional Act (1791), 241
contact(s): 'first', 21, 23; types of, 23
Cook, James, 21, 218–19
Cooper, William, 259–60, 261
Corbett, G.O., 436
Corn Laws, 302, 390
Cornwallis, Edward, 154, 181, 219, 221
Cornwallis, Kinahan, 445
Council of Assiniboia, 424
councils, colonial, 248–9
coureurs de bois, 96–8
courts, 386, 575

Coutume de Paris, 128–9
Craig, James, 253
Crawford, Isabella Valancy, 580, 583
Crease, Henry and Sarah, 342
Cree, 14, 16, 588
Creighton, Donald, 192
Crémazie, Octave, 578, 579
Croghan, George, 208
Crown Lands department, 377–8
Crozat, Antoine, 159
Crozier, L.N.F., 592
culture: in British North America, 340–59, 473–98; after 1867, 579–83; high, 340, 350–5; infrastructure of, 473–82; in New France, 131–9; popular, 134–7, 340, 355–8, 494–7
Cunard, Samuel, 304, 307, 308
Cunningham, Robert, 436
curling, 356
currency, 117–19, 310–11, 574

Dalhousie, George Ramsey, 282
Dalhousie College, 348
dance, 489
D'Aulnay, Charles de Menou, 75, 76
Davies, Robertson, 482
Davies, Thomas, 290
Davis, John, 56
Dawson, J.W., 584
Dawson, Simon James, 442
De Cosmos, Amor, 563
Dee, John, 55
Deerfield, MA, 176–7
Delgamuukw case, 194
Denison, George, 560
Denison, John, 318
Dennis, John Stoughton, 555
Denonville, Marquis de, 130, 172
DesBarres, J.F.W., 203, 252
Dewart, E.H., 479
Dick, John, 155–6
Dièreville, Sieur de, 144–5
diet, 138, 306–7
disease: Aboriginal peoples and, 23, 441
divorce, 327
Dobyns, Henry, and William R. Swagerty, 193
documentation: Aboriginal history and, 193–5; historical, *xii–xiii, xv*
Dogrib people, 18
Dollard des Ormeaux, Adam, 92
Dollier de Casson, François, 89–90
Domagaya, 48, 50, 51
domesticity, 340–4
Dominion of Canada, 538, 547; completion of Confederation and, 548–71; expansion of, 553–5; intellectual development and, 578–83; national identity and, 578–94; national policies and, 572–6
Dominion Day, 468
Dominion Lands Act, 585
Dominion Lands Survey, 585
Dominion Note Act, 574
Donnacona, 48, 51, 52
Dorion, A.-A., 534
Dorion, Jean-Baptiste-Eric, 533
Dorset people, 10, 18
'double majority', 373, 376–7, 529
Douglas, James, 373, 396, 443–6, 563

Drake, Francis, 54
Draper, William Henry, 371
Dumont, Gabriel, 592
Duncombe, Charles, 265, 268
Dunkin, Christopher, 524, 576
Dunlop, William ('Tiger'), 289
Dunphy, James, 463
Duplessis, Marguerite, 132
Durham, John George Lambton, Earl of, 247, 249, 268, 270, 379; report of, 288, 365, 369–70
Duval, Jean, 81, 83

Eastern Townships, 454–5
economy: Aboriginal, 33, 35–7; in British North America, 295–316; foreign investment in, 295, 401–2, 574; industrialization and, 421, 499–521; in New France, 113–21
Eddy, Jonathan, 214
education, 579, 582–3; as cultural institution, 340, 347–50; higher, 480–2; Loyalists and, 241; in New France, 92–3, 109, 109, 129–30, 134, 138; public, 349, 381, 383–4, 582–3; reforms in, 381–4; systems of, 349–50; see also schools
Edward VII (Prince of Wales), 406–9
elections: colonial, 249, 250, 257–8, 259; united Canadas and, 371
Elgin, Lord, 371–2, 374, 421
elites: colonial government and, 248–9, 251–3, 254–5, 264; commercial, 317, 320; governing, 317, 318–21; regional, 321–2
Elizabeth I (England), 45
Ellice, Edward, 289, 395
Ellis, C. Douglas, 14
England: colonization and, 59, 61–2, 64–6; empire and, 141, 143; exploration and, 45–7, 55–7; New France and, 110–13; sovereignty and, 30; see also Britain
English Shore, 66
Enjalran, Jean, 133
Eric the Red, 41
Eriksson, Leif, 41–2
Escheat Party, 261
ethnohistory, 193
Europeans: Aboriginal contacts and, 21–39; views on Aboriginal peoples and, 30–3
Évanturel, François, 532
Ewing, Juliana Horatia, 484–5
exploration: Aboriginal peoples and, 26–7, 195; early European, 40–58; English, 55–6; French, 47–55, 158–9; inland, 96, 158–9; Norse, 40–4

Fagundes, Juan, 46
Family Compact, 248–9, 257–9, 346
Fanning, Edmond, 237
Fenians, 536, 537, 572
filles du roi, 99, 106, 125, 129, 131
Fingard, Judith, 361
fires, 514–15
fisheries, 295, 296–8, 572–3; Acadia and, 145; cod, 46, 55, 64–6; inland, 378; Newfoundland and, 157–8; population and, 458; reciprocity and, 422
Fitzgerald, James E., 396
Five Nations, 12, 83, 91, 170, 172
Fléché, Jessé, 67, 69
Fleming, Michael, 463
folksongs, 135–6, 489
'foreign Protestants', 154–6, 202–3
Fort Beauséjour, 181
Fort Cumberland, 214

Fort Garry, 556, 557, 560
Fort La Tour, 73, 75–7
Fort Vancouver, 300
Fort William, 433–4
France: colonization and, 59, 61–4, 66–77, 79–103; empire and, 141, 143; exploration and, 45, 47–55; Hudson Bay and, 164; restoration of Canada and, 201; sovereignty and, 30; war with Britain and, 170–91
François I (France), 45, 47
Franklin, John, 450–1
Fraser, Simon, 298
Fréchette, Louis-Honoré, 579
Free Public Education Act, 582
free trade, 388, 389–91
Frobisher, Martin, 45, 54–6
Frontenac, Louis Buade de, 107, 173
Fugitive Slave Law, 293, 416, 417
fur trade, 166, 295, 298–302, 432–4; New France and, 79, 81, 83, 89, 98, 113, 120–1; after Seven Years' War, 215–19

Gage, Thomas, 210
Gagnon, Ernest, 489
Galt, Alexander Tilloch, 501
Galt, John, 288, 289
games, early Victorian, 494–7
Garden, George, 250
Garneau, F.-X., 481
garrisons, 399–400
Gaspé, 297–8
Geological Survey of Canada, 492, 493
geology, 493, 494
Gérin-Lajoie, Antoine, 454
Gesner, Abraham, 477, 493
Giffard de Moncel, Robert, 86
Gladman, George, 442
Gladstone, William, 394
Glenie, James, 252–3
Globensky, Hortense, 249
gold, 443–50, 509; Cartier and, 52; Frobisher and, 56
Gordon, Arthur Hamilton, 525
Gourlay, Robert, 256–7, 261
government: administrative, 377–86; British colonial, 246–53; Colonial Office and, 393–8; in New France, 104–10; representative, 372–3, 374; responsible, 260, 365, 367–73, 393–4; society and, 318
Governor General's awards, 584
grain, 295, 304–6; exports of, 390; reciprocity and, 422
Grand Trunk Railway, 401, 425, 428, 499, 501, 519
Grant, George Monro, 584
Granville, Lord, 565–6
Gravé Du Point, François, 67
'Great Coalition', 528
Great Farini, 484
Great Peace of 1701, 112, 161
Great Western Railway, 424–5, 429, 499
Greer, Allan, 130
Grenville, George, 201–2
Grey, Lord, 399
Grits, 374, 376
Groseilliers, Médard Chouart Des, 98, 164–5
Gros Ventre people, 16
Guadeloupe, 201
Guercheville, Antoinette de Pons, Marquise de, 69
Guillemot, Guillaume, 92

Gulf Islands, 416
Guthry, Richard, 70, 72–3
Guy, John, 64, 66
Gwich'in people, 18
Gyles, John, 34, 130
Gzowski, Casimir Stanislaus, 501

Haida, 17–18
Hakluyt, Richard, *xvi*, 52
'halfbreeds', 440
Haliburton, T.C., 340, 351–3, 479
Halifax, 153–6
Hamilton, Henry, 215
Hamilton, ON, 506–8, 512–13
Happy, Jesse, 329
Harmon, Daniel, 343, 353
Hart, Julia Catherine, 354
Harvey, John, 372
Hawke, Edward, 179
Hayman, Robert, 65
Haythorne, Robert, 551–2
Hazen, Moses, 223, 225–6
Head, Edmund Walker, 524–5, 376
Head, Francis Bond, 264, 336
Head-Smashed-in Buffalo Jump, 14
Hearne, Samuel, 26–7, 218
Heavysege, Charles, 482, 483
Hébert, Louis, 83
Heck, Barbara Ruckle, 235
Helmcken, John, 563, 564–5, 566–8
Henri IV (France), 61
Henry VII (England), 45
Henry VIII (England), 46–7
Hincks, Francis, 375, 376
Hind, Henry Youle, 442–3, 479
historiography, *viii*
history: conventions of, *xiii–xiv*; new interpretations and, *xiv–xv*; quantification and, *xv*; value of, *viii–x*
Hochelaga, 50, 52
hockey, 356, 358, 496
Hocquart, Gilles, 120
holidays, civic, 467–9
'homeguards', 324
Hope, BC, 449
Hopson, Peregrine, 181
Hore, Richard, 47
Hornby, Edmund, 425, 428
horse: industrial Canada and, 513
hospitals, 87, 94–5, 109
House of Commons, 530
housing, 325–6; early Victorian, 491–2; in New France, 137–9
Howatt, Cornelius, 552
Howe, Joseph, 335, 351, 357–8, 398, 478; Confederation and, 537, 548–50, 553; Red River and, 555; reform and, 259–60, 262–3
Howison, John, 307
Hoyles, Hugh, 535
Hudson, Henry, 56
Hudson Bay, 141, 158, 164–6; discovery of, 56; war and, 176
Hudson's Bay Company (HBC), 141, 164–6, 298, 299–302, 432–4; Britain and, 394–6; Red River and, 434–42, 554, 557; Vancouver Island and, 396
Hunt, Thomas Sterry, 584
Hunt, William Leonard, 484
hunting: Aboriginal peoples and, 14, 33; as sport, 495; *see also* buffalo

Huronia, 87, 89–92
Huron people, 12, 89, 160

Iberville, Pierre Le Moyne d', 159, 172–4, 176
ice ages, 7, 8
Iceland: immigrants from, 586
Île Royale (Cape Breton Island), 141, 142, 146
Île Saint-Jean (PEI), 141, 146
Illinois, 161–3
immigration: 'advice' and, 275; assisted, 284, 285–8; British Isles and, 273–5, 279, 280–2, 283–92, 402–6; ethnic groups and, 585–6; government-assisted, 285–6; to New France, 123–7; to Nova Scotia, 153–6; poverty and, 324; private assistance and, 286–8; private land companies and, 288–9; from 1791–1860, 273–94; transportation and, 290–2, 403–6; unassisted, 291–2
Indian Act, 192, 588–9
'Indian policy', 333–4, 336
industrialization, 421, 499–521; cities and, 512–15; infrastructure for, 500–1; labour and, 510–12; law and, 518–19; new resource industries and, 509–10
Inglis, Charles, 237, 241, 346
Inglis, John, 346
Ingstad, Helge, 42
Innu, 12
Institut Canadien, 463, 475
Intercolonial Railway, 528–9, 535–6
'interior French', 208, 215, 217
investment, foreign, 574; Britain and, 295, 401–2; US and, 295
Ireland: immigrants from, 461–2, 285–6; *see also* British Isles
Iroquois, 12; as Loyalists, 228, 230, 236–7; missionaries and, 98; New France and, 83, 88–92, 110–13; war against, 170, 172; *see also* Five Nations
Isbister, Alexander, 394
Island of Saint John (PEI), 202, 203, 230, 239

Jackson, W.H., 591
James Bay, 56
Jameson, Anna Brownell, 354–5
Jansenism, 95–6
Jarvis, Edward, 342
Jessop, John, 382–3
Jesuit Relations, *xvi*, 84–5, 88
Jesuits, 67, 69; expulsion of, 201; marriage and, 161; New France and, 84–5, 86–92, 98
Jesuits' Estates, 378
Johnson, George, 61
Jolliet, Louis, 158
Jones, Eliza, 337
Jones, Peter, 336, 337
Jones, William Harris, 478
journalism: Loyalists and, 244; *see also* newspapers
Judicature Act, 519

Kalm, Peter, 104, 115, 127, 131, 134, 138
Karlsefni, Thorfinn, 43
Kaskaskia, 161–2
Kaské, Charlot, 210
Keefer, Thomas Coltrin, 423–4, 428–9
Kelsey, Henry, 164, 166
Kennedy, Arthur, 373
Kennewick Man, 5
Ketchum, Jesse, 258
Killian, Bernard, 536
King George's War, 177–80

King William's War, 172–6
Kirke, Sir David, 66, 70, 71
Kirke brothers, 84, 96
Klilnck, Carl, 479
Knight, James, 165, 166
Knights of St Crispin, 511
Kohl, Johann Georg, 489
Kootenay people, 18
Kwakwaka-wakw people, 18

La Barre, Joseph-Antoine Le Febvre de, 172
labour, organized, 510–11
Lachine Canal, 311, 510
lacrosse, 358, 495
La Dauversière, Jérôme Le Royer de, 88
La Fontaine, Louis-H., 371, 372, 375
Lalemant, Charles, 88, 89, 97
Lampman, Archibald, 583
Lancaster, Joseph, 350
land: Crown Lands department and, 377–8; development of, 322;
    immigration and, 284, 285, 286, 287, 288–9, 585–6; policy and,
    284–9, 585–6; price of, 396–7; Prince Edward Island and, 397–8;
    section of, 585
Land Purchase Act, 398
Langton, John, 380–1
language, 578; Aboriginal, 5, 11, 16, 18, 25, 29–30, 97; British North
    America and, 273; civil service and, 379; Loyalists and, 243; New
    France and, 131
L' Anse aux Meadows, 40–4
La Roche de Mesgouez, Marquis de, 61, 62–3, 66
La Salle, René-Robert Cavelier de, 158–9
'last spike', 547, 594
La Tour, Charles, 67, 70, 73, 76–7
La Tour, Claude de Saint-Étienne de, 67, 70, 73, 75, 76
La Tour, Françoise-Marie Jacquelin, 75, 76
Laurier, Wilfrid, 594
Laval, François de, 98–9
La Vérendrye, Pierre Gaultier de Varennes et de, 28–9
La Vérendrye family, 166, 168
law: Aboriginal peoples and, 441–2; colonial, 326–9, 328–9; economic
    development and, 518–19; French civil code, 326; master-ser-
    vant, 327–8; practice of, 460; in Quebec, 206; reforms in, 385–6;
    women and, 326–9
Lawrence, Charles, 154, 156, 181, 183, 203
Law Society of Upper Canada, 460
Leacock, Stephen, 457, 587
Le Ber, Pierre, 134
Leblanc de Marconnay, Hyacinthe-Poirer, 486–7
Le Febvre de La Barre, Joseph-Antoine, 111
Légaré, Joseph, 478
legislatures: colonial, 246–7, 249, 251–3, 257–8; local, 530–1
Le Jeune, Paul, 84, 86–7, 92
Lemay, Léon-Pamphile, 579
Lépine, Ambroise, 559–60, 561–2
Lescarbot, Marc, 67
Levasseur, François-Noël, 120
Lévis, François, 188–90
Liberals, 376
libraries, 473–6
Lincoln, Abraham, 430
Lind, Jenny, 488
literacy, 480, 579
literature, 340, 351–5, 357–8, 479–80, 482, 579, 580–1, 583, 584;
    French-language, 480, 481; fur trade journals as, 343, 355

Logan, William Edmund, 477–8, 493
Lok, Michael, 55, 56
Lorne, Lord, 584
Louisbourg, 146–7, 179, 180, 181, 184
Louisiana, 158–9, 201
Lount, Samuel, 267, 268
Lovell, John, 479
Lower, Arthur, 192
Lower Canada, 241; agriculture in, 306; Americans in, 280; govern-
    ment in, 246; political parties in, 252–3; rebellion in, 264–5,
    268–71; riots in, 261; union with Upper Canada and, 369–70,
    522–3
Loyal Electors, 252
Loyalist Claims Commission, 230, 237
Loyalists, 207–8, 223–45; Aboriginal, 223, 228, 230, 236–7; black,
    223, 232–4; compensation and, 229, 230, 231, 232, 233–4,
    237–8, 241; composition of, 229–32; elite, 237–8; ethnic, 235–6;
    impact of, 239–44; inhabitants' response to, 223–7; 'late',
    279–80, 305; settlement and politics and, 238–9; unification and,
    523–4; women as, 224–5, 232, 233–5
Lynch, John Joseph, 469

McClintock, Leopold, 451
McCulloch, Thomas, 340, 351
MacDonald, Helen (Nelly), 223–5
MacDonald, John, 203, 225
Macdonald, John A., 375–7, 380, 518, 548; British Columbia and, 565;
    Confederation and, 528, 529, 530, 538, 540; national policies
    and, 572–4, 575–6; North-West Territories and, 585, 589, 592;
    Pacific Scandal and, 574; provincial rights and, 576; Red River
    and, 556; Supreme Court and, 575
Macdonnell, Alexander, 344
MacDonnell, Richard, 537
McDougall, Duncan, 289
McDougall, William, 553–4, 556, 561
McGee, Thomas D'Arcy, 507, 525–6, 560
McGill, James, 348
McGill College, 348
MacGregor, John, 307, 390
Mackenzie, Alexander (explorer), 298, 353
Mackenzie, Alexander (politician), 551, 572, 574–5
McKenzie, Kenneth, 397
Mackenzie, William Lyon, 258–61, 313, 380; education and, 349; rebel-
    lion and, 264, 265, 267, 268; unions and, 510
McLane, David, 261
Maclean, Allan, 211, 213
MacNab, Allan, 375, 376, 425, 519
Mactavish, William, 555
magazines, 351, 478–80
Mair, Charles, 483, 438, 578
Maisonneuve, Paul de Chomedy de, 87, 88, 99
Major, Charles, 445
Maliseet people, 179
Mallepart de Grand Maison, Paul (dit Beaucour), 134
Mance, Jean, 87, 94–5, 137
Manitoba: creation of, 553–63; legal profession in, 460
Manitoba Act, 560, 562–3, 570
manufacturing, 308–10, 499–521; in New France, 120
Marguerie de la Haye, François, 96–7
Marie de l'Incarnation, 92–4, 99, 102, 110
Marquette, Jacques, 158
marriage, 327, 343; Aboriginal/French, 161–4; in New France, 129
Marwick, Arthur, xiii
Mason, John, 61, 63

Massé, Enemond, 69
Massey family, 505–6
Massey Manufacturing Co., 506
Matonabbee, 26–7
Matthews, Peter, 267, 268
Mechanics' Institutes, 510
medicine, 460
Meilleur, Jean-Baptiste, 383
Membertou, 69
mercantilism, 307–15, 388–90
merchants, 307–8, 320
Merchants' Bank of Canada, 505
Mercier, Honoré, 576, 594
Merritt, William Hamilton, 312, 420
Metcalfe, Charles T., 332, 371
Methodists, 347
Métis, 195, 434–6, 438–40, 585, 589–92; provisional government and, 557–8; resistance and, 555–63
Michilimackinac, 161
'Middle Ground', 253, 255
Middleton, Frederick, 592
Mi'kmaq, 10–11, 23, 179, 334–5
military: cost of, 398–401; criticism of, 175; in New France, 110–13
militia, 111–13, 172, 400–1
Mills, Antonia, 194
mining, 509; copper, 434; gold, 443–50
minstrel shows, 483
missionaries: Aboriginal peoples and, 61, 84–5, 92–4, 98, 130; in Acadia, 67, 69, 145–6; coureurs de bois and, 96–8; in New France, 52, 79, 84–5, 86–9, 89–92; women as, 87, 92–6
Mississauga people, 336, 337
Mohawk people, 83
Moir, Susan Louise, 449
Molson, John, 459
Molson family, 502–3
Monck, Frances, 489
Monitorial system, 350
Monk, George, 334–5
Montagnais people, 83
Montaigne, Michel de, 32
Montcalm, Louis-Joseph de, 119, 185–8, 189
Montgomery, Richard, 213
Montreal, 127, 311, 313, 314–15; industrialization in, 504–5, 512–13; population of, 455; surrender of, 190
Montreal Gas Light Co., 502
Montreal Medical Institution, 460
Montreal Ocean Steamship Co., 505
Montreal Telegraph Company, 365
Monts, Pierre du Gua, Sieur de, 62, 66–7, 79, 81
Moodie, Susanna, 354, 479
Moody, James, 241
Moody, R.C., 400, 448
Moogk, Peter, 32
Moose Fort (Moose Factory), 172–3
Morgan, Cecilia, 362
Morin, Augustin-Norbert, 375, 376
Morris, Alexander, 394, 525, 588
Mountain, Jacob, 346, 347
Mowat, Oliver, 575, 576
Mulligan, James, 436
Murray, James, 188, 190, 204–5
museums, 477–8
Musgrave, Anthony, 552, 565–6, 568, 570
music, 340, 355; early Victorian, 488–9; in New France, 132–3, 135–6

National Committee of the Métis, 555
National Gallery of Canada, 583
nationalism, 578
national policies, 572–6
National Policy, 575–6
natural resources, 295; new, 509–10; truck system and, 323–4
navigation, 40–1, 44–5
Nelson, Wolfred, 268
Neolin, 208–10
New Brunswick: anti-confederates in, 548–50; Confederation and, 535–6, 538; education in, 582–3; Loyalists and, 237, 238, 239; political opposition in, 251–3; shipbuilding in, 308; timber and, 302, 304
New Brunswick and Nova Scotia Land Company, 288, 289–90
'New England', 63
New England 'Planters', 203
Newfoundland, 141, 156–8, 295–7; American Revolution and, 214–15; colonization of, 63, 64–6; Confederation and, 534–5, 552–3; French in, 157; Loyalists and, 230; religion in, 375; responsible government in, 372–3; Vikings and, 40–4; war and, 173–4, 176
Newfoundland Company, 64–6
New France, 79–103; as Crown colony, 99–102, 104–110; culture of, 131–9; economic development and, 113–21; elite in, 113, 116; government of, 107–10; industry in, 120; invasions of, 173; military and, 110–13; political system of, 100–1, 107–8; population of, 123–7; protests in, 108; settlement patterns and, 127–8; social structure of, 130–1; society and, 127–31; war and, 170–91
'New Holland', 77
'New Scotland', 63–4, 73, 72–3
newspapers, 351, 436, 579; colonial, 252, 258, 262–3, 265, 269; Confederation and, 524, 525–6, 529, 532, 534, 535, 537, 550, 551; early Victorian, 478–80, 481, 488; in New France, 131–2
New Westminster, BC, 448
Nicollet, Jean, 86
Nolan, Joseph, 559
Nootka Sound, 219
North, Lord, 206
North West Company, 298–9, 300, 432–4, 437
North West Mounted Police, 586, 592
Northwest Passage, 45, 55–6
North-West rebellion, 592–4
North-West Territories, 554, 563, 584–94
Nova Scotia, 141, 246, 296: American Revolution and, 213–15; anti-confederates in, 548–50; black immigrants and, 282; colonization of, 63–4, 66–77; Confederation and, 537–8, 540; as cultural centre, 351; Loyalists and, 228–9, 230, 232, 238–9; politics in, 262–3; responsible government in, 372; settlement in, 148–56; after Seven Years' War, 202, 203–4; war and, 177–80; *see also* Acadia
Nova Scotia Repeal League, 549
Nuu-chah-nulth people, 18

O'Brien, Lucius, 584
Ochiltree, Lord, 70
Ojibwa, 12, 336–7
Okanagan people, 18
Oneida, 83
Onondaga, 83
Ontario: population mobility in, 455–8; provincial rights and, 576; *see also* Canada West; Upper Canada
Orange Order, 461–2, 464–5, 466–7, 560
Order of Good Cheer, 67
Oregon Boundary Treaty, 414–16, 418

Oregon Terrritory, 399
organizations: early Victorian society and, 466–7, 468; temperance, 470–1
Orontony, 160
Otter, William, 592
Owen, David, 351
Owen, William, 203

Pacific Scandal, 574
Paleo-Eskimo peoples, 10, 18–19
Paleo-Indians, 5–10
Palliser, John, 442–3
'Palliser's Triangle', 443
Palmerston, Henry John Temple, 398
Papineau, Louis-Joseph, 253, 259–60, 265, 268, 269, 297
Parker, Thomas, 554
Parkman, Francis, *xiii*, 87, 159
Parry, Edward, 450–1
Passamaquoddy people, 11
Paterson, James, 493
patriotism, 358
Patterson, Walter, 252
pays en haut, 141, 159, 208–10
Peake, James, 308
Peel, Robert, 390
Peminuit Paul, 335
Peñon Woman, 5
Pepperrell, William, 179
Perkins, Simeon, 223, 226
Perrot, Nicholas, 158
Perry, Adele, 362
Perry, Peter, 257, 259, 264
petroleum, 509
Petun people, 12
Petworth Emigration Committee, 286–8
Philipsburg Proclamation, 232
Phillips, Richard, 184
Picturesque Canada, 584
Pitt, William, 201
Plains of Abraham, 185–8, 189
Plains Cree, 588
Plessis, Joseph-Octave, 346–7
Pochahontas, 69
political parties: Canada East and West and, 374, 375–7; early, 252–3
politics: in British North America, 246–72, 367–77, 522–41; popular colonial, 261–3
Pond, Peter, 217
Pontiac, 210
Pontiac's Rebellion, 202, 210
Pope, J.C., 550–1
population: Aboriginal, 23, 193, 277, 332–3; in Acadia, 144–5; in British North America, 273, 277–9, 280; mobility of, 453–9; in New France, 123–7; transient, 458–9; *see also* census
Port-Royal, 63, 67, 69, 70, 72–3, 144, 145
Portugal: exploration and, 45–7; sovereignty and, 30
Post Office, 378–9
potlatches, 441
Poundmaker, 588, 592, 593
Poutrincourt, Jean de Biencourt de, 67
poverty: in British North America, 324–5; industrialization and, 515–18
Pownall, John, 202
prairies, 166–8; *see also* western region
pre-history, 3

Presbyterians, 344, 347
Prince Edward Island, 141, 146, 202, 203, 535; Confederation and, 531, 550–2; land question and, 397–8; politics in, 252, 261–2, 263; religion in, 375; shipbuilding and, 393
Prince of Wales: *see* Edward VII (Prince of Wales)
Privy Council, 575
Proclamation of 1763, 202–3, 204, 207, 215–16
professionalization, 460–1
prostitution, 328–9
Protestantism, 344–7, 375, 461–2, 465–6; *see also* specific sects
provinces: elites and, 321–2; rights of, 576–7; *see also* specific provinces
Prud'homme, Firmin, 486
Puget's Sound Agricultural Company, 397

Quebec: American invasion of, 211–13, 242; architecture in, 127; capture of, 71, 84; education in, 583; Loyalists and, 228; population mobility in, 453–5; provincial rights and, 576; restored, 84–9; Riel's death and, 594, 597; Roman Catholic Church in, 463; after Seven Years' War, 204–8; war and, 173, 185–8; *see also* Canada East; Lower Canada; New France
Quebec Act of 1774, 206–7, 217
Quebec Conference, 377, 529–34
Quebec Resolutions, 538
Queen Anne's war, 176–7
Queen's Birthday, 468

racism, 329, 578
Radisson, Pierre-Esprit, 97–8, 164–5
Rae, John, 451
railways, 365–6; British Columbia and, 568, 570; Confederation and, 574; costs of, 424–5, 426–7; financing of, 401–2, 423, 425; industrialization and, 499, 501; 'mania' and, 422–9; PEI and, 552
Ramea, 61
Rand, Silas Tertius, 11
Rankin, Arthur McKee, 486
rape, 329
Raudot, Jacques, 117–18, 132
Razilly, Isaac de, 73, 75, 76
Rebellion Losses Act, 372, 419
rebellions: North-West, 592–4; Upper and Lower Canada and, 247, 264–8
reciprocity, 420–9, 507
Reciprocity Treaty, 421, 506
records, historical, *xii–xiii, xv*
Red River settlement, 432, 434–42, 554–63, 585; responsible government in, 373
Reed, Hayter, 594, 595–6
Reformers, 371–2, 375–6; democracy and, 260; radical, 259–61; social, 470–1
religion: in Acadia, 148; black people and, 331; celebrations and, 467–9; conflict and, 461–2; as cultural institution, 340, 344–7; dissenters and, 346, 347; early Victorian society and, 461–6; education and, 347–50, 582–3; European and Aboriginal, 37–8; Métis and, 440; politics and, 374–5; Quebec Act and, 206; *see also* missionaries; specific sects
'rep by pop', 373, 529–30
Richelieu, Cardinal, 83–4
Richtot, Noel, 560
Riel, Louis, 547, 555–63, 585; North-West rebellion and, 591–2; trial of, 592–3
Ritchie, W.J., 583
Robb, James, 342–3
Roberts, Charles G.D., 581, 583, 584
Roberval, Jean-François de La Rocque, Sieur de, 52–4

Roberval, Marguerite de, 53–4
Robinson, John Beverley, 319, 320, 523–4
Robinson, Peter, 285, 287
Rolph, John, 257
Roma, Jean-Pierre, 146
Roman Catholic Church, 344, 346–7, 348, 461–5; Acadia and, 148; culture and, 132–3; lay movements and, 95–6; New France and, 98–9, 108–9; New World and, 52; reform and, 374, 375; *see also* Jesuits; missionaries
Ross, Alexander, 437
Ross, John, 450–1
Ross, William, 343–4
Rouges, 376
Royal Academy of Arts, 583–4
Royal Institution for the Advancement of Learning, 348
Royal Society of Canada, 584
Rupert's Land, 432
Rush-Bagot Agreement, 255–6
Russell, Peter, 318–20
Russia: immigrants from, 585–6
Rut, John, 46
Ryerson, Egerton, 350, 381, 382–3

Sable Island, 62, 66
Saguenay: 'kingdom of', 50–2, 54
Sainte-Marie-aux-Hurons, 87
Saint John, 238, 308, 311, 314
St Lawrence and Atlantic Railway, 423
St Mary's Foundry, 502
St Patrick's Day, 468–9
Saint-Pierre, Comte de, 146
Saint-Sauveur, 69–70
St Vallier, Jean, 109
Salish people, 18
Sangster, Charles, 479
San Juan Islands, 416–18
Sarcee people, 16
Saskatchewan, 563
Saskatchewan Valley: Métis settlement of, 590–1
Saunders, Charles, 185
Sayer, Pierre-Guillaume, 436
School Acts, 381, 383
schools, 340, 480–2; medical, 460; in New France, 92–3, 109; *see also* education
Schultz, Agnes Campbell, 436
Schultz, John Christian, 436, 557–8
Schuyler, Philip, 211, 224
science, early Victorian, 492–4
Scobie, Hugh, 478–9
Scotland: colonization and, 63; immigrants from, 273, 279, 280–2, 288; *see also* British Isles
Scott, Duncan Campbell, 583
Scott, Thomas, 558–60, 562
sculpture, 355–6
scurvy, 51, 52
sealing, 296
seduction, 328
seigneurial system, 86, 106, 113–16, 144, 422
Selkirk, Thomas Douglas, 257, 299, 326
Senate, 530
Seneca people, 83, 172
sentimentalization, 342
Seven Years' war, 183–90, 201
Sewell, Jonathan, 261

Seymour, Frederick, 450, 563, 565
shamans, 38
Shawnadithit, 334
Shea, Ambrose, 553
Shelburne, NS, 232, 238
Sherwood, Henry, 524
shipbuilding, 308–10, 356, 392, 500; in New France, 120
shipping, 458; transatlantic, 391–3; *see also* carrying trade
ships, explorers', 41, 44, 45
Shirley, William, 179
Simcoe, John Graves, 237–8, 318
Simpson, George, 394, 396, 437, 440
'Skraelings', 43
slavery, 282, 329, 416, 417, 430; Loyalists and, 232–3; New France and, 127, 130, 132
Small, H. Beaumont, 503
Smallwood, Charles, 493
Smith, A.J., 536
Smith, Adam, 389
Smith, Deborah, 234
Smith, Donald A., 557
Smith, William, 23, 241
Snell, John, 455
social reform, 470–1
Société Notre-Dame de Montréal, 87, 96
society: ethnic tensions and, 461–2; in British North America, 317–39, 453–72; in New France, 127–31; resource, 317–18
Sockett, Thomas, 286
sovereignty, European, 30, 35
Spain, 45
sports, 340, 356, 358, 494–7
Stadacona, 50–1, 52
Stanley, Lord, 397–8
Stark, John, 383
steam engine, 365, 423
Stephen, James, 332–3
Stevens, James, 233
Strachan, John, 257, 258, 320, 345–6, 347, 348, 349, 518, 523
Strange, James, 219
Sulte, Benjamin, 579
Supreme Court, 575
Swanton, John, 17–18
Sydenham, Lord, 379
'System', 248–9

Taché, A.-A., 555
Taché, J.C., 524
Tadoussac, 66–7, 71, 87
Taignoagny, 48, 50, 51
Talon, Jean, 99, 105–7, 113
technology, early Victorian, 492–4
Tecumseh, 253
telegraph, 365
temperance movement, 470–1
Tenant League, 550–1
Tenskwatawa, 253
Thanadelthur, 165–6
theatre, 476–7; amateur, 483–5, 487; English-language, 482–6; French-language, 486–8
Thevet, André, 53–4
Thom, Adam, 437
Thompson, David, 299
Thomson, James, 447, 457
Thorne, Robert, 46–7

Thorpe, Robert, 251
Thule people, 18, 43
Ticonderoga, 83
Tilley, Samuel Leonard, 471, 535, 564
timber, 295, 302–4, 325, 458
Tonge, William Cottnam, 251
Toronto, 311, 315, 512–13, 516
Toronto Typographical Society, 511
Toryism: Upper Canada and, 254–5
trade: colonial policy and, 295; free, 388, 389–91; New France and, 116–20; transatlantic, 388; *see also* fur trade
Traill, Catharine Parr, 325, 354
transportation, 365–6; immigrants and, 290–2, 403–6; internal development and, 388; transatlantic, 391–3, 403–6; water, 311; *see also* railways; shipping
Treaty of Ghent, 255, 412
Treaty of Paris, 220, 412
Treaty of Ryswick, 174, 176
Treaty of Utrecht, 111, 141, 147, 148, 170, 177
Treaty of Washington, 573
Trent affair, 527, 528
Troyes, Pierre de, 172
truck system, 323–4
'True Whigs', 241
Tsimshian people, 18
Tubman, Harriet, 417
Tucker, Josiah, 389
Tupper, Charles, 471, 572, 530–1, 537–8

Underground Railroad, 293, 416, 417
unification, 522–41
unions, labour, 510–11
United States: annexation and, 411, 419–20, 444–5; attitudes towards, 429–30; border with, 256, 411–19; Civil War in, 430, 527, 572; Confederation and, 527; fishery and, 296; immigrants from, 273, 279–80, 282; integration with, 365; investment from, 295; migrants to, 453–4, 458; relations with, 411–31, 572–3; War of 1812 and, 253–6; *see also* American Revolution
universities, 348–9, 480–2, 579; history and, *viii–ix*
University of King's College, 346, 348, 349
University of Toronto, 374
Upper Canada: Aboriginal peoples and, 336–7; agriculture in, 304; Americans in, 280; Loyalists and, 230, 241; petitioning in, 261; politics in, 254–5, 256–9, 263–4; rebellion in, 264–8; union with Lower Canada and, 369–70, 522–3
urbanization, 512–15
Ursulines, 87, 92–3

Vancouver Island, 432, 443, 563; as colony, 395–6, 432, 443; responsible government in, 373
Van Kirk, Sylvia, 361
Vaudreuil, Pierre de, 108, 161
Vaughan, Sir William, 63
Verrazzano, Giovanni da, 47–8
Viger, Benjamin, 264, 269
Viger, Denis-Benjamin, 371
Vikings, 40–4
Vimont, Barthélemy, 87, 89
Vinland, 42–4

violence: labour and, 510–11; political, 263–4; *see also* rebellions

Waddington, Alfred, 445
Wakefield, Edward Gibbon, 286
Wakefield System, 396–7
Walker, James, 194
Wandering Spirit, 592, 593
war: Aboriginal peoples and, 35; of the Austrian succession, 177–80; Britain and France and, 170–91; of 1812, 253–6; of the League of Augsburg, 172–6; Seven Years', 183–90; of the Spanish succession, 176–7; *see also* American Revolution
Warren, Peter, 179
Washington, George, 211
Webster-Ashburton Treaty, 411–14
Welland Canal, 311, 312–13, 501
Wentworth, John, 237
western region, 158–64, 166–8; American Revolution and, 215; from 1821 to 1868, 432–4; scientific expeditions and, 442–3; after Seven Years' War, 215–19
West Indies, 201
'Wheat Kings', 305
Whelan, Edward, 550
Whitbourne, Richard, 61, 63
White, John, 56
White Paper on Indian policy, 192
Wilberforce Settlement, 330–1
Wilcocks, John, 319
Wilkins, Frederick, 416
Williams, Eunice, 36, 176
Williams, John, 176
Wilmot-Horton, Robert, 286, 287
Wilson, Charles, 444
Wilson, Daniel, 479
Wilton, Carol, 261
Winslow, John, 183
Winthrop, John, 177
Wise, Jupiter, 233
witchcraft, 99
Wolfe, James, 185–8
Wolseley, Garnet, 562
women: Aboriginal, 435; celebrations and, 469; colonial economy and, 306–7; colonial law and, 326–9; colonial politics and, 249–50; domesticity and, 340–4; family farm and, 456–7; industrialization and, 512, 516–17; as Loyalists, 224–5, 232, 233–5; as missionaries, 87, 92–6; in New France, 125, 128–9; rights of, 327; as writers, 353–5; writing history of, *xi, xiv–xv,* 360–2
Wood, Edmund Burke, 578
Woodstock Riot, 462
Woodworth, Elihu, 322
Wright, Philemon, 305
Wuastukwiuk people, 11
Wyandot, 160

Yeo, James, 393
York, 311, 317–21
York Fort, 174
Young, George Paxton, 492

Zeller, Suzanne, 494